GW00597195

Self, Community and Psychology

Self, Community and Psychology

Editors:

Norman Duncan

Kopano Ratele

Derek Hook

Nhlanhla Mkhize

Peace Kiguwa

Anthony Collins

UCT
PRESS

Chapters 1, 2, 4, 5, 7, 9, 10 and 12 have been taken from *Critical Psychology*.
(copy editing and proofreading: John Linnegar)

Chapters 3, 6, 8 and 13 have been taken from *Social Psychology*
(copy editing: Stuart Douglas, Boltupright
and proof reading: Andrew van der Spuy)

Self, Community and Psychology has been compiled as a reader for Unisa students
© 2004 UCT Press
Reprinted June 2007
Revised reprint September 2008 (including References)
Reprinted August 2010
Reprinted November 2012

Juta & Company Ltd
First Floor
Sunclare Building
21 Dreyer Street
Claremont
7708

*This book is copyright under the Berne Convention. In terms of the Copyright Act 98
of 1978, no part of this book may be reproduced or transmitted in any form or by
any means, electronic or mechanical, including photocopying, recording or by any
information storage and retrieval system, without permission in writing from
the publisher.*

ISBN 978-1-91971-351-9

Project management: Fiona Wakelin
Cover design: Pumphaus Design Studio
DTP and design: Charlene Bate
Printed and bound in the Republic of South Africa by Bevan Litho, Somerset West

The author and the publisher believe on the strength of due diligence exercised that
this work does not contain any material that is the subject of copyright held by another
person. In the alternative, they believe that any protected pre-existing material that
may be comprised in it has been used with appropriate authority or has been used in
circumstances that make such use permissible under the law.

Contents

Contributors

Catherine Campbell is an External Professor at the University of KwaZulu-Natal, although she lectures in the Department of Social Psychology at the London School of Economics. Her current research interests focus closely on issues of community intervention and the politics of HIV/AIDS in Southern Africa. She is the author of *Letting them die: how HIV/AIDS prevention programmes often fail* (Double Storey/Juta, 2003).

Anthony Collins is a lecturer in Psychology at the University of KwaZulu-Natal. He is a Fullbright scholar with degrees in Psychology (Rhodes University) and Cultural Studies (University of California). He has a long-standing interest in critical psychology with a specific focus on violence and trauma in South Africa.

Norman Duncan holds a professorship in Psychology at the University of the Witwatersrand, where he currently also serves as the Head of the School of Human and Community Development. His research and publications are primarily in the fields of racism and community psychology. He has co-edited a range of volumes, including *'Race', racism, knowledge production and psychology in South Africa* (Nova Science Publications, 2001).

Don Foster is Professor of Psychology at the University of Cape Town. His main research areas are the psychology of interrogation and torture, policing and explaining human rights abuses. He has published many academic works in local and international journals, and presented papers at local and international conferences. His books include *Detention and torture in South Africa* (David Philip, 1987), *Mental health policy issues of South Africa* (MASA, 1997).

Derek Hook is a lecturer in Social Psychology at the London School of Economics and a research fellow in Psychology at the University of the Witwatersrand. The over-arching focus of his research concerns the attempt to develop an 'analytics of power' sufficiently able to grapple with the unconscious and psychological dimensions of racism and ideological subjectivity. He is the author of *Foucault, Psychology & the Analytics of Power* (Palgrave, 2007), the editor of *Critical Psychology* (UCT Press, 2004). In addition, he is one of the founding editors of the journal *Subjectivity* and the coordinator of *Psychoanalysis@LSE*, a multi-disciplinary research group based at the London School of Economics.

Peace Kiguwa lectures in gender studies and critical social psychology in the School of Human and Community Development at the University of the Witwatersrand. She is co-editor on *Critical Psychology* (UCT Press, 2004) and *The Gender of Psychology* (UCT Press, 2006). Her research interests include critical race theories, asymmetrical social relations, critical psychology and gender and sexuality.

Vuyisile Mathiti's research interests cover social identity, indigenous knowledge systems and sports psychology. His current research and community work is on HIV/AIDS and mentoring projects involving young people, using music therapy and other diversion programmes.

Nhlanhla Mkhize is a registered counselling psychologist and a professor of Psychology at the University of KwaZulu-Natal. His main areas of interest are indigenous psychologies, moral and ethical decision-making, and sociocultural psychology, especially those approaches informed by the works of Vygotsky and Bakhtin.

Oscar Tso Modipa is a community psychologist with interests in cross-cultural and social psychology.

David Neves is a researcher at the Programme for Land and Agrarian Studies (PLAAS) in the School of Government, at the University of the Western Cape. He is also member of the international Chronic Poverty Research Centre (CPRC). His work unites his interest in cognition and human development with a focus on poverty, land-based livelihoods and informal sector economic activity. He has conducted research for both the South African government and various international aid agencies.

Kopano Ratele is a Professor at the Institute of Social and Health Sciences (ISHS) at the University of South Africa. He has a range of scholarly interests spanning the areas of violence and fatal injury, psychology, men and masculinities, racial hatred, intergroup relations, sexualities, epistemology and research methodology. Prior to joining ISHS, Ratele held a professorship at the University of Western Cape where he taught in the Department of Psychology and in Women's and Gender Studies. Among other works, he has co-edited or edited the books *From Boys to Men* (UCT Press, 2007) and *Inter-group relations: South African perspectives* (Juta, 2006). He is Editor-in-Chief of *African Safety Promotion: A Journal of Injury and Violence Prevention* and books editor of *South African Journal of Psychology*.

Mohamed Seedat is Professor of Psychology and Director of the University of South Africa's Institute for Social and Health Sciences and its Centre for Peace Action. He has been centrally involved in several priority national research initiatives and collaborative cross-disciplinary research projects. He serves on several editorial boards and international conference organising committees, acts as external examiner on numerous master's- and doctoral-level research reports, and provides consultancy to various agencies in the psychology, injury prevention and development fields. He has published several articles in the areas of community psychology, racism, psychohistory and community development, and is chief editor of the first South African community psychology text, *Theory, practice and methods in community psychology: South African and other perspectives* (Oxford University Press, 2000).

Tamara Shefer is Director and Professor of the Women's and Gender Studies Programme at the University of the Western Cape. Her research and publications are primarily in the areas of (hetero)sexual relationships, HIV/AIDS, gender and sexual identities, masculinities, politics of knowledge production, authorship and higher education, and critical and feminist psychology. She has recently co-edited *The Gender of Psychology* (UCT Press, 2006) and *From Boys to Men* (UCT Press, 2007).

Thabani Ngonyama Ka Sigogo is a community psychologist. His interests lie in community activism and in Africanist perspectives on community psychology as it is practised in South Africa.

Garth Stevens is a clinical psychologist and senior lecturer at the University of the Witwatersrand. His research interests include violence and its prevention as well as studies in social inequality and difference in the context of racialised social formations. He is a co-editor of the book, *a RACE against time: Psychology and challenges to deracialisation in South Africa* (UNISA Press, 2006).

Ashley van Niekerk is a Specialist Scientist and Manager of the University of South Africa and Medical Research Council's Crime, Violence and Injury Lead Programme. His current research interests and publications involve descriptions and analyses of the occurrence and circumstances of childhood injury in and around under-resourced homes in South African cities. He is co-editor of *Crime, violence and injury prevention in South Africa* (Medical Research Council/UNISA Press, 2004).

Hilde van Vlaenderen obtained her PhD degree from Rhodes University, Grahamstown, where she lectured in research methodology for 12 years. She has worked in several African countries and her research and teaching interests focus on participatory community development, local knowledge and organisational development. She uses Activity Theory as a framework for much of her work. She currently lives in France, where she works as an independent international researcher and consultant.

Introduction

Puleng Segalo
D. Johan Kruger
Eduard Fourie
Matshepo Nefale
Martin Terre Blanche

A psychology of liberation requires a prior liberation of psychology, and that liberation can only come from a praxis committed to the sufferings and hopes of the people

(Martín-Baró, 1986, p. 32)

This reader was commissioned for the University of South Africa's undergraduate modules in community psychology. While there are some useful non-South African community psychology texts, our experience as teachers and practitioners is that in South Africa the discipline of community psychology has developed to such an extent that international texts are no longer suitable. To some degree this is true of South African psychology generally, in that in the last few decades there has been a flowering of approaches that not only address local issues, but also focus on transforming the discipline itself. This reflects broader developments in South African society where the transition from apartheid to democracy has enabled new forms of collective agency and social justice which promise to go beyond traditional "western" political and social structures.

The renaissance in South African psychology is increasingly reflected in locally authored textbooks in fields such as critical, developmental and social psychology. Seedat, Duncan and Lazarus's (2001) groundbreaking volume has helped to put the new South African approach to community psychology on the map and in the curriculum, but as yet there is no text specifically written for undergraduate community psychology students that suits the requirements of the Unisa community psychology modules. In this reader we have therefore brought together some of the best recent work written from critical, social constructionist, participatory and liberatory perspectives but first published in two volumes dealing with social psychology and critical psychology respectively (*Critical Psychology*, 2004, edited by Derek Hook, Peace Kiguwa and Nhlanhla Mkhize, and *Social Psychology: Identities and Relationships*, 2003, edited by Kopano Ratele and Norman Duncan, both published by UCT Press).

An important impetus for the development of community psychology has always been an ongoing critique of mainstream psychology and its practices. In his inaugural lecture Naidoo (2000) highlights the main points of critique against mainstream psychology, namely:

▷ Inadequate, inaccessible, inappropriate and discriminatory provision of mental health services
▷ A pre-occupation with providing services to a privileged minority;
▷ An inability to address political concerns
▷ A lack of a broader contextual focus.

The aims of community psychology as a critical response to the above short-comings, as set out by Lazarus and Seedat (1995), are as follows:

▷ Extend mental health services to all citizens
▷ Transform how psychosocial problems are conceptualised
▷ Transform psychological service delivery to be more contextually appropriate
▷ Redefine the role of psychologists to embrace advocacy, lobbying, policy formulation, community mobilisation, community networking.

Following this logic we selected chapters for inclusion in this reader to emphasise three streams in the undergraduate modules in community psychology:

1. the act of making knowledge about selves in communities
2. the discourses, ideologies and cultures that shape communities and how they are understood
3. change processes in the increasingly complex interaction between global and local.

The first three chapters in this volume provide a broad introduction to psychology, power and social formations and a liberatory response through critical analysis, self-definition and collective action. They also show the deficiencies of traditional approaches to knowledge-making and research in psychology and suggest more ethical and collaborative alternatives. Importantly, they show how the language we use not only describes psycho-social phenomena, but also brings them into being as social realities. To speak of "foreigners" (or *makwere-kwere*) is not only to point to a reality that already exists, but to co-create and sustain a reality where one can act in harmful ways to people who happen to be immigrants. Discourses (or ways of speaking) about the social world constantly create ruptures and connections among different groups, and results in harm or benefit to people.

The introductory chapters are followed by five chapters showing how these powerful discursive and ideological forces define the global status quo and shape communities everywhere. The first of these discourses or ideologies is mainstream psychology itself, which can be understood as a form of cultural colonisation, which perpetuates systems that set up the individual against the collective. In contrast to this, there are attempts to revitalise African world-views which see personhood as being necessarily embedded in the collective. Secondly, the chapters address ideologies of race that create a post-colonial reality which legitimises oppression and cultural dispossession. Finally, we include chapters dealing with ideologies of gender and sexual inequality, that help to set up a regime of white heterosexual male privilege.

We then turn to approaches that focus not only on analysing social structures, but on ways of bringing about change within a people-centred paradigm. Two chapters deal with approaches (Activity Theory and Participatory Action Research) that combine intervention and research and that seek to redefine the relationship between "researcher" and "researched". The final three chapters focus on key areas of local concern where change is needed – poverty (as reflected in the lives of street children), HIV/Aids and violence. Each of these chapters provides a critical analysis, drawing on the theoretical resources introduced in previous chapters, and then goes on to describe a community psychology of participatory action to overcome social challenges.

The global and South African social landscapes that we attempt to sensitise students to in this reader are of course far from stable. Indeed, the rapid transformation in our society and psychology lends vitality and urgency to being a community psychologist in South Africa today. Inevitably, some of the material gathered together here will therefore also relatively rapidly be overtaken by new social and disciplinary developments. Already, for example, some of the critiques in the chapter on HIV/Aids have been blunted by positive developments in government policy.

We trust that students and other readwers will find this text an exciting and inspirational introduction to the field of community psychology.

> Who knows, perhaps community social psychology as a discipline will come to embody the philosophy of *Ubuntu*. At this early stage, it seems to me that we do have the chance of treading carefully new, community social psychology paths, finding and making our way by walking with and through others ... a liberation of psychology (Kagan, 2002).

REFERENCES

Hook, D., Kiguwa, P., & Mkhize, N. (2004). *Critical Psychology*. Cape Town: UCT Press.

Kagan, C. (2002). "Making the road by walking it". Inaugural lecture. Manchester Metropolitan University.
http://homepages.poptel.org.uk/mark.burton/proftalk8.htm

Lazarus, S., & Seedat, M. (1995). "Community Psychology in South Africa". Paper presented at the Fifth biennial conference of the Society for Community Research and Action, University of Illinois, Chicago, United States of America.

Martín-Baró, I (1986). Hacia una Psicología de la liberación Boletín de Psicología, 5(22) 219-231 (English Translation found in Aron.A. and Corne, S. (1994 *Writing for a Liberation Psychology*: Ignacio Martín-Baró Harvard University Press).

Naidoo, A.V. (2000). "Community psychology: Constructing community, reconstructing psychology in South Africa". Inaugural Lecture. University of Stellenbosch.

Ratele, K., & Duncan, N. (2003). *Social Psychology: Identities and Relationships*. Cape Town: UCT Press.

Seedat, M., Duncan, N., & Lazarus, S. (2001). *Community psychology: Theory, method and practice. South African and other perspectives*. Cape Town: Oxford University Press.

1

Liberation psychology

Don Foster

*'... those who are enmeshed, involved in these power relations can,
in their actions, their rebellion escape them, transform them, in a word,
cease being submissive.'*

Michel Foucault (Interview, 1978)

LEARNING OUTCOMES

By the end of this chapter, you should be able to:

▷ Expand on how certain notions of psychology, power and 'social formations' might usefully inform the key concerns of liberation psychology

▷ Discuss the problems and objectives of notions of utopia and emancipation

▷ Debate the contributions and 'ills' of modernity

▷ Elaborate on the forms of 'crisis' which affected psychology in the 1960s and 1970s

▷ Expand upon the psychology of oppression, using notions of authoritarianism, social identity theory and social dominance theory

▷ Discuss possible psychological consequences of oppression

▷ Identify both a series of directions or strategies for an emancipatory psychology and a number of potential pitfalls/challenges for a liberatory psychology of the future.

INTRODUCTION

Questions of liberation

The topic of liberation, or liberatory psychology, may, on the one hand, be viewed as disarmingly simple, straightforward and tidy and, on the other hand, as fiendishly complex, difficult, elusive and messy, requiring a good deal of tricky theorising and an ability to cope with murkiness. In the simple version, liberation psychology involves questions of the psychological processes, dynamics, capacities and practices through which people may achieve emancipation, freedom, liberation and escape from particular power structures of oppression and exploitation.

In the more complicated version, many questions arise: What exactly is meant by freedom? Can we ever be entirely free from the enmeshment of power? How do people know when and if they are oppressed? What is the best way to think about these issues? Are there clear-cut theories to light our way? Are we all now 'liberated' in South Africa, some ten years after democratic elections in 1994? Writing at the time when American and 'coalition' military forces have invaded Iraq and the fledgling 21st-century world – a 'globalising' world, so they tell us – is frantically debating, arguing and protesting against or defending the merits of this war, the question of a liberation psychology appears to be trickier, more complex and murkier: people have different values, there are ferocious arguments for and against (Billig, 1987) and, in between, passions are ignited while bombs and missiles fall like rain. Elsewhere, say some writers, our contemporary situation (late-, or high-, or even post-modern) seems like a 'runaway world' (Giddens, 1999) in which things change at an increasing pace, threats lurk everywhere and there is even greater uncertainty about the future. What is to be done? This is the abiding question at the core of our topic. It has been asked before and will be asked again, repeatedly, in the future.

This chapter attempts the impossible, to chart a relatively simple version of what is at stake for a liberation psychology while confronting some of the complexities. Although the topic is a relatively recent one (there are still few systematic writings on the issue) its roots are far older, not least due to the important 19th-century works of Karl Marx. Despite older roots, it is only in the past fifteen years or so that notions of a 'critical' or 'liberatory' perspective in psychology have really come to the fore (Martin-Baro, 1994; Seedat, 1997; Parker & Spears, 1996). Later in this chapter we shall ask: Why this recent revival of older concerns?

> Liberation psychology involves questions of the psychological processes, dynamics, capacities and practices through which people may achieve emancipation, freedom, liberation and escape from particular power structures of oppression and exploitation.

Arguments of the chapter

The central argument of this chapter is threefold. First, I shall argue that there are different sites and forms of oppression, principally those of 'race', class and sex/gender. These forms of oppression, however, should be seen as intertwined and interlocking. Furthermore, this is not an exhaustive list, there are inequalities and discriminations due to illness and disability, sexual orientation, age and a range of ethnic and religious minorities. While it seems easy to describe the ways in which separate forms of oppression resonate with each other, it is a more challenging task than expected. As Donna Haraway has put it:

> It has seemed very rare for feminist theory to hold race, sex/gender and class analytically together – all the best intentions, hues of authors, and remarks in prefaces notwithstanding (1991, 129).

Secondly, I shall argue that there are links between large-scale social processes, such as **social structures**, institutions, and ideologies and personal subjectivities. These links are complex, however, and at times contradictory, although it is true to say that they always occur within particular historical or cultural epochs and configurations. For instance, there is no one-to-one, direct relationship between 'race' and 'class'; rather, they interact differently, and with different other forces, in each specific social and historical situation.

The third strand of argument to follow is that there are always possibilities of revolt, resistance, challenge or subversion of the prevailing social order, but that such resistance is uneven, possibly painfully slow. The outcome of such resistance is never inevitable, and it may be faced with draconian repressions; even when successful, it may continue to carry traces of former oppressions. Successful resistance will involve a transformation, a transcendence, of the existing relationships, producing change in both parties – oppressor and oppressed. Successful resistance will also bring about a transformation in the form of relations between people, so that prior subjectivities – bosses/workers, black/white, able/disabled, or feminine/masculine – are replaced with new psychological forms.

> **Social structures:**
> the underlying structures or organisation of society, the underlying social, economic and political relations that 'pattern' society.

CENTRAL CONCERNS

In locating a field or a terrain for liberation psychology, I suggest there are three cardinal areas of concern: the nature of social formations, questions of power, and issues of psychological subjectivity. Of course, the three areas are intertwined, but for clarity of exposition they may be dealt with separately.

Social formations

Societies everywhere take the form of **hierarchies** in which there are classes, layers or stratifications of people differentiated in terms of power, status, privilege, advantage, opportunities, skills, economic wealth and resources of various kinds (Moane, 1999; Sidanius & Pratto, 1999; Tajfel, 1981). The shape of the hierarchy is frequently in the form of a pyramid: a small minority at the

> **Hierarchies:**
> classes, layers, stratifications of people differentiated in terms of power, status, privilege, advantage, opportunities, skills, economic wealth and resources of various kinds.

top, the greater majority at the bottom. The world order may be depicted in the same form – a minority in US-America and Europe, that is the Western world and the North, and the majority of poor people in the East and South. They are characterised by inequalities of all sorts (See Box 1 for economic inequalities in South Africa).

Societies everywhere take the form of hierarchies in which there are stratifications of people differentiated in terms of power, status, privilege etc. The world order may be depicted in the same form – a well-off minority in US-America or Europe, that is, the Western world and the North, and the majority of poor people in the East and South.

BOX 1   Economic inequality in South Africa

Based on Income Distribution, Year 2001.

Percentage of total population		Percentage of income
Upper class	16.6	72.0
Middle class	16.6	17.2
Upper lower class	16.6	7.3
Very poor	50.0	3.3
Total	45.0 million	100.0

Source: Adapted from S. Terreblanche (2002).

Hegemonic orders

Societies may differ in terms of how easy it is to move from membership of one group to another (how easy or difficult it is for a person to pass from black to white, from male to female or to shift upwards in social class). There are also differences in the extent to which the social divisions are understood as being legitimate: whether they are thought of as natural, inevitable or justified. For instance, people may think that differences in wealth and property are justified if they hold the belief that wealth is the reward of hard work and poverty the natural consequence of laziness and incompetence. Often societies take the form of **hegemonic orders**, in which the divisions and hierarchies become taken-for-granted, assumed, unproblematic and accorded some degree of legitimacy. Manifest conflict within a particular social formation will vary according to the degree of legitimacy (sense of justice, fairness) and hegemony accorded by members. Although there may exist many different strata, the Marxist thesis holds that in particular historical circumstances conflicts **polarise** into two main classes, the bourgeoisie and the proletariat, so that, for instance, Western industrialised societies will primarily be characterised as **class struggles**. Other scholars claim that the central polarised cleavage is between coloniser and colonised or between black and white (Fanon, 1952/1967; Memmi, 1957/1967; Said, 1993), while feminists would claim even more primary and older struggles on gender/sex lines, the system of patriarchy.

Hegemonic orders: various social structures by virtue of which various kinds of division and hierarchy become taken-for-granted, assumed, unproblematic and accorded some degree of legitimacy.

The notion of hegemonic orders suggests that certain social hierarchies come to be taken for granted, assumed, unproblematic and accorded some degree of legitimacy.

The development of social hierarchies

A reasonable question would be to ask how these social divisions and hierarchies developed. Only sketchy answers can be given here, given limits of space. Again, different scholars would give varying emphases:

1. Marxists see the origins in the shift to industrial capitalist society, where most people have to work under exploitative conditions which make the rich get richer while the workers remain poor.
2. Colonialist scholars would point to the imperialist project, the gradual development of racism and nationalisms, and the colonial seizure of land along with genocidal destruction of native populations or their gradual

Polarise: to cause to concentrate about two strongly conflicting or opposed positions.

Class struggles: struggle between exploited and exploiters, which may take many forms – economic, political, ideological, theoretical, although each of these is subordinate to the political struggle. In Marxist thought class interests are thought to be irreconcilable.

subjugation and subordination through forms of violence and cultural annexation (see Derek Hook's chapter in this work on Frantz Fanon).

3. Feminists would point to a very gradual form of exclusion and subordination of women through changes in religion (patriarchal priesthoods), political and economic status differentiation between men and women, and division among women due to sexual status, 'respectable women' under male patronage and 'non-respectable' others; concubines and whores. Radical feminists would argue that male violence against women has played, and continues to play a major role. (In this respect see Peace Kiguwa's chapter in this work: Feminist critical psychology in South Africa and Tamara Shefer's chapter on heterosexuality.

How does domination operate?

Clearly these social formations are not merely hierarchical and unequal but involve various forms of domination. How does such domination operate? A variety of writers (eg Apfelbaum, 1979; Bartky, 1990; Therbon, 1980; Young, 1990; Sidanius & Pratto, 1999) have identified a range of forms of domination. In her analysis of both colonialism and women's oppression, Moane (1999) proposed a list of six processes involved in the establishment and maintenance of domination:

1. Violence, involving mechanisms such as military force, invasion, conquest and occupation of territory as well as rape, sexual assault, domestic violence and sexual harassment.

2. Political exclusion from voting, government office, representation and subtle alienation of women from the political terrain.

3. Economic exploitation involving a host of issues including income, wealth, poverty, tax systems, restrictions on trade, economic ownership, surplus value, as well as exclusion from employment and unpaid household labour by women.

4. Sexual exploitation including prostitution, rape, sexual slavery, control of women's sexuality, and a range of reproductive issues.

5. Control of culture including restriction on expressions of indigenous languages, history, art-forms, the loss of language, and lack of 'voice' on the part of women and minorities; control of representations by dominant group; stereotyping and stigmatisation of subordinated.

6. Fragmentation, including use of divisions (ethnic, religious, linguistic) to prevent united opposition; manufacture of competition and distrust among oppressed, and for women, fragmentation due to dependency on men, labour market insecurity (temporary, part-time jobs) and victim-blaming, for example, settling blame on mothers or black families for various ills.

All of these, it should be clear enough, would have considerable implications for psychological functioning.

Interrelationships between oppressor and oppressed

A pervasive theme among theorists on oppression, is to emphasise the interrelationship, the mutual independency and the complementary nature of the relationship between oppressors and oppressed. Perhaps it is put too strongly when Sidanius & Pratto (1999) claim, 'oppression is very much a cooperative game' (43) in which 'subordinates *actively* participate in and contribute to their own subordination' (43; original emphasis). One may certainly recognise the circular interrelationship, but it is in the *asymmetry* of the dynamics, rather than a *cooperation*, that the polarised dependencies occur.

The role of ideology

One term missing from Moane's (1999) list is the pertinent one of **ideology**, used here in the 'restricted and *critical* sense derived from its Marxist heritage to refer to ways in which meaning (signification) serves to create and sustain power relations of domination' (Foster, 1993a, 56). Despite some wariness of the term by Foucauldian scholars who distrust its implied notions of mystification, 'false-consciousness' and possibilities of unveiling the 'truth' lurking behind the masks, the concept need not be used in this manner, and it remains an important tool in the arsenal of critical analysts (Parker, 1992). Ideologies are stories, narratives, discourses as well as practices which construct subject-positions for both rulers and ruled. They assist in maintaining relations of domination, according to Therborn (1980), through discourses which say:

▷ what is the case ... ie creating a sense of *inevitability*
▷ what is good/bad ... creating a sense of *deference,* that is, a submission, or a yielding to the wishes, opinions, or judgement of another
▷ what is possible/impossible ... creating a sense of *resignation,* that is, a pessimistic view which *fails to see possibility of alternatives.*

In the view of Althusser (1971), ideology assists in domination by hailing persons as particular forms of **subjects**. The ideological operation of **interpellation** which means hailing, recognising or calling a person, such as in the remark 'Hey, you there!'. The person hearing this immediately responds by experiencing him- or herself in terms of the call – when the policeman says 'Hey, you there!', the person immediately wonders what they have done wrong. For example a wolf-whistle, which is a practice, an action, a meaning, and a hailing, places women in subjugated and objectified, perhaps dehumanised, positions in relation to men. But, further than this, it's not just specific addresses made to the person, but the way in which the whole system of ideo-

Ideology:
ways in which meaning (signification) serves to create and sustain power-relations of domination. Ideologies are stories, narratives, discourses as well as practices that construct subject-positions for both rulers and ruled.

Subject:
notion insisting that people cannot be abstracted out of their sociopolitical and/or historical contexts, that persons always exist *in relation to the structures or values of power.*

Interpellation:
ideological process in which a person is hailed, or called; in recognising this call, and in responding to it, that person is positioned as a *subject.*

Dialectics:
originally, the notion of dialectics referred to debate or, more particularly, to the art of *knowing the truth* through *overcoming the contradictions in an argument.*

logical meanings in society provides each person with particular ways of understanding who they are and what they can be.

Ideology is a relatively autonomous terrain, not just a reflection of economic or political forms – but may well be linked to them. It includes practices (that is, it is not merely beliefs, values, ideas or words) and is a dynamic ever-changing process which constitutes subjects, and is taken up by people as everyday 'lived experience' (Billig, 1991). Ideological processes are **dialectical** in that they construct relations between self and others, and work both *positively* – to qualify persons, as in the notion that you are qualified to speak on this topic, you have 'voice' – and *negatively*, to subject people to certain subordinate positions. For example, a final-year psychology student may be granted a certain authority to make psychological interpretations amongst his/her peers ('Oh, he's just an obsessive personality') while not being legally allowed to practise as a psychotherapist, nor perhaps, to contradict a psychology lecturer's interpretation in an exam paper. Certainly, ideology is a significant process in the formation and maintenance of domination, and is particularly important for understanding psychological forms of **subjectification**.

Ideological processes construct relations between self and others which work both positively – to qualify persons, to 'give them voice' – and negatively, to subject people to certain subordinate positions.

A word of caution. It is far too easy to see this picture in terms of homogenous groups, all of one piece and in terms of polarised binaries – oppressed and oppressors. Black feminists, for instance, have pointed out that black women's experience of being 'women' is necessarily different from that of white women (Mama, 1995). All categories are likely to be internally differentiated to some or other degree, and the relations between two conflicting categories may well contain all sorts of shades of grey.

Questions of power

Subjectification:
qualifying or positioning of persons as subjects where they have a 'speaking voice', an active social role to play, *but within* the overarching structures or concerns of a particular form of power.

It is tempting to think of power in terms of a thing, that one class or category possesses, and which is used in the manner of a force over another class in order to obtain compliance. This, indeed, is the ready taken-for-granted notion of power, the standard view. However, it is also possible to understand power in far more subtle and far-reaching terms, stretching as it were into the farthest corners of human relations. This is the view taken by Foucault (1980, 1982). It is not that power excludes the use of violence, nor the obtaining of consent, but for Foucault these do not constitute the principal or basic nature of power. Power occurs only when there is resistance, it is a 'total structure of actions brought to bear upon possible actions' (1982, 789). During the course of modernity, particularly around the 18th century, a new form of **pastoral** power emerged in which 'salvation' took on new meanings, no longer 'salvation' in the next world but salvation in this world: health, well-being, standards of living, protection, welfare. New institutions and officials of 'pastoral power' emerged – medicine, welfare societies, philanthropists, the family – which

Pastoral:
of or relating to a pastor, to a moral or spiritual guide, or a form of guidance.

developed new knowledge and disciplines (including, in the 20th century, psychologists, psychiatry, criminology – the 'psy' disciplines, Rose, 1990). These new knowledge forms operated power through 'disciplinary' means, involving setting of norms, standards, discourses, guidelines, warnings and techniques of 'surveillance' – a shaping of individuality – so that individuals involved themselves in self-regulation. Instead of forcing people to do anything, these disciplines produce ideas by which people voluntarily judge themselves – 'Am I normal (is my sexuality deviant, is my family pathological)'? Am I achieving my full potential (are my marks high enough, have I chosen the right career)? Through self-reflexivity and a self-scrutiny, a 'gaze' on themselves, individuals increasingly became involved in, as it were, a form of governance of self, according to the norms and standards of the institutions and officials of the new pastoral power. People then actively and willingly manage themselves according to these ideas. Power in this form is viewed in a more positive manner; it enables the capacity to act – in a relational form – upon the conduct of ourselves and others.

This approach implies that we cannot readily throw off, escape or evade power; power-relations seen in these 'capillary' terms are in part what enables us to constitute ourselves as subjects, always within an 'ensemble' of social relations, as the Marxists would claim (Marx & Engels, 1938). This view goes some way in accounting for why it is so difficult to change social conditions but it also, in positive ways, simultaneously reminds us that people are constantly active in forms of resistance, strategies of struggle 'to promote new forms of subjectivity' (Foucault, 1982, 785).

For our purposes here, we should be alert to two forms of power in manufacturing subjectivities. One is where we are subject to someone else's control, shaping and dependence. Let us not forget that political states, economic institutions and ideological forms such as racism and patriarchy still have considerable means of coercion, not excluding violence, and that subjugated people do not form themselves in their own image. The second is the Foucauldian view in which power is more pervasive, subtle, enmeshing, is impossible to break free of, but which may be transformed in terms of new power/knowledge and new relations of subjectivities. Both forms of understanding may be a requirement for an appropriate liberation psychology.

Questions of psychology

What forms of psychology, what images of persons, would be appropriate for a liberation psychology? This is where we run into some trouble. There are various different and competing pictures, theories, images of the person in contemporary psychology. Nevertheless, and to state the case overbluntly, the dominant view of the person is that of a 'self-contained individual', tightly

We should be alert to two forms of power in manufacturing subjectivities. One is where we are subject to someone else's control, shaping and dependence. The second is the Foucauldian view in which power is more pervasive, subtle, enmeshing, is impossible to break free of, but which may be transformed in terms of new power/knowledge and new relations of subjectivities.

What is the relationship between individual and society? Psychology takes two contrary views. One sees the individual as passive, the outcome of forces of socialisation, conformity and obedience. The second, as in humanistic views, takes the individual as the active source of action, a creature who can make choices and decisions impelled by inner states.

boundaried and sharply differentiated from other 'self-contained individuals'. The individual is the container of a range of dispositions and unique attributes which are held 'within': personality traits, attitudes, skills, thoughts, emotions, motives and potentials. This self-contained individual is the product of dynamics both inside and outside: 'inside' in the form of biological inheritances and unique dispositions (personalities, traits, tendencies) and 'outside' in the form of the environment, culture and mechanisms of reward and punishment, in a word the old 'nature-nurture' debate. What is the relationship between individual and society?

Here, psychology tends to vacillate between two contrary views: one takes the individual as passive, that is the outcome or the 'victim' of forces labelled as socialisation, conformity, obedience, rule-following; the second, as in humanistic views, takes the individual as the active source of action, a creature who has individual needs, tastes, wishes and who can make choices and decisions impelled by inner states. Either way, 'society' is held to be distanced, foreign and 'other' to the 'individual'. This version of the person is of course a relatively recent invention; it is the modern, industrialised, Western, liberal and largely masculine image of personhood.

Individual-social dualism

The central problem here is the philosophical conundrum of 'individual-social dualism' (Henriques, Hollway, Urwin, Venn & Walkerdine, 1984), itself a product of modernity and a legacy of Descartes. This view sees both 'individual' and 'society' as separate entities, in a rather antagonistic relationship, opposed to each other. If this view of the person is correct, then the task of a liberation psychology would be to throw off the shackles of 'society', extend the choices and liberties of individuals, increase the search for our 'authentic', inner selves. However, we are dependent on one another.

Emphasis upon the other 'social' extreme creates a further problem of the 'over-socialised' image of personhood. Here the person is nothing but a hapless outcome of 'outside' forces, as in radical behaviourism, and the solution would lie in social engineering of new environmental forces. Freud for one was cautious of such moves. In an appraisal of the Russian 'experiment' (communist rule in Russia) Freud argued that:

> ... a sweeping alteration of the social order has little prospect of success until new discoveries have increased our control over the forces of Nature and so made easier the satisfaction of our needs (1933/1973, 218).

Mainstream psychology, then, does not provide us with ready-made theories or images of the person to assist a liberation psychology, and the doctrine of 'individual-social dualism' looms as part of the problem. In particular, the individualism of Western psychology represents obstacles rather than solutions since any persons outside the norm of the dominant viewpoint are liable to be treated as 'others': deviant, dangerous, different, inferior and at best to be regarded as 'serviceable others' (Sampson, 1993a, 1993b).

Over the past fifteen to twenty years we have witnessed considerable efforts to construct new images of the person which would be more conducive to a critical or liberation psychology. Writers have drawn on traditions as varied as Marxism, feminism, dialogism, rhetorical views, post-structuralism, hermeneutics, discourse analysis, linguistics, cultural theory and psychoanalysis to fashion different constructs and attempt to overcome the dangers of 'individual-social dualism' and other pernicious dualisms (body-mind, self-other, nature-culture, reason-unreason) so characteristic of modernism. We shall return to this later in the chapter.

EMANCIPATION AND UTOPIA

One persistent, niggardly and difficult issue requires some attention before proceeding: the question of ideals, values, future images and utopias. All writers on critical and liberation psychology allude to the notion that for emancipation to be possible, people need alternatives; other social values, new ideals, images of a better social order. Martin Luther King expressed the yearning for other ideals in his famous speech 'I have a dream'. The Freedom Charter of the African National Congress in 1955 laid out alternative visions in some detail (see Box 2). In 1792 Mary Wollstonecraft set out new possibilities for women in her work *'A Vindication of the Rights of Women'*. In the mid-19th century, Marx and Engels gave hope and possibilities for the emerging proletariat in the

Communist Manifesto. From the 1960s in South Africa, Steve Biko's writings gave new ideals and strategies for blacks under apartheid (Biko, 1978).

There is little quibble with the idea that people set forward visions for a better life; indeed, as some writers claim (Moane, 1999), it may be a condition for the very possibility of emancipation. The issue is: What kind of vision? Whose values and ideals? For the perfect values of any one group may be anathema, indeed in conflict with, another group. For instance, in the eyes of at least some men, the emancipation of women may not be in the interests of men,

Liberation psychology alludes to the notion that for emancipation to be possible, people need alternatives: other social values, new ideals, images of a better social life, of 'a better life for all'.

BOX 2   The Freedom Charter, 1955

The Freedom Charter was adopted at the Congress of the People, a gathering of some 10 000 people held over two days at Kliptown, on 26 June 1955. From the oppressed people of South Africa, it proposed a vision of the type of society in which they would like to live. Apart from the Preamble which stated that 'South Africa belongs to all who live in it, black and white', the Charter consisted of ten clauses, the headings of which are listed below. The Preamble also claimed that:

'only a democratic state, based on the will of the people, can secure to all their birthright without distinction of colour, race, sex or belief;'

'we pledge ourselves to strive together, sparing nothing of our strength and courage, until the democratic changes here set out have been won.'

The headings of the ten clauses are:
1.   The People Shall Govern
2.   All National Groups Shall Have Equal Rights

BOX 2   The Freedom Charter, 1955 *(continued)*

3. The People Shall Share In The Country's Wealth
4. The Land Shall Be Shared Among Those Who Work It
5. All Shall Be Equal Before the Law
6. All Shall Enjoy Human Rights
7. There Shall Be Work and Security
8. The Doors Of Learning and Culture Shall Be Opened
9. There Shall Be Houses, Security and Comfort
10. There Shall Be Peace and Friendship

Nigh on 50 years later, we may ask ourselves how far we have come in achieving these noble aims and ideals.

---

hence the recent 'backlash' against the modest gains made by women over the past thirty years.

One feature of the 'visionary' ideas mentioned above is that they involve rigorous descriptions, analyses of and grievances against the prevailing conditions of **servitude**. Quite often there are no clear-cut blueprints for alternatives, no ideal state; rather, in the arguments against, and in analyses of, existing conditions, some alternatives appear. The meaning of the word 'critique' is more than merely 'being against' or critical of, but entails analysis of the forms and dynamics of existing social and political circumstances. Marxists in particular have been wary of and hostile to the idea of an abstract utopia, as a set of ideals or values unrelated to present circumstances, as a blueprint for a better life. Instead, Marxists have favoured the concept of '**immanent critique**' which gives attention to possible, feasible futures based on current conditions of possibility, including specifications of the agents of transfiguration; who, what category (workers, students, rural women) is likely to challenge existing oppressions.

Servitude:
lack of freedom, state of subjection.

Immanent critique:
Marxist, critical focus on possible, feasible, *better* futures based on current conditions of possibility and which includes the specification of the agents of transfiguration.

Whose ideals of freedom?

Whose values are put forward as ideals? Again, it is to be found in the voice(s) of those struggling in prevailing circumstances, not some abstract and arbitrary set of values. To be sure, there may be divisions, schisms, splits and disagreements among the subjugated – likely to be exploited by the ruling classes – but that is a matter for the struggle itself, not to be solved by abstract blueprints of utopia. Indeed, when visions are transformed into precise blueprints and a dogmatic set of beliefs, as was arguably the case in the communist Soviet bloc, we need beware of purges and draconian repressions in the name of that righteous canon. Sadly, recent history, particularly of the 20th century, is replete with horrendous events of this sort. If there are lessons to be learned, then blueprint utopias are to be avoided; there should be space for disagreements and debates, as in the feminist movements of recent years. There is still something to be learned from the original Marxist position on utopias.

BOX 3   Socialists comment on utopia

The opposite of utopia for Marx was not the pathological fantasy that the present will merely perpetuate itself, but what is generally referred to as 'immanent critique'. If Marxism has traditionally set its face against utopia, it is not because it rejects the idea of a radically transfigured society, but because it rejects the assumption that such a society could be, so to speak, simply parachuted into the present from some metaphysical outer space.
(Terry Eagleton, 1999, 33–34)

The socialist 'utopian goal' is built around realising our potential to be full human beings. What separates this ideal from its liberal roots is not only socialism's commitment to extending this principle to all members of society, but also its insistence that the flowering of human capacities isn't a liberation of the individual from the social, but is only achievable through the social.
(Leo Panitch & Sam Gindin, 1999, 5)

'Bad' utopia persuades us to desire the unfeasible, and so, like the neurotic, to fall ill of longing; whereas the only authentic image of the future is, in the end, the failure of the present.
(Terry Eagleton, 1999, 36).

MODERNITY AND ITS ILLS

For many writers (eg Sloan, 1996), modernity or modernism itself is part of the problem. Some claim, for instance, that the Holocaust did not occur against the spirit of modernity, it was not some fit of madness, but rather occurred directly as a result of certain features of modernity (Bauman, 1989). There are two tales of modernity; one which sees enlightenment, discovery, science, technology, the amelioration of human suffering and, above all, progress and hope; the other is a much darker tale of the rise of racism, colonialism, Western imperialism, new forms of economic exploitation in capitalism, the continued subjugation of women and a substantial increase in large-scale wars and genocide, while torture continues unabated in many countries. By the early 20th century more than three-quarters of the globe was dominated politically and economically by Western nations (Said, 1993) and the African continent was almost entirely conquered.

Defining modernity

What is meant by modernity? There are varying takes. Some would say it is that period, roughly 500 years, since the voyages of discovery and the colonisation by the West of distant lands in the East, Africa and the Americas, or alternatively the discovery of the printing press. Others would suggest the historical period of roughly 200 years since the French revolution with the rise of democracy and the development of the nation-state and nationalism. Yet others may suggest a 300 year period, the transformation from a feudal to an industrial and capitalist economy and/or the philosophy of Descartes. Some might point to the gradual displacement of religion by science. Others might claim it is the rapid technological developments and transformations in communication over the past century. Whatever the precise historical periodisation, and many would claim it is all of the above, the two-sided or contradictory view of modernism, progress and light versus despair and darkness, persists. It is not really a question of whether one story is more correct than another; it is rather the case that modernity, like one of its fruits, nationalism, is Janus-faced, it looks in opposite directions simultaneously, both good and bad. While modernity may have spawned all sorts of discoveries and achievements, these very developments – for instance of science and technology – have also produced potential threats, environmental degradation, possibilities for mass human destruction, and risks of all sorts, leading some to argue that our contemporary social formation is a 'risk society' (Beck, 1992).

Promises of modernity

Our epoch of modernity with its concomitant rise of science, technology and rational thought, emanating from 17th- and 18th-century Europe, seemed to offer hope and optimism for the improvement in conditions for humankind; a 'brave new world'. The premise of modernity was that through reason and rationality – in contrast to religion and dogma – human beings would be able to shape history and governance for the better purposes of humanity. The world could be more predictable, stable and ordered, a place in which justice, fairness and reasonableness would prevail. Technological advances and progress, a 'machine age', could potentially alleviate many of the crushing burdens – the daily grind and early death – of human toil. Human reason could better plan for improved futures and more enlightened forms of rule, such as the rule of law. Reason, progress and civilisation could shape greater control over nature and permit humans to rise above enslavement to their own 'base instincts'; culture over nature. Rich promises indeed. It hasn't quite worked out that way.

Oppositions to modernity

Numerous commentators have tried to work out why modernity has failed or at least partially failed (see Box 4). Responses to the discontents of modernity have taken three paths:

Globalisation: increasing interconnectedness of various parts of the world through communication technologies and trade. Globalisation has seen an increasing tendency for ideas, cultural products, material goods and, perhaps most importantly, capital to disregard national boundaries. Globalisation occurs to both the benefit and the detriment of local communities.

1. those who wish to turn the clock back, traditionalists and conservatives, who yearn for old customary ways, 'family values', and a return to harsh punishment and 'pure races';
2. those who wish to extend and hasten the enlightenment project in the form of better reason, more progress, new discoveries, expanding the reach of technologies, increased growth and development;
3. and those, perhaps called post-modernists, who hope to supersede modernism, by going beyond the founding ideas of modernism – the faith in 'reason', 'progress', 'science' – as well as the specific categories that shackle our modernist thinking in false dichotomies – mind–body, self–society, male–female, true–false, cause–effect. Neither do these three streams operate in pure forms; fierce contemporary debates, between 'fundamentalists' and 'cosmopolitans' (Giddens, 1999), about issues such as '**globalisation**', 'first' and 'third' worlds, wars, ecology, crime and sexuality, frequently intertwine differing aspects of these discourses. If modernity is part of the problem, then a psychology of liberation would do well to give careful scrutiny to what modernisation means. In the meanwhile, a range of theorists keep alerting us to the psychological consequences of modernism: alienation, insecurity, dehumanisation, 'internalised oppression', anxieties, narcissism, addictions, dual consciousness, fear, anomie, depression, helplessness and a radical increase in multiple disorders and pathologies.

BOX 4   Modernity and its disorders

A range of critics from a wide variety of perspectives have pointed out many problems associated with the rise of modernity: every sphere of life has been affected and the consequences, albeit in uneven ways, stretch across the globe. Some of the problems are:

Manichean: approach to culture in which all values and concepts are split into binary opposites, one that is positive (which is white) and one that is negative (black).

▷ Domination by the West and North: Western cultural hegemony
▷ Political colonisation and subjugation: **Manichean** worldview
▷ Male domination, militarism and male violence
▷ Economic alienation, Fordist production: deskilling, rigid routine, competition
▷ Capitalism and impoverishment of the masses: increasing gap between rich and poor
▷ Bureaucratic forms of administration and surveillance: dehumanisation
▷ Technical production and rise of instrumental rationalities
▷ Radical separation of lifeworld: work/home/leisure; public-private
▷ Loss of meaning: dependence on things, commodity fetishism
▷ Urbanisation and crowding: pace and complexity
▷ Ideologies of oppression: sexism, racism, nationalism, homophobia
▷ Performance principle: demands for further work, cooptation of proletariat

| BOX 4 | Modernity and its disorders *(continued)* |

▷ 'Master narratives' of progress, competition, success
▷ Environmental and ecological destruction

Modernity and the rise of 'techniques of resistance'

However, as suggested above, modernity is not all of one piece; it would be churlish not to mention some positive achievement, without which it would not be possible even to raise the idea of emancipation. Above all, there has been resistance; despotic regimes have fallen, workers have gained benefits, the lot for some women has improved, the tide of colonialism has been reversed, apartheid is behind us. Apart from its horrors, modernity has also spawned Marxism, socialism, feminism, anti-racism, democracy, trade unions, human rights, women's liberation, liberation theology, Négritude and Black Consciousness. If there are techniques and strategies of oppression, of 'governing the soul' (Rose, 1990), then modernity has also inventively produced many techniques of resistance: boycotts, martyrdom, strikes, go-slows, hunger strikes, sit-ins, pamphleteering, marches, slogans, protests, guerrilla warfare, passive resistance, disruptions, bra burning, consciousness-raising, self-help groups and charters of demands. In many cases, they heroically required that bodies be put on the front line. Such 'techniques of resistance' require positive attributes of humanity – courage, hope, communication, trust, togetherness, resilience, fortitude, effort, forgiveness, self-sacrifice, vision and collectivity of purpose. High ideals; and the very antithesis of the dark side of modernity. Yet these characteristics and values are also the fruits and legacies of that historical period we call the modern era. It is not for nothing that Nelson Mandela is so revered in so many parts of the modern world.

PSYCHOLOGY AND ITS VICISSITUDES

For many, the notion of a liberation psychology is something of an oxymoron. Psychology, as an institution, is, of course, an offering of modernity, and carries with it many of the contradictions of its parent. It is the dark side of psychology, however, its complicity with Western imperialism, its support of racism, its often bizarre views on women, its class bias and collusion with colonial regimes and conservative politics, that renders it – to some mirthful onlookers – as the very antithesis of critical, emancipatory endeavours. But the problem is not just that psychology has sometimes behaved badly, collaborating with racism, sexism and exploitation, but also that psychology almost by definition undermines critical social thinking through its idea of the individual who is made the source and focus of all problems, allowing the social world to fade into the background. How then to imagine a critical, liberatory psychology? One task for a liberation psychology is to be critical of psychology itself; it is part of the problem.

Critiques of psychology from within

Psychology has probably always had its critics from outside, but a significant shift took place from the late 1960s when the sharpest critics came from inside the discipline (Baritz, 1960; Gergen, 1994; Parker, 1989; Parker & Spears, 1996; Sampson, 1993a, 1993b). These critical writings, in both Britain and US-America increased sharply in the 1990s and were considerably enhanced by a rising tide of feminist psychologists (Bohan, 1992; Burman, 1990, 1998; Mary Gergen, 2001; Gergen & Davies, 1997; Hare-Mustin & Maracek, 1990; Gilligan, 1982; Hekman, 1995; Hollway, 1989; Kitzinger, 1987; Mama, 1995; Morawski, 1994; Squire, 1989; Wilkinson, 1996 to name only some of them). Influenced by many intellectual currents, mainly from outside of psychology such as the 'linguistic turn', feminism, post-structuralism, semiotics, cultural studies, and micro-sociology, these critics began to forge new directions under the broad labels of **social constructionism**, discursive psychology or critical psychology.

The 1960s and 1970s – new types of critique

How did this come about? A number of strands – some inside, some on the margins and some outside of psychology – both in US-America and Europe, contributed to the construction of a 'crisis', an intensive period of critical appraisal from the mid-1960s through the 1970s. I provide a brief list of some of the most substantial of such critical responses:

1. Crisis in social psychology. Within the political contexts of the civil rights struggles and anti-Vietnam war in the USA, student and worker revolts in Europe (eg 'Paris, 1968') and the revitalisation of 'second wave' feminism, commentators labelled a number of 'crises' in mainstream psychology. The crisis of 'relevance' referred to the lack of serious engagement with political issues of the day; the 'crisis' of methods saw problems in predominantly experimental methods, and problems due to discoveries of 'demand' and 'experimenter effects'. There were concerns about the ahistorical nature of the discipline and worries about the philosophy of science and individual-istic assumptions underpinning psychology. Psychology had simply uncritically adopted the dominant ideas of science and the individual, without any reflection on where these ideas came from or what interests they served. Some argued that psychology itself was ideological, serving to sustain and reproduce the dominant order. Much of this criticism came from scholars within the field of psychology.

Social constructionism: paradigm of knowledge based on the idea that events, objects and selves – including all the psychological stuff that goes on 'inside individuals' heads' – do not have a pre-given or essential reality, but are constituted through the language we use to describe them.

2. From Europe, in the early 1970s, leading scholars such as Tajfel, Moscovici and Rom Harré, criticised the American domination and its individualistic bias, calling for a more adequate *social* theory of psychology. New journals and new associations were formed in Europe to counter the American bias and domination. Among other achievements this led to the rise of alternative approaches such as 'social identity theory', 'social representations' and ethogenics.

3. The considerable influence of Thomas Kuhn's (1962) book on the philosophy of science, led many to see 'crises' and new 'paradigms'; despite fuzziness in the meaning of the term, the notion of 'new paradigms' became almost a slogan of the time.

4. The anti-psychiatry movement of the 1960s led to critical debates about the meaning of 'madness'. Writings by R.D. Laing, David Cooper, Goffman, Foucault and Szasz, from differing directions were influential in criticising mainstream thinking and practice. These could be regarded as writings from the margins of psychology.

5. The difficult reinterpretations of psychoanalysis by Lacan, pushed new debates and assisted in the 'linguistic turn'; more writings from the margins.

6. From outside psychology, Foucault, Derrida and Barthes assisted in drawing out new thinking on meaning, interpretation and discourse from semiotics and post-structuralism.

7. In Europe, in the wake of late 1960s uprisings, there was a revitalisation of, and intense debates about the contributions of Marxism, fanned further by cold-war politics. In the 1970s Freud's works were published in Penguin paperbacks and became readily available to a new generation of students.

8. From the margins of psychology, there was new interest in the micro-sociology of social ordering, particularly in the 'dramaturgical' views of Goffman and the 'ethnomethodology' of Garfinkel. Later works by Sacks put 'conversation analysis', another linguistic turn, on the map.

9. Anti-colonial struggles fed into this mix. For example the influential works of Frantz Fanon, from the Fifties, were only translated into English from 1967 and suddenly became widely available to greater audiences.

10. The emergence of new transdisciplinary areas such as cultural studies, influenced by a range of theories from Marxism, post-colonialism, feminism and semiotics, gave new impetus to rethinking racism and subjectivity through important writers such as Stuart Hall, Homi Bhabha, Edward Said and Paul Gilroy.

11. Cutting across all these currents, voices from feminists presented widespread criticisms of psychology: androcentric bias, misogyny, inadequate theorising on gender, sexuality, psychopathology and the body; problems of method. Spaces were offered for feminist standpoint theory and qualitative methods used in more participatory and democratic ways.

Social identity theory (SIT): psychological *and* social perspective on identity in which the formation of social identities, 'us' and 'them', was seen as the key ingredient in group domination. Here both individual processes – such as categorisation and comparison across groups – *as well as* social processes – the perceived legitimacy of group relations, the capacity to see alternatives, the rigidity or fluidity of boundaries between groups – were viewed as operative in the formation of social identities.

12. Most pervasive of all was the 'linguistic turn', which emphasised the para-
     mount importance of language, discourse, meaning and interpretation
     for the human and social sciences. Drawing on various scholars, both
     ancient – the Greek rhetoricians (Billig, 1987) – and modern, and
     different schools (semiotics, hermeneutics, post-structuralism), it was
     this turn that produced the new psychology of discourse, rhetoric,
     conversation, dialogism, constructionism, and provided new critical
     devices for ideology critique.

A 'new paradigm' of critique in the social sciences?

The gestation period took some time, from the 'crises' in the 1960s to the
'establishment' in the late 1980s of constructionist and discursive views.
Nevertheless, there is something approximating a 'new paradigm' here; nor is
it confined to psychology, it has swept across the human and social sciences. It
is still on the margins of psychology: mainstream psychology marches on;
disdainful, haughty, aloof – claiming that these new fangled ideas are not
'science'. It is also a hotly contested terrain. Marxists, socialists and some feminists are deeply suspicious of its philosophical 'idealism', the primacy given to
language rather than the 'materialism' of economic conditions. 'Realists' worry
about the potential slide into 'relativism' and the lack of a firm grounding for
political action (see Parker, 1998), and an underestimation of materiality and
history (Foster, 1999; Hook, 2001). Such debates are ongoing, but there is
enough of a meta-theoretical core for this to be regarded as a major challenge
to the positivistic methods and practices of mainstream psychology.

Social constructionism

What is the kernel of the social constructionist position? It appears to be
twofold. First, it has a critical agenda: if the social order is seen as constructed,
then it can be deconstructed – that is, analytically taken apart, disassembled,
to see how it was built up – in order to reconstruct it in a better way. Two
metaphors are at work here, one a building metaphor of a site of construction,
and the other a narrative metaphor, that of inventing a story-line, plot, characters and events, as in a novel, play, opera or dance. All could be investigated to
see how they are put together to constitute a whole piece, a pattern, an 'assem-
blage' (Foucault, 1982), the equivalent, if you like, of ideology critique.
Secondly, it has an epistemological agenda, an issue of the philosophy of
knowledge: How do we know things? If our only way of knowing is through the
vehicle of language, of re-presentation, then there is no other bedrock, there
are no external referents, there is no absolute scientific method for knowledge
claims. This also has an emancipatory implication, since it offers the promise
of unmasking other taken-for-granted knowledges which proclaim themselves

Meta-narrative: privileged form of explanation, an account, a story or a theoretical system that is treated as superior to all others in its explanatory abilities.

as self-evident truths. It also raises a whole raft of other problems which cannot be dealt with here (see Phillips & Jorgensen, 2002). Suffice to say there is a realist stance within constructionism, which holds that just because it is constructed does not mean it is not real in actuality or in consequences. Because racism and its postulated claim of different 'race' groups has been constructed over many centuries, it does not mean that it is not lived out as real. Furthermore, constructionism does not rule out in principle that material as well as discursive or ideological factors are involved, for instance, in the construction of racism or patriarchy.

An anti-essentialist view of subjectivity

This new critical psychology (the term has been deployed only in recent years, but has far deeper roots in the 'critical theory' of the Frankfurt School from the 1930s) holds an **anti-essentialist** view of subjectivity, that is to say, persons are not fixed, predetermined, immutable or unchanging essences. Rather, persons as subjects, self-aware and with capacities for action, are made up in relation to other persons; we are positioned, and also actively position ourselves, through 'investments' (Hollway, 1989) in certain kinds of selves. In this view, subjectivity is quintessentially social, and we manoeuvre positionings *between* discourses, other people and conditions of possibility. Selves are temporally and partially fixed locations or positions (spatial metaphors), not things or entities, and they can be relocated and repositioned in new configurations. In this view, subjectivities cannot break free of the spatialised locations, since we are constituted in and through them, but we can reconfigure and reconstruct the relational positions to make up new subjectivities. In short, change and transformation are possible.

Discerning readers might argue that change does not occur as easily as perhaps indicated above. Indeed, as we witness in everyday life, let alone in severely oppressive conditions, neither people nor social forms change speedily or readily. Akin to a language, which at any particular time is relatively fixed, and cannot merely be altered by free choice, transformation is historical, sometimes slow and always entails struggle. That it may be slow and difficult does not suggest as some pessimists pontificate, that change is not possible, that it is not in our 'nature' or that history inevitably repeats itself. On the contrary, change is everywhere, is rather inevitable since neither technology nor culture nor language remains static. The question is rather: What sort of change?, since oppressive relations continue to persist but constantly change their forms and disguises. Constructionist psychologies offer some analytical tools for genuine, if difficult, transfigurations.

Anti-essentialism: approach to subjectivity (amongst other things) which suggests that persons are not fixed, predetermined, immutable or unchanging essences. Rather, persons as subjects, self-aware and with capacities for action, are made up in relation to other persons; we are positioned, and also actively position ourselves, in certain kinds of selves. Subjectivity is taken to be quintessentially social; we are thought to manoeuvre positionings between discourses.

Psychology and critique in South Africa

What about psychology in South Africa? At first sight, it would appear that we are at the periphery and that psychology mainly happens elsewhere, particularly in US-America. Sadly, that is largely the case. Psychology has been, and currently still is, largely a Western practice and discipline, many of its products are exported all over the world; a form of cultural imperialism, if you like. Nevertheless, particularly from the early 1980s, a minority of South African psychologists began to develop a critical voice in response to apartheid.

Since its beginnings in the 1920s, psychology in South Africa has not evidenced much resistance to racism nor, after 1948, against apartheid. Many writers have attested to racism in psychology, and its complicity with apartheid (see Duncan, Van Niekerk, De la Rey & Seedat, 2001; Bulhan, 1993; Butchart, 1998; Durrheim & Mokeki, 1997; Foster, 1991a, 1993a; Nicholas & Cooper, 1990; Nicholas, 1993; Seedat, 1993). Very little, apart from MacCrone (1937, 1949) and Lambley (1980), was written on the psychology of apartheid, and for most of the century, psychology was in white, and male, hands (Seedat, 1997). Few black psychologists were trained, and it was only from the 1970s that a prominent black scholar, Chabani Manganyi (1973, 1977, 1981, 1991), as part of the Black Consciousness movement, began to write about the psychological experience of a black person, viewed as 'a prisoner in enforced confinement peeping through the keyhole of his desolate cell' (Manganyi, 1981, 1).

Organisations of a progressive psychology

It was from 1983 that alternative organisations, openly opposed to apartheid, and a progressive journal (*Psychology in Society*) were formed and even then most 'progressive psychology' remained largely in 'white hands'. Apart from Manganyi, it was only from the mid-1980s that psychologists produced work on racism and the oppressive situation in South Africa (Dawes, 1985; Foster, Davis & Sandler, 1987; Foster, 1991a; Nicholas & Cooper, 1990; Nicholas, 1993). It was only in this period that the history of psychology in South Africa began to be mapped (Louw, 1986; Foster, 1990) and feminist perspectives made a late appearance (Levett, 1988). A new organisation, free of the taints of the apartheid era, the Psychological Society of South Africa (PsySSA) was established in 1994 and black leadership quickly emerged. A special issue of the *South African Journal of Psychology*, entirely devoted to black scholarship, appeared in 1997, while other issues attending to post-modernism and gender issues appeared during the 1990s. The year 1997 saw the publication of the first volume directed to mental health policy issues (Foster, Freeman & Pillay, 1997), while matters related to children's adversity (Burman & Reynolds, 1986; Dawes & Donald, 1994) were dealt with by Donald, Dawes & Louw (2000).

Through the 1990s regular conferences on qualitative methods provided a forum for psychologists with a critical voice (see Hook, Terre Blanche & Bhavnani, 1999). Mohamed Seedat (1997) put out an agenda, 'a yearning and quest for liberatory psychology' (267) which among other issues called to 'resist the imposition of Euro-American epistemological and philosophical domination' (263).

Although the trajectory and the issues were different from those in Europe and US-America, it was over roughly the same period, the past twenty years, that a critical and potentially liberatory psychology developed in South Africa. The direct context was struggle against apartheid and codified racism, but there was also an awareness of the wider spheres of anti-imperialism, the plight of low-income countries and the rising tide of feminism. Throughout this period there were repeated calls for 'relevance', for a 'progressive' psychology which would deliver 'appropriate' and more community-oriented (Seedat, Duncan & Lazarus, 2001) social services to the oppressed and victims of apartheid. There were attempts to deliver supportive services to political detainees, to poor communities, to rape survivors and to children. The 'progressive' psychology organisations aligned themselves with major political movements. Psychologists gave evidence on behalf of the oppressed in political trials. Forums were established to develop the 'voice' of black, women and marginalised scholars (De la Rey, Duncan, Shefer & Van Niekerk, 1997). Advocacy was stepped up and called for appropriate attention to 'cultural' and local aspects (Swartz, 1997) and for the indigenisation and Africanisation of psychology. Books and articles appeared which set psychology in the local southern African context, a turn against cultural imperialism. Local progressive psychologists formed alliances with critical counterparts elsewhere in the world, and after the academic boycott era there was increased dialogue (see Levett, Kottler, Burman & Parker, 1997). Although the process has been uneven and has involved a minority of psychologists, a reasonably significant gain has been made in South Africa towards a genuinely critical and emancipatory voice. There is still, of course, much to be done.

In the next two sections, our attention is turned to questions about the psychology of oppression as well as the consequences of domination and oppression. Has psychological theory given us much of an understanding of these processes?

THE PSYCHOLOGY OF OPPRESSION

Since an earlier section has discussed the general contours of oppression, this section will limit its focus to psychological approaches. Taken across the broad face of psychology, it is not surprising, given its individualistic bias, to find that not much attention has been given to oppression and social domination.

Nevertheless there are some interesting views that bear mention, and three approaches are briefly covered here: authoritarianism, social identity theory and social dominance theory.

Authoritarianism

In efforts to explain the rising tide of fascism in Europe from the late 1920s, a number of influential thinkers from the Frankfurt School (Fromm, Horkheimer, Adorno) drew on the notion of **authoritarianism** as a mediating construct between economics, politics and psychology. At the most general level, authoritarianism denotes a tendency to submit willingly to strong authority figures above and to act abusively to weaker groups below. In its earlier formulation it is one of few theories that attempt to link economic and subjective factors. Capitalism required docile and submissive workers; one way to achieve this was through an authoritarian culture, and the family was its vehicle. Harsh, punitive and overbearing family processes formed the socialisation soil for this kind of social character, in which potential hostility to higher authority figures was channelled safely away by means of ego defences such as displacement and projection onto purportedly inferior out-groups. As a result, authoritarians are characterised by fierce ethnocentrism (in-group patriotism and submissiveness to strong in-group leaders) and a generalised tendency towards discrimination and hostility to out-groups or allegedly inferior 'others'.

After the publication of the influential volume by Adorno and others in US-America in 1950, the theory sadly took an individualistic turn. In the hands of psychologists who viewed the construct as a 'personality type', it lost its links to social processes, and was endlessly measured without bringing much further light. There was more fussing about the measurement device (the F-Scale) than there was about the theoretical links to capitalism, the state or generalised political culture. The theory seemed to be in decline. Billig (1978), for instance, in a study of actual fascists in Britain, claimed that it was only partially useful, but couldn't account for the propensity for violence and the 'conspiracy mentality' that characterised real fascists.

Right-wing authoritarianism

Fortunately, the careful and measured research of Canadian Bob Altemeyer (1981, 1988, 1996) has revived the concept under the label of '**right-wing authoritarianism**' and found robust links with **ethnocentrism**, prejudice, support for conservative policies and anti-democratic tendencies. In South Africa, authoritarianism was steadily investigated from the 1950s as an explanation for apartheid, with mixed fortunes. John Duckitt (1992), influenced by Altemeyer, found solid links between right-wing authoritarianism and anti-

Authoritarianism: tendency to submit willingly to strong authority figures above and to act punitively towards weaker groups below. In its earlier formulation it is one of few theories that attempt to link economic and subjective factors.

Right-wing authoritarianism: form of authoritarianism with robust links to ethnocentrism, prejudice, support for conservative policies and anti-democratic tendencies.

Ethnocentrism: belief in the superiority of one's own ethnic group.

black racism, in-group propensities and resistance to democracy. Duckitt, however, saw authoritarianism as an intergroup orientation, in the manner of social identity theory, and not as a personality type. There may be something, after all, in the theory first introduced in fascist Germany in the 1930s.

Social identity theory (SIT)

Disappointed with, and in reaction to the individualism of American thinking, Tajfel (1981) – notably a member of the underground resistance in wartime Europe – and colleagues developed a view which incorporated both psychological and social perspectives. The formation of social identities, 'us' and 'them', was seen as the key ingredient in group domination. Both individual processes such as categorisation and social comparison across groups, as well as social processes – the perceived legitimacy of the group relations, the capacity to see alternatives, the rigidity or fluidity of boundaries between groups – were viewed as operative in the formation of social identities. If neither side perceived of alternatives, and ceded a degree of legitimacy to the situation, then intergroup domination would remain intact. A strength of the SIT approach has been to go beyond mere description of the status quo and to theorise about various strategies of resistance, ranging from redefinition of social identities to physical rebellion. It has been used with some success to account for the intergroup conflict in apartheid South Africa (Foster & Louw-Potgieter, 1991), and remains a useful tool in analysis of both domination and social change. Its central argument is that change requires a substantial shift in the *relations* between groups, not within individuals; social change involves *collective activity*. Two areas of weakness are evident: perhaps it does not have a sufficient account of ideology or of power, and it is inadequate in explaining gender or class relations.

Social identity theory (SIT): sees both individual processes and social processes as operative in the formation of 'social identities'. Importantly, SIT goes beyond simply describing the status quo; it actively theorises strategies of resistance, from the redefinition of social identities to actual physical rebellion.

Social dominance theory (SDT)

Working towards a general intergroup theory of social hierarchy and oppression, Sidanuis & Pratto (1999) argue that there are three basic systems of disproportionate social power based on age, gender and arbitrary-set systems (eg based on 'race', class, ethnicity, caste, class, estate, region, religion or any other constructions). Dominance, that is to say, is driven by three main processes:

▷ *aggregated individual discrimination* – daily, simple, quite inconspicuous individual acts;

▷ *aggregated institutional discrimination* – group rules, procedures and actions of institutions, which also involves systematic terror; violence and threatened violence, particularly when subordinates are directly challenging;

Social dominance theory (SDT): general intergroup theory of social hierarchy and oppression which claims that dominance is driven by three main processes: *aggregated individual discrimination*, *aggregated institutional discrimination* and *behavioural asymmetry*.

Social dominance orientation (SDO): general orientation through which people favour hierarchically structured and non-egalitarian relationships between groups.

▷ *behavioural asymmetry* – involving differences in behavioural repertoires of group members at different levels of the hierarchy, in which subordinates evidence 'both passive and active cooperation with their own oppression' (43) and it is this which provides oppressive hierarchies with 'their remarkable degrees of resilience, robustness and stability' (43). Phenomena in this category include out-group favouritism or deference and self-debilitation.

The most psychological notion is the construct of **social dominance orientation** (SDO), 'defined as the degree to which individuals desire and support group-based hierarchy and the domination of "inferior" groups by "superior" groups' (48). Social dominance orientation is seen to vary in terms of four factors: first, dominant group members are likely to be higher; secondly, socialisation issues such as education, religion and personal experiences; thirdly, temperamental predispositions such as empathy; and fourthly, gender, in terms of which males are likely to evidence higher levels of SDO (see Box 5).

BOX 5   Social dominance orientation (SDO)

SDO is a general orientation through which people favour hierarchically structured and non-egalitarian relationships between groups. (Groups here constructed on any criterion.) Social dominance orientation is a unitary construct. It is weakly correlated with political conservatism and authoritarianism, but remains a distinct construct. The roots of SDO lie in three major influences: *socialising experiences, situational contingencies and temperament*.

Those high on SDO show:
▷   strong endorsement of the legitimising ideologies (in the USA, for example)

▷   strong endorsement for racism, sexism, nationalism, cultural elitism, patriotism, anti-Arab racism, anti-Asian immigrants
▷   a propensity for cruelty
▷   a negative relationship to empathy, communality and tolerance.

Who are those high on SDO? Men and boys are consistently higher than women and girls. Those in high-status groups are higher on SDO than those in lower-status groups. Men, whites and heterosexuals score higher on SDO than blacks, Hispanics, gays, lesbians, women and bisexuals.

Source: Sidanius & Pratto (1999).

This is a recent and promising approach to the psychology of oppression, and it has already established a good deal of empirical support. It claims to be distinct from authoritarianism. This is an important point, because the authoritarian claims submission to in-group authority whereas, in contrast, SDO refers to relations *between* groups. More wide-ranging than SIT, its strength lies in a claim of dealing with *all* forms of oppression. Its reference to the role of masculinity in all forms of dominance sets it apart from other mainstream approaches. Some, particularly constructionists, would carp at its reliance on mainstream positivist research tools, but it remains a theory to be followed with interest.

Other approaches to the psychology of oppression

The three approaches above do not exhaust psychological views on domination. Freudian psychoanalysis has long given other angles: the social order is stabilised through introjection of authority figures (the 'law of the father'), repression of hostile urges towards authorities, renunciation of libidinal urges enacted in various rituals (such as the incest taboo and totemic representations), and projection of hostility to figures lower in the hierarchy. Feminist scholars have used psychoanalysis to theorise the complexity and ongoing conundrums of gender/sex domination (Benjamin, 1988; Butler, 1990). A potential problem with the three dominant psychological views described here is that they may ride roughshod over nuances, subtleties and unconscious processes which could be precisely where the tenacities of oppression actually occur.

PSYCHOLOGICAL CONSEQUENCES OF OPPRESSION

There is a surprisingly long history of writings on the consequences of oppression, beginning in the 1920s with work on the negative effects of stereotyping (see Foster, 1993b for an overview). Each successive decade seemed to bring new concepts and terms from a wide variety of writers and diverse contexts, yet across the span of the 20th century we are able to witness 'remarkable convergences in patterns identified' (Moane, 1999, 83). I shall provide a hasty historical tour here (all references to be found in Foster, 1993b).

Oppression and identity

In the 1930s, Stonequist suggested a 'marginal personality' (characterised by self-pity, identity conflicts and insecurity) among those caught between two conflicting groups. In the 1940s, Kenneth and Mamie Clark produced research which claimed that black children suffered from 'misidentification', a form of out-group preference and identification. This introduced a line of six decades of work which generally supported the original findings (see Foster, 1994). Also in the 1940s Bruno Bettleheim claimed a form of defence among Nazi concentration camp victims described as 'identification with the aggressors'. In the late 1940s both Sartre and Kurt Lewin spoke of Jewish 'self-hatred' as a response to anti-Semitism.

The 'mark of oppression'

In 1951, psychiatrists Kardiner and Ovesey published a book entitled *Mark of Oppression*, claiming that black Americans suffered a range of problems emanating from low self-esteem and aggression, producing anxiety, self-abnegation, ingratiation, denial of aggression with a cover of humour and affability, passivity and general constriction of emotions. This became a hotly contested work, since the majority of their black 'subjects' also happened to be psychotherapy patients. In the following year 1952 Frantz Fanon produced his celebrated *Black skin, white masks*, which described adverse consequences of colonialism. In 1957 Memmi reported on negative aspects of colonial stereotyping.

The 'damage thesis'

During the 1960s in America, numerous scholars continued to report on the 'damage' thesis, but with the rise of the civil rights, anti-colonial and black power movements, writers such as Tom Pettigrew, Robert Coles, Grier & Cobb, Malcolm X, Kenneth Clark, Carmichael & Hamilton, and the later 'sociogenic' writings of Fanon also reported on resilience, 'moving against', strength, resistance and 'black rage'. While some were seeing strength and uprising, others in the 1960s saw the origins of damage thesis in blacks themselves – in the black family, in black subculture, in the black ghetto – a form of victim-blaming. It was a contested decade.

Theorising resistance to oppression

Since the 1970s there has been heaps more evidence on the damage thesis, renewed by the added voice of feminists claiming 'fear of success', damaged sexuality, an orientation to others and low self-worth, but there have also been sustained efforts to revise and reformulate the 'mark of oppression' claim. At the core of this revision has been an effort to restore a more positive conception of oppressed people, to emphasise pride, solidarity and activity. Revisionist theories also produced arguments and research which emphasised coping, buffering and protective processes of the self and oppressed communities. The post-1970s literature also emphasised resistance, defiance and rebellion, no longer just a passive form of subjectivity. Subjectivity was viewed as multiple and complex rather than totally self-contained. For instance, racism should be:

> ... seen as texturing subjectivities rather than determining black social and emotional life ... race is only ever one among many dimensions of subjectivity and it never constitutes the totality of an individual's internal life (Mama, 1995. 111–112).

Rather than offering a passive conceptualisation of subjectivity, Revisionist theories of the 1970s produced arguments and research which emphasised coping, buffering and protective processes of the self and oppressed communities.

Psychological defence and identity development

With a focus on the concept of 'alienation', which carries with it a sense of critique – criticism of social conditions which stunt the full potential of humankind – Bulhan (1985) gave a synthesis of the revisionist thesis in terms of three major forms of psychological defence and identity development among oppressed people:

▷ *Capitulation*: involving defensive processes akin to identification with the aggressor, enhanced assimilation into dominant culture and rejection of own group culture. This is the classic 'mark of oppression' phenomenon.
▷ *Revitalisation:* resilience and resistance, and active repudiation of dominant culture and a defensive romanticism of indigenous cultures.
▷ *Radicalisation*: synthesis of the earlier 'moments' along with an unambiguous commitment to radical change.

In Bulhan's view these three strategic moments could also be seen as historical stages. The three psychohistorical moments or patterns will vary across time, space and specific social conditions. For Bulhan, all three forms may co-exist in each person or among a generation of oppressed people. Alternatively, one pattern may predominate, but not eclipse entirely the other tendencies. The co-variation of these tendencies holds serious implications for the degree and form of alienation but also for resistance and praxis.

Implications of the 'scars of bondage'

What is the upshot of our brief historical tour of the 'scars of bondage' (Alverson, 1978) thesis? First, the mark of oppression is not simply a psychological state that exists, or is there, but rather a formulation which operates in a sea of discourses about such a purported state. These discourses change over time, and vary due to politicocultural conditions. Secondly, it embodies a paradox; claims of 'damage' and claims of strength, positive qualities and active resistance. Bulhan's (1985) view captures this paradox and offers a useful synthesis. Thirdly, the more recent revisionist notions come chiefly from among dominated groups, and it is these 'voices' which have recognised strength, pride and resistance along with the 'scars' and 'marks'.

Is it possible to provide a cogent integration of views on the psychological consequences of oppression? Given the remarkable convergence of themes, it does seem feasible; Moane (1999) suggests four main themes. Presented in a slightly adapted form, these four consequential themes are:

1. *Subjectivity*: Top of the list is the notion of doubling, a division in self-consciousness, of a Manichean worldview (Fanon, 1952/1967) – dividing the world into 'us' and 'them', good and bad. On the one hand, the oppressed is oriented towards the oppressor, partially taking on those values, assimilating the language and cultural practices of the colonisers;

the notion of out-group identification. On the other hand, owing to negative stereotypes, the oppressed take on negative views of self, acting in accordance with myths of superiority; denial and perhaps hatred of blackness, in Fanon's view. Feminists have pointed to similar themes. Women are oriented towards others, attuned to the mood of the dominant group, thus less aware of own needs, creating dependency and a sense of inferiority, stigma, shame and anxiety.

2. *Emotional expression*: Strong emotions such as anger and rage are inhibited and constricted or denied due to fears of ridicule, retaliation or claims of overreaction. Emotions linked to anxiety, fear, uncertainty and ambivalence predominate.

3. *Intragroup relations*: One of the most widely reported consequences of oppression is that of horizonal hostility or lateral violence; due to difficulties of directing violence towards the dominant group it is turned against the in-group, including domestic violence. South Africa under apartheid was no exception to this pattern and it still appears to manifest in the forms of gangster violence, hostile criminality, rape and domestic abuse. Interpersonal relations among oppressed people are contradictory: on the one hand, solidarity, empathy and understanding due to shared experiences; on the other hand, a pattern of hostility and aggression. These contradictory patterns carry over into sexual relationships.

4. *Mental health issues*: It is not surprising that among those who have the least resources and who face the greatest hardships of daily living, the rate of mental health problems is likely to be elevated. Women, for instance, are reported to manifest higher rates in a range of disorders including depression, neuroses and anxiety-related problems. Addictions and extensive substance abuse create spirals of despair and helplessness. Direct violence from state-related agents in the form of shootings, detention and torture set up further cycles of mental health problems. Harassment and surveillance by security police create climates of fear, stress and suspicion. Stressors of daily living take their toll and susceptibility is arguably greater among the more vulnerable: the unemployed, children, youth and women. Analysing the lives of township youth in the violence-torn zones of mid-1980s South Africa, Gill Straker (1992) described a situation of continuous, relentless traumatic stress and numerous signs of disturbance, including substance abuse, psychosomatic symptoms, anxiety and chronic post-traumatic stress disorders, 'sufficiently severe to interfere with their functioning in life' (1992, 34). Yet a minority among these black youths, both girls and boys, showed strength and resilience, were symptom-free, and 'represent strongly functioning individuals in their communities' (1992, 33). Mental health issues do constitute problems for oppressed people, exacerbated by a lack of support and services, but some also show

courage, resilience and resourceful leadership in meaningful acts of rebellion. In similar fashion, Robert Jay Lifton (1993) has shown that the very multiplicity and fluidity of selfhood – a Protean self, after the Greek sea god of many forms – enables people to transcend vicious hardships. He reports numerous cases of people who despite pain and trauma, were able to 'transmute that trauma in various expressions of insight, compassion and innovation' (Lifton, 1993, 7).

Dialogical oppression and effects on oppressors

The topic of consequences for the oppressed would be incomplete without raising two further issues. The first refers to the *relational* aspect of oppression. There are two sides; it is **dialogical** in form. The apartheid state reacted to uprisings in black townships by further cycles of repression and violence, creating a spiral of violence. Oppressors are dependent upon the oppressed, and their supposed inferiority, for their own self-image of superiority. The second issue refers to consequences for the oppressors; they may differ in form, but there are at least three areas implicating psychological patterns. One area suggests a **Nero complex** involving obsessions with establishing legitimacy and self-justification (Moane, 1999). This may involve self-delusions, arrogance, narcissism and a sense of entitlement (Foster, 2000). A second area involves processes of dehumanisation and objectification, a form of emotional blunting, if you like. Oppressors lose feelings and empathy for the disadvantaged, and transform this into discourses of victim-blaming (the poor are idle, lazy and indolent), and frequently advocate further punitive treatment for those labelled as inferior. Oppressors lose a sense of justice and fairness.

Dialogical:
taking the form of a dialogue.

Nero complex:
obsessive preoccupation with establishing legitimacy and justification for one's acts and oneself, accompanied by delusions of arrogance, entitlement and narcissism.

The denial of oppression

A third area entails denial in many forms – turning a blind eye, seeing what we want to see, blocking out awareness. Those in dominant positions commonly deny the extent or even the occurrence of atrocities. Recently, Stan Cohen (2001) has written wisely on this matter of denial. It takes various forms: outright denial (it didn't happen); discrediting the source and method of report (biased, gullible); renaming and retelling (it was not quite like that); and justification (it did happen, but it was morally defensible). This was standard fare in apartheid South Africa. When my own research on torture in South Africa appeared in the turbulent mid-1980s, both the state and the Afrikaner press went to considerable lengths to deny the matter, using rhetorical devices of outraged denial along with discrediting the research and the researcher (Foster et al, 1987). Denial serves to justify a lack of any action. Dominant orders become blind to the suffering of others.

Jingoism

Jingoism:
extreme types of nationalism characterised by both fierce patriotism and an aggressive attitude to other countries or nationalities.

Over a hundred years ago, Hobson (1901) wrote an interesting book on 'Jingoism' – a term not much heard these days – which tells us a good deal about the psychology and rhetoric of dominant classes (see Box 6). Jingoism involves self-deceit, justification of brutality, a one-sided view, arrogance, bizarre reasoning, no empathy for the other, dishonesty, denial and the active silencing of alternative perspectives. This orientation was manufactured and fuelled by institutions; rhetoric from the press, political platforms and from the clergy. Although the style, language and expression is very different from that of Cohen's (2001) analysis of denial, both tell us much about the psychology of continuing oppression. These books ring out clarion calls at the present time of war in Iraq. Two books, exactly a hundred years apart, with remarkably convergent insights; this should make us reflect anew!

BOX 6   The psychology of Jingoism

In a book highly critical of English views which promoted and pushed the Boer War, J.A. Hobson in 1901 set out the main principles of **Jingoism** – a 'coarse patriotism', a feeding of a 'neurotic imagination', a form of 'national hate'. It is a product of 'civilised' communities, and involves an 'astonishing credulity' of the educated class, fed by a biased press, by political platforms and the 'bishops and clergy' who are 'so impressed by the "cleansing", "bracing", "fortifying" influences of war' (60).

Jingoism is characterised by:

▷ Vainglory – which credits the one side of the story, entails an 'infantile vanity', the 'mind of the people is swollen with pride' and 'boastful claims'.
▷ Lack of heed to 'instructive criticism' by others of the dominant group.
▷ Mental 'collapse' and mental confusion exhibiting itself in 'grotesque reasoning' (73).

▷ Eclipse of humour – particularly that humour which aids reason in 'detecting palpable inconsistencies and absurdities'.
▷ An appeal to 'the inevitable' – as in the notion that the 'superior nation inevitably gets the upper hand'; as in the 'inevitability of conflict' (90).
▷ An attitude of dishonesty – 'profess to be convinced from evidence' but 'refuses to apply reasonable tests' to the 'evidence' of one side.
▷ A conspiracy mentality – readily sees conspiracies as the source of evil among 'others'.
▷ A silencing of opposition voices – an 'abuse of platform and pulpit' in which people opposed to war were 'subjected to personal assaults and insult, their property was damaged, and the law gave them neither protection nor redress – full license for expression on one side, contumelious repression on the other' (127).

Source: J.A. Hobson (1901). *The psychology of Jingoism.*

TOWARDS AN EMANCIPATORY PSYCHOLOGY

What is to be done; how do we go forward? Big questions; perhaps only little answers. I think we recognise, now, in the early phases of the 21st century that the idea, the ideals, of emancipation stretch way beyond the 'big five' – political oppression, patriarchy, economic exploitation, cultural imperialism and ecological destruction – to many 'smaller' sites and regions of domination such as sexuality, spirituality, health, aesthetics, mental status, technology, disability and age (the list could be a long one; see Box 7). Questions of emancipation would stretch even further, as Freud richly recognised, to the capillaries of our psychic lives, the bonds that enslave us – neuroses, anxieties, addictions, **habitus**, appetites, debilitating emotions. Indeed, it is the central thesis of this chapter that the 'large' and the 'small' are intertwined; the 'personal is political', as feminists have taught us. In this regard, many of the Psy disciplines (Rose, 1990, 1996) are part of the problem.

Habitus:
a mediating link between objective social structures and individual action. It involves a set of dispositions that incline agents (persons) to act and react in certain patterned and fairly habitual ways.

BOX 7   Constitution of South Africa

The chapter on the Bill of Rights of the new Constitution of South Africa states that neither the state nor any person may 'unfairly discriminate directly or indirectly' against anyone on grounds including:

> race, gender, sex, pregnancy, marital status, ethnic or social origin, colour, sexual orientation, age, disability, religion, conscience, belief, culture, language and birth (para 9(3)).

The Constitution further established rights in terms of freedom of expression, assembly, demonstration, association, movement and residence, freedom of trade, occupation and profession, children's rights and property rights. It also sets out expression of good intent in terms of the environment, water, health care, housing and social security, education and access to information, all linked to a range of legal and justiciable rights.

This new Constitution may not be perfect, but this is a rather substantial list of protective rights.

Collective support in resistance

If there is one central lesson to be learned from psychology, mainstream or alternative, it is that resistance entails *collective* activity. From the conformity studies of Asch in the 1950s, from Milgram's research on obedience in the 1960s, from Moscovici's (1976) work on minority influence, and from Roger Brown's (1986) account of social change, we learn one thing, that we need the support of others to resist top-down influence. Although crowds were earlier seen as negative and dangerous, as in the notion of 'mob mentality' (Le Bon, 1896), over the course of the 20th century we began to see crowd action, literally bodies being put on the line, as the source of resistance, change and innovation. Crowd action played a significant part in resistance against apartheid (Foster, 1991b). Solidarity and communality provide the source for resistance, while new alternatives and strategies for action emerge only

Resistance entails collective activity, just as liberation requires praxis, that is the combination of political forms of reflection and action.

Praxis: notion that both *reflection* (awareness, self-consciousness, consciousness-raising) and *action* (visible protests, marches, taking-up-arms) are required to effect social transformation.

through collective discourses. There is a second major lesson to be learned, this time primarily from revolutionary and critical writings: that liberation requires **praxis.** The notion of praxis suggests that both *reflection* (awareness, self-consciousness, consciousness-raising) and *action* (visible protests, marches, taking-up-arms) are required to effect social transformation.

Common requirements of a liberatory psychology

Is it possible to discern themes or clusters of prerequisites for a liberatory psychology? Drawing on a wide range of writings, there does appear to be a convergence towards a consolidated scenario of requirements. This is an attempt, despite misgivings, at an integration across all sites and forms of oppressions – gendered, political, economic – while recognising that each site would entail varying specifics. As heterosexual feminists oft remind us, 'sleeping with the enemy' entails quite different dynamics from those involved in, say, opposition to racism in which men and women may struggle in solidarity. Such cautions should be noted; nevertheless, I suggest five clusters of common requirements:

Critical analysis

This involves awareness, insight, consciousness of the prevailing oppressive situation. It demands analysis as well as discerning alternatives. It is not for nothing that Karl Marx, Frantz Fanon and Simone de Beauvoir laboured chiefly to provide detailed and critical analyses of their respective situations. This is the task of ideology critique: analysis of and challenge to existing social conditions. It asks for a naming, or rather, a renaming of the immediate situation along with new narratives, without resorting to abstract utopias of political futures. It entails alternative 'voices', from the margins, from the contradictions and gaps of hegemonic discourses. It is a process of debunking, unveiling, unmasking and of demystification.

Self-definition

This is a politics of subjectivity. Subordinated people will have to provide self-definitions; a self-determination of naming, labelling and badging. Illustrations of the process often appear as slogans: 'black is beautiful', 'lesbian/gay pride', 'strike a woman, strike a rock'. It frequently involves a double movement, reaching back to past cultural heritages, retelling the past, as well as providing new futures, as suggested by Bulhan's (1985) synthesis. A cultural component entails challenging and confronting negative stereotypes, stigmatisation and mystifications. It is a movement of recovering pride, resilience, strength; of 'coming out of the closet', of constituting alternative forms of self-consciousness. Self-defining often recognises a strategy to overcome exisiting divisions among the oppressed, as in South Africa under apartheid when the inclusive term 'black' was employed strategically to negate apartheid divisions of Bantu, Coloured and Indian. A process of self-definition already implies a consciousness of the possibility of resistance.

Collective organising

A characteristic of any period of significant change is that numerous new organisations appear on the landscape. In South Africa from the 1960s onwards, countless alternative organisations were formed. Most academic disciplines made new societies, progressive journals mushroomed, an alternative press arose, resistant trade unions were formed and there was active organising among collectives as diverse as churches, students, scholars, women, teachers, unions, journalists, academic, business, communities, workers, artists, musicians and even ethnic groupings (eg. Jews for Justice). Many of these organisations combined in 1983 under the umbrella political stance of the United Democratic Front, which aligned itself with the Congress movement. Such organising requires time, labour, resources, activity and co-ordination of effort. Organisations also became a home, a refuge, a form of pride, a source of innovative discourses, and a means of reaching out across existing divisions. The call in South Africa was for 'grassroots organisations', a form of local activity, while also forming alliances with other groups, in joint campaigns, so constituting a network of co-ordinated resistance. Organisations formed the bases from which concrete tactics, projects, campaigns and strategies could be developed. Collective organising constitutes the very stuff of praxis; a co-ordination, a coming together, of analysis, reflection, shifts in self-consciousness and concrete activity. For those who suffer the ills of oppression, this modality of collective organising comes to be a vehicle of psychotherapy – arguably better than that offered by the Psy disciplines – providing both safe haven and launching pad for bright possibilities via a non-alienated form of concrete activity.

Collective action

The distinction between collective organising and collective action is a fine one; the former may be seen as more behind-the-scenes, the latter in terms of public visibility, action as spectacle. Such action may take a variety of forms; from lobbying, marches, protest, pickets, through joyous carnivals and public partying, to armed struggle and guerrilla warfare. Writing and speaking are forms of public action. Forms of political action will vary across differing sites of subordination and will be shaped by available resources and conditions of possibility, not least due to the tactics and surveillance of authorities. Public action is a risky business; it raises the ire of dominant strata and authorities who are likely to retaliate. Public action, particularly in highly repressive regimes, could be illegal, and risks retribution in the form of imprisonment, beatings, exile, torture or death. As Therborn (1980) reminds us, the imposition of fear and of reigns of terror is a powerful weapon in the arsenal of oppressors. Public action is a war-like zone; as Fanon and Foucault have shown, it should be understood through the metaphors of war, manoeuvres, strategies and tactics. Collective action is risky in that it can go awry and rebound back on subordinates.

Two further issues require mention: alliance and violence. Remaining with the metaphor of war, a crucial tactic for vulnerable groups and for resistance in general is forming alliances with other sites of subordination. During the anti-apartheid struggle, the formation of alliances across multiple groupings enabled the formation of a broad common 'front'. Alliances turn on the issue, once again, of collective action (Kelly & Breinlinger, 1996; Klandermans, 1997); the broader the collective, the greater the probability of legitimacy of action. Also remaining with warfare metaphors is the question of the use of violence by the oppressed, most notably expressed by Fanon (1961/1967) in the case of anti-colonialism. Since the zone of contact between oppressor and oppressed was policed by violence, Fanon saw violence by the oppressed as a means for unification, overcoming fragmentation and breaking inhibitions. It could also serve to regain agency and self-respect, demand self-recognition and act as a decisive rejection of colonial values – a clean break, not a compromise. Fanon regarded counter-violence as a vehicle for political education through action. The South African struggle included counter-violence in a circum-scribed form. These are noble ideals, but the world doesn't always work this

Collective action may take a variety of forms: from lobbying, marches, protest and pickets through joyous carnivals and public partying to armed struggle and guerrilla warfare.

way, thus the negotiated settlement, a form of compromise, in South Africa. It depends on local and particular conditions of possibility. Nevertheless, counter-violence, which always carries risks of legitimacy, remains a critical device in the tool-kit of subordinated people.

Spatial re-formations

Spatial dimensions are not often given mention in emancipatory discourses, but in recent years there has been increased recognition of spatial and bodily aspects of subjectivity. A momentary reflection reveals a significant spatial dimension to all forms of subjugation. Indeed, the whole arena of oppression is entirely shot through with spatial metaphors: exclusions, borders, hierarchies, boundaries, dividing lines, buffer zones, safe havens. All forms of subjugation involve spatial remoulding: seizing land, segregating, separating, spatial restrictions, rezoning, apartheid, fencing, walls, enclosures and barriers. Places, such as prisons and military barracks, constitute the dividing lines of colonialism. Land invasion of colonists was seen akin to the plunder of women's bodies, 'entering virgin territory' (McClintock, 1995). Feminists have long recognised the spatialisation of patriarchy; rape as invasion; qualification for some spaces (kitchen and boudoir), disqualification from others (boardroom and podium). In short, emancipatory endeavours necessarily will involve retrieval of stolen spaces, opening of closures, transcending divides, dismantling Berlin walls or Iron Curtains. How exactly this is to be done requires more space than we have here. It will certainly be a difficult task. The prison gates of apartheid may have closed behind us, but the spatial legacies of colonialism and apartheid remain virtually undisturbed.

Apart from challenging the materiality of space, tearing down barriers to enable a liberated circulation of bodies, we also need to question the dominant spatial discourses of subjugation, which revolve around three major polarities of metaphors: hierarchy (up and down), distance or centrality (core and periphery; centre and margins) and sphere (public and private). Various subaltern identities map slightly differently onto these binaries; feminists for instance have different concerns with the public-private dimension than, say, socialists although the issue is clearly pertinent for both. It may mean different things for socialists and feminists. In raising such distinctions, the central purpose, however, is to propose a transcendence, and not a mere inversion (despite its temptations) of positioning. For if East merely disposes West, if women are up and men are down, then little is gained. Transcendence could imagine a levelling of hierarchy, a contraction of distance, opening a space between spheres, a celebration of the 'other', a cheer for diversity.

Moreover, while these dominant mappings of subordination are not without value, they tend to capture only the cruder depictions of power, criti-

Since the zone of contact between oppressor and oppressed was policed by violence, Fanon saw violence by the oppressed as a means for unification, overcoming fragmentation, breaking inhibitions. It could also serve to regain agency and self-respect, demand self-recognition and act as a decisive rejection of colonial values – a clean break, not a compromise.

cised by Foucault, the notion that power is something one party has and another does not. These spatial metaphors may not be the most fruitful for dealing with capillary power. For a genuinely emancipatory psychology, attention should be given to imagining the spaces in between, third spaces, movements across boundaries, spatial mutuality, alternative inclusion zones. Mixing language and the spatial, we require new discourses of space, and new spaces for dialogue.

There is a significant spatial dimension to all forms of subjugation. The whole arena of oppression is shot through with spatial metaphors: exclusions, boundaries, borders, divisions, separations, spatial restrictions etc.

Phases of an emancipatory psychology

Closely intertwined with space is time. We map space through time; backwards and forwards. There are temporal, historical and developmental dimensions pertinent to the possibility of an emancipatory psychology. Seedat (1997) in the wake of Bulhan (1985), and in a survey of the South African psychological terrain, provided a temporal, developmental grid consisting of four interlocking phases. Briefly, these phases are:

▷ Disillusionment – disenchantment with Eurocentric psychology at all levels; a sense of alienation and 'foreignness' contributes to immobilisation.

▷ Reactive critical engagement – ambiguous strands of accommodation and resistance; vacillation between 'progressive' and mainstream positions; good intentions, but some progressive voices are insufficient.

▷ Constructive self-definition – a proactive endeavour; aims to locate psychology within parameters of the political economy; integrating experiences of other-than-Euro-American into the centre; resisting the imposition of European and US-American philosophical domination; redress silence and secure inclusion of marginalised – in concrete terms strive for the inclusion of black, women, Islamic psychologists; set dynamic agendas and systematic programmes.

▷ Emancipatory discourse, praxis and immersion – draw on paradigms that emphasise diversity and pluralism; ensure that producers of knowledge represent full human diversity; participatory democratic research; explore other culturally appropriate ways of knowing; psychology should immerse itself in the struggle of oppressed people to enable transformation and reconstruction aiming for autonomy, self-determination, independence; focus on people 'other-than-white, other-than-Euro-American, or other-than-Judaeo-Christian' (266).

This is a useful framework; most of us would recognise that liberation is a developmentally unfolding process, not an instant achievement. The key focus of Seedat's perspective is a clear call for the indigenisation of psychology in terms of (1) the study of 'uniquely African psychosocial phenomena' and (2) the 'extension of culturally appropriate mental health services to the under-served majority South African population' (261). These are indeed laudable aims; few would quibble with them. Recently, in similar vein, Swartz (1997) and Holdstock (2000), albeit from different angles, have called for Africanisation and indigenisation of psychology.

Two comments on Seedat's approach, both aimed to extend his agenda, are appropriate. First, while it is correct to propose a key focus on marginalised 'others', it should not be the exclusive focus. Attention could also be directed to those in more dominant positions, since they are a central part of the problem. Recent South African research by Melissa Steyn (2001) on the problem of 'whiteness', and by Rob Morrell (2001) on males and 'masculinity' as a problem (Luyt & Foster, 2001) has started to open up a 'gaze' on the psychology of dominant groups. Secondly, while it is crucial to focus on the local, the indigenous and the African context as well as on other low-income countries, it should not be a restrictive agenda. Liberation psychology is a transnational project, we should seek strategic alliances with critical psychology elsewhere, where useful. Caution against cultural imperialism is imperative, but emancipatory resources may also be gleaned through dialogue with critical scholars in European and US-American societies (Gilroy, 1993).

> Seedat calls for the indigenisation of psychology in terms of (1) the study of uniquely African psychosocial phenomena and (2) the extension of culturally appropriate mental health services to the underserved majority South African population.

Legacies of the past

This section has provided an agenda for a liberatory psychology through attention to five main clusters labelled as critical analysis, self-definition, collective organising, collective action and spatial reformations, with additional commentary on temporal, historical aspects and calls for indigenisation and

Africanisation. In terms of this scheme, the people of South Africa, as well as some aspects of psychology in South Africa, have come quite a long way over the past twenty years or so. South Africa offers something of a beacon, a guiding beam; its constitution, even if too liberal for some, sets out noble ideals. Yet simultaneously we witness everywhere the legacies of the past in the form of continuing patriarchy, racism, exploitation and inequalities. Suffering remains widespread in terms of poverty, unemployment, rape, domestic battery, illness, endemic violence and unaltered spatial divides. We have yet a long way to go. The brief final section will allude to some difficulties that lie ahead.

PITFALLS AND OBSTACLES

Although the early contours towards a liberatory psychology are appearing, numerous obstacles lie in its path. This section touches quite briefly on some of the difficulties, in order to extend an agenda for further debates. A key question lurks in many dark corners: why is it so difficult to effect transformation; why do people appear to be reluctant to change? Be wary, there are two sides; on the one hand everywhere there is change, people ineluctably shift, move, seek out new challenges, live identities as ever-shifting life projects; on the other hand, tyrannies abound, the poor become poorer, it seems difficult to change men, oppressive regimes fall only to be replaced with equally corrupt ones, environmental despoliation grows worse. We will have to live with this paradox; human beings have the tendency for both stasis and change. Here are some issues.

Globalisation

This is part of the paradox; globalisation is Janus-faced. It offers remarkable opportunities, yet may lead to increased problems. However uneven, globalisation is part of our everyday worlds, its reach is considerable. On the up side, democracy has spread rapidly in recent years, women have made significant gains in many places, and telecommunications offer possibilities of enormous communication transformations. On the down side lies immiseration of increasing masses, rampant capitalism in the hands of tiny minorities, life-sustaining resources are gobbled up by the wealthy spheres, local customs and communities disappear, and women still get more raw deals. No solutions here; this phenomenon requires careful analysis. Put it on the agenda.

Psychological investment

Why are people resistant to change? Writing nearly twenty years ago in the important volume by Henriques *et al* (1984), Wendy Hollway suggested the notion of psychological 'investment'. Theorising from both discursive and psychoanalytic directions, she argued that owing to life-developmental experiences and positionings, people were sufficiently invested in their own subjectivities to resist major changes. We shall not take this further here, but it warrants further exploration.

Relational politics

With the rise of new critical psychologies, and the 'rhetorical-discursive turn' more generally, the focus has shifted to relational politics. It suggests that transformational potentials lie in the dynamics in between people, in third spaces, in negotiated positionings, in 'third ways of knowing', through dialogue, via 'joint action', in collective discursive reconstructions, through disruptions of taken-for-granteds. All very well, and these new discourses offer exciting alternatives. But there are difficulties: people don't quite understand how to 'do' these new ways. Furthermore, owing to psychological investments, people may resist entry into negotiated positionings; men and women may have differentiated rather than 'joint' investments. Possibilities abound in these new ways of knowing; it is less easy to see exactly how they will be achieved. Watch this space, carefully.

Psy disciplines

The practices, methods, truths and ways of knowing of the Psy disciplines writ large form part of the problem. Mainstream knowledge and practices – psychological assessment, individual therapy and counselling, managerial bias of organisational psychology, focus on 'adjustment' to the social status quo and its attendant view of subjectivity as 'self-contained individualism' – remain dominant; while on the increase, critical psychologists are still on the edges. A liberation psychology cannot simply take existing mainstream psychology, with its non-democratic, patriarchal and managerial tendencies, and 'apply' it to underserviced people. The Psy disciplines themselves require transformation. Critical stances are well underway, as we have seen in this chapter; this aspect needs to be kept on the agenda.

Spatial-material transformation

Put starkly, this has been hard to achieve. Put simply, nearly ten years after democratic elections in South Africa, there are no additional jobs, unemployment is rampant, the gap between rich and poor has remained or even grown (Terreblanche, 2002), housing shortages remain and spatial arrangements between black and white have been little altered. Nor are there short-term prospects for rapid transformation on these fronts. Why? There are undoubtedly many, complex reasons. This is an area for much concern, which any emancipatory endeavour would have to place permanently on any agenda.

Nearly ten years after democratic elections in South Africa, there are no additional jobs, unemployment is rampant and the gap between rich and poor has remained.

Challenging violence

Violence is another arena which seems hard to 'do', difficult to change. Despite the best intentions and mountains of research, we appear to have a dim grasp of the wellsprings, undoubtedly rooted in social circumstances themselves, of numerous manifestations of violence. We are all aware that the extent of violence in South Africa is unacceptable. The recent spate of child rapes and children killed in gangsterism crossfire has horrified the nation, but these horrors are not new ones. Violence, locally and globally, always a constituent of oppression, continues to be a vital obstacle and remains an agenda item.

Forgiveness and reconciliation

The final report of the Truth and Reconciliation Commission of South Africa was in April 2003. Parliament has pronounced on it. How do divided people reconcile? Is genuine forgiveness possible? Under what circumstances? Where lie the obstacles in the way of reconciliation? Important questions. Considerable work has come from the TRC and academic scholarship around the TRC process. Some corners of psychology have recently started to investigate the neglected area of 'forgiveness'. In some significant work in the areas of both violence and forgiveness, Gobodo-Madikizela (2000, 2003) has written most sensitively both about the possibilities for healing and the obstacles in the way of genuine forgiveness. There is much to be learned in this area, and those with a 'yearning and quest for liberatory psychology' (Seedat, 1997, 267) would profit from exploring such avenues. Please add the puzzle of reconciliation to our, hopefully, 'joint' agenda.

The organisers wait for thousands of whites to apologise for apartheid.

Some corners of psychology have recently started to investigate the neglected area of 'forgiveness'. In some significant work in the areas of both violence and forgiveness, Gobodo-Madikizela (2000, 2003) has written most sensitively about both the possi-bilities for healing and the obstacles in the way of genuine forgiveness.

CONCLUDING REMARKS

This has been a tour of the potential terrain of a liberation psychology. Some parts of the ground have been reasonably well worked and have begun to yield fruits, other parts lie in vacant plots awaiting the gardener's attention. The tour has covered processes involved in oppression, rumination on utopia, spots from which to survey psychological views on oppression, the psycholog-ical consequences for both subordinates and the dominant, and a preliminary view of activities involved in resistance. It has also provided passing glances at the issue of power and the institution of psychology itself. Some obstacles and rocks, standing in the path of fertility, were recognised and were then added to the agenda of what a liberation psychology might seek to tackle.

In this yearning and quest we have also to deal with ourselves. There are two paths we can follow. One tempts us towards despair and pessimism: there is just too much continued suffering, misery and ugliness in our world. The others suggest that we can stand together, strive in joint actions towards a better space: it offers optimism, tumultuous togetherness and hope. I would suggest the second pathway only because the first is too ghastly to contemplate.

Critical thinking tasks

1. Think of a practical plan of action in which you initiate a campaign to change some major social problem (eg HIV/Aids, or the problem of rape, or criminal violence) in South Africa. How would the 'ingredients' outlined in this chapter assist you.

2. Why is it so difficult to get people to change? Review this chapter and look for clues.
3. What would you do to change the problem of poverty? What kind of theory would assist you?

Recommended readings

To grasp the three central forms of oppression – that is, economic, gender and racism or colonialism – the classical works of Karl Marx, Simone de Beauvoir and Frantz Fanon remain important reading matter. On South Africa, the writings of Steve Biko in *I write what I like* are insightful.

For a good introduction to the ideas of discourse analysis and social constructions see Ian Parker (1992) *Discourse dynamics* and V. Burr (1995) *Introduction to social constructionism.*

For a useful introductory work on oppression, the book by G. Moane (1999) *Gender and colonialism* is quite accessible.

Critical reflections on community and psychology in South Africa

Thabani Ngonyama Ka Sigogo & Oscar Tso Modipa

'South African researchers should be less concerned with chasing
Nobel Prizes than getting their hands dirty with the less fame-producing
but more essential process of doing work relevant to the vast problems
posed by our own needs as a third world community.'

Dutkewitz (in Dawes, 1986, 44)

LEARNING OUTCOMES

After studying this chapter, you should be able to:

▷ Describe and explain critical views in community practice in the context of community psychology

▷ Discuss an Africanist perspective on community

▷ Understand challenges to community practice within the African context

▷ Critique community practice within an Africanist perspective.

INTRODUCTION: THINKING ABOUT 'COMMUNITIES'

Community psychology in this chapter focuses on issues of subjectivity and on how communities in South Africa are influenced by sociocultural, socio-economic, political and historical events. The concept 'community' refers to a sense of coherence that enables people to make sense of their social actions, social interactions and thought processes. Shared experiences among people gathered in 'community' contribute to the creation of a 'common character'. Recently, in the South African context, the term has acquired political meaning and reflects the political histories and beliefs of people in a given sociopolitical context (Butchart & Seedat, 1990). In addition, the concept is used to refer to African communities, in their diversities, interacting with different political environments.

Problematising 'communities'

It is important here, at the very outset of this chapter, that we discuss some of the possible connotations of this term. It seems that the use of the term 'community' in South Africa has come almost automatically to refer to economically disadvantaged groups, which, given the history of apartheid, and the ongoing economic divisions characteristic of the post-apartheid era, are typically those of black South Africans. As a result, we need to be aware of how the idea of 'community' can come to operate as a code for race and, more than this, how it might start to work as a term that connotes certain ideas of racial difference. This is one objection to the term – that it might be a way of discretely anchoring a sense of racial differences (for how often does one speak of 'white communities', particularly within the domain of South African community psychology?). This example in fact directs us to a second possible objection to the use of the term 'communities' – that it might be seen as playing a *role in a greater discourse of avoidance of issues of race and privilege.* Again, the fact that one hardly ever hears mention of 'white communities' in South African psychology should alert us to the fact that there is a pressing history of structural privilege and dispossession in South Africa that should not be neglected in imagining that all social groupings in South Africa have shared the same social, political and economic benefits. Every community provides an opportunity for the development of practices that are critical of power, and the task of critical psychology is to introduce reflexive critique into the heart of the community itself.

The state of the discipline in South Africa

There have been concerted efforts among practitioners of mainstream psychology to reflect on the state of the discipline in view of social and political changes that have taken place particularly in South Africa. Questions about the discipline's legitimacy have revolved around its relevance and commitment to addressing the practical needs of marginalised communities (Dawes, 1986; Ivey, 1986). For example, psychology is criticised for failing to engage actively in the struggle to change the circumstances of the poverty-stricken and oppressed majority within the African context. Holdstock (2000) notes that often the agendas of practitioners and the priorities of communities differ. Other authors accuse psychology of exploiting rather than serving the needs of African communities (Berger & Lazarus, 1987; Bulhan, 1985; Nicholas, 1990; Nsamenang 1993, cited in Bakker, 1996). These authors in turn have called for a psychology that will serve as an instrument of liberation, with an emphasis on restructuring and developing communities which have suffered under exclusionary political and economic systems (Martín-Baró, 1994).

Challenges to community psychologists

Rhoads (1997) challenges practitioners to (1) situate their practice within the communities they serve, (2) rethink their relationships with these communities and (3) focus on social transformation. **Social transformation** refers to the initiatives that are aimed at helping to reorganise human relationships through challenging oppressive structures or relationships and changing the systems that represent injustice (Prilleltensky & Nelson, 1997). In addition, Bakker (1996) believes that in Africa psychologists themselves are alienated, oppressed and in need of liberation. In order for the psychologists to remedy this situation, Bakker challenges them to take their services to communities.

> **Social transformation:** refers to the initiatives aimed at helping reorganise human relationships through challenging oppressive structures or relationships and changing the systems that represent injustice.

It is of particular importance that community psychology has only relatively recently been introduced into South Africa (Bhana & Kanjee, 2001), and not in Africa as a whole for a long time. However, despite the importance of the novel perspective reflected in this understanding of psychology, it must not undermine the longstanding practice of community work of black African people evidenced until recently, by their communal lifestyles, their values, and their traditions. To claim that community practice or community work is new among African people would be exaggerating and mystifying our role as academics in the project of knowledge-production. Academics have been criticised for engaging in knowledge-production that is self-serving with little regard for the role of the communities in these processes. Seedat (1997) critiques the tendency of psychologists to exclude marginalised groups at the level of knowledge-production. Equally significantly, he notes that the psychologies of Europe and US-America are cultural derivatives of Western value systems. African communities are rich with practices that are not adequately documented and often inaccurately represented in mainstream psychological literature. For example, *indabas* – traditional courts and cleansing ceremonies – are a familiar social restoration process among the people of southern Africa. They have been part of African societies for centuries. Folklore, as another example, has sustained and enriched the learning process of African children. One challenge for psychologists seeking to value these contributions would include the careful documentation of such practices and, where possible, participation in the reconstruction of local or indigenous knowledge. This process of knowledge reconstruction is thus informed by the traditional cultural practices of the peoples about whom we write. Their traditional practices are the ordinary ways of doing things or, in the words of psychologists and sociologists, the everyday practices of daily living among people who have grown to understand, value, and accept themselves and their ways of being and doing.

BOX 1   Sociocultural rituals

Certain sociocultural rituals bring a sense of relief and well-being into communities. Such rituals may act as means of psychosocial adjustment in the face of continued misfortunes. Particularly important here is the spiritual symbolism of rites that enable people to communicate with the celestial world. For example, beer brewing is practised in some African communities to cleanse a family from bad luck. When there are several unexplained deaths in the family or accidents that are perceived to be too frequent, such rites are engaged in to rebuild confidence and a sense of well-being in the family. **Ukuthethela** is a long-standing tradition among the Nguni people. The ceremony is usually conducted after a harvest. The beer for the ceremony is usually made by an elderly woman in the community. Specific seeds from sorghum are selected from the harvest to brew this kind of beer. The seed would be put in water to soak and the owner of the homestead would call all the relatives to report to the ancestors that the family is in the process of preparing the special beer for the ritualistic ceremony. If there is any woman occupying the position of a grand mother, she will be requested to bless the ceremony. The owner of the homestead wakes up early in the morning and approaches the spiritual beast in the kraal (*inkomo yamadlozi*) to report on the occasion of the ceremony, including its purpose. The beast symbolically stands as a medium of communication between the living and the ancestral spirits. (For a more detailed discussion of these issues, see Ndlovu, Ndlovu & Ncube (1995).

Ukuthethela: pleading for spiritual well-being and support from ancestral spirits.

Community psychologists can play a useful role in fostering community narratives that re-present such practices – thereby safeguarding historic traditions and revitalising local practices and communities.

Community psychologists can play a useful role in fostering and reflexively questioning community narratives that re-present such practices – thereby revitalising local practices and communities. We must situate ourselves in the context of writing the stories narrated by local people without denying a human face to the stories that we hear nor the reality that we are able to see through collaborating with these informants. This chapter brings these issues to the fore through articulating community practice, theory and methods of conducting such practice, as informed by critical psychology.

PHILOSOPHICAL ASSUMPTIONS

Within the broad framework of community psychology, community psychology practitioners can choose from a range of intervention strategies, each of which has implications for the relationships that the practitioner can and will develop with the communities with whom they work. Such choices are influenced by the practitioners' values, belief systems, and professional orientations. For example, some practitioners adopt the position of advocate or activist, with a focus on challenging the state's policies in relation to affected communities.

Community practice as activism

This chapter seeks to address community practice as advocacy or activism, types of community practice that are all too often taken for granted or dismissed as nostalgia for the past. One reason for this dismissal is that some mainstream psychologists view any reference to the past as 'idealised retrospection'. We would argue, in contrast, that this position prioritises European and US-American psychology at the expense of indigenous psychologies. There is a relationship of dis-ease between the emerging indigenous knowledge system grounded in the African experience and academic knowledge systems, with the latter subjugating the former. Academic knowledge has a distinct advantage in this relationship, particularly because of being written and well documented. A post-modern or contemporary psychology is thus challenged to seek dialogue with practitioners of local customs and traditions and generators of indigenous or local knowledge, towards developing an understanding of their underlying subjectivity and meaning-making. Academic psychological knowledge must recognise the importance of learning about local cultures and of understanding them from within their 'own frame of reference' (Kim, 1990, 379). Towards that goal we identify and discuss several major assumptions about community as well as selected local or traditional practices emergent from a number of African communities. We clarify some of the ways in which the practice of community psychology as advocacy and activism helps us value these communities while elucidating the meaning of their practices for Western psychological understanding.

African social life is richly contradictory, and experience is relayed through proverbs that maintain and challenge how a community understands itself (see Box 2).

Ritual as a socialisation rite

One of the major assumptions about community in an African setting is that social behaviour is greatly influenced by practices that have a long-standing historical origin. Despite external, modernising influences, certain traditions

BOX 2   Ndebele proverbs

Proverb	Translation	Meaning
Emuva kuphambili	What was behind is now in front	Past deeds often have a way of catching up with a person; so one must take heed how one acts here and now. Be pleasant to people now so that they have pleasant memories of you. Treat someone badly today, tomorrow he may seek a way of getting his revenge
Induku kayilamuzi/ Induku kayakhi muzi	The knobkerrie has no kraal/home The knobkerrie does not build a home	One who keeps beating his wife will end up with no wife and no children
Inkunzi emnyama iyawona amathole	A black bull spoils the calves	A bad leader wields bad influence
Kwabo kagwala akulasililo	There is no mourning at the place of the coward	A coward would not place himself in danger in any campaign, but he would then preserve his life. Discretion is better than valour. Prevention is better than cure
Ubukhosi ngamazolo	Kingship is dew	Use your power or authority wisely lest it disappears and you suffer the treatment you dished out to others under you
Inkomo ehambayo kayiqedi tshani	The beast on the move doesn't eat all the grass	Don't be worried when the unexpected visitor turns up; he won't 'eat you out of house', so entertain him with kindness
Isisu somhambi kasinganani, singangophonjwana lwembuzi	The stomach of a traveller is not large, it's only the size of a small horn of a goat	When a traveller found himself in a strange place, and was hungry, he would approach a kraal, enter and greet the occupants with this greeting, thus explaining his needs. Don't refuse to help a stranger who asks for sustenance
Kusinwa kudedelwana	It is danced and then they give way to others	This is the way a dance goes, each person in turn showing his or her skill and then giving way to the next. Be fair and let others have a turn (to speak, to act etc)
Umunwe kawuzikhombi	A finger doesn't point at itself	One who points the accusing finger at others in order to avoid admitting his own faults or crimes

Source: Adapted from Pelling (1977).

and customs have been passed on from one generation to the next and continue to be valued by the community. For example, circumcision in the Xhosa community has been regarded by those who practise it as having major psychosocial implications in the development of personhood for young men within the community. As an initiation rite it informs and is informed by socialisation beliefs and practices for young men. Current distortions that criticise the practice as being dangerous notwithstanding, a closer look at the underlying value of this practice shows that it plays an important educational role and should not be reduced to its biological function, that is, the cutting of the fore skin. Such initiation processes inform us about the development of a person to a stage of being given responsibilities that adult life demands of a member of the community. During the initiation the person is taught how to handle social responsibilities such as taking care of the homestead, how to communicate with other people and nurture relationships (Ncube *et al*, 1995). The social and cultural significance of this event – as in the Hebrew tradition of circumcision – cannot simply be dismissed. Social transformation of this practice may engage the community in looking at the conditions under which the practice is done, including the instruments used, in order to safeguard young boys undergoing the ritual.

BOX 3   Nguni death rituals

Given that adult life is considered sacred to the Nguni people, the death of a member of the social community is viewed as something of a threatening event. This is particularly the case given that adults are seen as playing an important role as protectors or 'shields' of the community. If the person is very old and happens to be sick, both the person and the community are helped to prepare for the death. All the children of the ill person are called and informed about the possible end of life. Historically, and depending on certain circumstances, a cow would be slaughtered and the sick person given its liver in the belief that her or his spirit was waiting, or needing, to be given some blood before the ascension to the next world. If the person does not die after this event, then one of the pieces of wood (*uthungo*) that support the roof directly above the door entrance is broken. After the eventual death of the person in question, their eyes are immedi-ately closed, and their knees bent into a squatting position. The person is not buried the same day she or he dies for the sake of relatives who need to bid farewell. If the deceased is the owner of the homestead, the person would be buried next to the kraal before his cattle are taken for grazing. He or she would be covered with the skin of the cow that is slaughtered during the preparation for death ceremony. Historically, the slaughtering of the beast is viewed as extremely significant, as it is believed that the person is going on a long journey to another world different from the earth. She or he needs something to eat on the way or to carry food for those people ahead of the deceased. People would eat after the burial. All the tools used for the burial are kept under a granary waiting for cleansing, which is accompanied by cleansing beer (*utshwala bamanzi*). (For a more detailed description see Ndlovu, Ndlovu & Ncube (1995).)

Collectivism

Another important assumption underlying African community and well-being is the sense of collectivism. This sense of collectivism has implications for the

Ilima:
social gathering of neighbours to work on an activity or project on behalf of their neighbour which is usually followed by feasting and social drinking of beer or refreshments.

social interaction of members of the community and is perceived as fostering social harmony and social continuity. Continuity here refers to the need for the community to see itself extending in generations through various social formations. The importance of collectivism is thus reflected in multiple community practices. For example, individual decisions are very powerfully informed by the wishes of the significant others within the family and the community. Practices such as collective rearing of children and **ilima** have direct implications for survival and continuity within the African communities. Problems within families are hence as much the concern of the extended family as they are of the broader community. Any disruption in the nuclear family is viewed as unsettling the broader community, and this opens the opportunity for something new to appear.

The needs and concerns of rural African communities have for far too long been marginalised by Eurocentric forms of psychology.

Multiple forms of life

In a reciprocal and dialectic manner, the issue of personhood has direct implications for collectivism and, more particularly, for harmonious social relations within the community. Problems are resolvable through community systems and structures that interpret social behaviour within its sociocultural meaning systems. Moreover, there is a strong sense of connectedness between human life, nature and the spiritual and celestial world. It is a common understanding 'that physical and mental illness is a result of a distortion or disturbance in the harmony between' human nature and the cosmos (Ebigbo 1989, 91). Ebigbo (1989) suggests further that there is a sense of harmony – between the various facets of living and non-living, natural and supernatural, health and disease.

(For further discussion of African metaphysics, see Nhlanhla Mhkize's chapter Psychology: An African perspective.)

African meaning-making

This brief discussion of assumptions underlying life within some African communities is introductory, not comprehensive. We offer it as a starting point for community psychology practitioners who seek to develop relationships with local African communities. We argue that these community psychologists must also adapt a critical point of departure and work as advocates and activists. This is necessary because the sense of meaning-making and of being in African communities or what other psychologists have called the African worldview has been silenced, distorted and disparaged by the colonial discourse. Practitioners and theoreticians seeking to develop a critical psychology within an African context need to engage this material and local communities with a certain degree of curiosity – and humility. The task of a critical community psychologist is to be able to speak with members of a community against oppressive practices, not to lecture them about where they have gone wrong.

CRITICAL COMMUNITY PRACTICE

Community professionals

Many professionals engage in community practice, while no profession has claimed it exclusively as its own. Social workers are involved in projects that reach out to communities with the intention of assisting them in dealing with their problems (Lombard, Meyers & Schoeman, 1991). Public health practitioners focus on developing strategies for ensuring that the public benefits through health promotion, a subfield now known as 'community health promotion'. Notions of **empowerment** are now more explicitly used in the public health arena than ever before (Butchart & Kruger, 2001). By empowerment here we mean to refer to those processes by which structural conditions are modified so that a reallocation of power is made possible; this process also involves a subjective component, a sense of personal empowerment, through being able to take on a great social agency for social change and power. These are among some of the many professions that are currently regarding community practice as central to the appropriate delivery of services.

Community psychology offers multiple resources for engaging in community practice. Some practitioners have developed a combination of methods and strategies that draw families, groups and communities together in order to articulate needs and problems through processes that draw on their local practices and beliefs. For example, popular theatre that is culture-specific has been used in certain communities to help them express their needs and identify strategies for confronting the problems being faced (see, for example, Hinsdale,

Empowerment: the simultaneous development of a certain state of mind (feeling powerful, competent, worthy of esteem) and modification of structural conditions in order to reallocate power (eg modifying the structure of opportunities open to people).

Lewis, & Waller (1995) or Mda (1993)). Alternative methods and strategies for engaging the community challenge models for conceptualising and responding to the needs of the community that treat the community as objects of investigation rather than as subjects of their own realities (Lykes, 1997; Lykes, 2000).

Developing an identity for community psychology

In South Africa the practice of community psychology has struggled to develop its identity. The professional practice of psychology, primarily clinical treatment of white affluent patients, has attracted suspicion from the liberatory-oriented academics for some decades (Seedat, 1997; Seedat, 1998). For community psychology to be accepted, it had to express itself differently, creating a discernible distance from more conservative practices of psychology. The introduction of a critical community perspective on practice offers community psychologists a set of assumptions for developing a praxis that has the potential to render liberatory services with and for the community. These assumptions question the established ways through which human service practitioners view community practice and their traditional strategies for developing relationships with the communities and of collaborating with other professionals from other disciplines. This understanding also calls for redefinition of the roles of human service providers, as it requires of them to take on multiple roles as direct service providers, consultants, trainers, advocates and activists. This approach further calls for practitioners to be critical of and address the systemic and/or structural sources of human and community problems, and to 'strive for promotion of enlightenment, [while] condemn[ing the] psychic mutilation of the individual by sociopolitical structures' (Ivey, 1986, 24).

The political challenges of community psychology

The challenge of developing a truly critical community psychology can be seen within a three-decades-old historical debate calling for a relevant community practice within the African context (Dawes, 1986). Psychologists such as Dawes (1986) have called for continued dialogue and debate that informs praxis, emphasising issues of accessibility and the appropriateness of practice. For example, some have argued that the political struggles of the past four decades have justified and contributed to the development of relevant and accessible community psychology in South Africa (Swartz & Gibson, 2001). Others point out that despite some changes, psychology remains predominantly white and the services are to a large extent not accessible to the majority of black people in South Africa (Seedat, 1998). Still others point out that in order to be successful, community practice must be South African (Swartz & Gibson, 2001). Yet South Africa is diverse, with more than 22 languages and many cultural traditions. Thus some challenge this call for the Africanisation of psychology, arguing that it reflects intolerance of what is regarded as non-African.

While attempts are being made to correct the wrongs of the past, contemporary practitioners and academics seem to have difficulties shaking off the politics of exclusion, which have been typical of apartheid South Africa. Critical community practice is challenged to recognise that inclusion is a central tenet of progressive psychology. This core value of theory and practice is reflected in, for example, work with African immigrants who are often treated as outsiders. They constitute South Africa as much as South Africa constitutes what is African. This core value of a critical community psychology intersects with the African tradition of hospitality towards outsiders, as exemplified in African wisdom (***amazwahlakaniphileyo***). Thus we see, in this concrete example of work among immigrant communities a possible articulation between critical community psychology and indigenous practices, reflecting the integration of two knowledge systems towards the development of a third. Moreover, through this example, we argue that any psychological practice that does not articulate South Africa's connections with the rest of the continent can never be described as progressive, critical or liberatory.

Amazwahlaka-niphileyo:
words of wisdom.

Xenophobia – that is, the fear or hatred of other nationalities or immigrants – features as a dominant problem of social prejudice in contemporary South Africa. It is one of the many political issues that is of crucial concern to community psychologists.

Critical community psychology and political correctness

Community practice discourse must transcend political correctness and a sense of being part of political movements. Clearly, community psychology

Critical community psychology needs to be aware of the exclusionary kinds of practice and discourse that surround political situations such as African immigrants seeking exile in South Africa. Such a critical community practice would need to be aware of how the concept of 'otherness' comes to be perpetuated and reified around exactly such political situations.

should avoid becoming merely the instrument or the handmaiden of a political party, and should keep its allegiances firmly fixed on the basic needs of the members of the communities in which it works. Highly proclaimed political movements that were identified with the people's struggles in one historical moment can become reactionary and out of touch with the realities of everyday life in African communities today. One might take the example of the ANC government's contrary position to supplying anti-retroviral drugs to sufferers of HIV/Aids or, as another example, the seemingly xenophobic attitude of the Department of Home Affairs to African immigrants seeking exile in South Africa.

In diverse sociocultural environments such as South Africa, a critical community psychology must rescue itself from an ideology which problematises otherness in the absence of a praxis of constructive social engagement across diversities. A critical community psychology would want to be aware of the exclusionary kinds of practice and discourse that surround political situations such as the above, of African immigrants seeking exile in South Africa, of the cause of sufferers of HIV/Aids. And, furthermore, such a form of critical community practice would want to be aware of how the concept of 'otherness' comes to be perpetuated and reified around exactly such political problems. Within this framework community practitioners enter local contexts with certain risks and are prepared to do things differently from their 'comrades' of the recent past. Such positioning not only requires a certain level of ideological sophistication but also a courage and humility that is almost absent in the writings of scientific and mainstream psychology.

Multiple challenges in local communities

Community practice is multi-layered and involves multiple challenges. It is understandable, for example, that community health workers are known internationally for their 'short stays' in local communities. Several factors have been attributed to high turnover in the practice of community work, including overload and scarce resources (Binedell, 1991). One might conclude from this that the practice of community work has been hindered by a lack of appreciation of the complexities and the diversity of the problems that are found in the local community. Some suggest that community practice largely depends on role clarity and the availability of resources. Others view such arguments as naïve and justifications for quitting the field.

Transcending professional roles

In addition to these more practical challenges, critical community practice in psychology must continue to transcend rigid professional roles to address issues of ethnicity, gender and race, while remaining politically inquisitive and socially engaged. The practice looks above the possibilities of psychological treatment that are guided by rigid relational boundaries with individuals and small groups. Without politicising its practice – at least not in a partisan sense of *politicising* – critical community workers must sustain political awareness and develop a critical understanding, with local people, of their histories. Political understanding – that is, a broad and well-developed understanding of social structures of power and oppression in a given sociocultural and historical setting – will give us the tools to analyse the workings of power as well as the social origins of psychological difficulties (Smail 1994). The methods of investigation need to be rooted in a sociopolitical analysis. There is a pressing need not to see social impediments and inequities as separate from the difficult political histories of the communities that we seek to accompany to their destinies.

The project for the restoration of the dignity of the unheard and oppressed people within the African contexts will continue to compete with other needs coming from other role-players who may be more privileged. This means that problems and needs will continue to be addressed on the basis of a politics of marginalisation. We need to be highly aware here that efforts at transformation may be influenced by *competitive* needs for social justice from a variety of role-players, some of whom may have previously been involved in the destruction and distortion of the values and traditions of black people. This will make the project of rewriting the histories of the community ever challenging in that we need to be well aware of the insidious levels of racism that, for instance, elevate the needs and concerns of white constituencies over those of black groups.

Zapiro's cartoon draws attention to the fact that a variety of constituencies are calling for forms of reparation or special consideration in the new South Africa. Some of these constituencies may previously have been involved in the destruction and distortion of the values and traditions of black people.

AFRICANIST COMMUNITY PRACTICE

Sociocultural problems and their solution

There is a common saying which alludes to the fact that the lenses through which one looks at the world will determine how one understands and responds to that world. Put differently: the perspective one takes towards a particular phenomenon to a large extent influences one's understanding of and response to that phenomenon. For example, communities who perceive the death of young, educated adults in their neighbourhood as the 'work of the people' (ie caused by jealous people, relatives or neighbours) are likely to respond by consulting a traditional doctor to determine whether anyone is responsible for such events. This type of problem and its 'solution' are prevalent among indigenous African people and a reflection of the inextricable link between the individual and his or her sociocultural environment, on the one hand, and the link between the conceptualisation of problems and attempts at solving them, on the other.

Intergenerational traditions

Within an Africanist perspective one foundational principle is reflected in the statement, 'if you raise your child correctly, the child will look after you in the future.' If that intergenerational connection is broken, there is a lack of satisfaction and a sense of self-blame for this failure. The same principle extends to the community at large, that is: if you look after me well, I will do the same in turn. However, such an expectation is not expressed through spoken language but rather through behaviours. Moreover, when a stranger asks for help, it is

one's duty to take care of the stranger. This creates a sense of community continuity. These implicit rules govern the behaviour of members of the community
and are taken as givens. A child learns these rules through everyday living and
is expected to follow familial norms and values as doing his or her part in
fostering the continuity of the family and to learn that the family is not always
the best model of what a community is.

Community engagement

Community involvement or engagement is a major feature of African commu-   *w*
nities. If there is work to be done at home, one calls community members to
help while having a social drink, referred to above, called '*ilima*'. The
ploughing of fields is a key social event in this regard; indeed, traditional
African communities pride themselves on this event. Here, the sense of
community is further demonstrated by the fact that excess in one family's
harvest means that neighbours will not starve. Neighbours are invited to
collect baskets of food for their children, thereby ensuring the community's
continuity while acknowledging its co-existence. It is normative that in the
event that one does not have mealie meal, in such community contexts, one
asks one's neighbour for assistance. In situations such as this, one is typically
welcomed with a basketful of food, regardless of what time you arrive. When
the harvest improves, you can always do the same in the return of the basket as
an expression of reciprocity and gratitude. This acknowledgement extends to
those outside of the community, as the insistence is to be embracive because 'a
traveller's stomach is smaller than the horn of goat'. Rhoads (1997) says that
'[h]ow we serve others and what we do in action with and for others needs to
reflect what they desire and what they see as important' (130).

Creating partnerships: Local African community and critical community practitioners

Critical community practitioners recognise that community members are an
invaluable source of information. They are 'experts' of their communities in
terms of their lived experiences and thus can no longer be seen as passive recipients of services. Any form of intervention, if it is to have the desired impact
needs to be planned with community members and implemented by them.
Mutual participation in defining the issues and finding solutions to their
problems can have a number of positive spin-offs, such as creating a sense of
community, 'group spirit' among community members, as well as an awareness that they have the knowledge, power and skills to change conditions in
their communities (King, 1999; Santiago-Rivera, Morse & Hunt, 1998). As
Bakker (1996) notes, this could also have reciprocal benefits in helping
'psychologists become connected to communities, no longer marginalised but

Community research as it has been practised over the years tended to objectify communities, particularly communities marginalised from power and resources (ie the poor, the illiterate, the disabled).

be recognised as important role players in community building' (5). Lewis, Lewis, Daniels & D'Andrea (1998) argue that the greatest contribution practitioners of psychology can make to society rests in their willingness and ability to foster the development of healthy communities. However, Berkowitz & Wolff (1996) note that the track record of psychology as a profession in building and empowering communities is unimpressive. This they attribute to, amongst other factors, forms of professional training which do not engender the spirit of critical practice.

Africanist communities thus offer critical community psychologists multiple resources and multiple challenges. We have identified some of these resources and several of these challenges. In what follows we discuss specific methods that can be helpful towards developing a psychology that integrates an Africanist perspective and a critical community psychology towards transformational praxis.

CRITICAL COMMUNITY RESEARCH METHODS

Community research as it has been practised over the years tended to objectify communities, particularly communities marginalised from power and resources (ie the poor, the illiterate, the disabled). Such communities were frequently sites where practitioners tested their theories, with total disregard of the benefits to those communities. Critical community practice questions this approach to community research. In his discussion of the notion of a relevant psychology in South Africa, Dawes (1986) raised the interesting question of whether any African community can afford the luxury of engaging in research activities which provide no immediate relief to pressing needs. In response to Dawes, we propose that researchers who accord the marginalised communities an opportunity to articulate their problems must also take into consideration the material needs of the people whose stories constitute the subject of their investigations. For people in marginalised situations, the research may be viewed as an opportunity to bring about tangible change, but this must not accord the researcher an opportunity to exploit the people's subjectivities and experiences. As Dutkewitz (cited in Dawes, 1986, 44) has noted, 'South African researchers should be less concerned with chasing Nobel Prizes than getting their hands dirty with the less fame-producing but more essential process of doing work relevant to the vast problems posed by our own needs as a third world community.'

Research offers a context for developing an understanding of the relationships between the definition of social problems and the community's attempts at resolving them. For a long time research in psychology seems to have been conceived of as a tool for making 'scientific discoveries' about human behaviour and a way of advancing in the professorate. As a result, the researcher wielded so much power that the 'subjects' were at her or his mercy. In particular, the marginalised who were in certain instances regarded as 'deviant cases' were researched with no consideration of their status as potential beneficiaries. A call for the reconceptualisation of research methodologies in the light of general developments in the field of psychology poses serious challenges to those conducting research in culturally diverse communities, as is the case in Africa.

A continual concern of a critical community psychology is that of the marginalisation, or 'otherisation', by psychology and other value systems, of minority groupings within society. Women, and particularly poor black women, are one of the groups that most frequently suffers this kind of marginalisation. The same holds for people who have special needs, or apparent 'disabilities'.

Five principles underlying community research

The 'expert researcher' is therefore challenged to collaborate with the community through participatory approaches to research. Critical community research practice requires that researchers take cognisance of the potential impact that their research may have on the community involved in the study – always striving to ensure that community members benefit from the research undertaken with and in their communities. Dalton, Elias & Wandersman (2001, 80) identified five principles that *should* (authors' emphasis) underlie community research:

▷ Community research is stimulated by community needs.
▷ Community research is an exchange of resources.
▷ Community research is a tool for social action.
▷ Evaluation of social action is an ethical imperative.
▷ Community research yields products useful to the community.

As Calvino (1998) cautions, the study of the community should not be a goal in itself, that is, community research should not be solely about contemplation

The study of the community should not be a goal in itself, that is, community research should not be solely about contemplation and knowledge construction about communities. Rather, it should focus on helping communities to transform and improve themselves.

and knowledge construction about communities. Rather, it should focus on helping communities to transform and improve themselves. Calvino (1998) alludes to the fact that the training of psychologists tends to centre on psychological variables and this seems to blind practitioners to other necessary dimensions of the community such as economic, political and cultural factors, as well as to the traditions that have sustained the lives of community residents. One strategy for dealing with this 'professional deficit' is the introduction of multidisciplinary teams, by which other professionals would address other dimensions of the problems identified.

Collaborative researcher-community relationships

As noted in the introduction to this chapter, critical community practice suggests that practitioners from various fields need to develop even closer working relationships among themselves to facilitate a collaborative relationship with community members. Yet multidisciplinary team efforts pose serious challenges and are often difficult to develop and sustain due to, amongst other things, competition between various professions. It is against this background that community practitioners are challenged to put professional interests second to community interests. The ultimate goal in critical community research should be social restoration and transformation through strategies that ensure citizen representation and engagement. Social restoration will entail, amongst other things, re-evaluation of personhood, values, traditions, customs and belief systems, with a view to revitalising those social systems.

SUMMARY

Debates on the relevance of community psychology need to continue. Such debates must include the communities' needs to access any assistance that they may require from academic institutions. However, this desire for access should not be interpreted by academics as an invitation to institutionalise community-based knowledge-production. The knowledge generated within local communities should remain under the control of the people who are co-generating it. Appropriate tools for creating wider access to that knowledge should be influenced by a genuine interest among community psychologists to participate in a helping process. Political awareness of the people's circumstances is vital for this process to be successful. Critical community practice in collaboration with African communities needs to be broadly envisioned. It should not be a vehicle for charity but rather an attempt by practitioners and communities to collaborate in order to meet the immediate and long-term needs of individuals, groups and communities. Helping communities make connections between immediate difficulties they experience and larger sociopolitical and cultural forces is an integral aspect of critical community practice. The ultimate goal is ensuring social restoration and transformation that is guided by citizen representation and involvement.

Critical thinking questions

1. How do we foster a community's belief in itself, that is, that its knowledge is still critical to ensuring its continuity and development?
2. How do we educate practitioners who are expert in facilitating the community's capacity to initiate projects and develop itself, without creating an expectation that the practitioner is indispensable or that the community must expect the practitioner to do things for it?
3. How can critical community practice help communities appreciate and celebrate diversity without overemphasising differences among communities?
4. In what ways can community praxis within African communities inform the development of a critical community Africanist psychology that is both liberatory and transformational?

Acknowledgement

The authors thank Brinton Lykes for her detailed comments and suggestions on an earlier draft of this chapter.

Social Psychology and Research Methods

Anthony Collins

OUTCOMES

After having studied this chapter you should be able to answer the following questions:

- What are the advantages and disadvantages of experimental design as a research method in social psychology?
- How do discourse analysts understand the nature of language and how does this differ from traditional views of language?
- What are discourses, and why should we study them?
- What important discourses have been identified in local research on gender and HIV/AIDS?
- Based on this research, what can be done to reduce the spread of HIV/AIDS in South Africa?
- What can you do with discourse analysis methods, and what can't you do with them?

SOCIAL PSYCHOLOGY has a long history of debate about the best ways of doing research. From the outset, the academic discipline of psychology was defined in terms of its commitment to scientific methods, and social psychology followed this example. This meant that the ideal research design was the scientific experiment: the researcher created a controlled environment where s/he could change one detail and observe the effects that followed. A good example of this kind of research design is Milgram's famous investigation of obedience to authority (Milgram, 1963; 1974). Milgram asked volunteers to take part in what they were told was an investigation into the effects of punishment on learning. The volunteers had to give electric shocks to learners whenever they made a mistake in recalling words from a list. In fact the learners were just acting and no real shocks were being given – what was really being investigated was how far the volunteers would go in obeying the experimenter's instructions even while they thought they were giving increasingly painful and dangerous shocks. This obedience to authority was what was really being measured (*ibid.*).

Experimental design in social psychology

An experimental design allows a researcher to create a controlled situation where s/he can ensure that the results are not influenced by uncontrolled factors.

Why is this a good example of an experimental design? It allows the experimenter to create a controlled situation where s/he can ensure that the experimental results are not being influenced by other outside factors. Confounding factors – influences beyond the experimenter's control that change the results – could be kept to a minimum as it was easy to ensure that conditions were the same each time the experiment was run: the same instructions, the same learners' reactions, and so on. The only changes were those that were deliberately introduced by the experimenter, so it was easy to conclude that it was those changes that caused the different results. Hence, clear relationships of cause and effect could be identified.

Confounding factors: Influences beyond the experimenter's control that change the results of an experiment in unknown ways.

Very importantly, the results could be quantified. Human social life doesn't always just happen in convenient isolated units, so it is very important for the experimenter to turn it into specific behaviours that can be observed and measured. In this case, the degree of obedience to authority could be directly translated into the voltage at which the volunteers refused to carry on giving shocks. There was thus no need to get into the murky area of trying to interpret their internal psychological states or make inferences about their motives. Thus the experimenter could claim that the results were objective – based on simple direct observation, without having to resort to subjective interpretations that would be hard to verify. Also, because the results were in measurable units, statistical methods could easily be used to show various relationships between the findings.

It was also a good experimental design because it was easy to create variations on the original experiment to see what the effects would be. This is exactly what Milgram and others then did: in different versions they changed the person giving the instructions from a scientist to a civilian, they introduced physical contact between the person giving and the person receiving the shocks, and they had other volunteers in the same room refuse to give the shocks. Each change had different results and they were thus able to draw important inferences about what factors make people more or less inclined to obey authority. A further advantage of this design was that it was easy to reproduce, and anyone anywhere else could repeat exactly the same experiment to verify the results.

A quick examination of mainstream social psychology journals shows that this experimental ideal is still the goal of most research in the field. In fact, one is sometimes left wondering if most research is not more about the idea of experimental design and related displays of statistical calculation than about understanding the most urgent questions regarding human social life. Against this trend it has been argued that experiments are sometimes trivial because in the attempt to create controlled conditions, the situations that are produced are so artificial and unlike the everyday world that they undermine the meaningfulness of the results. The criticism here is that the experiments might not have ecological validity, that is to say, that the findings in the laboratory might not hold true in the complex social worlds in which people live their actual everyday lives.

Beyond experimental design

Many alternatives have been proposed. It has been argued that social psychologists could instead focus on studying people in their ordinary social worlds. The clear advantage here is that it avoids the contrived artificiality of the laboratory, but by the same token it loses the element of control and it becomes harder to determine exactly what causes are responsible for exactly what effects. It has been suggested that perhaps social psychologists should be less concerned with measuring behaviours and take note of the fact that what is essentially human and psychological about people is that their actions are meaningful, and that it would thus be more appropriate to study how people understand what they do, rather than treating them as machines that just respond automatically to external stimuli. It has also been proposed that social psychologists move towards a much more encompassing notion of the social – not just how individuals can influence other individuals in small social groups, but how people can be deeply influenced by the entire culture, society and history in which they find themselves.

The aim here is not to explore these arguments and the many different theoretical approaches and research methods that have emerged from them, although they make a fascinating area for further study. Instead I will exclusively focus on one of the recent approaches that has tried to respond to these problems and that is becoming increasingly influential amongst people who believe that a social psychology that is serious about tackling the challenges of contemporary South African society will need to move beyond is roots in USA-based and -derived experimental science.

Although it is relatively easy to move from experimental design to naturalistic observation, the shift from observing individual behaviours to investigating broader social processes is a more complex one. It is easy to measure behaviour, but it is not so easy to observe a meaning or a social process. Social psychologists have also tended to shy away from broad social theories that attempt to explain relationships between people and their social worlds. Thus, many of the critical challenges to traditional social psychology have focused on the need to develop a stronger theoretical framework in this area. Although there is little agreement on the best way to proceed, the example below will illustrate how discourse analysis has been found useful by some social psychologists.

> Although it is relatively easy to move from experimental design to naturalistic observation, the shift from observing individual behaviours to investigating broader social processes is a more complex one. It is easy to measure behaviour, but it is not so easy to observe a meaning or a social process.

Social psychology should study people in their ordinary worlds.

If we want to find out about people's experience rather than just their behaviour, speaking is probably the best, if not the only, tool we can use.

Language and discourse analysis

I wish to begin by arguing that if we want to find out about people's experience rather than just their behaviour, speaking is probably the best, if not the only, tool we can use. Language is after all, a specialised tool developed precisely for people to communicate their experiences with each other. While question-naires and interviews have long been an established way of doing this kind of research, more recently an approach known as *discourse analysis* was developed by people interested in studying the relationship between society and the individual.

Discourse analysis or conversation analysis

Confusingly, there are two different approaches in psychology, both called discourse analysis. It is not necessary that you understand the complex technical differences between them, but just in case you encounter them later in your studies, it might be useful to state that the version I am referring to here comes from cultural studies and looks at how language structures people's thought in ways that reflect the particular social system. The other version, also called conversation analysis, draws on linguistics and is less concerned with the way the social world is organised and how this affects people.

To understand discourse analysis, we need to grasp some important ideas about language that are very different from our traditional understandings.

Discourse analysis attempts to work out from what people say what underlying system of ideas is structuring their thoughts, words and experiences.

The traditional view assumes that reality consists of things (like dogs, cats and rats) that exist independently of our perceptions of them, and that words are just useful name tags that people use to refer to them. Similarly these things have properties and interact in specific ways that we can observe and then describe using language. In this view, science is the business of making rigorous observations and then carefully building theories to explain these observations. The important concern is that the observer should see and describe exactly what is taking place in the external world, and not allow his or her perceptions to be influenced by any errors, distortions or personal bias.

> Discourse analysts argue that language is not simply a set of labels that we use to refer to things we experience, but rather that languages are systems of organisation that shape the way we experience things in very important ways.

Discourse analysts take an alternative view, and argue that language is not simply a set of labels that we use to refer to things we experience, but rather that languages are systems of organisation that shape the way we experience things in very important ways. They organise our perceptions and thoughts by giving us the categories, concepts and systems of explanation that we use to interpret sensory information. Experience is not just the awareness of what is going on outside us, but an interpretation of those things. Our cultures give us these interpretations by providing us with language, which is here taken in the very broad sense of not only words, but all the symbols, myths, customs, rituals and systems of explanation that we use to make the world meaningful.

To give a very simple example, the word *dog* is not simply a convenient label for those four-legged things that yap when we walk past. Rather, it is because we have the word *dog* to think with that we automatically see idiotic Maltese poodles, vicious Rottweilers, and friendly Labradors as a fundamentally similar group of creatures, quite different from, say, cats or rodents. Another culture might have a completely different system of organisation, where instead of differentiating dogs, cats and rodents it might have categories which rather differentiate friendly animals (including spaniels, Siamese cats and domesticated mice), and dangerous animals (like pit-bulls, tigers and cane rats). In this culture, creatures within each of these two groups (friendly vs. dangerous) would automatically be experienced as having more in common with each other than they have with members of the other group, and the differences we make between the various members of each group would seem quite arbitrary, strange and unnecessary. The real difficulty is for us to imagine that our system is not the only possible one, and to realise that the main reason we tend to think that ours is more sensible, obvious or correct, is simply because it happens to be more familiar to us.

> If languages do not simply label the objects in the world, they do reflect something else that was not fully appreciated before: the way in which that society structures the experiences of individuals.

The next important idea is that if languages do not simply label the objects in the world, they do reflect something else that was not fully appreciated before: the way in which that society structures the experiences of individuals. For instance, a racist society will provide categories for dividing people into racial groups. When members of this society are in the presence of others, their experience will be shaped by those racial categories. They will not be aware of this process, but will simply experience people as belonging to particular races – race will be seen as an intrinsic property that can be clearly observed in people, and it will not be noticed that it is in fact a set of social categories that are shaping what is being seen. The racist society will probably also provide a whole system of explanation of these racial categories, with details of the qualities of each race, where they came from, what their position in the society is or should be, and how different races should interact with each other. Here again, any given individual will not necessarily be consciously aware of these ideas, but will automatically use them for thinking, and their experience of others will be structured by these ideas.

These clusters of ideas are what we call *discourses*. In doing discourse analysis we attempt to work out, from what people in a particular group say, what underlying system of ideas is structuring the way they think and experience things. These individuals are usually not consciously aware of the discourse, and the researcher has to notice the patterns in what is said in order to identify the structure that is shaping the way they think. Unlike a survey which investigates how many people say a particular thing, discourse analysis tries to get underneath the specific things that are said, to understand the way underlying organisation of ideas produces the beliefs or behaviours that people report. So a survey might find that, for example, despite awareness of AIDS, 38 per cent of sexually active South African university students say that it is not necessary to use condoms when having sex with a partner with whom they have a long-term relationship. Discourse analysis would try to go further than this claim, getting people to talk more about relationships, sex and related matters and then examine the patterns that emerge and how these reflect whole systems of thinking that shape their sexual experiences and behaviour. This analysis might then be able to identify underlying cultural ideas, such as romantic love, showing how it includes feelings of trust and safety that cause individuals to misjudge their risk of HIV infection, leading them to unsafe sexual practices in their long-term relationships.

Discourse analysis is of course not limited to spoken accounts – it can be done on material where meaning can be uncovered, be it written articles, adverts, TV programmes, fashion trends, social customs, or any other behaviour where underlying conventions shape the meanings of what is done.

One of the difficulties in doing discourse analysis is that we tend to take the way we think as being just common sense, so obviously true and right that we can't even ask questions about it. To do discourse analysis we need some distance from which to critically reflect on our own thinking. This can be done in various ways, for instance by contrasting the way a society has thought about something at different periods in time, by comparing different cultures, or by looking from a different position within the society. It is often easier for an outsider or someone from a marginalised group to see what the underlying patterns are than for a person for whom everything seems natural and familiar.

It is important to note that in any society there are different discourses contradicting and competing with each other. Contradictions exist between groups and within individuals. For instance, although racism was a dominant discourse in South Africa for a long time, there was at the same time a contradictory discourse of universal human rights, and another of Black consciousness. Different individuals juggled these competing discourses

Discourses are systems of meaning that operate at individual, social, cultural and historical levels and inform how we interpret and understand our lived experiences. They are not the speeches and conversations, but the broad patterns of talk, systems of statements, or clusters of ideas that underlie and inform particular speeches and conversations.

In doing discourse analysis we attempt to work out, from what people in a particular group say, what underlying system of ideas is structuring the way they think and experience things.

Discourse analysis is of course not limited to spoken accounts – it can be done on material where meaning can be uncovered, be it written articles, adverts, TV programmes, fashion trends, social customs, or any other behaviour where underlying conventions shape the meanings of what is done.

differently depending on aspects of their experience. For instance, it was easier for Whites to identify with racist discourse which justified their social privilege, than for Blacks, to whom it was degrading. Nonetheless, some White South Africans identified with universal human rights against racism, and some Black South Africans in certain ways internalised the negative images of themselves circulated by apartheid. But more than this, individuals had to resolve the tensions between these discourses within themselves in various ways, and might have found themselves using different discourses in different situations or creating hybrid mixtures to try and negotiate their way through the problems of everyday life. For instance, as an employee, someone might support equality in the workplace, but as a father, the same person might fall back on racist ideas regarding who his daughter should date.

Discourse analysis has been especially useful for developing social critiques because of the way in which it goes beyond what people think to show the hidden implications and consequences of their thought, and because it not only highlights contradictions and shortcomings, but in so doing also creates the possibility of thinking differently from the way we ordinarily do.

> Discourse analysis has been especially useful for developing social critiques because of the way in which it goes beyond what people think to show the hidden implications and consequences of their thought.

Two research examples

Two recent South African studies which we will now discuss investigated discourses of gender and AIDS in South Africa. Because HIV infection is very easy to avoid but expensive to treat and still cannot be cured, from the outset of the pandemic it was believed that providing people with information about prevention would be the best course of action. Education programmes had already been in place for some time, but what become clearer during the 1990s was that simply providing people with information about how HIV was transmitted and the medical consequences of AIDS would not automatically lead them to avoid situations where there was a high risk of HIV infection. Although people increasing came to know that AIDS was an incurable sexually transmitted disease that could very easily be avoided by either not having sexual intercourse or simply by using condoms when having sex, many continued to have unprotected sex and HIV continued to spread very rapidly.

Another aspect of the pandemic that became clearer during this period was the ways in which the social and economic structure of the society was affecting the spread HIV/AIDS. Poor people were at a higher risk for a number of reasons including their often already impaired health from poor nutrition, conditions of urban overcrowding with poor sanitation, and lack of access to both medical treatment and current health information.

It became important to investigate why AIDS education programmes where not working as well as had been hoped, and to examine the social and psychological factors affecting the spread of the pandemic. With this in mind,

Strebel and Lindegger (1998) did a study of discourses of women and AIDS in the Western Cape. They ran 14 *focus groups*, mostly with women recruited from a variety of different settings including clinics, community organisations, domestic workers, tertiary education students, and teachers.

Focus group

A focus group is a small group, usually of about six to twelve people, that has a focused discussion on a particular issue in which all group members are encouraged to participate and openly share their feelings and ideas. For research purposes, the discussion is often tape-recorded and then written up for analysis.

A similar study based on this one was later done by Hoosen and Collins (2001). The second study closely followed the methods suggested by Strebel and Lindegger (1998), and the striking similarities in the results strongly supported the original. However, the Hoosen and Collins (2001) study was with women from a poor community in KwaZulu–Natal, where HIV infection rates were known to be very high at that time. The study included a wide range of age groups and different situations with respect to relationships and children.

While the first study found that most of the women had a good idea of what AIDS was and the principles of how to avoid infection (but that these principles were more difficult to put into practice), the second study contradicted most previous research. The second study discovered that many of the women in fact had only a little knowledge of HIV and how to prevent sexually transmitted diseases. But the study made very similar findings to the first study in revealing how difficult it was for women to put the knowledge they did have into practice. This may indicate that there are large differences in levels of AIDS awareness in different areas, perhaps especially between rural and urban areas. It is worth noting that researchers, especially in universities, often research whoever is closest at hand, meaning that more research is done on students and their immediate social groups than on the general population. Hence, groups from different economic, cultural or geographical contexts are often not included in research, producing unrepresentative results.

The research identified two important groups of ideas in what was being said about why people did or did not practice safe sex, namely discourses of power and discourses of responsibility. Firstly, there was a discourse of male power, a whole set of ideas that revealed the underlying belief that men have the right to decide what happens in relationships, specifically that they can put themselves and their partners at risk by having multiple sexual partners and refusing to use condoms, and that the women simply have to accept this behaviour. Several factors were found to work together to produce this power.

Because of social discrimination, women were more likely to be unemployed, to be less educated, and have fewer and worse paid employment opportunities, which made them economically dependent on men and thus forced by them to tolerate abusive behaviour. In addition, certain ideas about masculinity supported these arrangements: the idea that men cannot help having multiple sex partners because of an uncontrollable sex drive that they need to express, the idea that men need to prove their manhood by having many different sexual encounters, and the idea that men need to prove their virility by having children, so they can reasonably object to the use of any contraception. There was also distressingly widespread acceptance of the idea that men could physically assault their partners if their partners objected to this behaviour.

At the same time there was a discourse of women's power. In their accounts, the women were not just victims or objects of a male sex drive, but could make their own decisions and sexual choices, both when it came to choosing sexual partners and in asserting themselves within relationships. At the same time it was made clear that the main problems they faced were created by the social position of women, and that the entire society needed to continue changing to give women equal rights and opportunities. There was also an indication that women as a group had the power to act collectively to change their situation, as they had in previous political struggles.

There was a discourse of women's power in Hoosen & Collins' (2001) study that revealed that women as a group had the power to act collectively to change their situation.

The other significant discourse to emerge was the discourse of responsibility. It was understood that individuals all need to take responsibility for their own sexual practices to protect themselves and others. It was understood that women need to be more assertive in raising issues of safe sex, such as insisting on the use of condoms and limiting promiscuity. There was also a reference to traditional practices of non-penetrative sex as a safe-sex alternative. At the same time it was clear that taking this responsibility was not always easy, and that several factors worked against it. Not only did women sometimes find that they themselves were reluctant to raise sexual issues and use condoms, but they faced the problem that often men not only fail to take responsibility for safe sex, but even actively resist changing their dangerous behaviours. Women found themselves not only economically and emotionally vulnerable at the hands of men who threatened to leave them if they insisted on safer sex practices, but often feared being physically beaten by their partners if they asserted themselves.

The gender roles provided by society in some ways empowered women by making them think about themselves as caregivers who needed to take responsibility for health issues, but also worked destructively by allowing men to be irresponsible, and even to be threatening and violent in asserting their lack of concern. The social position of women also made them more likely to be unemployed, less formally educated and trained with job skills, and paid less when they did have work. In addition they were more likely to have the responsibilities of caring for children and elders. For many this meant that they had to submit to their partner's dangerous and abusive behaviour out of sheer economic necessity and lack of social support. For these reasons women often felt individually powerless, but also at the same time felt strength in the solidarity of their shared social position, and the possibility of collectively engaging in social change.

This research made it clear that avoiding AIDS is not simply a matter of education, nor simply of understanding the psychology of the individual's reaction(s) to AIDS education, but rather of understanding the social arrangements which empower and disempower people. This means simultaneously understanding how people get the basic material necessities of survival, including examining social arrangements such as inequality in the workplace and the overall distribution of wealth in the society, and at the same time looking at the ways in which discourses structure their thinking about who they are and can be, such as the way in which ideas of gender lead men to be irresponsible and women to be submissive. The important thing to understand is how these two sides influence each other, and to grasp the ways in which discourses both reflect a system of social organisation and shape the identities of the individuals within that system.

This means that psychologists need to address not only the psychological problems of specific individuals, but also the problems in the psychological effects of the way the society is organised. In attempting to change sexual practices, they need to intervene in the different discourses that shape people, using

Avoiding HIV/AIDS is not simply a matter of education nor simply understanding the psychology of the individual's reactions to HIV/AIDS education, but also of understanding the social arrangements which empower and disempower people.

the positive possibilities against the negative. This means changing the emphasis in gender roles to safe sex as an expression of female care giving and away from risky practices that result from feminine submission. It also requires changing masculinity towards responsibility for protecting others rather then the irresponsible assertion of a 'male sex drive'. It would also entail arguing against the idea of condoms as a disruption to sexual intimacy, and instead present safe sex as a form of caring appropriate for intimate relationships. Thus this analysis leads us to both critique gender arrangements, and to use aspects of current thinking to bring about transformation in people's behaviour.

What discourse analysis can and cannot do

In these examples, discourse analysis was useful because it allowed the researchers to go beyond the idea that safe sex behaviour is simply a rational response to knowledge of HIV transmission. It also went beyond the idea that behaviour is simply caused by psychological attitudes and beliefs, and instead highlighted how the culture and society provide people with both the actual conditions in which they live, and the fundamental ideas that structure how they experience themselves and the situations they have to deal with. It further showed that these ideas are not simply abstract concepts, but shape the very way that people experience who they are and what they can do. In this case it determined something a basic as whether individuals could choose to practice safe sex.

But discourse analysis also does not allow us to reduce everything to social conditions – we cannot simply say that women don't use condoms because they are economically dependent on men. Nor can we argue that society creates discourses that control people like puppets.

Beyond discourse analysis? How the social psychologists got their facts: A post-colonial tale – part 1 [1]

This is script for a video, prefaced with an explanation, which was developed as the opening lecture of an introductory course in social psychology. The aim of the video was to destabilise the ways in which social psychology is imported and marketed as an authoritative body of knowledge, typically without reflecting too deeply on the problems and limitations it might face in being implemented in local contexts. As explained here (in the preface), the strategy chosen was not to contest the arguments and findings of social psychology, but rather to subvert its method of self-presentation. Hence the video is a children's fable, a post-colonial 'Just So' story, this time told by the native, about the process of colonisation by the Western academy.

> The history which bears and determines us has the form of a war rather than that of a language: relations of power, not relations of meaning (Foucault, 1980:160)

The empire strikes back [2]

In any war over a domain of academic knowledge, a crucial site of tactical engagement is the introductory textbook. For it is here that the basic training takes place: it is the ritual of initiation that defines the battleground for the hearts and minds. The textbook is a crucial ideological apparatus in the maintenance of the bureaucracies of academic knowledge. Ostensibly its aim is to provide an introduction to the content of a particular field. In fact, its role is to constitute that field by offering a narrative that produces an effect of coherence – presenting a clearly bounded, internally consistent, meaningful and authoritative network of practices, circumscribing the domain and organising the content of the field. Not simply reflecting the field, but (re-)producing it.

The real lesson of the textbook is hidden, which serves primarily to make it unassailable. While seeming to present an overview of significant theories and research findings, it is in fact presenting the exemplars that covertly structure what is admissible in the field. Specifically, it claims to present content, while in fact trading in

method. It is not the arguments but the rules of argument; not the findings, but the research designs, that are being set in place.

As with all initiation, it is a lesson in power: not just a humiliation, but a practical assertion of who must be respected. And a second lesson: the only way to engage it is to attempt to systematically become that authority by submitting to it and proceeding to ascend its internal hierarchies. You will be assimilated. Resistance is futile. Like the nation-state, under normal conditions disciplines tacitly agree not to engage in acts of war, leaving each one to occupy itself with its own domestic administration and policing. The discipline is thus protected from outside attack by implicit non-aggression pacts, and from inside attack by the establishment of the rules of engagement that radically limit the modes of internal opposition.

Conventional war implies that the adversary accepts the rules of engagement. But in the case of an oppositional grouping that lacks a fully developed institutional military apparatus, there is the possibility of guerilla war. The guerilla army, knowing it is massively outgunned, articulates new rules of engagement. The effectiveness of the guerilla war is determined by the degree to which it manages to analyse and attack the hidden mechanisms of power, while winning popular support by exposing the way those mechanisms of power are in fact being used against the domestic population. The guerilla attack on social psychology can proceed using these very principles. Rather than accepting the tacit rules of argument and research procedures of the discipline, it should seek both to reveal these regulations, and to reveal them for what they are: the mechanisms by which the discipline excludes radical internal critique and maintains its domestic policing against other possible modes of organisation.

In the case of the introductory textbook, the attack should not contest the arguments and findings on their own terms, but expose the hidden rules of rationality and assumptions about research methodology by which it asserts its authority. This entails identifying an underlying conceptual hierarchy, in which certain terms and concepts are taken as markers of authority, while others are rendered dubious and illegitimate. Some elements may include:

science	myth
history	story
rational	emotional
objective	situated/subjective
facts	interpretations
first world	third world
man	woman
White	Black
adult	child
serious	humorous
dispassionate	manipulative
etc.	

The textbook presents its narrative as the history of scientific findings. Here science is precisely that method that avoids the mistakes of religion, superstition and myth. While these systems of ideas offer interpretations, science offers the facts. The facts are established most securely by experimental design and statistical inference. Scientific methods allow unmediated access to the material world that exists prior to human perception, and thus eliminates the distortions of subjective experience. In this way it claims the ultimate authority: it is, quite simply, and by definition, true.

The textbook's narrative is first of all rational, and emotion would be out place. It is serious and dispassionate, neither entertaining nor deliberately designed to shift your thinking in a specific way. It is told by nobody in particular and to everybody in general, as it is simply the neutral vehicle of objective truth. This is its authority, its condition of truth.

> While people are influenced by discourses, discourses do not exist except as they are used by actual people in specific situations, and people have the ability to change and challenge discourses.

While we can show how deeply people are influenced by discourses, it is also clear that discourses don't exist except inasmuch as they are used by actual people in specific situations, and that people also have the ability to change and challenge discourses, to use different discourses against each other, or to use different parts of a discourse against other parts. Thus, while women can feel powerless to insist on safe sex practices because they believe they should be sexually submissive, they can also be motivated to change this because of their responsibilities towards their children. While they can feel powerless because of their economic dependency, they can also feel empowered by their ability to act collectively and challenge their oppression.

It is necessary to move away from the simple idea of a mechanical cause, and instead look at the ways in which systems are sustained by complex factors that interact with each other: how social conditions produce ideas, as well as how ideas produce social conditions; how beliefs shape behaviour but also how behaving in specific ways shapes what people can believe about themselves. Discourse provides a key concept in bringing these elements together, filling the gap between the social structures and individuals, without attempting to reduce either one to the other. It thus provides a useful tool for a social psychology that attempts to take both society and individuals seriously, avoiding the reductionism that has so often limited the scope of traditional scientific research in the field.

Beyond discourse analysis? How the social psychologists got their facts: A post-colonial tale – part 2

In the face of this apparently seamless fortification of knowledge, what is the guerilla to do? The first strategy is to reject the terms. In other words, and against this formidable seriousness, to play a joke. Against this science, a myth. Against this abstract truth, a local situated account. Against this dispassionate information, a deliberate intervention. Against this rational adult history, an imaginary children's story. Against the invisible White male voice, a Black woman speaking: not to a universal audience, but for our children. Against the tanks in the streets, some graffiti scribbled on the walls:

Many years ago, before you were born, even before your grandparents were born, maybe when your great-great-grandparents were still living, the greedy people in a faraway land devised a new plan for making money. The people of this land were crazed by money, and had tried everything to get richer and richer. They had gone around the whole world, taking everything they could find and selling it. Often they even sold things they had stolen back to the people they had stolen them from. So shameless were these people, that they even stole people and sold them, shipping them across the sea and selling them like animals to work in the fields and factories.

They kept inventing new things to sell, and made machines that could make things faster and faster so that every day there was more to sell. These machines were hungry and had to be fed all the time, so the people of this land had to look further and further for the materials to feed the machines. They spread all over the world, invading many countries, taking what they could find and forcing the inhabitants to work for them to make supplies for their devouring machines.

But our story is about a new way of making money that they invented. These people had realised that some kinds of knowledge were useful for making money, especially the technical knowledge that could be used for making new machines and new things to sell. So they became great scientists, with knowledge of all the material things in the world. And although they neglected the wisdom of other matters of life, their scientific knowledge brought them great power and wealth, riches and splendour which had never before been seen in this world. But even then they were not content, so some of them devised the plan to make

money out of understanding people.

Now every culture has its ways of understanding people, and its wisdom about human matters, but these people wanted a different kind of knowledge. They had wise elders with knowledge of philosophy and religion, but they wanted their knowledge of people to be like their scientific knowledge. This knowledge should not just be the wisdom of their culture, based on everyday truths observed by people in their daily lives, or the results of debates amongst the wisest of them. It should instead be based on the experiments of scientists, like their knowledge of machines and material things in which they had already excelled. It should not just bring them sympathetic ways of understanding people, but rather technical and scientific ways of understanding how to change people.

They realised that if they could tell those in charge of the factories how to make the people who work for them work harder and more efficiently, and those in charge of countries how to make their citizens more obedient and productive, their knowledge would be worth a lot of money. So they grouped together and invented a new profession, which they called psychology.

Now all this took place in Europe and the United States of America about one hundred years ago. This new profession of psychology quickly became powerful, especially in the United States, where industry was growing at a rapid rate, and the new techniques for making workers more productive were very popular with the bosses. But the real success of this psychology came with the outbreak of fighting between some of these countries. We must remember that these people were not only insatiably greedy, but inclined to great violence, and just when it seemed that they had finished conquering all the other countries of the world, they turned on each other. Believing, as they did, that they were the centre of the world, they called this terrible outbreak of White-on-White violence World War I.

In this war the American army recruited many thousands of new soldiers, and then had to work out how to fit each person into a job they could do properly. This was difficult as these Americans were mainly an uneducated bunch, many of whom could not even read or write, and some who hardly spoke English. Here the new psychologists showed themselves to be useful. Taking the idea from IQ testing, which had already been developed for placing learners in different classes, they made tests for assessing people and streaming them according their skills and abilities, and thus helped assign the new troops into suitable positions. It soon became clear that this skill could be just as useful in the workplace, and out of this testing the field of industrial psychology was born. For the psychologists who had been dealing with emotionally disturbed people, the war was also good for business, and they had many victims of shell-shock (or post-traumatic stress disorder as it has become known) whom they could now treat and use to develop their treatments. These years were so important for American psychology that by the end of World War I, they could proudly announce that:

> As we have put more psychology into this war than any other nation, and as we have more laboratories and more men than all others, we should henceforth lead the world in Psychology ... the future of the world depends in a peculiar sense upon American psychologists (Hall, 1919:49).

As psychology grew from strength to strength, it had to show how it was different from other professional approaches to studying people. Just as it had claimed to be better than philosophy because it used experimental methods, psychology also tried to make itself separate from other area of study like anthropology, sociology, and politics by studying individuals on their own rather than groups of people. This concern with the individual fitted very well with the culture of these Europeans and Americans, who were an individualistic, selfish and uncaring people, with little sense of community. Their greedy and aggressive nature made them compete against each other to try and be richer and have more possessions, and those that were very successful in this striving liked the psychological approach most of all, because it told them that they were successful because they had greater abilities and

higher intelligence. This let them ignore the fact that the rich almost always started out with wealth and privilege, and that the poor were poor not because of laziness or stupidity, as the rich liked to believe, but because their society did not offer them the same opportunities that the wealthy were given.

So psychology carried on ignoring the problems in the culture and society, and instead looked for problems inside each individual. Psychology became powerful, as it always had friends among the privileged, and in each country the psychologists formed professional societies so that they could control who could become psychologists and how much they would get paid. Psychology grew to have large departments in the universities, with a multitude of researchers publishing in many different academic journals, and developed specialised knowledge and training in several professional areas such as clinical, educational and industrial psychology. Only a privileged few could complete these training programmes, with the hope of lucrative career ahead of them.

But because psychology was concerned only with studying individuals, a problem remained. It is obvious to us that people live in a social world, but the psychologists, having cut themselves off from the other social sciences, did not know how to think about this properly. This was a common mistake in their culture, and their greatest philosophers had said 'I think, therefore I am', not realising, as we all do, that we do not just exist in our thoughts, but in our culture, and in our relationships with those around us. Psychologists had turned this mistake into a profession, and now had to try and think of ways of solving the problems it created.

Thus, in their discipline the psychologists invented a small area called social psychology, to investigate how social groups influence individuals. They avoided questions about how cultures and societies work, and concentrated instead on studying small groups of people. Because they wanted to seem scientific, they devised experiments to examine how people would behave in different situations. Although they did many thousands of different experiments, nobody really seemed very interested in the results, and it was only after the next major outbreak of White-on-White violence (this time they called it World War II) that things started getting interesting.

This long and brutal war left the Europeans and Americans in a state of shock. Finally they realised that the science and technology that they had believed would solve all their problems could also be used destructively, and that the brutal methods that they had developed for conquering other parts of the world could just as easily be used at home. They were especially shocked by the concentration camps, realising with horror that they could treat each other the way they had previously only treated other races, and by the atomic bomb, which gave them the ability to destroy each other completely.

Finally the social psychologists became interested in why they could inflict so much harm on each other, and why violence was so common in their societies. They designed new experiments to investigate these problems, several of which became quite famous because of their disturbing results. One such experiment was done by Stanley Milgram (1963), in which he asked people to take part in a study of punishment and learning. To repeat what is outlined at the beginning of this chapter, the participants were told to give stronger and stronger shocks to learners every time they made a mistake remembering groups of words. Milgram really wanted to see how severely the participants would shock the learners before refusing to carry on with the experiment. Most of the people he asked beforehand thought that the participants would not give very strong shocks at all, but in the actual experiment most of them carried on making the shocks stronger and stronger until they were giving extremely dangerous and potentially lethal shocks to the learners when the experimenter finally told them to stop.

Another psychologist called Philip Zimbardo (1974) and his associates did a study of how people's behaviour is affected by the social roles in which they find themselves. Zimbardo's researchers got students at the elite Stanford University to set up a mock prison, where some of them played the parts of prisoners and others were guards. The participants started acting as if their parts were real, and after a few days Zimbardo had to stop the whole study because the guards were becoming so abusive to the prisoners, who had quickly become scared and depressed.

In another famous study, Muzafer and Carolyn Sherif (Sherif *et al.*, 1961) and their colleagues took some young boys to a holiday camp to study the ways in which conflict between groups developed. The boys were divided into two groups who competed for prizes in various games and activities. The Sherifs and their colleagues found that the boys from the different groups became increasingly hostile to each other, and that this hostility carried on even when they were not competing with each other any more, and that it was very difficult to find was of reducing this conflict once it had started (Sherif & Sherif, 1969).

You might think that these disturbing findings made the social psychologists start worrying about the consequences of their culture, built as it was on ruthless competitiveness and exploitation. But this was not the case. Because they did not know how to think about culture and society, they just assumed that they had discovered the universal laws of human nature, which applied to all people everywhere. They believed that all people would behave in the destructive ways that they had seen in their experiments. They never thought about the fact that almost all their studies were done on and with middle-class White American men, and usually university students at that. But soon afterwards, some voices of discontent started to be heard in American society. Black Americans and women had grown angry that they did not have the civil rights that America so proudly claimed for all its citizens. The official discrimination against women and Blacks was challenged, and as they gradually managed to take up professional and academic positions in the field, the White men who had always run psychology were faced with criticism about the way they had assumed that their limited perspectives could explain all of human existence.

At the same time there was a bit of a squabble going on between American and European psychologists. The Americans had always been greatly impressed with the advances of the physical sciences, and had thought that the only way for psychology to become a respected field was to use the methods of the physical sciences as guidelines for their work. That is to say, that they should at all times use experimental methods in their research. Now the European psychologists argued that there were two problems with this belief. Firstly, an experiment relies on results that you can see and measure, which is a problem when you are trying to understand people, because you can't see and measure their thoughts and feelings. So all you can study is their behaviour, and it was argued that restricting yourself to examining behaviour without being allowed to talk about people's experiences meant missing the whole point of studying psychology. Secondly, the Europeans argued that people need to be understood in the social environment in which they exist, not just as isolated individuals in artificial laboratory settings. They were more influenced by ideas from the social sciences, like sociology and anthropology, than by the physical sciences. So the European social psychologists wanted to study people in real-life situations, and speak to them about their experiences.

The European social psychologists wanted to find out more about how people think, and were more willing to pay attention to the influence of culture and society in these matters. They said it was more important to study things like language and ideology, to find out how society shaped the way people think. They showed that the way in which people think about themselves and the world they live in was greatly influenced by the culture and society in which they live. These findings were very interesting, but the European social psychologists kept trying to justify their work by getting caught up in complicated philosophical arguments about language and the nature of reality, and so most of the time people didn't really understand what they were talking about.

In any case the American social psychologists were not very concerned with these arguments. Although they also wanted to make their work relevant for current social issues, nobody really paid much attention to them, and they had to get on with the business of making money. All that was left for them to do was to design more and more experiments and publish them in academic journals, which nobody else really read. But at least this helped them to get jobs in universities, teaching learners about all these experiments that they had done. Some of them even wrote big textbooks, with glossy pages and pictures, telling of all the things they had found. They sold these textbooks all over the world (even here), where university lecturers prescribed them for students of psychology. If you look around, you are sure to see them.

So now when you see learners weighed down with big books on social psychology, looking very confused by all the strange ideas, you can explain to them where these things come from, and tell them our story of how the social psychologists got their facts.

Exercises for critical engagement

1 Suggest several other areas where discourse analysis would be a useful research method. Briefly explain how you would go about doing the research in each case.

2 The chapter suggests that it is difficult for people to see the discourses which they use in their thinking. Can you identify some examples of this kind of 'common sense' that people simply take for granted? How are you able to identify them more easily than other people?

3 What additional discourses (over and above the ones identified in the research) do you think might affect safe sex behaviour in your community. How can you identify these discourses?

4   The research suggests that people need to think differently about what it means to be men or women. How is it possible for psychologists to try and get people to change in this way?

5   Based on the research and theories in this chapter, make practical suggestions for an intervention to reduce HIV infection.

Endnotes

1   The 'Post-colonial tale', Parts 1 and 2, first appeared in an article in *Psychology in Society* in 2001. Permission to use this is gratefully acknowledged.

2   At the initial presentation at the South African Psychology Congress, a member of the audience argued that the video was problematic in representing a paranoid account of the emergence of social psychology. At the time (and suspecting the unwitting invocation of the rhetorical rule developed for deligitimising oppositional discourse), I somewhat facetiously defended the importance of paranoid interpretations. A double task then emerged: how to write an introduction to the video script for this publication, and how to explore the utility of a paranoid standpoint. Methodologically, there was also the problem of avoiding replicating the rhetorical structure of academic writing, which is one of the things that the video sought to problematise. Given that military paranoia seems to be the prototypical paranoia of our age, the solution presented itself: it must surely be an *act of war*.

Recommended reading

Bannister, P., Burman, E. & I. Parker (Eds.) (1994). *Qualitative Methods in Psychology: A Research Guide.* Buckingham: Open University Press.

Breakwell, G., Hammond, S. & C. Fife-Shaw (Eds.) (1995). *Research Methods in Psychology.* London: Sage.

Burman, E. & I. Parker (1993). *Discourse Analytic Research: Repertoires and Readings of Texts in Action.* London: Routledge.

Burr, V. (1995). *An Introduction to Social Constructionism.* London: Routledge.

Foucault, M. (1980). 'Power/knowledge'. In Gordon, C. (Ed.) *Power/Knowledge: Selected Interviews and Other Writings by Michel Foucault, 1972–1977.* New York: Pantheon Books.

Hepburn, A. (2002). *An Introduction to Critical Social Psychology.* London: Sage.

Parker, I. (1989). *The Crisis in Modern Social Psychology – and How to End It.* London: Routledge.

Parker, I. (1992). *Discourse Dynamics: Critical Analysis for Social and Individual Psychology.* London: Routledge.

Parker, I. & the Bolton Discourse Network (1999). *Critical Textwork: An Introduction to Varieties of Discourse and Analysis.* Buckingham: Open University Press.

Potter, J. & M. Wetherell (1987). *Discourse and Social Psychology: Beyond Attitudes and Behaviour.* London: Sage.

Potter, J. (1996). *Representing Reality: Discourse, Rhetoric and Social Construction.* London: Sage.

Terre Blanche, M. & K. Durrheim (Eds.) (1999). *Research and Practice: Applied Methods for the Social Sciences.* Cape Town: UCT Press.

Wetherell, M. & J. Potter (1992). *Mapping the Language of Racism: Discourse and the Legitimation of Exploitation.* London: Harvester Wheatsheaf.

Willig, C. (Ed.) (1999). *Applied Discourse Analysis: Social and Psychological Interventions.* Buckingham: Open University Press.

Wilton, T. (1997). *Engendering AIDS: Deconstructing Sex, Text and the Epidemic.* London: Sage Publications.

Psychology: An African perspective

Nhlanhla Mkhize

'The concept of culture I espouse ... is essentially a semiotic one. ... Man [sic] is an animal suspended in webs of significance he himself has spun. I take culture to be those webs, and the analysis of it to be therefore not an experimental science in search of law[s] but an interpretive one in search of meaning.'

Geertz (1973, 5)

LEARNING OUTCOMES

By the end of this chapter, you should be able to:

▷ Critically discuss the context of psychology in developing societies

▷ Distinguish between indigenous psychology and indigenisation

▷ Define worldviews and the four dimensions of worldviews, illustrating each dimension with examples from traditional Western and indigenous societies

▷ Illustrate the counselling and healthcare implications of the notion of worldviews, preferably with your own examples

▷ Critically discuss the core components of an African metaphysical system, including a critical appraisal of the notion of a person-in-community.

INTRODUCTION

Traditional Western approaches to psychology are based on certain pre-suppositions about the person and the world. They also claim to be free of roots in particular philosophical and value systems. Western-derived theories, which are assumed to be universal, have been imposed on non-Western populations. Indigenous theoretical frameworks, on the other hand, have been marginalised.

This chapter critically reviews the context of psychology in developing societies. A critical, emancipatory psychology, it is argued, should take into account indigenous people's languages, philosophies and **worldviews**. It is through these worldviews and philosophies that people make sense of themselves and the world. A traditional African metaphysical framework is presented. This framework provides a basis for an African-based psychology. Its inclusion in teaching and research will give voice to marginalised African perspectives. This will empower marginalised communities as active participants in the knowledge-generation process, rather than spectators.

Worldview: set of basic assumptions that a group of people develops in order to explain reality and their place and purpose in the world. Worldviews shape our attitudes, values and opinions, as well as the way we think and behave.

THE CONTEXT OF PSYCHOLOGY IN DEVELOPING SOCIETIES

Modern psychology as we know it is essentially a Western product. It was brought to developing countries as part of the general transfer of knowledge and technology (Sinha, 1986). In the quest to emulate the natural sciences, psychologists construed their discipline as an objective, value-free and universal science. Eager to demonstrate the universality of psychological processes such as motivation, perception and emotion, psychologists saw culture as an impediment (Gergen, Gulerce, Lock, & Misra, 1996). Traditional psychology seeks to uncover underlying, universal structures of human functioning. It assumes that psychological processes are fixed and 'deeply hidden' within individuals. Its purpose is to go beyond 'superficial differences', resulting from varying cultural contexts, so as to isolate basic underlying psychological mechanisms and describe the invariant laws of their operation (Shweder, 1991). In line with this universalistic orientation, psychologists have attempted to understand people in developing societies with reference to conceptual categories and theories developed in the West. The same situation applies to research conducted in developing nations. The research tends to be initiated by psychologists in developed societies. Attempts are made to replicate studies conducted in developed societies, using imported theoretical frameworks (Sinha, 1990).

Cultural colonisation

The vertical – that is top-down, one-way – transfer of knowledge, ideas, values and practices from developed to developing societies is a form of cultural colonisation (Gergen *et al*, 1996; Sinha, 1990). It ensures that the developed world continues to produce and market psychological knowledge and technology (eg psychological tests) to developing societies. The latter, on the other hand, remain consumers of Western ideas and technology. The end product is that contemporary research and theorising in developing nations are largely irrelevant to the needs of the local populations. These are needs such as eliminating poverty and illiteracy (Nsamenang, 1992; Sinha, 1990).

Dissatisfaction with the assumptions and values embedded in Western psychology has increased in the past two decades or so. It has been argued that psychological science is based on Western cultural presuppositions about the knowing subject and the nature of knowledge (Gergen *et al*, 1996; Greenfield, 1997; Laubscher & McNeil, 1995). Traditional Western psychology is premised on an independent view of the **self**. It also assumes that knowledge is value-free.

Self:
in traditional psychology, regarded as a bounded, autonomous entity: it is defined in terms of its internal attributes such as thoughts and emotions, independently of social and contextual factors.

THE KNOWING SUBJECT: THE SELF IN TRADITIONAL PSYCHOLOGY

Traditional Western ways of knowing draw sharp distinctions between the knowing subject and the object of her/his knowledge (Greenfield, 1997). The knower is a solitary, disinterested subject. He or she is stripped of all particularities such as gender, culture, position, his or her existence in space and time, and the like (eg Rawls, 1972). The self in traditional psychology is regarded as a bounded, autonomous entity: it is defined in terms of its internal attributes such

Psychic unity:
assumption that human beings are all the same. It purports that there are universal, underlying psychological processes that are inherent in all individuals. From this perspective, the aim of psychology is to go beyond superficial differences (eg culture) so as to uncover these processes.

The self in traditional psychology is regarded as a bounded, autonomous entity: it is defined in terms of its internal attributes such as thoughts and emotions, independently of social and contextual factors. A collectivist approach to self, by contrast, adopts a context-based view, and sees self as defined in terms of one's relationships with others, such as family, community, and status or position within the group.

Collectivist self: view of the self shared by many indigenous societies and non-Western culture in which the self is fundamentally context-based, defined in terms of one's relationships with others, such as family, community, and status or position within the group. Also understood as the **interdependent** notion of self.

as thoughts and emotions, independently of social and contextual factors. Where relationships with others and the social order exist, they are thought to be established through discretionary choice (Shweder, 1982). This view of selfhood is also known as *self-contained individualism* (Hermans *et al*, 1992; Sampson, 1988) or the *independent* view of self (Markus & Kitayama, 1991, 1994).

The abovementioned view of the self contrasts sharply with conceptions of the self in indigenous societies and non-Western cultures in general. The self in these societies tends to be context-based (Shweder, 1991). It is defined in terms of one's relationships with others, such as family, community and status or position within the group. The goal of socialisation is not to be autonomous but to harmonise one's interests with those of the collective. This view of selfhood is also called the **collectivist** or **interdependent** self (Markus & Kitayama, 1991, 1994).

THE NATURE OF KNOWLEDGE: WESTERN PSYCHOLOGY AND THE PLACE OF VALUES

Materialism: theory that physical matter is the only reality and that everything, including thought, feeling, mind and will, can be explained in terms of matter and physical phenomena.

Traditional Western approaches to science seek *objective knowledge*. Knowledge is not supposed to be affected by the knower's values and meanings. The knower stands apart from that which is to be known, uninterested. Objective knowledge can be arrived at by anyone who has engaged in the necessary thought processes or experimental procedures. This way of knowing, also known as 'separate' (Clinchy, 1996), is neither timeless nor universal. It is a product of the scientific revolution in the 16th and 17th centuries (Cushman, 1990; Richardson, Rogers & McCarroll, 1998). During this period the Western world witnessed a gradual shift from a community/religious orientation to an unprecedented scientific and **materialistic** position. This was accompanied by a rebellion against traditions and customs, which were seen as a threat to individuality and freedom (Richardson *et al*, 1998). Thus emerged the view that individuals could be sharply distinguished from the world and each other, and from their customs, traditions, and the social realm in general (Richardson & Fowers, 1998).

Cultural psychology: study of the way cultural traditions and social practices regulate, express, and transform the human psyche, resulting less in **psychic unity** for humankind than in ethnic divergences in mind, self and emotion.

Cultural psychology

Cultural psychologists, among others, have criticised the notion of value-free knowledge. Shweder (1991) defines **cultural psychology** as 'the study of the way cultural traditions and social practices regulate, express, and transform the human psyche, resulting less in **psychic unity** for humankind than in ethnic divergences in mind, self, and emotion' (73; emphasis added). Cultural psychology also postulates that 'subject and object, self and other, psyche and culture, person and context, figure and ground, practitioner and practice, live together, require each other, and dynamically, dialectically, and jointly make each other up' (Shweder, 1991, 73). Thus, while traditional psychology seeks objective knowledge, cultural psychology assumes that the subject (scientist) and his or her object of knowledge are *interdependent*.

Like Shweder (1991), Bruner (1990) emphasises that an important part of a human psychology is '*meaning* and the processes and transactions involved in the construction of meanings' (33; original emphasis). These meanings are not realised by individuals acting in isolation. They result from participation in the symbolic systems afforded by the culture (Bruner, 1990; Shweder, 1991). From a cultural psychology perspective, psychology cannot be value-free. It needs to engage with the values and meaning systems of scientists or researchers and well as those of local actors.

LINKS WITH CRITICAL PSYCHOLOGY

The abovementioned objections to traditional Western psychology are consistent with the goals of critical psychology. Parker (1999) contends that critical psychology aims to reflect upon the diverse ways in which men and women of various cultures and classes create meaning in their lives, including the manner in which they reflect upon their **lived experience**. Because the explanations and concepts of psychology feature so strongly in such accounts, an important part of such an exercise is an examination of how dominant forms of psychology operate here, and operate ideologically in the service of certain interest and power groups. What becomes important here is that we consider the reflections on life of the marginalised groups in society – those reflections typically ignored by psychology – because these reflections may help us to upset some of the ideological uses of certain psychological notions and the interests of power that they serve. Furthermore, critical psychology also maintains that all forms of psychological knowledge are grounded in social, cultural and historical contexts (Maiers, 1991; Parker, 1999; Tolman, 1994).

Critical psychology is also opposed to the abstract-isolated notion of the self, so characteristic of traditional psychology. Rather, it aims to restore concreteness to our understanding of psychological functioning by locating human values, motivations and behaviours in their cultural context (Martin-Baro, 1994; Maiers, 1991; Tolman, 1994). In line with the goals of critical psychology, then, this chapter argues that the hegemony of Western psychological science can be overcome if we turn our attention to indigenous conceptions of psychology (Nsamenang, 1992).

INDIGENOUS PSYCHOLOGIES

The call for indigenous approaches to psychology stems from the realisation that indigenous peoples of the world were never passive recipients of experience. Long before colonisation, indigenous peoples were actively creating

Objective knowledge: notion that knowledge is not supposed to be affected by the knower's values and meanings.

Lived experience: term closely associated with phenomenology, a school of philosophy that seeks to study human phenomena, focusing entirely on them by suspending all presuppositions. In its most basic form, 'lived experience' refers to real life, as opposed to laboratory or hypothetical, experiences. Thus, one can study the lived experience of being sexually abused or the lived experience of being racially discriminated against.

From a cultural psychology perspective, psychology cannot be value-free. It needs to engage with the values and meaning systems of scientists or researchers as well as those of local actors.

psychosocial and other forms of knowledge. Every group is confronted by challenges and problems in the course of its historical development. These are challenges such as illness and death. Over a period of time concepts, worldviews and assumptions are developed to address these problems (Lock, 1981). Likewise, indigenous communities had to develop practices and conceptual frameworks to deal with problems they encountered in life.

Heelas (1981) defines **indigenous psychologies** as 'the cultural views, theories, conjectures, classifications, assumptions, and metaphors – together with notions embedded in social institutions – which bear on psychological topics' (3). Among these are conceptions of what it means to be a person (self-definition) and statements pertaining to how to relate to others and the natural environment. Ho (1998) also considers indigenous psychologies to be 'the study of human behavior and mental processes within a cultural context that relies on values, concepts, belief systems, methodologies, and other resources indigenous to the specific ethnic or cultural group under investigation' (94). Thus, indigenous psychologies refer to forms of knowledge that arise out of the *social* and *cultural* realities of the people concerned. They are not imposed from outside. They also investigate mundane (everyday), rather than experimental (laboratory), behaviours. Finally, indigenous psychologies aim to address the needs of the people under investigation (Sinha, 1993).

Indigenisation

The definitions of indigenous psychology offered above focus narrowly on the role of local frameworks in the interpretation of human experience. Other frameworks cannot be ignored, however, given that people do not live in impenetrable cultural enclaves. To take this into account, a distinction should be made between indigenous psychologies and **indigenisation**. Indigenisation is an attempt to blend imported theoretical and methodological frameworks with the unique elements of the culture in question (Sinha, 1993). It aims to transform foreign models to make them suitable to local cultural contexts.

According to Kumar (cited in Sinha, 1993), indigenisation may take place at the *structural, substantive,* and *theoretical* levels. *Structurally,* indigenisation refers to the nation's organisational and institutional capabilities to produce and disseminate relevant knowledge. For example, Nsamenang (1992) laments that the growth of indigenous knowledge in Africa is hampered by limited publication and technological resources. *Substantive* or *content* indigenisation could be achieved by applying psychology to address national policy issues (eg health and educational policies) (Sinha, 1993; Nsamenang, 1992). Finally, *theoretical* indigenisation seeks to develop conceptual frameworks and metatheories that are consistent with the sociocultural experiences, worldviews and goals of the people in question. This includes the use of locally derived reference systems as well as borrowed theoretical frameworks that

---

Indigenous psychologies: cultural views, theories, conjectures, classifications, assumptions and metaphors – together with notions embedded in social institutions – which bear on psychological topics.

Indigenisation: attempt to blend imported theoretical and methodological frameworks with the unique elements of the culture in question. Indigenisation aims to transform foreign models to make them suitable to local cultural contexts. Indigenisation can occur at structural, substantive and theoretical levels.

---

have been transformed to suit the needs of local populations (Sinha, 1993). While recognising the importance of other forms of indigenisation, this chapter focuses on theoretical indigenisation.

The worldviews of a society

The chapter provides a conceptual framework to facilitate the indigenisation of psychology in Africa. This is based on the realisation that it is not possible to arrive at a balanced understanding of psychological processes in developing societies without a critical awareness of these societies' assumptions about life. A proper understanding of a people should begin with an examination of the philosophies, languages and worldviews through which they experience the world (Huebner & Garrod, 1991; Simpson, 1974; Vasudev & Hummel, 1987). Psychology in general is based on the worldviews of the white middle class, to the exclusion of the worldviews and values of people in developing societies (Nsamenang, 1992).

DO WE NEED AN AFRICAN-BASED PSYCHOLOGY?

Contesting ideas of a 'dated' worldview

Before going any further, I should like to address the possible objection that the worldview propounded here is dated, given the widespread influences of acculturation and globalisation. To address this objection, I begin by posing the typical Bakhtinian (1981) questions: *Who* says that the worldview is dated? Based on *what* information? And *whose* voice/perspective and interests does he or she represent? Far from being dated, the worldview continues to guide the lives of many people in traditional sectors of African society. Unfortunately, psychology in developing societies tends to be confined to the modern sectors. It has hardly permeated the majority of people in rural settings (Nsamenang, 1992). Rural inhabitants, who hardly, if ever, participate in studies conducted by psychologists, continue to rely on indigenous theories of illness and interventions, among others. What right do we, as psychologists, have to proclaim that these ways of life are 'dated'? If rural inhabitants abandon their 'dated' ways of life, can we guarantee that they will be able to participate in and benefit from modern psychology, among others? Or are we creating doubly marginalised people, deprived of their own cultural heritage and yet unable to partake meaningfully in modern ways of life? Let me leave the reader to ponder these questions.

Selective acculturation and the racism of Western philosophy

The selective **acculturation** of urban Africans into European ways of life tacitly reinforces the assumption that European experiences and philosophical traditions explain the totality of human experiences all over the world. The fact that

Self-contained individualism: traditional psychological view in which the self is regarded as a bounded, autonomous entity – defined in terms of its internal attributes such as thoughts and emotions, independently of social and contextual factors. Like the idea of the **knowing subject**, the self-contained individual is stripped of all particularities such as gender, culture, position, and of his or her existence in space and time.

Acculturation: modification of the culture of a group or an individual as a result of contact with a different culture.

Rural inhabitants, who hardly, if ever, participate in studies conducted by psychologists, continue to rely on indigenous theories of illness and interventions, among other things. What right do we, as psychologists, have to proclaim that these ways of life are 'dated'?

Unilateral:
relating to, involving or affecting only one side.

acculturation tends to be unidirectional perhaps bolsters the view that Western ways of life are better, and African ways superstitious and backward. (Psychologists have never adequately addressed the question why acculturation in South Africa tends to be **unilateral**, with blacks being assimilated into white ways of life, rather than bi-directional.) In a way, this is consistent with the views of some major European philosophers, who contended that nothing of note ever came out of Africa (Laubscher & McNeil, 1995; Onyewuenyi, 1993). For example, Hegel (1956) argued that '[Africa] ... is no historical part of the world; it has no movement or development to exhibit. Historical movement in it – that is in its northern part – belong to the Asiatic or European world' (99). Likewise, Hume is quoted as follows: 'I am apt to suspect the Negroes ... to be naturally inferior to whites. There never was a civilised nation of any complexion other than white' (cited in Serequeberhan, 1991, 5). These philosophers had a major influence in the history of Western ideas, including psychology. It could thus be inferred that their views laid a foundation for the marginalisation of African philosophical and other knowledge systems.

The danger of importing Western systems of understanding

If one considers that critical psychology is concerned with the manner in which men and women *in various classes and cultures* construct and reflect upon their action and experiences in the world (Parker, 1999), then there must be a place for indigenous conceptions of human development in psychology. It does not make sense to explain exclusively the psychological needs and experiences of people in developing societies with reference to conceptual categories and philosophical systems imported from the West. These knowledge traditions 'reflect the needs, intellectual and otherwise, of developed rather than developing societies' (Moghaddam, 1993, 121). Although there is some degree of universality in the challenges facing human societies in the course of their development (eg the need for self-definition, dealing with birth and death), cultural variations exist in the way these challenges are resolved (Heelas, 1981). Most importantly, it is usually the most disadvantaged segments of the population, with limited access to modern healthcare, who rely most on services premised on traditional African worldviews. For example, according to the World Health Organisation, about 80% to 90% of people in developing societies rely on traditional healers for healthcare. Marginalisation of these perspectives thus contributes to the oppression of the people who rely on them.

The oppression of traditional African sociopsychological frameworks

Why do social scientists in developing societies favour Western theoretical frameworks? Is it because indigenous frameworks have fallen out of favour among the local people? I concur with Moghaddam (1993) that 'traditional cultural systems survive in traditional sectors of Third World societies [that are] supported by traditional industries and the social and psychological knowledge provided by traditional religions and philosophies' (121). Traditional African sociopsychological frameworks are not used because, like the people who espouse them, they belong in the category of marginalised knowledge. These knowledge systems are oppressed in the same way that women's concerns were oppressed in psychology (Belenky, Clinchy, Goldberger & Tarule, 1986). Far from being dated, African conceptions of sociopsychological processes have been rendered invisible by the competition between cultural systems, of which the Western is the most dominant. The question is: *Whose* interests does this situation serve?

Focusing on the needs of a society

The process by which new subjectivities are created does not end with undergraduate education (see discussion in Box 1 below): it continues at the postgraduate level. Writing with respect to Iranian psychologists, Moghaddam (1993) laments the separation of indigenous psychologists from the traditional sectors of their society. He maintains that the teaching, research and professional practice of psychologists 'is oriented toward, and more in tune with, the modern sector' (Moghaddam, 1993, 125). Through the process of training, a new (African) elite, whose views and lifestyles are similar to those of middle and upper class Westerners, who are their mentors, and different from those of their own (traditional) societies, is created (Moghaddam, 1993). The same could be said of the training of psychologists in South Africa. Even at the level of research, there is a tendency to encourage students to pursue research questions that are more relevant to the needs of the modern sector (eg human-computer interactions). On the other hand, problems of illiteracy, the disintegration of extended

---

BOX 1   Oppression of African knowledge systems in education

A reflection on the oppression of traditional African knowledge systems cannot be complete without a brief overview of the complicity of the educational system and the African elite. The training of psychologists, for example, initiates (indigenous) students into a new way of thinking about the self and the world. It creates specific subjects who do things in a particular way, as mapped out by their discipline. Let me illustrate this by reflecting briefly on my first encounter with psychology as an undergraduate student. I, like many others in my cohort, was initiated into an individualistic way of thinking about the self and the world. At first this was strange and alienating, given my largely communal upbringing. We had to master theories such as behaviourism, psychoanalysis, and humanistic approaches. Apart from being Western in origin, these theories take the individual as the primary unit of analysis. The context in which the person is embedded is ignored. For example, behaviourism focuses on the relationship between stimuli and responses, while psychoanalytical and humanistic approaches seek to help individ-

uals to realise their innermost potential through the process of individuation (separation) and self-actualisation.

The training was alienating because it was the opposite of the socialisation I had received in the process of growing up. This socialisation had emphasised the relational nature of personhood. This is captured in the saying '*Umuntu ngumuntu ngabantu*', which roughly translates as 'A person becomes a human being through other human beings'. African conceptions of experience and the world were conspicuous by their absence. Even to date, the teaching of African knowledge systems in South African institutions of higher education has been largely left to traditions such as philosophy and theology (eg Louw, 1999; 2001; Shutte, 1993, 2001; Teffo & Roux, 1998) rather than psychology. Consciously or unconsciously, psychological training creates new subjectivities, characterised by an individualistic and disembedded orientation towards the self and the world. Again, the critical question is: To *whose* advantage?

> A critical psychology should not only be concerned with the way in which cultural and institutional practices shape individual development: it should produce research that furthers the needs of developing societies. This includes research into poverty, illiteracy and alienation caused by globalisation.

family systems, and learning under conditions of abject poverty, take a back seat. Those who do tackle such issues run the risk of having their research ignored because it does not address 'hard-core' psychological issues.

Agendas of an African critical psychology

The Aids pandemic has aptly brought home the importance of conducting relevant research in developing societies. Earlier intervention efforts, based on research conducted in developed societies, focused on changing people's cognitions. The assumption was that cognitive change would result in behavioural change. These efforts failed miserably because they did not take into account the sociocultural context of people in developing societies. A critical psychology should thus not only be concerned with the way in which cultural and institutional practices shape individual development: it should produce research that furthers the needs of developing societies. This includes research into poverty, illiteracy and alienation caused by globalisation, among other things. It is only then that critical psychology will achieve its emancipatory project.

Possibility of dialogue between theoretical frameworks

I have written at length about the relevance or otherwise of Western-derived theoretical frameworks. These frameworks are not irrelevant in an absolute sense (Tolman, 1991). As Tolman (1991) argues, even Watson's stimulus-response behaviourism was relevant to the interests of capital and its managers. Western theoretical frameworks do have a relevance of some sort in developing societies. My objection to them is based on the view that they cannot be exclusively used to explain human needs across cultures and across time. In the past, this has been done, to the exclusion of local people's attempts to account for their own life experiences. Neither is it implied that African frameworks are a **panacea** to resolve all sociopsychological problems among Africans. Rather, the purpose is to show that a critical psychology should be willing to engage in a dialogue with theoretical frameworks emanating from the life perspectives of the people in question.

The dynamic interpenetration of worldviews

Let me hasten to address a common criticism of attempts to introduce indigenous knowledge systems to academic and other forms of discourse. The objection is often raised that this reifies culture. (Paradoxically, this criticism is never levelled against Western psychology, which is supposedly free of cultural influences.) This criticism fails to take into account the dynamic nature of **cultural meaning systems**. The ideas presented in this chapter are neither static nor the sole determinant of African thought systems. Cultural meaning systems are always in dialogue with other bodies of knowledge. They are thus capable of undergoing innovation and renewal. This has been the case with independent Christian churches in Africa. These churches have successfully interwoven traditional African and Christian belief systems (Oosthuisen, 1989). One cannot talk about African belief systems without taking history into account. Changes and adaptations resulting from colonisation, Western-type education, industrialisation and exposure to Western media need to be accounted for. Exposure to multiple worldviews means that there cannot be a simple, one-to-one correspondence between a meaning system and how it is employed in real life. To understand the complexity of human experience, we have to take into account the dynamic interpenetration of various worldviews. Rather than arguing for a complete break with cultural meaning systems, or a complete immersion in them, attention should be paid to processes by which they unfold or fail to unfold over time, as they come into contact with other bodies of knowledge (Maffi, 1998).

No *one* unifying African metaphysics

It is important to note that the views presented here are not necessarily shared by all Africans. African scholars are not in agreement about the existence of a

Panacea:
kind of remedy, cure for diseases, ailments, difficulties, problems; a sort of 'cure all'.

Culture:
generally refers to knowledge that is passed on from one generation to another within a given society, through which people make sense of themselves and the world. It incorporates language, values, assumptions, norms of behaviour, ideas about illness and health etc. This body of knowledge is organised systematically and is known in anthropology as 'cultural meaning systems'.

unifying African worldview or metaphysics. As a result, there has been a tendency of late to approach metaphysical issues in a culture-specific way (eg Wiredu, 1984, 1991, 1992). Although there may not be a unifying African metaphysics, there is nevertheless an approach to reality shared by a number of Africans (Nsamenang, 1992; Teffo & Roux, 1998) and other indigenous societies. Its central tenets are beliefs about God, the universe and notions of causality, person and time (Myers, 1988). Historically, these views have been associated with large parts of Africa. Thus, they can be regarded as typical of African metaphysical thinking, especially in the regions south of the Sahara.

What is a worldview?

A worldview is a set of basic assumptions that a group of people develops in order to explain reality and their place and purpose in the world. These assumptions provide a frame of reference to address problems in life. Worldviews provide responses to a set of core questions that people in all cultures have had to respond to in the course of their development (Sue & Sue, 1999). These are questions about the nature of the world (what is the world like?) and the meaning of personhood, among other issues (Jensen, 1997). Worldviews shape our attitudes, values and opinions as well as the way we think and behave (Sue, 1978).

The spread of Western concepts and categories of understanding – particularly in psychology – has excluded or marginalised the lived experience of others, especially Africans.

Worldviews contain the following components: *time orientation; people-nature orientation; activity orientation;* and the *relational orientation* (Jensen, 1997; Lock, 1981; Sue & Sue, 1999). The table overleaf shows general cultural differences in worldviews.

To say that there is an African worldview does not mean every member of a culture should subscribe to it, in the same manner that not every European subscribes to individualism as a way of life. The worldview described is an attempt to explain human reality from an indigenous African perspective (Myers, 1988). Ignoring alternative worldviews limits practitioners' ability to deal with people from different cultural backgrounds, especially in counselling and healthcare (see Boxes 1 and 2).

AN AFRICAN METAPHYSICAL SYSTEM

Defining metaphysics

Metaphysics is concerned with a people's conceptions of reality, their position in the universe, and their relation to others and the environment. It represents

Metaphysics: branch of philosophy concerned with our conceptions of reality, position in the universe, and our relation to others and the environment – our grappling with time, space, causality and existence.

Table 2.1 Components of a worldview

Description	Examples
Time orientation A culture may emphasise history and tradition, the here and now, or the distant future. Time and space orientation are intertwined. Self-awareness involves an appreciation of where one is coming from, the present, as well as where one is likely to be in the future	Western societies tend to emphasise the future. Time is organised into linear segments, marked by what people are doing at a time (Hall, 1983; Hall & Hall, 1990). Traditional communities, on the other hand, concentrate on the past and the present. It is not the passage of time per se that is important, but the relationship one has with ancestors (the past) and one's fellow human beings (the present). The ideal is to live harmoniously with ancestors, the family and the community. Paying attention to context and relationships is thus more important than the mathematical division of time.
Orientation to nature This dimension answers the question: How is the relationship of people to nature to be understood?	For cultures that emphasise the past, external forces beyond one's control determine life (eg God, ancestors, and fate). For cultures that emphasise the present, people and nature co-exist, living harmoniously with each other. Most indigenous African societies emphasise both the past and the present. (Myers, 1988). Future-oriented cultures, on the other hand, emphasise mastery and control over the environment, a situation that holds in many Anglo societies. (Ivey, Ivey & Simerk-Morgan, 1997)
Human ˙activity The human activity dimension answers the question: What is the preferred mode of human activity?	Traditional Western cultures place value on doing over the being or being-in-becoming (the process) mode of activity. This emanates from the belief that one's value as a person is determined by personal accomplishments (Sue & Sue, 1999). Other cultures, on the other hand, emphasise being or being-in-becoming. This mode values harmony with others and the social milieu, as well spiritual fulfillment. (Sue & Sue, 1999)
The relational orientation This is concerned with how the self is defined in relation to the Other and the environment	Traditional Western cultures regard the self as a bounded entity. People are defined in terms of internal attributes such as thoughts and emotions. This view of selfhood is also known as self-contained individualism (Sampson, 1988, 1993; Hermans et al, 1992) or the independent view of self (Markus & Kitayama, 1991). On the other hand, indigenous cultures define the self in terms of one's relationships with others, such as family, community and status or position within the group. Children are socialised to harmonise their interests with those of their family and the community.

people's attempts to grapple with fundamental questions pertaining to existence, space, time and causality (Teffo & Roux, 1998). Metaphysical systems may be seen as cultural models (Quinn & Holland, 1987) or meaning systems (Miller, 1997). These are the taken-for-granted models through which people make sense of the world and their behaviour in it.

Metaphysical **ontologies** not only prescribe what is but also incorporate ideals of what can be, the ideal cosmic and natural order, and its possible defects. For example, traditional African societies believe that there should be harmony and interdependence between elements in the cosmos. Disconnection between parts comprising the whole is undesirable and immoral or

Ontology: describes the nature of reality to be studied, and what can be known about it. For example, traditional African worldviews described in this chapter posit a world in which everything is inter-connected.

unethical. Thus, awareness of this framework is indispensable if one were wanting to understand a people's conception of moral reasoning. Traditional Western theories, on the other hand, conceive moral development individual-istically. Moral actors are abstract subjects who derive moral principles rationally and independently of history and time (Kohlberg, 1981, 1984; Rawls, 1972). Given the abovementioned differences between traditional African and European understandings of the relationship between the person and his or her environment, it is unfair to declare one culture morally deficient based on the conceptual categories of another (Simpson, 1974).

BOX 2   Worldviews, conceptions of illness, and counselling

The following case study illustrates the impor-tance of worldviews in counselling. The client presented at a Student Counselling Centre at one of the local universities. He was finding it difficult to concentrate on his studies. Thus, he was not making satisfactory academic progress. His name and identifying particulars have been altered.

Bheki is a 29-year-old, single black student. He resides in one of the townships surrounding a major urban city. He was referred to the Student Counselling Centre by one of his lecturers, who had noted that he was sometimes 'day-dreaming' in class. Bheki is the 6th eldest in a family of nine children. They all live with their mother, who is a pensioner. Except for the eldest sister, who now lives independently, all his siblings are unemployed. Prior to returning to university, Bheki had been a teacher for 5 years. He decided to pursue further studies to improve his education. This would in turn improve his income, enabling him to support his siblings better. He maintained that whenever he tried to study he became drowsy and fell asleep. He attributed this to family problems. He had felt like this since 1994, but the situation had become more pronounced over the years.

Bheki's father, Mr Nkosi, passed away in 1994. He was born in a polygamous family. There was always tension within the family. Mr Nkosi decided to get married and stay away from his original family. He moved away from Nkandla, in Northern KwaZulu-Natal, to the city to escape 'bewitchment' by members of his extended family. Unfortunately he died before

he could make peace with them. Bheki believes that someone interfered with the transition of his father's soul from the world of the living to the spiritual world. He maintained that his father's soul was being held captive by *umthakathi* (a sorcerer), who had turned his father into a zombie. He was worried that his father's soul was wandering aimlessly, without finding peace. He was also worried that, as the eldest son, the same fate would befall him if he happened to die before rectifying the situation.

Bheki came to the Student Counselling Centre reluctantly because he knew that coun-sellors 'did not understand traditional problems'.

I've cited this case study to show that the client relied on a different worldview to account for his experience. This worldview espouses a different theory of illness. It is based on a con-nected, rather than an abstract, view of the self. The case study is about relationships, responsi-bilities, and consequences to the self and others. To make sense of it, one needs to understand the nature of human relationships in traditional African societies. This worldview is not part of formal psychological training in many institu-tions. No wonder the client felt the counsellors 'did not understand traditional problems'. When presented with this case, many students are quick to argue incompetence, preferring to 'refer the person to a traditional healer'. From an ethical perspective, that might be an appropriate thing to do. However, one way to address this shortcoming is to incorporate indigenous world-views into the training of psychologists.

Metaphysics and psychology

A related issue is the relationship between metaphysical ontologies and psychological topics. Much & Harré (1994) maintain that a culture's psychological discourse is a reflection of dominant local metaphysical ontologies. From these ontologies are derived theories of the person, the social context, and the natural order. All psychologies are somehow 'connected to underlying metaphysical ontologies which ... order things in specific ways with regard to what is "good" and "bad", "right" and "wrong" about conditions of life' (Much & Harré, 1994, 308). Unfortunately, the Western history of ideas has created an illusion that psychological theories are objective, universalisable and free of roots in historically particular metaphysical systems. (See Much & Harré, 1994, for an account of how spirit and, later, the mind, came to be valued over the body in Western thought.)

Metaphysical ontologies are central to traditional African understandings of the world. Akbar (1984) and Nobles (1972) have argued that they can serve as a foundation of an African-based psychology. In the next section, four interdependent philosophical assumptions bearing directly on psychological topics are discussed. These are (a) the hierarchy of beings, (b) the notion of vitality, (c) the principle of cosmic unity, and (d) the communal view of personhood. The worldview presented below extols connection and interdependence, and is hence oriented towards **concrete (particular)** existence. It differs from traditional Western worldviews, which prize an **abstract**, **generalised view** of the self.

> Much & Harré (1994) maintain that a culture's psychological discourse is a reflection of dominant local metaphysical ontologies. From these ontologies are derived theories of the person, the social context, and the natural order.

BOX 3   Marginalised worldviews in healthcare

The fact that a worldview is marginalised does not mean that it ceases to function. People continue to rely on it, sometimes secretly. The following excerpt is from Gambu (2000). Gambu studied ethical decision-making in the nursing profession. She was interested in how traditional African worldviews influence nurses' understanding and application of ethics. Nurses are guided by a professional Code of Ethics. Professional codes emphasise *autonomy,* which is the freedom of individuals to hold and act upon their own opinions provided they do not violate others' rights; *beneficence,* which requires professionals to protect patients from harm and to promote their welfare; and *justice,* which requires that people be treated according to what is fair or due. Professional codes of ethics are based on Western assumptions about the person. They do not give guidelines on how to act ethically in particular circumstances.

The nurses interviewed were black Africans who saw mainly black patients.

The following extract involves an ophthalmic nurse who saw a 50-year-old partially blind patient. The nurse's initial examination revealed no organic basis for the patient's blindness. Her own beliefs about Zulu traditions then came to the fore. Rather than referring the patient for further assessment, as expected, she secretly advised her to consult a traditional healer:

Gambu: What was the ethical dilemma for you in that situation?

Nurse: The conflict was that I really did not know what to do. *Should I refer* this woman for further assessment or *should I advise her to consult a*

BOX 3   Marginalised worldviews in healthcare *(continued)*

traditional healer? The conflict was also the fact that *we as black people* have our own beliefs and customs while at the same time, in our training we are taught what to do, which is different to our beliefs. But, *we at the same time know that there are customs* which we should follow, so the [ethical dilemma] for me was in not knowing what to do.

Gambu: What did you eventually do?

Nurse: *I secretly told her to consult a traditional healer whom I knew,* and she eventually confessed that she had been to see a traditional healer before.

Gambu: How did your decision make you feel emotionally?

Nurse: It was a *very difficult decision* for me but I consoled myself that I had done the right thing because I knew that *there are things that cannot be cured at the hospital.* I have worked in rural

areas before, *people there believe strongly in traditional customs.* We also saw many instances where traditional healing was beneficial. (Gambu, 2000, 68; original emphasis)

This extract has been cited not because the nurse acted ethically (or otherwise). The aim is to highlight the shortcomings of a universalistic approach to ethics. Had traditional African worldviews, including theories of illness, been part of medical discourse, the nurse would have freely discussed the issue with her colleagues (rather than acting secretly). This shows that marginalised worldviews do not die out. They continue to operate underground. It is thus important to engage openly with them. Useful aspects of African worldviews should be incorporated into patient treatment. This way, the many indigenous people who rely on them to make sense of their experiences will be empowered. Open dialogue with this perspective will also enhance ethical conduct.

The hierarchy of beings

Traditionally, Africans believe that all things in the universe are connected ontologically to one other. Beings and objects in the universe are organised hierarchically (Mbiti, 1991; Ngubane, 1977; Ruch & Anyanwu, 1981). Intricate webs of relationships exist between organisms and objects in the hierarchy (Figure 2.1). Each object or organism is dependent upon and capable of influencing and being influenced by others. The nature and direction of influence is determined by the amount of life force (energy or power, see discussion below) possessed by each object or organism.

Different levels of being

Intermediate world: level in the hierarchy of being in African metaphysics that consists of human beings.

Inanimate objects and plants occupy the lowest level on the hierarchy. They have very little life force of their own. As a result, they have no direct influence on superior beings such as human beings. Animals occupy the level immediately above that of objects and plants. The next level, which Ngubane (1977) calls the **intermediate world**, consists of human beings. Human beings can communicate directly or indirectly with the living-dead (ancestors) (Mbiti, 1991), who occupy the next level on the hierarchy. According to Ngubane

(1977), the world of the ancestors is divided into two. First, there is the world of the recently deceased. They do not proceed directly to ancestorhood; initially they remain in an in-between state, until their relatives have performed rituals of integration on their behalf. While in this state, they are incapable of interceding with God on human beings' behalf. However, they can make their concerns known to their relatives through dreams. Then there is the world of **integrated ancestors**, those who have had rituals performed for them. Integrated ancestors are capable of communicating with God on behalf of their relatives. Ancestors, whose world is both analogous and contiguous to that of human beings, continue to interact with, and remain interested in the affairs of, their relatives (Teffo & Roux, 1998). Human beings maintain a link with their ancestors through acts of libation and sacrifices. It is through the ancestors that human beings communicate with God, who is rarely invoked directly.

Generalised versus concrete self: view of the self as the 'generalised other' requires us to see all individuals as rational beings with the same rights and duties we would ascribe to ourselves. It is what we have in common that matters, rather than the *individuality* or *concrete identity* of the other. If we adopt the standpoint of the self as the 'concrete other', on the other hand, people's individuality, history, and concrete identity take centre stage, while what we have in common recedes to the background.

Integrated ancestors: ancestors who are capable of communicating with God on behalf of their relatives, and for whom rituals are performed. Ancestors, whose world is both analogous and contiguous to that of humans, continue to interact with, and remain interested in the affairs of, their relatives.

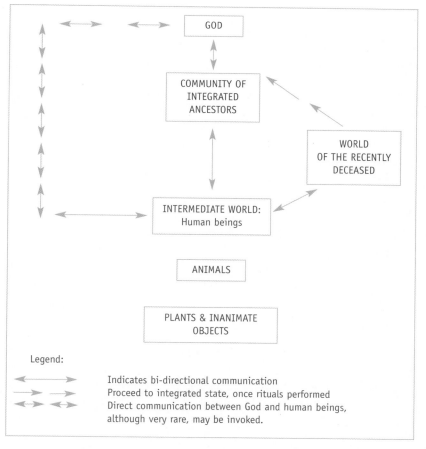

Figure 2.1 **Relationships between elements in the hierarchy of beings**

The role of ancestors

The notion of ancestors has caused a great deal of confusion in African scholarship, resulting in the misrepresentation of African belief systems. This confusion is often reflected in the view that Africans worship ancestors (Dzobo, 1992; Ejizu, 2000; Mbiti, 1991). The situation is complicated by the fact that in English the word 'ancestor' means any person from whom one is descended (Geddie, 1901/1964; Swannell, 1992). However, Africans conceive ancestors differently. Who is an ancestor, from an African point of view? To begin with, I propose that the word *iinyanya* or *izinyanya* (plural for isiXhosa and isiZulu respectively) be substituted for ancestors, because of connotations associated with the English word. Not every person qualifies to be an *inyanya* (singular).

Inyanya

Only those who lived a life characterised by high moral standards can be elevated to the status of an *inyanya*. These standards include promoting interdependence and harmony within one's family and community. Once rituals of integration – *ukubuyisa,* literally, to return the spirit of the ancestor home – have been performed, the deceased who were good moral exemplars join the community of *iinyanya.* This is a spiritual community of other family members who lived exemplary lives. Sometimes a person does not have to die to be considered *inyanya* (Dzobo, 1992). Older members of the family, whose lives are worthy of emulation, may be referred to as *iinyanya.* Nevertheless, it usually remains essential that integration rituals be performed after death, to bring their *ubu-nyanya* (ancestorhood) to completion.

Izinyanya and the living

The relationship between the living and *izinyanya* is one of interdependence. The latter need the former to perform rituals on their behalf. This elevates them to an influential status, thus giving them audience with God. This means that they can now negotiate with God on behalf of their descendants. Connection with God through *izinyanya* is considered essential for family unity and prosperity (Ngubane, 1977).

The *iinyanya* are moral paragons or exemplars of good conduct. Their superior moral values and principles continue to be cherished. These are adopted as normative standards of conduct. It is believed that the world of *iinyanya* is no different from that of human beings. *Izinyanya* continue to live an exemplary life in their world. They also remain interested in their families' affairs. As guardians of morality, *izinyanya* sanction bad conduct by withdrawing their interest in family matters. The withdrawal of *izinyanya* is undesirable. It breaks the chain of communication between individuals and

God. The family is effectively cut off from God, the source of all life. Rituals and acts of libation are not ancestor worship. They ensure that through *izinyanya* one remains connected to God, the highest source of life.

A holistic worldview

God is at the apex of the hierarchy. Although at the apex, God is not apart from the rest of the world. Together with the world, God 'constitutes the spatio-temporal totality of existence' (Teffo & Roux, 1998, 140). That is, God does not rule the world from a distance, but permeates everything in it. For example, the fact that human beings participate in the Divine is captured by the Sotho saying, *'motho ke Modimo'*, which means 'The person is (the) Divine'. God's omnipresence is consistent with the **holistic** worldview; an account of the world in which everything is interconnected in such a way that elements of the whole are contained in each part (see discussion of cosmic unity below).

Holistic/holism: account of the world in which everything is interconnected in such a way that elements of the whole are contained in each part.

THE NOTION OF VITALITY OR LIFE FORCE

Beings and objects in the hierarchy are endowed with a life force. The notion of life force has been a source of great controversy in African scholarship since Tempels (1959) propounded it. According to Myers (1988), **life force** refers to the energy or power that is the essence of all phenomena, material and immaterial. Everything is endowed with 'energy', spirit, or creative force. The idea of life force as 'spirit' does not imply ghost-like, inner powers of an occult nature. It refers to dynamic creativity, thought to be the most precious gift from God. This creativity descends hierarchically from God to *izinyanya*, elders, human beings, and all that is created (Kasenene, 1992). The creativity of God's power is manifest in the changing seasons, birth, the cycles of nature and in human achievements. It is extended to *izinyanya*, human beings, and other creatures and creations lower in the hierarchy, in descending order. The Basotho/ Tswana refer to a person's life force as *seriti*, while the Nguni call it *isithunzi*. Literally, both terms mean 'the shadow'. Human beings are capable of influencing events in the world to a certain degree, because they partake in this creative life force. Ideally, it is expected that one will always use life force to maintain vital connections and interdependence between the family, the community and the rest of nature.

Life force: energy or power that is the essence of all phenomena, material and immaterial.

Distinguishing life from *life force*

A crucial distinction needs to be made between the principle of *life force*, the principle of *life* (as in being a living organism), and being *full of energy* (vitality as in liveliness). The principle of life force cannot be reduced to the quality of being alive, given that both the living and the deceased participate in this vital

When the Nguni and the Sotho of southern Africa say a person *uyaphila/o ea phela* (he or she has life), they are not referring to biological life. They refer to the relationship between individuals and their milieu. It is their lived experience, as evidenced in the day-to-day relationships with others, that is at stake.

union. When the Nguni and the Sotho of southern Africa say a person *uyaphila/o ea phela* (he or she has life), they are not referring to biological life. They refer to the relationship between individuals and their milieu. It is their lived experience, as evidenced in the day-to-day relationships with others, that is at stake. It is expected that one will live harmoniously and interdependently with others. From an African point of view, life is a never-ending spiral of human and communal relationships. It is defined in terms of reciprocal obligations (Dzobo, 1992; Mbiti, 1991). All individuals are expected to promote vitality in the community by fulfilling their duties and responsibilities, according to their positions or roles (Kasenene, 1992).

An organic view of the universe

Separate and connected ways of knowing: terms popularised by Belenky *et al* (1986). Separate knowing is characterised by a skeptical, distanced, and impartial stance toward the object of one's knowledge. It takes an adversarial, argumentative stance to new ideas, even if they appear to make intuitive sense. Connected knowing, on the other hand, tries to accommodate new ideas, searching for what is 'right' even in what might initially appear to be wrong.

Traditionally, it is assumed that human beings will live harmoniously with animals and nature. This organic view of the universe, the principal feature of which is to think ecologically, making little or no distinctions between nature and culture, is common among indigenous societies (Howard, 1994; Maffi, 1998). Living harmoniously with the natural environment requires that it be harvested to the extent that it is necessary to support human needs. This had to be done respectfully and religiously. For example, religious rituals accompanied the planting and harvesting of crops. Respect for the principle of life is also illustrated by the practice by traditional healers to pray before harvesting plants for medical purposes. It is believed that not only does this make the plant more effective; failure to do so could cause it to fail to regenerate. Harvesting the plant in a disrespectful manner will cause it to die. This means that it will not be available to support human life in the future. Recently, indigenous communities working with Western-trained scientists to find a cure for HIV/Aids have voiced the view that plants should be collected respectfully and religiously (Burford, Bodeker, Kabatesi, Gemmill, & Rukangira, 2000). Behind this concern is respect for the principle of life. It also affirms the interdependence between the natural and the human environment.

The causes of things

Life forces are constantly in interaction with each other. It is possible for unknown forces to intervene in the order of events, without our awareness. The nature of this intervention is beyond our conscious understanding. For this reason Africans deny the possibility of events happening by accident. For example, in the event of a personal tragedy, cause is sought as to how individual, the family or a sinister force might have brought about the undesired consequence. This stems from the belief that the creative life force may be manipulated for sinister purposes. Witchcraft is an example (Ngubane, 1977). It is believed that a witch can manipulate life force to bring about an unfortunate event to someone. The tendency among Africans to prefer **teleo-logically** inclined explanations stems from the view that life force can be manipulated. Teleological orientations assume that 'reality hangs together because of aims, and is driven by aims' (Teffo & Roux, 1998, 134). Consequently, questions are directed not only towards why events happen. Of most interest is why they happen to *someone* at a *particular locality* and at a *certain point in time.*

In review, then, life force is the creative energy, extending directly from God to all that is created. Through life force all share in God's creative energy or spirit, although not to the same degree. The creative power descends vertically to *izinyanya,* human beings, and all that is created. The principle of life force requires coexistence with and strengthening of vital relationships, in the community and universe (Kasenene, 1992; Ruch & Anyanwu, 1981). Severance of vital relationships constitutes the opposite of the Good, and is undesirable. Whether life force exists or not is irrelevant for our purposes. What is important is that a number of people share this belief. The belief continues to influence their perception of the world.

Teleology: derived from the Greek words *telos* (end) and *logos* (discourse), seeks to explain the universe in terms of final (rather than immediate) causes. It is based on the view that the universe has a purpose or design. To understand the cause of things, one needs to understand the final cause, which is the purpose why the phenomenon exists or was created.

THE PRINCIPLE OF COSMIC UNITY

Knowing through participation

Cosmic unity is closely related to the notion of vitality (Anyanwu, 1981; Kasenene, 1992; Kinoti; 1992; Verhoef & Michel, 1997). It is sometimes referred to as a holistic conception of life. Cosmic unity means that there is a connection between God, *izinyanya,* animals, plants and inanimate objects (Mbiti, 1969; Verhoef & Michel, 1997). Within this system, everything is perpetually in motion, influencing and being influenced by something else. This is another principle shared by a number of indigenous societies. Indigenous societies, for the most part, do not view the world in a mechanical, cause-effect manner (Howard, 1994; Maffi, 1998). They tend to subscribe to a holistic view of the world. This means that units of analysis are not abstracted from their context. What has evolved from this point of view is the idea that knowledge *through participation,* rather than separation and abstraction, is to be prized. One does not know by standing and observing at a distance. To know is *to participate in the dynamic process involving interaction between parts and the whole.* Analysis of discrete elements in isolation from their context cannot account for the flux of becoming (Myers, 1988). Rather, becoming can be accounted for only by a holistic approach that relates individual elements to the total system. Again, this differs sharply from traditional Western ways of knowing. From a Western perspective, the knower stands apart from the object of his or her knowledge.

Cosmic unity: idea that there is a connection between God, *izinyanya,* animals, plants, and inanimate objects. Within this system, everything is perpetually in motion, influencing and being influenced by something else.

Dynamism between parts and whole

The dynamism between parts and the whole, characteristic of the African world-view, is illustrated in the following quotation from Senghor (1966). Senghor draws contrasts between traditional European and African worldviews:

> [T]he African has always and everywhere presented a concept of the world, which is diametrically opposed to the traditional philosophy of Europe. The latter is essentially static, objective, dichotomous; it is in fact dualistic in that it makes an absolute distinction between body and soul, matter and spirit. It is founded on separation and opposition, on analysis and conflict. The African on the other hand, conceives the world, beyond the diversity of its forms, as a fundamentally mobile yet unique reality that seeks synthesis. (4)

Senegalese poet and Africanist scholar, Leopold S. Senghor.

Observer as part of the system

Myers (1988) argues that a holistic conception of life is compatible with the new physics (quantum and relativity theories). Unlike classical physics, the new physics sees the world in terms of interacting, inseparable components, which are perpetually in motion. The observer or scientist is integral to this process, rather than detached. Similarly, Capra (1988) has drawn parallels between the new physics and the mystic philosophical traditions of the East and other traditions. He argues that mystical thought 'provides a consistent and relevant conception of the world in which scientific discoveries can be made in perfect harmony with spiritual and religious beliefs' (11). Although writing about Eastern belief systems, Capra maintains that his views apply equally to all mystically based belief systems.

The holistic conception of life means, to reiterate, that one cannot look at individual units in isolation from their context. This is particularly so if one is working in indigenous societies. Because everything is perpetually in motion, influencing and being influenced by something else, social science research can no longer afford to follow the fragmented, disinterested model of the natural sciences. This model is inadequate, especially in communities that subscribe to a holistic worldview. What we know about the world and ourselves is inseparable from our worldviews or *ways of knowing* (Belenky *et al*, 1986; Howard, 1994). Likewise, we need to understanding psychological processes with reference to the frameworks of the people concerned. It is high time that the world open up to traditional African lenses of viewing the world, in the same way that it has considered similar mystic philosophical traditions from the East.

COMMUNAL LIFE AND PERSONHOOD

'An organic relationship between component individuals'

Another important principle underlying traditional African thinking is that of *communal life*. Personhood in African thought is defined in relation to the community. It is important to discuss briefly understandings of the term 'community' in African scholarship. Community does not mean a 'mere collection of individuals, each with his [sic] private set of preferences, but all of whom get together nonetheless because they realise ... that in association they can accomplish things which they are not able to accomplish otherwise' (Menkiti, 1984, 179). It does not refer to a collection of **atomistic** individuals who gather together to pursue common goals. Community refers to an organic relationship between component individuals (Menkiti, 1984). Coetzee (1998) defines it as 'an ongoing association of men and women who have special commitment to one another and a developed (distinct) sense of their common life' (276).

Atomistic:
consisting of many separate, diverse or disparate elements.

Community as characteristic way of life

Community results from a shared understanding of a characteristic way of life. A sense of community exists if people mutually recognise the obligation to be responsive to one another's needs. The tendency among traditional societies to regard a number of people as members of one's family, irrespective of the actual genetic relationship, stems from this understanding of community (Nsamenang, 1992). Extension of terms such as mother and father to others goes hand in hand with an obligation to act responsively, in a manner that is befitting of these terms (Verhoef & Michel, 1997). For example, parental responsibilities may be assumed by anyone through the practice of collective rearing of children (Mkhise, 1999). This is informed by an understanding that the child will grow and develop leadership and/or other qualities that will enhance the life of the community as a whole. The entire community is thus expected to play a vital role in raising children.

Personhood relationally defined

Because of the interdependence between individuals and the community, personhood cannot be defined solely in terms of physical and psychological attributes (Menkiti, 1984). It is through participation in a community that a person finds meaning in life (Kasenene, 1994; Kinoti, 1992; Menkiti, 1984; Verhoef & Michel, 1997). The importance of the community in self-definition is summed up by Mbiti's (1969) dictum 'I am because we are, and since we are, therefore I am' (214). The rootedness of the self-in-community is reflected in sayings such as *Umuntu ngumuntu ngabantu* (Nguni), or *Motho ke motho ka batho babang* (Sotho). These roughly translate as: 'One becomes a human being through other human beings.' Similarly, the Xhivenda equivalent, *Muthu u bebelwa munwe* ('a person is born for the other'), points at the interdependence between self and other.

Personhood in African thought is defined relationally. A person does not exist alone. Rather, he or she belongs to a community of similarly constituted selves. Belonging carries with it a dynamism or 'dance of harmony [because] everyone who belongs is continuously moving, adjusting to the rhythm of life within the community' (Ogbonnaya, 1994, 77). This occurs as individuals attend to their responsibilities to others and the natural environment. The *ilimo* and *ukusisa* practices are good examples. *Ilimo* is a practice by which neighbours join together to help till another's fields. It is extended to other activities such as building a house. *Ukusisa* refers to the act of loaning someone cattle so that he or she can plough the fields and milk the cows. Activities such as these maintain communal equilibrium, thus strengthening the community.

> Because of the interdependence between individuals and the community, personhood cannot be defined solely in terms of physical and psychological attributes.

> The importance of the community in self-definition is summed up by Mbiti's (1969) dictum 'I am because we are, and since we are, therefore I am' (214).

CRITICISMS OF THE 'SELF-IN-COMMUNITY'

Ikuenobe (1998) raises some plausible criticisms of the African conception of the person. He notes that it may be construed as an account in which individuals are under the totalitarian control of the community. However, the notion of the person-in-community does not deny individuality (Myers, 1988; Ogbonnaya, 1994). Individuals can transcend the perspective of the community in creative ways. It is expected, however, that the achievements of outstanding individuals will transform the community to a higher level of functioning. The relationship between an individual and the community is thus a multi-directional one. Ogbonnaya (1994) argues that 'the community is preserved and enriched by the "highest riches" of the person ... just as the person is continually enriched by the experience of emergent selves in the persona-communal' (78). This is a vindication of the principle of interdependence between parts and the whole: individuals are part of a collective (community) that they create and which, in turn, creates them (Myers, 1988).

The relationship between individuals and community is not always smooth. Tensions are likely to occur (Gyekye, 1984). Ideally, tensions should be resolved in a way that restores interdependence, and perhaps even advance the community to a higher level of functioning than before. This could be the case with creative individuals who invent novel ways of doing things. Initially, these inventions may be viewed with suspicion. However, once the invention has been shown to benefit the community as a whole, the individual is acclaimed as a model to be emulated. Dzobo (1992) refers to the symbol of the fingers and the hand to illustrate the interdependence between an individual and a community. Fingers represent free, unique, independent members of society. However, they are firmly rooted in the hand (the whole). On the other hand, the community (the hand) is incomplete without the fingers. The view of the self-in-community recognises the possibility of tensions between the person and the community. The ideal is that they will be resolved in a way that enhances both individual and community.

THE FAMILY COMMUNITY

If the community in general is important, then the family community is of utmost significance. It forms an essential element of an individual's social reality and personal identity, apart from which personhood is almost inconceivable (Paris, 1995). It should be noted that 'family' is not restricted to the Western notion of a nuclear family. It constitutes a closely knit community of relatives, including both the living and the deceased (*izinyanya*) (Moyo, 1992). Deceased family members continue to partake in the day-to-day affairs of their families. Through the totemic system, family could be extended to plants, other non-living objects, and anything connected with human relationships

Totem: animal, plant, or natural object that serves among traditional peoples as the emblem of a clan or family.

(Mbiti, 1969). In the **totemic** system, an animal (eg a particular snake) is adopted by the family or clan as its emblem. The animal is treated as a member of the family. The family, as defined above, is *the* most important aspect of self-definition. To be disowned by family is to cease to exist.

The family is hierarchically organised, from the oldest member to the youngest child. Members are bound together by a reciprocal understanding of their roles and responsibilities. These depend on position and status in the hierarchy. The elder, usually the oldest member of the family, has the all-important responsibility to ensure that the family remains a thriving, cohesive unit. He or she is thus highly respected. Older members have the most complete memory of the family's lineage, and are considered to be much closer to *izinyanya* (Mbiti, 1991). The injunction to respect elders, common in traditional societies, emanates from an understanding that a person of an elder's status and position will act in a dignified and *responsible* manner. Elders earn their status in the community by virtue of the richness of their knowledge and experiences. They are expected to bring their wisdom to bear in decision-making (Ikuenobe, 1998; Paris, 1995). For example, elders play a critical role in resolving marital and other forms of conflict. Failure to act responsibly diminishes the elder's status. Irresponsible elders may in turn be censured by *izinyanya*, who do not look kindly upon family members who neglect their responsibilities (Moyo, 1992).

PERSONHOOD AS A PROCESS

It has been mentioned that the concept of a person in African societies is that of a person-in-relation, a 'being-with-and-for-others,' and not an isolated, atomistic individual. To attain personhood, it is not sufficient to be a biological organism with physical and psychological attributes. Personhood does not follow automatically simply because one is born of human seed. Rather, it must be earned (Menkiti, 1984; Ruch & Anyanwu, 1981). Menkiti (1984) refers to this as the 'processual' nature of being. Children are first born into a family community. They then undergo rituals of incorporation, culminating in some societies in the rites marking the passage from childhood to adulthood.

Personhood as earned

It could be argued that the 'processual' nature of personhood means that one becomes a person as one 'goes along' in society. Indeed, Menkiti (1984) takes this position. He maintains that children are not fully human. Following Gyekye (1992), however, I would argue that the fact that personhood must be earned is not a denial of personhood to children. It is an affirmation of the view that *personhood is an ongoing process* attained through interactions with others and one's community. It requires one to affirm ideals and standards thought to be constitutive of the life of a community. These are standards such as generosity, benevolence and respect (Gyekye, 1992). A number of sayings in some African societies refer to people who have failed to meet standards expected of a fully human person. These are sayings such as *ga e se motho* (Tswana) or *a ku si muntu* (Nguni), literally meaning 'he or she is not a person'. Because one can fall short of these standards at any stage in the life cycle, personhood could be regarded as a *becoming*. It is an unpredictable, open-ended process during which personhood may be achieved, lost, and regained, depending on a person's circumstances. In the following chapter, the idea of personhood as becoming is revisited and discussed with reference to the soci-ocultural approaches to the self.

Ubuntu

It should be emphasised that standards of personhood are not of an abstract, theoretical type. Possession of the qualities of personhood is reflected in people's relationships with others and their milieu. It is referred to as *ubuntu* in Nguni, and *botho* in Sotho/Tswana. *Ubuntu* is inferred from a person's knowledge of his or her duties and responsibilities within a community of other, interdependent human beings. Further, to *know* one's duties is not enough. **Ubuntu** is the *concrete* or *practical* realisation of this knowledge and not a cognitive appraisal of it. However, because a person is always a being-with-and-for-others, failure to attain personhood points blame at the individual, his or her family and his or her community. Just as it is a collective responsibility to raise children, an individual's shortcomings reflect poorly on his or her family and the community. This is consistent with the notion of person-in-community, discussed above.

Ubuntu: concrete or practical realisation of the knowledge that the possession of the qualities of personhood is reflected in people's relationship with others. *Ubuntu* is characterised by caring, just and respectful relationships.

CONCLUSION

An African critical psychology

Critical psychology situates psychological functioning in its societal and histor-ical context. It attends to different voices, especially those that have been marginalised for ideological and political reasons. This chapter has attempted to achieve some of the aims of an African critical psychology by highlighting the value of indigenous worldviews in psychological discourse. Attention to marginalised voices is particularly important, given the long history of the cultural subordination of African points of view in South Africa.

A framework for an African-based psychology

The chapter has presented a philosophical framework that could serve as a basis of an African-based psychology. According to this framework, objects and organisms in the universe are organised hierarchically, from inanimate objects at the bottom, to God at the apex. A dynamic interdependence exists between all elements within the system. These elements are capable of influencing and being influenced by others, depending on their life force. This dynamism means that reality can be understood by studying the system as a whole, rather than isolated parts. Similarly, personhood cannot be conceived independently of the relationship between the individual and the community. Implications of this framework for counselling and health-care provision were briefly illustrated.

A dynamic relationship of worldviews

However, the modern world is characterised by rapid changes. Cross-pollination of ideas between cultures occurs more rapidly than in the past. In the same way that Western psychology cannot afford to ignore African worldviews, it will be shortsighted of African scholarship to remain insulated in one conceptual framework. It is imperative to take into account the many factors that influence individual development. As mentioned previously, people are exposed to multiple perspectives. Once incorporated into people's ways of thinking, these perspectives are capable of entering into a dynamic relationship with each other. This process may result in the emergence of new perspectives out of the old. It is this dialogue between perspectives that is of psychological significance. The dialogue should address questions such as how African worldviews interface with new ideas such as Christianity and individualism. Do they exist simultaneously with these worldviews? Does exposure to new ideas affect men and women, the young and the old, in the same way? New theoretical frameworks are needed to account for psychological processes resulting from the interpenetration of various worldviews.

The task of acknowledging multiple influences in psychological development is made possible by the sociocultural approaches advocated by Vygotsky (1978) and Bakhtin (1981, 1990), among others. Sociocultural approaches enable us to account for an existence of African psychological perspectives alongside other orientations. They also offer conceptual tools to critically engage with tensions and power dimensions involved in psychological development. These theoretical frameworks are discussed in the following chapter.

Critical thinking tasks

1. Traditional Western psychology has been criticised because of its underlying assumptions. Revisit one or two mainstream psychological theories you are most familiar with (eg Rogerian approaches) and critically discuss each theory's assumptions about (a) the nature of the knowing subject (the self) and (b) the relationship between the knower and the object of his or her knowledge.

2.   Distinguish between indigenous psychologies and indigenisation.

3.   Mention and briefly discuss local/indigenous practices, values and beliefs that could contribute to an indigenous African psychology. To help you get started, three examples are given: *communal child-rearing practices, conceptions of illness* and *ways of handling grief.*

    ▷ Discuss the psychological significance of the three practices mentioned above with a colleague who is familiar with African practices and value systems. (For example, your discussion answers questions such as: How do traditional African communities raise children? What is the nature of the self that is encouraged by raising children this way?)

    ▷ Working with your colleague again, generate three additional African practices, values, or beliefs, and critically discuss their psychological significance.

4.1   Critically discuss the main components of the traditional African metaphysical system presented in this chapter.

4.2   In what ways does this metaphysical system differ from traditional Western approaches to psychology? Discuss with reference to healthcare or any relevant aspect of psychology, illustrating with examples.

Recommended readings

Holdstock, T.L. (2000). *Re-examining psychology: Critical perspectives and African insights.* London: Routledge.

Myers, L.J. (1988). *Understanding an Afrocentric worldview: Introduction to an optimal psychology.* Dubuque, IA: Kendall/Hunt Publishing.

5

Sociocultural approaches to psychology: Dialogism and African conceptions of the self

Nhlanhla Mkhize

'The single adequate form for verbally expressing authentic
human life is open-ended dialogue. Life by its very nature is dialogic.
To live means to part cipate in dialogue: to ask questions, to heed,
to respond, to agree, and so forth. In this dialogue a person participates
wholly and throughout his [sic] whole life: with his eyes, lips, hands, soul,
spirit, with his whole body and deeds. He invests his entire self in
discourse, and this discourse enters into the dialogic fabric of
human life, into the world symposium.'

(Bakhtin, 1984/1993)

LEARNING OUTCOMES

By the end of this chapter, you should be able to:

▷ Describe the relationship between higher mental functions and social life

▷ Critically discuss and apply Vygotsky's account of human development to the South African context

▷ Compare and contrast Vygotskian and Bakhtinian approaches to psychological mediation

▷ Critically discuss the notion of a dialogical self

▷ Compare and contrast dialogical and traditional African approaches to selfhood.

INTRODUCTION

The social basis of psychological processes

Critical psychology locates psychological functioning in its social, historical and cultural contexts. Sociocultural approaches to psychology, as exemplified by the works of Vygotsky (1978) and Bakhtin (1981), provide the necessary tools to explore critically the thesis that psychological processes such as self-understanding emerge from the social basis of life. These approaches also enable us to theorise about the co-existence of, and interface between, indigenous and traditional Western psychologies. In a world characterised by a high degree of movement and contact between cultures, dichotomous explanations of human development, in terms indigenous *or* Western psychological concepts, are no longer tenable. In this chapter, I propose that Bakhtin's (1981) literary writings, particularly his notion of **dialogism**, provide fertile ground to study the emergence of psychological processes from a myriad of social and cultural influences.

Mediation and internalisation

Before introducing Bakhtin, it is important to review Vygotsky's account of human development briefly, so as to introduce concepts that are central to the understanding of Bakhtin's work. The two authors have a lot in common and, although the argument will not be pursued at length here, Bakhtin's work could be seen as a logical extension of Vygotsky's ideas. The chapter thus begins with a brief discussion of Vygotsky's view that higher mental functions such as thinking originate from social activity. Two concepts central to Vygotsky and Bakhtin, mediation and **internalisation**, are presented. Bakhtin's notion of existence as dialogue is then introduced. The view of selfhood emanating from this conceptualisation of life, namely the **dialogical self**, is discussed. Comparisons are drawn between the notion of the dialogical self and traditional African views of selfhood. The chapter concludes with the view that dialogism provides a framework for reconciling the individual-society dichotomy, namely the view that psychological development is influenced *either* by individual *or* by societal factors (Wertsch, 1995).

VYGOTSKY AND THE SOCIAL ORIGINS OF MENTAL FUNCTIONING

The general genetic law of cultural development

Vygotsky (1978) located the origins of higher mental functions in social life. This was against the then dominant social science view that psychological functions can be studied in isolation from their context (Wertsch, 1991; Wertsch & Stone, 1985). Instead, Vygotsky argued that **ontogenesis** (individual development) originates from social, cultural and historical forms of

---

Dialogism and the dialogical self: for dialogism, there is no singular, fixed and pre-given meaning. Rather, meaning is emergent. It arises dialogically, from our encounter with others, and when we interact with the social environment. This view leads to the dialogical self, which results from social and interpersonal interactions. It is characterised by a high degree of multiplicity, flexibility and change.

Internalisation: processes originally outside of people's control become part of their intrapsychological world. It does not describe a geographic transfer of activities from the social to the internal world of the individual. Rather, it represents the process by which higher mental functions are formed.

Ontogenesis: study of individual development.

life. This view is captured in what is known as the 'general genetic law of cultural development' (Vygotsky, 1981). This law posits that:

> Any function in the child's development appears twice, or on two planes. First, it appears on the social plane, and then on the psychological plane. First it appears between people as an interpsychological category, and then within the child as an intrapsychological category. This is equally true with regard to voluntary attention, logical memory, the formation of concepts, and the development of volition. We may consider this position as a law in the full sense of the word, but it goes without saying that internalisation transforms the process itself and changes its structure and functions. Social relations or relations among people genetically underlie all higher functions and their interrelationships. (163)

For both Vygotsky and critical psychology more generally, psychological functioning cannot be properly understood outside of the social, cultural, historical and economic contexts in which it occurs.

From interpsychological to intrapsychological

According to the 'general genetic law of cultural development', higher psychological functions such as thinking first represent relations between people (the social or interpsychological plane). Later, these relations become part of the individual's inner world (the intrapsychological plane). This does not mean that individual mental processes are a mere copy of outside social life, however. Rather, Vogotsky's position is that processes that appear on the interpsychological plane, between people, can also be carried out on the intrapsychological plane, within the person (Wertsch, 1991). For example, when an adult gives a child instructions to solve an arithmetic puzzle (an activity between the child and an adult), the child can later use the same instructions to instruct herself, independently of the adult. Self-instruction could take the form of a rehearsal, which could be done verbally or silently (see egocentric speech). When this happens, the same activity is now being carried out at the intrapsychological plane.

For Vygotsky, any function in the child's development appears twice, or on two planes. First, it appears on the social plane, and then on the psychological plane. First it appears between people as an interpsychological category, and then within the child as an intrapsychological category.

Cultural tools

The 'general genetic law of cultural development' implies that for psychology to be truly social, historical and cultural, it needs to take into consideration social relations and practices: the things people do and say. It needs to address itself to **forms of life** valued in various cultural contexts. These forms of life are reflected in activities such as plays, songs, cultural narratives and proverbs, which collectively constitute the cultural tools through which psychological processes are mediated.

Mediation

It has been mentioned that higher mental functions were once relations between people. Higher mental functions are mediated by cultural tools, which are eventually internalised to direct our own behaviour (Shotter, 1989; Wertsch & Stone, 1985). Mediation is a process by which individuals or groups employ cultural tools such as language, stories and proverbs to carry out their actions (Wertsch, 1995). For example, children in traditional African societies are socialised to the moral values thought to be important to the community through storytelling. The stories are imbued with moral and other lessons that children must internalise to become competent members of their societies. Vygotsky was of the view that human agency cannot be understood by analysing individuals or mediational means in isolation. Rather, it involves 'humans ... *acting with mediational means*' (Wertsch, 1990, 69; original emphasis). This view differs from traditional Western approaches to psychology, which assume that the individual is the primary unit of analysis. Hence, traditional Western approaches seek to isolate social and cultural factors so as to uncover what are thought to be the underlying bases of human behaviour (Shweder, 1991).

'Self-talk'

We shall further illustrate mediation by contrasting Piaget and Vygotsky's understanding of the role of 'self-talk' in child development. Piaget (1924/1969) viewed children's 'self-talk' as an indication of immaturity or lack of social interest. He expected this tendency, which he termed 'egocentric speech', to disappear as children matured cognitively and socially. Vygotsky (1966), on the other hand, argued that children use 'egocentric speech' as a tool to solve problems. He noted that 'egocentric speech' repeats earlier social relations between children and adults. It marks the beginning of a process by which children begin to converse with themselves in the same way that they had earlier conversed with others. Initially, children require external assistance to solve problems. Gradually they begin to guide themselves through problem-solving while verbalising instructions previously given by adults or competent peers. Eventually the language used by others is incorporated into children's

Forms of life: in its most simplistic form, the term refers to social relations or practices, the things people do, or ways of relating to each other and responding to life experiences that are tied to particular contexts. For example, *ukubona*, the tradition by which relatives and community members visit a family after the death of one of its members, constitutes a form of life to handle grief.

psychological world (ie internalised). It becomes a tool that directs their behaviour (Shotter, 1989; Wertsch & Stone, 1985). From a Vygotskian perspective, the 'disappearance' of 'egocentric' speech means that the social relations it represented have become part of the inner world of the child. Thus, social relations between children and their social environment provide insight into psychological functions such as thinking.

The zone of proximal development

A critical question is how do activities happening between people get transferred into the intrapsychological realm? To answer this question it is necessary to revisit Vygotsky's account of learning and development in children. Vygotsky drew a distinction between two levels of development, namely the 'actual developmental level,' and the 'potential' or 'zone of proximal development' (ZPD) (Vygotsky, 1978). 'Actual development' refers to mental functions that are already fully matured. It is indicated by children's ability to solve problems independently. It could be regarded as the end product of development (Vygotsky, 1978).

The ZPD, on the other hand, refers to maturing functions. It is determined by what the child is capable of doing with the assistance of adults or other competent children. Formally, it is defined as 'the distance between the actual developmental level as determined by independent problem solving and the level of potential as determined through problem solving under adult guidance or in collaboration with more capable peers' (Vygotsky, 1978, 86). Development takes place in the ZPD as adults and competent peers interact with children to support them to master the values and skills that are essential in order to become competent and mature members of their society (Tappan, 1998). This view has found support from Rogoff (1990, 1995), who also maintained that children advance their understanding through 'apprenticeship' with others in culturally organised activities.

Internalisation

Internalisation means that processes originally outside of people's control become part of their intrapsychological world. By resorting to '**inner dialogue**', these processes can be recalled and used to construe, inform, and direct our behaviour (Shotter, 1989). Internalisation does not describe a geographic transfer of activities from the social to the internal world of the individual. Rather, it represents the very process by which higher mental functions are formed. Shotter (1993a, 1993b) further contends that internalisation enables children to learn to do on their own what they initially did under the supervision of adults. Through internalisation, 'the child learns to practice with respect to himself [sic] the same forms of behavior that others formerly practiced with respect to him' (Vygotsky, 1966, 39–40). Internalisation may be

Inner dialogue: we are continually engaged in dialogues with others. For example, a mother resorts to dialogue to teach her child to write (eg 'You hold the pen like this, and then draw a circle.'). These dialogues can be repeated internally, within ourselves, even when we are alone. In other words, we can engage in inner dialogues with the various, internalised parts of the self, representing important Others in our lives.

construed as a transformation in our responsibility for things (Shotter, 1993a, 1993b). It is a process by which individuals assume responsibility for activities that were initially under others' control.

> Through internalisation, 'the child learns to practice with respect to himself [sic] the same forms of behavior that others formerly practiced with respect to him' (Vygotsky, 1966, 39–40).

Internalisation as ethical-moral process

Internalisation is an indispensable part of becoming a person (the development of self-understanding). Self-understanding emerges against the background social practices provided by the culture at large. Shotter (1993b) argues that internalisation involves an ethical-moral transformation of the self:

> In learning how *to be* a responsible member of a certain social group, one must learn *to do* certain things in the right kind of way: how to perceive, think, talk, act, and to experience one's surroundings in ways that make sense to the others around one in ways considered legitimate. (73; original emphasis).

Shotter's (1993b) reinterpretation of internalisation paves a way for the emergence of personhood from the collective forms of life. Internalisation is an ethical-moral process because it involves acquiring ways of understanding oneself as a human being in relation to others. The ethical-moral nature of this process lies in the fact that these ways of being are not ours. They have always been there, serving other people's purposes (eg the internalisation of dominant gender relationships). This view finds support in MacIntyre (1984), who argues that 'the self has to find its moral identity in and through its membership in communities' (143). This does not mean, however, that we need to accept uncritically the limitations of forms of self that are prevalent in our communities (McIntyre, 1984). These ways of talking and sense-making need to be critically debated in order to determine their liberating and constraining effects (Prilleltensky, 1997). Bakhtin's dialogical account of human functioning, discussed below, provides the necessary theoretical tools for such a critique.

Beyond Vygotsky

Vygotskian psychology provides fertile ground for studying the sociocultural origins of psychological processes. Rather than focusing on processes occurring within the individual, Vygotsky was more concerned with what happens at the boundary or zone between the individual and his or her social and cultural context.

Positioning

However, perhaps due to his rather short career, Vygotsky's experimental work was limited to small group interactions, such as parent–child dyads. He did not spell out the relationship between cultural, historical and institutional settings and various forms of mediated action (Wertsch, 1991). Neither did he take into account influences of positioning in the process of individual development.

Positioning refers to 'a complex cluster of generic personal attributes, structured in various ways, which impinges on the possibilities of interpersonal, intergroup and even intrapersonal action through some assignment of such rights, duties and obligations to an individual as are sustained by the cluster' (Harré & Langenhove, 1999, 1). For example, a person who is positioned as knowledgeable in a particular field (eg law) will be accorded more say should issues pertaining to that field be discussed. People are positioned in various ways in society, depending on gender, race, and age, among other things. For example, traditional African communities accord more status and respect to elders (Paris, 1995). Vygotskian psychology cannot account for the power resulting from one's positioning within a social field. In this respect, it can benefit from the ideas of Bakhtin (1981), who was concerned with influences of broader social and cultural factors on individual development.

> **Positioning:** refers to the process by which personal attributes such as gender influence intrapersonal, interpersonal or intergroup actions.

> We are all socially positioned in complex and multiple ways. How we are positioned plays a vital role in the importance and status we are given. An example of this is the status and respect generally accorded elders in traditional African cultures.

BAKHTIN'S DIALOGISM

The starting point in understanding Bakhtin's ideas is the notion of dialogue, which is an interchange of ideas between two equally responsive subjects. For Bakhtin, meaning is not pre-given, nor does it arise internally, from within the person. It is constructed actively and dialogically, in our encounter with the other (Bandlamudi, 1994). It also emanates from the person's encounter with his or her social world.

Logical relationships

Relationships characterised by dialogism are better understood in comparison with logical relationships (Hermans & Kempen, 1993). Logical relationships constitute a closed system. They do not allow for further commentary beyond what is permissible in terms of the rules by which the statements are related. Bakhtin (1984/1993) showed this by drawing a comparison between two identical statements, namely 'life is good' and 'life is good' (see also Hermans, 1996; Hermans & Kempen, 1993; Vasil'eva, 1985). From the point of view of Aristotelian logic, the two statements are *identical*. Similarly, the statements 'life is good' and 'life is not good' only express a relationship of negation. Logically, the statements can be understood independently of who utters them.

Dialogical relationships

Dialogical relationships, on the other hand, presuppose (and recognise) the *other*, with whom one can agree or disagree. A dialogical relationship between the above pairs of statements exists if they are uttered by two embodied beings, either in agreement or disagreement with each other. The meaning of the statements can be fully grasped *only in the context of the relationship between speakers*. Dialogism extends beyond interindividual processes to include how the person engages with her or his social and cultural world.

Living language and the study of human life

It should be noted that Bakhtin was a literary analyst: he analysed relationships between characters and the author in written works. However, he was interested in *living language*, which is speech as spoken by concrete individuals, and addressed to immediate as well as distant audiences (Skinner, Valsiner & Holland, 2001). He took the Russian cultural tradition as his point of departure. This tradition regarded the creative process and, in particular, the creation of literary texts (eg writing a novel) as a model for the study of human life (Kozulin, 1991). Bakhtin drew parallels between the process of writing (production of literary texts) and living. He proposed an account of individual development (becoming) based on the concept of 'life as authoring' and existence as dialogue (Holquist, 1990; Kozulin, 1991).

Life as authoring

The idea of life as authorship is premised on the understanding that 'the world is not given but conceived' (Clarke & Holquist, 1984, 59). This means that we cannot have direct access to the world because it is not 'out there', to be discovered independently of our experiences/actions. We make sense of the world and ourselves through an active process of engagement. We engage with the world, and hence come to know it and our place in it through activities such as thinking, doing and communicating (Kozulin, 1991). It is for this reason that Bakhtin (1981) argued that human life parallels the process of literary authorship. Clarke and Holquist (1984) expressed the relationship between authorship and living as follows:

Life as event presumes selves that are performers. To be successful, the relation between me and the other must be shaped into a coherent performance, and thus the architectonic activity of authorship, which is the building of a text, parallels the activity of human existence, which is the building of a self (64).

Literary authorship and life

Let us consider the analogy between literary authorship and living in detail. Writing a novel, for example, is an active process. It involves building ideas into a text. The novelist has to create characters, the plot and points of view. Further, authors do not invent everything anew when they write: their works are situated within the context of established literary genres (writing styles such as drama and prose), which must be taken into account during the writing process. Then there is the question of the point(s) of view, which is the reason the work of art is created. Thus, we can ask ourselves: What was the author trying to communicate to us in this novel? Novelists express their opinions, thereby *authoring* their point of view, through their works.

Similarly, we inevitably express (author) our points of view in our responses (actions) to challenges in life. The exemplary lives of former South African president, Rolihlahla Nelson Mandela, and Black Consciousness activist, Bantu Steve Biko, illustrate this. In response to apartheid, both men sacrificed their careers/lives to engage in the struggle for liberation. Biko died in jail, whereas Mandela was to spend 27 years of his life in prison, most of which were spent doing hard labour (digging lime in the quarries). The question is: What were these men (and many other men and women) trying to achieve by their actions? What were their points of view? The answer to this question is perhaps found in Mandela's closing remark during the Rivonia trial in 1964. Their actions were driven by a desire to establish a democratic society in which people live together in harmony and as equals, with equal opportunities. This, among other viewpoints, was the point of view behind their actions.

Horizons of understanding

Literary authorship and living are also similar because, in the same way that novelists situate their work within established literary genres, so do human actions take place within the sphere of culture. We live in a world that is already pre-configured in a particular way. We do not reinvent the world anew every time we do something. Thus, our actions must take into account the **horizons of understanding** (Gadamer, 1975), what has already been established within a given sphere of communication (Kozulin, 1991; Shotter, 1993a). These horizons constitute the background against which we act. For example, Mandela and Biko's actions above could be understood with reference to colonialism and its defeat in other parts of Africa.

We make sense of the world and ourselves through an active process of engagement. We engage with the world, and hence come to know it and our place in it, through activities such as thinking, doing, and communication (Kozulin, 1991).

Horizon of understanding: term based on the philosophy of Gadamer (1975), who maintained that understanding does not occur in isolation. Rather, it is perspectival. That it, there is always a background, or horizon, against which we see anything. As psychologists, our theories and social backgrounds constitute our horizons of understanding.

With the analogy of 'life as authorship' Bakhtin laid a foundation for a meaningful understanding of psychological functioning through the study of people's life experiences. Life experiences cannot be studied out of context, however, given that by definition, our lives unfold in a world populated with other people.

The utterance as the unit of analysis

If life parallels the process of authorship, then what should the units of analysis be in psychological studies? It should be noted that, although he studied literary texts, Bakhtin was concerned with language as a living process: the manner in which language expresses relationships between real embodied people, and their life conditions in general. For this reason Bakhtin positioned himself against the prevailing linguistics of his time, which was dominated by Saussurian linguists. Saussurian linguists studied grammatical units such as sentences, phrases, words and phonemes as a means to uncover underlying and stable patterns of language. These units were studied independently of the context of their users. Sentences are abstract because they do not belong to anyone and are not addressed to anyone. Bakhtin argued that such units are inappropriate because they cannot tell us anything about actual relationships between embodied beings.

To understand language as a living process, Bakhtin turned his attention to the study of the whole **utterance** (Holquist, 1983; Vasil'eva, 1985; Wertsch, 1990). Utterances are real responsive-interactive units (Shotter, 1993a). Bakhtin (1986) defined the utterance as:

> a unit of speech communication ... determined by a change of speaking subjects, that is, a change of speakers. Any utterance – from a short (single-word) rejoinder in everyday dialogue to the large novel or scientific treatise – has, so to speak, an absolute beginning and an absolute end: its beginning is preceded by the utterances of others, and its end is followed by the responsive utterances of others. ... The speaker ends his utterance in order to relinquish the floor to the other or to make room for the other's active responsive understanding (71).

Utterance: any unit of communication characterised by a change of speaking subjects. Utterances always seek or elicit a response from those to whom they are addressed. A command is an utterance, as is an article appearing in a journal.

Unlike sentences, words, and phrases, utterances always belong to 'individual speaking people, speech subjects' (Bakhtin, 1986, 7). They are thus consistent with a model of human understanding based on people as performers. Utterances not only belong to real, embodied people: they also elicit a *response* from the one to whom they are *addressed*. Bakhtin (1986) referred to this as the *responsiveness* and '*addressivity*' of utterances.

The responsiveness and 'addressivity' of utterances

Utterances presuppose someone with whom one can agree or disagree. Bakhtin (1986) found the study of utterances attractive because they indicate the gaps or boundaries in the flow of speech between speaking subjects (Shotter, 1993a; Wertsch, 1990). Once the utterance of one speaker has been finalised, the other speaker can assume a *responsive* attitude toward what has been said.

> When the listener perceives and understands the meaning ... of speech he [sic] simultaneously takes an active, responsive attitude toward it. He [sic] either agrees or disagrees with it ... augments it, applies it, prepares for its execution and so on. ... Any understanding of live speech, a live utterance, is inherently responsive, although the degree of this activity varies extremely. Any understanding is imbued with response and necessarily elicits it in one form or another: the listener becomes the speaker (Bakhtin, 1986, 68).

The role of the addressee

Utterances are, by definition, dialogical. Participants can state their point(s) of view in response to what has been said by the other. This is because, unlike sentences, which are abstracted from their conditions of real use, utterances are always addressed to someone, a process Bakhtin termed the 'addressivity' of utterances (Bakhtin, 1986; Wertsch, 1991). Whenever an utterance is made, there is always an actual or imaginary audience of listeners (Hermans, 1997; Wertsch, 1991). Every utterance has an addressee or a 'second party' whose responsive understanding is being sought. The notion of 'addressivity' follows from the fact that people are not passive in their conversations with others. Quite on the contrary, they engage in activities such as negotiation, agreeing, disagreeing and questioning (Sampson, 1993; Shotter, 1995). The very composition and style of the utterance will depend on the audience for whom it is meant and must, of necessity, take into account the effect it will have on them (Bakhtin, 1986).

'Addressivity' extends beyond actual participants in a dialogue to include real or imagined Others for whom the utterance is meant and from whom some responsive understanding is sought (Bakhtin, 1986). For example, when we contemplate doing something that our parents do not approve of, we may engage in an internal dialogue with them, even if they are not there. It could thus be argued that higher mental functions such as thinking do not constitute the activity of the solitary thinker. Instead, the internal world of the person is 'populated' with others. Arendt expressed a similar view:

> the thinking process ... is not, like the thought of pure reasoning, a dialogue between me and myself, but finds itself always and primarily, even if I am quite alone in making up my mind, in an anticipated communication with others with whom I must finally come to some agreement (cited in Bernstein, 1983, 218).

Oriented towards others

The fact that 'addressivity' includes imagined others highlights that we cannot claim to be alone in what we are doing, even in our thoughts. Our actions must

It could thus be argued that higher mental functions such as thinking do not constitute the activity of the solitary thinker. Instead, the internal world of the person is 'populated' with others.

always be oriented toward others, and anticipate their responses, in order to be meaningful. Traditional psychological theories of human development, on the other hand, posit that people reason in isolation from others and the social context (Sampson, 1993). For example, in the cognitivist paradigm, higher psychological functions, such as the development of moral and ethical reasoning (eg Kohlberg, 1981, 1984), are envisaged to be a matter of individual legislation, with reference to internally held principles (Day & Tappan, 1996). This process is envisaged to occur independently of others, history and time (Benhabib, 1992). Bakhtin's dialogism opens up the possibility of studying the role played by others, real or imagined, in the development of higher mental functions.

The notion of 'addressivity' alerts us to the importance of others' *responses* to what we have to say. Utterances are always addressed to someone else, and every utterance has an addressee whose responsive understanding is being sought. An example of this might be the telling of a joke. Here the speaker attempts to elicit a response of humour; if the addressee laughs, then the speaker has been successful.

The superaddressee

Bakhtin (1986) also maintained that the 'addressivity' of utterances might be extended to a 'third party' or a '*superaddressee*'. This is an indefinite audience, such as a system of ideas or beliefs, an appeal to God, or scientific knowledge, to which we appeal to justify our claims or actions. For example, psychology in South Africa has not only lived in tandem with racism: it blossomed during apartheid because it could be used to justify the policy of the Nationalist government.

BOX 1   The discipline of psychology as a superaddressee

Psychology, like other forms of scientific knowledge, can function as a superaddressee. That is, we can appeal to psychological knowledge to justify our actions. For example, 'racial differences' in IQ have been used to justify educational and employment inequities. In the United States, Ferguson (1916, cited in Richards, 1997) commented as follows on the performances of black and white children on intelligence tests:

> The negroes ... were slow to warm up, quick to lose interest, difficult to stimulate except through flattery, irregular, moody, vacillating in attention, inaccurate, envious of each other's progress, given to mumbling, grumbling, humming, saying funny things while at work. ... *the very fact that the negroes were not interested as were the whites possibly points to a deficiency in the colored group* (cited in Richards, 1997, 85).

Ferguson went on to conclude as follows:

> [I]t is very clear that by far the greater number of writers who have dealt with the problem of the relative mental ability of the white and the negro take the view that the negro is inferior. This is particularly true of those investigators who have used quantitative methods. The negro has not shown the same capacity as the white when put to the test of psychological or educational experiment, and the racial differences revealed have been considerable (cited in Richards, 1997, 85).

In South Africa, Holdstock (2000) commented as follows on the position of psychology during the apartheid era:

> The flourishing of psychology in South Africa during the apartheid era is an equally telling example of how a scientific discipline can come to serve the political ends of those in power. It also calls for a close examination of the values underlying the practice of mainstream psychology. ... The parallels between contemporary psychology and the political system of apartheid are striking. Although there will certainly be those in psychology who object to such a comparison, an uncanny commonality nevertheless exists between the political system and the professional discipline. The scale of the political experiment was just grander than could ever be envisaged by even the most inclusive of research projects in psychology. In fact, the political experiment approached the ideal of eliminating sampling statistics by involving the total population. The entire country became a laboratory. It is not surprising therefore, to find critical descriptions of psychology that fit the homelands policy of the nationalist government like a glove (57–58).

Both Holdstock (2000) and Richards point us to the fact that psychology is not neutral. Rather, psychological claims can be used to justify oppression.

The chainlike nature of utterances

It is also important to note that the meaning of utterances cannot be deciphered in isolation, independently of the history of ideas and social relations (Bakhtin, 1986; Holquist, 1983; Shotter, 1993a). Utterances are already imbued with meaning, associated with the way they have been used historically within a given sphere of communication. By 'sphere of communication' is meant historically particular contexts in which utterances have been used, such as the family, work and scientific spheres. Bakhtin (1986) expressed this feature, which he termed the *chainlike nature* of utterances, as follows:

> Utterances are not indifferent to another, and are not self-sufficient; they are aware of and mutually reflect one another. ... Every utterance must be regarded

primarily as a *response* to preceding utterances of the given sphere ... Each utterance refutes, affirms, supplements, and relies upon others, presupposes them to be known, and somehow takes them into account ... Therefore each kind of utterance is filled with various kinds of responsive reactions to other utterances of the given sphere of communication (91).

On the value of the utterance as the psychological unit of analysis

Given that utterances are linked to other utterances before them, we should study them with reference to the *perspectives, worldviews* and *positions* associated with a given topic. It is from positions already available to them in their social settings that speakers seize meaning, making the utterance their own. For example, suppose a community worker is teaching men about having one partner as a strategy to reduce the spread of HIV/Aids. If one of these men responds by saying: 'I am a man!', how are we to understand him? This response can be understood only with reference to the already established meanings of manhood (masculinity) in his social setting. Most likely, having multiple partners is an important part of this man's identity. Thus, interventions that do not tackle the relationship between social identity and sexuality are likely to fail. By studying utterances, we would be able to discern how people engage with **voices** from their social and cultural worlds – which voices are already imbued with others' meanings and intentions – to develop new ways of understanding themselves and their world (Skinner, Valsiner & Holland, 2001).

Voice: speakers have a voice when they use utterances to communicate their personal meanings or points of view.

The study of utterances would appear to be an appropriate subject-matter for a critically oriented psychology. Traditional, mainstream psychology posits that the knower and the object of his or her knowledge are beyond time and history (ie objective, timeless and universal). Haraway (1991) contends that the traditional assumption of objectivity represents a 'view from above, from nowhere, from simplicity' (195). The utterance draws to our attention that psychological and other forms of knowledge can only be articulated by *embodied*, living subjects. These subjects can be differentiated on a number of dimensions, such as race, gender, class, and ethnicity. Thus, knowledge always represents 'views from somewhere' (Haraway, 1991, 196). The utterance enables us to situate speakers and knowledge in social and cultural contexts. It empowers us to pose critical questions about the knowledge production process. These are typical Bakhtinian (1981) questions such as: *Who* speaks/ writes/conducts research about *whom?* From *which* theoretical vantage positions? Under what *social, historical* and *cultural* circumstances? (Brown & Gilligan, 1991). These issues have not been adequately addressed in South African psychological discourse.

Utterance and voice

Utterances also differ from abstract linguistic units such as sentences because they are inherently tied to the notion of '**voice**' (Holquist, 1983; Holquist &

Emerson, 1981; Vasil'eva, 1985; Wertsch, 1990). Holquist & Emerson (1981) define 'voice' as 'the speaking personality, the speaking consciousness' (434). Every utterance exists in so far as it can be produced by someone (Wertsch, 1990). An utterance is endowed with a voice when speakers adopt an *expressive, evaluative attitude* towards the subject of their speech (Bakhtin, 1986). The evaluative nature of the words we use in language is realised only in particular concrete situations, when we employ them for our purposes. Bakhtin argued that 'words belong to nobody, and in themselves … evaluate nothing … [T]hey can serve any speaker and be used for the most varied and directly contradictory evaluations on the part of the speakers' (Bakhtin, 1986, 85). Meanings, ideas, and thoughts are voiced when they are expressed by someone to communicate a personal (ie authorial) position with respect to a particular subject (Vasil'eva, 1985). The term 'voice' generally applies to the speaking subject's perspective, worldview and belief system with regard to written and other forms of communication (Wertsch, 1990). It is the very condition for the existence of dialogue, an alternation of subjective points of view between partners (Vasil'eva, 1985).

> 'Words belong to nobody, and in themselves … evaluate nothing … [T]hey can serve any speaker and be used for the most varied and directly contradictory evaluations on the part of the speakers' (Bakhtin, 1986, 85).

Studying voicelessness

In *I write what I like*, Biko (1978) comments critically on circumstances that led to voicelessness among black people in South Africa. Suppose that a 'garden boy' or 'maid' is angry with his or her superior but smiles, pretending to be happy in his presence. He or she lacks voice to express his or her point of view. Critical psychology, it could be argued, should also study voicelessness among the oppressed. This includes studying processes through which the mind becomes colonised (see Hook's chapter on Fanon, this work). It should also investigate means to decolonise the mind, thereby reclaiming voice for the people. One way of doing this is to explicate the various ways through which the oppressed have contributed to world civilisation and the history of ideas. This chapter is an attempt to contribute to that process.

Collective voices

Bakhtin was concerned not only with utterances of individual, speaking subjects; he paid attention to *types of speech* produced by certain groups in society. He referred to these types of speech as *collective voices* (Bakhtin, 1986; Wertsch, 1990). The term 'collective voices' refers to opinions, points of view and perspectives that reflect the views of our social and cultural communities. These voices can also be reflected in the way individuals speak about themselves. Bakhtin's dialogism extends beyond face-to-face interaction. It includes the process by which a person's utterance incorporates voices of social groups and institutions. Bakhtin (1981) referred to this process as *ventriloquation*.

It is important to note that collective voices are not neutral: they are imbued with expressive meanings. This is because utterances do not belong entirely to individual speakers. They have always existed 'out there', belonging to other people and social groups. Words cannot be 'neutral' because they have always been used for particular purposes. They thus carry with them traces of meanings associated with their use in particular spheres of communication (Bakhtin, 1981; Shotter, 1993). Bakhtin (1981) expressed this as follows:

> The word in language is half someone else's. It becomes 'one's own' only when the speaker populates it with his [sic] own intention, his own accent, when he appropriates the word, adapting it to his own semantic and expressive intention. Prior to this moment of **appropriation**, the word does not exist in a neutral and impersonal language ... but rather it exists in other people's mouths, in other people's concrete contexts, serving other people's intentions: it is from there that one must take the word, and make it one's own (Bakhtin, 1981, 293–294).

Appropriation: utterances, argued Bakhtin (1981), are already imbued with others' meanings. Bakhtin used the term 'appropriation' to indicate a process by which we give voice (intonation, accent, personal meaning/intentions) to the utterance or a particular subject/topic.

Collective voices and psychological mediation

The notion of collective voices enriches our understanding of psychological mediation. Higher mental functions are also mediated by collective forms of life. This observation ties psychological functions (eg self-understanding, identity formation) to the social and cultural context. For example, a man who believes that he is superior to women is not only expressing his point of view. Most probably, he is ventriloquating patriarchal views in his society, which he has assimilated into the self. Identity development involves a struggle with others' voices. This may result in the person uncritically accepting others' views, or giving new meanings to them (in Bakhtinian terms, 'appropriating' them), thereby authoring his or her own point of view. Thus, when a person is speaking, we can ask the question: 'Who is speaking?' In other words, whose ideas are being ventriloquated in the person's speech? In what ways has the person made sense of these views for himself or herself (ie appropriated them)? As discussed below, such an analysis takes us beyond the *individual–society dichotomy* (Wertsch, 1995). It focuses on the dialogical interchange between the individual and others' voices.

Three types of collective voice are critical for our purposes: *national languages, social languages* and *speech genres*.

National languages

For Bakhtin, these are the traditional language units such as IsiZulu, Tshivenda and Afrikaans. National languages are characterised by coherent grammatical and semantic forms (Wertsch, 1991). Bakhtin noted that there is a dialogical interaction between national languages in the sense that one language may be used at home, another one in the school, and perhaps even another for religious purposes (Wertsch, 1990). The interaction between national languages is of vital importance in South Africa. For example, many African schoolchildren are taught in English and yet use an African language at home. The impact of this on their understanding of scientific and other concepts has not been fully explored.

The dialogic relationship between national languages is also important to understanding relationships between various groups. For example, while it is a status symbol of some sort for Africans to be fluent in English, French or Portuguese, the reverse (eg fluency in Tswana) does not hold for people of European descent. In meetings full of African people, I have observed speakers automatically switching to English immediately when a person of European descent arrives. The same does not hold if a non-English-speaking African enters a hall full of English people. It should be noted that this is not about languages per se, but about the position and power of the people who speak them. Despite the potential benefit of studying dialogic interanimations between national languages, Bakhtin paid more attention to social languages.

Social languages

Bakhtin noted that within a single national language there might exist many social languages. Social languages represent the social position of the speaker. Examples are the languages of various professional groups, urban and rural dialects, as well as the languages of various age groups or generations. Speakers never produce utterances in isolation. Even if alone, they enter into dialogue with the social and other languages, representing various interest groups in society.

The fact that we speak in social languages has several implications for us as social scientists. We need to engage critically with the voices embedded in our practices. We need to be aware that our theories, methodologies, and intervention methods are tied to particular social languages. The language of psychology is consistent with the values of the dominant (white) middle classes. For example, it has been argued that traditional psychotherapy is class bound. It values verbal and emotional expressiveness on the part of the client. It also distinguishes between the mental and physical needs of the client, and chooses to focus on the former. Sessions are usually limited to 50 minutes, tend to be unstructured, and the focus is on long-term rather than short-term goals (Sue & Sue, 1999). The higher dropout rate in psychotherapy among minorities has been attributed to this fact, among other factors.

The fact that our practices are imbued with class-bound social values calls for *dialogical reflexivity* in practice. Reflexivity is 'a process of explicitly turning one's critical gaze on oneself as well as the professional, historical, and cultural discourses that empower and constrain one's capacities to think and act in the

The fact that we speak in social languages has several implications for us as social scientists. We need to engage critically with the voices embedded in our practices. We need to be aware that our theories, methodologies and intervention methods are tied to particular social languages.

context of a relationship' (Hawes, 1998, 105–106). Reflexivity will enhance the ability of psychologists and other social scientists to understand and interpret others' lives meaningfully.

Speech genres

While the distinguishing feature of social languages is the social position of the speakers, speech genres are characterised by the *typical situations* in which they are invoked. They are the '*generic* forms of the utterance' (Bakhtin, 1986, 78), such as greetings and intimate conversations between friends. For example, the man who declared 'I am a man!', cited earlier, is expressing himself through a *speech genre*. This expression might be invoked in typical situations where one's sexuality or manhood is at stake. Speech genres are products of a community's history and collective way of life. They are acquired from our concrete experiences with those around us. Speech genres are more changeable and diverse. They take into account not only the context and personal interrelations of the speakers but also their social positions (Bakhtin, 1986). An individual may resort to many genres, depending on the context and position of those being addressed.

It has been argued that *interindividual*, small-group and broader collective forms of life mediate psychological functioning. Given the importance of the concept of the self in psychology, we shall now turn to the view of selfhood emanating from a dialogical account of human functioning. Dialogism, it is argued, enables us to theorise about the relationship between the individual and society without falling victim to the individual–society antithesis (Wertsch, 1995).

THE DIALOGICAL SELF

Bakhtin's dialogism leads to a self that is always engaged in relationships with others and the social context. Bakhtin regarded communication as an essential aspect of personhood. For him, 'the very being of man [sic] ... is a *profound communication. To be* means to *communicate*. ... To be means to be for the other; and through him [sic] for oneself' (Bakhtin, 1984/1993, 287; original emphasis). The dialogical self is not pre-given. It emerges from exposure to others' voices. Once internalised, these voices continue to dialogue with each other on an ongoing basis. The dialogical self is decentralised. It is composed of multiple characters, capable of engaging each other (Hermans & Kempen, 1993). Although multiplicity of selves has been proposed by others (eg Higgins, 1987; Markus & Nurius, 1986; Markus & Wurf, 1987), Bakhtin's approach comprehensively explains the emergence of self from collective forms of life.

To understand fully the dialogical basis of selfhood, it is important to revisit four main characteristics of the dialogical self, namely *polyphony*, *spatialisation*, *self-renewal* or *innovation*, and *power relationships*. Parallels are drawn between a dialogically conceived self and the traditional African view of selfhood.

Polyphony and the dialogical self

Bakhtin's (1984/1993) analysis of Dostoevsky's literary works and, in particular, the relationship between characters and the author in his novels provides a basis for understanding polyphony in the dialogical self (see also Hermans, 1996, 1997; Hermans et al, 1992; Vasil'eva, 1985). To understand fully Bakhtin's ideas regarding the polyphonic novel, it is important to contrast the position of the characters and the author in *monological* and *polyphonic* literary works.

Monological versus polyphonic works

Monological works are characterised by the privileged position of the author as the sole proponent of the truth. The author retains the power to express the truth directly and there is only one truth: that propounded by him or her. Each character's position is measured against the ideological position of the author. Thus, the author and the characters are not on the same plane; they do not interact as equals. The characters serve as mouthpieces to convey the author's position. The right to mediate between the characters and the readers remains solely with the author. He or she retains the power to synthesise the various insights and propositions into a coherent system. Once the ideas have been synthesised, they are deinvested of their individuality, that is, they are rendered independently of the characters who created or uttered them or of the context of their discovery (Bakhtin, 1993; Morson & Emerson, 1990).

Contrary to the traditional, monological novel, Bakhtin (1984/1993) noted that Dostoevsky created a special kind of novelistic genre, namely, the *polyphonic* novel. A polyphonic novel does not contain only one authorial viewpoint. Instead, there are several characters, with independent and mutually opposing voices. The characters are continually engaged in a dialogical relationship with each other. The author's perspective is just one of many. The characters are capable of authoring (expressing) and defending their views and perspectives. Each character is 'ideologically authoritative and independent; he [sic] is perceived as the author of a fully-weighted ideological conception of his own, and not as the object of Dostoevsky's finalising artistic vision' (Bakhtin, 1984/1993, 5). This leads to a '*plurality of independent and unmerged voices and consciousness, a genuine polyphony of fully-valid voices*' (Ibid, 6; original emphasis).

A plurality of independent voices

The metaphor of the polyphonic novel leads to a conception of the self that is radically different from the traditional, unitary self. The traditional Western view of the self assumes that there is only one centralised thinker responsible for the thinking process (Hermans, 2001). Polyphony, on the other hand, makes it possible to envisage different voices in dialogue within a single person. These voices are capable of engaging in a relationship of questioning and answering, agreement and disagreement, with each other. In other words, the dialogical self is characterised by a plurality of independent voices or perspectives. A person is capable of telling different stories from different vantage positions, reflecting the multiple worlds in which he or she has grown up.

The voices comprising the dialogical self need not be in agreement with each other. Rivalry or tensions between different selves may occur. Bakhtin (1993) showed that once an inner thought of a character has been transformed into an utterance, dialogical relationships between this utterance and the utterances of real or imagined Others occur spontaneously (Hermans & Kempen, 1993). Bakhtin (1993) illustrated this by referring to Dostoevsky's novel, *The double.* In this novel, Dostoevsky creates a second hero (the double) to act as an externalised, interior voice (thought) of Golyadkin, who is the first hero. Once the thought of the second hero is externalised, dialogical relationships between this voice and the first hero become possible. This makes it possible to study the internal world of one individual with reference to the relationship between the multiple voices comprising the self (Hermans, 1996; Hermans, 1997; Hermans & Kempen, 1993). For example, tensions may occur between the social self, defined in terms of one's membership in a particular group, and the person's own intentions (see Box 2).

Spatialisation in the dialogical self

At this point, it is necessary to discuss briefly Bakhtin's understanding of the relationship between an idea and a person holding it. For Bakhtin, an idea represents a person's point of view: it cannot be separated from the / (person) voicing it. Likewise, the person holding it becomes a fully fledged personality by virtue of that idea (Morson & Emerson, 1990). Because it is the idea that defines the person, it is possible to externalise it metaphorically, in order to give it its own 'personality'. Spatialisation refers to an idea that has been endowed with a personality of its own through externalisation. Once externalised, the idea tells its own story, from its own vantage position (eg in Dostoevsky's novel *The double,* referred to above). The dialogical self could thus be conceived *spatially* as a multiplicity of autonomous authors in an imaginary landscape. Each author is capable of telling different stories from different perspectives (Hermans, 1996; 1997). For example, people can tell various stories, perhaps from the vantage position of their parents, their grandparents, and even deceased relatives. The stories are ideologically independent and hence can engage dialogically with each other (Hermans, 1997; Josephs, 1997).

To illustrate the spatialisation of the dialogical self, Hermans, Kempen & Van Loon (1992) conceived of the dialogical self as a play of positions in an imaginary landscape. They maintained that:

> The *I* has the possibility to move, as in space, from one position to the other in accordance with changes in situation and time. The *I* fluctuates among different and even opposed positions. The *I* has the capacity to imaginatively endow each position with a voice so that dialogical relations between positions can be established. The voices function like interacting characters in a story. Once a character is set in motion in a story, the character takes on a life of its own and thus assumes a certain narrative necessity. Each character has a story to tell about experiences of its own stance. As different voices, these characters exchange information about respective *Me(s)* and their worlds, resulting in a complex, narratively structured self (28–29).

The dialogical self is not limited to one centralised position, towards which every voice gravitates. Rather, the person can move from one position to another, in response to changes in situation and time (see Box 2).

BOX 2   Relationships between voices in the dialogical self

The following interview extract was taken from the author's ongoing work on moral and ethical decision-making. It illustrates many aspects of the dialogical self. The narrator had been pressurised by members of his family to take part in an effort to avenge a family murder.

Interviewer: Anything that came to your mind?

Narrator: Yes. In my mind there was a great debate, which I could not resolve. When I tried to convince them [family members] otherwise, they said: 'Don't worry, you will just drive. You won't be involved.' So, we arrived at this place called Y. We looked for an area called N, but we could not find it, and it was getting dark and dangerous. So, eventually we went back home, as we could not find them that day. So, I tried another plan. I said: 'Why don't we contact the police? ... *But at the same time, as I was giving this opinion, I did not want to appear as a coward*. I had to avoid that; otherwise, they would think being educated has turned me into a coward. So, I gave this opinion in a matter-of-fact way. We contacted the police but at the same time we were scared, as they could have been in cahoots with the criminals. ... Even though we contacted the police, we continued our search the next day. So, as we were traveling, [my conscience] was killing me inside, that I am driving a car, carrying would-be murderers. But at the same time they had to be punished because they had done wrong. He who lives by the sword dies by the sword! Inside, I wanted them to be punished, but I did not want to be personally involved. ... But somehow they had to feel the pain that we felt. We were looking

The dialogical self can be described only in terms of becoming. It is always oriented towards the future, and is continually challenged to reposition itself in the light of new information.

BOX 2   Relationships between voices in the dialogical self *(cont)*

for them again, but [my conscience] was against what we were doing. 'Why Me! Why should I be the one driving the car?' ... So, that is the most difficult situation I faced in my life, having to decide whether to withdraw or not, and the meaning the family would attribute to my withdrawal. What would they say? They would say I am forsaking him (the deceased) because he is dead? At the same time I thought: 'What about me? If I do not think of myself as a member of the family, do I like what is happening?' And you find that inside; that is against your feelings, that I am doing this because they say I must do it. Although I do not want to do it, I do not want to show the Me [his real views]. Because, my inside, it is weak compared to my outside, which is what I show.

This extract could be analysed in terms of the dialogical interchange between perspectives. The narrator was torn between his views as an individual (his 'conscience'), and the part of the self representing his family (anger, pain, desire to punish, social identity). He vacillates between the two. He was also concerned with preserving his image as a brave man in his society (his positioning). The voice representing the family seems to dominate. Thus, he does not want to voice his views explicitly.

The dialogical self and innovation

Innovation or self-renewal is another critical feature of the dialogical self (Hermans, 1996, 1997). The dialogical self is always challenged by questions, disagreements, and confrontations. Owing to the interchange of voiced perspectives, it is possible for the person to reposition himself or herself, leading to innovation. That is, the dialogue between voices can lead to a new way of seeing oneself and the world (Hermans, 1996). The dialogical self can never be fixed in advance. It is characterised by a high degree of openness. This is sometimes referred to as the '*unfinalisability*' of the self (Hermans, 1996, 1997). The notion is taken from the behaviour of characters in a polyphonic novel. Characters in such a novel are highly unpredictable. They continually ridicule attempts to turn them into voiceless objects at the mercy of others' finalising descriptions. That is, the characters 'sense their own inner unfinalisability, their capacity to outgrow ... from within and to render *untrue* any externalizing and finalizing definition of them' (Bakhtin, 1993, 59; original emphasis). Meaning in a polyphonic novel is not given *a priori*: it unfolds during the process, as the author and the characters continually address each other in the present (Morson & Emerson, 1990). Likewise, the dialogical self can be described only in terms of becoming. It is always oriented toward the future, and is continually challenged to reposition itself in the light of new information.

Hierarchy, power and the dialogical self

Given the multiplicity of voices comprising the dialogical self, the question of their positioning with respect to each other, becomes inevitable. The multiple voices comprising the dialogical self are not necessarily equal. Dialogue is not only ordered horizontally, but vertically as well (Hermans, 1996). Referring to Linell's (1990) work, Hermans (1996) and Hermans & Kempen (1993) showed that conversations between interlocutors are characterised by emergence of symmetrical and asymmetrical (dominance) relationships between voices. Although conversation usually requires turn taking between interlocutors, and hence alternation between dominance versus subjectivity, it is possible for one conversant, or groups, to hold perpetual power over others. This follows from the fact that positions emerging in a conversation 'can be partly understood as reproductions of culturally-established and institutionally congealed provisions and constraints on communicative activities' (Hermans & Kempen, 1993, 73). For example, a conversation between a madam, usually a white woman, and a maid, usually a black woman, in South Africa, can be understood in terms of the power relations between these two groups in society. Likewise, the relationships between voices comprising the self are not equal. For example, the voice representing one's social group or family may take precedence over the one representing the person's aspirations (see Box 2).

THE DIALOGICAL SELF: COMPARISONS WITH AFRICAN APPROACHES

It has been argued that the dialogical self is saturated with others' perspectives. The characteristics of the dialogical self, mentioned above, also apply to traditional African conceptions of the self. The view of a multiple, dialogically constituted self is not new to African scholarship. The self in traditional African thought is, by definition, dialogical.

The social and relational origins of the self

The view that the self emerges from relationships is consistent with African conceptions of personhood. From an African perspective, the human being is never alone. He or she is always in dialogue with the surrounding environment. Thus, selfhood cannot be defined individualistically in terms of a person's thought processes. This finds support in Zahan (1979), who argues that African psychology conceptualises the self in much broader and richer terms. Communication between the self and the world is the order of the day:

> [The human being] enters into the surrounding environment, which in turn penetrates him [sic]. Between the two realities there exists a constant communication, a sort of osmotic exchange, owing to which man finds himself permanently listening, so to speak, to the pulse of the world (Zahan, 1979, 9).

From a traditional African point of view, 'the human being lives in close contact with the universe; he [sic] lives in symbiosis with it and does not artificially separate himself from it at any moment of his existence' (Zahan, 1979, 20). As the passage cited above indicates, there is always interpenetration between the self and the external environment. Such a conceptualisation renders questions about what is inside or outside of the person (the individual-versus-society debate) inadequate. Rather, we should focus on how, through mediation, social and cultural processes become part of the person's internal world.

The dialogical implications of 'Umuntu ngumuntu ngabantu'

Dialogism in African thought incorporates relationships between people. Let us reconsider the saying: *Umuntu ngumuntu ngabantu.* Although quoted very often, the dialogical implications of this saying have never been fully grasped, especially in psychology. This saying can be interpreted as: 'A human being is a human being because of other human beings'. In other words, it points at the fact that selfhood emerges dialogically, *through participation in a community of other human beings.'* Further support is found in the Tshivenda equivalent, *muthu ubebelwa munwe.* This translates as: 'a person is [already] *born for the other.'* Both sayings highlight that the self cannot be conceived independently of social relationships.

Louw (1999, 2001) points out that the saying *umuntu ngumuntu ngabantu,* as a dialogical principle, is a call for human beings to respect the individuality and particularity of the other. This does not refer to individuality in the abstract sense, synonymous with the **Cartesian view of the self**. The Cartesian self exists 'prior' to society; it is thus inconsistent with a dialogical, socially immersed self. 'Individuality' here refers to the concreteness of the other. It refers to *particular* individuals who, by virtue of their *particularity,* are capable of voicing their own perspectives.

The abovementioned interpretation of *umuntu ngumuntu ngabantu* also finds support in Van der Merwe (1996). He interprets the saying as follows: 'To be a human being is to affirm one's humanity by recognizing the humanity of others in its infinite variety of content or form.' (1). Alternatively, the saying could be envisaged to mean: 'A human being is a human being through (the otherness of) other human beings' (1). Thus, it is through our encounter with another, fully voiced consciousness that we gain self-understanding. We cannot claim to fully understand who we are when we deny others the right to mean or speak.

The saying '*umuntu ngumuntu ngabantu*' is a call for us to enrich our own self-understanding through contact with, and recognition of, the Other who is different from us. This requires that we come to terms with the Other's points of views, or lenses through which he or she makes sense of the world. As Bakhtin argued, people become fully fledged personalities by virtue of their ideas or points of view (Morson & Emerson). To deny others the right to mean

Cartesian (unitary) self: traditional Western view of the self that defines the person in terms of his or her thoughts or psychological attributes. It draws sharp distinctions between the self (inside) and the non-self (the outside). The Cartesian self is unitary: it proclaims only one centralised thinker.

(voice) is to deny them individuality. Recognising others' views is also important because it is through them that we come to be conscious of who we are.

The notion that 'we are because of others' is central to many African cultures, as in the saying *'Umuntu ngumuntu ngabantu',* which may be interpreted as: 'A human being is a human being because of other human beings.'

Personhood and becoming in African thought

Selfhood in traditional African thought is also conceptualised in space and time. The person in African thought is never a finished product; he or she is perpetually in the making (Sow, 1980). This means that human beings can be defined only in terms of becoming (Ramose, 1999; Sow, 1980; Zahan, 1979). People achieve full selfhood once they have undergone 'certain physical transformations or ... perform[ed] ... rites designed to admit [them] into adult society as a new member' (Zahan, 1979, 10). Sow (1980) captures this view of the self in the following paragraph:

> [T]he human person/personality is not a 'completed' system (already at three to five years of age); the human being, as such, is perpetually 'in the making'. From the psychological and psychopathological point of view, difficulties and conflicts are always present, seen in a context of ceaseless development, for the personality is continually evolving in a life that is felt to unfold in an orderly fashion, dominated, at its highest point, by the ideas of seniority and ancestry. The basic ideas or phases of life (codified through rituals and traditional practices, including initiation) permit progressive integration into a well-ordered universe. ... The status of full person is really acquired only with old age, which takes on an ancestral quality (126).

Selfhood in traditional African thought is also conceptualised in space and time. The person in African thought is never a finished product; he or she is perpetually in the making.

The passage above indicates that personhood in African scholarship can only be defined in terms of becoming. Conception and birth are not enough to ensure humanhood (Menkiti, 1984; Zahan, 1979). Instead, it is through participation in the community of others, which in some societies includes rituals of transformation, that one becomes fully human (Sow, 1980; Zahan, 1979). These are ritual practices such as *imbeleko,* a sacrificial offering performed by Nguni groups to introduce a newborn child to the family, the community of integrated ancestors (*izinyanya*) and, by extension, to God. Similar offerings are made during various stages in life, culminating with the rituals of burial, which mark the person's transition from the world of the living to the spiritual world.

Vigilance regarding oppressive ritual practices

At this point, it is necessary to pause to address some possible, and justified, objections to initiation rituals. I have in mind practices such as 'female circumcision', which, in some African societies, marks the transition to womanhood. It is not my intention to portray all forms of ritual initiation as positive. Indeed, all cultural practices carry with them complex contradictions. These contradictions can be exploited for other purposes, including gender and other forms of oppression. Critical social science has no room for oppressive cultural practices: its very existence is predicated on the eradication of such practices, among other practices. The theory of dialogism allows us to critically debate cultural practices, so as to eliminate their oppressive elements, while retaining positive ones.

For the purposes of my argument, which is to demonstrate that personhood is conceived in terms of becoming in African thought, the analysis of transformation rituals is limited to their social and spiritual significance, rather than the visible, outside criteria. This is based on the view that outside criteria can be eliminated, without compromising the hidden social and spiritual meanings attached to the practice. Indeed, some African societies do not have initiation rites, and yet retain the social and spiritual meanings associated with them (Zahan, 1979).

Initiation: passage from exteriority to interiority

Following Zahan (1979), I would argue that initiation represents a process by which people discover themselves (who they are) through others and their communities. It represents 'a slow transformation of the individual, a progressive passage from exteriority to interiority' (Zahan, 1979, 54). The reference to the '*passage from exteriority to interiority*' does not mean that knowledge developed through initiation is of an abstract, individualistic type, as in the self-contained view of the self (Hermans *et al*, 1992). Rather, it points to the fact that self-knowledge is the basis of all forms of knowledge in African thought (Myers, 1988; Zahan, 1979). Self-knowledge does not result from the maturation of internally held principles, however. It ensues from a person's relationships with others, including the social environment. Thus, it moves from the direction of the social environment (social relationships and practices) to the internal world of the individual. One can never completely master the external environment, and hence, self-knowledge is always oriented toward the future. As Zahan (1979) argues, initiation (to self-knowledge) 'becomes a long process, a confrontation between man [sic] and himself which ends in death. It becomes an experience which is enriched with every passing day, being in principle more complete in an elderly person than in an adult, and more in an adult than in a child' (55). Because one can never attain full (complete) **self-knowledge**, it could be argued that the self in African thought is always distributed at the boundary between the self and the non-self.

Ubuntu as a process

Finally, I should like to reflect on the open-ended, dialogically oriented view of the self in African thought by analysing the meaning of the terms *ubuntu* (*botho*) and *umuntu* (*motho*). It should be noted that the term *ubuntu* has complex philosophical and ethical implications. For the purposes of my argument, only the linguistic analysis is presented here. Although similar terms are found in a number of South African languages, I limit the analysis to the Nguni equivalents.

Ubuntu, often interpreted as 'humanness' in English, is about becoming. The word can be broken down to the prefix *ubu-* and the stem *-ntu.* Ubu- belongs in the group of nouns indicating a process or becoming. The stem *-ntu,* on the other hand, indicates a human being (*umuntu*). This means that, linguistically, *ubuntu* indicates a being that is always oriented toward becoming. According to Ramose (1999), *umuntu,* from which *ubuntu* is derived,

> is the specific entity which continues to conduct an inquiry into experience, knowledge, and truth. *This is an activity rather than an act. It is an ongoing process impossible to stop.* On this reasoning, *ubu-* may be regarded as be-ing becoming and this evidently implies the idea of motion (51; emphasis added).

The idea of personhood as becoming, (movement) as reflected in the writings of Bakhtin (1984/1993) and those of Hermans and colleagues (Hermans, 2001a, 2001b; Hermans & Kempen, 1993), is consistent with traditional African conceptions of the self. The fact that this idea is reflected in African languages and proverbs indicates that it predates the psychological literature about dialogism. Further, this view is not something the African reads about in the literature (and hence, comes to know only cognitively). It is an indispensable part of lived experience or *ubu-ntu.* Becoming, or *inkambo* ('life journey' or lived experience) is manifest in the relationship between the person and others, including the surrounding environment. Our analysis of the saying '*umuntu ngumuntu ngabantu*' already testifies to this.

Pluralism and the African self

The traditional African worldview also conceptualises the self in pluralistic terms (Ogbonnaya, 1994; Sow, 1980; Zahan, 1979).

Self-knowledge is the basis of all forms of knowledge in African thought. Self-knowledge does not result from the maturation of internally held principles. It ensues from a person's relationships with others, including the social environment. It moves from the direction of the social environment (social relationships and practices) to the internal world of the individual.

Sow (1980) wrote as follows on that subject:

Inseparable from his [sic] social dimension, the individual in Africa ... *appears composite in space, multiple in time, extending and testifying to a culture of rich complexity.* ... Only an anthropological perspective that views the person as a living system of social relations and a system of interaction with the realm of the symbolic will enable one to grasp the way in which Africans experience the self (Sow, 1980, 126; emphasis added).

To illustrate further the multiple nature of the self in African scholarship, Sow (1980) cites from the work of Thomas & Luneau (1975), who wrote as follows:

The concept of person sums up and brings together ideas and principles of traditional Negro-African thought. Indeed, one finds there the necessity of pluralism, the networks of participation and correspondence that bind the subject to the group and to the cosmos, the verbal dimensions, the dynamic and unfinished quality, the richness and the fragility, the important role assigned to the milieu, and the inevitable reference to the sacred (Thomas & Lineau, 1975, cited in Sow, 1980, 127).

Like the dialogical self, personhood in African thought is pluralistic. It is extended in space and time.

The human being as a 'community of selves'

If the self in African thought is multiple, what is the nature of that multiplicity? Zahan (1979) argues that the self cannot be separate because, physiologically and psychically, human beings always carry within themselves their own genitors and ascendants. That is, human beings carry with them the ancestral (spiritual) component, the present self, as well as selves that are yet to be born. Ogbonnaya (1994) expresses the same view when he argues that 'the human person must be seen as a community in and of itself including a plurality of selves' (75). He does not refer to a community outside the person. Rather, this is the community of selves constituting the internal world of the person. He maintains that:

the person in African worldview should be visualized as a centrifugal force capable of emanating other complex selves that can interpermeate each other as well as other selves generated from other persona-communal centers. This centrifugality of the person reaches into all directions and touches all events that contribute to the full person – the mythical past, the generational past, the ever present nature, and the self in the process of being born (Ogbonnaya, 1994, 79).

The plurality of selves envisaged in African thought is expressed differently, depending on one's cultural group. For example, the Balong of Cameroon believe that a person is born with different souls, some representing the parents, the ancestors, God and other spiritual beings (Ogbonnaya, 1994). Similarly, most traditional societies in South Africa believe that over and above unique 'individual selves' people are born with a spiritual self, representing their *izinyanya* (ancestors). The spiritual self is thought to be more pronounced in those called to become traditional diviners and healers (*izangoma*). This indicates that multiplicity of the self is integral to traditional African ways of thinking.

Most probably, plurality of selves applies to most cultures. However, the people or internal 'audiences' (Day, 1991) inhabiting our worlds will differ from culture to culture and from person to person. For some, these may be angels (Christians), and for others, ancestors, and even movie heroes for others (especially children). Further, our internal audiences may change as we move from one cultural setting to another. The critical question is not only about who constitutes our internal world, but how internal audiences are formed and transformed over time (Day, 1991).

Tensions or rivalry between selves

Ogbonnaya (1994) brings to our attention that selves within the person are always engaged in interplay with each other. The relationship between internal communal selves resembles the one between the individual and the community. Ideally, the various selves should work together interdependently, without the loss or sacrifice of other aspects of the communal self. However, problems of power and dominance between selves arise, threatening to destabilise the community of selves. That is, the selves can be in conflict with each other. This is exemplified by someone called by *izinyanya* (ancestors) to assume a healing function in society. Because the call is involuntary, it sometimes results in a struggle between the spiritual self and the individual personality. The former seeks to dominate the latter by directing it to assume a healing function. With the assistance of a highly trained spiritual medium, it is possible for an individual to enter into a dialogue with the spiritual self and, through the medium of **impepho**, request it to forgive him or her for not accepting the call to heal.

Impepho: traditional incense used by traditional healers to communicate with the ancestors.

Should the individual accept the call to heal, the spiritual self becomes capable of holding an independent conversation with the individual self. It can be consulted for healing purposes. It is the general view that the spiritual self speaks with its own voice, independently of the voice of the healer. Because the healer is not aware of what the spiritual self is saying (through him or her), the service of an interpreter is usually solicited. This lends support to the view that the multiple selves within a person can be engaged in a dialogical interplay with each other.

Implications and conclusion

Dialogism has several implications. This principle always recognises another, with whom one can agree or disagree. It emphasises processes taking place at the zone or contact between the person and his or her environment. Dialogism provides a meaningful framework for exploring the role of social, historical and cultural factors in development, making it an important theoretical perspective for critical psychology.

Through the principle of dialogism, influences of the contact between various worldviews on development can be explored. It acknowledges that local (indigenous) and Western worldviews can coexist within a single person. These worldviews can engage dialogically with each other, and people are capable of moving between both worlds. The lived experiences of many African (and other) people are already characterised by a need to continually shift self perspectives. An old man who works as a sweeper in the mines may be a highly respected *induna* (headman) in his rural community. Likewise, Holdstock (2000) reports on many highly educated Africans who successfully shift between modern and traditional ways of life. Because we live in a world characterised by connections (eg between the local and the foreign, the national and the transactional), focusing on the interplay between these worldviews is more fruitful. This, argue Hermans & Kempen (1998), requires the notion of a dialogical self.

> Dialogism emphasises processes taking place at the zone or contact between the person and his or her environment. Dialogism provides a meaningful framework for exploring the role of social, historical, and cultural factors in development.

Methodological individualism versus methodological collectivism

Another advantage of dialogism is that it makes it possible to move beyond the individual-society dichotomy, or what Wertsch (1995) calls *methodological individualism* and *methodological collectivism*. Methodological individualism reduces social and individual phenomena to facts about the individual. Everything depends on the individual. Methodological collectivism, on the other hand, explains human behaviour in terms of societal factors. Everything depends on society. Dialogism breaches this dichotomy through the concept of *mediated activity*. Mediation explains how what is outside the individual (the social and cultural realm) becomes part of his or her functioning through internalisation.

The dichotomy between the individual and society is also reduced by the notion of *ventriloquation,* by which people speak in collective voices. Indeed, Bakhtin (1981) argues that the word is neither fully ours nor fully someone else's. We make it our own when we appropriate it (from others and the social and cultural sphere) by populating it with our own intentions and accent.

The need to generate intercultural dialogue

In conclusion, it has been argued that the sociocultural tradition in psychology facilitates incorporation of local worldviews into psychological discourse. It has been shown that African conceptions of the person have many parallels with those emanating from Bakhtin's dialogism. A truly dialogical account of knowledge should take into account the Other's worldviews and perspectives.

Psychological science needs to generate *intercultural dialogue* between the indigenous and the Western, the local and the international (Gergen *et al*, 1996). If it fails to do so, it runs the risk of becoming monological. We also need to capitalise on the innovative quality of the dialogical self. Always oriented toward the future, this self is ready to reinvent itself in the light of new information. Because meaning *emerges* at the point of contact between 'bodies' of knowledge (Holquist, 1990), psychology will benefit from attending to processes at the zone between indigenous and Western worldviews.

Critical thinking tasks

1. List two higher psychological functions (eg thinking, memory). How are these functions mediated in your cultural community? (eg memory may be mediated by the use of stories).
2. Collective forms of life play an important role in self/identity formation. With reference to some of the cultural tools in your community (eg children's comic books, newspaper clippings, songs), critically discuss the process by which we come to understand ourselves as men and women (gender identity formation).
3. 'African conceptions of the self are inherently dialogical.' Discuss this statement critically, with reference to the key characteristics of the dialogical self.
4. Find an extract from any text (eg journal, newspaper clipping, song, book). Highlight voices or conceptions of the self in the text. What is the relationship between these voices or selves? Discuss this with one of your classmates.
5. Although we may not be consciously aware of it, our lives are characterised by dialogism. That is, most of us have to negotiate self-understanding (who we are) continually as we move from one context or locality to another. Give a few examples illustrating dialogism from your own life experiences. Discuss these with one of your classmates.

Recommended readings

Hermans, H.J.M., & Kempen, H.J.G. (1993). *The dialogical self: Meaning as movement.* San Diego, CA: Academic Press.

Hermans, H.J.M., & Kempen, H.J.G. (1998). 'Moving cultures: The perilous problems of cultural dichotomies in a globalizing society.' *American Psychologist*, 53: 1111–1120.

Ogbonnaya, A.O. (1994). 'Person as community: An African understanding of the person as an intrapsychic community.' *Journal of Black Psychology*, 20: 75–87.

Sow, I. (1980). *Anthropological structures of madness in black Africa* (Joyce Diamanti, trans). New York: International University Press.

Frantz Fanon and Racial Identity in Post-Colonial Contexts

6

Derek Hook

OUTCOMES

After having studied this chapter you should be able to:

- define the concept of identity
- qualify what is meant by 'the post-colonial'
- explain concepts of racial alienation, cultural dispossession and double consciousness, as well as Fanon's ideas of 'lactification', 'pathologies of liberty' and the lack of synchrony between culture, nation and family
- discuss the identity-dynamics of racism, including the notions of essentialised identity and the binary logic of whiteness and blackness, and
- explain and elaborate Bulhan's stages of marginal identity and his ideas of cultural 'in-betweenity'.

Thinking post-colonial identity

THIS CHAPTER will focus on a particular approach to the question of identity, an approach that may be characterised as *post-colonial*. Identity here will be understood as that set of social and cultural understandings through which we come to *know* and *experience* ourselves. These understandings play an important role in constituting *who we are* – that is, in who we, and others, *understand ourselves to be*.

There are four important aspects of this approach to identity that are worth emphasising. Firstly, this definition presents identity as *necessarily social* – as contingent on a variety of social factors, be they material, political, economic or ideological. I am talking here both of *social meanings*, on the one hand – ways of talking, ways of making sense of the world – and of *actual structural conditions* of day-to-day life, that is, the material circumstances that define and limit where and how one lives. Secondly, given that identity has here been understood in terms of experience and self-knowledge – terms that seem reasonably flexible and mobile – we can see that this approach views identity as potentially shifting, *as open to negotiation and change*. Then again,

> **Identity:**
> A set of social and cultural understandings through which we come to know and experience ourselves.

and this is the third point, given that this approach emphasises the *contingency* of identity on a variety of social and political factors, on relations of power, we need to understand that *identity is not simply free-floating or arbitrary*, but is significantly *delimited and conditioned by social (and material) relations of power*, by ideology and by historical patterns of privilege. Fourthly, we might say that individual or group identity has a given amount of cultural resources available to it. Here we are referring to a collection of narratives, values, ideals, types of knowledge, discourses, social practices and beliefs, which are *shared*, and which maintain a sense of sameness, or continuity, across different contexts within that culture. This is the framework *without* which, as Bulhan (1979) notes, social identity fails to have meaning. What is important to understand about this *cultural dimension* to identity is that it is not equally shared across society. Different groupings of people – and this is especially so in situations of cultural dominance – have differing resources of identity available to them.

Integral to the critical perspective on identity that this chapter will put forward are questions of race, culture and power, all of which play an important role in the works of the revolutionary writer Frantz Fanon (1968; 1970; 1986; 1990), around which an increasing body of contemporary scholarship has come to centre (see particularly Alessandrini, 1999; Gordon *et al.*, 1996; Read, 1996). Fanon was a psychiatrist and revolutionary, born in the French colony of Martinique, who dedicated much of his life to the liberation of

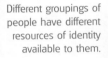

Different groupings of people have different resources of identity available to them.

Algeria from France (see Julien, 1996; Macey, 2000a). Amongst others, he was responsible for the massively influential books *Black Skin, White Masks* (1986, originally published 1952) and *The Wretched of the Earth* (1990, originally published 1961). The first of these texts will form the basic touchstone of this chapter. Also important here is the writing of Hussein Abdilahi Bulhan (1979; 1980a; 1980b; 1985), who has provided one of the most valuable commentaries on Fanon. Bulhan's work will also feature strongly in what follows.

Identity is necessarily social, open to negotiation, but not simply free-floating, and has a given amount of cultural resources open to it.

Defining the post-colonial

A further qualification that needs be made here concerns a definition of 'the post-colonial'. As both Ashcroft *et al.* (1995) and Williams and Chrisman (1994) have reiterated, this term has come to mean many different things to many different people, so much so that the term is in danger of losing its effective meaning altogether. Perhaps the most basic use of the label of 'post-colonial' is simply to indicate the historical period immediately following the age of European colonial expansion, an age which began its decline at roughly the end of World War II. This is the period in which colonial powers increasingly began to grant independence to former colonies. (It should be noted that this itself was often a period of great conflict and violence, however.) Importantly, however, the granting of independence does not simply bring colonial politics to an end. As Ashcroft *et al.* (1995:2) warn: 'All post-colonial societies are still subject in one way or another to overt or subtle forms of neo-colonial domination, and independence has not solved this problem.' So although the terms of Fanon's analysis are principally those of the colonial situation, they still usefully inform post-colonial periods, which are never fully separable from their colonial past.

Post-colonial refers to the historical period following European colonial expansion when former colonies gained political independence. But in addition, post-colonial means a particular critical orientation to understanding the relationship between the coloniser and colonised.

More than just a historical period, the term 'post-colonial' denotes a particular critical orientation to understanding the relationship between colonisers and colonised, and the psychological, material and cultural effects of these relationships. Indeed, in this respect, *post-colonialism* – as a particular *theoretical* form of reading and critique – pays particular attention to the relationship between *the personal-subjective* and *the socio-historical* domains in the construction of individual identity. Van Zyl (1998) provides one of the most useful shorthand definitions of the post-colonial from within a South African perspective. She views post-colonialism as *a critical perspective* that aims to understand the relationships of *domination* and/or *resistance* that manifest when one culture (typically Western) 'owns' or controls another (typically Eastern or African) culture, *even after the era of formalised colonialism has ended* (*ibid.*). Key concerns in this connection are issues of cultural dispossession/integration, racial identity and the self–other dynamic of inter-group relations, all of which are discussed by Fanon.

It is important we realise the importance of this approach to South Africa. For, as Bertoldi (1998) points out, apartheid may be considered a particular extension or variation of the basic politics and conditions of colonialism. Similarly, Wolpe (1975) considered South Africa a 'colonial society of a special type', and saw apartheid as a form of 'internal-Colonialism'. In a similar way, we might consider the current post-apartheid period as a particularly South African variant of the broader post-colonial era. An important word of caution stems from this last point. I am not here seeking to reduce the current historical period of post-apartheid South Africa simply to a 'post-colonial' characterisation. There are clearly unique historical circumstances present within post-apartheid South Africa which differentiate it from other post-colonial contexts. Similarly, broader political forces like globalisation, as one example, and the growing and differing intersections between race, class, gender, ethnicity, religion, as another, would seem to call for more detailed forms of analyses than those outlined here, under the label of 'the post-colonial'. Furthermore, again emphasising the lack of any rigid demarcation between the colonial and the post-colonial, we need be aware that certain dynamics of race, racism and identity formation that were present in apartheid South Africa no doubt *still* feature in what counts as a *post*-apartheid situation. In view of this, I suggest that 'the post-colonial', as either historical period or critical perspective, should not be viewed as *all-encompassing*, but rather as one element within many potential others through which we may read, attempt to understand, and critique, the social-political life in previously colonial contexts.

One last qualification: we should beware of attempting to apply too easily, too directly, the terms of Fanon's analysis to the South African situation. Ultimately we should undertake our own forms of analysis and critique of racial identities in the *particularity of the post-apartheid South African context*. However, this is not to say that Fanon's concepts do not provide us with a valuable starting point, a basic conceptual vocabulary that we can draw on, where appropriate. (Both Fanon [1986; 1990] and Bulhan [1979; 1980a; 1985] do in fact make repeated reference to apartheid South Africa in their writings.)

Post-colonialism:
A theoretical perspective that seeks to understand the relationships of domination and/or resistance that manifest when one culture 'owns' or controls another culture even after the era of formal colonialism has ended.

How racial oppression affects identity

The *lived experience* of the Black man/woman

The task Fanon sets himself in *Black Skin, White Masks* is that of describing, as vividly as possible, *the lived experience of the Black man*. In attempting to do this, Fanon is not merely looking at experience in the banal everyday sense of the term. The notion of experience here suggests a deep engagement with the world around the subject, a profound sense of feeling and 'living through' the social conditions that define a particular time and place (Macey, 2000a). One way of understanding how Fanon means 'lived experience' here is through the idea of a *political consciousness*, that is, an acute awareness both *of how one is crucially a part of the world and its conditions* – and not easily separated from them – and a critical attention to exactly how much of that world is conditioned, or even determined, by political circumstances (such awareness and attention forms the basis of one's political project).

Such a political consciousness entails a careful consideration of what Fanon, following Sartre, refers to as *facticity*, in other words, those seemingly 'concrete' factors that define my situation in the world, such as the actual physical environment in which I live, the time of my birth, my class membership, the facts of my nationality, my body, my race, etc. These are the conditions within which I live, that cannot simply be transcended, merely 'wished away'. In fact, it is vitally important that they not be under-estimated when one starts to formulate one's political project. A broader understanding of what 'lived experience' means to Fanon helps us think about exactly why, for him, identity is always in dynamic negotiation with the world around it, always in relation to other people, structures and conditions, and remains eternally potentially changeable, despite the facticity of these elements.

Racial alienation

The search for Black identity, and racial identity, is the abiding concern of *Black Skin, White Masks*. Although for Fanon both White and Black races are locked within the constraints of colour, his particular emphasis, as Wyrick (1998) suggests, is on the formation, meaning and effects of 'Blackness'. Fanon is trying to understand both Blackness *and* Whiteness, *as inseparably linked*, and as always in relation to one another. If *lived experience* is the basis on which Fanon begins his exploration of racial identity in colonial contexts, then *racial alienation* proves to be his chief problematic. It is this notion – of alienation – that provides Fanon with his principal means of 'thinking' racial identity and its cultural challenges within colonial contexts. 'Alienation', is a very dense theoretical concept, one with a formidable history. As such, it is important that we be clear on how Fanon used the term. Both Zahar (1969) and Bulhan (1985) will be useful to us here, although principally the latter.

Alienation is a dynamic concept, one which relates experience to social conditions in a way that enables us to produce critique (Bulhan, 1985; Zahar, 1969). It is also a concept with a certain amount of synthesising power, by which I mean to say that it can be applied in a number of different levels of experience (Zahar, 1969). Bulhan (1985) introduces his qualification of the term by emphasising its usefulness as a means of linking *personal-subjective* and *socio-historical* domains. Already, then, we get a sense of the importance of the term to Fanon; it gives us a way of thinking the connections – or articulations – between the *internal world of the individual subject*, and the *external world of the constraining social, economic or political structures* that surround and contain that individual.

Estrangement

A second basic aspect of the notion of alienation is the idea of estrangement. This idea features centrally in what is perhaps the best-known account of alienation, that of Karl Marx. For Marx, alienation is the result, particularly characteristic of modern capitalism, of the separation of the worker from the products of his or her labour. In his conceptualisation, what the workers produce they do not own or ultimately have control over. Their labour hence takes on a life of its own, which is alien, and even threatening. The products produced by the worker are lost to her or him and appropriated by the employer, which leads to a sense of estrangement and alienation on the part of the worker. This alienation of labour leads, as Macey (2000b) summarises, to a loss of reality, to the situation where human beings are estranged from their own bodies, from the natural world and from their potentially universal essences.

The concept of alienation then emphasises a sense of rupture in the relationship between the self and those things, objects and people around us. This estrangement is not only that of the self from the world, but also, in a very powerful way, *that of the individual person's estrangement from him- or herself.* Here it is important to pay attention to how Fanon adapts the concept of alienation to suit his purposes. For Marx, the root causes of alienation reside in the substructure of society, and particularly in the alienation of productive labour engendered by a capitalist mode of production. Therefore, when the worker's labour is alienated, so too is his or her 'humanness'. In different terms, because of alienated labour, the being of the worker remains alien to him and all others.

For Fanon, *race*, and the various social practices and meanings attached to it, proves to be the pivot of alienation, rather than productive labour. As Bulhan (1985) rightly notes, Fanon's application favours *psychological* and *cultural* dimensions rather than *economic* and *class* dimensions. Clearly, as a psychiatrist, Fanon was interested in an exposition of alienation from a *psychological* perspective (*ibid.*). As individuals, we can then be estranged, from our 'humanness', from our own body and sense of self, from a sense even

> The concept of *racial* alienation seeks to show the sense of separation in the relationship of the Black self and things, objects and others around itself.

of belonging to our people, *all on the basis of race*. In many ways, this is perhaps the most consistent theme throughout *Black Skin, White Masks*, that of dehumanisation, that of the inability, because of various forms of racism and cultural dispossession, to settle on any kind of authentic identity.

The pathology of the colonial context

The juxtaposition of the Black and White races in post-colonial contexts creates, for Fanon, a collective form of mental illness, a 'massive psycho-existential complex' (1986:12). I must be clear on what Fanon means here; he is by no means suggesting that racial contact is inherently pathological, that races should not seek contact. Rather he means to emphasise how problematic, *pathogenic* even (in the sense of inducing psycho-pathologies, inauthentic forms of identity), such racial contacts prove to be in contexts in which one racial group maintains a powerful degree of aggressive dominance over the other. (And this dominance may be realised in concrete physical, economic or cultural terms.) In such contexts, the potential for psycho-pathology, at least in the sense of compromised identity formation, is omnipresent. Hence Fanon's assertion that 'a normal black child who has grown up in the bosom of a normal family will be made abnormal by the slightest contact with the white world' (1986:117).

Pathogenic:
Causing or tending
to cause disease,
illness, or
psychological
disturbance.

One of Fanon's most profound points in the thinking of Black identity is to suggest that the material effects of racism and colonialism have large-scale *identity effects*. We need to think of colonialism, and for Fanon (1986; 1990), its lingering after-effects, not only as a means of appropriating land and terri-tory, but of appropriating culture and history themselves, that is, as appropriating the means and resources of identity. Here we get a sense of how the material practices of colonialism, to use Wyrick's phrase (1998), *translate a denial of history into a displacement of culture and language*. The colonisation of a land, its people, its culture, in short, is a 'colonising of the mind', in Ngugi wa Thiong'o's (1986) famous phrase.

Cultural dispossession: Alienation through language

One of the most direct routes of racial alienation is through the adoption of the language of the oppressor. To speak a language, for Fanon, is 'to assume a culture, to support the weight of a civilization' (1986:17–18). More than this, the colonised Black subject 'will be proportionately whiter – that is, he will come closer to being a real human being – in direct ratio to his mastery of the [coloniser's] language' (*ibid.*:18). Fanon here is emphasising the role of language within the objectifying and dehumanising qualities of colonial practice. He is also aware, however, of the two-part process of alienation, whereby the process of assuming another's culture typically necessitates the giving up of one's own.

Simply put, the Black man or woman's mastery of the coloniser's language may increase their acceptance by Whites, but it alienates them from their root culture – taking on of the coloniser's language can erase their own cultural memory. An assumed language can both reinforce feelings of racial inferiority in the colonised, and emphatically mark their dislocation from the black community. In Bulhan's words: 'The fact of having to speak nothing but the other's language when this other was the ... oppressor was at once an affirmation of him, his worldview, and his values; a concession to his framework; and an estrangement from one's history, values and outlook' (1985:189).

Lactification

What starts to become apparent here is the idea of the possibility of moderating one's race, of lessening the degree of one's Blackness, a desire which Fanon refers to as *lactification*, toying with the word's associations to milk and Whiteness. He considers this, the wish to be White, to be a very powerful – and damaging – desire in colonised subjects, so much so that he poses (then answers) what is perhaps *the* question of racial identity and desire for the Black colonised subject: 'What does the black man want?... The black man wants to be white' (1986:8–9).

This is a pathological desire that is forced upon Black subjects by White civilisation and European culture. The effect of racist culture is to affirm supposedly global standards of value, which are really those of a select White American/European/Western group, as universal. In other words, the Black subject is, right from the start, 'predetermined' to fall short of these norms, by virtue of how culturally specific they are. 'Black people, then, abandon themselves individually and collectively in quest of white acceptance. The quest is inherently and ultimately futile; it results primarily in solidifying deep and disturbing feelings of inferiority' (Wyrick, 1998:29). This notion of internalised kinds of inferiority, of socially induced inferiority complexes, is one of the most important ways in which Fanon thinks about the damage, on the level of identity, the mass victimisation, enforced by dominant racist cultures on those they colonise. It is in this connection that he quotes Aimé Césaire: 'I am talking of millions of men who have been skilfully infected with fear, inferiority complexes, trepidation, servility, despair, debasement' (Fanon, 1986:12).

Practices of hair-straightening, skin-lightening, the attempt to earn a White spouse at all costs, and the enthusiastic adoption of the accent and language of the oppressor, all of these are examples of *inauthenticity* for Fanon. They are voluntary kinds of masking, symptoms of what is wrong in the colonised subject's psyche. These are negative bids at identity – processes of negation – that constantly *affirm* the coloniser's culture as the superior term, and dismiss the colonised culture as inferior. Importantly, these are *self-objectifying* practices in which the Black subjects comes to implement a kind of racism *from within*, so to speak, *upon themselves*. It is due to these internally reproduced kinds of racism that Fanon (1986:8) asserts that 'I propose nothing short of the liberation of the man of colour from himself.'

'Degrees' of race: The whitening of the Black subject

What Fanon's idea of lactification suggests, perhaps contrary to our expectations, is that race need not work simply as an 'all or nothing' category. In certain instances, it would seem that we are working with a *hierarchy* of racial identities, with *degrees* of Whiteness and Blackness. The Black subject hence, for Fanon (1986) becomes proportionately White, and closer to being a real human being, in direct ratio to his or her mastery of a White language, his acquisition of White culture, the attaining of a certain level of wealth. Put differently, one might say that the dynamics of race intersect with dynamics of class, such that it is understood that 'one is white above a certain class' (Fanon, 1986:44). European accents, figures of speech, fashions, modes of dress, all of these come to act as 'signals of class', which contribute, in the colonised subject, to a feeling of equality with the European, to an apparent *lessening* of one's Blackness. As true as these observations might seem one should point out that where racial categories have been essentialised (as to be discussed below) then race becomes an inescapable category. So even if one is able to lessen considerably one's Blackness, one will never be totally White, totally accepted by the colonising culture. Of course it is also important to mention here that a dynamics of race is overlaid not only by dynamics of gender, class and sexuality, but also by a dynamics of ethnicity, such that Fanon notes that in the Antilles it was understood that Senegalese were considered to be *more Black*, so to speak, that is less civilised, than the native inhabitants of Martinique. In this sense one is able to see how a racist culture begins to set up levels of separation, differential degrees of Blackness, in this case, *hierarchies of prejudice*, within a given population.

Dispossessed identities

To be the subject of cultural oppression/racism, is to be continually fed with cultural understandings *which are not our own*, which are primarily hostile towards us, *and which consistently de-evaluate us and our culture*. It means to exist in a state of few or no cultural resources of my own, because they have been eradicated by the cultural imperialism of the coloniser. More than this, it means to internalise the coloniser's stereotypes as a means of *knowing self*. Simply put, for each step with which I try to understand myself, I am actually further alienated, because I am using pre-determined and loaded terms that always dispossess and devaluate me, and serve the dominant group culture.

What Fanon is here attempting to impart to the critical consciousness of his readers is an awareness of the continual sense of dissonance within the colonised subject, which occurs between ego and culture, self and society. There is a continual mismatch here – a sense of alienation rooted in race, or how race has been *socially produced* and *practiced* within a given culture – which results in a dislocation between the ideals, the norms of the valorised Western culture, and what I, by distinction, am (namely the *other* of all of these values). This constant and recurring slippage is pathogenic, it causes a deeply-rooted sense of inferiority, a constantly problematised sense of identity which is split and at war with itself, causing 'pathologies of liberty' as Fanon (1990) calls them.

'Double consciousness'

Black identity is hence typically marked by self-division, and can be characterised as a kind of *double consciousness*, which is essentially the result of the attempt *to configure Black identity within the coordinates of (racist) White culture.* For Fanon then, the Black subject has two dimensions, one with the other Black man/woman, and another with the White subject. As previously noted, the more the colonised subject comes to succeed in the culture of the coloniser, the more he or she is distanced from the home culture, the more the difference, the incomprehension and the disharmony between the two sides is increased. This situation presents as a double bind; despite the costs in terms of cultural alienation of identifying with the world of the coloniser, this colonising culture will never accept the colonised subject completely. And of course it is understandable that the colonised subject would want to speak the language of the oppressor, to attain competence in his or her culture, because it 'can open doors which were still barred to him [sic] fifty years ago' (Fanon, 1986:38). Fanon dramatises this double bind with the following comment: 'I'm beginning to wonder *if I haven't been betrayed by everything around me*, as the white people do not recognize me as one of their own, and with the black people virtually rejecting me' (cited in Macey, 2000a:197, own emphasis).

> ### What is 'double consciousness'?
>
> Double consciousness has become a useful, shorthand critical term used to evoke a sense of *looking at one's self through someone else's eyes*. Gilroy (1994; 2000) describes it as a state of 'being and not belonging', *of being an outsider on one's self* by virtue of the fact that the various norms, templates and categories for understanding and making sense of self have been set by a dominant class to which one does not belong. The term originates in the writing of W.E.B. du Bois (1995), who suggested that marginal groups in society are denied a 'true self-consciousness' because the dominant culture constantly devalues them, looks at them, their history and their traditions, with contempt. As a result they feel a divided sense of self, a *double consciousness*, with an allegiance to the valued world of their family and traditions, but also looking at themselves and their world through the eyes of the dominant culture.

Synchrony between culture, nation, family

Alienation of the sort of which we have been speaking happens at multiple levels, many of which reinforce one another. As a way of emphasising the depth and complexity of such alienation, Fanon expounds briefly on the ideal situation, on what it means to be 'at home' within a culture, nation and family. Here, as Bulhan (1985) paraphrases him, the family and the nation turn on the same axis; both are governed by essentially the same values, laws and principles. In such a situation, the values children internalise, the parental rules they observe, the forms of self-expression they are permitted, all of these guide them along a normative course of socialisation (*ibid.*). An ego-syntonic view of the self arises, as does a shared sense of belonging, hence 'The child grows in ... [a] stable family constellation and later emerges from that intimate circle to encounter a wider social world governed by similar values, laws, and principles' (*ibid.*:190).

Hence, where goes the nation, so follows the family, and ultimately the child. In short, these senses of home, of belonging, and meaning – all of which of course are vital sources of identity – are commensurate and resonant, echoed and reiterated across the levels of family, nation, culture. Situations of social or political oppression present us with a very different picture. Here one finds, in Bulhan's (1985:190) words,

> The colonial situation fosters ... neither continuity between the nation and family nor synchrony between the family and the identity of its members. The social structure exists primarily for the purpose of exploitation. Violence, crude and subtle, brought it into existence and maintains it. This violence, pervading the social order, in time affects the life of the colonized in a most fundamental way. The indigenous social structure is dislocated. The family institution subsequently is disrupted. The identity of its members also is constantly assaulted. In situations of prolonged oppression ... the oppressor had long obliterated the culture, language, and history of the oppressed. It is here less a question of discontinuity of the social structure and the family and personal identity than of a massive swamping of the family and a profound intrusion into the psyche.

Violence internalised

I am speaking here not only of how family structures are destroyed by oppressive systems, such as that of the migrant labour as necessitated by policies of separate development within apartheid South Africa. I am also speaking of how families may be destroyed from within. Bulhan (1985) here is referring to a traumatic tearing apart – one that exists within individual identities also – which occurs as a result of violent and oppressive cultural dislocations. What Bulhan is speaking of here is an extremely insidious process of negation in which one's loved ones and family members have 'unwittingly been enlisted as instruments of the prevailing social order' (*ibid.*:191).

Bulhan's objective, obviously extending Fanon, is to emphasise the overwhelming and ubiquitous violence of the colonial social order. Even if family conflicts of the sort described above are avoided, colonised subjects will sooner or later 'come up against massive social forces that undermine and sometimes overwhelm their development' (Bulhan, 1985:191). In this way the transition from childhood to adulthood, from the intimate circle of the family to broader spheres of social interaction, almost unavoidably involves personal conflicts and turmoil.

What is so valuable about the way in which Bulhan (1985) has elaborated Fanon's basic position is that it conveys how unavoidable some or other kind of conflict is within the marginalised identity of the colonial subject. Put slightly differently, we might suggest that the identity of the oppressed subject has violence at its core, a violence that duplicates itself on the level of how that individual attempts to know and experience self, between the individual and significant others, within families, within intimate relationships.

In closing this section, it is important not to over-emphasise Fanon's pessimism. While it is true that he argued that the disjuncture between what happens in the Black family and broader (racist) society may lead to psychic disarray, Fanon, specifically when writing on the Algerian family, also implied that the disruption of the Black family which is provoked by racism simultaneously also serves to co-create with various other processes the conditions for the destruction of racism. For Fanon, racist oppression does not only lead to inestimable psychic maiming, but the phenomenon ineluctably also generates the conditions for its own undoing. Indeed, it is sometimes within the contexts of the worst and ostensibly most invincible forms of racist oppression that the seeds of a new social order are sown.

The 'identity dynamics' of racism

Blackness essentialised

Fanon's analysis suggests that race often comes to act as an *essential* and *determining* quality of identity, perhaps *the* essential and determining quality of identity. European existentialist Jean-Paul Sartre, a prodigious influence on Fanon's writings, famously announced that 'existence precedes essence', meaning to suggest, amongst other things, that we should not tie our identity, or that of others, to predetermined qualities, prejudices or stereotypes. The experience of living as a minority (racial or otherwise) within a dominant or racist culture is to live the reverse of this adage – to live the experience of our '*essence preceding [our] existence*'. In this connection Fanon (1986:111–12) relates an incident where a White child sees him on a train:

'Look, a Negro!' It was an external stimulus that flicked over me as I passed by ...

'Look, a Negro!' It was true. It amused me ...

'Mama, see the Negro! I'm frightened!' Frightened! Frightened!

Here Fanon feels himself radically objectified, imprisoned by his race. His subjectivity, along with his ability to represent or define himself, is evaporated, destroyed. Hence, 'it is not I who make a meaning for myself, but it is the meaning that was already there, pre-existing, waiting for me' (1986:134). The Black subject, as such, becomes 'the eternal victim of an essence, of an appearance for which [he or she] is not responsible' (*ibid*.:35).

What is particularly important for Fanon here is the *inescapability of an individual's Blackness*. He refers to Sartre's thoughts on anti-Semitism, which suggest that because Jews have come to internalise the stereotypes others have of them – even if only to try and contest them – they have become 'over-determined' from within. They have come to understand themselves in the objectifying terms provided by the racist and hostile culture in which they live. There is a crucial difference here, though: whereas the Jew can 'be unknown in his Jewishness ... [and can] go unnoticed', because, after all, he is White, the Black subject cannot but be seen and identified, hence defined by his race. What Fanon is emphasising here is that Blackness comes to function as a fixed essence both in speech *and appearance*, one comes to 'speak' one's race, as well as to visually embody it. One cannot mask one's race, conceal it. Hence one is 'overdetermined from without' (Fanon, 1986:16). The evidence of the Blackness of a person's identity is there, unalterable, to 'torment ... pursue ... disturb ... anger' the Black subject (*ibid*.:117).

Qualifying, categorising, problematising the racial subject

What Fanon is suggesting here is that racist thinking defines individuals not only in terms of their race, but in terms of all the associations, stereotypes and values that such racial categories involve. All of these associated qualities themselves come to be virtually inescapable, *essentialised* qualities of identity. Fanon's point here is apt. If we want to problematise a woman, a Black man, a homosexual, or any minority, we do it exactly on the basis of what is taken to be most essential about them. So women are problematised on the basis of their femininity (which is, seemingly, by 'nature' irrational), Black people on the basis of their Blackness (which is by 'nature' primitive, dangerous, unintellectual), the gay man on the basis of his gayness (which is by 'nature' perverse and/or promiscuous), etc. These qualities are taken to be unchanging and timeless, and come to be locked into circular and self-confirming ways of thinking about particular types of personhood. Put differently, these ways of thinking, these prejudicial discourses, give birth to categorical ways of thinking, which come to order our world.

What we see operationalised here are the prejudicial terms of privilege and dispossession which systematically protect and idealise one (dominant) class of people, while derogating or problematising another (dominated) class. Hence the tendency always to qualify 'the other'; the White woman is referred to as *a woman*, the Black man as *a Black*, the Black woman as *a Black woman* whereas the White man is thought of as just *a person* (Edley & Wetherell,

1995). The Black subject, the woman, the gay person, etc. always needs be understood *through* the terms of these categorical groupings, that is through how they are thought to *differ* from the norms of the dominant culture. Put differently, this is a categorical fixing of certain identities that ties them to a set of prejudicial stereotypes. Note of course that dominant classes are not qualified in this way – they are not to be understood in terms of such a prejudicial fixing of identity – their acts, achievements, characteristics need not be understood against, or in terms of, such a basis or essence.

How Whiteness defines Blackness

The trauma of Blackness, as Wyrick (1998:37) puts it, paraphrasing Fanon, 'lies in its absolute Otherness in relation to white men'. Not only then must the Black man be Black, 'he must be black in relation to the white man' (Fanon, 1986:110). What Fanon is driving at here is the fact that the racial categories of Whiteness and Blackness are necessarily related to one another in the sense that they are *mutually dependent* terms, each coming to define and delimit the other. Simply put, the apparent superiority of Whiteness requires *the systematic devaluation of Blacks*. It is in this sense that Fanon (1986) argues that it is 'the white man who creates the black man' – his meaning here of course is not literal, his suggestion is rather that the White man creates the Black man as *an object of racism*.

In order to present itself as a superior term, Whiteness relies on something other than it, something it defines as inferior and problematic, and against which it may be qualified as preferable, morally, intellectually, culturally superior. *Black Skin, White Masks* is full of references to what Fanon calls a *Manichean way of thinking*, that is a binary logic which splits all concepts into pairs of opposites, one which is negative (typically *Black*), one which is positive (typically *White*). Fanon hence underscores an important logic of racist thinking, and at the same time demonstrates how the racist, in an odd sort of way, comes to be reliant on the object of his or her hatred and racism as a means of qualifying and affirming his or her own supposed superiority.

Manicheanism:
A way of thinking, based on the religious system of Persian founder Manes, that believed in the supposed primeval conflict between light and darkness, God and Satan.

In the same vein, Fanon's suggestion is that Blackness does not come to be experienced as a predominant dimension of identity – and certainly not in the derogatory sense implied by racism – in pre-colonial contexts. It is only after contact with White culture that the native is 'led to ask himself whether he is indeed a man ... because his reality as a man has been challenged' (Fanon, 1986:98). His supposed inferiority only comes into being through the mediation of the White other. Blackness is hence predicated on the fact *of not being White*. In Fanon's own words: 'I begin to suffer from not being a white man to the degree that the white man imposes discrimination on me ... robs me of all worth, all individuality' (*ibid.*).

Blackness is predicated on the fact of not being White, according to Frantz Fanon.

Identity development in oppressive contexts

Stages of marginal identity

Bulhan (1979; 1980a; 1980b; 1985) has usefully extended Fanon's work by proposing a stage theory of identity development in oppressive contexts. Clearly, these stages hold only for those racial, cultural or minority 'others' who have experienced prolonged periods of oppression or alienation, although this oppression need not necessarily be characterised by physical violence. Each stage in this theory of identity development is essentially a mode of *psychological defence*. What we view at each level is a struggle between two ways of being in the world, two kinds of knowing and acting. Put slightly differently, each stage represents a mode of existence and of action in a hostile, unaccommodating, or alienating world. Furthermore, and as a result, each stage is characterised by its own particular risks of alienation and its own distinct social rewards.

Bulhan refers to the first stage of this form of identity development as *capitulation*. The defensive mechanism that predominates in this stage is *identification with the aggressor*. What occurs here, as has been described above, is the individual's increasing *assimilation* into/by the dominant culture, an assimilation that results in his or her increased detachment from the root culture. For this reason Bulhan (1980a; 1985) argues that this stage involves a pattern of *compromise*. Here cultural and racial alienation is at its highest; the standards, values and ways of knowing and understanding our self are almost exclusively those of the dominant culture. This stage involves 'relegation to objecthood' (Bulhan, 1979:260). Accordingly, the potential for an interiorised sense of identity, for tendencies to self-estrangement and auto-destruction, is very high. As a result, psycho-affective injuries are frequent and

Psychological defence: Processes which defend or protect the self from threats or anxiety and whose major goal is to keep what is in the unconscious out of conscious awareness.

extreme. Fanon (1990) refers to these marginalised or colonised subjects as 'without horizon', anchorless, colourless, rootless.

Revitalisation is the term with which Bulhan (1980a; 1985) names the second stage. This is a period characterised by a powerful reactive repudiation of the dominant culture. The defense mechanism entailed here is that of the *romanticism of the indigenous or accommodating culture*. The example Bulhan (1985) gives here is the literature of negritude, which, as explained above, is a celebratory approach to Black Africanness and its distinctive forms of expression and culture. This stage is thought to involve a pattern of *flight* from the dominant culture. A transitional phase, this level of identity development can be painful and difficult to accomplish; it remains nonetheless necessary, however, if viable forms of racial and cultural identity are to be established (Bulhan, 1979). The possibilities for cultural and racial alienation have been alleviated here somewhat, chiefly because of the availability of new cultural resources of identity that are not wholeheartedly owned and defined by the oppressive socio-political domain.

The third stage is that of *radicalisation*. It signals an 'unambiguous commitment to radical social change' (Bulhan 1985:193), and is characterised by a willingness to *fight*, to claim a just and equitable place for ourselves within our current social-political location. The pattern of adaptation in this stage is that of *synthesis*. Here the emergence of individuation and autonomy becomes a real possibility for the colonised/marginalised subject. Bulhan (1979; 1980a; 1985) considers this to be a period of potentially revolutionary action, one in which the individual or group significantly understands and in fact changes the root causes of social reality.

The dynamics of cultural 'in-betweenity'

Bulhan (1979; 1985) warns that one should not conceptualise these stages in a static fashion: 'whether considered as stages, tendencies, or patterns, it is important to note that none of them exist in a "pure state" nor is any one ... exclusive of the others' (1985:194). All three of these stages are taken to coexist in each marginalised individual, with one or another being dominant in a given moment, situation or era. Ordinary people will remain in the phase that is prevalent in their particular time and social milieu (Bulhan, 1979; 1985). Furthermore, Bulhan (1985) suggests these stages may characterise a given generation, which, for example, remains in a position of *capitulation* during a particular historical era. Because these stages overlap, and because they refer to historical eras and groupings as much as to individuals, Bulhan (*ibid.*) prefers to represent them not in a separable, sequential fashion, but together, as cultural trajectories, directions, that are linked in a relationship of dynamic tension.

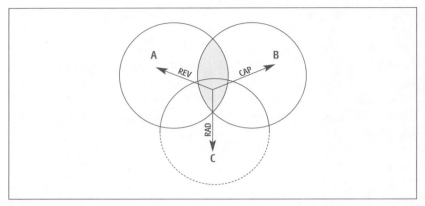

Figure 6.1
Bulhan's (1985) dynamics of 'cultural in-betweenity': The shaded area represents spaces of cultural overlap, confrontation and/or mutual influence.
The arrows indicate different routes of identity development or adaptation within marginal groups in oppressed contexts, REV, CAP and RAD.

Bulhan's (1985) diagrammatic representation of these stages (above) consists of the following – three overlapping circles, one of which represents the dominated culture (A), another the dominating culture (B), and a third culture (C), as of yet unformed and which is still coming into being. The three arrows REV (revitalisation), CAP (capitulation) and RAD (radicalisation) indicate the patterns of reaction or stages of identity development of marginal groups in oppressed contexts. The dominated culture (A) is made up of all the values, beliefs, norms and ideals that have historically characterised that culture, despite the fact that they are under threat by the dominant culture. The dominant culture (B) is that vast system of knowledge, representation, values and politics that has come to be imposed on the oppressed in a variety of different ways. The third, emerging, culture (C) is partly made up of a synthesis of aspects of the dominant and dominated cultures. It is more than just this, however. Part of the reason that Bulhan (1985) represents this new culture with broken lines is to suggest that this situation of cultural hybridity brings with it the potential to form new, unique, hitherto unprecedented cultural forms.

The shaded areas in the diagram indicate the region of cultural contact – or 'cultural in-betweenity' as Bulhan (1979; 1985) refers to it – typically characterised by confrontation and/or mutual influence. These spaces of cultural overlap vary greatly according to time and place, depending, obviously, on the type and strength of one culture's oppression of another. As Bulhan (1985:193) points out, frequently it is less a question of overlap of cultures than 'the obliteration of one and the supplanting of the other'. Bulhan is particularly interested in this area of 'cultural in-betweenity', in which 'new' and 'old', 'modern' and 'indigenous' coalesce, 'one modifying the other and each losing in consequence its original character' (*ibid.*:193–4).

Critiques of Fanon

Before closing, it is important to draw attention to certain shortcomings within Fanon's theory of racial identity. In this regard one of the most obvious problems with Fanon's work, despite its heightened sense of race-based oppression, is its implicit, and at times quite *explicit* sexism. A large part of *Black Skin, White Masks* deals with the question of sexual desire across the lines of race. For Fanon it is the case that the Black female's desire to marry a White man is inauthentic, it is a detestable example of negative, self-depreciating identity. The Black male subject's desire for the White female subject is portrayed in very different terms, as containing an almost redemptive political value: 'When my restless hands caress those white breasts, they grasp white civilization and dignity and make them mine' (Fanon, 1986:63). Fanon has been rightly criticised for this sexist double-standard in his work (Fuss, 1994; McCulloch, 1983; Wyrick, 1998).

While Fanon portrays the Black female's desire to marry a White man as a detestable example of negative, self-depreciating identity, he depicts the Black male subject's desire for the White female as containing an almost redemptive political value.

Fanon is sometimes criticised as representing the colonial relationship as one of *complete dominance and control* (Moore-Gilbert, 1997; Young 1990). The claim here is that Fanon undervalues the various forms of resistance and opposition that colonised individuals and groups can offer colonisers, and that he stereotypes the nature of these relationships. The first part of this suggestion is not always true, although a book like *Black Skin, White Masks* does spend far more time emphasising the degree and dynamics of colonial/racist control, than it does the possibility of resistance. *The Wretched of the Earth* is a useful counterpoint here, in that it is exactly a revolutionary text focusing on the possibility, and in Fanon's terms, the *inevitability* of an eventual overthrow of, colonial dominance. Perhaps the point is that whereas *Black Skin, White Masks* rather pessimistically prioritises relations of domination and control in its analysis – because it does not want these processes to be *underestimated* – *The Wretched of the Earth* far more optimistically prioritises the prospects of revolutionary resistance.

A further criticism of Fanon is to argue that he himself involves essentialist and static categories – 'the Black', 'the White', 'the colonised', 'the coloniser', and so on, as Caute (1970) suggests. To a certain extent this is true. Fanon does appear to make sweeping observations and remarks at this level, and does seem to tie certain categories of personhood to certain necessary forms of experience, or identity. The strongest version of this critique is to suggest that Fanon enforces a kind of victim blaming, by emphasising how Black subjects, in their grasping at White culture are making only 'inauthentic' and self-objec-tifying bids for identity. The idea that Black subjects perpetuate a form of internal racism against themselves seems to do much the same.

It could be argued that the reason that Fanon makes the kinds of arguments that he does is exactly to emphasise the insidious and pervasive nature of the effects of racism on identity, effects that had not previously been examined, and particularly not from a perspective of *internalised psychological damage*. Does this mean that the terms of Fanon's analysis may be somewhat stark, somewhat caricatured, that his understanding of the 'Black subject' allows for little diversity within itself? Very possibly, but many would argue that Fanon provides us with the *starting point* for the analysis of post-colonial contexts, one that is elaborated on in increasingly sophisticated terms by later post-colonial theorists such as Homi Bhabha (1994). Similarly, Fanon's objective is not to do further racist damage by recourse to a form of victim blaming, but to warn those he empathises with precisely of the damaging effects of internal-ising racist, objectifying terms of identity. Hence one might argue that Fanon's project is a fundamentally liberatory one.

Conclusion

This chapter has discussed marginal identity in post-colonial contexts. Such forms of identity, it has been suggested, are necessarily social, and exist in negotiated states which are at the same time informed by cultural resources and delimited by them, especially in those cases where forms of oppression have obliterated, undermined or devalued such cultural resources. The chapter has tried to illustrate what a political consciousness meant to Fanon, and to describe the dynamics of oppressed identities, particularly with reference to the ideas of racial alienation and cultural dispossession. Also important here were ideas of double consciousness, of racist disruptions of identity, or 'pathologies of liberty' as Fanon called them. Questions regarding the essentialisation of racial identity, of the mutually dependent relation of Whiteness and Blackness, and of the ways in which categorical thinking and prejudicial discourse problematise minority identities, were also discussed. The chapter closed with a brief elaboration of Bulhan's stages of marginal identity development in oppressed contexts, and with a description of his notion of the dynamics of 'cultural in-betweenity'.

It is worth noting that how Fanon has thought of the problems of Black identity in hostile cultural environments may inform how we understand marginality in society more generally. Of great importance here is Fanon's assertion that in the presence of a dominant and/or oppressive culture, minority groups, who do not significantly share in the power holding of a society, must make sense of themselves, *understand* themselves in terms of the racist and inferiority-inducing terms and values of that society, terms that are evaluative and pre-set so as to affirm Whiteness over Blackness, masculinity over femininity, heterosexuality over homosexuality, and so forth. *Black Skin, White Masks* is nothing if not this, a dramatisation of such a process of *ongoing* psychic damage, where exactly the practices of identity are beset *with a systematic devaluation of self.* Just as we should not underestimate the extent of such oppressive practices on identity, however, so we should not underestimate the possibilities of resistance to them, of cultural revitalisation and radicalisation as forms of social change. Without this lesson, we have not properly grasped Fanon.

Steve Biko and Black Consciousness in South Africa

One of the most important Black leaders to oppose the apartheid government in the late 1960s and early 1970s was Steve Biko. Biko was the founder of Black Consciousness in South Africa, a movement that both echoed, and was strongly indebted to, Fanon. Biko's view of Black Consciousness called for the *psychological* and *cultural* liberation of the Black mind as a prerequisite for political freedom — in his own words: 'mental emancipation as a precondition to political emancipation' (Biko in Arnold, 1972:xx). Hence a large part of the struggle, for Biko, was exactly 'the *psychological* battle for the minds of the black people' (*ibid.*, emphasis added). As Biko described it in May 1976:

Black Consciousness refers itself to the Black man and to his situation ... [to the fact that] the Black man is subjected to two forces in [South Africa]. He is first of all oppressed by an external world through institutionalized machinery, through laws that restrict him from doing certain things, through heavy work conditions, through poor education – these are all external to him – and secondly ... the most important, the Black man in himself has developed a certain state of alienation. He rejects himself, precisely because he attaches the meaning White to all that is good ... (Biko in Arnold, 1979:22).

In opposition to such self-negating ways of thinking, Biko called for solidarity among Blacks, emphasising the need for oppressed groups to identify with *themselves* and to advance the liberation struggle on this basis. The challenge confronting Black consciousness was to reverse years of negative self-image and to replace it with an affirming and positive – if not *angry* – Black identity. 'Black' here, as Arnold (1979:xxv) points out, was more a state of mind than an expression of origin: 'The use of the word was a deliberate attempt to lay both the intellectual and emotive base for ultimate political unity between the Africans [Blacks], Coloreds and Asians[/Indians] of South Africa.' 'Blackness' here is a form of solidarity, a collective form of hope and security, a way for Black people to 'build up their humanity' (Biko in Arnold, 1979:34).

The key strategy of Black Consciousness was *conscientisation*. Conscientisation involves what Biko referred to as 'protest talk', talk about circumstances of oppression. It involves the repeated attempt to

make reference to the conditions of the Black man and the conditions in which the Black man lives. We try to get Blacks in conscientization to grapple realistically with their problems ... to develop what one might call an awareness, a physical awareness of their situation ... to be able to analyze it, and to provide answers for themselves (Biko in Arnold, 1979:33).

Black Consciousness was an extremely positive form of politics, one which maintained that the very conditions of oppression were what would often bring a group of people together, embolden and invigorate them in their resistance to power. In Biko's own words (in Arnold, 1979:xx):

The call for Black Consciousness is the most positive call to come from any group in the Black world for a long time ... The quintessence of it is the realization by blacks [that] ... they have to use the concept of group power ... Being an historically, politically, socially and economically disinherited and dispossessed group, they have the strongest foundation from which to operate. The philosophy of Black Consciousness ... expresses group pride and the determination by the Blacks to rise and attain the envisaged self.

One of the most powerful lessons of Black Consciousness for Biko is contained in 'the realization by Blacks that the most potent weapon in the hands of the oppressor is the mind of the oppressed' (in Arnold, 1979:xx). This, of course, is a weapon that can be reclaimed.

Exercises for critical engagement

1 Is it the case that race can exist as a matter of degree? Motivate your answer with examples.

2 Think of other forms of 'double consciousness' and use them to further illustrate the concept.

3 If it is the case, as Fanon suggests, that Whiteness defines Blackness, is it also the case that Blackness defines Whiteness?

4 Bulhan is careful to qualify that his stages of identity development can also be applied to an entire nation. At what stage of development would you locate post-apartheid South Africa, and why?

Recommended reading

Bulhan, H.A. (1985). *Frantz Fanon and the Psychology of Oppression*. New York & London: Plenum Press.

Fanon, F. (1968) [1961]. *Toward the African Revolution.* New York: Grove.
Fanon, F. (1970) [1959]. *A Dying Colonialism.* New York: Grove.
Fanon, F. (1986) [1952]. *Black Skin, White Masks.* London: Pluto.
Fanon, F. (1990) [1963]. *The Wretched of the Earth.* London: Penguin.
Macey, D. (2000a). *Frantz Fanon: A Life.* London: Granta.

Acknowledgements

I would like to thank Peace Kiguwa, Garth Stevens and Norman Duncan for their critical input on earlier drafts of this chapter. I am also indebted to the Center for the Study of Public Scholarship at Emory University; it was during a fellowship granted by the Center to the author that final work on this chapter took place.

Derek Hook was a Rockefeller Scholar at the Center for the Study of Public Scholarship, Emroy University, Atlanta, whilst when he did a large part of the editorial work on the manuscript of Critical Psychology. He is particularly grateful to Professors Ivan Karp and Cory Kratz for their support in this respect. He was also the recipient of both a University of the Witwatersrand Research Office grant and a larger University Research Committee Grant – the Sellschop Award – during this time, awards that likewise greatly enabled the project. A special thanks to Solani Ngobeni for initiating and managing the project, and for his commitment to encouraging the production of a 'discourse of the South' in South African publishing, and to Professors Burman and Parker for advice and editorial input.

7

Feminist critical psychology in South Africa

Peace Kiguwa

---

*'Feminism. You know how we feel about that embarrassing
Western philosophy? The destroyer of homes. Imported mainly
from America to ruin nice African women.'*

Ama Ata Aidoo (1986, 22)

*'That feminism is many and not one is to be expected
because women are many and not one.'*

Rosemarie Tong (1998, 7)

LEARNING OUTCOMES

By the end of this chapter, you should be able to:

▷ Understand feminisms as a diverse range of approaches

▷ Discuss some major theoretical and research trends of feminist research in
psychology

▷ Explore how alternative 'routes' to exploring gender issues may be applied in local
contexts

▷ Use the notion of 'difference', along with essentialism, in thinking about, and
doing, psychology

▷ Discuss some of the major agendas of a critical psychology and the role of an
African feminism within these agendas.

INTRODUCTION

Feminism as action

Feminism is often mistaken for an exclusively academic pursuit, where feminists (usually women) debate issues of gender and women's oppression. Feminists are certainly committed to studying gender relations and how gender as a cultural construct can be manipulated as a tool of oppression, where men are able to occupy positions of social power over women. But there is also another aspect to feminism that may not always be understood as an extension of feminist theory, and that is that *feminism is also action/behaviour*. Feminist practice is not just about studying gender and gender relations. It is also about trying to *change* those constructs and relations that are seen to reinforce women's subordination to men.

Feminists do not all agree on the exact cause of gender inequality. Depending on one's theoretical orientation, it is possible to have a range of different commitments and agendas that one would deem necessary to remedy women's unequal status in society. In other words, feminist theories tend to differ on what they consider to be the *causes* of women's oppression as well as the *means* by which such oppression can be eliminated.

Gender: social, cultural and psychological differences between men and women.

Plural feminisms

The original feminist idea of **Sisterhood** – the idea that all women share some kind of 'kindred' interest – has come under increasing attack and discredit by women (eg so-called 'Third World' feminists such as Chandra Mohanty) traditionally excluded from mainstream (that is, European and US-American) feminist debate. We now generally accept that common political, economic and social goal(s) cannot be ascribed to women as a group feminist commitment has come to mean different things to different women and has taken many forms in different places (see Table 7.1). Hence it is appropriate to talk of feminisms as plural rather than singular. This invites the question of how these multiple feminist perspectives and interventions may or may not engage with psychology.

Asymmetrical relationships between groupings of people have come to be cemented through ostensibly authoritative forms of knowledge such as psychology. The above description of feminism therefore becomes doubly important in an African context, because, quite simply, not all feminisms are equally responsive to the particular political and substantive issues facing African women. This chapter is spread over a wide set of theoretical and political agendas. This is not only so as to grapple with what an African feminism might be, but also to establish what an African feminism of critical psychology might be.

Sisterhood: notion that all women share the same kind of 'kindred' interest by virtue of being women.

Table 7.1 'Feminism and its differences': Brief summary of major feminist schools of thought

Stand-point	Background	Key ideas and agendas	Strengths	Weaknesses
Liberal feminism	▷ Traced back to the 18th century, most notably with the publication of what has come to be considered one of the key texts of the women's suffrage movement – Mary Wollstonecraft's (1759–99) *A Vindication of the Rights of Women* and also in the 19th century, John Stuart Mill's *The Subjection of Women* in 1869	▷ There is no fundamental difference between men and women. And therefore no real basis for the unequal sharing of resources and opportunities ▷ Women's oppression an inevitable outcome of a systematic denial of *opportunity* for women as enjoyed by men ▷ Female subordination thus a direct result of the *legal constraints* women are subject to in patriarchal society ▷ Works from within the structure of mainstream society to integrate women into that structure	▷ Liberal feminist agendas have been particularly instrumental in the establishment of more gender equity laws, which have arguably improved the quality of lives of many women. South Africa's post-'94 Constitution, for instance, has opened the way for many women, traditionally marginalised, to pursue career interests in politics, law, entrepreneurship, etc. In the words of Tong (1998): '... such reforms are to be neither trivialised nor memorialised as *past* accomplishments' (44)	▷ The interplay of *power* in sustaining unequal gender relations not fully emphasised. A liberal feminist agenda could, for example, be inadequate in accounting for ongoing male violence in South African society ▷ The pervasive effects of past discriminatory gender practices not fully considered, such that those previously disadvantaged are in many ways still disadvantaged in the present ▷ As is often the case with any liberal agenda, 'working from within' the system may often mean getting very little accomplished by way of radical social change
Marxist feminism	▷ Emerged in feminist critiques of the left post-1968	▷ Attributes women's oppression to the capitalist/private property system (see Marxism chapter in this edition) ▷ The only way to end such oppression is to overthrow the capitalist system of economy ▷ Theorises the role of domestic labour as part of class system ▷ Problematises the public/private sphere division ▷ Challenges sexism within structures, forms and relations of left organizations; later versions concerned with intersections of class, race and sexuality	▷ Contemporary Marxist feminists have allowed us to move beyond reductionist economic/class analysis and gender oppression to a holistic approach, such as questioning the interrelatedness between institutions such as the nuclear family and broader economic structures (Tong, 1998)	▷ Underemphasises the interplay of non-material forces of power that equally sustain female subordination in society, such as culture. In other words, female subordination is debated and given priority only in so far as it can be linked to a wider economic analysis of society

Standpoint	Background	Key ideas and agenda	Strengths	Weaknesses
Radical feminism	▷ Post-liberal era ▷ Cutting edge of feminist theory between 1967 and 1975 ▷ Emerged from the gay rights movements	▷ Patriarchy (rather than class as for Marxist/socialist feminism) is the most fundamental cause of women's oppression ▷ Women's oppression exists in *any* society – capitalist/socialist, communal/individualistic etc ▷ This system of oppression includes even the most common and popular of institutions, such as marriage and the family ▷ This system of oppression is not easily eradicated by changing legislation or abolishing capitalist economy in society ▷ Patriarchal system cannot be reformed – and must therefore be *rooted* out completely ▷ Seeks to question gender roles, eg why must women adopt certain roles such as 'mother' by virtue of their biology and men alternative roles also by virtue of their biology? ▷ We must problematise gender behaviour by drawing distinctions between biologically vs culturally determined gender behaviour	▷ Radical feminist emphasis on *social* as opposed to *natural* difference between men and women has encouraged the deconstruction of social/cultural constructions of gender difference	▷ Argues that the patriarchal system must be destroyed completely – but does not say *how* this is likely to occur ▷ Rather impractical to presume that a system so pervasive as patriarchy can simply be 'rooted' out of existence. Female subordination is both practised and experienced at multiple and intertwining levels, eg ideological, economic, social and sexual. Rooting out one level does not necessarily translate into women's liberation ▷ Tendency to romanticise and universalise women's position and experiences, without taking account of other structural inequalities between women

Standpoint	Background	Key ideas and agenda	Strengths	Weaknesses
Psychoanalytic feminism	▷ Stemmed from Freud's theories about sexuality ▷ In the 1970s feminists contested the biological reductionism of Freud's construction of femininity and masculinity, arguing that femininity/masculinity are in fact socially constructed ▷ Psychoanalytic feminists attempted to reinterpret Freud by 'telling the Oedipal tale in a non-patriarchal voice' (Tong, 1998, 138), by focusing on pre-Oedipal as opposed to Oedipal stage ▷ Juliet Mitchell's key book *Psychoanalysis and feminism* argues that psychoanalysis provides a description of gender relations under patriarchy, including the constitution of sexed/gendered difference, rather than a prescription for it. This opened the way for a radical re-engagement with psychoanalysis as a way of theorising resistance, both against oppressive conditions and to change	▷ Fundamental explanation for women's behaviour is rooted deep in women's psyche ▷ Relies on Freudian concepts of pre-Oedipal stage and the Oedipal complex ▷ Gender inequality rooted in a series of early childhood experiences resulting in both men's and women's perceptions of themselves as masculine/feminine. Argue that patriarchal society constructs and values these perceptions differently ▷ Theorists such as Chodorow have focused on the need to change contexts of early childrearing as a means of reconfiguring gendered subjectivities	▷ Emphasises the role and function of the psyche in women's self-liberation. Can therefore speak directly to post-colonial theory's focus on 'mental decolonisation' (see also Fanon's 'double consciousness' and Biko's 'Black Consciousness' debate, in this work) ▷ Offers a universalist theory of psychic construction of gender identity on basis of repression. By so doing, it gives specific answers to how we acquire our gender identities as well as how we internalise gendered norms and values	▷ Underplays the role of legal, political and economic institutions and structures in sustaining women's oppression in patriarchal society ▷ Tendency to universalise

Standpoint	Background	Key ideas and agenda	Strengths	Weaknesses
Post-structuralist feminism	▷ Stemmed from post-structuralist theoretical assumptions about **language/ meaning** and **subjectivity** (see the discursive practice chapter in this work) ▷ Linked to a variety of theoretical positions developed from the works of theorists such as Lacan (1977), Foucault (1978) and Kristeva (1981)	▷ No such thing as a universal gender experience ▷ Not so much concerned with particular cause or solution to women's oppression, as with the ways in which women experience gender – and oppression – *differently* ▷ Uses post-structuralist notion of language, discourse, social processes and institutions to understand gendered power relations and identify strategies for change ▷ Through concept of discourse post-structuralist feminism seeks to explore the working of power as well as resistance to power (see Wilbraham & Hook, in this edition)	▷ Recognises the interplay of social factors such as race, class, sexuality in influencing how women may experience gender ▷ Seeks to de-essentialise gender identity ▷ Emphasises the social constructedness of gender identity through discursive reproductions ▷ Emphasises the power interests behind these constructions ▷ Focuses on practice of **resistance** in the construction of identity. This is necessary in attempting a theory for 'mental decolonisation' (see also 'Black Consciousness') ▷ Able to explain where our gendered experiences come from, why we may experience these as contradictory and why/how these may also change ▷ Able to account for the political limitations of change at the level of individual consciousness through its emphasis on material relations ▷ Can explain the assumptions underlying the agendas of other feminist theories, thus making their political assumptions more explicit ▷ Can indicate the types of discourse underlying particular feminist questions and locate these both socially and institutionally ▷ Can also explain implications of these discourses for feminist practice	▷ Tendency to be too abstract and not very accessible, also very Eurocentric ▷ Tendency to universalise ▷ Ignores differences of structural relations

Standpoint	Background	Key ideas and agenda	Strengths	Weaknesses
Black feminism	▷ First formulated in US-America through fiction-writing in the works of many African-American women, as a direct result of dissatisfaction with anti-racist movements (largely dominated by black men) as well as feminist movement (equally dominated by white women)	▷ Feminist politics among black women is – unlike Western and mainstream feminisms – rarely seriously explored ▷ Black female researchers should seek to develop new theories and concepts which capture actual lived experiences of 'Third World' women in Africa ▷ Identifies white feminism as misrepresentative and oppressive to black women	▷ Explicitly addresses the racial discourses of knowledge-production as well as emphasising the relevance of categories such as 'black woman'. This is a distinct category. For example, a 'poor black woman' relates neither to poverty nor to racism in the same way a 'poor black man' does. Interlocking categories of race, gender and class are significant tools of analysis in trying to understand the totality of her experience as a woman ▷ Provides a basis for consciousness-raising among black women as well as emphasising emotional and psychological empowerment	▷ Tends to rely on an essentialist position in its claim that black women exclusively have insight into their experiences by virtue of their socio-economic, cultural and biological heritage
Womanism	▷ Origins of womanism lay in black women's dissatisfaction with the white feminist movement ▷ Often associated with black feminism in its theoretical framework ▷ Has also been linked to the theoretical frameworks of Marxism, feminism and Pan-Africanism/Black Consciousness (see Biko chapter in this work)	▷ A woman is never simply a woman: she has a racial and class identity, which also influences and sometimes determines the ways she will experience herself as a woman ▷ Similar to black feminism in its definition of racism and sexism as not just an expression of denigratory ideas with no foundation but also as theoretical and practical exclusion of black women's experiences ▷ Developed a theoretical space – one that is void of the term 'Black' – to explore any marginalised woman's identity and gender experience. It is in this one respect that womanism can be distinguished from black feminism	▷ A more comprehensive view of gender oppression. Emphasises the interlocking categories of race, class and gender in analysing women's experiences ▷ Places the reality and experience of black women at the centre of theoretical feminist debate and activism (see also Black feminism)	▷ Tendency towards romanticism and mysticism of black women's experiences ▷ Tends to essentialise women and blacks into fixed attributes

Standpoint	Background	Key ideas and agenda	Strengths	Weaknesses
Womanism *(continued)*	▷ In South Africa, the womanist movement has remained largely unpopular. Gquola (1998) has argued that a key reason for this might lie with the 'absence of the word "feminist" in the name adopted by the womanist movement. It is the coining of a name which shows no loyalty to feminism which makes womanism suspect to its critics' (quoted in Abrahams, 2002, 61)	▷ 'Womanism' – while acknowledging the psychological necessity of **self-naming** – simultaneously seeks to go beyond a reassertion of 'blackness' ▷ Not a separatist movement (unlike Black feminist agenda), that is, not focused on separatism but more 'centring'. In other words, a womanist framework is more concerned with placing African and other so-called 'Third World' women at the centre of theoretical debate ▷ Concerned with the psychological, existential and mystical meanings of strong black womanhood – ie the spiritual welfare of black women as the basis of the struggle for social justice	▷ Allows for a nuanced approach to exploring many black women's experiences. For example, where traditional mainstream feminism would target traditional maternal role as a key site of female oppression, a womanist approach would seek to show how the role of motherhood has been experienced by many black South African women as both ambiguous and liberating – even in the face of stereotypical mothering (Hendricks *et al*, 1994). In the words of bell hooks (1984): '... because the family is a site of resistance against racism for black women, it does not have the same oppressive meanings for them that it has for white women' (cited in Hendricks *et al*, 1994, 221)	
African feminism	▷ Has been linked to Africanist movements which dominantly construct a pre-colonial Africa that is free from any form of oppression	▷ Focus on a reconstruction of pre-colonial history as a period in which black women experienced considerable political and social power	▷ Like black feminism and womanism, African feminism seeks to construct anti-imperialist knowledge systems which emphasise an independent and positive sense of identity for many 'Third World'/ black women ▷ Strategic in its subversion of colonial constructions of racial inferiority of black people. Plays a mentally decolonising role. Thus is of important and necessary psychological value (see Fanon/Biko chapters in this work)	▷ Like womanism, African feminism often falls prey to a romantising and essentialising tendency in its nostalgic call for a pre-colonial Africa ▷ By so doing it also ceases to be sufficiently critical of pre-colonial history and the traditional patriarchy that characterised this history

Source: Table assembled from various sources.

CRITICAL PSYCHOLOGY AND FEMINIST PRACTICE

The powers of psychology

A critical psychology agenda is both cognisant and critical of the different uses and abuses of psychology and the ways in which these have been complicit in the perpetuating of oppressive social relations. The discipline of psychology exercises power through both its methods and its forms of knowledge . Psychologists must therefore be constantly critical of their practice and of the ways in which they produce and reproduce knowledge about the people they study and seek to help.

This continual interrogating of the use and abuse of psychological power must include not just how knowledge about people is produced but also the notion that psychology can represent everyone in its construction of knowledge. A critical psychology is one that resists any temptation to 'speak for' all groups precisely because it recognises that the philosophical underpinnings of psychology are far from universal and may in fact be oppositional to other philosophies and forms of practice. Mhkize (in this work) discusses the ways in which African belief systems may be philosophically and ontologically different from a Western belief system, such that even the notion of 'identity', for instance, may be understood in conceptually different ways. This difference may be attributed to the 'communal' versus 'individualistic' ways of knowing and theorising identity. Because mainstream psychology is rooted in European and US-American philosophies, psychological practice and theory may be irrelevant and misrepresentative of non-Western contexts and people.

Who psychology has excluded

Because marginalised voices have traditionally been excluded from any generation of psychological knowledge, a more critical approach would seek to redress this exclusion – *not* by presuming to speak for such marginalised groups (which would just be another effective and powerful way of further silencing them) but, instead, allowing them to speak for themselves as legitimate and equally crucial to understanding the individual self. A critical psychology should open itself up to other non-mainstream knowledge systems if it is to be critical of traditional psychological practice and be more relevant to the people it is meant to serve.

Challenging identity

Perhaps even more crucial is the notion of the individual self, implicit in psychological theory, which asserts that our identities are fixed and connected to an '**essence**'. In psychology the notion of 'identity' implies a singular, individual subject. Much essentialist construction of knowledge has stemmed from this understanding of identity as both *unchanging* and *universal.* It is precisely this conceptualisation of a stable and universal identity that has given much legitimacy to psychology's presumption to represent and consider its theoretical constructs as unquestionably applicable to all human groups. Mama (2002) has argued that 'identity' as a concept has no distinct meaning (as would be understood psychologically) in most African languages simply because Africans tend to define themselves in communal terms that indicate their clan or ethnic origins. Psychology's conceptualisation of identity thus remains a vexing one to many Africans precisely because it cannot be pinned down. Shefer (1997) has shown how women's gender identity may be expressed differently depending on the rural or urban setting in which the individual finds herself, where one setting requires a more 'traditional' presentation of self as a married woman would not require this and the subject is free to discard and adopt a different identity. Identity therefore becomes something that can be changed and adopted depending on the situation we may find ourselves in. We cannot therefore go with the assumption that our identities are unitary and constant.

Essence: true nature of objects, people. May be understood as any category that is assigned to objects, people and experiences that are seen to be the one defining nature or characteristic of that person or experience.

Critical feminist practice and the 'universal woman'

Having considered some of the defining characteristics of what a critical psychology must entail, we turn now to the agenda of critical feminist practice and the ways these speak directly to the agendas of a South African critical psychology. Because feminism is necessarily political in the sense that feminism is geared toward actual change in social relations, whether at the economic or political or sociocultural level, it addresses one of the key tenets of a critical psychology, which is that the psychological practice can and has been put to political use and has been employed to serve specific power interests.

Traditional feminist practice has largely focused on the 'universal woman' as oppressed. This conceptualisation has relied on a universalist under-standing of identity/experience/oppression and gender. All women were perceived to share similar experiences of gender and oppression by virtue of being women. Such conceptualisation downplayed other equally crucial categories that may differentiate women's experience of gender and oppression. Categories of race and class, for example, may influence the ways in which a poor black woman's experiences of gender may be dramatically different from a middle class white woman's for instance. In other words, while **patriarchy** is universal the ways in which women may experience this are far from universal and any such universalising practice inevitably means the exclusion and/or marginalisation of certain women's experiences. This is another way in which theoretical and disciplinary power operates.

Identities of flux

Critical feminist practice therefore constantly seeks to interrogate its own forms of knowledge-production. Traditional feminist ideas of gender identity have largely come from psychology's constructions of these concepts, which have generally tended to view these as stable and unchanging, following a set developmental pattern. These terms have, however, come to be redefined by more critical theorists such as Judith Butler and Michel Foucault, who have theorised identity to be in constant flux and lacking in a fixed essence.

Inasmuch as feminist theory has been criticised for its marginalisation of many women from mainstream debates, it is important to note that this is an injustice that has been increasingly readdressed by many feminists – both Western and non-Western. Mama (2001) makes this point too (see Box 4), arguing that it would be both redundant and theoretically limiting for non-Western feminists to focus only on the marginalisation of so-called 'Third World' women's lived experiences from mainstream debate. It is important to note here, then, that feminist theory is in a process of re-evaluation: traditional constructs and methodologies are increasingly being re-examined, and alter-native voices are being explored for their multiple value that could be enriching for feminism in general.

While patriarchy is universal, the ways in which women may experience this are far from universal and any such universalising practice inevitably means the exclusion and/or marginalisa-tion of certain women's experiences.

Patriarchy: defines the personal, physical and institutional power that men exert over women. Although it takes many forms, patri-archy is universal. It is important to recognise the cultural, social and political diversity between patri-archies, but this should not under-mine the fact that women experience oppression *as* women first and foremost.

The 'concrete material reality' of cultural constructions

Hoff (1996) has argued that a focus on *how* we come to know gender may displace equally significant questions of *what* needs to be known about women's lives. In a manner of speaking, we recognise that gender relations may be discursively constituted, but this should not detract from the fact that these relations also have a concrete material reality. This can be illustrated with a very common example: Cultural constructions may position women as 'submissive' and 'nurturing'. On the one hand, we have a romanticised and idealised image of women – a glorified image of womanhood, if you like. A feminist analysis can deconstruct and show the ways in which such construction has been socially constructed or created, such that women are once again essentialised and controlled through patriarchal discourse. But, on the other hand, we also have a concrete reality in which women's identities and lives are experienced within such a framework, and their oppression as women stems directly from this framework and construction. The 'nurturing mother' who fails to bear any children or, in some instances, sons *for her husband* is ostracised precisely because she has not conformed to a culturally prescribed role. While we may acknowledge the gendered roles that are certainly inherent in such construction and explore the 'constructedness' of such gender prescriptive behaviour and identities, we cannot ignore the fact that this is both an actual lived and oppressive experience for many women. Ramazanoglu (1996) has described this overemphasis on the discursive construction of gender as a subtle means by which feminist knowledge disempowers itself.

Localised forms of oppression

Perhaps what a critical feminist agenda needs to engage with is not how gender oppression is a universal phenomenon but rather the ways in which such oppression can be experienced on different levels and how it is embedded in different institutional structures and policies of a society – in other words, the ways in which gender is a crucial oppressive category in areas such as HIV/Aids and health policy or cultural practices that are meant to symbolise the coming into one's manhood/femininity etc which may be inherently oppressive to women. An example that comes to mind here is the virginity-testing rites that many young African girls often have to submit to.

QUESTIONING RESEARCH

Research that constructs identities

The paucity of gender research in psychology and the theoretical and methodological limitations attaching to it has been researched and documented in what is fast becoming a wide range of feminist criticisms and explorations of gender bias in social science research (see for example, Shefer, 2001 and in this work; Hollway, 1989; Weisstein, 1996; Eagle, 1999). Previous research into gender issues was generally limited in theoretical and methodological approach. In trying to construct a universal gender identity and define the essence of womanhood many feminist and non-feminist studies tended to employ essentialist notions of gender identity.

Decontextualised gender identities

In addition, methodological frameworks were such that they never really captured women's gendered narratives. Why? This is largely as a result of a compliance with traditional positivist social science paradigm with its emphasis on objective and valid research. The nature of social reality is seen to be stable, with pre-existing patterns just waiting to be discovered (Neuman, 2000). Social research is seen to be void of any subjective value and/or political agendas. The result is that theories on gender identity and oppression remain decontextualised from the social, economic, political and ideological environment. Thus psychological theories such as Erikson's eight stages of identity development (see Hook, Watts & Cockcroft, 2002) may argue that contexts of gender development can and do differ but nevertheless still follow a set pattern or process. However, a young South African child from a rural environment, living in poverty, may not be said to share similar patterns of gender identity development. It is reasonable to assume that other influential factors may play significant roles in her gender identity (Shefer, 1997).

Positivist science: belief that social science can and should only know what can readily be observed. Social reality is what we can see (observe) to exist.

The problems of positivist science for feminist research

Feminist critique of traditional gender research has generally focused on the methodological limitations of the notion of a *value-free* science that can be *objective* in its approach to studying gender issues. Social reality is characterised by a stable pre-existing pattern or order that can be discovered (Neuman, 2000) and therefore it is quite feasible for a researcher to be objective and value-free when doing research. There is no place for values in research because science is by nature value-free. Explanations of events that one studies must also be based on factual evidence. Such issues, related to the myth of objectivity as well as the position of the researcher as superior in relation to subjects have been questioned by many a feminist analysis of research methodologies in psychology (Mama, 1995).

The positivist and/or experimental approach in most psychological studies has generally tended to undermine or downplay the workings of any sociopolitical factors in a given context. With regard to studies with female subjects this approach has been especially narrowly focused, largely because significant

'Psychology is one version of the power of the narrative. As with any power, it can be misused to wield power rather than to empower others' (Apter, 1994, 41).

factors that should be considered when trying to understand the experiences of women still remain underresearched (Unger, 1979) and reinterpreted from the [usually male] researcher's own framework, with subjects having little or no space to control her own narrative: 'Psychology is one version of the power of the narrative. As with any power, it can be misused to wield power rather than to empower others' (Apter, 1994, 41). Because psychologists generally tend to occupy more powerful positions in the research process than the subjects they study, any agency for subjects to determine the form their narratives will eventually take is drastically reduced and sometimes even non-existent. The final outcome may thus often be the researcher's own interpretation of events and meaning. This inevitably raises some ethical questions about the conduct of research.

Subjective, explorative research

Collins (1990, 207) has argued that objective positivist research is problematic with particular reference to studying minority women's experiences: 'Such criteria requires (sic) ... women to objectify ourselves, devalue our emotional life ...It seems unlikely that black women would use a positivist epistemological stance in rearticulating black women's standpoint. Black women are more likely to use an alternative epistemology for assessing knowledge claims, one using different standards that are consistent with black women's criteria for substantiated knowledge and with our criteria for methodological adequacy' (cited in Abrahams, 2002, 66).

The dominance of the positivist approach to research was later to be contested by the *interpretive* approach, which focused on more subjective explorative research. In seeking to understand and describe women's lived experiences feminists researchers with more interpretative worldviews focused on the ways in which women generated and sustained meaning. This new approach was quite welcome for its emphasis on value-laden research as desirable. This was a marked shift from the positivist 'value-free' stance. Interpretive research also allowed for more alternative approaches to doing research with women, for instance the use of the autobiography as a valid form of data collection.

Showing up structures of oppression

This interpretive approach to research was, however, problematic in its disregard of the political context within which women may generate and sustain meaning. This paved the way for theorists with far more *critical* agendas. Social science research was not only value-laden but the task of feminist researchers was to challenge the illusions and false beliefs that tended to hide gendered power relations in society. Social change can be achieved only when women are able to question the structures and institutions in their society that sustain oppression. Social research is also political and feminists are equally concerned with the political dimensions of most psychological research on gender issues.

THE 'LIBERAL' TRADITION IN PSYCHOLOGY
How gender has been linked to genetics

The liberal approach in gender research is a crucial one to discuss precisely because it has been the most influential and has helped to recuperate and de-radicalise feminist interventions. Liberal trends in researching gender issues in psychology represent a marked opposition to previous traditional research that represented gender (when considered as a 'variable' in particular research) as nothing more than a natural category that could be brought to bear in an analysis. The traditional treatment of gender – approached as sex differences – presented differences between men and women (whether behaviour, personality or roles) as *biological* and therefore *natural*. For example, Kimball (1981) and Aper (1985), both cited in Goldberg (1996), focused on the various ways in which 'sex differences' have been studied in psychology by linking gender to genetic differences in the brain as well as in cognitive functioning.

Psychology's move from such blatantly reductionist approaches to more egalitarian ways of doing gender research can be described as a move towards a more 'liberal' psychology. This trend has also arguably been influenced by early liberal feminist notions of gender equality (see Table 7.1).

Points of similarity rather than difference

Psychologists with a liberal agenda have tended to move from theorising *gender as difference* to highlighting *similarity*. In fact, the proving of similarity, and hence the need for equality, was seen as a key objective in this respect. This was particularly so, given that gender differences – and the idea of women's characteristic roles, skills, positions, preoccupations – were typically understood to indicate *deficits* in women relative to men. The purpose of this research was overwhelmingly that of *redressing* such representations of women, avoiding the 'discourse of difference' so as to argue for equality.

We might take the work of Carol Gilligan as something of a *counter-example* here (see Gilligan, 1982; Grant, 2002). Her critique of Kohlberg's stages of moral development seems to suggest that women and men are morally different in orientation, despite the fact that an understanding of equality in difference, a kind of equal but separate view, is asserted. The liberal tradition takes a very different approach in the emphasis and approach of its research. It would suggest, in the case of moral development (to extend the example), that men and women *are not* particularly likely to be morally different from each other than is supposed. This would then be a move away from presumed natural – and therefore – biological gender difference to emphasise commonality or even the universal transcendence of gender.

Universalising the gender experience

This liberal trend in theorising gender does not just encompass relationships between men and women but also between women themselves. Women and men are seen to be equal but so also are all women in relation to each other. Gender research is therefore seen as applicable and relevant for every woman, regardless of race, class, sexuality, and geographical location, for example. This can be described as a *universalising of the gender experience*, that is, the assumption that all women share the same experiences of oppression and gender by virtue of being women.

Such theoretical practice is not only misleading in its representation of gender as universal but also effectively serves to further silence many women already marginalised by their race, class and sexuality. What may be termed 'triple oppression' is exemplified in the lives of many domestic servants in South Africa for instance. Poor and lacking in any worthwhile education, these women are often oppressed at the level of their race, gender and class. In attempting to explain female subordination, the discipline of psychology has focused almost exclusively on sexism and gender issues and as a consequence has had little or no applicability to the special position of *black* women in a white social structure. These, however, are the women who are subject to the effects of racism, sexism and class bias in combination (Howitt & Owusu-Bempah, 1994).

In attempting to explain female subordination, the discipline of psychology has focused almost exclusively on sexism and gender issues and as a consequence has had little or no applicability to the special position of black women in a white social structure.

'Triple oppression' is the term that has been coined to describe the situation in which many black South African women find themselves: oppressed in terms of race, class and gender.

> **BOX 1** **'The Invisible Man'**
>
> The American sociologist Michael Kimmel tells a revealing anecdote about one of his graduate classes in Women's Studies in which he heard a dispute going on between a white and a black woman. The white woman was arguing that the **universal oppression of women** by men bound black and white women together in a common plight. The black woman disagreed and asked, 'When you wake up in the morning and look in the mirror, what do you see?'
>
> 'I see a woman,' the white woman replied.
>
> 'That's precisely the problem,' said the black woman. 'When I wake up in the morning and look in the mirror, I see a *black* woman. My race is visible to me every day because I am not privileged in this culture. Because you *are* privileged, your race is invisible to you.'
>
> Kimmel was very much struck by this exchange because he realised that when he looked in the mirror he saw neither his whiteness nor his masculinity. All he saw was a simple human being.
>
> Source: Kimmel, quoted in Wetherell & Griffin (1991).

FOCUSING ON DEVELOPMENTAL PSYCHOLOGY

While the discipline of psychology as a whole has been instrumental in legitimating certain forms of power in knowledge-production the field of developmental psychology represents a special interest to us here. In the words of Morss (1996), 'developmental psychology has told us what development is' (1). Theories of development have enabled us to define what 'normal' as opposed to 'abnormal' human development is. It has provided norms and guidelines through which we can assess healthy psychological and social development. It is because we have some pre-set notions of what children are like, for instance, that we set up specific laws for their protection. Developmental psychology may therefore be seen to have a crucial importance in reiterating forms of social or structural power.

The importance of developmental issues for feminism

Burman (1994) identifies developmental issues as crucial for any psychological feminist analysis because the developmental process of the individual, from birth to death, is one that has been *gendered* by the discipline of psychology, with passivity, dependence and emotionality culturally associated with femininity as well as immaturity, and autonomy, activity and rationality associated with masculinity. Further additional responsibilities for 'successful development' are borne by women as mothers. The healthy development of the child is constructed as dependent on several key factors and influences, the most significant being that of the *mother's presence* in the child's life.

For many black South African women, psychological theories of child development arguably have more significant implications than may be normally supposed. Escalating crime (perpetrators understood to be mainly the black male) – as well as the sociocultural contexts in which these occur – bring to the fore specific and implicit understandings of black family culture and the specific roles black women are seen to play in creating the pathological black male. Phoenix (1987) has explored the ways in which a dynamic of homogenised absence/pathologised presence structuring the representation of black families, and especially black women, has been a dominant trend in psychology.

A critical African feminist approach to psychology is aware of how mothers are typically made to bear responsibility for the 'successful development' of their children.

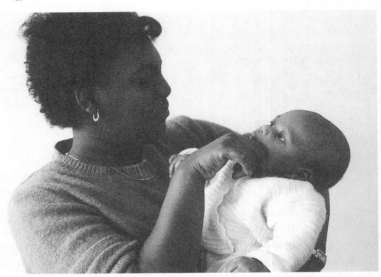

| BOX 2 | 'Monstrous mothers and selfish mothers': How women carry the burden of gender |

Alldred (1996) has questioned psychology's constructions of the 'traditional' and 'non-traditional' family with specific focus on female-headed households. She argues:

> Making links between psychology and popular culture allows psychological research practice to be contextualised in the broader cultural and political issues of its time, and highlights the implications of psychological discourses as they operate in everyday life ... Images of the *monstrous mother* have included the overprotective mother who refuses to relinquish the child and so smothers or subsumes them ... the fears evidenced in this particular cultural moment are about women bearing and rearing children without men, and the danger of these 'monstrous females' breeding 'monstrous children'.
>
> In much the same way that heterosexuality is seen to require no justification or cause, neither is the 'traditional' family. The label 'non-traditional' is one

> **BOX 2** **'Monstrous mothers and selfish mothers': How women carry the burden of gender** *(continued)*
>
> that is used to 'set outside the norm, and render [...] oppositional to those seen as traditional'. The term 'traditional' evokes a history, by virtue of which the object is then naturalised. This then confers a moral weight so that it becomes possible to argue that it *ought to be* simply because it *has been* ... the image that is evoked is of white families, leaving black families already positioned as Other. The supposedly general concept of family is actually fairly narrow.
>
> Source: Alldred, Pam. (1996). '"Fit to parent"? Developmental psychology and "non-traditional" families.' In Burman *et al Challenging women*.

The family structure and the scapegoating of women

Howitt *et al* (1994) focus on several key areas of mythical 'knowledge' generated by psychology about family structure, and do so in a way that draws attention to the maternal role and how women are often scapegoated by patriarchal discourse. Why is the focus on the family such an important one for the promulgation of racist/patriarchal stereotypes? Well, the family and its structures of power are taken to have and extend the beliefs and values of one's society or culture. Furthermore, it is taken to be the social institution where enculturation, or rather the fragmentation (or lack thereof) is thought to occur.

The black family living in South Africa is commonly assumed to follow a matriarchal family structure, one that is dominated by females who have taken on traditional male roles, inherently transgressing 'normal' family structure. The value that psychology has placed on the 'father figure' as role model for the male child (Weiten, 2002) has in many ways been detrimental for single, female-headed families. Studies have been conducted to stress the importance of the father to a child's motor and mental developmental tasks (for example, Pederson, 1979) and social responsiveness (Parke, 1979).

These families are implicitly assumed to embody some form of fragmentation and difficulty in enculturation. Children from such families are assumed to have been denied proper socialisation skills and find it difficult to integrate fully within broader society as psychologically healthy and fully functioning individuals. Psychopathology is deemed to be the inevitable outcome of such an 'abnormal' family pattern.

FEMINISM IN AN AFRICAN CONTEXT

'... Psychology has nothing to say about what women are really like, what they need and what they want, essentially because psychology does not know.'

Naomi Weisstein *Psychology constructs the female* (1996)

BOX 3   Post-natal depression as an expression of rebellion against the maternal role

'She loved, she tried to love, she screamed and was not heard, because there was nothing and no one in her surrounding that saw her plight as unusual, as anything but the homemaker's plight to her home. She became a scapegoat, the one around whom the darkness of motherhood is allowed to swirl, the invisible violence of the institution of motherhood.'

Welburn (1998, 132)

An exploration of 'invisible violence of the institution of motherhood' exposes how the feminine is highly enmeshed with the 'homemakers plight to her home'. The maternal as a natural feminine entitlement, is one that has indeed 'scapegoated' women through biological discourse, psychological theory and culturally mediated social practice. An alternative exploration of post-natal depression is offered for women who have 'tried to love', 'screamed' and are 'not heard' because clinical theory has negated to explore the patriarchal assumptions from which it is born. Socially motivated biological assumptions may often become biological realities by which women's childbearing capacities align themselves with child-caring responsibilities and maternal traits (Chodorow, 1978). Motherhood is a role women are expected to adopt and accept readily. This has infringed upon their own personal nourishment and their ability to construct own femininities.

Psychology's object relational theory has further trapped women in maternal obligations (Doane & Hodges, 1992). It is the maternal

instinct which is crowned queen by psychology. The 'fathering' of a child (Lupton & Barclay, 1997, 27) does not ensure its healthy development (Holmes, 1993). Psychiatry cannot be applauded for objective clinical diagnosis as it pulls the patriarchal proverbial corsette strings of social control of the feminine subject. Women are not allowed to extrapolate from its pre-definitions of the maternal. The feminine is playdough in the hands of culture, which assumes to construct her psychopathology. Women are taught to be depressed rather than defiant. Chesler (1974) suggests that good mothers 'will resolve to be more patient and cling more tightly to what passes for sanity'. Chesler (1974) suggests that women's psychopathology is an expression of the 'devalued feminine role'.

> The scapegoat is also an escape valve; through her the passions and blind raging waters of suppressed knowledge are permitted to churn, so that they need not emerge in less extreme situations as lucid rebellion (Welburn 1974, 132).

Women who show resistance to motherhood may become scapegoats, so that the 'blind raging waters' of suppressed feministic rage does not emerge as lucid rebellion.' The invisible violence of the institution of motherhood swelling in the belly of the feminine and the patriarchal perils of psychiatry cannot offer an objective understanding of post-natal depression.

Source: Kruger, Monique. (2002). *Post natal depression as an expression of rebellion against the maternal role.*

The experiences of marginalised women

We have seen that women can hardly be said to constitute a homogenous group. Solidarities are broken along the lines of 'race', ethnicity, class, language, rural/urban divisions and sexuality, as well as almost every other social identity marker that exists. Feminism as modelled upon Western and Eurocentric philosophy thus becomes somewhat problematic for a non-Western context. What is certainly needed is a feminism that does not just acknowledge but also actively engages with every woman's perceived 'difference' and resulting subjective experience of gender. Hendricks *et al* argue this same point in their emphasis on the need to 'reassess the concepts, methods and models used for defining feminism, and to develop new ways of identifying and charting marginalised women's unique engagement with feminism' (225).

In July 2001 a workshop hosted by the African Gender Institute and feminist academic journal *Agenda* was organised. It was aimed at reflecting on the multiple meanings of feminism in Africa. Essof (2001) reported on the distinct understandings that were put forward regarding the theory and practice of African feminism: '... there are those who argue feminism is not African and thus has no relevance to Africa's political, social and economic realities. Rather, it is seen as an elite, bourgeois phenomenon, an invention of the West with no real value, or meaning for African women' (124–125).

The damage of being named

The alternative practice to theorising feminism is to suggest that while feminism is very much an important ideology relevant to all women, it is also one that needs to be *renamed* by marginalised women. Gqola (2001) and Mama (2002) have ascribed this to the 'damaging power of being named', by which as colonial subjects, Africans for a long time have not only been told who they were but the ways in which these terms of reference – 'natives', 'kaffirs', 'negroes' etc – have been used as sites of oppression and dominance. Indeed, the labels chosen seem to testify to a specific affirming essence, the need to define and possess an identity that we have freely chosen for ourselves and which in some ways foreground and prioritise our own particular lived experiences as specific subjects, so that we have **post-colonial/Black/African/Womanist** feminisms (see table 7.1), in the words of Mama (2002, 1): '...for many of us, identity remains a quest, something in-the-making.'

> While feminism is very much an important ideology relevant to all women, it is also one that needs to be renamed by marginalised women.

An African feminism of sociocultural and political contexts

A critical feminist practice explores issues and concerns of women by situating them within the political and sociocultural contexts. An African feminist agenda in this regard is to address and explore the gender-related experiences of African women in acknowledgement of the fact that many African women's experiences of gender and identity development have not been fully represented in psychological theory. Also, an African feminism would consider the political/economic and sociocultural contexts to be crucial to theorising and exploring gender identity development. Emphasis would be on those areas of social and political life that implicitly are influenced by gender, such as health, and which are implicitly oppressive, within patriarchy, to women. The Aids pandemic in Africa would thus be one such area of focus for feminist research.

| BOX 4 | 'Talking about feminism in Africa': Elaine Salo speaks to Amina Mama |

The following extract is adapted from an interview with Professor Amina Mama, an activist scholar and academic in feminist theory and practice at the University of Cape Town (UCT). Elaine Salo lectures at the African Gender Institute at UCT.

ES: Would you say that **womanism** has any relevance for African feminists?

AM: ... I have no problems with womanism but changing the terminology doesn't solve the problem of global domination. I choose to stick with the original term, insist that my own reality inform my application of it. Words can always be appropriated, for example there is not just womanism, but Omolara Ogundipe-Leslie's Stiwanism and Catherine Obonulu's Motherism – but this does not get away from the main problem, namely white domination of global politics and northern-based white women's power to define. We should define our own terms. To put it bluntly, white feminism has never been strong enough to be 'the enemy' – as the way that, say, global capitalism can be viewed as an enemy ...

The constant tirades against 'white feminists' do not have the same strategic relevance as they might have had 20 years ago when we first subjected feminism to anti-racist scrutiny. Since then many Westerners have not only listened to the critiques of African and other so-called 'Third World' feminists – they have also re-considered their simplistic paradigms and come up with more complex theories. Postcolonial feminism owes much to African, Asian and Latin American thinkers. Western feminists have agreed with much of what we have told them about different women being oppressed differently, and the importance of class and race and culture in configuring gender relations. Having won the battle why would we want to abandon the struggle, leave the semantic territory to others, and find ourselves a new word?

Source: (2001) *Agenda 50*: 58–63.

PROSPECTS AND CHALLENGES FOR FEMINIST THEORY AND PRACTICE IN AFRICA: FOCUS ON HIV/AIDS

'Culturally prescribed gender scripts that legitimate sexual violence against women lie close to the roots of the current Aids epidemic in South Africa.'

Leclerc-Madlala *WHP Review* (2001, 6)

The 'gendering' of HIV/Aids in South Africa

An African feminist agenda involves prioritising and exploring those features of African cultural practice and tradition that emphasise the most human and enduring aspects in the lives of women living in Africa. In this regard a critical South African feminist psychology should seek to explore and deconstruct those features of African culture which function to the detriment and subordination of African women. The intention must be one of strengthening and adapting traditional values that promote or enhance African women's empowerment, seeking to promote their needs through opening up further the discursive space and strategies inherent in indigenous culture and resisting those customs that oppress and degrade women.

Virginity testing

Nowhere is this more necessary than in the cultural constructions of female sexuality which function to tie many African women to the dominant and oppressive patriarchal system, through such gendered practices as virginity testing (Leclerc-Madlala, 2001). An essentialised construction of female sexuality as pure and chaste may, for instance, position many African women as moral guardians for their respective cultural values and traditions. They are imbued with constructions of an 'ideal' womanhood with sole responsibility for maintaining the moral sexual equilibrium as well as reinstalling lost cultural values of 'chastity'. The invoking of a lost value system that needs to be 'regained' is inherent in a growing number of male African constructions of an 'African renaissance'. Even more disturbing is the self-regulation this pervasive discourse achieves, with many African women themselves actively promoting and organising virginity-testing ceremonies. Such practices are in effect culturally prescribed gender-scripts that legitimate sexual violence against women. By placing emphasis on women's gender roles, men are effectively absolved from any sexual responsibility, not just with regard to curbing the spread of HIV/Aids but also in widespread deviant sexual behaviour such as rape.

> By placing emphasis on women's gender roles, men are effectively absolved from any sexual responsibility, not just with regard to curbing the spread of HIV/Aids but also in widespread deviant sexual behaviour such as rape.

BOX 5   Five-year sex ban for young Swazi women

Agence France Presse

In September 2001 the Swaziland government announced a five-year sex ban for young women in a bid to combat the spread of HIV/Aids. The ban was announced by the leader of Swaziland's young women, Lungile Ndlovu, who said the elders of the nation deemed it fitting.

'During this period you will be expected to observe a five-year sex ban. No shaking of hands with males, no wearing of pants and you will be expected to wear woollen tassels wherever you go for the next five years,' Ndlovu said at the end of the lengthy celebrations to mark the Swazi king's 33rd birthday. Ndlovu did not specify what age group the ban targets, but said women in relationships and older than 19 would be expected to wear red with black tassels. Those who are still virgins will wear blue with yellow tassels. Her announcement was met by howls of protest.

The ban follows an announcement by King Mswati III that Swaziland will revive the *umchwasho* chastity rite to preserve virginity among girls and to combat Aids. [...] Ndlovu said the tradition of preserving a maiden's chastity, known as *Imbali YeMaswati* (Flower of the Nation), will be policed by traditional chiefs who still rule over much of Swazi society ...

Source: *Women's Health Project Review* (2001) 7.

Challenging violence against women

'It is an implicit assumption that the area of psychology which concerns itself with personality has the onerous but necessary task of describing the limits of human possibility. Thus when we are about to consider the liberation of women, we naturally look to psychology to tell us what 'true' liberation would mean: what would give women the freedom to fulfill their own intrinsic natures. Psychologists have set about describing the true natures of women with a certainty and a sense of their own infallibility rarely found in the secular world.'

Naomi Weisstein *Psychology constructs the female* (1996)

The widespread nature of women's oppression

All identities are gendered (Mama, 2002). Any psychological theory about women's liberation in Africa needs to be aware of gender-oppressive discourse that seems to be finding voice in many indigenous traditionalist calls for a pre-colonial African customary-law system. The inherent danger of such a sex-gender system is that gender oppression is, in retrospect, constructed as non-existent in indigenous customs as opposed to Western society. This is in fact not the case. While patriarchy is far from universal in form, it is a social fact that women are globally subordinated on the basis of their gender. In any society – socialist/capitalist, communal/individualistic – a built-in power inequality can be said to exist between men and women. Many African cultural practices, for instance, still define intellectual pursuit as an exclusively male domain. Male education is thus prioritised over female education, enabling men to have far more competitive career opportunities than women.

The gender dimension to experience and politics

Psychological research now increasingly takes into account the gender-specific influences of social phenomena and at almost every turn seeks to incorporate gender as necessary to understanding social phenomenon (see, for example, Harris, Lea & Foster, 1995). Gender relations in South Africa alone are seen to have much significance for a nation-building agenda and issues pertaining to gender have already received much political focus (Beyond Racism Report, 1994). But there are varieties of experiences and events that still need to be acknowledged and explored as legitimate questions for psychological research, such as cultural constructions of sexuality and how these have very often been employed in legitimating a patriarchal system.

Links between race, gender, class

A feminist critical psychology in South Africa needs to engage with culture-specific practices that are inherently gender-specific as well. Most research topics inevitably require a gender focus and it seems theoretically limiting to separate other significant categories such as race, class and physical location from this focus of analysis. Hollway (1984, 1989) has shown how specific gender discourses on male and female sexuality have served to legitimate both male and female gender roles. In explaining differences between men and women, psychological theories of biological determinism operate alongside a society's framework of constructing gender relations. This is another way of saying we sometimes cannot begin to deconstruct a culture's normalisation of gender norms without also deconstructing the 'expert' theoretical framework that either builds or supports it.

Gender in the South African Constitution

South Africa's post-'94 Constitution – particularly its gender equity laws – is certainly one of the most liberal in the world. This is also one instance where we clearly see an influence and the workings of the liberal feminist agenda, that is, the notion that all gender equality must begin with a change in the legislation:

> Gender justice, insist liberal feminists, requires us, first to make the rules of the game fair and, second, to make certain that none of the runners in the race for society's goods and services is systematically disadvantaged ...' (Tong, 1994, 2):

But this change in legislation has not done much for women's liberation from male domination. Not every woman has access to better a livelihood despite the equality laws that have been enshrined in the new Constitution. There are other equally significant social categories that still stand in many women's way, such as class, education, poverty etc. In other words, many women previously discriminated against under apartheid still experience discrimination precisely because they are still disadvantaged in multiple ways in post-apartheid South Africa.

Male violence against women

In addition, many South African women are still plagued by ongoing male violence. Legislation may have been erected that is meant to enforce women's protection, such as the new law that says rapists should get life sentences for raping someone more than once (*Beyond Racism*, 1994). However, it is now becoming increasingly obvious that female subordination does not stem exclusively from legal constraints imposed on women. Women's oppression is so much more deeply entrenched than mere legislation:

The concepts and categories that developmental and other psychologists generate very often have a deep impact on how societies function, as well as the laws and legal identities that are constructed (Hook, 2001). The 'normalising' character of models of human development has significant meaning for who and what we tend to consider right or wrong ways of living and developing or mobilising notions of 'normal' and 'abnormal'. To quote from Hook (2001):

> The danger of these scientific categories of 'normal' and 'abnormal' is that they become very loaded terms.
>
> ... this scientific language is doing little more than replacing notions of good/bad, right/sinful with new categories normal/abnormal (146).

Rape

This is especially crucial in a context and notion of rape as a social control practice, and in many ways one that is socially sanctioned. Stereotypical views about female and male sexuality are often employed in explaining the incidence of rape, such as the idea that many rape victims 'ask' to be raped by virtue of the fact that they are sexually active or promiscuous (the implicit understanding being that the active sexual person is naturally male), or that sexual aggression is merely another instance of men acting out their hormonal natures (see Hollway, 1989). In South Africa a judge handed down a light sentence on a 54-year-old father accused of raping his 14-year-old daughter after his action was considered to embody no signs of any sexual deviance 'outside the family unit' by the ruling judge (*Sunday Times*, October 1999). In another case, a young man was also given a light sentence for the repeated rape of two 15-year-old girls, which was attributed to the man's 'virility' and also because one of the girls had been 'stout' (naughty) because she had had sex with someone else two days before (*Sunday Times*, August 1999).

The above incidences seem to indicate a deep-seated shared understanding about sexual aggression toward women, including to what degree this is considered to be a matter to be sympathised with. The labelling of 'normal' and 'abnormal' behaviour is proving to be a site where women's continued oppression is allowed to continue, and one where feminist psychology can begin to question the normalising practices a society might have. This is no more evident than in the controversial anti-rape advertisement shown on South African television and banned a few years ago after a group of men accused the advertisers of 'discrimination against men' (*Monitor*, 1999).

Representations of rape in patriarchy

While the inherent message conveyed in the advertisement was that of rape being endemic in South Africa precisely because so few men seem to take it seriously and because it raised the crucial question of male complacency in so pervasive a crime against women and children, many angry men complained to the advertising board that they were being 'smeared', 'insulted' and 'unfairly labelled rapists'. As one young man put it: 'I don't want to be lumped with them.' This labeling of 'normal' (us) and 'abnormal' (them) men effectively camouflages the complicity and complacency of many so-called 'normal' men – and legal institutions – in the abuse of women (see Harris, Lea & Foster, 1995). Through forms of social arrangement and cultural traditions gender relations are contextualised and accepted as 'normal' and 'abnormal'. The system of patriarchy thus maintains and sustains structures of male dominance through systems of collective ideas, and shared assumptions about gender.

ESSENTIALISM IN THEORY: PSYCHOLOGY'S ENGAGEMENT WITH DIFFERENCE

What is essentialism?

Fuss (1989) defines **essentialism** to be a 'belief in the real, true essence of things, in the variable and fixed properties which define the "whatness" of a given identity' (9). In other words, essentialism is the idea that our identities are somehow *fixed and unchangeable*, that specific physical and social facts about who we are (such as gender, class and race) come to determine our identities. Now while such facts are certainly relevant in trying to understand and explore identities – recognising the multiplicity of our identities – it would be essentialist for us to define these identities as *determined* by these categories or facts. Identity invariably has more to do with *how* we choose to behave and the kinds of resource (discursive and material) that might be available to us.

The word 'essence' may be understood to refer to what is natural – *already existing*, but that can be subjected to some or other kind of shaping. Reality is therefore just waiting to be discovered. The social science researcher can go out and 'discover' identities, for instance. The word 'construct', on the other hand, implies *building from scratch*. We cannot just go out and discover identity, we must pay attention to the multiple, shifting and very often contradictory meanings people draw upon and reproduce to understand themselves and their social environment. We can do this only by having no preconceived notions of what people's lived experiences must be like – because people are not defined by their race or class or gender or sexuality etc. We cannot simply use these categories as determining the 'whatness' of people's identities.

Essentialism: mode of thought that defines individual existence as secondary to an essence. Essentialism assigns essences to people and/or experiences as a means of defining and explaining them, either through science or philosophy/religion or politics, the assumption being that people and objects have an essential or inherent nature that can be discovered.

Essentialism versus social constructionism

Essentialism is different from **social constructionism** in quite specific and significant ways. In essentialism knowledge is discovered through *experience*, that is, we come to acquire and know certain things as a result of having undergone a particular event or situation by virtue of our experiences as *specific individuals*. For example, a young black woman will experience markedly different life events from, say, a middle-aged white man. The social constructionist view, however, is that knowledge is *constructed, deconstructed* and *reconstructed* through ideological discourse. We are not limited into specific roles of race or class or gender, for instance. Our sense of who we are is in no way connected to an essence. And because 'experience' is subjective in nature – meaning we attribute meanings to events based on the theoretical resources available to us – it becomes difficult to tie knowledge and/or experience to an essence or fixed property. After all we do not always share the same resources in constructing knowledge. This is irrespective of gender, race etc. Multiple and shifting

Social constructionism: there are many different interpretations of this concept. The common meaning underlying the different ideas is a concern with the processes by which human abilities, experiences, common sense and scientific knowledge are both produced and reproduced in human communities.

resources may also mean that knowledge may sometimes be dominantly operative at specific historical points in time. The central notion here is truth as universal (essentialism) versus truth as arbitrary (social constructionism).

Why is essentialism undesirable?

> 'If it's natural we can't change it.'
>
> Lieven (1981, 203)

> Essentialism hinders any real and worthwhile social change. It does this quite simply by constructing oppressive social relations as natural and, by default, unnecessary to have to submit to any radical change.

Essentialism is undesirable for crucial reasons. Perhaps most significantly, essentialism hinders any real and worthwhile social change. It does this quite simply by constructing oppressive social relations as natural and, by default, unnecessary to have to submit to any radical change. Foucault (1984) has described the ways by which women have been controlled historically by being defined as either 'hysterical' or 'frigid'. This was effectively legitimated through an employment of medicalised discourses of sexuality. While this understanding of female sexuality may now be generally unpopular and regarded as unscientific, other equally essentialist constructions of a natural female sexuality may still be effective and dominant in patriarchal society. For instance, it is not uncommon to hear women described as maternal, intuitive, vain, seductive and sometimes irrational.

The 'discourse of nature' as a means of oppression

These are all constructions that make use of a *nature* argument to define female sexuality. Women are defined as naturally different. And it is because they are *naturally* maternal that nurturing and familial roles are prescribed for them. It is because they are *naturally* seductive to men – to the extent that they may unwittingly 'invite' male sexual aggression – that their sexuality needs to be controlled and watched over. If women are *naturally* irrational, then they certainly cannot be allowed to occupy leadership positions over men. On the contrary, they are in dire need of having decisions made for them by more *naturally* rational (male) minds.

Guillaumin (1995) has argued that the surest route to legitimising any illegitimate power over any group of people is to use the nature discourse – the *essence* of what it means to belong to a particular racial or gender group is futile to oppose what is natural. And trying to redress social injustice is of little significance and a waste of economic resources precisely because we cannot change nature. Because female subordination is seen to stem directly from *biological* differences as opposed to *social relationships* themselves, it is perceived to be both natural and unchangeable: '... if we are ever oppressed or exploited, it is the result of our nature. Or, better still, our nature is such that we are oppressed, exploited, appropriated' (Guillaumin, 1995, 225).

The essentialising of identity

This essentialising of identity is not only restricted to gender. Fanon (1952) has argued that racist language often employs such naturalist discourses as a legitimating tool for racial oppression. Racist language may *'infantilise'*, *'primitivise'*, *'decivilise'* and *'essentialise'* the black man by making him 'the eternal victim of an essence for which he is not responsible' (Fanon, 1952, 35). Being defined and understood solely in terms of an essence means that we become, again in the words of Fanon, 'trapped' in categories we are unable to reject, we are reduced to that one defining category of 'black', 'woman', African' etc. This is a trap many feminists have been unable to get out of and one that proponents of an African feminism should continually be aware of. The term 'African woman' is a social category just like any other, and while we need to engage with the varied and multiple life experiences of many African women, we also need to beware of universalising these experiences and identities.

> Theory is a necessary tool for the transformation of both private and public consciousness, and this may hopefully lead to a disempowering of deeply entrenched power structures in people's lives.

How race and gender combine in oppression

Any feminist agenda that seeks to explore and redress female subordination should pay attention to the varied social realities of race, class and other social categories, acknowledging these as different aspects of gender relations. A feminist critical agenda is especially well placed to open up dialogue within which these categories can be analysed in relation to gender identity. This process would mean having to re-evaluate the old theoretical models that have constructed and promoted the notion of a unitary model of women's identities and experiences. Feminist and critical race theorists often treat gender and race separately, to the detriment of both feminist and anti-racist psychologies. African feminist practice is significant in its emphasis on race as a critical aspect of female subordination.

The dominant trends in gender research

Finchilescu (1995) identifies two dominant theoretical trends in gender research in South African psychology: *essentialism* (biological and social differences) and *social constructionism*. The first kind of essentialism in theorising gender is classified as biological essentialism, in which the purpose and underlying theory of psychological research was to prove the significance of biological differences between men and women, that is genetic and/or hormonal explanations for sex-related behaviour. Research such as this relies on a notion of 'nature' to explain and justify gender relations (Goldberg, 1996; Guillaumin, 1995). Thus we might have studies seeking to explain male sexual aggression in such biological terms as male hormones in overdrive (Hollway, 1989) or a naturally intuitive or maternal trait (Alldred, 1996).

The second kind of essentialist theorising is that which defines gender difference as *social* as opposed to *natural* (Finchilescu, 1995). Gender roles are recognised to be socially constructed and having some significant implications for the way men and women live in society. This approach seeks to redefine the negative connotations surrounding the notion of gender difference, with the true essence of women constructed in positive terms. Another underlying notion in this approach is the idea that all women are the same – in their essence – and there is no major difference to be spoken of.

Social creativity: attempt to redefine existing group characteristics in positive terms, as a means of changing the negative social identity of in-group members. A common example of this is the popular 'Black is beautiful' movement which seeks to define black culture in more positive terms than it has historically been defined.

Social creativity

The above approach employs Tajfel's (1959) notion of **social creativity** as a form of **cognitive alternative**. This notion basically argues that members of an out-group may sometimes employ a strategy of altering the negative stereo-types of the group by redefining some group characteristic in more positive terms. For example, previous assumptions of women as naturally maternal (which may have conveyed negative connotations) may be redefined by some women as something positive and of value.

The immediate problem with the above approach is that it does not seek to question the notion of a *natural* difference between men and women. This is taken as a given. Thus the term 'gender' itself is not seen to be a social construct (see Shefer, 2001) and the category 'woman' is uncritically assumed. Further-more this approach is often devoid of much politically progressive social psychology in the sense that it does not consider the social, political, cultural, economic and historical factors of social contexts (Foster & Louw-Potgieter, 1992).

Cognitive alternative: perception that the status relations between groups are changeable to the extent that a complete reversal of such status is feasible. Change in social identity is rooted in an individual's first *perceiving* that such change is possible.

Social context in gender

The second trend in psychological research is the social constructionist approach which emphasised the construction of the social context and the separating of gender behaviour from the actor (Finchislescuieu, 1995). Gender identity was now seen to be something constantly changing and in multiple forms so that it becomes theoretically limiting to assume that all women are the same. Identity was not something that could easily be stamped on an individual.

Awareness of how 'difference' might imply kinds of essentialism

Hollway (1989) has, however, cautioned against an essentialising practice when theorising any form of identity. This is a crucial and ever-present pitfall to be constantly aware of whenever one engages with the notion of 'difference'. However much we need to explore the gender experiences of marginalised groups, we must be careful about reproducing essentialist constructions.

BOX 6   'All The Women Are White, All The Blacks Are Men, But Some Of Us Are Brave'

The above title is taken from a fairly recent anthology by black American female writers, exploring their discontent with mainstream theoretical tendency to prioritise race over gender and vice versa. Indeed, psychology's reluctance to engage directly with issues simultaneously relating to both gender and race – thereby emphasising the multiple forms of identity – has largely worked to the detriment of many marginalised women. At the World Conference Against Racism (WCAR) held in Durban in 2001, attention was given to the double and triple discrimination many women face globally because they were of a racial, class and religious minority: '... women who are at risk of both race and gender discrimination are also "doubly at risk of violence", particularly if they are from marginalised communities' (report by Christina Stucky, *Sunday Independent,* 2001). The idea is not to exclude one form of identity over another, but rather to point out the impracticality of privileging and exploring one way of *being-in-the-world* as a human being. Different societies accord varying levels of importance to race, class, gender, ethnicity etc, and therefore it makes sense to assume that gender is experienced differently by women all over the world.

Another way of saying this is that in the quest to be 'different' feminists may reproduce differences that are even more harmful than previous constructions of differences. This is irrespective of approach. Hendricks *et al* (1994, 218) emphasise this point further in their assertion that '[f]eminists who have worked under the banner of "African Feminism" have developed essentialist ideas very similar to those of womanists'.

More than this, we continually need to guard against a one-dimensional approach to theorising gender issues in which a 'romanticised' view of the social system only serves to further distort gender relations. This is in particular reference to feminist theories that have been developed as counter-arguments to the mainstream, and which may often be in danger of misrepresenting and silencing marginalised women's experiences of gender. While mainstream representation of a universal patriarchal system presents a distorted lens of gender experience, it is equally misleading to assume that a universal African patriarchal system exists or, even worse, was non-existent until the advent of colonialism and neo-colonialism. Ogundipe-Leslie (1994, 216) has questioned: 'What is feminism in the context of Africa ...? We must define specificities ... we cannot generalize Africa.'

The central tenets of African Feminism at times seem to reinscribe the very forms of cultural essentialism for which mainstream feminism has been condemned. This is even more evident in the assumption that Western, white feminists are unable to know or even represent African women's experiences in a truthful or sympathetic manner. This assumption in effect says 'only black African women can research their own experiences of gender'. This is a misguided notion that inevitably may prove theoretically limiting for many marginalised women. Post-colonial theorist Edward Said criticises this notion as well when he says: 'I certainly do not believe the limited proposition that only a black man can write about blacks, a Muslim about Muslims, and so forth' (cited in Moore-Gilbert, 1997, 53).

BOX 7 **'Beyond the Essentialism of (some) Constructionists'**

French feminist scholar Colette Guillaumin (1995) has questioned the tendency towards essentialism evident not just in mainstream psychological theory but also amongst feminist social constructionist debates. Many constructionists equally fail to escape essentialism (Fuss, 1989). The practice is to

> take diversity into account by fragmenting the subject into multiple identities: women of colour, white women, bourgeois women, proletarian women, black proletarian women, and so on. But this operation [...] specifies, and does not counteract essentialism, as each sub-category is seen as possessing its own self-referential essence' (16–17).

As a means of guarding against such reductionism we would need to engage continually in a deconstructionist process regarding any knowledge system that attempts to theorise identity and social relations. The focus here is on contextualised knowledge-production, that is, the need to approach all knowledge of identity-gender – as instances of discursive practice. It is through an acknowledgement of power as embedded within all representations that we can really begin to trace key origins of female subordination.

FEMINIST PSYCHOLOGY AND POST-COLONIAL THEORY

Double consciousness

> **Post-colonial theory:** orientation critical to understanding the relationship between colonisers and colonised, and the psychological, material and cultural effects of these relationships.

It is also here that **post-colonial theory** can be applied as a particularly effective means for deconstructing Eurocentric knowledge systems, as well as in seeking to explore marginalised women's identities. Gilroy (1994) uses the notion of a 'double-consciousness' to explore that sense of marginal identity by which an individual from an oppressed group seeks to understand him- or herself through the eyes of the dominant culture, thereby fostering and sustaining a sort of self-loathing. This phenomenon of a double consciousness can be doubly experienced by many black women who would have to engage with subjective inferioritisation on more than one level – manifested through racial and patriarchal ideology. Post-colonial theory can be deployed to explore this double internalisation process by seeking to subvert racist and sexist constructions, and at the same time emphasise the worthiness and autonomy of black women – a process Hendricks *et al* (1994, 224) refer to as 'mental decolonization'.

The post-colonial woman's experience of gender is inextricably tied to social categories of 'race', class and political inferiority. Both post-colonial theory and feminism seek to explore and interrogate dominant power structures that continue to oppress historically marginalised groups in society. Although the *two schools of thought can hardly be said to be complementary* – certain post-colonial theorists would suggest that Western feminism has itself served implicitly colonial interests (Gandhi, 1998) – they can arguably be deployed in several respects to form an even stronger force than they traditionally might be on their own.

The phenomenon of a double consciousness can be doubly experienced by many black women who would have to engage with subjective inferioritisation on more than one level – manifested through racial and patriarchal ideology.

A black womanist vision of humanity

This understanding of gender identity is one that has further been adopted by Womanist theorists who emphasise the power of resistance inherent in any act of self-naming. Womanist theory seeks to promote an awareness of African women to the empowering process of self-definition: 'Fundamental to womanism is the realisation that to merely invert the terms of reference is not, in itself, a successful mode of struggle' (Abrahams, 2002, 60). Asserting one's femininity or Blackness must involve a process of defining for oneself a black 'womanist vision of humanity'.

Critical psychology can promote an understanding and critical engagement of how gendered and racially minoritised bodies can and do negotiate their identities and policies across varied historical and contemporary domains. Hendricks *et al* (1994) have observed that the feminist trend as is currently played out in South Africa is something resembling a contestation of experience and not collaboration. On the one hand, white women feel caught in a defensive position within which they need continually to reaffirm their right to represent everyone – white and black – and, on the other hand, black women testify to personal oppression as their right to speak for marginalised groups.

Womanist theory seeks to promote an awareness of African women to the empowering process of self-definition: 'Fundamental to womanism is the realisation that to merely invert the terms of reference is not, in itself, a successful mode of struggle' (Abrahams, 2002, 60).

The dangers of ignoring difference

It is important to reiterate: if one ignores differences one distorts reality. Choosing to ignore the power relations that have been built on these perceived differences, however well intentioned one may be, would merely reinforce these relations of power in the interests of those holding power. At the same time, while we should avoid theorising such simplistic ideas of global sisterhood and ignore relative power dynamics, this practice and principle must also apply to any notion of a supposed sisterhood among 'Third World' women.

What is certainly needed is a reconceptualising of the notion of 'difference' between women. That is, we should seek to eradicate all difference between women in the name of global sisterhood and yet, simultaneously, explore and acknowledge the diverse national and cultural identities separating women. It is with this same principle that Mohanty (1987, 31) has questioned: '*Can I speak of difference without speaking Difference?*' For her, contemporary feminism needs to ground itself in a 'self-conscious politics of location'.

The interrelatedness of gender and race as factors of oppression

Perhaps we also need to move beyond an attempt to locate or pinpoint priorities of oppression (race versus gender) but rather seek to explore the interrelatedness of these two aspects of oppression as well as their interdependency. Critical psychology's strength should lie in a centring of the experience of minority women in a variety of social sites, thereby seeking to invite a broader examination of social space as well as avoid a homogenised and typified construction of subjects we seek to represent – and in doing so further 'othering' them. One way to counteract such a pitfall would be for trained gender researchers to seek to involve untrained black women in research as a means of sharing skills-research and theoretical concepts. Van Niekerk (1991) has suggested a focus on trying to develop a broader range of research and communication techniques. This is particularly significant in the light of the fact that many rural African women do grapple with illiteracy and most indigenous cultures are characterised by oral and dramatic traditions of expression. Feminist theory can certainly be enhanced in such attempts at exploring the worldviews of many marginalised women, especially in discovering new and challenging gender identities.

CONCLUSION

Finally, by way of conclusion, Hendricks *et al* (1994, 217) re-adapt postcolonial feminist Chandra Mohanty's guidelines for exploring identity and meaning. These are challenging issues worth repeating here:

▷ How do different communities of women define feminism?
▷ Whose history do we draw on to chart women's engagement with feminism?
▷ How do questions of gender, 'race', nation and other identities intersect in determining feminisms?
▷ How do we produce knowledge about ourselves and others, and with what assumptions?
▷ What methods do we use to identify and describe different women's subjectivity and self-interests?
▷ What are the politics of the production of this knowledge?
▷ Which conventions limit our production of this knowledge?

Perhaps subscribing to the notion of African feminisms is like that of feminist psychology in *naming* a site of critique, contestation and debate between its terms, rather than claiming an integration or harmony between the two standpoints. Feminist arguments necessarily challenge prevailing patriarchal structures, while African-centred perspectives need to continue to press feminists to address the cultural and political implications of frameworks that bear the history and cultural privilege of their European and US-American origins.

Critical thinking tasks

1. 'Perhaps the paradox is inherent: in challenging a system of subordination by gender, feminist psychologists have attempted to re-mediate a sex bias in research and to demonstrate a uniquely feminine experience. But construing gender as a property of individuals, rather than as a set of interactive processes that form a system of subordination, leads back to

questions about the nature and meaning of difference that have preoccupied feminist psychology for so long' (Crawford in Gergen & Davis, 1997, 281).

Using this quotation as a springboard, critically discuss the range of debates that feminist researchers are compelled to engage with in pursuing their research (and its consequences) as a form of feminist activism.

2. 'Anti-essentialism is the key to democracy.'

Critically discuss the ways in which feminist psychology, including the theories of black and 'Third World' women, may be seen sometimes to reproduce essentialist notions of gender and experience and how theory can seek to avoid such a non-liberating approach to theorising gender experiences.

3. 'The destabilisation and uncertainty of accommodating difference and deconstructing stable categories and concepts have generated anxiety about whether feminism will abandon its political thrust' (Hendricks & Lewis, 1994, 63).

In what ways can a South African critical feminist psychological agenda be seen to address and speak directly to the particular needs of South African women while also addressing original feminist principles of a universal oppression shared by women?

Recommended readings

Squire, C. (1989). *Significant differences: Feminism in psychology*. London: Routledge.

Tong, R. (1998). *Feminist thought: A more comprehensive introduction*. 2nd edition. Oxford: Westview Press.

Burman, E., Alldred, A., Bewley, C., Goldberg, B., Heenan, C., Marks, D., Marshall, J., Taylor, K., Ullah, R., & Warner, S. (eds) (1996). *Challenging women: Psychology's exclusions, feminist possibilities*. London: Open University Press.

Mama, A. (1995). *Beyond the masks: Race, gender and subjectivity*. London: Routledge.

Ogundipe-Leslie, M. (1994). *Re-creating ourselves: African women and critical transformations*. Trenton, NJ: Africa World Press.

Acknowledgement

The author acknowledges the contribution of Erica Burman to this chapter.

Heterosexuality

8

Tamara Shefer

OUTCOMES

After having studied this chapter you should be able to:

- understand the current context of heterosexual practices in local communities through a review of the literature
- see the critical role that gender and other forms of power inequality such as age, class and 'race' play in heterosexual relationships
- look critically at what picture of men, women and heterosex is being promulgated in the literature, and
- reflect on what is required towards creating more equitable heterosexual relationships.

THIS CHAPTER explores the practices of heterosexuality in contemporary South Africa as they are portrayed within current research and literature. The chapter highlights how heterosexuality has received little critical attention, particularly within psychology, as it has been assumed to be normal and natural. More recently, however, due to the efforts of feminism, and the global imperative to address the HIV/AIDS pandemic, heterosexual practices have come under scrutiny. The chapter discusses heterosexual sexuality (heterosex) within five main themes drawn from the literature: gender and power inequalities in sexual relationships; male power and women's lack of negotiation in sexual relationships; coercive and violent practices in sexuality; the developmental and social context of masculinity and femininity in understanding heterosexual power relations; and the impact of HIV/AIDS on heterosex. The chapter also presents a critical discussion of some of the more negative implications of the current ways in which gender and heterosex are presented in the literature.

Heterosexuality under scrutiny

Jabu was shortlisted as a candidate for the Masters in Clinical Psychology Programme. At the interview he felt that it was important to identify himself as gay when asked if he had anything that he would like to share about himself. None of the heterosexual candidates, however, identified themselves in relation to their sexual orientation.
- What does this experience tell you about heterosexuality?
- What comes to mind when you think about sex?
- Why is it that when we think about sex, we immediately assume that it refers to sex between men and women?
- Why is it that when we think about sex, we immediately assume that it refers to heterosexual penetration?

Heterosexuality has historically been a silent partner to its binary opposite, homosexuality. Like Whiteness in respect of Blackness, or 'man' in relation to 'woman', the normative identity is always assumed to be unproblematic. The institution of heterosexuality has been idealised, romanticised and naturalised, while in many cultures homosexuality remains a marginalised, pathologised and stigmatised sexual orientation. Thus, as many have pointed out, heterosexuality has been relatively untouched and untheorised across most disciplines (Kitzinger & Wilkinson, 1993; Richardson, 1996). Yet, over the last few decades, heterosex has been increasingly problematised. Feminist work since the 1960s, and the urgency of the HIV/AIDS pandemic since the 1980s, have seen an increasing global focus on exploring sexuality between men and women. It has been widely argued and empirically illustrated that heterosexuality (as both institution and ideology) is a central site for the production and reproduction of gender power inequalities, with women having little power to assert their needs or negotiate for their safety or pleasure (see, for example, Holland et al., 1990; 1991; Jeffreys, 1990; Kitzinger & Wilkinson, 1993; MacKinnon, 1989; Rich, 1980; Richardson, 1996; Vance, 1984). Furthermore, it has now been well recognised that central to understanding the barriers to challenging HIV/AIDS through safe sex practices are the taken-for-granted sexual practices and sexual identities of the two genders.

> Heterosexuality (as both institution and ideology) is a central site for the production and reproduction of gender power inequalities, with women having little power to assert their needs or negotiate for their safety or pleasure.

Given the high rate of HIV infection in sub-Saharan Africa and the fact that heterosexual relations are the primary mode of infection in these countries, research on (hetero-) sexuality has accelerated over the last decade in South Africa. As a consequence we now know quite a lot about the gender power inequalities that manifest in heterosexual relationships in local South African contexts.

As a discipline, psychology has been fairly silent on the issue of heterosexuality, at least with respect to theorising power inequalities in heterosexual practices. While sexual development has been theorised in psychology, from psychodynamic theory to social constructionism, much of the work has focused on the development of (heterosexual) identity or on topics such as inter-personal sexual attraction as in traditional social psychology. Much of this work has assumed heterosexuality as a normative outcome of sexual development and psychology has been criticised for pathologising homosexuality (see, for example, Butler, 1990a, 1990b). There is a growing body of critical feminist psychological work that has begun exploring such dynamics (e.g. Wilkinson & Kitzinger, 1993).

Feminist work has shown that heterosexuality is a central site for the reproduction of gender power inequalities, with women largely having little power to assert their needs or negotiate for their safety or pleasure.

Gender and power inequalities in sexuality

At an international level, there is a large body of work in disadvantaged countries that views gender inequality and women's sexual and economic subordination as central to HIV infection and women's reproductive health generally (e.g. McFadden, 1992; Schoepf, 1988; Seidel, 1993; WHO, 1994). With the *feminisation of poverty*, particularly evident in Africa, women, through the intersection of economic and gender power inequalities, are especially vulnerable to HIV infection.

Such dynamics clearly play a significant role in the South African context too. The economic context, cultural prescriptions and gender power inequalities all intersect to create barriers for women in the negotiation of heterosex, and the imperative for women to be involved in sexual relationships for economic gain has been illustrated (NPPHCN, 1995; Simbayi *et al.*, 1999; Strebel, 1993). Furthermore, the colonial heritage of poverty, war and physical dislocation (such as migrant labour systems) have been found to further impact on women's ability to protect themselves from HIV infection. In South Africa, as with the rest of Africa, the impact of the migrant labour system on the spread of HIV has been illustrated (see, for example, Hunt, 1989; Campbell, 2001; Campbell *et al.*, 1998).

Feminisation of poverty:
Poverty affects women more than it does men, and women globally are poorer than men. In Africa and other third world contexts, the majority of women are poor as a consequence of the colonial heritage and due to international gender inequalities. In South Africa Black, working-class women have historically been at the bottom of the economic hierarchy, occupying the lowest earning and most undervalued positions.

The articulation of gender with age and class positions young, poor women as particularly vulnerable to HIV infection and sexual abuse. South African studies illustrate that young women frequently get involved with older men for access to money and/or status (NPPHCN, 1995; Varga & Makubalo, 1996). Similarly, there is some anecdotal evidence that men are seeking younger women to have sex with in order to avoid sexually transmitted illnesses, which may be contributing to coercive sexual practices (Simbayi *et al.*, 1999). Another current example of the overlap between age and gender in South Africa and elsewhere in the region has been the rape of young girls and babies, which has been presented in the media as resulting from the apparently widely accepted belief that sex with virgins is a way of curing or protecting against HIV/AIDS (LoveLife, 2000; Vetten & Bhana, 2001).

Psychology has been fairly silent on the issue of heterosexuality, especially with regard to theorising power inequalities in heterosexual relations.

Male power and women's lack of negotiation in sexual relationships

In the search for understanding the vast barriers to 'safe' sexual practices, much research has highlighted the inequitable nature of 'normal' heterosexual relationships. It has been fairly widely reported that even if women have knowledge about HIV/AIDS or wish to protect themselves against pregnancy, they frequently are unable to successfully negotiate this (Shefer, 1999; Strebel, 1992; 1993; Varga & Makubalo, 1996).

On the other hand, traditional gender roles together with or outside of socio-economic factors clearly play a significant role as barriers to safe sex practices. The central role that cultural practices of gender power inequality play in creating barriers to the negotiation of safe and equitable heterosex has been increasingly theorised and researched in an international context. Similarly in South Africa, a number of key studies have highlighted the way in which gender power relations manifest in the negotiation of heterosex (see, for example, Miles, 1992; Shefer, 1999; Strebel, 1993). These studies show how women's lack of negotiation is strongly associated with socialised sexual practices where it is expected of women to be passive, submissive partners, while men are expected to initiate, be active and lead women in the realm of sexuality (Shefer, 1999; Varga & Makubalo, 1996). Men are viewed as in control of relationships and sexuality. Much of this is related to the cultural constructions of male and female sexuality. A number of qualitative studies highlight a popular construction of male sexuality as overwhelmingly strong, urgent and uncontrollable (Shefer & Ruiters, 1998; Shefer & Foster, 2001; Strebel, 1993). This

Heterosex:
This term is used to refer to sexual practices between men and women. In most popular culture we simply use the term sex to refer to heterosex. This however assumes that all sexual activity takes place between men and women, and ignores homosexual sexuality.

has elsewhere been named the '*male sexual drive discourse*' (Hollway, 1989) that seems to play an important role in women's lack of negotiation in heterosex.

Emerging from the assumption that men are highly sexual is the construction of the domain of sexuality as masculine and a male preserve. Women are viewed as 'asexual', and therefore 'strangers' to matters related to sexuality. Women are understood to be waiting on men to 'show them the ropes'. They are expected to be focused on relationships and 'love', and sexuality is only legitimised for them if attached to these. A number of authors, both internationally and locally, emphasise the lack of a positive discourse on female sexuality – in other words, women do not appear to be able to express or view their sexuality or their sexual desires and pleasures as positive (Holland et al., 1991; Hollway, 1995; 1996; Lesch, 2000; Shefer & Foster, 2001; Shefer & Strebel, 2001). Thus, there is an increasing call for the articulation of women's voices in the realm of sexuality. It is asserted that if women cannot 'say yes' to sexuality, and 'own' their sexuality and sexual desires, then they certainly cannot assertively 'say no' and negotiate what they desire in their sexual relationships with men.

Linked to the above is the reported pervasiveness of the traditional *double standard* where men are encouraged to actively pursue sexuality and take multiple partners (NPPHCN, 1995; Wood & Foster, 1995). On the other hand, women are punished for being sexually active, and constructed as 'loose' and promiscuous. Even having knowledge about sexuality, and admitting to having had sexual experience, appears to be taboo for women (Shefer, 1999).

'Male sexual drive discourse' refers to the construction of men as highly sexual and always ready for sex (Hollway, 1989).

Studies show how women's lack of negotiation in heterosexual relationships is associated with socialised sexual practices where it is expected of women to be passive partners and men are expected to be active.

A focus on condom use, in particular, has highlighted the problematic dynamics of heterosexual negotiation. In South Africa, studies show how condoms are generally not viewed positively by either men or women, are frequently seen as symbolising a lack of trust or infidelity, are seen as 'unmacho' by men and unromantic by women and contrary to their traditional female role ('women who carry condoms are promiscuous') (see, for example, Abdool Karim et al., 1992a; Abdool Karim et al., 1992b; Abdool Karim, et al., 1992c; Lesch, 2000; Strebel, 1993; Varga & Makubalo, 1996; Wood & Foster, 1995). It is also more than evident from empirical findings that men's sexuality is privileged in decisions regarding condoms, with women fearing the loss of their partners, anxious about their men not enjoying sex with a condom, and fearing that a request for condoms will be interpreted as a lack of trust in the men or as an admission of their own infidelity (Bremridge, 2000; Campbell et al., 1998; Shefer, 1999; Strebel, 1993; Wood & Foster, 1995). While there is a definite increase in calls for women-centred methods of protection against HIV infection (e.g. female condom and spermicides) in South Africa (e.g. Rees, 1998), there is little research on the efficacy of such methods and there is much resistance to these methods (Richards, 1996; Strebel & Lindegger, 1998).

Discourse on condom use also highlights the traditional prescriptions for female sexuality within the *whore-madonna dichotomy*. Qualitative research in South Africa, mirroring international literature (e.g. Waldby et al., 1993), shows how men distinguish between 'clean' and 'unclean' women (Bremridge, 2000; Shefer, 1999; Wood & Foster, 1995), in which 'unclean' women constitute those who step outside prescribed feminine sexuality ('promiscuous' women and prostitutes). Condom use is therefore constructed by both men and women as inappropriate in long-term relationships where faithfulness is assumed. Clearly condoms are not neutral objects, but embody stigmas, which may differ from context to context and from one relationship to another, but nonetheless reflect dominant discourse on gendered power relations and serve to inhibit negotiations around 'safe sex'.

Excerpts from focus groups with UWC psychology students talking about heterosex

The 'male sexual drive' discourse:
It is no use us hiding away or ... denying it ... Men have got a very powerful urge ... sexual urge ... more than women have ... that is nature ... (Female participant)

Sex as a male domain:
I think that the men actually consider sex as a man's thing and not a woman thing ... Like if they get satisfied, then that's fine ... (Female participant)

Woman as passive and asexual:
Nice girls don't initiate ... and are passive (Female participant)

Male participant 1: What actually embarrasses men [is] ... if a lady is too active sexually they tend to label that lady. They tend to say ...

Male participant 2: ... that she's a bitch.

Male participant 3: Sometimes it's just her fear of exposing her knowledge about sex, especially during that first time. If she did during the first time, she could give him the wrong impression about her ... being a bitch.

Whore-madonna dichotomy:
If you change boyfriends from this one this month and next month another one, then you'll be labelled a bitch ... But if you have a steady affair for a long time, then you will be respectable ... (Female participant)

Culture and gender roles:
Male participant (following discussion of 'double standards'): I would think that maybe it's ... it's our culture [agreement from other men]

Female participant: But you cannot blame *the culture* all the time!

Male participant: What ... who said that men should be approaching the women? Nobody knows. But it is a fact ... it is what always happens ... in fact everyone knows that a man should do the proposal ... (Mixed group of participants)

Source: Shefer, 1999

While cultural constructions are found to play a huge role in the reproduction of unequal sexual practices, some authors are more critical of the way in which 'culture' may be used as a way of excusing problematic male behaviour and male power in sexual relationships (Shefer, 2002; Shefer *et al.*, 1999; Shefer & Foster, 2001). These authors point out how notions of 'tradition' and 'culture' are frequently used to rationalise and legitimise such practices as the 'double standard' (discussed earlier) and male promiscuity (based on notions of historical polygamy), as well as male lack of responsibility for contraceptives and safe sex practices.

Feminist writers have pointed out how notions of 'tradition' and 'culture' are frequently used to rationalise and legitimise double standards, male promiscuity, as well as male lack of responsibility for safe sex practices.

Coercive and violent practices

Given the high rate of violence against women in South Africa, much attention has been paid to this problem over the last decade. There has been a proliferation of research in South Africa on violence against women, and an increasing focus on the links between violence and heterosexuality and HIV/AIDS infection. Sexual violence against women and girls, whether by known or unknown rapists, is widespread. Coercive sexual practices and abuse have been increasingly reported in studies exploring heterosexual negotiations and practices. In this respect, girls and women are clearly more vulnerable to HIV/AIDS and other infection, as well as unwanted pregnancies. It has become apparent that for South African communities, violence and heterosex are inextricably interwoven (Shefer *et al.*, 2000). A recent spate of research among adolescents and children has revealed that their sexual experiences are bound up with violence and coercion (Buga *et al.*, 1996; NPPHCN, 1995; Richter, 1996; Varga & Makubalo, 1996; Wood *et al.*, 1996; Wood & Jewkes, 1998).

Reporting having sex against their will
- 28 per cent of Black, Coloured and Indian/Asian urban youth (Richter, 1996)
- 71 per cent of adolescent Black women in peri-urban Cape Town (Maforah in Wood *et al.*, 1996)

Coercive sexual practices
- A study in the rural Eastern Cape found that the most frequently cited reasons for women beginning sexual activity were coercion by a partner (28 per cent), and 'peer pressure' (20 per cent) (Buga *et al.*, 1996)
- A CIETafrica survey (in Vetten & Bhana, 2001) in Greater Johannesburg found that 27 per cent of young women and 32 per cent of young men did not see forced sex with someone they know as sexual violence
- When asked to write down the first experience that comes to mind when thinking about heterosex 22 per cent of UWC psychology students wrote of their own or others' experiences of violence and coercion, and a further 21 per cent spoke of issues of male power and women's lack of control (Shefer, 1999)

Everyday coercive practices in heterosex are also found to be common, particularly in interactions involving older men who are in more powerful social positions, and young women. Thus it is not only overt sexual violence that is commonplace. Rather, more subtle forms of coercion and pressure appear to be endemic to heterosexual relationships. Discourses of love and romance play a significant role in sexual coercion. This appears to be particularly salient for girls or women who speak of 'giving in' to male pressure for sex because of 'love', commitment and fear of loss of the relationship (Shefer, 1999; Varga & Makubalo, 1996; Wood *et al.*, 1996). In these studies, it is evident that girls' sexuality is constructed as responsive to and in the service of male sexuality. Even when young women are aware of power inequalities and double standards within discourses of love and sexuality, there appears to be little space for resistance given peer pressure and male violence (Wood *et al.*, 1996). A number of South African studies also highlight the widespread nature of coercive sexuality or unprotected sexuality linked to economic factors such as poverty, financial dependence, and job security (e.g. Jewkes & Abrahams, 2000; Vetten & Dladla, 2000).

A growing body of research is beginning to establish a strong link between violence against women and HIV/AIDS (see Vetten & Bhana, 2001 for a review). One of the significant areas hinges around condom usage in safe sex practices. Violence plays a role in negotiations around condoms, with women speaking of the fear and actual experience of angry or violent responses if they insist on condom use (Strebel, 1992; 1993; Varga & Makubalo, 1996; Shefer *et al.*, 2000). The link between violence and HIV/AIDS also emerges around the disclosure of HIV status, and attempts to practise safe sex by HIV-positive

Discourses of love and romance play a significant role in sexual coercion.

women. Although mostly anecdotal, there is evidence of male violence following women's disclosure of their HIV status in South African communities (Mthembu, 1998; Vetten & Bhana, 1991).

Developmental and social contexts of masculinity and femininity in understanding heterosexual power relations

This is still a fairly poorly subscribed area of research (Shefer, 1998), but there is wide acknowledgement, as elaborated below, of the significance of early gender development to heterosexual behaviour. Social and sexual inequalities that are powerfully implicated in young people's constructions of sexuality, love and relationships, are promulgated during childhood and adolescence.

With respect to girls, some of the salient issues are related to puberty and the beginnings of their menstruation. One central thread is the lack of knowledge and access to reliable and constructive information that young people, at all corners of the globe, have through the process of their development. Young women in particular appear to lack basic knowledge about their bodies, reproductivity and sexuality (Bassett & Sherman, 1994; Bhende, 1995; Uwakwe *et al.*, 1994; Vasconcelos *et al.*, 1995). This lack of knowledge appears to be reinforced by global moralising and gendered discourses on female sexuality, where virginity and sexual naivety are prescribed for girls (Weiss *et al.*, 1996). Thus, even if women have sexual knowledge, they face social pressure to maintain an image of innocence, particularly with men, who may interpret knowledge as past sexual activity (as mentioned earlier). Consequently, it is very difficult for women to protect themselves against sexually transmitted infections (STIs) and AIDS, given that such measures will imply 'the outward appearance of an active sexual life which is not congruent with traditional norms of conduct for adolescent girls' (*ibid.*:9). In this way, dominant constructions of femininity act to decrease women's power in the negotiation of heterosex.

In the South African context, both historical and contemporary studies point to the protective construction of girls as sexually vulnerable to 'dangerous' male sexuality at the onset of menstruation (Lesch, 2000; Mager, 1996; Shefer, 1998). Practices of forcing and placing girls immediately on contraception, and warnings against boys and men are apparently common in many South African communities. In this way, young girls are taught of their passivity and vulnerability to men or boys and their menstruation is constructed as a negative, dangerous transition (Shefer, 1998; 1999). As a consequence young women are often unprepared for sexual relationships, lacking not only useful knowledge but also a positive sexual identity (Thomson & Scott, 1991).

Boys, on the other hand, appear to be socialised positively into their 'manhood', with puberty signifying a transition to active (hetero-)sexuality.

Social and sexual inequalities that are powerfully implicated in young people's constructions of sexuality, love and relationships, are promulgated during childhood and adolescence.

Nonetheless, manhood appears to be rigidly associated with heterosexuality and the ability to be sexual with multiple women. Thus, those who do not conform or are not successful in this realm may be punished or stigmatised. Alternative sexualities, either homosexual or those resistant to traditional macho masculinity, are still not well tolerated in South African communities. For men and boys, the feminist argument of the close ties between heterosexual and masculine identity are borne out by empirical studies. For example, when asked what it means to be a boy, a 12-year-old boy replied '... to have sex with a woman' (NPPHCN, 1995:35). The female answer from a 14-year-old girl is similarly stereotyped and makes no mention of sex: 'To be a mother ... to have a husband and to look after children' (*ibid.*:36).

While masculinity studies have been fairly marginalised in South Africa, there is clearly a growing emphasis on understanding the role of masculinities in contemporary South Africa (see, for example, Morrell, 2001), including a focus on the masculine in heterosexual relationships (e.g. Dunbar Moodie, 2001; Shefer & Ruiters, 1998).

> Manhood appears to be rigidly associated with heterosexuality and the ability to be sexual with multiple women.

The impact of HIV/AIDS on heterosex

Few studies specifically focus on this, yet through using such a lens to look at contemporary findings it is evident that more work is needed to explore the impact of HIV/AIDS on heterosex. One would expect that the increased focus on heterosex and the attempt to popularise information on HIV/AIDS and safe sex practices would facilitate a move to more equitable sexual practices. Earlier studies have however found that in spite of increased knowledge and awareness, there has been little evidence of a change in gender power relationships in heterosexual practices (e.g. Perkel *et al.*, 1991). On the other hand, more recent calls for the inclusion of issues of gender relationship and specific skills of negotiation and assertiveness within educational and lifeskills interventions may lead to more concrete changes in this area. More research is required, in particular evaluation studies on interventions that are currently in process.

> Early studies around HIV/AIDS found that in spite of increased knowledge and awareness, there was little evidence of a change in gender power relationships in heterosexual practices.

Some pointers to a more negative impact of HIV/AIDS on heterosex include the now widely publicised 'virgin rape' phenomenon, mentioned earlier. The widespread belief that having sex with a virgin or with a young woman may lead to a cure for HIV/AIDS appears to have particular salience in Southern Africa (LoveLife, 2000). Although there is no proof that such a belief has lead to an increase of child sexual abuse, a number of sensationalised media cases have certainly established such a link in the public eye. Furthermore, it stands to reason, as has been reported elsewhere, that the attempt to escape HIV/AIDS may lead to an increase in sexual practices between older men and younger women or girls. More research is clearly needed in this area to establish whether there is a more definitive relationship between HIV/AIDS and child sexual abuse.

Another area where HIV/AIDS may be impacting negatively on heterosex centres on the *stigmatisation* of HIV/AIDS and other STIs (Ratele & Shefer, 2002; Simbayi *et al.*, 1999). The continued silencing and stigmatisation of STIs in South African communities is believed to perpetuate unsafe sex practices, with men and women afraid to reveal their status and rather risk infecting their partners. Some studies even report a vindictive promiscuity among those who are infected in order to 'punish' others (Simbayi *et al.*, 1999). Also, given reports of violent retribution from male partners when women reveal their HIV status, mentioned above, it is expected that they may resist disclosure and avoid the insistence on safe sex out of fear of male violence.

Critical evaluation of contemporary findings on heterosexuality

The proliferation of research and the educational emphasis on heterosexual relationships is extremely important. It may even be argued that, disastrous as it is, the HIV/AIDS epidemic has opened up a significant space for challenging gender inequality as it manifests in heterosexual relationships, as well as gender roles and inequality more broadly. On the other hand, there are also problems and potential concerns with the way in which heterosexual relationships are currently viewed.

In relation to women, it is arguable that while it is important to highlight women's lack of negotiation in heterosex, the dominant picture of women emerging is that of inevitable victims of male power. Nobody would argue against the significance of acknowledging women's lack of power in heterosex, but it is also important that we do not inadvertently reproduce the dominant stereotype of women's passivity. Contemporary feminist writers have begun challenging the way in which feminist theories on heterosexuality have historically constructed power as the inherent preserve of (all) men, and women as inevitably disempowered victims of male power (Hollway, 1995; Jackson, 1996; Smart, 1996). Smart (1996), for example, speaks of a conflation of the penis with the phallus, in which she maintains all power is seen as male, and all males are seen as having access to power. She argues that both of these are problematic assumptions, given a post-modern understanding of the multiple, contextual and fluid nature of power. In this way, while most feminists distance themselves from biological determinism, she argues that power and gender are inadvertently essentialised, globalised and decontextualised.

What is probably most problematic about the continued emphasis on women's vulnerability, passivity and powerlessness, is that this emphasis serves to silence the many times that women *do* resist male power and *do* challenge men. Furthermore, the stereotyped image of women is ultimately

Contemporary feminist writers have begun challenging the way in which feminist theories on heterosexuality have historically constructed power as the inherent preserve of (all) men, and women as inevitably disempowered victims of male power.

What is probably most problematic about the continued emphasis on women's vulnerability, passivity and powerlessness, is that this emphasis serves to silence the many times that women do resist male power and do challenge men.

reproduced, with no space given to alternative images and discourses of women as strong, assertive and powerful agents. Importantly, as mentioned, the predominant picture of women remains one of asexual victims of male desires, and women's own sexual desires and a positive female sexuality are seldom represented in the literature.

The flipside of women being constructed as inevitable victims is the reproduction of the stereotype of men as inevitably powerful and controlling in relation to women in heterosexual relationships. While some authors have pointed out the salience of a 'male sexual drive' discourse in talk on heterosex, the literature itself appears to reproduce this stereotype. Clearly there is a silence around alternative ways of being men. There is very little literature that highlights men's resistance to traditional masculinity, or speaks of men's vulnerability to women and their difficulties with hegemonic masculinity. In some research, fragments of male vulnerability and the pressure on men to conform to hegemonic masculinity are beginning to emerge (see, for example, Shefer & Ruiters, 1998. Nonetheless, there is still little work that gives a voice to the different ways of being men, and offers alternative and more nuanced versions of maleness in heterosexual relationships.

Finally, it is significant to note that while heterosexuality continues to be the normative sexual practice, idealised and romanticised in the public eye, the literature on heterosexuality overwhelmingly presents a picture of an oppressive, inequitable and often violent institution. While this has been an important step in the struggle towards gender equality, it is problematic that heterosexuality is presented as a homogeneous, unitary and singular experience in the literature. The literature appears to assume only one way of being heterosexual, and presents heterosexuality as an institution that inevitably reflects and reproduces power imbalance. Furthermore, most work seems to accept a construction of heterosex as centred on penetrative sexuality, again reproducing, rather than challenging, the social stereotypes of what heterosex is. As with masculinities, alternative pictures and experiences of heterosexuality and heterosex are silenced and/or marginalised. It could be argued that if we are not presented with alternative images and discourses on heterosex, there is no way in which we can challenge the current oppressive context of heterosexual relationships.

> While heterosexuality continues to be the normative sexual practice, idealised and romanticised in the public eye, the literature on heterosexuality overwhelmingly presents a picture of an oppressive, inequitable and often violent institution.

Conclusion

For the most part, the current picture of heterosex emerging from research in South Africa, as it is globally, is one imbued with much negativity. We have seen how heterosex is interwoven with gender power inequality, in which both men and women are engaged in reproducing the traditional roles of masculinity and femininity. It has become evident that such roles and power inequality between men and women mean that they do not negotiate sexuality very successfully or equitably. Given the dangers associated with heterosex, including unwanted pregnancies, STIs and HIV/AIDS, the opportunity for men and women to negotiate their sexual practices safely is an imperative. Yet, by all accounts there are major barriers, related to the power inequalities of gender, class and age that stand in the way of open and equitable sexual negotiation.

It is important to begin to expose different experiences of heterosex and developing new ways of thinking about relations between women and men.

On the other hand, we need to be cautious about the way in which the current focus on heterosexuality may itself perpetuate this problematic pattern of behaviours. Given this negative picture of heterosex, it is evident we need to find ways to create new identities and ways of relating sexually as men and women. This means that we need to move beyond criticising and highlighting the inequities of heterosex to also exploring the alternatives and resistances to this dominant mode of relationship. Thus, while we need to be cautious of denying the problematic reality of heterosexuality for many women (and men), and the way in which it currently facilitates women's vulnerability to HIV/AIDS, STIs and unwanted pregnancies, we also need to allow for the development of an alternative picture of men, women and heterosex. It is important to begin exposing different experiences of heterosex and developing new ways of thinking and talking about the sexual relationships between men and women. An important way of doing this involves highlighting the marginalised experiences and voices on sexuality, such as those of men who resist taking power and control in heterosex, and of women who resist passivity and have positive experiences of their sexuality with men. We need to begin documenting some of the experiences which contradict our 'normal' image of men and women – such as men who enjoy affection without sex, and examples of women's strength and agency in resisting male power in heterosex. Men need to be encouraged to admit to their vulnerability in sexual relationships, just as women need to begin to assert their sexual desires and own their sexuality. Finally, we need to be able to expose images of a positive heterosexuality as well. In order to challenge the current problematic context of heterosex, we need to be able to imagine a more equitable and mutually enjoyable experience.

Exercises for critical engagement

1 Reflect on your own growing up as a girl or boy. What were the messages you received about your gender and sexual identity?

2 Think about your community and how it responds to a woman who initiates a sexual relationship. How does this differ for a man who does? Why is this so?

3 What are the barriers to safe sex practices in your community? What do you think would facilitate safe sex practices?

4 Do you agree with the statement: 'If women could express their own desires for sexuality, they would be better equipped to say "no" when they don't want sex'?

5 How do you think other forms of inequality impact on gender inequalities in sexual relationships? Think of some examples from your own community.

Endnote

1 Also see the section entitled *The impact of HIV/AIDS on heterosex* for a critical comment on this perception.

Recommended reading

Butler, J. (1990). *Gender Trouble: Feminism and the Subversion of Identity.* New York: Routledge.

Foucault, M. (1981). *The History of Sexuality, Vol. 1: Introduction.* Harmondsworth: Penguin Books.

Richardson, D. (Ed.) (1996). *Theorising Heterosexuality.* Milton Keynes: Open University Press.

Segal, L. (1994). *Straight Sex: Rethinking Heterosexuality and the Politics of Pleasure.* London: Virago.

Shefer, T. (1999) *Discourses of Heterosexual Negotiation and Relation.* Unpublished doctoral thesis, University of the Western Cape, Cape Town.

Wilkinson, S. & C. Kitzinger (Eds.) (1993). *Heterosexuality: A Feminism and Psychology Reader.* London: Sage.

Activity Theory as a framework for psychological research and practice in developing societies

Hilde van Vlaenderen & David Neves

'It is not the consciousness of men that determines their being, but, on the contrary, their social being that determines their consciousness.'

Marx (1859/1977)

'The profound crisis which has afflicted bourgeois psychology during the past few decades has assumed new acute, ugly and repulsive forms, hitherto unknown in the history of psychological science ....'

Vygotsky (1934/1994)

LEARNING OUTCOMES

By the end of this chapter, you should be able to:

▷ Elaborate on traditional psychology's lack of involvement in matters of societal development

▷ Debate critical psychology's role in the developing world, particularly in terms of an emancipatory or socially transformative agenda

▷ Discuss and explain the people-centred paradigm

▷ Explain the basic tenets of Activity Theory as a form of psychological theory and practice

▷ Give examples, in the applied context of the transformative programme described in the chapter, of some of the potential difficulties/problems of the mediation process.

INTRODUCTION

Ideology: complex term concerned how ideas and culture are expressed in (and connected to) societal and political structures. For Marxists the term often denotes the false ideas that obscure the reality of underlying socio-political arrangements.

This book contemplates various interpretations and practical applications of critical psychology in a South African context. The chapters of this entire text catalogue a variety of ways in which critically minded psychologists concern themselves with both the theoretical underpinnings of their discipline and the manner in which these underpinnings are translated into practice. Several themes recur across the chapters, including critical psychology's attention to questions of **ideology**, power dynamics, reflexivity and the ethical dimensions of psychological practice. Critical psychology is generally regarded as an expansive enterprise that seeks to interrogate many of the 'taken-for-granted' assumptions concerning reality, human nature and knowledge, which are simultaneously reflected and perpetuated by psychology. In the words of Nightingale & Neilands (1997, 76) critical psychology is sensitive to the fact that 'the stance we take towards the nature of the world (**ontology**) and our considerations of our knowledge of this world (**epistemology**) have particular implications for the **methodology** we use'.

Epistemology: branch of philosophy concerned with knowledge – it examines the rules for what, and how, we know what we know.

This chapter, and the chapter that follows, are embedded in the tenets described above, although both are predicated on the belief that the development of a critical psychology relevant to the South African context needs to go beyond furnishing critiques of psychology's ideological allegiances, theoretical assumptions and dominant practices. If critical psychology is to serve an emancipatory and socially transformative agenda fully, responsive to the demands of a developing society, it needs also to consider new methods, novel techniques and emergent theories. This and the following chapter are focused on this task. We hope to achieve the task by drawing attention – within this present chapter – to a perspective which is relatively unknown and occasionally misunderstood within psychology, namely Activity Theory. The next chapter explores the emancipatory potential of Participatory Action Research (PAR).

Ontology/ ontological: branch of philosophy concerned with fundamental questions of being and existence. We make ontological assumptions (either explicit or implicit) about what kinds of thing can be said to exist (eg gravity, ghosts, atoms) and the relationship between these entities.

In this chapter we advocate Activity Theory as an analytical framework for socially relevant research and practice and elaborate on how this framework provides opportunities for potentially emancipatory social activity. We further provide an example of how the theory was used towards emancipatory ends in a rural African development context. The structure of the chapter is as follows: we briefly discuss psychology's traditional lack of involvement in matters of societal development within so-called '**Third World**' societies and consider the reasons for this; a people-centred paradigm for development is then proposed, as is the requirement for a socially relevant psychological practice within such paradigm; we then present Activity Theory as a powerful theoretical resource for research and practice. The chapter is concluded with an illustrative case study.

THE IRRELEVANCE OF PSYCHOLOGY

Despite a general recognition that developing countries have been, and still are, grappling with a morass of sociopsychological problems related to poverty, political exclusion and rapid social change, psychology has largely remained outside the orbit of societal development in these settings (Moghaddam, 1990; Sloan, 1990; Nsamenang, 1993). Psychological research has historically been dominated by issues that are of interest to the '**First World**', and very little research has been geared towards explaining the processes of rapid social change characteristic of most developing countries (Van Vlaenderen, 1993). (One should note here that 'First World' is a term that deserves critical attention, in that it may be taken to imply a moral evaluation of the 'First World' as superior to the 'Third World'. The term 'Third World' is likewise problematic in suggesting the inferior status of those parts of the world nominated as such). This problem is to a large extent structurally embedded in the nature of knowledge-production in the West, which predominantly aims to enrich a pool of abstract scientific knowledge rather than to provide knowledge that is directed at improving the everyday lives of underprivileged communities.

However, during the last 35 years, some debate has been generated around the role and relevance of psychology in developing countries (Jahoda, 1973; Korten, 1980; Sinha, 1984; Van Vlaenderen, 1993). In these debates it is acknowledged that in developing societies, where resources are scarce, psychologists are faced with the challenge of providing knowledge and services that contribute to development. However, suggestions as to how psychologists can put their knowledge and skills to the benefit of development have been scant, varied and often contradictory. This is partially due to the fact that they are divided by their adherence to different, and often irreconcilable, development paradigms.

PEOPLE-CENTRED DEVELOPMENT AS A PARADIGM FOR THE CRITICAL PSYCHOLOGIST

In this chapter we argue for a people-centred development approach as a paradigm for critical psychological practice in service of social development. David Korten (1990), who is one of the most prominent theorists of this paradigm, defines the people-centred approach as a development vision in which the well-being of people and the living systems of the planet, which they inhabit, come first. He defines development as 'a process by which the members of society increase their personal and institutional capacities to mobilise and manage resources to produce sustainable and justly distributed improvements in their quality of life, consistent with their own aspirations' (Korten, 1990, 67). Although this perspective sits very uncomfortably with the

'First World': also termed the 'West' or 'North' and designates developed and industrialised countries whose populations enjoy a high standard of living (North America, Europe and regions of Australasia). It is considered derogatory by many, implying that the 'Third World' is inferior to the 'First World'.

'Third World': also termed the 'South' or 'underdeveloped' world, refers to developing countries in Africa, Latin America, the Middle East and Asia. The term sought to distinguish these countries from postwar 'First (ie developed) World' and 'Second (ie communist) World'. It is considered derogatory by many, implying that the 'Third World' is inferior to the 'First World'.

Inclusiveness: inclusion is the notion of the desirability of the participation by all people in a system (such as decision-making, health or education).

anti-humanistic social constructionistic tradition from which much critical psychology is drawn, this definition does emphasise the process aspect of development and draws attention to questions of personal and institutional capacity. It furthermore encompasses the principles of sustainability, social justice, **equality** and **inclusiveness**. It acknowledges, first, that only the affected people themselves can define what they consider to be improvements in the quality of their lives and, secondly, that development demands the balancing of power differentials between all those involved in the process. For the people-centred development approach to succeed, the local beneficiaries of development need to be empowered to participate in their development process. This requires a **capacity-building** process based on their local knowledge and resources. What follows is a discussion of the concepts of **participation** and **empowerment** and how these impact on psychological practice and research for development.

BOX 1   Development and its discontents

Throughout its hundred-year existence the concept of development has been subject to numerous interpretations and controversies. With its roots in 18th- and 19th-century notions of material and economic progress, development was, in the early 20th century, theorised in terms of modernisation theory. This perspective held that underdeveloped societies ought to simply emulate the systems, values and technologies that historically drove economic growth in the West. In this process the benefits of development would hypothetically 'trickle down' to the lowest and most deprived sectors of society – a proposition that is not particularly well supported by evidence. Modernisation theory was rebutted by the Dependency theorists (Mehmet, 1995; Rodney, 1988), whose ideas ascended to prominence during the period of rapid decolonisation following the Second World War. Motivated by varying degrees of anti-colonial sentiment and Marxist sympathies these theorists argued, with some justification, that 'First World' development and industrialisation were built on the exploitation and underdevelopment of the 'Third World'. Dependency theorists therefore view development rather circumspectly and point to the way in which 'development'

tends to converge with prevailing economic and political interests. Certainly development has in many of its manifestations reflected or worse still, perpetuated deep-rooted colonial-era inequalities. This critique of development still has enormous force and is shared by those who decry the rapacious globalisation, growing global inequality and environmental degradation of the present day. It is important to note that various theories of development tend to lead a somewhat quarrelsome political and conceptual coexistence. Parallel with and in some respects broadly complementary to dependency theory is the 'people-centred' (Cohen & Uphoff, 1977; Korten, 1990) theory of development. Within this approach, notions of participation, empowerment and socially transformative action are vaunted as key components of development. The usefulness of the people-centred perspective is that it confers a useful 'micro-perspective' (Graaff, 2001) on development thereby providing an alternative to the overarching economic and political focus that has often characterised development theory. The people-centred perspective therefore provides a way of understanding development in terms of its nuanced local and relational micro-dynamics.

SOWETAN 1 9-98 ZAPIRO

Critics of globalisation argue that the increasing inter-connectedness of various parts of the world takes a form that is fundamentally inequitable, and that favours the 'First World'.

Capacity-building: in the context of development, the term argues that the ability to utilise opportunities and resources needs to be actively engendered within stakeholders.

The need for participation

Axiomatic to the people-centred development paradigm is the notion of **participation**. Analysis of a range of authoritative definitions of participation reveals that the core component of participation is decision making (Cohen & Uphoff, 1977; Oakley & Marsden, 1985; Mathur, 1986; Rajakutty, 1991). People participate to the extent that they are able cognitively, affectively and physically to engage in identifying, planning, establishing, implementing and evaluating national and local development initiatives. As such, participation can be regarded as a decision-making process, occurring at both the individual and the social level, but, in order for people to make the necessary decisions with regard to their own development, they need to be empowered to do so.

Participation: decision-making process, occurring at both the individual and the social level. It suggests that in order for people to make decisions regarding their own development, they need to be empowered.

Building capacity for empowerment

Swift & Levin (1987) believe that empowerment refers simultaneously to the development of a certain state of mind (feeling powerful, competent, worthy of esteem) and to the modification of structural conditions in order to reallocate power (eg modifying the structure of opportunities open to people). In other words, empowerment refers to a subjective experience and objective reality and is both a process and a goal (Yeich & Levine, 1992).

At macro-level and meso-level, empowerment can be defined in terms of group possession of actual social influence, political power and legal rights (Swift & Levin, 1987, 72). It relates to people's power with respect to access and control of the national resources necessary to protect their livelihood (Mathur, 1986; Yeich & Levine, 1992). According to Shaeffer (1994), empowerment

Equality: foundational assumption of democracy which holds that everybody (and everybody's voice) is equal (eg before the law or when voting in elections).

Empowerment: simultaneous development of a certain state of mind and modification of structural conditions in order to reallocate power.

means that communities become more explicit in asserting rights and responsibilities in determining the direction of their own development. This power is formal and legitimate.

At the individual level empowerment conveys a sense of personal control or influence (Zimmerman, 1990). For empowerment to take place, two interrelated changes are required. First, people, individually or in groups, must develop a greater sense of self-worth, self-confidence, self-reliance and recognition of their own skills and resources. This implies less dependence on external inputs and greater pride in the significance and validity of personal and collective knowledge and experience. Second, there must be a change in people's perceptions of their relations with others and with the institutions that define their social world. This change involves both an understanding of how the broad social world has defined their lives and the potential they have actively to influence their own environment. Together these changes position people to determine their own needs and to assume the right to change their world so that it is more responsive to these needs (Vanderslice, 1984).

Dependency theorists argue that 'First World' development and industrialisation has been built on the underdevelopment of the 'Third World'.

The concept of 'empowerment' is useful for critical-minded psychologists because it encourages them to conceptualise their actions in socially transformative (changing society) rather than simply ameliorative (tweaking social relations) terms (Prilleltensky & Nelson, 1997). Traditionally psychology has been oriented towards the former at the expense of the latter.

There is a **dialectical** relationship between empowerment and participation. People need to have the capacity and the power to participate in decision making, at the same time they need opportunities to participate in decision making in order to build capacity and to empower themselves (Prestby, Wandersman, Florin, Rich & Chavis, 1990). Empowerment needs to be facilitated rather than imposed on people. This involves building individual and group capacity in local people to participate fully in decision-making processes that influence their lives.

Rethinking the psychologist's task

Psychologists' role in the people-centred development approach is regarded as one of facilitation and mediation between the various **stakeholders** in the development process, with a particular focus on exposing power differentials between the local people and the other stakeholders in the development process. Psychologists ought to fulfil the role of facilitator in a process in which stakeholders' different knowledge bases are explicated. In particular they need to focus on the explication of local people's knowledge, thereby rebuilding their confidence in the value of their own knowledge and cognitive abilities. Simultaneously, psychologists are well placed (but often neglected) to expose the prejudices of development professionals and agencies about the cognitive and other capacities (or rather, perceptions of the lack of capacities) of local communities. Gilbert (1997) argues that the empowerment of local communities in development endeavours involves the facilitation of joint activities for developer and local community, which allows for the emergence of shared goals, the construction of a shared knowledge base and leads to further joint practice.

ACTIVITY THEORY

To this point we have described people-centred development as a complex ethical and political endeavour. We have furthermore suggested a particular role for psychologists within this task. We now turn to Activity Theory as a conceptual resource for engaging in a critical psychology responsive to the requirements of participatory development and social transformation.

Although Activity Theory is a rich resource for critical work within psychology, it is not easily summarised for a number of reasons. First, it is a multi-method, interdisciplinary endeavour that has only in the last three

---

For empowerment to take place, people must develop a greater sense of self-worth, self-confidence, self-reliance and recognition of their own skills and resources. There must also be a change in people's perceptions of their relations with others and with the institutions that define their social world.

Dialectical: philosophical concept which argues that theory, society or reality advances through an idea or force (a thesis), which elicits a counter-idea, or force (an antithesis), which is then integrated or resolved in a synthesis.

Stakeholder/ stakeholder groups: people or groups who have a responsibility for and/or would benefit from a particular community programme.

Dependency theory: approach to development that suggests that 'First World' development and industrialisation were built on the exploitation and underdevelopment of the 'Third World'. Strongly influenced by Marxist and anti-colonial sentiments, dependency theorists point to the ways in which 'development' tends to converge with prevailing economic and political interests, and point out how certain forms of development reflect or perpetuate deep-rooted colonial-era inequalities.

decades overcome a host of ideological and language barriers and received attention within the dominant European and American psychological orthodoxy. Secondly, and related to its relatively recent critical reception in the West, Activity Theory is still in the process of defining itself. It therefore remains somewhat elusive and subject to multiple and conflicting interpretations. Thirdly, and possibly most significantly, Activity Theory is rooted in philosophical assumptions fundamentally different from those at the foundations of much mainstream psychological practice. The truly radical quality of Activity theoretical insights is not readily apparent unless we understand these assumptions.

Contextualism and materialism

Activity Theory grew out of the Soviet sociohistorical (or cultural-historical) tradition, formulated in the first three decades of the 20th century. Activity Theory therefore has its roots in an intellectual context far closer to the realities of contemporary developing societies than in the affluent, individualistic and developed West. Activity Theory's earliest theorists included Vygotsky, Luria and Leont'ev, thinkers who were heavily influenced by the prevailing philosophical trends of their era and who attempted to formulate a Marxist psychology. At this point it is useful to signpost that Marxism is both a political philosophy and, more generally, a theoretical orientation. It is the latter, rather than the former, which is of interest to us here. Marxism or, more accurately, 'historical materialism' is a form of theoretical critique concerned with questions of ideology and organised around the core idea of **materialism**. This materialism, from which Activity Theory grew, denies that consciousness or mental or psychic states can be viewed as ontologically distinct from the material conditions and forces in society; instead, these material conditions serve to determine social conditions and, ultimately, individual psychological functioning. Hence a profound contextualism and materialism reside at the heart of Activity Theory.

'Object-orientated action'

As the term itself suggests, Activity theorists embrace activity as being at the explanatory core of human behaviour and subjectivity. For instance, Lev Vygotsky (1978, 40) elaborated on how psychology's focus ought to be on 'object-orientated action mediated by cultural tools and signs', rather than individually located entities such as consciousness. The consequences of understanding and analysing psychological functioning and social relations in this way are as revolutionary and **methodologically** innovative today as they were in Russia almost a hundred years ago. This approach allowed Activity theorists to steer a middle course between a mechanistic, behaviouristic (or, in the Russian tradition, reflexological) psychology, on the one hand, and the

Methodology/ methodological: refers to the methods and techniques used to answer a particular research question and generate valid knowledge.

introspective-mentalistic continental tradition, on the other (Kozulin, 1986). These traditions represent two halves of the same duality, two sides of the same coin, because the first seeks to study behaviour without mind, while the second examines mind without behaviour. Activity Theory serves to transcend the dichotomy between the individual subject and the objective social conditions. It provides a theoretical antidote to the well-worn (and often decidedly unhelpful) opposition between the individual and society, or subject and object. Activity Theory's enduring contribution to critical psychology, therefore, is that it confers a new meta-psychology – a new basis for psychological theorising.

Praxis

Distinct **methodological** implications flow from Activity Theory: human activity is not analysed in terms of context-free 'scientific' principles; instead it is to be understood in terms of **praxis** and the broader, contextually located activity. Activity theorists view theory and method as inextricably intertwined. Kozulin notes that: 'The term **methodology** has a somewhat different meaning in Russian, referring to meta-theoretical or philosophical study of the method used in a particular science' (1986, 264–265). Activity Theory can helpfully be described in terms of three themes, all of which are clearly evident in the work of Vygotsky. The first is the notion of genetic or historical analysis. The second is the proposition that human psychological functioning and subjectivity can be understood only if we consider its roots in the interaction of social life. The third idea is that to understand the interactions within social life we need to consider the mediating functions of tools and signs (Wertsch, 1990). These themes are amplified in what follows.

Praxis:
translation or implementation of ideas and theories into practice.

Materialism:
in everyday use, it usually means someone has an exaggerated concern with acquiring material goods; but materialism also has alternative socio-logical and philosophical meanings. It is the idea that social struc-tures and human relations are to a large extent deter-mined by our interactions with, and in, the material and economic world.

BOX 2   Is mediated activity discourse by another name?

If Activity Theory's emphasis on mediated activity creates an analytic unit that sounds suspiciously similar to notions of discourse (which are well represented within the critical psychology tradition) you might justifiably ask: Isn't mediated activity simply discourse by another name? This is a complex issue, but we maintain the short answer to this question is 'No.' Granted, Activity Theory and discursively oriented approaches share several basic ideas such as the notion that we are embedded in a world of sign systems and that these come to structure our consciousness, subjectivity and social relations. Furthermore, both Activity

theoretical and discursive approaches have affinities for the kind of socially transformative and emancipatory work that is central to a critical psychology – even though they are rooted in very different intellectual traditions (Soviet historical materialism and Continental post-structuralism, respectively) and epistemo-logical stances (critical realism, on the one hand, and social constructionism, on the other). We maintain that an activity theoretical orientation serves to counter several weak-nesses within a discursive approach. For instance, while many of the proponents of discursively oriented approaches are at pains to

---

BOX 2 **Is mediated activity discourse by another name?** *(continued)*

argue that the abstract discursive practices they explicate need to be connected to institutions and material relations of power (Burman, Kottler, Levett & Parker, 1997; Painter & Theron, 2001; Parker & Burman, 1993) this is done with varying degrees of success. Therefore the criticism that discursive approaches both tend to **reify** language and are inattentive to questions of materiality remains difficult to escape. Conversely, Activity theoretical approaches can be criticised for their narrow instrumentality and, sometimes, naïve conceptualisation of language. It is hence unhelpful to suggest that any one **methodology** is inherently and inviolably 'critical', because criticality resides not in particular methods but rather in the epistemic assumptions in which they are grounded and the ends to which they are used. No method makes one 'more critical than thou'. Instead, Activity Theory introduces methodological diversity into critical psychology, which has historically been forged from discourse analysis and various standpoint theories. This may be Activity Theory's most substantial contribution to a critical psychology.

Reify/reification: philosophical error that occurs when we treat something abstract and hypothetical as though it were real and concrete.

A South African critical psychology needs to go beyond critiquing psychology's ideological allegiances, theoretical assumptions and dominant practices. If it is to serve fully an emancipatory and socially transformative agenda, responsive to the demands of a developing society, it must consider new methods, novel techniques and emergent theories.

The Vygotskian approach

Activity is historically located

The first theme flows from Activity Theory's insistence on genetic or historical analysis. (It is important to note here that we do not mean genetics in the contemporary biological usage, instead this term is closer to the Latin root *genus*, which means 'origins' or 'birth'.) This Marxist notion of historicity refers to the belief that 'the essence of any phenomenon can be captured only through studying its origin and development' (Blanck, 1990, 46). We cannot understand practice unless we understand the history of practice. This is in contrast to orthodox psychology, which tends to be ahistorical and relatively inattentive to the history of its practice (Harris, 1997; Hayes, 1989). Attending to questions of power therefore entails understanding the historical trajectory of the exercise of power. For instance, we cannot engage with a community if we do not have some appreciation of the historical forces that have shaped it. Certainly the notion of assuming a historically informed perspective is well articulated in critical psychology, for example, various kinds of genealogical analysis often conducted under the rubric of discourse analysis.

Activity requires internalisation of the social

The second theme contained within Vygotsky's work concerns the internalisation of the social world and human relations. Vygotsky describes a process whereby society is 'taken in' or internalised in the individual. Vygotsky postulated (1978, 57) '[a]ll the higher psychological functions originate as actual relations between human individuals'. This occurs in the critical space between the sociocultural and individual realms – a gap in which development occurs and subjectivity is forged. However, internalisation is not simply the transferral of external activity into a pre-existing internal plane of consciousness. It is instead the very process by which the inner mental plane is formed (Leont'ev, 1978). In this respect there are broad conceptual affinities between Activity theoretical and other varieties of critical psychology theorising which attempt to 'change the subject' (Henriques, Hollway, Urwin, Venn & Walkerdine; 1984) or dethrone the sovereign individual consciousness, which historically resides at the centre of the discipline. Much critical psychology is therefore suspicious of claims about human beings having an inner realm, a pristine interiority, which is forged somehow independently of the larger social context.

Activity uses various mediational means

The question 'How exactly does what is outside come to be inside the individual?' brings us to the third theme delineated in Vygotsky's work. He contends that what fundamentally determines the sociogenesis of the higher psychological functions is the use of historically evolved **semiotic** systems (sign systems). Wertsch (1995, 89) defines these **mediational** means as 'the socially based entities or resources that people employ when acting in order to achieve some goal'. He further argues that mediational means embody a tension between the potential they have to shape action in accordance with cultural convention, on the one hand, and the unique use of these cultural means with all the accompanying unpredictability and creativity, on the other. Mediational means include (but are not limited to) various linguistic and numerical systems, maps, technical drawings and mnemonic techniques.

There is a mounting awareness of this general notion of mediation within critical psychology-oriented work. Critically minded psychologists recognise and devote much attention to the constitutive effects of language and discourse. However, in contrast to language-oriented approaches, Activity Theory's unit of analysis remains mediated action rather than language itself. In what follows we consider now how activity can be used as an analytical tool.

From activity to activity system

Engeström (1993) expounds on the notion of socioculturally mediated action, introduced by the early Activity theorists, through his introduction of the notion of **activity system**. The utility of Engeström's approach is in providing an analytical framework that links the intrapsychological plane of mental functioning to the broader cultural, historical and institutional matrix, simultaneously integrating and distinguishing the two elements. Engeström's activity system schema consists of several components including a subject, an object, a community, tools, rules and a division of tasks and power. Figure 9.1 presents Engeström's notion of a human activity system.

Semiotic(s): discipline of the study of signs and sign systems. The concept of signs is here understood expansively and can include diverse sign systems such as language, road traffic signs, mathematical algebra, fashion styles or even gestures.

Mediation/ mediated: in the Activity Theory tradition mediation refers to the processes and artefacts by which the external world is taken or 'internalised' within the human being.

Activity system: integrated account of the actions, subjects (participants) and mediational means (both material and non-material artefacts) directed towards a goal. The activity system consists of several components, including subject, object, community, tools, rules and a division of tasks and power.

Figure 9.1
**Human activity
system (adapted
from Engeström
1987, 8)**

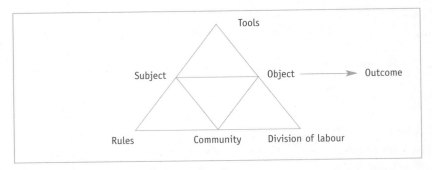

Division of labour:
a concept from
Marx, it emphasises
the notion that in
any stable organi-
sation individuals,
or groups of indivi-
duals, engage in
different yet
integrated tasks.

The subject of an activity is an individual or a group whose viewpoint is used in analysing the activity. The object refers to the 'problem space' at which the activity is directed and which is transformed into outcomes with the help of physical and symbolic tools. The community comprises the multiple individuals and/or subgroups which share the same object of the activity and the **division of labour** relates to both the division of tasks and power between the members of that community. The rules refer to the explicit and implicit regulations, norms, values and conventions that constrain (and enable) actions and interactions within the activity system. The activity system provides an integrated account of the actions, subjects (participants in the system) and mediational means (embracing both material and non-material artefacts) directed towards a goal.

BOX 3   Which activity system are you in?

Engeström's notion of the activity system provides what might be thought of as a kind of analytic scalpel for investigating the structure of complex social practices. This approach draws on Activity Theory and has been used to understand practice in a range of settings including legal (Engeström, Brown, Christopher & Gregory, 1997), industrial (Engeström, 1999), health (Engeström, 1993) and educational (Thomen, 2002) contexts. Using the activity system approach means that collective human activity is not understood as the sum of individual actions; it is instead connected to collective practices, communities and institutions. Have you ever found yourself working within a group or institution and suddenly doubting whether the people around you understand the group or institution's objectives in the same way as you? Or perhaps you've wondered whether you understand the objectives they appear to be

working towards? This is partially because, as Engeström (1999) explains, 'in complex activities with fragmented division of labor, the participants' themselves have great difficulty in constructing a connection between the goals of their individual actions and the object and motive of collective activity' (173). Examining a community development project in the rural Eastern Cape, Neves (2002) found that the object or intended outcome of the development intervention was understood and acted towards in highly disparate ways by the three main sets of stakeholders involved. In fact, viewed in terms of the commonality of their activity, it was quite questionable whether they were participating in the same activity at all! These insights are helpful because an important part of critically reflecting on practice entails understanding how understanding is not always shared.

Learning by expanding: Something new from something old

Engeström argues that activity systems do not exist in isolation but should be seen as historically embedded. He further argues that activity systems are not stable and harmonious but evolve historically through the resolution of their inner contradictions and tensions. These tensions take specific forms, located in each component of the activity (rules, tools etc). For instance, in a community development project, tension may be experienced between the rules and values of a local community (ie a reliance on local practical knowledge) and the tools used by the development agency (training methodologies based on formalised disembedded knowledge).

Moreover, each activity system is connected to other activity systems through all its components and, according to Engeström, secondary contradictions arise from the injection of new elements into any one of the components of the activity system, which in turn requires modification of the other components. For instance, the incorporation of new development strategies (ie a gender analysis) may create tensions in the various components of the system, including division of labour (change in gender balance in local community structures). Engeström (1993) argues that those contradictions are the driving forces in a process of what he terms 'learning by expansion'. Expansive learning refers to learning something new, which is generated from the old (Engeström, 1987). It is a process of constructing a new object for an activity involving the participants in the system. The object construction begins with analysing the existing situation and the contradictions inherent in it. After the analysis, instruments are jointly modelled for transforming the activity. These new models are applied to the activity at hand and gradually new, more developed and sustainable activity will occur on the basis of the old (Kontinen, 1999).

DEVELOPMENT INTERVENTIONS AS ACTIVITY SYSTEMS AND THE ROLE OF THE PSYCHOLOGIST IN 'LEARNING BY EXPANDING'

Development interventions can be conceptualised as processes in which different stakeholders interact in a common activity which has a particular object, uses particular tools and strategies, adheres to certain rules, and in which each of the stakeholders assumes specific roles and tasks. Development programmes, however, typically involve stakeholders from very different socio-cultural backgrounds. As a result, their perceptions of the object of the development programme (the activity) in which they are initiated, the role they apportion to the stakeholders and the values they bring to the programme, may be divergent and conflicting. Often, the interpretation of the most powerful stakeholder (ie the donor or the development organisation) becomes dominant, thereby suppressing the perspectives and experiences of the other stakeholders (2001). This may create obstacles to the participation of all stakeholders in the programme and ultimately the transformational potential of development efforts.

Congruent with the notion of empowerment, argued for earlier in this chapter, the transformation of the activity system, through the explication, analysis and negotiation of the contradictions in the activity system needs to be particularly sensitive to the needs and demands of the least powerful stakeholders (often the local communities). It is argued that the contribution of the critical psychologist in the realm of development ought to be framed in terms of a facilitation of this transformation process. In the next section a case study is presented that illustrates the facilitation of a process of learning by expanding in an African development context.

CASE STUDY: FACILITATING DEVELOPMENT

The case study refers to a conservation training programme in Africa (Van Vlaenderen, 2001) which was funded by two international donor organisations involved in conservation funding and run by a training consortium, composed of representatives of a US-American non-profit organisation (including a resident expatriate) and a local African organisation. The stated goal of the programme was to build research capacity in the service of conservation in the African country. The programme involved the establishment of a network of trained fieldworkers with the capacity to assist conservation organisations with the collection of botanical data. Nine young, local people (seven men and two women) from rural areas were recruited by the training consortium in collaboration with project managers of five local conservation organisations, each of which employed one or more of the trainees. The programme involved attendance at six 14-day workshops which extended over an 18-month period. These included theoretical sessions as well as practical exercises. In the periods between the workshops the trainees worked in their local conservation organisations and put into practice their newly acquired knowledge and skills. During those periods the trainees were visited at their sites by the training staff to provide further individual guidance.

The facilitation process

The first author of this chapter was engaged by the programme as an evaluator, with the specific brief of monitoring the training process with the aim of optimising the quality and sustainability of the programme. What follows is an account of the process that took place with the stakeholders of the programme.

Explicating the activity system: The stakeholder identification and goal-setting procedure

At the start of the programme, all the people involved in it came together in an initial workshop in which participants were required to identify themselves in different stakeholder groups. Stakeholder groups were defined as 'groups who have a responsibility for and/or would benefit from the programme'. Four main stakeholder groups were identified: The local African organisation, the US-American non-profit organisation, the local trainees and the conservation organisations employing the trainees. Each group subsequently expressed its perceptions and expectations of the programme. There were overlaps in stakeholder expectations as well as differences. The trainees and the African organisation emphasised the importance of personal opportunities, enhancement of personal status and quality of life. The US-American funding organisation and the conservation organisations emphasised organisational gain. All stakeholders agreed that the programme was about botanical training and enhancement of conservation efforts in the African country. This process of identifying goals and expectations made explicit to all participants that the programme consisted of a joint activity with different actors (subjects), with potentially different perceptions of the course (object). It is argued that in order to improve a programme through the negotiation of its inner contradictions, there needs, first, to be an explicit acknowledgement of possible internal differences and, secondly, an acceptance by all stakeholders that these differences are valuable and worthy of affirmation.

After the stakeholder analysis, the notion of an ongoing, joint goal-setting and reflection process was introduced. It was explained that a series of workshops would be held where stakeholders would come together to communicate their needs, goals, proposed strategies (tools) and expectations of themselves and one another (division of labour). This emphasised the importance and responsibilities of all stakeholders in the programme.

Joint planning and reflection workshops – learning by expanding

In subsequent workshops, which took place at regular intervals and which were facilitated by the evaluator, the stakeholders reflected on their activities up to date and the activities of the others, based on the criteria they had set for themselves and the expectations of the others. Issues discussed related to practical (tools) as well as more ideological (rules, division of labour) and strategic (tools, division of labour) concerns. The stakeholders occasionally made use of stories, songs, simulation games and short theatrical pieces to present their problems and achievements. Reflection was followed by suggestions for improvement and ultimately each stakeholder group set goals for the next period and reidentified their responsibilities and their expectations of the other stakeholders.

In between the workshops, the evaluator conducted interviews and group discussions with the different stakeholders in their specific activity settings. Analysis of this data was compiled in reports and distributed to all stakeholders. These reports provided stakeholders with additional knowledge about each other and enabled them to gain deeper insight into the dynamics and contradictions of the programme. This facilitation process comprised several functions with respect to a process of learning by expanding. The evaluator mediated the activity in the sense that she created and manipulated a space for stakeholders to analyse and discuss viewpoints and emerging contradictions. The evaluator was particularly instrumental in creating a space for the least powerful in the programme (the trainees) to have their voice heard. The use of songs and other cultural tools enabled the different stakeholders to embed the programme activities within their particular sociocultural value systems and facilitated the explication of value differences. The regular occurrence of the evaluation and goal-setting workshops enabled a gradual process of change in the programme activities as well as in the relationships between the stakeholders and in the stakeholders themselves. This strengthened the notion of progress in a joint activity.

Emergence of inner contradictions in the programme

Throughout the duration of the programme, as a result of the facilitation, inner contradictions in the activity system were revealed. It is not within the scope of this chapter to discuss all of those; however, some examples are presented below.

Differences in research conventions and practice: Contradictions in tools and rules

A contradiction between the US-American non-profit organisation and the local conservation organisations with respect to their expectations of the programme and their underlying value system was encapsulated in the trainees' role confusion. The US-American funding organisation trained the trainees to use specific research methods and conventions which are in compliance with international scientific standards and research protocols. These were, however, regarded by the conservation organisations as 'non user friendly'. The conservation organisations' commitment to their specific conservation projects and their limited previous exposure to the methods and techniques advocated in the training programme placed the responsibility for transforming the knowledge of the course into a directly accessible tool for conservation strategies on the trainee. This led to confusion about the role, accountability and allegiances of the trainees as well as in their understanding of the relation between what they were taught in the programme and their conservation work.

Status and power: Contradictions in division of labour

The trainees were ambivalent about their status in the programme. On the one hand they saw themselves as pivotal to the programme for various reasons. First, they provided the link between the conservation organisations (and the larger local conservation community) and the US-American funding organisation (and the international community). Secondly, the US-American funding organisation instilled a sense of pride in them as important contributors to conservation in their country. Third, the conservation organisations implicitly relied on them to make their acquired knowledge accessible to conservation. However, at the same time they were the least powerful actors in the programme. Strict authority lines limited their impact on the activities in their organisations. Their accountability to and dependence on the training organisation and their employing organisation, for all their needs (eg financial, educational), made their involvement in the course predominantly one of target group rather than contributors.

Scientific and local knowledge: Contradictions in object and rules/values

There were tensions between the different types of knowledge relied upon in the programme. On the one hand, by becoming part of the programme, the trainees and the conservation organisations demonstrated their aspiration to embrace the formal **disembedded knowledge** of botanical and conservation sciences. At the same time they regarded the local knowledge of rural people and local experts appropriate and even primary to their work. The local knowledge provided them with grounding in their daily activities.

Disembedded knowledge: knowledge that is abstract and not exclusively related to a specific context. Generally, formal academic and scientific knowledge is of this kind.

Networking: Contradictions in division of labour and object

Staff of the US-American organisation and the African organisation experienced role confusion. Although all stakeholders regarded the African organisation as the appropriate agent to do the networking between all the local stakeholders in the programme, it was the US-American organisation, which did in fact most of the networking. Several factors may have contributed to this. First, the staff of the African organisation expected to have their capacity built rather than to take initiatives in the running of the programme. Secondly, strict authority lines at the African organisation made initiative amongst its staff difficult.

Summative reflection: Has the activity expanded?

The facilitation process culminated in a final workshop, in which the achievements of the programme, the contributions of the different stakeholders and the fulfilment of expectations was reviewed as well as future plans discussed. Analysis of the summative reflection revealed that the process of acknowledging and negotiating the contradictions (some of which are described above) had led to some degree of transformation.

An important change pertains to the resolution of the contradictions in the status of the trainees. Towards the end of the programme, as a result of continuous renegotiation of goals and roles, the trainees initiated plans to found an independent society of botanical conservation workers. The aim of the society was to provide the trainees with an anchor for their ideas and needs, outside their employment and beyond the immediate training programme. Although they would still need financial and other support from the training consortium to start their society, they changed the programme by expanding its tools (a society of trainees) and its division of tasks and power (an independent society). The trainees changed from being almost exclusively recipients to contributors in shaping the scope and direction of the programme. They developed a greater confidence in their own abilities and knowledge, which empowered them to contribute to the future course of the programme.

The mediation of the contradictions in the programme between the value apportioned to scientific versus local knowledge led to a workshop in which the stakeholders, as well as members of the wider conservation community discussed those contradictions. It was resolved that the African organisation would co-ordinate the compilation of a database on ethno-botanical information, which would integrate local and scientific botanical knowledge in one centre. Secondly, ideas were developed for conservation projects which outlined how the scientific data and local knowledge collection could be combined in function of conservation. As a result of the mediation, the division of labour had been changed in that the conservation organisations started to contribute more significantly to the object of the programme. It also enabled a redefinition of the values and rules (local versus scientific knowledge) underlying the programme.

A third impact of the facilitation process was the change in perception of all stakeholders with respect to the programme. The process had enabled them to conceive of the programme as an activity system, and to appreciate their role in its existence and change.

Having highlighted the positive changes created by the evaluation process towards transformation in the programme, it is important to point out some of the problems and threats to such a mediation process. It needs to be emphasised that these positive changes were embryonic in nature and as such fragile. Consolidation of the changes is dependent on the nature of the follow-up programme. The time available to the evaluator, to develop the notion of 'joint activity' with the stakeholders; and subsequently, to facilitate a process of analysing and negotiating the inner contradiction in the activity, was too short to ensure lasting transformation. A question can also be posed as to how long a mediation process should be continued before the stakeholders manage their own transformative process?

A second potential barrier to successful mediation is the cost of such a process. The organisation of joint meetings and workshops, as well as site visits in the context of a developing country, even though of vital importance to the success of the approach, are very costly. Additionally, to facilitate a programme successfully, the evaluator needs to remain close to the programme throughout its life span, which is time-consuming and costly.

CONCLUSION

In this chapter we have sought to show the potential contribution of an Activity theoretical perspective to conceptualising, implementing and researching social interventions in developing societies. We hope that we have also conveyed a sense of our excitement at this particular theoretical and methodological orientation, the revolutionary potential of which has only relatively recently been recognised. In this way we hope we have given you a sense of how a critically oriented psychology can contribute to the imperatives of societal transformation and development that continue to be keenly felt within contemporary South Africa.

Critical thinking tasks

1. Either individually or in a group, devise a historical time-line of development. On a large landscape sheet of paper draw a horizontal time-line, extending from the 19th century to the present, calibrate it in five- or ten-year increments. Either individually or in your group, brainstorm important historical events (such as wars, technological advances and political developments) and plot these on your time-line. Then, using the ideas discussed in Box 1 and whichever other sources you have access to, list the emergence of particular schools of development.

2. Using the printed mass media as a source, construct a spider map of globalisation. Carefully examine the daily and weekly newspapers (including the finance sections!) for a period of at least a week, noting all references to globalisation. (You might also want to examine weekly news magazines.) Write the world '**globalisation**' in the centre of a large sheet of paper and enumerate all the concepts, issues, controversies and implications of globalisation. Sketch the links between these various elements to fill in your spider diagram.

3. Describe an activity system of which you are, or have been, a part. (Think of an institution-directed or goal-directed activity that you are associated with.) Using the figure in the text, 'map' the activity system's various components. Where and what are the contradictions (carefully consider the rules, tools and object)?

Globalisation: increasing interconnectedness of various parts of the world through communication technologies and trade. Globalisation has seen an increasing tendency for ideas, cultural products, material goods and, perhaps most importantly, capital to disregard national boundaries. It occurs to both the benefit and the detriment of local communities.

Recommended readings

Coetzee, J.K., Graaff, J., Hendricks, F., & Wood, G. (2001). *Development: Theory, policy and practice.* Cape Town: Oxford University Press.
A good overview of development with a strong South African flavour.
Kozulin, A. (1986). 'The concept of Activity in Soviet psychology.' *American Psychologist*, 41(3): 264–274.
A seminal article which gives an overview of Activity Theory's origins and core concepts and contextualises them within the Soviet tradition.
Rahnema, M. & Bawtree, V. (1997). *The post-development reader.* Cape Town: David Philip.
A diverse and engaging compilation of readings on development, this work serves as a good introduction to several contemporary debates and controversies.
Vygotsky, L.S. (1978). *Mind in society.* Cambridge, MA: Harvard University Press.
A readable introduction to Vygotsky's thinking.

In terms of journals, *Mind, Culture and Activity* is probably the flagship journal for Activity Theory and cultural-historical psychology. Peruse your library for any of the various development journals in print.

Acknowledgement

We should like to thank The MacArthur Foundation for funding the evaluation and the US-American and African organisations as well as the trainees for their cooperation.

10

Participatory Action Research and local knowledge in community contexts

Hilde van Vlaenderen & David Neves

'For apart from inquiry, apart from praxis, individuals cannot be truly human. Knowledge emerges only through invention and re-invention, through the restless, impatient, continuing, hopeful inquiry human beings pursue in the world, with the world, and with each other.'

Freire (1972)

LEARNING OUTCOMES

By the end of this chapter, you should be able to:

▷ Describe the various paradigms which historically have shaped social development

▷ Discuss the role of the psychologist in these various development paradigms

▷ Explain the concept and importance of local knowledge

▷ Elaborate on the value and key theoretical precepts of Participatory Action Research

▷ Reflect critically on some of the tensions inherent in conducting psychologically based interventions within community settings.

**Ideological/
ideology:**
ideology is a
complex concept,
but is generally
concerned with the
manner in which
ideas and culture
are expressed in
(and ultimately
connected to)
societal and
political structures.
In the Marxist
tradition the term
'ideology' often
denotes the false
ideas that obscure
the reality of
underlying
sociopolitical
arrangements.

**Participatory
Action Research
(PAR):**
three-pronged
process involving
social investigation
with the full and
active participation
of the local commu-
nity; an *educational
process* of mobilisa-
tion for develop-
ment, and *a means
of taking action for
development*. It
aims at the develop-
ment of a critical
consciousness of the
people designated
as the recipients of
development, at
improving their life
conditions, and at
transforming their
social structure.

INTRODUCTION

In the preceding chapter we suggested that the development of a critical psychology, relevant to the demands of the South African context, requires more than the **ideological** critique that has often marked the critical endeavour. An emancipatory critical psychology requires the development of new conceptual resources and forms of action. Accordingly, Activity Theory was discussed as a conceptual framework for a socially transformative psychology. Insights from Activity Theory were applied to understanding societal development in terms of the *people-centred paradigm* and its atten-dant concepts of *participation*, *empowerment* and *capacity-building*.

Motivated by the same ethos and understanding of critical psychology, the present chapter considers other theoretical resources for conducting research in order to support socially transformative interventions; or perhaps, more accurately, it suggests that *research can be conceptualised as a form of intervention* by means of a **Participatory Action Research** (PAR) approach. This chapter furthermore indicates the importance of local knowl-edge in relation to PAR.

The structure of the chapter is as follows. First, the manner in which psychologists have traditionally responded to the demands of (societal) devel-opment is described and located relative to the three dominant paradigms that have historically informed development. PAR is then introduced as an approach congruent with a people-centred approach, which affirms local knowledge. PAR is finally discussed and illustrated by means of a case example.

PSYCHOLOGY AND DEVELOPMENT

This section considers three perspectives on the contribution of psychological knowledge to the imperatives of societal development. It is suggested that perspectives on the role psychology can play in development (and its resultant rapid social change) vary considerably between psychologists of different persuasions (Van Vlaenderen, 1993).

Development as modernisation

The main paradigm for psychological practice in developing countries has traditionally been derived from modernisation theory. **Modernisation theory**, as introduced in the previous chapter, holds that underdevelopment of 'Third World' societies is due to the absence of certain conditions, which are present in technologically advanced Western societies (Kindervatter, 1979). Social development is here defined as a process of rapid economic growth attained through industrialisation and the adoption of modern scientific agricultural techniques (Sinha, 1983). Oakly & Marsden, proponents of this approach, write that

[d]evelopment strategies based on this traditional modernisation approach emphasise centralised planning and control over the distribution of resources. The focus is on providing infrastructure and institutions to facilitate the progression towards a Western model and to tackle obstacles on the way (1985, 5).

The writings of Durganand Sinha (1973, 1984) and Harry Triandis (1972, 1984) provide us with some of the earliest examples of psychological practice conceptualised in terms of a modernisation approach. The change towards a Western model is valued because, it is argued, people in developing countries are impatient to catch up with the developed world, often within the span of a single generation (Sinha, 1984). This involves a process of rapid change in traditional social institutions and relations, which can have both desirable and undesirable consequences. Sinha (1984) argues that this rapid change engenders instability and can lead to many sociopsychological problems. Changing aspirations and increasing discrepancy between aspiration and achievement lead to dissatisfaction, a higher incidence of **psychosomatic** ailments, and challenges to personal identity. Triandis (1972) enumerates commonly observed ill-effects of rapid socioeconomic development, such as an increasing incidence of suicide, violence, social instability, substance abuse, crime and delinquency, as well as a greater incidence of psychosomatic ailments and mental health problems. Accordingly, Sinha (1983) argues that the psychologist's task in national development is threefold: to analyse the factors conducive to desirable changes ('facilitators'); to analyse the factors that act as impediments to change ('inhibitors'), and to determine ways of mitigating the psychological dislocations occasioned by rapid development.

A large body of psychological research in the context of development focuses (often rather uncritically) on impediments to change. Modernisation psychologists tend to look at how local attitudes and values differ from those required in the desired 'modern' society. Surveys on the presence or absence of the requisite 'modern' attitudes amongst people in developing countries represent a major avenue of psychology research into development. These studies are then used as a basis for educational programmes intended to prepare people for the 'take off' stage towards modernisation (Kagitcibasi, 1973; Sinha, 1986; Williamson, 1982).

Psychological practice within a modernisation approach has a number of shortcomings, most notably that it provides little space for the expression or application of indigenous values, knowledge and skills of developing communities. This is particularly the case when such values deviate from the fixed goal of modernisation. It therefore creates limited opportunity for dialogue between the psychologist and the local people; as a result, interventions may lead to further alienation and social dislocation among local communities.

In its undertaking to assist people to attain a Western lifestyle the modernisation approach is further based on an assumption of the superiority of

Modernisation theory: perspective that holds that underdeveloped societies ought to emulate the systems, values and technologies which drove economic growth in the West. Social development is defined as a process of rapid economic growth attained through industrialisation and the adoption of modern scientific agricultural techniques.

Participation: expansive, yet often poorly theorised concept, participation embodies the idea that people ought to take part inclusively in the planning and implementing of interventions that impact on their lives.

Psychosomatic: psychological ailments or disorders which have psychic (mental) and somatic (bodily) components; these two aspects interact with and influence each other.

Sinha (1983) argues that the psychologist's task in national development is threefold: to analyse the factors conducive to desirable changes ('facilitators'); to analyse the factors that act as impediments to change ('inhibitors'), and to determine ways of mitigating the psychological dislocations occasioned by rapid development.

Western values. It often demands of the psychologist an alliance with the government of the developing country or a foreign development agency. Therefore, at its core, people are considered passive recipients of an imposed development process that strives to adjust people to an imposed change. The psychologist's task is hence *remedial* rather than *proactive*, and focused on the individual rather than on communities or groups.

Dependency theories

Since the 1960s development programmes worldwide have been evaluated and frequently found to be ineffectual. Often they have neither reduced poverty nor addressed underdevelopment and large numbers of people in developing countries continue to live in absolute poverty and deprivation (Oakley & Marsden, 1985; Korten, 1990; World Bank, 1992).

The failure of development programmes based on the modernisation approach has inspired the emergence of alternative development paradigms such as **dependency theory**. The top-down process of the modernisation approach and its presumption that people in developing countries are unable to meet their own needs is criticised by dependency theorists. Historical analysis of the 'Third World' conducted by the dependency theorists during the 1970s asserted a causal relationship between the development of some coun-

Dependency theory: approach to development which suggests that **'First World'** development and industrialisation were built on the exploitation and underdevelopment of the **'Third World'**. Strongly influenced by Marxist and anti-colonial sentiments, dependency theorists point to the ways in which 'development' tends to converge with prevailing economic and political interests and call attention to how certain forms of development reflect or perpetuate deep-rooted colonial-era inequalities.

tries and the parallel 'underdevelopment' of others. Underdevelopment was attributed to the unequal power relationship between technologically advanced and 'Third World' countries (Frank, 1975; Harrison, 1982; Hoogvelt, 1976) and is a direct result of the way in which the West relies heavily on large-scale exploitation of the 'Third World'. The structural inequalities of international trade and investment benefit the technologically advanced countries of the 'First World' and create a weak bargaining position for 'Third World' societies, thereby leading to dependency (Frank, 1975; Hoogvelt, 1976).

The 'total trauma' that results from dependency is described by Goulet as follows:

> The trauma is total because the desire mechanisms of an entire population are altered before it possesses control over the social institutions which would enable it to gain effective use of resources needed to meet these new desires. Those who do not possess the resources or enjoy access to them understandably assist the development efforts of others only to the degree that such an activity enhances their own objectives. Since they are technologically and economically more powerful, transfers of resources, information and personnel consolidate the dominant position of the strong and further accentuate the dependency of the weak (quoted in Kindervatter, 1979, 29).

Concurrent with this alternative analysis of development, the concept of development was revisited and enlarged. Dependency theorists argue that different

Historical analysis of the 'Third World' conducted by the dependency theorists during the 1970s asserted a causal relationship between the development of some countries and the parallel 'underdevelopment' of others. Under-development was attributed to the unequal power relationship between technologically advanced and 'Third World' countries and is a direct result of the way in which the West relies heavily on large-scale exploitation of the 'Third World'.

societies pursue different goals, depending on their own values (Hoogvelt, 1976). Hence development is not a fixed cluster of benefits given to people in need, but rather a process by which a society acquires a greater control over its own destiny (Goulet, cited in Kindervatter 1979). In this context development involves overcoming the relationship of dependency with technologically advanced countries.

Limited psychological work has been inspired by the dependency theory. Its implicit concern with politics and political empowerment does not generally synchronise with psychology's traditional orientation. Psychologists' training

People-centred approach: approach to development which emphasises the *process* aspect of development and draws attention to questions of personal and institutional capacity. It confirms that only the affected people themselves can define what they consider to be improvements in the quality of their lives.

Sustainability: argues that development needs to endure and occur without despoiling the physical environment or consuming overly large amounts of resources.

David Korten (1990) describes social development as 'a process by which the members of society increase their personal and institutional capacities to mobilise and manage resources to produce sustainable and justly distributed improvements in their quality of life, consistent with their own aspirations' (67).

prepares them to focus on the individual instead of the group and therapeutic concerns rather than social struggle. The few psychologists who have worked within the dependency theory paradigm have used their skills to assist people in political activism towards gaining more political and economical power. These activities range from psychodynamic practices encompassing political analyses of the clients' position in society, to assistance with group mobilisation as part of a broader political struggle.

The people-centred development approach

During the 1980s, the **people-centred approach** to development, which took cognisance of the dependency theories' critique of development, gained increased popularity. It acknowledged the power differentials between the 'First World' and 'Third World' identified by the dependency approach, but criticised dependency theory for its overemphasis on economic and political factors and neglect of local social and ecological factors. Consequently it argued for a definition of development in which 'quality of life' is not solely defined in economic terms.

In a much-cited definition, David Korten (1990) described development as 'a process by which the members of society increase their personal and institutional capacities to mobilise and manage resources to produce sustainable and justly distributed improvements in their quality of life, consistent with their own aspirations' (Korten, 1990, 67). He contrasts 'people-centred' sustainable development with the 'growth-centred' development that characterised the modernisation (and, to some extent the dependency approach) that puts economic growth ahead of people and the environment. His alternative vision of development embraces the principles of sustainability, social justice and inclusiveness described in the preceding chapter.

Working in Latin America, Max-Neef, Elizalde & Hopenhayn (1989) elaborated on what they called 'human scale development'. This approach is based on the satisfaction of fundamental human needs and on the generation of self-reliance. Adherents of this approach emphasise an ecological focus and the symbiosis of global processes with local activity. They further advocate a balance between central planning and autonomy, between the powers of civil society and those of the state.

In putting the people-centred approach into practice, several problems have been identified, such as its heavy reliance on grassroots voluntary associations. Experience shows that, while such associations are fairly easily mobilised for protests around issues of common concern, sustained effort towards development is more difficult to attain, particularly when no immediate monetary rewards are provided. Secondly, the people-centred approach assumes that people in developing countries value sustainability over rapid economic advancement – which may well not be the case.

Psychologists working within the people-centred paradigm see their task as facilitators and capacity builders in a process informed and managed by the communities within which they work. Their work includes: teaching local people basic research and problem-solving skills to enhance their capacity to deal with the development process in their everyday situations; facilitating the formation and functioning of organisations, and enhancing the participation of formerly excluded groups, such as women. However, psychological practice within the people-centred approach has revealed that communities are not homogenous. Power differentials exist not only between national and local levels but also within local communities, between gender groups, class groups etc.

Social justice: suggests the desirability of equality and the inclusion of all people in social relations.

Psychologists adhering to a dependency approach or a people-centred approach do not accept Western values as a necessary model for developing countries. Recognising the pivotal signifi-cance of political and economic power differentials in development, they see their role as facilitator and capacity builder of local communities in their endeavour to take charge of their own development, according to the local values. These practi-tioners draw on a conflict model and consider working with power struggles both at national level and at local levels (within communities) as central to their work. They reject the notion of the 'value-free scientist' and acknowledge the political nature of their work.

An obstacle to psychological practice within the dependency and people-centred approach is the absence of an appropriate research paradigm and techniques that prepare psychologists for the kind of activist work detailed up to this point. So psychologists working within a people-centred approach are often torn between abandoning psychological practice to become activists or abandoning the activist role to return to a more traditional psychological practice.

Practitioners in the field need to be aware of the power differentials that exist within communities.

Photograph by A Gilbert

THE ROLE OF LOCAL KNOWLEDGE IN PEOPLE-CENTRED DEVELOPMENT

In this chapter an argument is made for psychological work within a people-centred development approach. This particular approach relies on several of the theoretical precepts discussed in the previous chapter, including partici-pation, capacity-building and empowerment. The process of participation,

Enabling environment: environment that allows for errors to be made without disastrous effects and which encourages continued evaluation.

Local knowledge: general term for the *situated* knowledge of ordinary people. It is the common-sense wisdom that comes from everyday life rather than formal book learning. It arises from practical activity with others in a particular sociohistorical-cultural context. It is constantly changing and contains knowledge on what is, or exists, as well as on how things ought to be done. It refers to the whole system of knowledge, including concepts, beliefs and perceptions, as well as the stock of knowledge and the process by which it is acquired, augmented, stored and transmitted.

capacity-building and empowerment can be understood in relation to the notion of local knowledge, which we shall now go on to describe.

Van Vlaenderen & Gilbert (1993) argue that the multi-faceted task the psychologist is faced with is harnessing participation in a capacity-building process for empowerment. This requires facilitation of an analytical process in which local people can articulate their needs, knowledge, skills and resources. It also involves assistance with the establishment of local community networks and the strengthening of local leadership, to take responsibility for development. In this process the psychologist needs to impart human-resource and problem-solving skills and create an **enabling environment** to practise these newly acquired skills. An enabling environment is one that allows for errors to be made without disastrous effects and which encourages continued evaluation. Lastly, this process requires different role-players in the development process (both local communities and the development agents) to bring their views together.

Defining local knowledge

An important aspect of empowerment is the acknowledgement of people's **local knowledge**. In the context of development, people's knowledge is variously referred to as 'indigenous knowledge' (Brokenshaw, Warren & Werner, 1980), 'rural people's knowledge' and 'local knowledge' (Chambers, 1985). 'Local knowledge' is used as a general term for the situated knowledge of ordinary people (it straddles the terms 'indigenous knowledge', 'rural people's knowledge' and 'everyday knowledge'). Local knowledge is the common-sense wisdom that comes from everyday life rather than formal book learning. It arises from practical activity with others in a particular sociohistorical-cultural context and is constantly changing. It contains knowledge on what is, or exists, as well as on how things ought to be done (Gilbert & Van Vlaenderen, 1995). It refers to the whole system of knowledge, including concepts, beliefs and perceptions, as well as the stock of knowledge and the process by which it is acquired, augmented, stored and transmitted (Gengaje & Setty, 1991).

Local knowledge is an essential ingredient of empowerment in a people-centred development approach because it represents successful ways in which people have dealt with their environment in the past, and provides a basis to build on. Korten (1980) argues that indigenous people have well-established systems and carefully developed methods, which have over many years allowed them to survive under adverse conditions. Local knowledge can therefore serve as a guiding force for the local community's behaviour and helps in shaping their mental maps. Building on local knowledge and resources reduces the likelihood that a development intervention will 'de-skill' people and increase their dependency on external experts (Korten, 1980). On the contrary, it empowers people by increasing their self-reliance.

BOX 1 Local knowledge and cognitive psychology

The concept of 'local knowledge' is often described in the cognitive psychology literature as everyday cognition or situated cognition. Soviet sociocultural theorist Lev Vygotsky (1978) pioneered the situated cognition approach and contended that in order to understand people's thinking one has to look at their thinking within actual, everyday life (see the preceding chapter for a discussion of Vygotsky and Activity Theory.) Working within the field of situated or everyday cognition, contemporary authors such as Rogoff (1984), Lave (1988) and Cole (1995) extended these insights. They examined acts of everyday thinking and knowledge construction not in the laboratory but rather in naturalistic contexts such as homes, tailor shops and supermarkets. Knowledge in the situated cognition approach is not constructed within the head of the autono-mous, individual, information-processing subject; it is instead socially defined, interpreted and supported. Furthermore,

> what is regarded as logical problem-solving in academic settings may not fit with problem solving in everyday situations, not because people are 'illogical' but because practical problem-solving requires efficiency rather than a full and systemic consideration of all alternatives. In everyday situations thought is in service of action (Rogoff, 1984, 7).

Situated, local or everyday knowledge is therefore dynamic, functional and formulated to meet the demands of the context in which it is generated. We ignore it at the risk of having a greatly impoverished understanding of how people think and act in everyday life.

Using local knowledge

Using people's local knowledge as inspiration for the development process does not, however, imply an uncritical acceptance of all local knowledge as worthy of preservation and a rejection of all external knowledge (ie the knowledge that is brought to the development process by the development agency) as inferior. There are many examples of the shortcomings of local knowledge as well as the pragmatic usefulness of external knowledge in development (Chambers, 1985). Instead, what is argued for here is the need to start valuing local knowledge as an important knowledge source within the context of development. A well-managed development process ought to assess the relative strengths and weaknesses of outsiders' and local people's knowledge, and should attempt to combine the strengths and neutralise the weaknesses of both (Chambers, 1985).

Psychologists can play an important part in this process. They can facilitate a process in which local people explicate their local knowledge as a group, thereby rebuilding their confidence in the value of their own knowledge and cognitive abilities. Simultaneously, psychologists can expose the prejudices of development professionals about the cognitive capacities of the local people. They can also mediate between local knowledge, which is highly contextualised and specific, and expert knowledge that tends to be formalised and abstract, in order to bridge the gap that exists between them. This involves the creation of an environment in which both types of knowledge can merge. It requires the facilitation of initial communication between expert and local groups, based on equality and mutual respect. Gilbert (1995) argues that it also involves the facilitation of joint activities for developer and local community, which allows for the emergence of shared goals, which will lead to further joint practice.

PARTICIPATORY ACTION RESEARCH

The task of the psychologist within the above-sketched framework is one of facilitator and capacity builder rather than of traditional researcher and trainer. This requires a reorientation of values and strategies to those traditionally used by psychologists. This reorientation has been operationalised by a group of social scientists in what has come to be known as Participatory Action Research (PAR). It is important to stress that this is not simply a new research methodology or a paradigm; it is rather a holistic approach to social science practice.

Conscientisation

For Freire conscientisation is a process of dialogue which enables the individual to transform him- or herself in relation to others and critically reflect on him- or herself in society. It is a process of learning to perceive social, political and economic contradictions and to take action against the sources of oppression.

PAR has arisen mainly out of the experience of developing countries (Maguire, 1987); it has been influenced by three movements. The people-centred approach towards development, elaborated on in some detail above, is one of them. A second movement is based on Brazilian intellectual Paolo Freire's (1972) conscientisation approach to adult education and social activism. According to Freire, **conscientisation** ought to be the basic aim of adult education. He sees conscientisation as a process of dialogue which enables the individual to transform him- or herself in relation to others and critically reflect on him- or herself in society. It is a process of learning to perceive social, political and economic contradictions and to take action against the sources of oppression. The process of conscientisation, therefore, involves the active participation of people in transforming themselves by engaging in a dialogue through which they identify their problems, reflect on why the problems exists and take action to address these problems. Freire advances a formula of dialogue in which teachers and students collaborate together in exploring new questions and new alternatives, rather than a situation in which the teacher is an expert, which encourages dependency of the student upon the teacher.

Conscientisation: associated with the work of Paulo Freire, this describes the process of facilitating the development of a critical self- and social awareness in oppressed or marginalised people.

Challenging the dominant social science paradigm

A third influence on PAR came from a debate within social science practice in developing countries which challenged the compatibility of the dominant social science paradigm, traditional social research methods and the role of the researcher in relation to the development needs and problems of 'Third World'

BOX 2   Methods for conscientisation

Brazilian intellectual, social activist and educationalist Paulo Freire not only theorised the nature of oppression experienced by the dispossessed and marginalised. He enumerated a number of practical tools to challenge the oppressed's 'culture of silence' (Freire, 1972) and facilitate the development of a critical awareness, or conscientisation. The manner in which Freire combined incisive social analysis with practical methods for transformative action is probably his enduring legacy. Freirian **generative codes** are one such practical method.

Generative codes are developed from the stock of symbols, metaphors or tales the focal community draws on. These could be recurrent images, verbal expressions or narratives. These codes are usually developed in conjunction with co-researchers who come from, or have a very keen sense of, the focal community. Generative codes are intended to be comprehensible yet ambiguous, in order to create a stimulus for

the oppressed respondents to respond to. A generative code can be concretised in the form of an acted-out scenario or poster, which is then reflected back to the broader community in order to stimulate discussion about the issue or social problem concerned. A generative code is therefore a kind of Rorschach inkblot devised with the intention of encouraging a group of oppressed people to reflect on their experiences – in other words, to conscientise them.

Using the code as a stimulus, multiple interpretations are elicited from the community and, through skilful facilitation, connected to their everyday existence. These discussions and (ideally) plans for action come to provide the basis for socially transformative action. These actions might be ploughing an unused field, sending representatives to petition a government agency or initiating a local clean up campaign, but they need ultimately to emerge from the oppressed themselves.

---

societies (Walters, 1983). Orlando Fals-Borda (1981), one of the early thinkers within the PAR approach, criticises the community of Western specialised scientists who have attempted to monopolise the idea of what science and scientific methodology are. He argues that, generally speaking, the scientific community defends the interests of the dominant classes of the societies to which it belongs. Fals-Borda contends that the basic premise of PAR is a conception of science that departs from the usual academic presumptions. From this vision of science, action researchers start their work and establish their social and political commitments. The popular science paradigm therefore combines theory and practice in a bundle of praxis and seeks to produce radical changes in society for the benefit of exploited and oppressed social classes (Fals-Borda, 1981). This leads Walters (1983) to suggest that what binds people involved in PAR together is their shared dissatisfaction with the existing social order, a commitment to improving the social conditions of the poor, and their desire for a research and education process which involves the active participation of local people.

Generative codes: one of Freire's practical methods for transformative action, generative codes are images, expressions or narratives, developed from the stock of symbols, metaphors or tales that a local community draws on. They are comprehensible yet ambiguous in order to create a stimulus for the oppressed respondents to respond to.

The characteristics of PAR

PAR can be defined as a three-pronged process involving social investigation with the full and active participation of the local community in the entire process, an educational process of mobilisation for development and a means of taking action for development (Greenwood, Whyte & Harkory, 1993; Van Vlaenderen, 1993). As such, it aims at three types of change, namely, the development of a critical consciousness of the people traditionally designated as the recipients of development, an improvement in their life conditions and a transformation of the social structure in which they operate (Maguire, 1987). The process (Van Vlaenderen & Nkwinti, 1993) is characterised by the following features:

▷ It is a method of social investigation of problems, involving the participation of ordinary people in the process of problem posing and solving. Throughout the PAR process – including the identification phase, the data-gathering and data-analysis process, the use and dissemination of the results – full participation by all those involved is required. Investigation is demystified by involving people in deciding what to investigate, how to gather information and how to organise and use information.

▷ It is a collective process. Collective forms of inquiry build up group ownership of knowledge as people move from being mere objects of scrutiny to active subjects of their own investigation process.

▷ An analysis of the local community history forms the basis for any PAR intervention. The researcher therefore needs to play an active role in the process of tapping local knowledge, indigenous technologies, survival skills and resources, which serve as a foundation for the development of an appropriate action plan.

▷ It relies and builds on the capacity and legitimacy of local community organisations.

▷ It combines investigation with education. The researcher assists people to develop skills in collecting, analysing and using information. However, the researcher is regarded as only one of the contributors in the investigation and problem-solving process, and is continually informed and educated both by the people she or he works with and by the process.

▷ Within PAR the combination of data gathering, education, action and evaluation provides a direct link between research activity and problem solving (for development). The direct link between research and action is perhaps the most distinctive feature of PAR. Combining the creation of knowledge about social reality with concrete action extinguishes the traditional research dichotomy between knowing and doing. The important point here is that those involved in the production of knowledge are involved in the decision making regarding its use and application to their daily lives.

The practice of PAR

As can be gleaned from the above, PAR requires a strong commitment from the researcher to certain values and to participatory methods and principles. In practice, these methods and principles can be **operationalised** in a variety of ways and, depending on the real-life circumstances, are usually more or less successful in achieving the ideals of participation and empowerment. In order to illustrate this and highlight the constraints and problems related to the practice of PAR, an example is provided from one of the author's involvement in development work. It is important to note that the case discussed below has been abbreviated and simplified due to the constraints of space.

Village profiles: Using self-surveys for PAR development planning

This example refers to the first author's involvement in a project that aimed at conducting a participatory **needs analysis** of development needs in a rural district of the Eastern Cape region of South Africa (see Van Vlaenderen & Gilbert, 1993). The project formed part of a larger Educational Research Project based within the Psychology Department of a regional university and run by a team of three researchers. To enable the reader to understand the dynamics of the process that took place in this project, it is important to provide some background information and to describe the chronology of the process.

The case study

The district consists of 14 villages. The villagers make a distinction between the east and the west part of the district. This is partially due to the **topography** and existing transport routes within the area, which limit communication between the two sides. It is also accentuated by the fact that east historically acted as a link to the outside world. As a result of these and other factors, different social dynamics exist across these villages.

In July the researchers were invited to a meeting in the district at which they were requested by a donor organisation and the local district trust to conduct a needs analysis in all the villages of the district. It was explained that a needs analysis was required to identify and prioritise the development needs of the area, in order to access funds which had been set aside for the district. The researchers were further informed that the communities in the district were interested in an analysis of their needs.

In August of the same year the researchers were invited to address a meeting of the Umbrella Body of the district Residents' Association (which included all the villages) to discuss the needs analysis. The meeting resolved that individual villages should take the initiative to invite the researchers to conduct the research in their community, if they deemed it necessary. The researchers were approached by the villagers of Umzekelo. These villagers argued that their needs were greater than those of the other villages, since they were the only resettlement village populated exclusively by people displaced under apartheid. In addition, this village's infrastructure was the most

Operationalised: refers to the process of making operational. In the context of the research process this entails specifying precisely how the particular entity or phenomenon under investigation (eg malnutrition, depression or social capital) is defined, in order to be able to indicate how it will be measured or explored.

Needs analysis/needs assessment: first step in an evaluation, a needs assessment entails the systematic appraisal or investigation of the needs or requirements of the target group.

Topography: detailed description of the structure of the physical environment or landscape.

Brainstorm(ed):
colloquial term referring to a problem-solving technique in which as many and as diverse solutions to a problem as possible are generated either by an individual or a group. These solutions are only later subjected to testing or evaluation.

underdeveloped. Extensive discussions between the researchers and the local Residents' Association Committee of Umzekelo led to the design of a basic socioeconomic survey. The committee **brainstormed** the different areas of village life in which needs and problems were encountered, and with the researchers' assistance devised a questionnaire to elicit information on these issues. The local youth league administered the questionnaires to every household and the researchers analysed the questionnaires and prepared a preliminary report, which was taken back to the committee for discussion and amendments. A final draft (in English and Xhosa) was eventually returned to the community. The Residents' Association Committee organised a community meeting at which they presented the report.

In September, the researchers contacted the chairperson of the Umbrella Body of the district to enquire about progress in the other villages, as there was no word from any of them. The chairperson informed them that they should start work in all villages, since approval for collaboration had been obtained at the general meeting earlier in the year. However, during their visits to the different villages, it became increasingly apparent that the district did not consist of a coherent community and that the perceptions towards the researchers' role and involvement in the area differed markedly amongst the villages. The researchers eventually worked in eleven of the fourteen villages, with three villages indicating a lack of interest in the project. Eight of the 11 villages in the west indicated that they wanted to work as a group under a unified umbrella body. The chairpersons and secretaries of the Residents' Committees of those eight villages formed the West District Forum and received a mandate from their villages to represent them in the project.

PAR facilitators work with existing community structures.

Photograph by A Gilbert

A process of collaboration between the researchers/facilitators and the forum ensued. During a first workshop with the forum, the needs, resources and skills of the communities were brainstormed. It was identified that additional information was needed from the communities to establish what the specific and general needs were for each of the villages. The use of a survey was suggested by one of the forum members. He mentioned that a questionnaire had been used in one of the other villages in the district earlier in the year (the Umzekelo village). After discussion, the forum accepted the need for a survey. It was also resolved that, based on the survey data, a development plan for the Western district should be devised. The researchers argued that the forum would need to possess the capacity to deal with this process of doing research and developing development strategies. The forum members responded that they would find two people in each of their communities who would be willing and had the time to take part in the forum to replace them since, as Resident's Association Committee members, they did not have the necessary time to carry the process through. New members were accordingly mandated by the communities to take part in the forum.

Subsequently, several workshops were held which dealt with the content and the format of the questionnaire. The researchers' role was to facilitate this process by eliciting ideas, critically evaluating suggestions and providing advice when requested. There was lively debate on the kind of information required, the type of questions that needed to be asked and how these needed to be formulated. Eventually a final draft of the questionnaire was compiled in the group and the researcher/facilitator project team subsequently typed and duplicated it (having access to the required facilities). The questionnaires were then returned to the forum members of each of the villages, who called community meetings in their villages to explain the aim of the questionnaire and the procedure for completing the forms. The youth organisation of each of the villages conducted the survey and the forum members brought the questionnaires back to a workshop for analysis. In the workshop the researchers explained how questionnaires are analysed and subsequently jointly (forum members and researchers/facilitators) analysed all the questionnaires in a series of workshops. The researchers discussed the format of the reports and decided on how the village profiles should be presented. The reports were completed, printed and returned to the forum members for scrutiny and amendments before a final copy was produced.

During the same period, surveys were conducted in the three villages which did not form part of the West District Forum. Owing to a lack of interest, a less participatory process enfolded and the questionnaires developed by the West District Forum were administered by the youth leagues of the three villages, after which the researchers/facilitators analysed the data, wrote the reports and presented these to the villagers.

NGO:
abbreviation for Non-Governmental Organisation, the term embraces a wide range of civil society organisations, many of which have a long legacy of involvement in issues of development.

The forum reported back on the research in a round of village meetings in all eight villages of the west of the district, to which the facilitators were invited as guests. During those gatherings the idea arose to organise a conference at which all the villages would present their village profile to invited guests from local and international **NGOs** and donor organisations.

From September onwards the forum, and the facilitators, started to prepare for the conference. Several subcommittees were formed to deal with different aspects of the conference, such as administration, catering, the programme and funding. These subcommittees met on their own or with the facilitators (when they required assistance). Whenever the researchers' input was requested, they organised a meeting in which they could workshop the issues and problems and arrive at solutions.

In November, the West District Forum ran the conference in one of their villages. Representatives of several national and international development agencies attended. After presentations by the villages of their profiles and development needs and introductions by the development agencies, discussion took place on how the development agencies could get involved in the area. The conference marked the end of the researchers formal involvement in the district. However, further informal follow-up revealed that, as a result of the conference, a water development scheme was introduced and several other NGOs had plans for further involvement.

Case study: Successes and shortcomings

The district project managed to implement the ideals of a PAR approach in several ways. It combined *data gathering* on development needs with informal *training* and *action*. In order to collect data, forum members were trained in conducting a survey and in order to use the data for action (through the conference) the forum was trained in the skills necessary to organise the conference. Furthermore, the process relied on *the local knowledge* of the people. The focus and wording of the questionnaires was largely determined by the forum members as a result of discussions and workshops, facilitated by the researchers.

The process relied on *local leadership and local organisations*. The Western District Forum devised the questionnaires and prepared for the conference and the local youth leagues administered the questionnaires. Also, the workshops which led to the development of the questionnaire enabled *communal analysis* of the development issues in the district. The conference enabled the district to make contact with important role-players in the development field and thereby contributed to the *empowerment* of the villagers.

Local people participated in the *management* of the project. They made the majority of decisions about the research process, including the survey, the conference and the need for workshops.

However, several shortcomings can be identified in the PAR process within this study. The process in which the researchers were engaged was terminated because they had no further funds to continue their work. This may have resulted in a lack of sustainability of the process they had embarked on and eventually may have led to a sense of disempowerment. Although aiming to work with the communities in all the villages, the researcher/facilitators inter-acted mainly with the Western District Forum, and relied on them to report back to their communities as a whole. Hence the researchers worked with a very *specific subgroup*, namely those who had most power and most education and who were predominantly men. As a result the concerns of other, less powerful groups may not have been encapsulated in the process.

Whilst the researchers worked together with the forum to develop and analyse the reports, the researchers took the rough data analysis of the ques-tionnaires with them to refine it and to prepare the reports. When they brought the reports back, there was a feeling of *'disownership'* of the reports by the forum members. They had difficulty making the connection between the analytical data they compiled and the reports subsequently prepared on the basis of that data. Hence the facilitators were not able to build their capacity in all the aspects of the research process and a lot of effort was needed to bring the reports 'back' to the community. Similarly, despite the success of the video project (discussed in the box which follows), the lack of community technical facilities and skills may have contributed to a sense of disempower-ment and dependency.

BOX 3   Just picture it: Using video in PAR

Video was used to great effect in Umzekelo village, in the same project detailed in this chapter (cf Van Vlaenderen & Nkwinti, 1993; Van Vlaenderen, 1999). At an early meeting the villagers expressed doubts about the effective-ness of a research survey; they argued that for the researchers and outside world to really grasp the community's situation we needed to 'take a look' at how the villagers lived. A villager suggested a video would be able to 'show' the community's problems and strengths; so at the meeting it was decided that the Resi-dents' Association would write a script for the video and the researchers would provide the necessary assistance with the filming. The 'Umzekelo Video Project' was presented to the whole village for approval and met with great enthusiasm.

The filming was regarded as an important event in the village and a large group of villagers were present throughout. The majority of the filming was done by a professional camera operator engaged by the researchers/facilitators, although several villagers had a go at filming. After editing, a 45-minute video narrated by the chairperson of the Residents' Association was produced. It consisted of interviews and a tour of the village, where it examined the communal gardens, a village water tap, a villager's corru-gated iron house, communal village land, small business projects, the local youth choir and soccer association and the defunct primary health care clinic. The video reflected on the problems and successes of these various aspects of village life.

| BOX 3 | Just picture it: Using video in PAR *(continued)* |

The researchers/facilitators returned to the village with the video and all the equipment necessary to screen it (including a generator, as the village was not electrified). Packed into the church hall, the audience responded extremely emotionally to the first video viewing, especially those who saw themselves on the screen. Requests for a second and third viewing were followed by a lively discussion. The villagers felt that their living circumstances were well reflected in the video and plans were made to form various working groups and elicit development assistance. At the end of the day, when the time arrived for the researchers to leave, there was a feeling of disappointment in the community, who indicated a desire to have several more viewings. Two copies of the video were left with the villagers and additional viewings and meetings were planned for a future date.

The video project inspired confidence for action and the initiation of several activities. Working committees were revived or formed around issues such as transport, a poultry project and health care. With renewed confidence the community took the initiative to contact donor agencies who were invited to the village and presented with copies of the video and project proposals. Several of these community projects were subsequently funded.

Members of the Residents' Association also set up an action committee to liaise between the village and the local government with regard to water issues in the village. The video showing villagers struggling uphill with wheelbarrows to carry water provided them with a powerful image of their plight. A proposal for taps in the streets close to their homes was presented to local government, quite independently of the research team. Furthermore, the process of producing the video was in many respects more important than the final (video) product itself. For instance, it led to the resolution of a community dispute over the use of some communal land far outside the village. The men of the village wanted to use the land to build a school, but the women felt the school would be too far away. The video production process encouraged the women to reopen debate and seek external mediators. After discussion between the different stakeholders it was decided to allocate the land for grazing purposes.

CONCLUSION: THE CHALLENGES OF BEING A PARTICIPATORY ACTION RESEARCHER

We conclude on a more personal, reflective note by considering several of the critical tensions experienced by researchers/facilitators working in the PAR paradigm.

▷ PAR researchers are continuously torn between allegiances to those who pay their fees and the communities with whom they choose to work (due to their personal and political convictions). Moreover, PAR researchers' dependence on financial support from external sources sometimes compels them prematurely to disengage from these communities.

▷ PAR researchers frequently feel limited in their attempt to facilitate empowerment in the communities because, as psychologists, their skills are confined to building human skills and capacity in the community. Psychologists do not have the means to facilitate the enhancement in material or technical capacity, which is the other essential component in the empowerment process. At times, enhancing people's political analysis of a situation and skills, without facilitating access to material improvements in their lives, leads to a sense of disempowerment in the communities and even in ourselves.

▷ Related to this is the fact that it is difficult for a participatory researcher to combine the roles of facilitator, catalyst, capacity-builder and researcher as communities tend to classify the researcher in a particular category (usually that of trainer), which often limits the researcher's other roles (such as that of facilitator).

▷ Finally, as an outsider in a community it is often difficult to gain access to all the different stakeholders and subgroupings within the community. Gatekeepers often attempt to confine the researcher to the elites of the community; as a result, the most disempowered community members may not have their voice heard in the participatory process.

These critical tensions are not readily resolvable nor can they easily be eliminated; they are inherent to the practice of PAR. They therefore need to be continually negotiated and managed throughout the PAR process – a process which enables the psychologist to engage critically with socially transformative change.

Critical thinking tasks

1. Participatory methods often draw on and legitimate existing forms of authority within local communities. These authorities, in turn, often reflect existing power relations within the community – power relations often determined along the lines of gender, age and class. In the light of this, critically discuss *whether* and *how* PAR researchers should and could encourage broader community participation.

2. Set yourself the task of researching unfamiliar local knowledge. Either by yourself or in groups of two or three, explore and document a body of local knowledge that you are unfamiliar with. Where do you find local knowledge? Well, ask somebody who engages in an activity, solves problems (and even makes money) without necessarily drawing on formal 'book' learning. Ideas for sources of local knowledge include a traditional healer, a craftsperson or tradesperson of some sort (a basket weaver or informal roadside car exhaust welder, for instance), a small-scale farmer, or even a surfer! You could ask the traditional healer about how illness is understood and cured; the craftsperson or tradesperson or farmer how they create their product or deliver their service; or the surfer, how they predict the conditions of the sea. From your informal interviews and observations describe the local knowledge in terms of the following:

   (a) the contexts in which this knowledge is used, and

   (b) the most important components of this knowledge.

3. With the proliferation of social science research in contemporary South Africa many groups of people have become repeatedly researched or even 'overresearched'. Speak to someone who has been a participant in research and research the process of being researched by asking them the following:
   (a) What did they have to do, or what they were asked by the researcher?
   (b) Why was the research conducted or what was the research for?
   (c) Do they think they benefited from participating in the research?

Recommended readings

Brokenshaw, D., Warren, D.M., & Werner, O. (1980). 'Introduction.' In D. Brokenshaw, D.M. Warren & O. Werner (eds), *Indigenous knowledge systems and development*. New York: University Press of America.

This is an interesting text that explores the role of local or indigenous knowledge in relation to the practice of development.

Lave, J. (1988). *Cognition in practice: Mind, mathematics and culture in everyday life*. Cambridge: Cambridge University Press.

Do not be deterred by the reference to mathematics! Well illustrated with case examples, this text sketches out the notion of cognition and knowledge as situated, socially embedded acts.

Freire, P. (1972). *Pedagogy of the oppressed*. Harmondsworth: Penguin.

A seminal and accessible text in which Freire explains both his valuational assumptions and practical methods by which the oppressed and marginalised can develop a critical understanding of their situation.

Fals-Borda, O., & Rhaman, M.A. (eds). (1991). *Action and knowledge: Breaking the monopoly with participatory action research*. New York: Apex Press.

This valuable resource text details several studies that use PAR.

Kelly, K., & Van Vlaenderen, H. (1996). 'Dynamics of participation in a community health project.' *Social Science and Medicine*, 42(9): 1235–1245.

This South African study documents several of the challenges inherent in a participatory approach.

Street Life and the Construction of Social Problems

11

Vuyisile Mathiti

OUTCOMES

After having studied this chapter you should be able to:

- discuss the limitations of the distinction made between children of the streets and children on the streets
- describe the state of the quality of life of street children
- critically discuss the theoretical perspectives used in understanding how social problems are constructed
- discuss how discontinuities in socialisation affect identity formation, and
- explain three models used when planning interventions for street children.

THE PRESENCE of an ever-increasing number of street children is generating concern. This concern is informed by their low position on the power ladder relative to other interest groups in South Africa. But they constitute an important social group. Despite difficulties in determining the exact number of street children, attempts to derive estimates continue. Agnelli (in Chetty, 1997) estimates that there are 30 million street children world-wide. A significant proportion of this number – seven to eight million – is found in Brazil (Dimenstein, 1991). In Vietnam, the number of street children is estimated at 2 000 (Barr, 1995). The figure of 4 000 in Rwanda is thought to have increased due to an influx of people to Kigali after the 1994 war (Spry-Leverton, 1996). Swart (in Donald & Swart-Kruger, 1994) estimated the presence of over 10 000 street children in South Africa. That the number of street children has increased since Swart's estimates, seems reasonable.

The first part of this chapter will examine conceptual problems in defining street children. The second part offers an overview of the state of the quality of life of street children. The third part looks at how social problems are constructed. The context used to explore theoretical approaches to the

construction of social problems is street life. Implications for identity formation are examined.

Children *of* the streets and children *on* the streets

Although the use of the concept of street child is credited to a newspaper
article in 1957, the first known record of street children in South Africa was in
the form of a report published in 1917 by the Society for the Protection of Child
Life (Peacock in Hansson, 1991). The scientific community developed interest
much later in the phenomenon of street children. According to Scharf *et al.*
(1986) the first research findings on the phenomenon of street children were
published in 1986, even though the work for that study had started a few years
earlier. It was not until the late 1980s that the phenomenon that is known
world-wide as 'street children' began to arouse interest in some sections of the
public and academic community (Hansson, 1991).

The term 'street children' is one coined by outsiders (Hansson, 1991). The
children to whom the concept is applied have a different nomenclature. For
example, according to Scharf *et al.* (1986) and Swart (1990), in Johannesburg
and Durban they call themselves *malunde* (those of the streets) and
malalapipe (those who sleep in the pipes), whereas in Cape Town they call
themselves *strollers* (those walking on the streets).

When defining the concept of street children, a distinction is often made in
the literature between children *on* the streets and children *of* the streets. This
distinction, first introduced by Ennew (in Scharf *et al.*, 1986), seems to have
universal acceptance (Barr, 1995; Dimenstein, 1991; Richter, 1988; Scharf *et
al.*, 1986; Smith, 1996; Swart, 1990). According to Richter (1988:7), children
on the streets are defined as those who 'go into urban areas in order to earn or
beg money and who then return home. These children contribute all or most
of their earnings to their families. Importantly, children on the street are
attached to, and integrally involved with, their families.' Children *of* the
streets, on the other hand, are defined as those '... who have abandoned (or
have been abandoned by) their families, schools and immediate communities,
before they are 16 years of age, and drifted into a nomadic life' (*ibid.*). It is for
the latter group that the term 'street children' has been reserved.

The distinction used to categorise the experiences of an increasing number
of children who are making a living on the streets is artificial, convenient and
spurious. According to Richter (1988), children on the streets return home and
contribute most or all of their earnings to their families, whereas children of
the streets have no contact with their families. However, this distinction is
problematic. A noteworthy proportion of street children has contact with
family and does not sleep on the street permanently. For example, some of the
children in a study conducted by Mathiti (2000) maintained contact with their

families despite being considered children of the street. They reported visiting their families once in a month or once in two months. This contradicts an important criterion that children of the streets do not maintain contact with their families.

In response to the inadequacies of this distinction, Smith (in Hansson, 1991) introduced the concepts of full-time and part-time street children. These concepts no longer use the criterion of sleeping on the streets as a distinguishing factor. They instead use relative time spent on the street. Children of the streets will be those who are on the streets full-time whereas children on the streets will be those who are on the streets part-time.

The activity pattern of most street children defies this methodical categorisation. Although the children in a study by Mathiti (2000) were living at shelters, few (4 per cent) reported sleeping on the streets occasionally, 38 per cent were regularly involved in income-generating activities, and 68.8 per cent had access to educational services, and many still returned home for short periods. Some of the children reported that some members of their families visited them at the shelters. Hansson (1991) also noted this activity pattern, which clearly contradicts the currently accepted distinction between children on the streets and children of the streets. After a review of studies conducted by Smith and Keen, Hansson noted that most of the females who were strolling (engaging in activities that characterise street children) part-time showed different activity patterns at different times.

> During term-time, they strolled after school, or at times truanted in order to stroll during school time, but generally they returned home at night to sleep. At weekends and during school vacations, however, they typically strolled and slept on the streets at night (Hansson, 1991:7).

If we were to accept the distinction between children of the streets and children on the streets, this would mean, for example, that children on the streets would be defined as such during the week and differently during school vacations and weekends. This is an untenable proposition indeed. Hansson (1991) further noted that although 71 per cent of the females interviewed by Smith strolled full-time, 35 per cent had intermittent contact with their families, and that only a few of the females who were on the streets claimed to contribute their earnings directly to their families. This pattern further contradicts the current distinction between children of the streets and children on the streets.

A further problematic aspect of this distinction is that it promotes the neglect of the needs of the children on the streets. That these children have to earn an income is seldom denounced as an inadmissible pursuit.

It can be argued that children on the streets are more vulnerable to chronic abuse and neglect than children of the streets because the possibility of getting help is better for the latter than the former group. Nonetheless, that these children have to provide for their own and their families' needs is a flagrant violation of both their rights and moral precepts. The majority of South African children, especially street children, are disappointed with the adult community, given the pervasive nature of the violation of their rights. Experiences such as physical and sexual abuse, neglect, abject poverty, HIV/AIDS and family violence reinforce their perception that an adult-dominated world is indifferent, pernicious and untrustworthy. Escaping this domination is perceived as a desirable goal and when attained, a significant achievement.

The quality of life of street children

An analysis of the condition of street children suggests that they experience social, health, emotional and educational difficulties (see the box below). Some of their difficulties include the distressing realities of increasing separation from their families and loss of access to basic facilities such as health, education and recreation (UNICEF, 1986). Their social, health, physical, emotional and educational difficulties have been well documented (Barrette, 1995; Bourdillon, 1995; Cockburn, 1994; Donald & Swart-Kruger, 1994; Smith, 1996; Swart, 1990).

> Ben (not his real name) is a quiet 12-year-old youngster. His parents divorced four years ago when he was eight years old. He has not seen nor spoken to his father since the divorce. His mother remarried when he was ten years old. His relationship with his stepfather can be described as stormy. He believes that his stepfather does not like him and he says he does not like him either. According to Ben, his stepfather treats him differently to his two siblings. For example, he does not shout at them or call them names. His mother has tried to intervene in order to improve his relationship with his stepfather. He has expressed displeasure with the lack of a relationship with his paternal relatives.
>
> He has expressed a wish to stay with his uncle, but his mother refused. That the mother is unemployed means that the family has to rely on his stepfather to meet their needs. According to Ben, it is rare for the family to have three meals per day. Sometimes they have to do with one meal per day. As a result, he started stealing money to buy food. He admitted that he stole money from his stepfather and uncle a few times. His uncle caught him on one occasion and had a serious talk with him about the consequences of theft. He decided to go to the city to beg for money and food. He could no longer attend school and was sad to drop out of school because he will no longer be a doctor (a dream he has cherished since he was six). Although he says it is tough on the streets and that he does not like it, he says it is better than staying with his stepfather. He says he misses his mother and siblings and cries when he misses them. His greatest wish is to have a relationship with his father.

Donald and Swart-Kruger (1994) have observed that these children face emotional problems such as loss of relationship with an adult caregiver, anxiety and depression. They have to deal with feelings of being unloved, unwanted and rejected (Cockburn, 1991; Swart, 1990). The lack of nurturance contributes to emotional insecurity, self-blame, and warped development of a sense of relating to and engaging with others. That unmet affectional and dependency needs are acutely experienced by street children is shown in a study conducted by Richter (in Donald & Swart-Kruger, 1994), where she found that street children displayed higher than normal rates of enuresis, regressive behaviour, anxiety and depression.

Street children are socially marginalised and rejected by many segments of society (Smith, 1996). They constantly face violence, harassment and abuse. On the whole, they are exploited and victimised social reprobates whom society loves to hate. Police brutality is not an uncommon experience for many street children. Besides the antagonism, hostilities and violence they face, they also experience hunger, cold, sexual abuse and sexually transmitted diseases (Chetty, 1997).

A study by Jansen *et al.* (1990) documented the effects of glue sniffing by street children. They had multiple deficits, which included visual-spatial diffi-culties, visual scanning problems, language problems, motor coordination, memory and concentration deficits. These cognitive deficits are related to a number of factors, such as the use of various drugs. A number of studies have highlighted the use of drugs by street children (Chetty, 1997; Cockburn, 1995; Donald & Swart-Kruger, 1994). For example, in her study in Durban, Chetty (1997) found that most of the street children smoked dagga (23.3 per cent) followed by glue sniffing (22.8 per cent), benzine sniffing (16.6 per cent) and use of alcohol (16.6 per cent). There were also children sniffing petrol (16.1 per cent) and inhaling paint thinners (7.8 per cent). It seems as if dagga, glue and alcohol are some of the drugs most widely used by street children. These drugs are sometimes used to provide a cushioning effect against hunger, cold, illness, fear and insecurity (Chetty, 1997). A study by Richter (in Moran, 1994) suggests that approximately 30 per cent of the street children who experiment with solvents become chronic users.

A compromise in their sense of safety is another source of vulnerability. These children are exposed to cold, rain and storms. Often they do not have sufficient protective clothing. They are also at risk of pedestrian traffic acci-dents, particularly after glue-sniffing episodes (Donald & Swart-Kruger, 1994). That so many children are neglected and uncared for by their families, commu-nities and government is a flagrant violation not only of their rights, but also of moral and religious precepts (Chetty, 1997). Despite a review of existing literature suggesting that street children are 'at-risk children', many of them have survived the harsh realities of their environments. The resilience displayed by these children has given rise to a pervasive paradox between the evidence of developmental vulnerabilities across social, emotional, cognitive and physical areas of development, on the one hand, and the evidence of tenacity, resourcefulness and ingenuity, on the other (Chapman, 1997; Donald & Swart-Kruger, 1994).

Even though they face multiple stressors, such as malnutrition and under-nutrition, illness, injuries, anxiety, social rejection, violence and lack of protective clothing, some of these children are able to overcome these adversities. Although the mechanisms of protection and preservation used by these children are not yet fully understood, 'research findings on the whole support the notion that young people are potentially resilient and that ... they have the capacity to resist being overwhelmed by [their experiences] in the long term' (Smith, 1996:94). Mathiti (2000) observed that social support, however limited, was a mitigating factor.

Developmental implications of a poor quality of life

Emotional development

Donald and Swart-Kruger (1994) assert that the greatest emotional risk most street children face is the loss or lack of an adequate relationship with an adult figure. Due to disappointment with the primary caregiver, most of the street children have adopted a sceptical, disengaging way to relate to adult figures. They experienced disappointment with their primary caregivers for their inability or unwillingness to meet their affectional and dependency needs. High levels of physical (50 per cent) and sexual (17 per cent) abuse by the primary caregivers were reported by Cockburn (in Chapman, 1997). In terms of Erickson's theory (in Meyer *et al.*, 1997), the loss of a relationship with an adult figure has profound implications for trust, shame, guilt, inferiority and identity confusion. Successful resolution of these developmental tasks contributes to healthy psychological functioning. Failure to resolve these tasks can lead to a sense of mistrust, low self-esteem, identity confusion and social alienation. Unsuccessful resolution of these tasks can predispose street children to serious psychological and social problems.

Against the background of these emotional developmental risks, and as mentioned earlier, street children are more likely to develop anxiety, depression, enuresis and regressive behaviour (Richter in Donald & Swart-Kruger, 1994). The results of a study by Richter (in Chapman, 1997) showed that street children who have retained some links with their families showed more emotional disturbance than those who have broken off completely. Even though the reasons for this finding are not entirely clear, it is hypothesised that the conditions that motivated the children to leave home resurface when they meet their families. They are exposed to unremitting circumstances. The perception that their primary caregivers show unwillingness to change their 'old ways' can be experienced as demoralising and can contribute to feelings of anger, bitterness and resentment. This finding has implications for programme development in that programme developers must assess the family environments before the children are reconnected with their families. However, groups of street children have supported each other physically and emotionally. The group is important in ensuring the satisfaction of affectional needs.

Social development

Street children face rejection from many segments of society. They face violence, harassment and marginalisation. They are outcast. Their position as 'social rejects' is likely to put a positive social identity and feelings of self-worth at risk. This is likely to lead to 'victim identity' (Donald & Swart-Kruger, 1994:172).

Generally, street children are exploited and victimised reprobates whom society loves to hate.

Their clothing and unkempt appearance are factors that contribute to premature judgements by people. The rejection that results from such judgements reinforces the street children's negative self-perception. Although these children often have contact with people who evaluate them negatively, they avoid these contacts and seek people whose evaluations are anticipated to be positive. Consequently, their social contact becomes circumscribed. Their *affiliation needs* are often not met given the constraints imposed on their social contacts, and the group is often regarded as a resource to satisfy psychological needs. The fluid and erratic nature of the composition of groups and relationships is likely to negatively affect the establishment of permanent relationships and the benefits that flow from these (Donald & Swart-Kruger, 1994).

Street life as a social problem: Theoretical perspectives

This section focuses on two theoretical perspectives, namely, the positivist and constructionist, that help to explain the social position of street children and the implications for identity formation.

Positivist perspective

According to Stefan (1993:2), *positivism* suggests that 'social problems are conditions that can be objectively identified as having some intrinsic harmful effects'. From this perspective, a social problem is considered as an individual, group, condition or activity that is apparently troublesome, threatening or perilous. A significant element of a social problem is its high public risk value.

According to Chetty (1997), the incarceration of street children is partly motivated by their public nuisance value. Their unkempt appearance, tendency to beg for food and money and sleeping on the streets undermine the efforts of city managers to build 'marketable brands' and can hasten neighbourhood decline. This perception is racially inspired. Furthermore, the possibility that they will beg from tourists is regarded as a problem in that it might annoy the tourists or even 'scare' them away. This has the potential to undermine the local economy. From the positivist perspective, street children are regarded as a social problem because they can delimit local economic growth and threaten environmental health. The assistance of the police is often solicited to deal with this 'social problem' because it threatens law and order.

Furthermore, a street life is considered a social problem because it is considered to be inconsistent with societal norms that expect children to be under parental care and supervision. The constitutionally guaranteed rights in the *Bill of Rights* (The Constitution, 1996) and the United Nations' (1993) *Convention on the Rights of the Child* (CRC) document the provisions that should be made for children. When these provisions are not met, the condition of the intended recipient is regarded as a social problem. This perception is motivated by a desire to protect the individual from him- or herself and to protect society. In this way, social order and balance can be maintained.

Children's rights

SECTION 28 (South African Constitution)

1. Every child has a right
   a. to a name and nationality;
   b. to family care or parental care, or to appropriate alternative care when removed from the family environment;
   c. to basic nutrition, shelter, basic health care services and social service;
   d. to be protected from malnutrition, neglect, abuse or degradation;
   e. to be protected from exploitative labour practices;

    f.   not to be required or permitted to perform work or provide services that
        i)   are inappropriate for a person of that child's age; or
        ii) place at risk the child's well-being, education, physical or mental health or spiritual, moral or social development;

    g. not to be detained except as a measure of last resort, in which case, in addition to the rights a child enjoys under sections 12 and 35, the child may be detained only for the shortest appropriate period of time, and has the right to be
        i)   kept separately from detained persons over the age of 18 years; and
        ii) treated in a manner, and kept in conditions, that take account of the child's age

    h. to have a legal practitioner assigned to the child by the state, and at state expense, in civil proceedings affecting the child, if substantial injustice would otherwise result; and

    i.   not to be used directly in armed conflict; and to be protected in times of armed conflict.

2. A child's rights are of paramount importance in every matter concerning the child.

3. In this section 'child' means a person under the age of 18 years.

Constructionist perspective

Some authors have expressed dissatisfaction with the positivist perspective. Stefan (1993:2) has observed that 'not all apparently dangerous, threatening or troublesome conditions are considered social problems, while other unimportant issues have become major concerns for the media and society'. Mills (1978:19) put it succinctly when he stated that 'not child labour but comic books, not poverty but mass leisure are at the centre of concern'. The dissatisfaction has led to the consideration of social problems as the result of social constructionism (Blummer, 1971). In other words, the social constructionist's perspective suggests that a phenomenon or condition is conceived and defined as a social problem rather than objectively determined to be one.

In line with a constructionist perspective on social problems, Schneider (in Stefan, 1993) believes that the claims and claim-making activities, and not the objective condition, constitute a social problem. In other words, social problems are what people claim they are and are not defined in terms of their truthfulness. Schneider maintains that a situation or phenomenon will be considered a social problem if it is viable, which is to say, functional for those with power on their side. A difficulty or abnormality needs to be usable and valuable once it has been defined as a social problem. What makes a successful problem would be the viability rather than the validity of claims (Schneider, 1985). This view is also shared by Anderson (in Stefan, 1993:3) who observed that 'for a certain situation to be regarded as a "problem" rather than a mere "condition" or "the way things are", there must be some reason or interest in creating it'.

The operation of divergent and conflicting interests, intentions and objectives results in the construction of a plethora of contesting problems that compete for attention and recognition as legitimate social problems (Blummer, 1971). Entry into the arenas of public discourse is a selective process involving conflict over recognition, confirmation and rejection of claims (Hilgartner & Bosk in Stefan, 1993). The success with which an issue enters the arena of public discourse and consequently transforms into a social problem, is also influenced by its 'credentials' and legitimation (Blummer, 1971). The rise to prominence of a social problem will invite the attention of government agencies, social action groups, political campaigns, news media and the academic community. The notability of a problem helps to create ameliorative conditions.

Perhaps the greatest emotional risk most street children face is the loss or lack of an adequate relationship with an adult figure.

Media discourse plays a significant role in the construction of social problems. The process of news selection, emphasis on expert opinions and objective reporting means the content of media discourse is not reflective of divergent views but promotes the opinions of politicians, experts and government officials. The emphasis on authoritative views promotes a single definition of a social problem (Stefan, 1993).

The viability criterion in defining social problems was met for child abuse to be defined as a social problem. Stefan (1993) observed that until 1988 child abuse and child sexual abuse were virtually unknown in South Africa except to a small esoteric group of paediatricians in Durban. The following year, in 1989, the issue of child abuse was useful in supporting the government's election campaign. Prior to the election, the police invited media representatives to offer coverage to the campaign to clamp down on crime by and against children. Stefan observed that 'during late 1989 and 1990 the coverage of child sexual abuse declined somewhat, but the issue was taken by secondary media such as popular, professional and academic magazines' (*ibid.*: 11). From a constructionist perspective, street life has remained out of public discourse and attention because, unlike child abuse, it is not usable. It cannot be used during election campaigns due to the negative public perception and social stereotyping of street children. The socially ascribed status of 'adult-child' also means the issue of street existence cannot compete with other children's issues. It cannot compete in the 'social problem's marketplace' against issues such as malnutrition, HIV/AIDS orphanage, abuse and neglect because it is considered to affect 'adult-children' as opposed to affecting children.

Another explanation for the entry of social problems into social discourse is the migration of an issue from a large centre to the periphery (Stefan, 1993). An issue of concern emerges in a large cultural centre and then moves to the perimeter. The sexual abuse of children *as a social problem* emerged in the United States in the 1960s, was diffused to Britain and other remote locations such as South Africa in the 1980s (Stefan, 1993). To aid the dispersion process, the group that occupies the highest strata often appropriates more power to itself. The media, wittingly or unwittingly, plays a crucial role in the dispersion process. For example, the South African public received an increasing number of reports on international concern about sexual abuse of children in the late 1980s (Robertson in Stefan, 1993). The media has treated street children with 'benign neglect'. In those instances that street children received media coverage, their representation was negative. They were often portrayed as violent, beggars or criminals.

Viewed in this light, street life has remained outside the arenas of public discourse because of the lack of power of claim-makers to diffuse it to the centre (decision-makers in national and international communities). In South Africa, the position of powerlessness has often been underlined by racial considerations (see Chapter 6). That an overwhelming number of street children come from the historically disadvantaged communities serves to disempower and undermine efforts to make street life part of the socio-political programme and public speeches and debates. The complex intersection of being a Black (a low social class) child (a low social class) who lives on the streets (a low social class) foils the entry of a street life in public discourse. Street life has been envisaged as a 'Black thing' considering that for a long time the South African media have been predominantly White-owned with a significant White audience (again, see Chapter 6).

Street life is also a gendered experience. Although it is accepted that females comprise a small minority of the street children in South Africa (Richter, 1988; Scharf *et al.*, 1986), some commentators believe that this under-representation reflects gender construction. For example, Hansson (1991) believes that the way in which the phenomenon of street children is defined reflects the typical experience of males. Females are excluded because their activity patterns do not fit the male-inspired definition of what it is to be a child. Consequently, an erroneous conclusion is reached that there are fewer females than males. One of the unfortunate consequences of under-representing the number of female street children is the neglect of their needs. Unlike their male counterparts, they are perceived to be in less need of assistance. This gendered perception has led to fewer programmes and facilities for this group.

> The predicament of the street girl is far more intricate due to her condition of abandonment and to her nature as a woman. In the streets she is more exposed to the consequences brought about by the role of women in society ... she is subject to the consequences of premature maternity, of abandonment and prostitution (Paulo Freire cited in Barrette, 1995:39).

The age restriction (females under 16 years of age) is a criterion that serves to exclude a large proportion of female street children. Fifty per cent of the sample in a study conducted by Smith and Keen were over the age of 16 (Hansson, 1991). Their finding suggests that females tend to start a street existence at a later age (in their early teens) than do males (10 years of age). Most of the female street children are soon disqualified because of age considerations. The choice of 16 years as the cut-off point is viewed with suspicion considering that the legal age marking adulthood is 18 years. That males start a street life earlier is an advantage that helps them to gain street experience and subsequently, status and power (Chetty, 1997). The lack of experience means that females do not meet an important requirement that would afford them status and authority.

A further gendered and devalued perception is that female street children are prostitutes. This identity attracts disgust and condemnation from society. The absence of low-risk, income-generating activities for females is considered as one of the possible antecedent factors. Parking cars, which is a relatively low-risk income-generating activity, is male-dominated. The territorial behaviour of males in this area is considered a defence mechanism against competition. This leaves females with a few high-risk alternatives, such as selling sexual services. Due to the possibility of assault and arrest, this activity is performed in less public places (Hansson, 1991). The male-dominated nature of a street existence has led to constructions that reflect male experience to the exclusion of female experience.

Discontinuity in socialisation and social identity

According to Erikson (in Meyer *et al.*, 1997), experiences at each life stage are an effective preparation for the next. The continuity in the socialisation process provides smooth transitions from one stage to another. The family, as a primary *socialisation* agent during the formative years, plays a crucial role in helping children learn skills and attitudes that enhance their social participation. The learned behavioural patterns prepare children to respond effectively to familial and societal demands at subsequent phases. Experiences of such continuities enable clarity of *social roles* and social integration.

However, a street life is marked by discontinuities that lead to social isolation and rejection. This rupture in socialisation is punctuated by a depressed quality of life experienced by street children (Chetty, 1986; Dimenstein, 1991; Mathiti, 2000; Smith, 1996; Swart, 1990). The ascribed 'adult-child' status serves to promote the discontinuities that are encountered. This status involves the display of both child and adult behavioural patterns. In other words, a child is expected to engage in normal child behaviours, and to shift his or her behavioural repertoire in the direction of adulthood. In a study on the quality of life of street children, Mathiti (2000) observed that one of the significant recreation and leisure activities of the street children was playing with toys. Recreation and leisure activities were undertaken after the execution of adult responsibilities such as searching for employment (mainly as parking attendants) and food. These discontinuities suggest that their role as children has been redefined in quite a radical way. As a result, the previously established childhood rhythms and patterns of engaging with the social world have been disrupted. Consequently, role confusion and fragmented identities are experienced. The production and recognition of the fragmented identity, 'adult-child', is problematic indeed. The fragmented identities and a constricted social network serve to undermine the development of a strong and normative sense of relating to self and others.

A number of studies have shown that street children have constricted social networks (Apteker, 1994; Bourdillon, 1995; Chetty, 1994; Dimenstein, 1991; Smith, 1996). The police are one of the few social institutions with which they have frequent contact. This contact has often been described as violent and brutal (Chetty, 1997). Besides the police, street children have limited, if any, contact with schools. The circumvention of their sense of belonging created poor and inadequate identification with their communities.

Studies have shown that street children have constricted social networks, with the police one of the few social institutions with which they have fequent contact.

The view that individual identity is a product of self-construction is problematic in the context of fragmented identities, because it discounts the role of social context in identity formation. The negative collective identity of street children is seen as a product of social construction. Their identity is therefore constructed and situated in a flow of social discourses (see Chapter 6 on how apartheid, considered an extension of colonialism, appropriated the means and resources for a positive identity). Some of the discourses involve their low position on the social ladder. Their low social class relative to other groups does not evoke honour and pride. Their powerlessness further serves to entrench their low social class with the resultant negative public perception and *stereotyping*. Their unkempt appearance, unconventional survival strategies, abandonment of family and status as a public nuisance reinforce this perception. Exposure to socially sustained negative discourses inevitably shapes the way street children look at and constitute themselves. Loneliness and rejection therefore facilitate the formation of a negative collective identity. However, tensions have been observed in this regard. The street children have resisted the imposed identities by their rejection of the name 'street children'. In a study conducted in Hillbrow, Swart (1990) noted that most of the children rejected the label of 'street children' and suggested various possible alternative names.

Although it has been argued in this section that identity is socially constructed and situated, this thesis should not be construed as support for *social determinism*. Identity is not viewed as a complete reflection of social circumstances but of the dynamic tensions within individuals and among contending social discourses.

The consequences of devalued identities

The person who is *stigmatised* is a person whose social identity calls his or her full humanity into question (Ratele & Shefer, 2002; Tajfel & Turner, 1979). The perception of others is that this person is marginal, secondary (at best), flawed and impaired. Such people are often the targets of negative stereotypes. In this section I examine the consequences of devalued identities for well-being, minority status and identification.

Well-being

There is a paucity of research examining the influence of group membership on well-being. According to Mathiti (2000), well-being is used in a rather broad sense to include a variety of temporary emotional states or moods (e.g. happiness, anxiety, depression), as well as more stable positive or negative feelings (such as self-acceptance and self-esteem). It can be assumed, from a theoretical perspective, that membership in a minority group with a devalued identity may be associated with negative feelings. First, membership in this group can attract negative reactions such as stigmatisation, social isolation and violence. The literature is replete with these experiences on the part of street children (Chetty, 1997; Richter, 1988; Swart, 1990). They can lead to negative emotions and ultimately undermine the emotional well-being of the street children. Second, the internalisation of devalued images can lead to undesirable psychological and behavioural consequences such as poor self-esteem, feelings of rejection and detrimental personality and value changes. Third, given that personal feelings of worth depend on the social evaluation of the *in-group* with which a person is identified, self-hatred and feelings of worthlessness tend to arise from membership of an outcast group (Tajfel & Turner, 1979). Fourth, members of groups that are devalued and are relatively small are disadvantaged when they need to solicit validations from *many* similar others (*ibid.*).

As a result, members of minority groups may feel less secure than members of majority groups. Although research findings examining the influence of group *status* and size on well-being are contradictory, there is also new evidence which confirms that, at least under some conditions, members of low-status minority groups differ in well-being from members of high-status majority groups (Tajfel & Turner, 1979).

Minority status

Tajfel and Turner (1979) maintain that membership of a minority group and membership of a majority group each constitute distinct socio-psychological situations for the particular member. Unlike majority members, minority members typically find themselves in what they call cognitive-affective cross-fire. On the one hand, being a small figure (minority) against a large (majority) makes membership of that group salient and members cannot forget their affiliation to such groups. They are reminded of their membership in a minority group by word or deed. As a result, their membership of this group becomes a central aspect for the minority (more so than for the majority). Furthermore, minority membership entails risks and stressful experiences that may be unknown to members of the majority group. The risks, which often lead to negative affective experiences, are increased if the image of the minority is devalued. Compared to majority members, there are strong forces pushing minority members towards their group or keeping them in it, while at the same time there are stronger affective forces pulling them away. As a result, minority members experience internal conflict. According to Tajfel and Turner (*ibid.*), they may opt for individual or group strategies. Individual strategies may involve dis-identification with or exit from their group. Assertive inter-group behaviour can be a possible collective strategy.

> Tajfel and Turner (1979) have argued that membership of a group constitutes distinct social-psychological states for members, and members of minority groups generally find themselves in cognitive-affective crossfire.

Identification

The impact of the group status is often moderated by the strength of the ties of the individual with the group. A review of experimental work on the effects of relative group status on the degree to which individuals identify with their groups shows that low group status generally results in lower levels of identification than high group status (Tajfel & Turner, 1979). This has been explained from a social identity perspective. According to this perspective, people are likely to resist membership or involvement with a low-status group because this may diminish the possibility of their achieving a positive social identity (*ibid.*). Decreasing the level of identification may help members to experience less negative emotions that may ensue as a result of membership in a lower status group.

Models of intervention

Health:
A state of complete physical, mental and social well-being and not merely the absence of disease.

Intervention programmes have been motivated by the observation that street life impacts negatively on street children's health. Health is seen in a broad sense as a state of complete physical, mental and social well-being, and not merely the absence of disease or infirmity (World Health Organisation in Parmenter, 1994). These programmes suggest that many street children could be helped to overcome the effects of their harsh environments.

Containment approaches are used in closed institutions where correctional measures are applied.

According to Cockburn (1995), intervention programmes can be divided into three broad approaches, namely, containment, cure and prevention. The *containment* approach usually occurs in closed institutions where correctional measures are applied. She believes that this approach is costly and ineffective. The second approach, *cure*, involves weaning children away from street life and gradually introducing them to mainstream society (see also Schurink, 1993). This approach is sometimes termed rehabilitative because it puts emphasis on resocialising the street child. The third approach, *prevention*, is aimed at preventing the occurrence of the street child phenomenon by attempting to identify the root cause of the problem (see Rapholo, 1996).

Curative approaches involve weaning children away from street life and gradually introducing them to mainstream society.

An assessment of these approaches by Cockburn (1995), Rapholo (1996) and Smith (1996) suggests that the containment approach is the least effective approach, the prevention approach the least explored, and the curative or rehabilitative approach the most moderately promising of the three. According to Cockburn (1993), the success or failure of these intervention programmes is partly dependent on the skills and training of service providers. Her advocacy of the use of trained service providers is borne out by the success of pilot projects using trained street workers in the Cape Town area. Chetty (1997) also shares this view. In an exploratory investigation of the street child phenomenon in Durban, she found that:

Preventative approaches are aimed at preventing the occurrence of the street child pheno- menon by attempting to identify the root cause of the problem.

> the majority of service providers had not proceeded beyond matriculation level, and that they advocated largely punitive measures in respect of street children ... Most agreed that street children were likely to become hardened criminals. Some of the reasons given in support of this statement were that the children refused to listen, they isolated themselves from the community (Chetty, 1997:177–178).

These views suggest that the service providers concerned did not really understand street children, and demonstrate the critical importance of professional, trained workers. Their perceptions, which leaned towards hard options, were inconsistent with the sympathy and understanding expected of them. This divergence is unhealthy for any intervention programme.

Conclusion

The phenomenon of a street existence is a complex one. The tendency is to treat those on and of the streets as an insignificant minority of problematic children. It has been argued in this chapter that street children constitute a significant social group that has, unfortunately, not been part of public debate. Their depressed quality of life is a source of concern. They are considered a social problem for reasons that do not promote their interests. The negative public perception has engendered a devalued negative identity.

Exercises for critical engagement

1 Provide a critique of the media coverage of street children in South Africa in the last few months to see how street children have been represented.
2 What are some of the factors that could explain the high representation of Black, male children on the street?
3 Discuss factors that put the development of a positive social identity for street children at risk.
4 Compare and contrast the positivist and constructivist approaches to street life.
5 With reference to street children, discuss three possible consequences of a devalued identity.
6 It has been suggested that street children have utilised effective coping mechanisms to deal with the harshness of their situation. Discuss some of the coping strategies used by the street children.
7 The aim of most intervention programmes for street children is often to reunite them with their family. Do you think this should be the aim of most or all interventions? Motivate your answer.
8 You have been appointed to a by the government commission into the investigation of the phenomenon of street children. Write a five-page report of the most significant findings and recommendations of your commission.

Recommended reading

Barrette, M. (1995). *Street Children Need Our Care.* Pretoria: Kagiso Publishers.

Chetty, V. (1997). *Street Children in Durban: An Exploratory Investigation.* Pretoria: Human Sciences Research Council.

Donald, D. & J. Swart-Kruger. (1994). 'The South African street child: Developmental implications'. *South African Journal of Psychology,* 24(4):196–174.

Swart, J. (1990). *Malunde: The Street Children of Hillbrow.* Johannesburg: Witwatersrand University Press.

12

The role of collective action in the prevention of HIV/Aids in South Africa

Catherine Campbell

'... individual change is most likely to come from projects in which people collaborate not only to change their own behaviour but also to understand and challenge the social circumstances that place their health at risk.'

Freire (1973/1993)

LEARNING OUTCOMES

By the end of this chapter, you should be able to:

▷ Explain what is meant by the concept of a 'health-enabling community'

▷ Identify and explain the psychosocial and community-level processes underlying the impact of collective action on health

▷ Illustrate how each of these processes operates in relation to the promotion of sexual health and the prevention of HIV/Aids

▷ Elaborate on the way in which each of these processes is shaped by the power relations associated with poverty, gender and stigma

▷ Justify why health-enhancing social change is most likely to be achieved through a combination of 'top-down' and 'bottom-up' efforts

▷ Speculate about what forms 'top-down' and 'bottom-up' changes might take to reduce HIV-transmission in the community in which you live and/or work.

INTRODUCTION: WHAT DO WE MEAN BY 'CRITICAL' HEALTH PSYCHOLOGY?

Stigma: attitudes of fear, contempt or disrespect for members of an out-group which are often associated with intolerant, and discriminatory behaviour towards out-group members. Members of stigmatised groups may 'internalise' these negative judgements, leading to increased lack of self-confidence and low self-esteem – which further exacerbates their situation of rejection and isolation.

The starting point of this chapter is the field of critical health psychology, with a particular focus on the role of psychology in understanding the HIV/Aids epidemic in South Africa. There are two ways in which the chapter seeks to be 'critical'. First, it seeks to be *critical of society*, drawing attention to the way in which social factors such as poverty, gender and **stigma** make it difficult for so many people to protect their sexual health. Secondly, it seeks to be *critical of mainstream health psychology*, which has sought to explain health-related behaviours (such as using condoms or accessing treatment quickly when a person has a sexually transmitted infection, or STI) in terms of properties of the individual, ignoring the role of social factors in shaping these behaviours.

In explaining high-risk sexual behaviours, mainstream health psychologists tend to focus on individual-level factors (Norman, Abraham & Conner, 2000; Rutter & Quine, 2002). Thus, for example, they might say that the likelihood of a person engaging in unsafe sex is determined by the accuracy of their knowledge of the risks of HIV/Aids or the extent to which they feel personally vulnerable to HIV/Aids. They might also focus on the individual decision-making processes underlying the decision to use a condom or on the degree to which a person feels confident or motivated to negotiate safe sexual encounters. There is no doubt that individual factors such as knowledge and confidence play a key role in shaping sexual behaviour. However, such individual factors are heavily shaped by the social context in which a person is located. Thus, for example, a man may choose not to act on information about the risks of HIV/Aids due to the social construction of masculinity, which dictates that a 'real man' should have sex with many women, and should not be afraid to take risks. A woman's confidence to assert her rights to sexual health may be undermined in contexts where she depends on gifts from male sexual partners to support herself and her children. A young person's motivation to attend a clinic for STIs may be reduced in a social context here adults (ranging from parents to clinic nurses) refuse to acknowledge the existence of youth sexuality and where STIs are heavily stigmatised.

Top-down social change: social change driven by powerful social actors (eg leaders in politics, industry or religion) or agencies (eg government, legal institutions). They use their power to influence social events and relations.

In a review of HIV-prevention science, Waldo & Coates (2000) highlight the way in which mainstream health psychology has hindered the HIV-prevention struggle. Individual-level explanations of sexual behaviour lead to individual-level interventions seeking to bring about *individual-level change*. Such interventions seek to change individuals by increasing their knowledge about HIV/Aids or their perceived vulnerability to infection or their ability to act assertively in sexual encounters. However, such interventions fail to take account of those features of social context that enable or support the individual's ability to act on this newly acquired knowledge or this increased sense of personal vulnerability to HIV/Aids or to transfer the lessons from

Zapiro's biting commentary on the government's HIV/Aids policy reminds us that macro-structures are a crucial part of any effective HIV/Aids intervention and that marginalised communities often have little political or economic influence over more powerful stakeholders.

assertiveness training courses to real-life contexts where factors such as gender and poverty limit their freedom to act. Individuals are social creatures; society has a key influence on the way in which we behave. If this is indeed the case, then attempts to change the behaviour of individuals need to go hand in hand with attempts to bring about *social change* – transformations in the social contexts that limit people's ability to act in ways that protect their sexual health.

Participation: taking part in a joint activity with other people.

WHAT ARE THE DRIVERS OF SOCIAL CHANGE?
Social change through top-down and bottom-up efforts

In short, ideally, HIV-prevention interventions should aim not only to change individuals but also to create health-enabling social contexts – environmental conditions that make it easier for people to act in ways that protect their sexual health (Tawil, Verster & O'Reilly, 1995). This involves the challenge of working to combat the impact of social factors such as poverty, gender and stigma on peoples' health-related choices. What strategies are needed to drive attempts to bring about social change of this nature? Social change needs to come through a combination of **top-down** and **bottom-up** efforts. *Top-down* efforts involve high-level efforts by powerful leaders, policymakers and agencies to develop strategies for social change through instruments of government, politics, law or economics. *Bottom-up* efforts involve the **participation** of members of marginalised communities (who usually suffer from the worst health) in **collective action** to improve their health. Such collective action involves collaboration by **grassroots** people in identifying the way in which social conditions undermine their health and well-being, and in working towards improving such

Bottom-up social change: social change driven by demands and initiatives of ordinary grassroots people. They mobilise themselves on the basis of common problems or discontents, and work from their position at the bottom of the social **hierarchy** to lobby for social changes.

Collective action: collaborative action by a unified group to fight for social changes that will realise their quest for better living and/or working conditions.

Grassroots: the majority of ordinary people who form the mass of citizens of a hierarchically structured society, lacking any exceptional social advantages or social power.

conditions. Such improvements, as will be discussed below, are most likely to result from the twin processes of (1) strengthening grassroots communities from within and (2) building bridges between such communities and more powerful actors and agencies in the public and private sectors and civil society who are best placed to assist them in achieving their goals.

The need to challenge power

This chapter is concerned with the bottom-up drivers of social change and, more particularly, with the issue of grassroots participation in collective action for change. This focus on the bottom-up dimensions is justified for two reasons. First, an emphasis on bottom-up drivers of change is important because the voices of grassroots communities have a key role to play in motivating social change (Beeker, Gray & Raj, 1998). This is because many of the social factors that shape peoples' health-related behaviour are linked to the unequal distribution of economic and political power – often in favour of a small group of highly educated and/or wealthy persons, mostly men. The social changes needed to promote health-enabling communities often involve an increase in the political and/or economic power of women relative to men, or of poor people relative to wealthier ones. As Bulhan (cited in Seedat, 2001, 17) has argued: 'Power is never conceded without a demand.' Elites rarely give up power without strenuous challenges from those who are exploited or oppressed. For this reason, the voices and demands of grassroots communities and their strategic allies have a vital role to play in struggles for sexual health.

Secondly, this chapter focuses on bottom-up drivers of social change because it is these that fall within the boundaries of critical psychology, the

Individuals are social creatures. Attempts to change their behaviour need to go hand-in-hand with attempts to bring about social change – transformations in the social contexts.

focus of this book. The top-down drivers fall within the boundaries of economics, political science, law, development studies and social policy. However, as this chapter's case study will illustrate, efforts to achieve social change through bottom-up strategies have little hope of succeeding unless they are supported by top-down efforts. For this reason there is a lot of room for collaboration between critical psychologists and colleagues from other disciplines in developing theories and strategies of change which support and reinforce one another.

HOW DOES PARTICIPATION IN COLLECTIVE ACTION IMPACT ON THE SEXUAL HEALTH OF A COMMUNITY?

Defining 'grassroots' and 'community'

The remainder of this chapter has two goals. First, it seeks to outline the social psychological and community-level processes underlying the potential impact of participation in collective action on the health of grassroots communities. Secondly, it seeks to provide an illustration of the way in which this framework has been used to evaluate a community-led participatory HIV-prevention programme in the South African mining community of Summertown. In this chapter, the term 'grassroots' is used to refer to the mass of ordinary people that make up the majority of citizens in any society and who generally have relatively limited access to political and/or economic power, despite their numbers. A community is defined as a group of people who live and/or work in a common geographical place. Whilst it is often argued that 'communities' are better defined as 'communities of interest' (eg the Christian community) than 'communities of place' (eg the residents of Summertown), for reasons related to pragmatism and resources, health-related community development projects usually focus their energies on geographically bounded spaces. For this reason, this is the definition preferred here. Geographical communities tend to consist of diverse groups of people, constantly debating and negotiating ways of living and working together in varying degrees of harmony and conflict.

Forms of community participation

Two forms of community participation are increasingly advocated in the field of HIV prevention. The first of these is the participation of grassroots people in the design and implementation of HIV-prevention efforts. A popular strategy within this tradition is that of community-led **peer education**, in which health programmes are delivered by 'peers' rather than health professionals (UN Aids, 1999). Ideally, peer education uses participatory and democratic educational techniques where educators and learners are seen as equals and where both parties are required to be equally active in the learning process. This approach stands in contrast to more traditional education techniques, where the

'Power is never conceded without a demand.' Elites rarely give up power without strenuous challenges from those who are exploited or oppressed.

Peer education: non-traditional educational approach where people are taught by their peers rather than by outside experts. Ideally, peer educators use participatory educational techniques – where learning grows out of democratic action, debate and discussion amongst learners and educators rather than through more powerful or learned educators instructing learners.

educator is active and the learner is passive, and where the educator is regarded as superior to the learner. Thus, for example, youth peer educators are trained in participatory education techniques, such as games, dramas or role-plays, which enable them to facilitate sexual health education with their peers. Peer educators seek to promote the sexual health of other youth of a similar age and social status rather than youth having to rely on the interventions of more distant adults such as teachers or nurses. Rather than telling their peers how to behave, peer educators aim to generate debate and discussion about the range of sexual behaviours available to young people and about the advantages and disadvantages of each of these options. Thereafter, programme participants are left to make their own decisions about which option they will pursue rather than being instructed how to behave by the educators.

The fight against HIV/Aids requires collaboration between colleagues from a variety of disciplines in developing theories and strategies of change, prevention and treatment that support and reinforce one another.

Q. What do these people have in common?

DOCTORS WORKING WITH HIV/AIDS... AIDS SCIENTISTS... THE MEDICAL RESEARCH COUNCIL'S AIDS RESEARCHERS... THE MEDICINES CONTROL COUNCIL'S AIDS EXPERTS... THE NATIONAL AIDS CONSORTIUM, REPRESENTING 230 NGOs...

A. They're all excluded from the government's brilliant new National AIDS Council.

Multi-stakeholder partnerships

Stakeholder: someone who lives and/or works in a particular community and has a commitment to the health, success and general well-being of other community members.

The second strategy of community participation involves what are often referred to as 'multi-**stakeholder** partnerships', in which representatives of key local constituencies (eg youth, women, churches, local health departments, schools, local industry and so on) work together to support and co-ordinate local HIV-prevention activities such as peer education, STI control, home-based care of people living with HIV/Aids and so on. The rationale for the partnerships approach rests on two insights. The first of these is the insight that the causes and impacts of the HIV/Aids epidemic are too complex and multi-faceted to be dealt with by any single constituency, and that communities have the best chance of effective responses if they pool the insights, resources and efforts of as wide a range of groupings as possible. The second insight is that an epidemic is an extraordinary event, which arises because existing understandings of health, and existing health services, are inadequate for addressing it. For this reason dealing with an epidemic involves innovative and creative responses which are most likely to arise through the cooperation of a wide range of actors, networks and agencies (Gillies, 1998).

TOWARDS A 'SOCIAL PSYCHOLOGY OF PARTICIPATION'

Psychosocial processes underlying the impact of participation on health

How might the very public activity of participation in collective action impact on the very intimate and private nature of the sexual act? The aim of this section is to outline the psychosocial and community-level processes that underlie the potential impact of participation in strategies such as peer education and stakeholder partnerships on sexual health. The case study of the Summertown HIV-prevention programme which follows below will seek to illustrate how each of these processes are enabled and constrained by the wider social context within which communities are located, with particular emphasis on the unequal power dynamics around which South African societies are structured – particularly the relationships between men and women and between rich and poor. The view of participation presented in this chapter is underpinned by the work of the Brazilian social theorist and activist Paulo Freire (1970, 1973). He argued that individual change is most likely to occur when people participate in collective action aiming not only to change themselves as individuals but also to challenge those negative social conditions that undermine their interests and well-being.

The causes and impacts of the HIV/Aids epidemic are too complex and multi-faceted to be dealt with by any single constituency. Communities have the best chance of effective responses if they pool the insights, resources and efforts of as wide a range of groupings as possible.

In critical community interventions it is crucial that we bear in mind the unequal power dynamics around which South African societies are structured – particularly the relationships between men and women.

Social identities

Social identity: knowledge that one belongs to a particular social group. This knowledge usually goes together with being engaged in a set of group-related behaviours. It may also be associated with a sense of emotional commitment to in-group values and a sense of solidarity with other group members.

Our social identities consist of those aspects of our self-definitions that arise from our memberships of social groups (eg age-linked peer groups or occupational groups such as mineworker or sex workers) or from our positioning within networks of power relationships shaped by factors such as gender, ethnicity or socioeconomic position. Different identities or positionings are associated with different behavioural options. Thus, for example, a male identity is associated with a different range of behaviours to a female identity. In many contexts, males are allowed to be open about their enjoyment of sex and to behave accordingly. Women are given far less opportunity for public expression of their sexual desire (the denial of the existence of female sexual desire is common in many contexts). A woman is far more likely to behave in a way that hides her sexual activities from the public eye, particularly if she has several partners. All of these identity-linked behaviours have a range of potential consequences for people's vulnerability to HIV/Aids.

Socially constructed norms and values

In contrast to mainstream psychological approaches, which explain health-related behaviours (such as sexual behaviour) solely in terms of individual choices or decisions, researchers in the **social identity** tradition emphasise that a person's sexual choices or decisions are often deeply influenced by the socially constructed norms or values of liked and trusted peers who share a common identity (Allen, 1997; Stockdale, 1995). Such norms and values are constructed and reconstructed in the ongoing interactions between a group of people united through a sense of perceived common interests or a shared social position. The peer education approach builds on this insight. Ideally, peer education provides a context in which a group of peers who share a common identity can debate the possibility of constructing new sexual norms and values which are less damaging to their sexual health.

Peer education

Thus, for example, a group of like-minded women who feel unable to insist on condom use with their (unfaithful) sexual partners may use peer education settings as a forum for sharing ideas about ways in which they might assert themselves in their relationships, or about developing income-generation strategies which make them less dependent on these men. Such discussions may form the basis of new systems of norms and values in which women have more confidence and power to protect their sexual health. To cite another example, peer education might result in a group of young men coming together to discuss the way in which the social construction of masculinity places pressure on them to indulge in high-risk sex (by perpetuating the notion that 'real men are not afraid to take risks'). They might make a group decision to challenge this stereotype, sharing their uncertainties about where to find condoms and how to use them, and engaging in role-plays to develop strategies for responding to friends who might tease them about their new risk-avoiding stance.

Reconstructing social identities

In other words, social identities are not necessarily static or permanent. In certain circumstances they can be changed, and collective action strategies such as peer education can serve as important strategies for bringing about such change (Melucci, 1995). In principle, it should be possible for a group of young men or young women to make collective decisions to reconstruct the old social identities that are not consistent with their health or well-being. However, as will be discussed below, there are variations in the degrees of freedom that people have to change their identities and associated high-risk behaviours. A woman whose sexual partners assist her in supporting herself and her children will have limited freedom to refuse sex with a condom-resistant partner. A young man whose confidence has been dented by repeated failure to find work might be reluctant to give up the **macho** identity and behaviours which place his sexual health at risk but which lead to the approval and admiration of his youth gang.

Given the close relationship between a person's social identity and the **power-relations** characteristic of the society in which they live, attempts to change identities are most likely to be successful if they take place hand in hand with attempts to challenge the social relations that limit people's degree of freedom to act in ways that meet their needs and interests. Ideally, as will be discussed below, peer education efforts should go hand in hand with more general efforts to improve people's material life circumstances or to raise the levels of respect and recognition they receive from other social groups, as women or as youth, for example.

Empowerment

The renegotiation of social identities and associated norms and values needs to go hand in hand with the development of people's confidence and ability to act on collective decisions to engage in **health-enhancing behaviour** change. People are most likely to feel they can take control of their sexual health if they have positive experiences of exercising control in other areas of their lives (Wallerstein, 1992). Many people, particularly those who are marginalised on the grounds of poverty or gender, may have had few such experiences. Peer education seeks to empower participants by transferring health-related knowledge and teaching methods – usually the province of health professionals and experts – into the hands of ordinary people. It also provides opportunities for the exercise of leadership (in local health initiatives) by members of tradition-

---

Macho:
description of identities or behaviours associated with an exaggerated interpretation of masculinity. In some cases these are positive (eg an exaggerated desire to provide support and protection for one's family). In others, they may be negative (eg exerting undemocratic power over women, or treating them as sex objects rather than as equals).

Power-relations:
relations between individuals or groups – in a hierarchically structured society – with different levels of access to wealth, political influence and/or symbolic respect and recognition.

Health-enhancing behaviour:
all behaviours (eg condom use, seeking appropriate treatment for other STIs) that reduce the chance of HIV-infection and promote good health.

Critical consciousness: understanding of the way in which social circumstances serve as obstacles to people's health and well-being. Ideally, such an understanding goes hand-in-hand with a vision of alternative social relations in which people's living and/or working conditions were better, as well as some insights into the strategies that might be used to make such changes happen.

ally excluded social groups – such as youth out of school or commercial sex workers. In so doing it gives people a sense of 'ownership' of the problem of HIV/Aids, and increases the likelihood that they will feel the problem is their own responsibility rather than the responsibility of the more distant agencies of government or health departments.

In addition to promoting a more general sense of **empowerment**, peer education should also empower participants more directly in relation to providing them with the practical skills they need to engage in safe sexual behaviour. For example, youth peer education may include role-plays and discussions seeking to enhance participants' assertiveness or sexual negotiation techniques, familiarising them with condoms, where to obtain them, how to use them, and so on. They may also include discussions of the importance of prompt and appropriate treatment for other STIs, as well as familiarising participants with the whereabouts of clinics and preparing them for the more embarrassing aspects of the STI clinic encounter, such as having to show one's private parts to a stranger or having to deal with a clinic nurse who is prejudiced against sexually active women or young people, for example.

Critical thinking

People are far more likely to be able to change their behaviour if they have a realistic understanding of the obstacles that stand in the way of behaviour change, a belief that such obstacles can be overcome and a vision of alternative behavioural options (Freire, 1970, 1973). Such understandings constitute a state of **critical consciousness** that Freire argues is a precondition for mobilising marginalised groupings in collective action to improve their health. In the context of HIV/Aids, this might involve a group of peers developing understandings of the ways in which factors such as the stigmatisation of sexuality and STIs, gender inequalities and poverty undermine their sexual health – and the development of a vision of social relations that were less damaging of their well-being. Thus, for example, a successful peer education programme might provide a group of men with the opportunity to discuss the way in which the achievement of masculine identities was limited by poverty and unemployment, as discussed above. Through debate and discussion these men may develop insights into the way in which they compensate for this by adopting an overly macho and controlling attitude to women in sexual relationships. Such understandings would form the starting point from which men could collectively work towards redefining their masculine identities in ways that were less endangering of their sexual health.

Freire sees a state of 'critical consciousness' as a precondition for mobilising marginalised groupings in collective action. 'Critical consciousness' involves a realistic understanding of the obstacles to behaviour change, a belief that such obstacles can be overcome and a vision of alternative behavioural options.

HIV/Aids stigma

A key obstacle to the HIV/Aids prevention struggle is the stigmatisation of people living with HIV/Aids (Vetten & Bhana, 2001) (see Box 1). The fear and loathing of HIV positive people serves to drive the disease even further 'underground', discouraging others from going for testing or from facing up to the possibility that they too could become infected and should therefore take precautions. It also causes untold misery for HIV/Aids sufferers. The area of stigma is an important arena for critical thinking and debate, in the interests of raising people's awareness of the way in which it serves as a key social obstacle to the prevention of HIV and to the support of people living with Aids. Ideally, peer education could raise participants' awareness of the importance of creating a climate of tolerance and compassion for people living with Aids and developing understandings of the way in which stigma indirectly serves to hinder people from taking control of their sexual health.

Empowerment: psychosocial state in which a group of people feel confident and motivated that they can achieve important goals they set themselves, and where they have the skills and opportunities to do so.

BOX 1   The social psychology of stigma

A combination of fear and ignorance has led to a situation in which many HIV/Aids sufferers are treated with high levels of disrespect and rejection. Joffe (1999) explains stigma in terms of the human fear of the random and uncertain nature of life and death, a fear that is dramatically exaggerated in the context of the HIV/Aids epidemic. She says that people cope with this situation by projecting their worst fears onto clearly identifiable out-groups, who are then subjected to prejudice and discrimination. This process of stigmatisation or 'othering' is said to result in feelings of comfort and security. It serves to distance people who hope that they are HIV/Aids-free from a sense of danger, giving them a sense of personal invulnerability to the threat of HIV/Aids, a threat that might otherwise appear too terrifying to contemplate.

Community: group of people who are united through a common identity, interests or geographical residence. The last of these is most frequently used in the field of public health and health promotion.

Community-level processes underlying the impact of participation on health

Dimensions of power

What are the **community** contexts most likely to facilitate the processes of identity reshaping, empowerment and critical consciousness outlined above? And what contexts are most likely to support the goals of participatory HIV-prevention strategies such as peer education? The arguments in this section rest on two assumptions. The first is that HIV/Aids often tends to flourish in marginalised social groupings (such as young people or women) (Barnett & Whiteside, 2002). These are the social groupings that often have the least access to three interrelated dimensions of power – *economic* power (access to money and paid work), *political* power (access to formal political influence) and **symbolic power** (access to respect and recognition from other social groups). For this reason it is extremely unlikely that groups of multiple-disempowered youth or women will have the power or influence to promote the development of health-enabling environments without the support and assistance of more powerful groups. For this reason it is vitally important that

Symbolic power: extent to which members of particular social or identity groups have access to respect and the recognition of their worth and dignity from other members of society. Lack of symbolic power may characterise the life situations of poor people in a materialist society, women in a sexist society, black people in a racist society, or people living with Aids in a context of stigmatisation.

community-based HIV-prevention programmes provide opportunities for the building of alliances or partnerships between local HIV-vulnerable groups and more powerful constituencies.

Micro- and macro-dynamics of power

The second assumption is that the HIV/Aids epidemic – with its roots in a series of complex processes ranging from the micro-dynamics of human sexual desire to the macro-dynamics of gender, economics and politics – is too complex a problem to be solved by any single constituency, such as peer educators or schools or health departments. Addressing the challenge requires the co-operation of a wide range of sectors both within local communities and between local communities and a range of national and even international actors and agencies. Building on these two assumptions, it will be argued below that efforts to engage grassroots communities in collective action to achieve improved sexual health are most likely to succeed in communities characterised by bonding and bridging social capital, and where strong organisational initiatives exist to support the mobilisation of collective action.

Social capital

Health-enabling community contexts

It has been argued that people are most likely to undergo health-enhancing behaviour change if they live in communities characterised by high levels of **social capital** (Baum, 1999). Such 'health-enabling community contexts' are believed to enable and support the renegotiation of social identities and the development of empowerment and critical consciousness outlined above. Social capital is defined in terms of participation in local networks and organisations (Putnam, 2000). These may include *informal networks* of friends and neighbours, *voluntary associations* linked with hobbies, leisure and personal development, or *community activist groupings* concerned with matters of local interest. Such participation is associated with increased levels of trust, reciprocal help and support and a positive local community identity amongst local community residents. High levels of local participation are associated with high levels of **collective efficacy** or **perceived citizen power** (see Box 2). This is a characteristic of communities where people feel that their needs and views are respected and valued and where they have channels to participate in making decisions in the context of the family, school and neighbourhood, as well as influencing wider political processes which shape their daily lives (Campbell, 2000).

Creating new social capital

An important determinant of the success of participatory health promotional interventions – such as peer education – is the extent to which they mobilise or

---

Social capital: community-level strengths or resources such as trust, mutually supportive relationships, a positive local identity and high levels of participation in informal and formal social networks of various kinds (eg friends or neighbours; voluntary associations linked to personal development; activist organisations).

Perceived citizen power: situation in which grassroots people believe they have the power to influence the laws, policies and events that shape key aspects of their lives.

> ## BOX 2   The impact of 'perceived citizen power' on health
>
> In a small pilot study of community-level influences on health in England, Campbell, Wood & Kelly (1999) compared levels of social capital in two communities that were matched in terms of socioeconomic status and employment levels. Despite these similarities, levels of health were higher in one community than the other. The most striking difference between the two communities lay in levels of 'perceived citizen power'. Residents of the less healthy community had little experience of local community activism and were seldom aware of the existence of organisations or channels through which people might express their views on local facilities, services or quality of life. In comparison, many residents of the healthier community expressed the view that ordinary people ought to get involved in local community politics. They cited examples of ways in which they might do this, and expressed the view that such activist involvement had the potential to yield benefits for both the individuals involved as well as other community members. The authors conclude that much research remains to be done in exploring links between perceived citizen power and health.

create social capital. Ideally, peer education programmes mobilise existing sources of social capital by drawing on existing community strengths and networks. Ideally, they also create new social capital in the form of strong and valued peer education networks. Such networks impact on health directly through their efforts to promote healthy behaviours. They also impact on health indirectly through creating generalised social cohesion and trust that not only increases the likelihood of positive health behaviours (eg condom use in relation to HIV prevention) but also reduces health-damaging stress (which may undermine the immune systems of people living with HIV/Aids).

Collective efficacy: power or ability of a group (or collection) of people to succeed in achieving goals of mutual interest.

Processes of enablement and constraint

However, social capital is not equally distributed in any community (Bourdieu, 1986; Saegert, Thompson & Warren, 2000). People who are marginalised by virtue of poverty or gender or social stigma may have reduced opportunities for positive and empowering participation in local community life. It is vitally important that policies and interventions that advocate participation as a means of promoting health are not blind to obstacles to such participation by socially excluded groups (Nelson & Wright, 1995). Different social groups hold different levels of power to engage in collective action and to construct life projects to meet their needs and interests (Kelly & Van Vlaenderen, 1996). Community development approaches and participatory strategies such as peer education tread a thin line between the processes of enablement (grassroots community agency) and constraint (structural obstacles resulting from unequal power relations or resistance to social change by powerful groups). It is often at the very moment that local community development programmes open up the possibility of the empowerment of local people to take control of

Social capital is not equally distributed in any community. People who are marginalised by virtue of poverty or gender or social stigma may have reduced opportunities for positive and empowering participation in local community life.

their sexual health that they simultaneously come up against a series of institutional barriers to such change.

Bonding social capital

Bonding social capital:
trusting, supportive relationships ('bonds') among members of a group who live/work in similar conditions, who feel a sense of commonness with one another and who have similar access to economic, political and symbolic power (eg young people in school; sex workers).

Jovchelovitch (1996) points to the 'double-edged' nature of power. Power can be a negative force, something that constrains people and holds them back. But it can also be 'a space of possible action', where previously marginalised local people can act together to maximise their collective voice and their collective impact. The concept of power is relevant to the distinction between bridging and **bonding social capital**. This distinction provides a useful way of conceptualising the types of local community relationship that might contribute to the development of a health-enabling community (Putnam, 2000). *Bonding* social capital refers to inward-looking social capital located within homogenous groups, whose members are united through a common social identity and similar levels of access to the three forms of social power outlined above ('within-group' social capital). Such social capital binds similar people together in strong horizontal peer groups characterised by trust, reciprocal help and support, and a positive common identity. Such relationships result in the benefits and resources that flow from close trusting relations with similar others.

Bridging social capital

Bridging social capital:
compared to bonding social capital, bridging social capital refers to 'bridges' between small local groupings and more powerful actors and agencies who have the political and/or economic power to help them meet their goals.

The second form of social capital is called **bridging social capital**. It refers to links that occur between diverse social groups. Such links bring together diverse groups with varying levels of access to economic, political and symbolic power ('between-group' social capital). Bridging social capital brings people in contact with the resources and benefits that result from having a wide and varied range of social contacts. It is associated with trusting and supportive relationships amongst groups whose worldviews, interests and access to resources might be very different but who have some sort of overlapping mutual interest.

Thus, for example, bridging social capital might bring together representatives of youth peer groups, local employers, local civic groupings and government health and education representatives. These groups may traditionally have little in common, but HIV/Aids provides a special context in which they are united by their mutual interest in promoting healthy sexual behaviour in the local community. Bridging social capital ensures that traditionally isolated and disadvantaged groups (eg young people or sex workers) are put in touch with vertical networks of political and economic influence and expertise that will assist them in maximising their efforts to address particular problems.

This bonding/bridging distinction is vital for clarifying those forms of participation and collaboration most likely to further the goals of community-led health promotion. It is through the development of bonding social capital that a group of people take the first step towards developing a critical consciousness of the economic, political and symbolic obstacles to their health and well-being and begin to develop both the insight and the confidence to address these obstacles.

Two forms of bridging social capital

However, it is vital that participatory projects also seek to promote the development of two forms of bridging social capital. The first is the development of bridges between small peer education groups with more powerful groups – in their local geographical area – who may have the power and resources to assist them in their quest to develop more health-enabling community contexts. These powerful groups might include local government representatives or local employers. The second form of bridging social capital links small local groups into networks of influence beyond the geographical location of the local community. Here we refer to the importance of developing channels through which umbrella alliances of small local peer groups can add their voices to extra-local debates about regional and national policies and interventions that are supportive of their local efforts. Local youth peer education networks might link into regional or national networks and channels through which they could pressurise the government to provide better skills training and employment opportunities for youth. More directly related to HIV/Aids, such youth groups might develop extra-community links through which they sought to pressurise health departments into providing more youth-friendly sexual health services, and in training STI clinic workers to treat sexually active youth with respect and tolerance. Local groups of people living with Aids might seek to link up with the national Treatment Action Campaign to lobby government to provide affordable drug treatment for Aids patients or to speed up the delivery of government grants to full-blown Aids patients.

According to Paulo Freire, a vital dimension of successful participation includes the development of opportunities for small local groups to influence wider initiatives for positive social change beyond their immediate community contexts. He argues that the activity of participation is most likely to be successful when it enables people simultaneously to change themselves, their local communities and the wider societies in which they live.

> A vital dimension of successful participation is developing opportunities for small local groups to influence wider initiatives for positive social change beyond their immediate community contexts.

Organisational initiatives

The role of an external change agent

What forces are most likely to initiate and drive forward the processes of individual and collective change that Freire cites as the hallmarks of successful community development programmes? Ideally the motivation and momentum for such changes should come from within the local communities themselves, who should get together to identify publicly the nature of the problem and then develop a collective strategy for addressing it. However, such motivation and momentum will not always be present, particularly in relation to a taboo topic such as HIV/Aids, where the high levels of stigma and denial around sexuality, death and STIs make it unlikely that those who fear they are at risk, or those already affected, will stand up in public and confidently and openly publicise their condition. In such a situation, an external change agent may be necessary to bring together local people and support them in working out ways in which the problem can best be identified and tackled. External change agents are generally organisations associated with government, the private sector or non-government organisations (NGOs).

Trust and confidentiality

The success of such organisations in mobilising local people to work for change to improve their sexual health will be influenced by at least two factors (Campbell, 2003). The first of these is the extent to which the organisation is trusted by local people. The second is the extent to which the organisation's goals and strategies resonate with the needs and experiences of local people. The experience of many NGOs working in the HIV/Aids field suggests that a great deal of time and effort is necessary to build such trust and to formulate goals and strategies that local people feel they are able to identify with and openly associate themselves with. In relation to a stigmatised disease such as HIV/Aids, trust is often closely linked to the extent to which people believe that the organisation's workers will respect the confidentiality of those who approach them for help.

The fact that many local people will often only associate themselves with such organisations in conditions of secrecy makes the organisations' goals of mobilising people for assertive collective action to address common goals a very difficult task. Some organisations have responded by attempting to disguise their focus on HIV-prevention and Aids-care, presenting themselves as youth organisations or health organisations for example. Support groups for people with Aids emphasise that their goals are to support people who are 'infected or *affected by* HIV/Aids', enabling those who wish to disguise their status to elicit the support they need under the guise of claiming that they are indirectly affected by the HIV-positive status of a friend or relative rather than being directly affected themselves. Much work remains to be done in addressing the stigma that makes people reluctant to be open about their sexual health needs, and that undermines the possibility of open and confident collective action by people who believe either that they are already infected or that their future sexual health is at risk.

Social factors such as poverty and homelessness make it difficult for many people to protect their sexual health.

CASE STUDY: PEER EDUCATION BY COMMERCIAL SEX WORKERS IN SOUTH AFRICA

This section reports on a three-year study of a peer education programme amongst commercial sex workers in an isolated 400-person shack settlement in a gold mining community, where more than six out of ten women were HIV positive (Campbell, 2003; Campbell & Mzaidume, 2001). Women lived in conditions of poverty and violence in makeshift tin structures without running water or sanitation. Most came from extremely deprived backgrounds characterised by physical or emotional abuse. Relationships between sex workers were often unsupportive and competitive in a context where women competed fiercely for a short supply of paying clients. They had little formal education and few skills. Sex workers made their living from the sale of sex and alcohol to migrant workers on a nearby gold mine. The harsh working conditions of underground mining led to strongly macho identities amongst mineworkers, associated with reluctance to using condoms in commercial encounters (see Box 3). Sex workers lacked both economic and psychological power to resist clients' wishes, and condom use was virtually non-existent at the start of the peer education programme.

Aims of the programme

At the psychosocial level, the aims of the programme, co-ordinated by a nursing sister employed by a local NGO, were threefold. These were: to increase knowledge about sexual health risks and a sense of perceived vulnerability to HIV infection; to encourage people to seek out early diagnosis and appropriate treatment of other sexually transmitted infections, which increase vulnerability to HIV; and to encourage the use of condoms, and make them

HIV-transmission:
spread of a
predominantly
sexually transmitted
virus through a
complex and multi-
layered series of
causes, ranging
from individual
behaviour to macro-
social relations.

BOX 3   Miners, masculinity and HIV-transmission

A study of **HIV-transmission** on the gold mines (Macheke & Campbell, 1998) examines why some miners continue to take risks with their sexual health, despite being well informed about the risks of HIV. Several aspects of the social construction of masculinity on the mines influence sexual behaviour. Thus, for example, regular flesh-to-flesh sex is seen as necessary for a man's good health as well as his pleasure. Macho identities serve as mechanisms by which men cope with the dangers of underground work. 'Real men' are regarded as brave, fearless and willing to risk death in order to fulfil their role as breadwinners. Associated with this macho masculinity is the notion of a man having a powerful drive to desire sex with many women. Within such a context, many miners choose not to use condoms.

freely available. The programme aimed to achieve these goals through the processes outlined above. The first of these was to provide opportunities for the renegotiation of the social and sexual identities that made it unlikely that sex workers would assert their health interests in the fact of client reluctance. This would involve examining the way in which both their identities as women, in a male-dominated society, and as workers in a highly stigmatised profession undermined their confidence and their negotiating power. The programme hoped to increase a sense of empowerment amongst women through placing health-related knowledge – usually the province of outside experts – in their hands, and through providing them with the opportunities to exercise leadership of an important health initiative. The dialogical nature of the peer education approach would encourage development of a sense of critical consciousness of the social obstacles to behaviour change, and of the need for collective action to begin to challenge the ways in which these impacted negatively on their sexual health.

Finally, and most importantly, the programme sought not only to build bonding social capital within sex worker communities but also to build bridging social capital to link sex workers to sources of power and influence beyond their marginalised local settings. This would be created in two ways. First, through putting this particular sex worker peer educator group in touch with other similar groups in the region. Secondly, through involving a wide range of more powerful local community 'stakeholders' in supporting the programme. These would include representatives of the provincial and national health departments, the largest local employer, namely the mining industry as well as a range of local civic, religious and political groupings. A central goal was to ensure that parallel peer education efforts were imple-mented amongst mineworker clients. This was because clients held both psychological power (as men) and economic power (as paying customers) over sex workers. Efforts to promote behaviour change amongst sex workers would have very limited impact without simultaneous efforts to promote such behaviour change amongst men. In addition, the programme sought to reduce women's total economic dependence on clients through providing opportunities for alternative forms of income generation (such as savings clubs and small business opportunities).

Challenges of setting up the programme

The nursing sister employed to facilitate the programme struggled against great odds to develop a strong and united team of peer educators. The shack community was run by a group of unelected armed men, who served as gate-keepers to the settlement, and much effort had to go in to getting their permission for the project to be set up. Women had little experience of working collectively to achieve mutually beneficial goals. Much work had to go into team building, and developing codes of conduct in the chaotic and conflict-ridden community, with high alcohol use and fighting, and low levels of trust. Despite many setbacks, the peer educator team developed into a strong and respected group of local women. They worked tirelessly to distribute condoms and to educate their peers about the risks of STDs, using participatory methods. It was through such methods that the programme sought to promote a critical awareness of the way in which gender relations and the stigmatisation of sex work undermined women's confidence and ability to protect their health.

STDs/STIs:
sexually transmitted diseases or infections, including HIV/Aids and other diseases (eg gonorrhoea, syphilis or herpes) which increase vulnerability to HIV-infection.

Disappointing outcomes: Varying impacts of poverty on people's ability to change

However, despite these efforts, the programme had little success in increasing condom use or reducing STDs over a three-year period. Programme evaluators have identified a complex array of reasons for its disappointing results at each level of analysis (Campbell, 2003). A detailed account is beyond the scope of a short case study, but some key points are raised here, all related in some way or another to the impact of poverty on people's abilities to change their life circumstances. The programme had great success in uniting a small group of women in a motivated and dedicated group who met regularly and worked tirelessly at promoting peer educational activities. They also actively involved themselves in regular meetings with similar sex worker peer education teams in the region, participating in the training of new peer educators in other regions, with teams from different local communities providing important support and advice for one another.

However, despite this partial success, some sex workers did not collaborate with the peer education team. In hindsight, in relation to its goal of providing contexts for the renegotiation of social identities, the programme probably began with the unrealistic expectation that women in such a divided, competitive and highly stigmatised community would automatically constitute 'peers', simply by virtue of the fact that they were all sex workers. The concept of a 'peer education' presupposes the possibility that a collection of people might have enough of a sense of a common identity and mutually defined interests to learn to work together in pursuit of collaborative goals. The forces dividing the programme's intended 'peers' were often greater than those uniting them. One major dividing force was the fierce competition for clients, which undermined the likelihood of women forming a divided front against condom-averse clients. If a sex worker refused to have sex without a condom, the customer would simply move on from shack to shack until he found someone who agreed, and in conditions of severe poverty turning away a paying client was not always an option.

Programme goals ran strongly against the strategies that some women had developed to deal with their harsh lives. One way in which some sex workers chose to cope with the stigma and contempt associated with sex work was to conduct their profession in secret. They loudly dissociated themselves from an openly sex worker led health promotion programme as part of their ongoing struggle to maintain an image of respectability. Ironically, the programme rationale of working with women to feel more open and assertive about their work as a means of improving their confidence succeeded with some sex workers, but had the unintended consequence of alienating others. In this community, the sale of alcohol was a key economic survival strategy, and the use of alcohol was a psychological strategy for dealing with ongoing stresses.

Yet people were far less likely to use condoms when they had been drinking. Another survival strategy in a context of poverty and violence – where women had little control over their lives – was an attitude of fatalism. This fatalism discouraged some women from believing that they had any power to control their sexual health.

Attempts to generate alternative means of income generation for women – through setting up child-care schemes or vegetable stalls in the local shack settlement – met with little interest. Sex workers pointed out that fellow shack residents had already exploited existing commercial opportunities to their utmost limit. They saw mainstream income-generating activities as unrewarding drudgery in comparison with sex work which, for all its disadvantages, yielded financial rewards which were not only immediate, but also far in excess of what could be raised in a small business.

Lack of collaboration by powerful community stakeholders

The greatest obstacle to programme success was continued mineworker refusal to use condoms. Despite its ambitious goals, in reality the project, under the auspices of a small and humble NGO, had little influence on the powerful mining industry. The latter group had little commitment to implementing peer education amongst the vast majority of mineworker clients. Mine medical doctors responsible for sexual health were unfamiliar with the social understandings of disease transmission and prevention which underlie the peer education approach. Within this context, they dismissed peer education as 'vague social science', and preferred to throw their HIV-prevention energies into biomedical STI-control programmes, which had little impact on reducing STIs amongst mineworkers over our three-year study period. Such attitudes, combined with a lack of mineworker trade union commitment to participating in project management, meant that the majority of miners were not exposed to peer education, as outlined in the original project proposal. Yet it was male miners who held both economic and psychological power in encounters with female sex workers. Much remains to be learned about the factors shaping the likelihood that powerful stakeholders will collaborate in partnerships with marginalised community groups in addressing social problems such as HIV-transmission (see Box 4). There is a need for insights into systems of incentives and accountability that might motivate powerful groupings to collaborate with marginalised communities who have little political or economic power or influence over more powerful stakeholders.

This case study has illustrated the way in which the conceptual framework outlined above served to inform the evaluation of a community-led peer education programme in a highly marginalised and disorganised community. In short, while the programme went some way to promoting bonding social capital amongst some women within this community, as well as bonds

> There is a need for insights into systems of incentives and accountability that might motivate powerful groupings to collaborate with marginalised communities who have little political or economic power or influence over more powerful stakeholders.

BOX 4 Maximising the potential of multi-stakeholder partnerships

In the HIV/Aids field there is currently a strong emphasis on the importance of involving a wide range of stakeholders in prevention efforts. Whilst such an emphasis makes excellent theoretical and political sense, much remains to be learned about the complexities of implementing multi-stakeholder projects, and how best to avoid the obstacles that inevitably arise when diverse groups of people seek to work together. Five factors are likely to maximise the success of multi-stakeholder HIV-prevention programmes (Campbell, 2003):

(1) There should be equal levels of *commitment* by all stakeholders.

(2) Programmes should not be dominated by biomedically trained people who do not always have a strong *understanding of the*

social dimensions of disease transmission and prevention.

(3) Programmes benefit when they have *skills and capacity* in areas such as organisational development, project management and conflict mediation – which are required to coordinate groups who may have very different skills and worldviews.

(4) Collaborative projects need to be backed up by *health systems infrastructure* to facilitate this coordination.

(5) Projects should ensure that there are well-established *incentives* and procedures to ensure the *accountability* of stakeholders to each other and to grassroots project beneficiaries.

A health promotional strategy of community participation should seek not only to change the behaviour of individuals but also to promote the development of 'health-enabling community and social contexts' which support people's efforts to be healthy.

between this group of women and similar sex worker peer educators in similar settlements in the region, its goals were crucially undermined by its lack of success in building bridging social capital, and in particular in mobilising support from more powerful local constituencies, such as the gold mining industry and its workers.

CONCLUSION

This chapter began by specifying the author's commitment to contributing to a health psychology that was 'critical' through its commitment (1) to highlighting how social conditions often make it very difficult for people to behave in health-enhancing ways; and (2) to broadening the individualistic focus of traditional health psychology to take account of this insight. Within this context the chapter has focused on community participation as a health promotional strategy which seeks not only to change the behaviour of individuals but also to promote the development of 'health-enabling community and social contexts' which support people's efforts to be healthy.

This interest in community participation has been located within the context of Freire's contention that individual change is most likely to come from projects in which people collaborate not only to change their own behaviour but also to understand and challenge the social circumstances that place their health at risk. The framework outlined in this chapter has drawn on the concepts of *social identity, empowerment, critical consciousness* and *social capital* as conceptual tools for a 'social psychology of participation', with particular emphasis on the way in which these processes are enabled and constrained by unequal *power-relations*. The chapter has illustrated the way in which this conceptual framework informed the evaluation of a community-led peer education programme amongst sex workers in South Africa. In this programme, peer education failed to achieve its intended effects in reducing levels of HIV and other STDs.

One of the many lessons arising from this case study relates to the importance of building bridging social capital. This lesson highlights the limitations of behaviour change programmes which focus narrowly on psychosocial and community-level processes without succeeding in mobilising more powerful actors and agencies (both inside and outside the community) to assist in working towards programme goals. The brief case study provided above sought to highlight the ways in which poverty, stigma and gender oppression undermined attempts to promote the collective identity and critical empowerment of sex workers that underlie successful peer education. Within such a context, it was unlikely that marginalised sex workers would succeed in improving their sexual health without significant efforts to change the behaviour of their psychologically and economically more powerful male clients, for example.

Hierarchy:
set of social relations characterised by an unequal distribution of economic power and/or political influence. In many societies hierarchical social relations can be symbolised by a triangle, with the numerical majority of less powerful people occupying the broad base of the triangle, and a decreasing number of increasingly powerful people occupying the space as one moves towards the triangle's sharp tip.

Collective action by members of marginalised social groupings is unlikely to be effective in the absence of alliances with more powerful social groupings, which have access to the economic and political power necessary for the success of programme goals. As stated earlier in the chapter, attempts to drive social change through 'bottom-up' strategies are unlikely to be successful unless they are reinforced by parallel 'top-down' efforts to promote the kinds of social changes which are necessary to maximise the possibility of health for all.

This emphasis on the need for a combination of bottom-up and top-down efforts to promote social change for health is consistent with the UN Aids (2000) analysis of the common features of initiatives that have succeeded in reducing HIV transmission. This analysis highlights the mobilisation and participation of local communities as a necessary precondition for successful HIV prevention. However, on its own, it is not a sufficient condition. Community action is not a 'magic bullet'. The UN Aids report emphasises that the potential for grassroots participation to bring about health-enhancing social change is shaped and constrained by the quality of the partnerships or alliances that local communities develop with a wide range of actors – in government, the private sector, civil society and (where appropriate) among project donors. Participants and facilitators of social psychological and community-level interventions – such as peer education – need to stand side-by-side with a much wider range of agencies and actors if they are to have optimal benefits in reducing health inequalities and improving the health of marginalised groups.

The UN Aids emphasis on the role of appropriate alliances and partnerships in successful community health interventions resonates with frequently voiced criticisms of many so-called community action programmes that seek only to promote local grassroots participation in community health projects. Such programmes are condemned for failing to pay adequate attention to the way in which the ability of marginalised communities to improve their health is constrained by political and economic power relations that lie beyond the boundaries or influence of local communities (Campbell & Mzaidume, 2001). They are also criticised for failing to take steps to challenge the political and economic inequalities that often prevent marginalised people from improving their health. They have also been charged with 'victim-blaming' through suggesting that politically and economically disempowered groupings are capable of taking control of their health – when in fact the social contexts in which they live make it unlikely that they can do so (Seedat, 2001). The sex worker programme outlined above illustrates the strength of this critique.

In short, while critical health psychologists have a vital role to play in contributing to understandings of the psychosocial and community-level aspects of health promotion and social change, they also need to have a realistic understanding of the limits of their discipline. Much work remains to be done in building links between critical health psychologists and thinkers and activists in terrains such as economics, politics, social policy and development studies. Such links are essential for the development of understandings and strategies for synthesising top-down and bottom-up efforts to create community contexts which are most likely to support and enable healthy sexual behaviours.

Collective action by members of marginalised social groupings is unlikely to be effective in the absence of alliances with more powerful social groupings, which have access to the economic and political power necessary for the success of programme goals.

Critical thinking tasks

1. Speculate about some of the economic, political and legal obstacles to effective HIV-prevention in South Africa. To what extent do existing laws and social policies (in fields such as health, welfare, education, gender and social development) provide an effective starting point for the fight against HIV, or to what extent are new laws and policies necessary? Which factors stand in the way of the implementation of those positive laws and policies that already exist?
2. What kinds of top-down social change are necessary to support the psychosocial and community-level processes underlying local collective action, particularly in relation to the challenges of reducing the spread of HIV and of providing better care and support for people living with Aids?
3. Many would argue that the key factors that facilitate HIV-transmission and the stigmatisation of people living with Aids lie beyond the disciplinary boundaries of critical psychology. Outline how you would respond to a critic who said that psychology had no role to play in the struggle to limit HIV-transmission in South Africa.
4. Speculate about the processes and mechanisms by which 'perceived citizen power' may (or indeed may not) impact on people's health – either in terms of reducing health-damaging stress or in terms of increasing the likelihood that people will engage in health-enhancing behaviours.

Recommended readings

For a fuller outline of the conceptual arguments laid out in this chapter see Catherine Campbell (2003) *Letting them die: Why HIV/Aids prevention programmes often fail* (Cape Town: Double Storey/Juta). This book also provides an illustration of the way in which this conceptual framework has been used to understand the challenges of HIV-prevention amongst youth and mineworkers, as well as the complexities of creating bridging social capital amongst the residents of marginalised local communities and more powerful social actors and agencies.

Paulo Freire's (1970/1996) *Pedagogy of the oppressed* (Harmondsworth: Penguin) provides a valuable account of the role and possibilities of collective action as a strategy for improving the life chances of marginalised social group-ings. While the author was an activist in the field of adult education rather than health, the book is full of generalisable insights.

Understanding and Preventing Violence

Garth Stevens, Mohamed Seedat &
Ashley van Niekerk

OUTCOMES

After having studied this chapter you should be able to:

- understand the historical location and importance of violence as a social phenomenon and as an object of social inquiry
- describe a range of social scientific perspectives and definitions of violence
- explain a range of psychological paradigms and definitions of violence, and
- critically apply the public health model as a health science framework within which violence can be described, analysed, theorised and prevented through various forms of social action.

Looking back: Violence as endemic to South Africa

THE PARTICULAR form and expression of contemporary South African society has undoubtedly been influenced and shaped by its violent history of racism and oppression. For the social scientist, locating current manifestations of violence within their ideological, historical and material contexts is therefore critical if comprehensive understandings of such manifestations are to be generated alongside appropriate forms of social action aimed at preventing them. Such a critical social analysis allows for scrutiny of the ways in which violence has mutated over time and in different social contexts, its various points of genesis within social formations, its cyclical impacts and residual effects on all sectors of society, and an ability to historically understand and develop interventions to address current manifestations of violence in South Africa. This is particularly important as we strive to develop scientific approaches that can make relevant contributions to the overall health, psychosocial well-being and development of the population, in ways that move beyond scientific rhetoric to concrete social action.

The endemic nature of violence within the history of South Africa was already evident in the period of initial 'discovery' and conquest that was premised on colonial expansion and slavery as far back as the mid 1600s (Banton, 1988; Callinicos, 1987; Miles, 1989). This was followed by concerted efforts to penetrate the interior of South Africa for a range of social and economic reasons, and was accompanied by wars of dispossession, slavery and indentured labour (Callinicos, 1987). These genocidal, controlling and exclusionary practices were most frequently justified through scientific racism and notions of 'bringing civilisation to African heathens' (Miles, 1989). Throughout this period, racism increasingly became institutionalised through the legislative processes, thereby enabling the development of White privilege through Black economic and social exploitation. The result was the emergence of an increasingly polarised society that facilitated the growth of White-owned and -controlled local and regional economies within Southern Africa. These processes and outcomes were further entrenched in the pre-apartheid years as economic independence from colonial powers was pursued, and the necessity to formalise 'racial' exploitation became an economic imperative. It ultimately culminated in the institutionalisation and legalisation of racism in the 1948 apartheid policy that advocated 'racial' segregation and separate development, and furthermore ensured White privilege through the legal, social, economic, political and military control of Blacks (Alexander, 1985; O'Meara, 1983; Terreblanche & Natrass, 1990; Wolpe, 1988).

While the effects of state-sanctioned violence have been well documented (see for example, Cooper, 1990; Duncan, 1991; Letlaka-Rennert, 1990; Reynolds, 1989; Straker 1992), it also spawned a history of resistance, counter-violence and liberatory politics. Examples of this counter-violence were most notably found in the anti-colonial uprisings amongst Blacks, the armed struggle waged by various elements within the liberation movement, and the range of historical uprisings that occurred throughout the turbulent years of apartheid. Despite the eventual formation of a 'non-racial' democracy in 1994 and the dismantling of the apartheid state apparatus, the social and psychological effects of prolonged repression and counter-violence also became readily apparent, even in post-apartheid South Africa (see for example, Dawes & Donald, 1994; Duncan & Rock 1994; Richter, 1994). Bulhan (1985:131) emphasises the historical connections between violence, oppression and racism, and argues that a 'situation of violence is essentially a cauldron of violence. It is brought into existence and maintained by dint of violence. This violence gradually permeates the social order to affect everyday living. In time, the violence takes on different guises and becomes less blatant and more integral to institutional as well as interpersonal reality.'

Living with the fallout: Violence in contemporary South Africa

The ongoing socio-economic inequities, social fragmentation, and individual socialisation patterns have been asserted as amongst the spectrum of causal agents complicit in the persisting prominence of violence in South African society (Butchart *et al.*, 2000). Despite the political and social reform that characterises present-day South Africa, violence has indeed continued to permeate our everyday realities. Violence remains a major cause of death, disability and psychic trauma, and prevails as a significant area of attention for the social scientist. While the impact of globalisation on South African economic policy and its negative effects on the living standards of the majority of South Africans may also be construed as a violent consequence (Bond, 1994; 2000), the more overt manifestations of contemporary violence tend to be dominated by intra- and inter-personal forms of violence that are not as overtly politicised as they were during the apartheid era.

The ongoing socio-economic inequalities have been seen by researchers and theorists as part of the spectrum of causal agents complicit in the persisting prominence of violence in South African society.

The violence epidemic

Annually more than two million people around the world die as a result of injuries arising from violent acts (WHO, 2001) and by the year 2020 injuries will be the second largest contributor to the global burden of disease. This pattern is likely to be emphasised in sub-Saharan Africa, due to the anticipated concentration of wars, regional conflicts and inter-personal violence (Murray & Lopez, 1996). Presently, wars are one of the leading injury-related causes of death in Africa (WHO, 2001).

In South Africa, data from the National Injury Mortality Surveillance System (NIMSS) shows homicide to be the major cause of death as a result of injury, accounting for approximately 46 per cent of all the cases recorded in the NIMSS. Firearms and sharp objects are the main external causes of death (Burrows *et al.*, 2001). Similarly, non-fatal injuries presenting at sentinel health facilities appear to be dominated by inter-personal acts of violence within South Africa (Peden & van der Spuy, 1998).

For those who survive the immediate effects of a violent assault, their injuries often result in permanent disability. While violence and the associated injury patterns vary across gender, age, region and income groups, the overall impact is tremendous human suffering, serious social consequences (e.g. heightened levels of perceived threat and fear), and a significant economic burden to families, communities and the country (e.g. loss of income amongst victims and their dependents, skewed patterns of health expenditure, etc.). In addition, violence is also often associated with a wide range of health and psychosocial problems (Bergman, 1992; Farrington, 1991; UNAIDS, 1999; WHD, 1997), such as eating and sleeping disorders, mental illness, unwanted pregnancies and sexually transmitted diseases (e.g. HIV/AIDS). Central to this cursory overview of violence in South Africa today is the fact that it remains a significant psycho-social and health priority requiring vital description, analysis, theorising and social intervention.

Making sense: Perspectives and definitions of violence

There is a range of ways to define and understand violence. One method is to frame its definition according to commonly identified key components. These components include, amongst others, the nature of the relationship between victim and perpetrator (e.g. intimate–stranger violence); the form of discipline that examines violence (e.g. psychology); the broader paradigm into which violence is inserted as a phenomenon (e.g. social constructionism); and the 'essential nature' of the violence (e.g. child abuse). While at present there is still no single broadly accepted typology of violence, the WHO Task Force's classification (WHO, 1996) provides a useful reference point. It distinguishes between three types of violence (see box below).

Types of violence

The WHO Task Force (WHO, 1996) distinguishes between three types of violence:

- *Inter-personal violence* encompasses violent behaviours that occur between individuals, but are not planned by any social or political groups in which they participate. It occurs in many forms, and can be grouped into three categories according to the victim-perpetrator relationship:

  - family and intimate violence (mainly child abuse and violence against women, but may also include violence against vulnerable groups such as the elderly and the disabled if this occurs in a family setting)

  - violence among acquaintances (e.g. in a social setting between 'friends')

  - stranger violence (e.g. homicide by a perpetrator unknown to the victim).

Violence between acquaintances and strangers also includes: workplace violence (including health-care institutions and prisons); violence in schools (including bullying); community-based violence (that does not further the aims of a formally defined group or cause); youth violence (that does not further the aims of a formally defined group or cause); sexual violence between strangers or acquaintances; and crime-related violence.

- *Self-directed violence* involves intentional and harmful behaviours directed at oneself. Suicide represents the most severe type of self-inflicted violence. Other types of self-inflicted violence include suicide attempts, and behaviours where the intent is self-destructive, but not lethal (e.g. self-mutilation).

- *Organised violence* is violent behaviour planned to achieve the specific objectives of a social or political group. It includes political violence involving carefully executed efforts to intimidate an opposing political faction violently. Genital mutilation of women and men in the name of religious and cultural rites of passage might also be considered a form of organised violence. As a last example, war is the most highly organised form of violence as it is often waged in a strictly regimented manner by military organisations specifically trained in undertaking violence.

In the following sections we highlight definitions derived from disciplines that take violence as their subject matter as well as the paradigms into which violence is inserted, and examine the consequent implications for prevention. These perspectives are by no means an attempt to provide an exhaustive account of discipline-specific approaches to violence. We illustrate the most prominent definitions that provide some indication of varied emphases that are often placed on the understandings and prevention of violence as a social phenomenon.

Paradigmatic approaches to violence within psychology

Degenaar (1980) provides a broad social scientific definition of violence in suggesting that it is an extreme force willfully carried out against a person, violating that person because it does not show respect for his or her intrinsic value. This definition highlights three key dimensions, namely, the intentionality behind the violence, the extreme force that violates the victim's integrity, and a value that is ascribed to the victim (Olivier, 1991). One psychological definition suggests that it involves the 'application of force, action, motive or thought in such a way (overt, covert, direct or indirect) that a person or group is injured, controlled or destroyed in a physical, psychological or spiritual sense' (van der Merwe, 1989:16).

Even though these definitions differ with regard to the exact description of what constitutes violence, the similarities can clearly be found in the relational nature of violence as well as the emphasis on psychic, intra-personal and subjective consequences for the victim(s). This section highlights such differences and contestations within psychology, by examining varied paradigms into which violence may be inserted and the implications for prevention efforts.

Individualistic approaches

Throughout the history of psychology, the study and understanding of violence and conflict have been central, particularly within social psychology.

The *individualistic* approaches tended to view violence as having an essentially intra-psychic basis. In South Africa, from as early as the 1890s through until the 1960s, psycho-dynamic approaches (with strong 'racialised' overtones) dominated understandings of violence (Butchart *et al.*, 2000). Common to psycho-dynamic approaches, violence was viewed as the conscious manifestation of unconscious wishes, drives and fantasies due to poor defense mechanisms within the personality structure and an inability to repress these unconscious impulses (Freud, 1938). At other points, violence was viewed as a specific deficit within the psychological constitution of individuals who were unable to control aggressive impulses due to heightened levels of frustration. This hypothesis also assumed that the root of violence laid in the inability of individuals to contain such levels of frustration within their personality structures (Dollard *et al.*, 1939). Others focused on specific authoritarian personality formations and configurations to explain the prevalence of violence in specific populations. This approach suggested that due to particular familial and parenting styles, children internalise a rigid and domineering style of relating, thereby promoting the development of authoritarianism and even the enactment of violence (Adorno *et al.*, 1950. Despite Bandura's (1977) attempts to infuse the individualistic approaches with an appropriate social context within which individuals learn through modelling the social behaviour of others, these approaches have by and large been consistently critiqued for the lack of historical, social and ideological content in their analyses of violence. The assumption that violence is essentially rooted in the personality and learning processes of individuals implicitly directs social scientists towards individualistic methods of prevention and control. In South Africa, adherents of this approach envisaged the individual's mind as the primary object of violence prevention interventions (Butchart *et al.*, 2000). This approach does not account for the fact that violence occurs as a relational phenomenon in a specific time, space and context, and that the personal experiences and actions of individuals interact with temporal, spatial and contextual events and processes that are in turn shaped by broader historical, ideological and material conditions. Furthermore, it has often been criticised for pathologising victims and sustaining oppressive socio-political structures (*ibid.*).

Group relations

In response to the limitations of the individualistic approaches, some theorists attempted to locate the study of violence within the context of *group* dynamics and relations. Here specifically, Sherif's (1966) *Realistic Conflict Theory* attempted to account for inter-group conflict as the result of competition between groups for scarce resources. Gurr (1970) went even further to suggest

---

Individualistic approaches to violence view it as having an essentially intra-psychic basis.

Psycho-dynamic views of violence describe it as the conscious manifestation of unconscious wishes, drives, and fantasies due to poor defensive mechanisms within the personality structure to repress the unconscious impulses.

that even in the absence of an objective scarcity in resources, when groups perceive themselves to be relatively deprived in relation to other groups, they tend to experience heightened levels of resentment and discontent, which may in fact result in violence being enacted at an inter-group level. In South Africa, the 1960s saw a similar shift in the conceptualisation of violence as a legitimate tactic of political struggle between the apartheid state and its opponents (Butchart *et al.*, 2000). A further approach that had attempted to examine the connection between individuals and groups within situations of group, crowd or collective violence can be found in deindividuation theory (Festinger *et al.*, 1952). Proponents of this theory essentially argued that within the context of collective violence, individual psyches tend to become less resistant to a group norm, and within this context, individuals tend to lose their individualised controls and subject themselves to the norm of the group. The anonymity generates a sense of safety and diffusion of responsibility that may encourage collective acts of violence that might not have been enacted had the individuals not been in the presence of the group (Foster & Durrheim, 1998). Many of these approaches made significant contributions to social psychology in their identification of group processes as being much more than the mere sum of individual psychological processes within groups. They also provided useful beginnings for social scientists to explore group conflicts. However, they too failed to provide a thorough analysis of why violence resulted within some groups and not in others, and how the salient causes related to group and/or collective violence are delimited by historical, material, ideological and cultural processes prevailing within the social context at that particular time.

> Realistic conflict theory accounts for inter-group conflict as the result of competition between groups for scarce resources.

> Deindividuation theory argued that within the context of collective violence, individual psyches tend to become less resistant to a group norm, and within this context, individuals tend to lose their individualised controls and subject themselves to the norm of the group.

Individual–social interactions

During the 1960s, an imperative for mainstream, experimental social psychology was to develop a theoretical position that allowed for the incorporation of both individual and group functioning within a single framework. Tajfel's (1981) *Social Identity Theory* seemingly provided an answer to the problem of individual–social dualism that had plagued psychology. This approach argued that all individuals simultaneously occupy positions within a range of individual and group identities, and that depending on the social context of interaction, these identities either become less or more salient. It therefore provided an analysis of the complexity and range of individual and group interactions that may at times be consistent and/or contradictory. In a recent South African application, Bornman (1998) explores a number of group–individual factors reported to exacerbate conflict amongst groups differentiated according to perceived ethnic, 'racial' or class membership, including group identification, the experience of relative deprivation, and conformity to group norms. However, despite attempts to link identities to the enactment of

> Social Identity Theory argues that all individuals simultaneously occupy positions within a range of individual and group identities, and that depending on the social context of interaction, these identities either become less or more salient.

violence through this approach, it failed to identify why group or individual identities become more or less salient within the social context at a given point in time and why violence is enacted at some points and not at others. Foster (1991) argued that an analysis of ideology in these studies was notably absent, and that the use of these analyses in understanding violence and conflict needed to be augmented with an examination of the role of ideology.

From contextual theories to social constructionism

In developments that were occurring relatively independently of this process, several theorists attempted to provide a more contextually sound view of violence through looking at historical, ideological and material social contexts of violence production. Fanon (1968) and Mannoni (1962) adopted approaches that attempted to understand violence within the framework of colonial oppression, racism and violence. They argued that the social conditions of structural, vertical violence gave rise to the generation of intra-personal, inter-personal and collective counter-violence. Others, such as Bulhan (1985), also focused on the social factors that constrained human development and ultimately resulted in violence amongst marginalised groups within oppressive contexts beyond colonial social formations. These approaches were more *sociogenic* in their understandings of violence and implicitly started to incorporate what we today know as the paradigm of *social constructionism*. They incorporated the idea that all psycho-social phenomena are representations that are constructed by and through the contexts from which they emerge. They therefore started to focus not only on social, but historical, material and ideological antecedents of violence. A recent South African example of this analysis is provided by Butchart *et al.* (2000). By extension, contextual approaches link violence prevention interventions to political and ideological processes that are aimed at fundamental and revolutionary social transformation.

> Sociogenic approaches have argued that the social conditions of structural, vertical violence give rise to the generation of intra-personal, inter-personal and collective counter-violence.

Postmodern developments

In recent years, an increasingly strong perspective has been to move beyond the frameworks of modernity and to view violence as more than being essentially derived from the structures of personalities, economic systems, political systems and so forth. *Postmodern* frameworks argue that the idea of violence simply being socially constructed is restrictive, and rather focuses on the individual's subjective experiences of social encounters within these historically, ideologically, materially, culturally and temporally specific contexts. The aim is therefore not to generate a single fundamental 'truth' or definition pertaining to violence, but rather to deconstruct understandings, social actions and cultural expressions related to violence and to generate understandings unique to its relational location in time and space (Curran *et al.*, 1996).

> Postmodern frameworks focus on the individual's subjective experiences of social encounters with the aim of deconstructing understandings, social actions and cultural expressions related to violence and to generate understandings unique to its relational location in time and space.

The above-mentioned paradigms have facilitated robust debate within psychology as to the description, analysis and theorising of violence, but the critical component of translation into relevant social action has most frequently been implied or even arbitrarily disconnected from such description, analysis and theorising. In many instances, violence prevention has been the exclusive domain of psychotherapists, or has been relegated to the fringes of community psychology, participatory action research, development work and social activism. However, the endemic nature of violence and its deleterious effects in many contexts is increasingly challenging researcher–practitioners to address violence comprehensively and concretely through prevention initiatives.

Related perspectives and definitions

The range of psychological approaches reflected above does not, however, constitute the only formulations of violence. An array of broader social scientific and health approaches to violence have also made significant contributions to understanding violence and its prevention in South Africa. We outline a selection of some of the more prominent contributions below.

Sociological perspectives and definitions

The sociological approach to violence broadly suggests that violence is not necessarily exerted by an individual but by social structures, created and/or perpetuated by custom or by law (Degenaar, 1980). Within this approach, these structures invariably curtail the freedoms of subjects or discriminate unjustly against certain sections of the population. This is premised on classical sociological theory that suggests that violence is a form of social deviance through which individuals and/or groups react to restrictive social control inherent to these social structures (Durkheim, 1998; Weber, 1969). Sociological understandings of violence clearly de-emphasise the role of the individual in the perpetration of violence and instead insist on the importance of analysing social structures in the origination and perpetuation of violence, and the subsequent transformation of these social structures in the prevention and control of violence. Such structural violence shows itself when resources and powers are unequally shared and are the property of a restricted number who use them not for the good of all, but for the domination of the less favoured. Furthermore, this form of violence causes harm through the inflexibility and rigidity of rules within the social structure in dealing with difference. Through gender, 'race', and class studies, we have become much more aware in recent years of the harm that can be caused without any given perpetrator, but by the existence of policies and rules that do not allow for differences.

> The sociological approach to violence broadly suggests that violence is not necessarily exerted by an individual but by social structures, created and/or perpetuated by custom or by law.

13-9

Criminological perspectives and definitions

Generally within criminology, violence is construed as the intentional and violent violation of law that is committed without defense or justification, and is sanctioned by the state as criminal, with the implicit consequence of enforcement and punishment through deterrence, incapacitation and incarceration (Keseredy & Schwartz, 1996). This approach generally emphasises the importance of individuals and/or groups and their intentional acts of violence which contravene social codes as embodied within the legal system (Smit & Cilliers, 1998). While criminologists certainly recognise the impact of social factors on the generation of violent behaviour, there is often a focus on the individual and/or group experiences of such social factors. In addition, psychological responses to these social contexts are frequently focused upon to construct understandings of the patterns of causation associated with violence. Furthermore, the response to violence within criminology tends to be underscored by processes and mechanisms that ensure minimal behavioural deviance amongst the population in relation to the law, thus the focus on deterrence and punishment.

Health perspectives and definitions

Recent years have seen a growing number of researchers, practitioners and decision-makers in the field of violence prevention and control locating violence within a health paradigm (Butchart *et al.*, 2000; Kruger *et al.*, 1998). Within this framework, violence is viewed as the 'intentional use of physical force or power, threatened or actual, against oneself or another, or against a group or community, that either results in or has a high likelihood of resulting in injury, death, psychological harm, maladjustment or deprivation' (WHO, 1996:3–4). This definition clearly focuses on violence as a significant social phenomenon, which impacts on morbidity, mortality and future risk factors that may negatively influence the overall population health status. The mainstream conceptualisation of violence and its prevention within this framework concentrates on the identification of patterns of intentional violence, the study of causal pathways and risks, and the elimination or minimisation of such risks. While social antecedents are certainly considered as risk factors within this framework as well, the dominant understanding of violence is constructed as an impingement on satisfactory health status. However, recent years have seen an increasing modification of this framework to accommodate for resilience factors and also to embrace an asset-based approach, as well as to incorporate both social–scientific and bio–medical methods into its application (Butchart & Kruger, 2001; Stevens *et al.*, in press).

The following section attempts to looks at one possible framework for violence description, analysis, theorising and social action directed at its prevention. In so doing, it endeavours to transcend disciplinary boundaries and to allow for truly scholarly interactions (Billig, 1988) that promote greater collaboration across disciplinary, methodological and theoretical boundaries. This is particularly critical, given the complex causal pathways and constructed meanings of violence that may necessitate the broadest possible range of health and social–scientific inputs to comprehensively prevent and control this social phenomenon.

Re-committing to social action: Adapting the public health approach

The increased utilisation of the public health approach in violence prevention (WHO, 2001), and its adaptation for use within communities in South Africa, are relatively well-documented features (see for example Butchart, 1996; Butchart & Kruger, 2001; Butchart *et al.*, 1996; Emmett & Butchart, 2000; Kruger *et al.*, 1998; Seedat, 1995). The following section provides the conceptual basis for reinterpreting a classic public health approach, and the manner in which this facilitates interdisciplinarity, methodological pluralism, theoretical diversity, community empowerment, and sectoral and inter-sectoral coalition-building.

As separate frameworks for research and intervention in the area of violence prevention, health and social scientific approaches are frequently driven by differing epistemologies, ontologies, methodologies and theoretical understandings. Because the public health model was initially developed in the context of high-income countries, a central challenge is therefore to determine its value and appropriateness for South Africa and other low-income countries. Given that large urban areas have complex causal relationships linked to violence, and the fact that this complexity increases with the decrease in income (Mohan, 1996), this framework cannot simply be transposed to the South African context. The public health framework essentially argues that many of the principles that are utilised with communicable and non-communicable diseases can also be applied to the control and prevention of violence (Butchart, 1996). Within the public health approach, violence is not only preventable, but its consequences and impact can also be contained. The public health approach recognises the psycho-social, neurological, physiological and cognitive components of violence. It views violent behaviour as a consequence of the interaction between environmental, socialisation and behavioural factors evident at the level of populations (Butchart, 1996). The utility of the public health approach is threefold. Firstly, it offers a four-step logic, representing an interactive process to focus on the *magnitude and causes* of violence (step 1 and step 2). In step 3, the focus is on developing and testing prevention interventions and in step 4 implementation of *what works* on a large scale (see Figure 13.1).

The public health approach views violence as a consequence of the interaction between environmental, socialisation and behavioural factors evident at the level of populations.

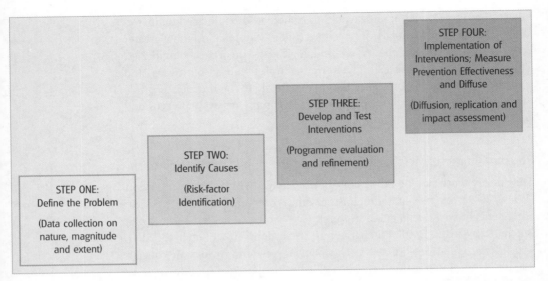

STEP FOUR:
Implementation of
Interventions; Measure
Prevention Effectiveness
and Diffuse

(Diffusion, replication and
impact assessment)

STEP THREE:
Develop and Test
Interventions

(Programme evaluation
and refinement)

STEP TWO:
Identify Causes

(Risk-factor
Identification)

STEP ONE:
Define the Problem

(Data collection on
nature, magnitude
and extent)

Figure 13.1
The public health
model

Secondly, the public health approach allows for an analysis of violence and the development of appropriate preventative interventions across two dimensions (Haddon & Baker, 1981). The first dimension, based on the idea that violent injuries are events located in time, divides violence into three stages: pre-event, event and post-event. The second dimension argues that violence is determined by both risk and resiliency factors (e.g. age, gender, physical strength, psycho-social skills), agent factors (e.g. perpetrator and weapon) and environmental factors (e.g. lack of socio-economic opportunities).

Thirdly, the public health approach accommodates for conscious interdisciplinarity (e.g. criminology, economics, psychology, urban planning, history) and cross-sectoral perspectives (e.g. health, criminal justice, transport, housing, NGOs, business) in our attempts to study violence and its magnitude, causes and prevention. Below we examine some of the benefits of the public health approach as one potential framework through which research can be translated into concrete action in the area of violence prevention.

Public health: A four-step logic

One of the more useful aspects of the public health approach and its application to addressing violence is in the basic four-step logic that it employs. This logic can be found in some form or another in most social-scientific and health-related disciplines, and therefore facilitates interdisciplinary approaches to understanding and preventing violence. Below, this four-step process is outlined, and we examine the manner in which it may contribute to holistic research and programme design that encourages the translation of research data into concrete practice.

Figure 13.2
Figure research and prevention utilising public health logic

PROBLEM ⟶ RESPONSE			
STEP ONE: Define the Problem (Data on nature, magnitude & extent) Collective needs assessment (Accessing, co-construction and description of community needs)	**STEP TWO:** Identify Causes (Risk-factor identification) Identify indigenous causal models (Elicit organic explanations and resilience factors)	**STEP THREE:** Develop and Test Interventions (Programme evaluation and refinement) Generate/evaluate Community responses (Action-reflection research)	**STEP FOUR:** Implementation of Interventions; Measure Prevention Effectiveness and Diffuse (Diffusion, replication and impact assessment) Social action for social change (Social mobilisation) Methodologies utilised
METHODOLOGIES UTILISED • Focus groups/ interviews • Rapid participatory appraisals • Descriptive content analyses • Surveillance (epidemiological) • Surveys	• Multivariate analyses • Case-control and case-crossover studies • Thematic and Discursive analyses • Participatory action research	• Participatory action research • Illuminative program evaluation • Evaluation research • Control studies • Cost-analyses	• Trend monitoring • Evaluation research • Materials development and documentation • Formal and informal training • Advocacy and lobbying strategies • Promoting social movements • Media utilisation • Interdisciplinary collaborations and theoretical diversity
INTERDISCIPLINARY COLLABORATIONS AND THEORETICAL DIVERSITY • Biostatisticians • Psychologists • Criminologists • Sociologists • Anthropologists • Epidemiologists • Historians • Economists • Health workers • Community-based knowledge brokers and key stakeholders	• Biostatisticians • Psychologists • Criminologists • Sociologists • Anthropologists • Epidemiologists • Historians • Economists • Health workers • Targeted community roleplayers	• Psychologists • Criminologists • Sociologists • Anthropologists • Historians • Economists • Health workers • Existing service deliverers • Recipients, community intervention roleplayers and boader community	• Biostatisticians • Psychologists • Criminologists • Sociologists • Anthropologists • Epidemiologists • Historians • Economists • Health workers • Lobbyists and advocates • Materials and media specialists • Broader community • Policy- and decision-makers • Multiple targets

PROBLEM			RESPONSE
MULTIPLE TARGETS			
• Women • Youth • Children • Income-defined groups • 'Racially'-defined groups • Other at-risk and high-risk groups, behaviors and environments	• Women • Youth • Children • Income-defined groups • 'Racially'-defined groups • Other at-risk and high-risk groups, behaviors and environments	• Women • Youth • Children • Income-defined groups • 'Racially'-defined groups • Other at-risk and high-risk groups, behaviors and environments	• Women • Youth • Children • Income-defined groups • 'Racially'-defined groups • Other at-risk and high-risk groups, behaviors and environments • Intervention levels
INTERVENTION LEVELS			
• Individual • Familial or household • School and workplace • Service delivery sites • Community • Provincial • National	• Individual • Familial or household • School and workplace • Service delivery sites • Community • Provincial • National	• Individual • Familial or household • School and workplace • Service delivery sites • Community • Provincial • National	• Individual • Familial or household • School and workplace • Service delivery sites • Community • Provincial • National

Magnitude: What is the problem?

In this step, the public health model examines the *how, when, where,* and *what* of violence. Thus, violence can be described in relational terms, including information on the number of cases, demographic characteristics of victims and perpetrators, the victim–perpetrator relationship, the mechanisms of violent injury, the involvement of products such as handguns and alcohol, and the temporal and geographical characteristics of violent incidents. Surveillance systems, as an example of routine sources of quantitative data, provide timely information on the who, what and when of violence, and inform population-based studies that are used to assess risks, triggers, and causes of violence. In addition, qualitative analyses may also be utilised to provide and augment information on specific populations that may be at risk of specific forms of violence, thereby promoting methodological pluralism (Stevens *et al.*, in press).

Risks, triggers and causes: What are the determinants?

Risk factor identification looks at the why of violence. Risk factors are factors that are shown to increase the possibility of exposure or experience of violence. In a study of risk factors we are interested, for instance, in the relationship between violence and variables such as age, gender, gun ownership, alcohol abuse, and inequalities in power. These and other such risk factors are often associated with both violent perpetration and violent victimisation. Risk factors are sometimes specific to certain types of violence. For example, ease of access to firearms increases the risk of homicide and violence between acquaintances and strangers.

Once we understand risk factors and the micro-, meso- and macro-causes, we can design specific prevention programmes to reduce violence and violent behaviour. For example, programmes may be targeted at young males, as they are a high-risk group for perpetrating and experiencing inter-personal violence. Other programmes target access to firearms or alcohol legislation, yet others focus on employment or empowerment activities to address inequalities in gender and wealth.

Within the public health approach we determine the risks, triggers, and causes of violence through analysis secured through routine information systems (e.g. injury and violence surveillance systems) or population based quantitative and qualitative studies (e.g. case control studies, cross-sectional studies, discursive analyses, etc.). Given public health's multi-disciplinary orientation, a feminist perspective may be introduced to understand how, for instance, patriarchy, gender inequality, and poverty contribute to femicide. Similarly, those interested in uncovering the discourses underlying our social constructions of violence may introduce critical theory to conduct an archival and historical analysis with a view to producing alternative explanations of violence. Likewise, researchers focusing on 'race' or ethnicity may place the accent on 'racialised' patterns of socio-political, economic and geographical exclusion in their explanations of violence and associated prevention measures. This step basically allows us to take a multi-disciplinary understanding as to the causes of violence, including all of the discipline-specific and paradigmatic approaches referred to above. At a theoretical level, contextual social analyses complement more technical analyses of specific determinants, risks and triggers prior to, during and after violent events. Violence can therefore be addressed at a macro-level as well as at the levels of individuals, families and communities. This allows for the possibility of moving beyond the restrictive definitions of violence that are situation- and event-specific (Haddon & Baker, 1981), to include political and ideological components that help to contextualise this phenomenon (Bulhan, 1985). This form of inter-disciplinarity is not only desirable, but imperative for a comprehensive understanding of the complex underpinnings of violence that are located within the subjective, cultural, ideological, material and historical realms that help to constitute social realities.

Develop and test interventions: What works?

Problem definition, risk factor analysis and the determination of causes help us to understand violence in relational terms, illuminating the association between people, products and the environments that promote the contexts of violence. Such understandings should then enable the design, implementation and evaluation of intervention programmes. In this step we are interested in the study of *what works*. Programmes may assume a singular or multiple focus (e.g. youth violence, child abuse, family violence), targeting one or more at-risk environments (e.g. schools, recreational facilities), or risk factors (e.g. poverty, life styles), and one or more at-risk groups (e.g. children, young men, the elderly, etc.).

An example of a schools-based violence prevention programme

Inter-personal violence disproportionately involves young people as both victims and perpetrators of violence. Of particular concern is the proliferation of violence and injuries within schools. Prevention of schools-based violence and injury is therefore a public health and educational priority. School violence is affected by levels of violence in communities and the broader society.

Safe schools programmatic summary

- Assessment, monitoring, surveillance and evaluation.
- Behaviour, conduct and discipline codes.
- Staff and student training.
- Student leadership and responsibility.
- Parental participation.
- After-school safety activities.
- Crisis management strategies.
- Broader community involvement.
- Environmental design.
- Policy formulation, adoption and implementation.

Interventions may also be directed at different parts in the chain of causation of violence and therefore interventions are also categorised under the *four Es*: Education, Environmental change, Engineering, and Enforcement.

The four Es of public health interventions

Education: Aimed at changing individual skills, knowledge, and beliefs.

Environmental: Aimed at modifying physical and social spaces that place people at risk of violence.

Engineering: Aimed at reducing risk by improving the safety of dangerous products.

Enforcement: Involves the development and enforcement of legal measures and practices that prevent violence.

Interventions may furthermore be classified as *passive* or *active* depending on the level of activity required of the group or individual being targeted. Whereas *active interventions* require deliberate action from the targeted group/individual (e.g. community mobilisation against firearm proliferation), passive measures require no individual action (e.g. policy formulation and enforcement that attempts to address violence at national, regional and international levels). This could conceivably incorporate strategies aimed at regional disarmament, demilitarisation and the development of more equitable global economic policies. Within the public health approach, prevention programmes may therefore assume varying intensities, focus on different target groups, target various settings including geographical locations, and socio-economically stratified groups.

Implement interventions: How is it done and what is its impact?

The fourth and final step in the public health model deals with implementation vis-à-vis those good practices that have been shown to be effective. Typically, good practice initiatives, including demonstration programmes, are utilised to inform public health policy and practice on violence prevention and containment. Institutional and funding support is vital for the adoption of known and evaluated good practices on a large scale. In short, focusing on *how do you do it?* addresses the translation of effective programmes into wide-scale prevention policy and practice. It should also consciously involve two additional Es, namely *Evaluation* and *Empowerment*. Here, the public health approach structurally incorporates the necessity for programme evaluation to assess the overall impact of such of programmes. In addition, it can also actively encourage the inclusion of communities in the prevention of violence through participatory processes that facilitate self-reliance, self-determination, ownership and empowerment to control the outcome of their everyday realities.

From the above, it becomes apparent that the public health framework can be utilised as a structural logic to ensure that research in the form of description, analysis and theorising is translated into conscious forms of evidence-led and evaluated social action. This adapted framework represents a matrix through which to engage in violence prevention work, and simultaneously accommodates for theoretical diversity, methodological pluralism, inter-disciplinarity and varied scientific philosophies (see Figure 13.2). It also allows for evidence-led interventions to be structured across micro-, meso- and macro-levels; with universal, targeted and specified populations and environments; and at primary, secondary and tertiary levels. However, it is important to note that this adapted matrix is not underpinned by a generic scientific neutrality that automatically accommodates for diverse philosophical foundations of science, but rather, that it allows for the conscious co-existence of varying ontologies, epistemologies and methodologies in the prevention of violence.

This is particularly important to emphasise, given the erroneous belief that the public health model is in and of itself an all-encompassing and scientifically neutral framework to accommodate for a range of diverse perspectives. The key element in this process is therefore the *conscious* introduction of alternative and complementary perspectives of science and their application to the resolution of violence as an obstacle to health, psycho-social well-being and social development.

Looking ahead

In conclusion, we argue that violence is a preventable social phenomenon and is not an intractable social problem or an inevitable part of the human condition. The wide variation in the form and extent of violence among and within populations over time suggests that violence is the product of complex, yet modifiable, subjective and social factors.

Within the public health approach, health and social science researchers and practitioners have an important role to play in providing a vision and leadership in the establishment of national social programmes and policies for violence prevention. This becomes an even more desirable prospect when one considers that it may occur within the context of inter- and intra-sectoral coalition-building, multi-disciplinary theorising, methodological eclecticism and a philosophy of empowerment. In so doing, the public health logic provides important entry points for researchers and practitioners to reflexively consider as they dynamically engage in processes related to describing, analysing, theorising and preventing violence.

Exercises for critical engagement

1 *Violence in South Africa constitutes a significant historical and current psychosocial and health priority.* Please discuss and substantiate your argument in relation to this statement.

2 Describe the main types of violence as defined by the WHO (1996).

3 Describe and critically discuss one psychological definition of violence.

4 Describe the main features and limitations of the individualistic, group relations, individual–group, contextual and postmodern psychological approaches to understanding violence.

5 Describe the key contributions and limitations of the sociological, criminological, and health perspectives on violence.

6 Provide a critical discussion of the public health approach to violence prevention.

Recommended reading

Bornman, E., van Eeden, R. & M. Wentzel (Eds.) (1998). *Violence in South Africa: A Variety of Perspectives*. Pretoria: HSRC.

Bulhan, H.A. (1985). *Frantz Fanon and the Psychology of Oppression*. New York: Plenum Press.

Butchart, A. & J. Kruger (2001). 'Public health and community psychology: A case study in community-based injury prevention'. In Seedat, M., Duncan, N. & S. Lazarus (Eds.) *Theory, Method and Practice in Community Psychology: South African and Other Perspectives*, pp. 215–241. Cape Town: Oxford University Press.

Emmett, T. & A. Butchart (Eds.) (2000). *Behind the Mask*. Pretoria: HSRC Publishers.

Foster, D. & J. Louw-Potgieter (Eds.) (1991). *Social Psychology in South Africa*. Johannesburg. Lexicon Publishers.

Stevens, G., Seedat, M., Swart, T. & C. van der Walt (2003). 'Promoting methodological pluralism, theoretical diversity and interdisciplinarity in a multi-levelled violence prevention initiative in South Africa'. *Journal of Prevention and Intervention in the Community*, in press.

References

1. The complete reference list for this reader can be found in:

   Critical Psychology
   Editor: Derek Hook
   UCT Press
   ISBN 1-919713-88-3

   and

   Social Psychology: Identities and Relationships
   Editors: Kopano Ratele
          Norman Duncan
   UCT Press
   ISBN 1-919713-83-2

2. The reference list is also available online:
   http://www.criticalmethods.org/community/refs.htm

Critical Psychology: References

ABC. (2000). *Audit Bureau of Circulation of South Africa.* December, 2000. Johannesburg: Newspaper Union.

Aboud, F. (1988). *Children and prejudice.* Oxford: Blackwell.

Abrahams, Y. (2002). 'We're here because we're here: Speaking African womanism', In Duncan, N., Gqola, P.D., Hofmeyr, M., Shefer, T., Malunga, F., & Mashige, M. (eds), *Discourses on difference discourses on oppression.* Plumstead: CASAS.

Adams, P.L. (1970). 'The Social Psychiatry of Frantz Fanon.' *American Journal of Psychiatry.* 126(6), December: 809–814.

Aggleton, P., Hart, G., & Davies, P. (1989). *Social aspects of Aids.* New York: The Falmer Press.

Airhihenbuwa, C.O. (1995). *Health and culture: Beyond the Western paradigm.* Thousand Oaks CA: Sage.

Akbar, N. (1984). 'Africentric social sciences for human liberation.' *Journal of Black Studies,* 14: 395–414.

Alldred, P. (1996). '"Fit to Parent"? Developmental psychology and "non-traditional" families'. In E. Burman, A. Alldred, C. Bewley, B. Goldberg, C. Heenan, D. Marks, J. Marshall, K. Taylor, R. Ullah, S. Warner, (eds), *Challenging women: Psychology's exclusions, feminist possibilities.* London: Open University Press.

Allen, C. (1997). 'Community development for health and identity politics.' *Ethnicity and Health,* 2(3): 229–242.

Allen, H. (1986). 'Psychiatry and the feminine.' In P. Miller & N. Rose (eds), *The power of psychiatry.* Cambridge: Polity Press.

Altemeyer, B. (1981). *Right wing authoritarianism.* Winnipeg: University of Manitoba Press.

Altemeyer, B. (1988). *Enemies of freedom.* San Francisco: Jossey-Bass.

Altemeyer, B. (1996). *The authoritarian specter.* Cambridge, MA: Harvard University Press.

Althusser, L. (1971). *Lenin and philosophy and other essays.* New York: Monthly Review Press; London: New Left Books.

Althusser, L. (1979). *For Marx.* London: Verso. (1965 French).

Alverson, N. (1978). *Mind in the heart of darkness.* Johannesburg: MacMillan.

AMPS. (2000). *All Media products survey.* December, 2000. Johannesburg: Markinor.

Anonymous. (1986). 'Some thoughts on a more relevant or indigenous counselling psychology in South Africa: Discovering the socio-political context of the oppressed.' *Psychology in Society (PINS),* 5: 81–89.

Anyanwu, C. (1981). 'The African worldview and theory knowledge.' In E.A. Ruch & K.C. Anyanwu, *African philosophy: An introduction to the main philosophical trends in contemporary Africa.* Rome: Catholic Book Agency.

Apfelbaum, E. (1979). Relations of domination and movements for liberation. In W. Austin & S. Worchel (eds), *The social psychology of intergroup relations.* 188–204. Monterey, CA: Brooks/Cole.

Arnold, M. (ed) (1979). *Steve Biko: Black consciousness in South Africa.* New York: Vintage.

Ashcroft, B., Griffiths, G., & Tiffin, H. (eds) (1995). *The postcolonial studies reader.* London and New York: Routledge.

Asmal, K. (2001). 'Address by the Minister of Education, Professor Kader Asmal, MP, to the 7th Annual Congress of the Psychological Society of SA.' *PsyTalk: A Newsletter of the Psychological Society of South Africa,* Issue 4: 1, 4.

Atkinson, R.L., Atkinson, R.C., & Hilgard, E.R. (1983). *Introduction to psychology.* New York: Harcourt Brace Jovanovich.

Babbie, E., & Mouton, J. (2001). *The practice of social research.* Oxford: Oxford University Press.

Bakhtin, M.M. (1981). *The dialogic imagination.* (trans C. Emerson & M. Holquist). Austin, TX: University of Texas Press.

Bakhtin, M.M. (1984/1993). *Problems of Dostoevsky's poetics* (ed and trans Caryl Emerson). Minneapolis, MN: University of Minnesota Press.

Bakhtin, M.M. (1986). *Speech genres and other late essays.* (trans V. McGee). Austin: University of Texas Press.

Bakhtin, M.M. (1990). *Art and answerability: Early philosophical essays.* (trans V. Liapunov). Austin, TX: University of Texas Press.

Bakker, T.M. (1996). 'An archaeology of psychological knowledge as technology of power in Africa.' Unpublished doctoral thesis: Unisa, South Africa.

Baldwin-Ragaven, L., De Gruchy, J., & London, L. (1999). *An ambulance of the wrong colour. Health professionals, human rights and ethics in South Africa.* Rondebosch: UCT Press.

Balibar, E. (1995). *The philosophy of Marx.* London: Verso. (1993 French).

Bandlamudi, L. (1994). 'Dialogics of understanding self/culture.' *Ethos,* 22: 460–493.

Banister, P., Burman, E., Parker, I., Taylor, M., & Tindall, C. (1994). *Qualitative methods in psychology: A research guide.* Buckingham: Open University Press.

Baritz, L. (1960). *The servants of power.* Middletown, CT: Wesleyen University Press.

Barker, P. (1998). *Michel Foucault an introduction.* Edinburgh: Edinburgh University Press.

Barnes, S. (1998). Paper presented at an International Workshop on Sexuality, Interventions and Possibilities. Sea Point, Cape Town, 26–26 June.

Barnett, T., & Whiteside, A. (2002) *Aids in the 21st century: Disease and globalisation.* Hampshire and New York: Palgrave MacMillan.

Bartky, S.L. (1990). *Femininity and domination: Studies in the phenomenology of oppression.* New York and London: Routledge.

Baum, F. (1999). 'The role of social capital in health promotion: Australian perspectives.' *Health Promotion Journal of Australia* 9(3): 171–178.

Bauman, Z. (1989). *Modernity and the holocaust.* Cambridge, UK: Polity Press.

Beck, U. (1992). *Risk society.* London: Sage.

Beeker, C., Guenther Gray, C., & Raj, A. (1998) 'Community empowerment paradigm and the primary prevention of HIV/Aids.' *Social Science and Medicine,* 46(7): 831–842.

Belenky, M.F., Clinchy, B.M., Goldberger, N.R., & Tarule, J.M. (1986). *Women's ways of knowing: The development of self, voice, and mind.* New York: Basic Books.

Bem, S. (1985). Androgyny and gender schema theory: A conceptual and empirical investigation.' In T.B. Sondegegger (ed), *Nebraska Symposium on Motivation 1984: Psychology and gender.* Lincoln: University of Nebraska Press.

Bengu, S.M.E. (2002). Address to the Bax Nomvete Inaugural Lecture, 17 April, Cape Town.

Benhabib, S. (1992). *Situating the self: Gender, community and postmodernism in contemporary ethics.* Cambridge, UK: Polity Press.

Benjamin, J. (1988). *The bonds of love.* New York: Pantheon Books.

Berger, J. (1972). *Ways of seeing.* Harmondsworth, UK: Penguin Books.

Berger, P., & Luckmann, T. (1981). *The social construction of reality*. New York: Fletcher.

Berger, S., & Lazarus, S. (1987). 'The views of community organisers on the relevance of psychological practice in South Africa.' *Psychology in Society*, 7: 2–6.

Berkowitz, B., & Wolff, T. (1996). 'Rethinking social action and community empowerment: A dialogue.' In M.B. Lykes, A. Banuazizi, R. Liem & M. Morris, (eds), *Myths about the powerless: Contesting social inequalities*. 296–316. Philadelphia: Temple University Press.

Bernardez, T. (1988). 'Gender based countertransference of female therapists in the psychotherapy of women.' In. M. Braude. *Women power and therapy*. 25–40. New York: Harrington Park Press.

Bernstein, R. (1983). *Beyond objectivism and relativism*. Philadelphia: University of Pennsylvania Press.

Bertoldi, A. (1998). 'Oedipus in (South) Africa?: Psychoanalysis and the politics of difference.' *American Imago*, 55(1), Spring 1998: 101–134.

Best, S., & Kellner, D. (1991). *Postmodern theory critical interrogations*. Hong Kong: Macmillan.

Bettelheim, B. (1986). *Freud and man's soul*. London: Flamingo.

Bhana, A. (1999). 'Participatory action research: A practical guide for realistic radicals.' In M. Terre Blanche & K. Durrheim (eds), *Research in practice: Applied methods for the social sciences*. 227–238. Cape Town: UCT Press.

Bhana, A., & Kanjee, A. (2001). 'Epistemological and methodological issues in community psychology.' In M. Seedat, N. Duncan & S. Lazarus (eds), *Community psychology: Theory, method and practice – South African and other perspectives*. 135–158. Cape Town: Oxford University Press.

Biesheuvel, S. (1958). 'Objectives and methods of African psychological research.' *Journal of Social Psychology*, 47: 161–168.

Biesheuvel, S. (1987). 'Psychology: Science and politics. Theoretical developments and applications in a plural society.' *South African Journal of Psychology*, 17(1): 1–8.

Biko, S. (1978). *I write what I like: Selected writings*. Chicago: University of Chicago Press.

Biko, S. (1998a). 'South African cultural concepts.' In P.H. Coetzee & A.P.J. Roux (eds), *Philosophy from Africa: A text with readings*. 26–30. Halfway House: International Thomson Publishing.

Biko, S. (1998b). 'The definition of Black Consciousness.' In P.H. Coetzee & A.P.J. Roux (eds), *Philosophy from Africa: A text with readings*. 360–363. Halfway House: International Thomson Publishing.

Billig, M. (1978). *Fascists*. London: Academic Press.

Billig, M. (1987). *Arguing and thinking*. Cambridge, UK: Cambridge University Press.

Billig, M. (1991). *Ideology and opinions*. London: Sage.

Billig, M. (1999). *Freudian repression: Conversation creating the unconscious*. Cambridge, UK: Cambridge University Press.

Binedell, J. (1991). 'Community health workers talk about their work.' Paper presented at the Association of Sociology of Southern Africa Conference, University of Cape Town, July 1991.

Bion, W. (1961). *Experiences in groups*. London: Tavistock.

Bion, W. (1962). *Learning from experience*. Northvale, NJ: Jason Aronson.

Blanck, G. (1990). 'Vygotsky: The man and his cause'. In E. Moll (ed), *Vygotsky and education: Instructional implications and applications of sociohistorical psychology*. 31–58. Cambridge, UK: Cambridge University Press.

Bohan, J.S. (ed) (1992). *Seldom seen, rarely heard: Women's place in psychology.* Boulder, Colorado: Westview Press.

Bottomore, T. (ed) (1983). *A dictionary of Marxist thought.* Oxford: Blackwell.

Bourdieu, P. (1986). 'The forms of capital.' In J. Richardson (ed), *Handbook of theory and research for the sociology of education.* 241–248. New York: Greenwood.

Braidotti, R. (1997). 'Comment on Felski's "The doxa of difference": Working through sexual difference.' *Signs*, 23(1): 23–40.

Brokenshaw, D., Warren, D.M., & Werner, O. (1980). 'Introduction.' In D. Brokenshaw, D.M. Warren & O. Werner (eds), *Indigenous knowledge systems and development.* New York: University Press of America.

Bronfenbrenner, U. (1979). *The ecology of human development.* Cambridge, MA: Harvard University Press.

Brown, L.M., & Gilligan, C. (1991). 'Listening for voice in narratives of relationship.' In M.B. Tappan & M.J. Packer (eds), *Narrative and storytelling: Implications for understanding moral development.* 43–62. San Francisco: Jossey-Bass.

Brown, P. (1973). 'Preface.' In P. Brown (ed), *Radical psychology.* xiii–xxii. New York, Evanston, San Francisco, London: Harper Colophon Books.

Brown, P. (1973). 'Sex roles.' In P. Brown (ed), *Radical psychology.* 386–389. New York, Evanston, San Francisco, London: Harper Colophon Books.

Brown, R. (1986). *Social psychology.* 2nd edition. New York: Free Press.

Bruner, J. (1990). *Acts of meaning.* Cambridge, MA: Harvard University Press.

Bulhan, H.A. (1979). 'Black psyches in captivity and crisis.' *Race & Class*, XX(3): 243–261.

Bulhan, H.A. (1980a). 'Frantz Fanon: The revolutionary psychiatrist.' *Race and Class*, XXI(3): 251–271.

Bulhan, H.A. (1980b). 'Dynamics of cultural in-betweenity: An empirical study.' *International Journal of Psychology* 15: 105–121.

Bulhan, H.A. (1981). 'Psychological research in Africa: Genesis and function.' *Race and Class*, XXIII(1): 25–41.

Bulhan, H.A. (1985). *Frantz Fanon and the psychology of oppression.* New York and London: Plenum Press.

Bulhan, H.A. (1993). 'Imperialism in studies of the psyche: A critique of African psychological research.' In L.J. Nicholas (ed), *Psychology and oppression: Critiques and proposals.*1–34. Johannesburg: Skotaville.

Bulhan, H.A. (1999). 'Revolutionary psychiatry of Fanon.' In N.C. Gibson (ed), *Rethinking Fanon: The continuing dialogue.* 141–178. New York: Humanity Books.

Bulmer, M., & Solomos, J. (1999). *Racism.* Oxford: Oxford University Press.

Burford, G., Bodeker, G., Kabatesi, D., Gemmill, B., & Rukangira, E. (2000). 'Traditional medicines and HIV in traditional medicine and HIV/Aids in Africa: Report from the International Conference on Medicinal Plants, Traditional Medicine and Local Communities in Africa.' Available: http://www.para55.org/ caretreat/trad_med_mine.asp [2001, 03 October].

Burman, E. (1991). 'What discourse is not.' *Philosophical Psychology*, 4(3): 325–342.

Burman, E. (1994). 'Development phallacies: Psychology, gender and childhood'. *Agenda,* 20.

Burman, E. (1994). *Deconstructing developmental psychology.* London: Routledge.

Burman, E. (1995a). 'Identity, subjectivity, and power in feminist psychotherapy.' In J. Siegfied (ed), *Therapeutic and everyday discourse as behaviour change.* 469–488. New Jersey: Ablex.

Burman, E. (1995b). 'What is it? Masculinity and femininity in the cultural representation of childhood.' In S. Wilkinson & C. Kitzinger (eds), *Feminism and discourse: Psychological perspectives*. 49–67. London: Sage.

Burman, E. (ed) (1990). *Feminists and psychological practice*. London: Sage.

Burman, E. (ed) (1998). *Deconstructing feminist psychology*. Thousand Oaks, CA: Sage.

Burman, E., Alldred, P., Bewley, C., Goldberg, B., Heenan, C., Marks, D., Marshall, J., Taylor, K., Ullah, R., & Warner, S. (eds) (1996). *Challenging women: Psychology's exclusion, feminist possibilities*. Buckingham: Open University Press.

Burman, E., Kottler, A., Levett, A., & Parker, I. (1997) 'Power and discourse: Culture and change in South Africa.' In A. Levett, A. Kottler, E. Burman & I. Parker. *Power and discourse: Culture, power and difference: Discourse analysis in South Africa*. 1–14. Cape Town: UCT Press.

Burman, S., & Reynolds, P. (eds) (1986). *Growing up in a divided society*. Johannesburg: Ravan Press.

Burr, V. (1995). *An introduction to social constructionism*. London: Routledge.

Busfield, J. (1996). *Men, women and madness: Understanding gender and mental disorder*. New York: New York University Press.

Butchart, A. (1996). 'The industrial panopticon: Mining and the medical construction of migrant African labour in South Africa 1900–1950.' *Social Science and Medicine*, 42: 185–197.

Butchart, A. (1997). 'Objects without origins: Foucault in South African socio-medical science.' *South African Journal of Psychology*, 27(2): 101–110.

Butchart, A. (1998). *The anatomy of power: European constructions of the African body*. London and New York: Zed Books; Pretoria: Unisa Press.

Butchart, A., & Kruger, J. (2001). 'Public health and community psychology: A case study in community–based injury prevention.' In M. Seedat, N. Duncan, & S. Lazarus (eds), *Community psychology: Theory, method and practice – South African and other perspectives*. 215–241. Cape Town: Oxford University Press.

Butchart, A., & Seedat, M. (1990). 'Within and without: Images of community and implications for South African psychology.' *Social Science and Medicine*. 31(10): 1093–1102.

Butler, J. (1990a). *Gender trouble: Feminism and the subversion of identity*. New York: Routledge.

Butler, J. (1990b). Gender trouble, feminist theory, and psychoanalytic discourse. In L.J. Nicholson, (ed), *Feminism/Postmodernism*. 324–340. New York and London: Routledge.

Butler, J. (1994). 'Gender as performance: An interview with Judith Butler.' *Radical Philosophy*, 67: 32–39.

CAL (Cape Action League). (1987). *Introduction to 'race' and racism*. Salt River: CAL.

Calvino, M. (1998). 'Reflections on community studies.' *Journal of Community Psychology*. 26(3): 253–259.

Campbell, C. (2000). 'Social capital and health: Contextualising health promotion within local community networks.' In S. Baron, J. Field & T. Schuller (eds), *Social capital: Critical perspectives*. 182–196. Oxford: Oxford University Press.

Campbell, C. (2003). *Letting them die: Why HIV/Aids prevention programmes often fail*. Cape Town: Double Storey/Juta.

Campbell, C., & Mzaidume, Y. (2001). 'Grassroots participation in health promotional projects: Peer education and HIV prevention by sex workers in South Africa.' *American Journal of Public Health*, 91(12): 1978–1987.

Campbell, C., Wood, R., & Kelly, M. (1999). *Social capital and health*. London: Health Education Authority.

Capra, F. (1988). *The tao of physics: An exploration of the parallels between modern physics and Eastern mysticism*. 2nd edition. New York: Bantam Books.

Chambers, R. (1985). *Rural development. Putting the last first*. London: Longman.

Chavajay, P., & Rogoff, B. (1999). 'Cultural variation in management of attention by children and their caregivers.' *Developmental psychology*, 35: 4, 1079–1090.

Chesler, M.A. (1976). 'Contemporary sociological theories of racism'. In P.A. Katz (ed), *Towards the elimination of racism*. New York: Pergamon Press.

Chesler, P. (1972). *Women and madness*. San Diego, CA: Harcourt Brace Jovanich.

Chodorow, N. (1978). *The reproduction of mothering: Psychoanalysis and the sociology of gender*. Berkeley and Los Angeles: University of California Press.

Clark, K., & Holquist, M. (1984). *Mikhail Bakhtin*. Cambridge, MA: Harvard University Press.

Clark, K.B. & Clark M.P. (1940). 'Skin color as a factor in racial identification of negro preschool children.' *Journal of Social Psychology*, 11: 591–599.

Clark, K.B. (1955). *Prejudice and your child*. 2nd edition. Boston: Beacon Press.

Clark, K.B., & Clark M.P. (1939). 'The development of consciousness of self and the emergence of racial identification in Negro pre-school children.' *Journal of Social Psychology*, 10: 591–599.

Clifford, J. (1993). 'Adlerian therapy.' In W. Dryden (ed), *Individual therapy: A handbook*. 86–103. Milton Keynes, UK, Philadelphia, PA: Open University Press.

Clinchy, B.M. (1996). 'Connected and separate knowing: Toward a marriage of two minds.' In N. Goldberger, J. Tarule, B. Clinchy, & M. Belenky (eds), *Knowledge, difference, and power: Essays inspired by women's ways of knowing*. 205–242. New York: Basic Books.

Cloete, N., & Muller, G. (1991). 'Human Sciences Research Council Incorporated (Pty) Ltd: Social sciences research, markets and accountability in South Africa.' In J. Jansen (ed), *Knowledge and power in South Africa*. Braamfontein: Skotaville.

Cloete, N., Muller, G., & Orkin, M. (1986). 'How we learned to stop worrying and love the HSRC.' *Psychology in Society*, 6: 29–46.

Cockcroft, K. (2002). 'Basic concepts and principles in developmental psychology.' In D. Hook, J. Watts & K. Cockcroft (eds), *Developmental psychology*. Cape Town: UCT Press.

Coetzee, C.J.S., & Geggus, C. (1980). *University education in South Africa*. Pretoria: HSRC.

Coetzee, P.H. (1998). 'Particularity in morality and its relation to the community.' In P.H. Coetzee & A.P.J. Roux (eds), *Philosophy from Africa: A text with readings*. 275–291. Halfway House, South Africa: International Thomson Publishing.

Cohen, J.M. & Uphoff, N.T. (1977). *Rural development participation: Concepts and measures for project design, implementation and evaluation*. New York: Rural Development Committee.

Cohen, S. (2001). *States of denial*. Cambridge, UK: Polity Press.

Cole, M. (1995). 'Culture and cognitive development: from cross-cultural research to creating systems of cultural mediation.' *Culture and Psychology*, 1(1): 25–54.

Cole, M., Gay, J., & Glick, J. (1968). 'Some experimental studies of Kpelle quantitative behaviour.' In J.W. Berry & P.R. Dasen (eds), *Culture and cognition: Readings in cross-cultural psychology*. London: Methuen.

Collins, P.H. (1990). *Black feminist thought: Knowledge, consciousness and the politics of empowerment*. Boston: Unwin Hyman.

Collins, T. (1997). 'Models of Health: Pervasive, persuasive and politically charged.' In M. Siddel, L. Jones, J. Katz & A. Peberdy (eds), *Debates and dilemmas in promoting health: A reader.* London: Macmillan Press.

Connell, R.W. (1987). *Gender and power: Society, the person and sexual politics.* Cambridge: Polity Press.

Connell, R.W. (1990). 'An iron man: The body and some contradictions of hegemonic masculinity.' In M.A. Messner & D.F. Sabo (eds), *Sport, men, and the gender order: Critical feminist perspectives.* 8–95. Champaign, IL: Human Kinetics Books.

Cooke, B., & Kothari, U. (2001). *Participation: The new tyranny.* London: Zed Books.

Cooper, D. (1967). *Psychiatry and anti-psychiatry.* London: Paladin, Granada.

Cooper, S., Nicholas, L.J., Seedat, M., & Statman, J.M. (1990). 'Psychology and Apartheid: The struggle for psychology in South Africa.' In L.J. Nicholas & S. Cooper (eds), *Psychology and apartheid.* Johannesburg: Vision Publications.

Couve, C. (1986). 'Psychology and politics in Manganyi's work: A materialist critique.' *Psychology in Society (PINS)*, 5: 90–130.

Coward, R. (1984). *Female desire: Women's sexuality today.* London: Paladin Books.

Crooks, R., & Baur, K. (1996). *Our sexuality.* 6th edition. Pacific Grove, CA: Brooks/Cole.

Crouch, S. (1998). *Always in pursuit: Fresh American perspectives, 1995–1997.* New York: Pantheon Books.

Cushman, P. (1990). 'Towards a historically situated psychology.' *American Psychologist,* 45(5): 599–611.

Cushman, P. (1992). 'Psychotherapy to 1992: A historically situated interpretation.' In D.K. Freedheim (ed), *History of psychotherapy: A century of change.* 21–63. Washington, DC: American Psychological Association.

Cushman, P. (1995). *Constructing the self, constructing America: A cultural history of psychotherapy.* Reading, Mass: Addison-Wesley.

Dalal, F. (1988). 'The racism of Jung'. *Race & Class,* 29(1): 1–22.

Dalton, J.H., Elias, M.J., & Wandersman, A. (2001). *Community psychology: Linking individuals to community.* Australia: Wadsworth/Thomson Learning.

Danziger, K. (1990). *Constructing the subject: Historical origins of psychological research.* Cambridge: Cambridge University Press.

Davids, M.F. (1996). 'Frantz Fanon: The struggle for inner freedom.' *Free Associations,* 6,2(38): 205–234.

Davies, B., & Harré, R. (1990). 'Positioning: The discursive production of selves.' *Journal for the Theory of Social Behaviour,* 20(1): 45–63.

Dawes, A. (1985). 'Politics and mental health: The position of clinical psychology in South Africa.' *South African Journal of Psychology,* 15: 55–61.

Dawes, A. (1986). 'The notion of relevant psychology with particular reference to Africanist pragmatic initiatives.' *Psychology in Society (PINS),* 5: 28–48.

Dawes, A. (1998). 'Africanisation of psychology: Identities and continents.' *Psychology in Society (PINS), 23*: 4–16.

Dawes, A., & Donald, D. (eds) (1994). *Childhood and adversity.* Cape Town: David Philip.

Day, J.M. (1991). 'The moral audience: On the narrative mediation of moral "judgment" and moral "action".' In M.B. Tappan & M.J. Packer (eds), *Narrative and storytelling: Implications for understanding moral development.* 27–42. San Francisco: Jossey-Bass.

Day, J.M., & Tappan, M.B. (1996). 'The narrative approach to moral development: From the epistemic subject to dialogical selves.' *Human Development, 39*: 67–82.

De Beauvoir, S. (1949/1982). *The second sex*. Harmondsworth: Penguin Books.

De la Rey, C. (1997). 'On political activism and discourse analysis in South Africa.' In A. Levett, A. Kottler, E. Burman & I. Parker (eds), *Culture, power and difference: Discourse analysis in South Africa*. 189–197. Cape Town: UCT Press.

De la Rey, C. (2001). 'Racism and the history of university education in South Africa.' In N. Duncan, A. van Niekerk, C. de la Rey & M. Seedat (eds), *'Race', racism, knowledge production and psychology in South Africa*. 7–15. New York: Nova Science.

De la Rey, C., Duncan, N., Shefer, T., & Van Niekerk, A. (eds) (1997). *Contemporary issues in human development*. Johannesburg: International Thomson.

Dean, M. (1994). 'A social structure of many souls: moral regulation, government and self-formation.' *Canadian Journal of Sociology*, 19(2): 145–168.

Dean, M. (1999). *Governmentality. Power and rule in modern society*. London, New Delhi, Thousand Oaks, CA: Sage.

Donald, D., Dawes, A., & Louw, J. (eds) (2000). *Addressing childhood adversity*. Cape Town: David Philip.

Donzelot, J. (1979). *The policing of families* (with a foreword by G. Deleuze). London: Hutchinson.

Drennan, G., & Swartz, L. (1999). 'A concept over burdened: Institutional roles for psychiatric interpreters in post-apartheid South Africa.' *Interpreting*, 4(2): 169–198.

Drennan, G., Levett, A., & Swartz, L. (1991). 'Hidden dimensions of power and resistance in the translation process: A South African study.' *Culture, Medicine & Psychiatry*, 15(3): 361–381.

Dreyfus, H.L., & Rabinow, P. (1982). *Michel Foucault. Beyond structuralism and hermeneutics*. New York: Harvester Wheatsheaf.

Du Bois, W.E.B. (1903/1996). *The souls of black folk*. New York: Penguin Books.

Du Toit, J.M., & Van der Merwe, A.B. (1976). *Sielkunde (Psychology)*. Cape Town: HAUM.

Dubow, S. (1995). *Illicit union. Scientific racism in modern South Africa*. Johannesburg: Wits University Press.

Duckitt, J. (1992). *The social psychology of prejudice*. New York: Praeger.

Duncan, N., & Hofmeyr, M. (2002). 'Academic authorship development in the social sciences in South Africa through self-empowerment collectives: Research report.' *UNISA Institute for Social and Health Sciences Occasional Paper 1*.

Duncan, N. (1993). 'Discourses of racism.' Unpublished doctoral dissertation. University of the Western Cape, Bellville.

Duncan, N. (2001). 'Dislodging the sub-texts: An analysis of a corpus of articles on racism produced by South African psychologists.' In N. Duncan, A. van Niekerk, C. de la Rey & M. Seedat (eds), *'Race', racism, knowledge production and psychology in South Africa*. 125–152. New York: Nova Science Publishers.

Duncan, N., Gqola, P., Hofmeyr, M., Shefer, T., Malunga, F., & Mashige, M. (eds) (2002). *Discourses on difference, discourses on oppression*. Plumstead: CASAS.

Duncan, N. (2002). 'Listen here, just because you think I'm a coloured ...: Responses to the constructions of difference in racist discourses.' In N. Duncan, P.D. Gqola, M, Hofmeyer, T. Shefer, F. Malunga & M. Mashige (eds), *Discourses on difference, discourses on oppression*. 113–137. Cape Town: CASAS.

Duncan, N., Seedat, M., Van Niekerk, A., De la Rey, C., Gobodo-Madikizela, P., Simbayi, L., & Bhana, A. (1997). 'Black scholarship: Doing something active and positive about academic racism.' *South African Journal of Psychology*, 27(4): 201–205.

Duncan, N., Van Niekerk, A., De la Ray, C., & Seedat, M. (2001). 'Race, racism, knowledge-production and psychology in South Africa: Editorial Introduction.' In N. Duncan, A. van Niekerk, C. de la Rey & M. Seedat (eds), *'Race', racism, knowledge production and psychology in South Africa*. 1–6. New York: Nova Science.

Durrheim, K. (2001). 'A defence of an "immanentist" account of social form and experience.' *South African Journal of Psychology*, 31: 9–11.

Durrheim, K. (in press). 'White opposition to racial transformation: Is it racism?' *South African Journal of Psychology*.

Durrheim, K., & Mokeki, S. (1997). 'Race and relevance: A content analysis of the *South African Journal of Psychology*.' *South African Journal of Psychology*, 27(4): 206–213.

Dzobo, N.K. (1992). 'Values in a changing society: Man, ancestors, and God.' In K. Wiredu & K. Gyekye (eds), *Person and community: Ghanaian Philosophical Studies, Volume I*. Available: http://www.crvp.org/book/Series02/II-01.htm. [2000, 18 September].

Eagle, G. (1999). 'Standpoint methodologies: Marxist, feminist and black scholarship perspectives.' In M. Terre Blanche & K. Durrheim (eds), *Research in practice: Applied methods for the social sciences*. Cape Town: UCT Press.

Eagleton, T. (1999). 'Utopia and its opposites.' In L. Panitch & C. Leys (eds), *Necessary and unnecessary utopias*. 31–40. Rendlesham, UK: Merlin Press.

Ebersohn, D. (1983). *Die sielkundige van die Republiek van Suid-Afrika* (*The South African psychologist*). Pretoria: HSRC.

Ebigbo, P.O. (1989). 'The mind, the body and society: An African perspective.' In K. Peltzer & P.O. Ebigbo (eds), *Clinical psychology in Africa (South of the Sahara), the Caribbean and Afro-Latin America*. Enugu, Nigeria: Chuka Printing Company.

Edley, N., & Wetherell, M. (1997). 'Jockeying for position: The construction of masculine identities.' *Discourse & Society*, 8: 203–217.

Ejizu, C.I. (2000). 'African traditional religions and the promotion of community living in Africa.' Available: http://www.afrikaworld.net/afrel/community. htm [2000, 12 December].

Elliot, A. (1992). *Social theory and psychoanalysis in transition: Self and society from Freud to Kristeva*. Oxford, UK and Cambridge, USA: Blackwell.

Engeström, Y. (1987). *Learning by expanding: An activity theoretical approach to developmental research*. Helsinki: Orienta-Konsultit.

Engeström, Y. (1999). 'Innovative learning in work teams: Analyzing cycles of knowledge creation in practice'. In Y. Engeström, R. Miettinen & R-L. Punamaki. *Perspectives on activity theory*. 377–406. Cambridge: Cambridge University Press.

Engeström, Y., Brown, K., Christopher, L.C., & Gregory, J. (1997). 'Coordination, cooperation, and communication in the courts: Expansive transitions in legal work.' In M. Cole, Y. Engeström & O. Vasquez (eds), *Mind, culture and activity: Seminal papers from the laboratory of comparative human cognition*. 369–385. Cambridge: Cambridge University Press.

Engeström, Y. (1993). 'Development studies of work as a testbench of activity theory: The case of primary care medical practice.' In S. Chaiklin & J. Lave (eds), *Understanding practice: Perspectives on activity and context*. Cambridge: Cambridge University Press.

Essed, P. (1987). *Academic racism*. Amsterdam: CRES Publications Series.

Fairclough, N. (1992). *Discourse and social change*. Cambridge: Polity Press.

Falso-Borda, O. (1981). 'The challenge of action research.' *Development: Seeds of change*, 1: 55–61.

Fanon, F. (1952/1967). *Black skin, white masks*. New York: Grove Press.

Fanon, F. (1952/1986). *Black skin white masks*. London: Pluto Press.

Fanon, F. (1959/1970). *A dying colonialism*. New York: Grove. (trans Haakon Chevalier).

Fanon, F. (1961/1967). *The wretched of the earth*. Harmondsworth, UK: Penguin.

Fanon, F. (1961/1968). *Toward the African Revolution*. New York: Grove. (trans Haakon Chevalier).

Fanon, F. (1963/1990). *The wretched of the earth*. London: Penguin. (trans C. Farrington).

Fanon, F. (1985). 'Psychology: Science or sorcery?' In H.A. Bulhan, *Frantz Fanon and the psychology of oppression*. New York: Plenum Press.

Fillingham, L.A. (1993). *Foucault for beginners*. New York: Writers & Readers Publishing.

Finchilescu, G. (1995). 'Setting the frame: Gender and psychology.' *South African Journal of Psychology*, 25(3): 133–139.

Foster, D. (1986). 'The South Africa crisis of 1985.' *Psychology in Society (PINS)*, 5: 49–65.

Foster, D. (1990). 'Historical and legal traces 1800–1990.' In S. Lea & D. Foster (eds), *Perspectives on mental handicap in South Africa*. 21–70. Durban: Butterworths.

Foster, D. (1991). 'Introduction.' In D. Foster & J. Louw-Potgieter (eds), *Social psychology in South Africa*. Johannesburg: Lexicon.

Foster, D. (1991). 'On racism: Virulent mythologies and fragile threads.' Inaugural Lecture, 21 August, University of Cape Town, Cape Town.

Foster, D. (1991a). '"Race" and racism in South African psychology.' *South African Journal of Psychology*, 21: 203–210.

Foster, D. (1991b). 'Crowds and collective action.' In D. Foster & J. Louw-Potgieter (eds), *Social psychology in South Africa*. 441–483. Johannesburg: Lexicon.

Foster, D. (1993, 1993a). 'On racism: Virulent mythologies and fragile threads.' In L.J. Nicholas (ed), *Psychology and oppression: Critiques and proposals*. 55–80. Braamfontein: Skotaville Publishers.

Foster, D. (1993b). 'The mark of oppression?' In L. Nicholas (ed), *Psychology and oppression*. 128–141. Johannesburg: Skotaville.

Foster, D. (1994). 'Racism and children's intergroup orientations.' In A. Dawes & D. Donald (eds), *Childhood and adversity*. 220–239. Cape Town: David Philip.

Foster, D. (1999). 'Racism, Marxism, psychology.' *Theory and Psychology*, 9(3): 331–352.

Foster, D. (2000). 'Entitlement as explanation for perpetrators' actions.' *South African Journal of Psychology*, 30(1): 10–13.

Foster, D., & Louw-Potgieter, J. (eds) (1991). *Social psychology in South Africa*. Johannesburg: Lexicon.

Foster, D., Davis, D., & Sandler, D. (1987). *Detention and torture in South Africa*. London: James Currey.

Foster, D., Freeman, M., & Pillay, Y. (eds) (1997). *Mental health policy issues for South Africa*. Cape Town: MASA Multimedia.

Foucault, M. (1972). *The archaeology of knowledge*. London: Tavistock; New York: Pantheon Books.

Foucault, M. (1977). *Discipline and punish: The birth of the prison*. London: Penguin.

Foucault, M. (1978). *History of sexuality. Volume 1: An introduction*. Harmondsworth, UK: Penguin.

Foucault, M. (1978/2002). 'Interview.' In J.D. Faubion (ed), *Michel Foucault. Volume 3: Power*. 239–297. London: Penguin.

Foucault, M. (1979, 1979b). 'Governmentality.' *Ideology & Consciousness*, 6: 5–21.

Foucault, M. (1979a). *Discipline and punish: The birth of the prison.* New York: Vintage Books.

Foucault, M. (1980, 1980a). 'Power/knowledge.' In C. Gordon (ed), *Power/knowledge: Selected interviews and other writings by Michel Foucault, 1972–1977.* 1–228. New York: Pantheon Books.

Foucault, M. (1980b). *History of sexuality. Volume 1: An introduction.* New York: Vintage Books.

Foucault, M. (1982). 'The subject and power.' Afterword to H.L. Dreyfus & P. Rabinow (eds), *Michel Foucault: Beyond structuralism and hermeneutics.* 208–226. New York: Harvester Wheatsheaf; Chicago: University of Chicago Press.

Foucault, M. (1982). 'The subject and power.' *Critical Inquiry,* 8(4): 777–795.

Foucault, M. (1986). *The use of pleasure: The history of sexuality. Volume 2.* New York: Vintage Books.

Foucault, M. (1988). 'Technologies of the self.' In L.H. Martin, H. Gutman & P.H. Hutton (eds), *Technologies of the self: A seminar with Michel Foucault.* 16–49. London: Tavistock.

Foucault, M. (1988a). 'Politics and reason.' In L.D. Kritzman (ed), *Michel Foucault: Politics, philosophy, culture, interviews and other writings 1977–1984.* London and New York: Routledge.

Foucault, M. (1988b). 'The ethic of care for the self as a practice of freedom.' In J. Bernauer & D. Rasmussen (eds), *The Final Foucault.* 78–109. Cambridge, MA: MIT Press.

Foucault, M. (1988c). 'Technologies of the self.' In L.H. Martin, H. Gutman & P.H. Hutton (eds), *Technologies of the self: A seminar with Michel Foucault.* Massachusetts: University of Massachusetts Press.

Foucault, M. (1988d). 'The political technology of individuals.' In L.H. Martin, H. Gutman & P.H. Hutton (eds), *Technologies of the self: A seminar with Michel Foucault.* Massachusetts: University of Massachusetts Press.

Foucault, M. (1990). 'Politics and reason.' In L.D. Kritzman (ed), *Michel Foucault: Politics, philosophy, culture, interviews and other writings 1977–1984.* New York and London: Routledge.

Foucault, M. (1997). 'The birth of biopolitics.' In P. Rabinow (ed), *Michel Foucault – ethics, subjectivity and truth: The essential works of Michel Foucault 1954–1984 Volume I.* New York: The New York Press.

Fouts, H.N. (2001). 'Weaning and the nature of early childhood interactions among Bofi foragers in Central Africa.' *Human Nature,* 12: 1, 27–46.

Fox, D. (2000). 'The Critical psychology project: Transforming society and transforming Psychology.' In T. Sloan (ed), *Critical psychology: Voices for Change.* 21–33. Basingstoke, UK: MacMillan Press.

Franchi, V. (2002). 'Affirmative action and the racialisation of organisational conflict: The challenge of symbolic racism for intercultural training.' *International Journal of Intercultural Relations,* 27(2).

Frank, A.G. (1975). *On capitalist underdevelopment.* Bombay: Oxford University Press.

Franklin, A.J. (1999). 'Invisibility syndrome and racial identity development in psychotherapy and counselling African American men.' *The Counselling Psychologist,* 27(6): 761–793.

Freeman, A. & Greenwood, V. (eds) (1983). *Cognitive therapy: Applications in psychiatric and medical settings.* New York: Human Sciences Press.

Freire, P. (1970/1996). *Pedagogy of the oppressed.* Harmondsworth, UK: Penguin.

Freire, P. (1973/1993). *Education for critical consciousness.* New York: Continuum.

Freud, S. (1933/1973). *New introductory lectures on psychoanalysis.* Harmondsworth, UK: Penguin.

Frosh, S. (1989). *Psychoanalysis and psychology: Minding the gap.* Houndmills, Basingstoke and London: Macmillan.

Frosh, S. (1991). *Identity crisis: Modernity, psychology and the self.* Houndmills, Basingstoke and London: Macmillan.

Frosh, S. (1999). 'What is outside discourse?' *Psychoanalytic Studies,* 1(4): 381–390.

Fuss, D. (1989). *Essentially speaking: Feminism, nature and difference.* New York: Routledge.

Gadamer, H-G. (1975). *Truth and method.* New York: Continuum.

Galton, F. (1892). *Hereditary Genius.* New York: MacMillan.

Gambu, S.Q. (2000). 'Cultural issues in the understanding of ethics in the nursing profession: Implications for practice.' Unpublished Masters dissertation, University of Natal, Pietermaritzburg, South Africa.

Gandhi, L. (1998). *Postcolonial theory: A critical introduction.* New York: Columbia University Press.

Gates, H.L. (jnr), & West, C. (1996). *The future of the race.* New York: Alfred A. Knopf.

Geddie, W. (ed), (1901/1964). *Chambers twentieth century dictionary.* London, UK: W. & R. Chambers, Ltd.

Geertz, C. (1973). *The interpretation of cultures: Selected essays.* New York: Basic Books.

Geertz, C. (1979). 'From the native's point of view: On the nature of anthropological understanding.' In P. Rabinow & W.M. Sullivan (eds), *Interpretive social science.* Berkeley: University of California Press.

Gengaje, R.K., & Setty, E.D. (1991). 'People's image of development: Development implications.' *Journal of Rural Development,* 10(3): 311–332.

Gergen, K. (1994). *Realities and relationships.* Cambridge, MA: Harvard University Press.

Gergen, K.J., Gulerce, A., Lock, A., & Misra, G. (1996). 'Psychological science in cultural context.' *American Psychologist,* 51: 496–503.

Gergen, M., & Gergen, K.J. (1993). 'Autobiographies and the shaping of gendered lives.' In N. Coupland & J. Nussbaum (eds), *Discourse and lifespan identity.* 28–54. Sage: Newbury Park.

Gergen, M.M. (2001). *Feminist reconstructions in psychology.* Thousand Oaks, CA: Sage.

Gergen, M.M., & Davis, S. (eds) (1997). *Towards a new psychology of gender.* New York: Routledge.

Ghent, E. (1992). 'Foreword.' In N. Skolnick & S. Warshaw (eds), *Relational perspectives in psychoanalysis.* Hillsdale, NJ & London: The Analytic Press.

Gibson, K., & Swartz, L. (2000). 'Politics and emotion: Working with disadvantaged children in South Africa.' *Psychodynamic Counselling,* 6(2): 133–153.

Giddens, A. (1992). *The transformation of intimacy: Sexuality, love and eroticism in modern societies.* Cambridge, UK: Polity Press.

Giddens, A. (1999). *Runaway world.* London: Profile Books.

Gilbert, A. & Van Vlaenderen, H. (1995). 'The need for individual and organisational capacity building among stakeholders in rural development.' Paper presented at the UNCRD Conference, University of Transkei, Umtata, 30 Sep./Oct.

Gilbert, A. (1995). 'Small voices against the wind: Local knowledge and social transformation.' Paper presented at the 4th International Symposium on the contributions of psychology to peace, University of Cape Town, 25–30 June.

Gilbert, A. (1997). 'Small voices against the wind: Local knowledge and social transformation.' *Peace and Conflict: Journal of Peace Psychology,* 3(3): 275–292.

Gillies, P. (1998). 'The effectiveness of alliances and partnerships for health promotion.' *Health Promotion International*, 13: 1–21.

Gilligan, C. (1982). *In a different voice: Psychological theory and women's development.* Cambridge, MA: Harvard University Press.

Gilman, S.L. (1985). *Difference and pathology: Stereotypes of sexuality, race and madness.* London: Cornell University Press.

Gilroy, P. (1993). *The black Atlantic.* Cambridge, MA: Harvard University Press.

Gilroy, P. (1994). *The black Atlantic: Modernity and double consciousness.* Cambridge, MA: Harvard University Press.

Gobodo-Madikizela, P. (2000). 'Legacies of violence.' Unpublished PhD thesis, University of Cape Town.

Gobodo-Madikizela, P. (2003). *A human being died that night.* Boston: Houghton-Mifflin.

Goffman, E. (1968). *Asylums: Essays on the social situation of mental patients and other inmates.* London: Peregrine.

Goffman, E. (1973). 'The medical model and mental hospitalization.' In P. Brown (ed), *Radical psychology.* 25–45. New York, Evanston, San Francisco, London: Harper Colophon Books.

Goldberg, B. (1996). 'In a bad humour with psychology.' In E. Burman, A. Alldred, C. Bewley, B. Goldberg, C. Heenan, D. Marks, J. Marshall, K. Taylor, R. Ullah, & S. Warner (eds), *Challenging women: Psychology's exclusions, feminist possibilities.* London: Open University Press.

Gough, B. (1998). 'Men and the discursive reproduction of sexism: Repertoires of difference and equality.' *Feminism and Psychology*, 8(1): 25–49.

Gqola, P. (1997). 'What's in this womanist shit? Naming self as resistance, or my name is a womanist issue.' Unpublished Conference Paper. UCT.

Gqola, P. (2001). '*Ufanele uqavile*: Black women, feminisms & postcoloniality in Africa.' *Agenda*, 50: 11–23.

Graaff, J. (2001). 'Theorising development.' In J.K. Coetzee, J. Graaff, F. Hendricks & G. Wood. *Development: Theory, policy and practice.* 5–11. Cape Town: Oxford University Press.

Gramsci, A. (1978). *Selections from political writing.* London: Laurence & Wishart.

Grant, J. (2002). 'Kohlberg's theory of moral reasoning.' In D. Hook, J. Watts & K. Cockcroft (eds). *Developmental Psychology.* Cape Town: UCT Press.

Greenfield, P.M. (1997). 'You can't take it with you: Why ability assessments don't cross cultures.' *American Psychologist*, 52(10): 1115–1124.

Greenwood, D.J., Foot-Whyte, W., & Harkory, I. (1993). 'Participatory Action Research as a process and as a goal.' *Human Relations,* 46(2): 175–192.

Grosz, E. (1990). *Jacques Lacan: A feminist introduction.* London & New York: Routledge.

Grunseit, A., Kippax, S., Aggleton, P., Baldo, M., & Slutkin, G. (1997). 'Sexuality education and young people's sexual behaviour.' *Journal of Adolescent Research*, 12(4): 421–453.

Guillaumin, C. (1995). *Racism, sexism, power and ideology.* London: Routledge.

Guillaumin, C. (2002). *L'idéologie raciste.* Mesnil-sur-l'Estrée, Fr: Gallimard.

Gyekye, K. (1984). 'The Akan concept of a person.' In R.A. Wright (ed), *African philosophy.* 199–212. University of Toledo: University Press of America.

Gyekye, K. (1992). 'Person and community in African thought.' In K. Wiredu & K. Gyekye (eds), *Person and community: Ghanaian Philosophical Studies. Volume I.* Available: http://www.crvp.org/book/Series02/II-01.htm. [2000, 18 September].

Hall, E.T. (1983). *The dance of life: The other dimensions of time.* Garden City, NY: Anchor Press/Double Day.

Hall, E.T., & Hall, M.R. (1990). *Understanding cultural differences.* Yarmouth, ME: Intercultural Press.

Hall, G.S. (1905). *Adolescence: Its psychology and its relations to physiology, anthropology, sociology, sex, crime, religion and education.* London: Sidney Appleton.

Hall, S. (2001). 'Foucault, power, knowledge and discourse.' In M. Wetherell, S. Taylor & S. Yates (eds), *Discourse theory and practice: A reader.* 72–81. Sage: London.

Hall, S., Critcher, G., Jefferson, T., Clarke, J., & Roberts, B. (1984). *Policing the crisis: Mugging, the state and law and order.* London: MacMillan.

Halton, W. (1994). 'Some unconscious aspects of organizational life: contributions from psychoanalysis.' In A. Obholzer & V.Z. Roberts (eds), *The unconscious at work: Individual and organizational stress in the human services.* 11–18. London: Routledge.

Hamber, B., Masilela, T.C., & Terre Blanche, M. (2001). 'Towards a Marxist community psychology: Radical tools for community psychological analysis and practice.' In M. Seedat, S. Lazarus & N. Duncan (eds), *Community psychology: Theory, method and practice. South African and other perspectives.* 51–66. Cape Town: Oxford University Press.

Haraway, D. (1991). *Simians, cyborgs and women.* London: Free Association Press.

Haraway, D.J. (1991). 'Situated knowledges: The science question in feminism and the privilege of partial perspective.' In D.J. Haraway, *Simians, cyborgs, and women: The reinvention of nature.* 183–202. New York: Routledge.

Hare-Mustin, R.T., & Maracek, J. (1992). 'The meaning of difference: gender theory, postmodernism and psychology.' In J.S. Bohan (ed), *Seldom seen, rarely heard: Women's place in psychology.* 227–249. Boulder, Colorado: Westview Press.

Hare-Mustin, R.T., & Maracek, J. (1990, 1990a). 'On making a difference.' In R.T. Hare-Mustin & J. Maracek (eds), *Making a difference: Psychology and the construction of gender.* 1–21. New Haven, CT: Yale University Press.

Hare-Mustin, R.T., & Maracek, J. (1990b). 'Gender and the meaning of difference: Postmodernism and psychology.' In R.T. Hare-Mustin & J. Maracek (eds), *Making a difference: Psychology and the construction of gender.* 22–64. New Haven, CT; Yale University Press.

Hare-Mustin, R.T., & Maracek, J. (1990c). 'Beyond difference.' In R.T. Hare-Mustin & J. Maracek (eds), *Making a difference: Psychology and the construction of gender.* 184–201. New Haven, CT: Yale University Press.

Harré, R., & Van Langenhove, L. (1999a). 'The dynamics of social episodes.' In R. Harr´e & L. van Langenhove (eds), *Positioning theory.* 1–31. Oxford: Blackwell.

Harré, R., & Van Langenhove, L. (1991). 'Varieties of positioning.' *Journal for the Theory of Social Behaviour,* 21: 393–407.

Harris, B. (1997). 'Repoliticizing the history of psychology'. In D. Fox & I. Prilleltensky. *Critical psychology: An introduction.* 21–33. London: Sage.

Harris, E., Lea, S., & Foster, D. (1995). 'The construction of gender: An analysis of men's talk on gender.' In *South African Journal of Psychology,* 25(3): 175–183.

Harrison, D. (1981). *The white tribe of Africa.* Los Angeles: University of California Press.

Harrison, P. (1982). *Inside the 'Third World': The anatomy of power.* Harmondsworth, UK: Penguin.

Hawes, S.E. (1998). 'Positioning a dialogical reflexivity in the practice of feminist supervision.' In B.M. Bayer & J. Shotter (eds), *Reconstructing the psychological subject.* 94–110. London: Sage.

Hayes, G. (1986). 'The politics of industrial psychology.' *Psychology in Society (PINS),* 7: 67–77.

Hayes, G. (1989). 'Psychology and ideology: The case of Althusser.' *South African Journal of Psychology,* 19(2): 84–90.

Hayes, G. (1995). 'Editorial.' *Psychology in Society (PINS),* 20: 1–3.

Hayes, G. (1998). 'We suffer our memories: Thinking about the past, healing and reconciliation.' *American Imago,* 55: 29–50.

Hayes, G. (2001). 'Editorial: Critical psychology.' *Psychology in Society (PINS),* 27: 1–2.

Hayes, G. (2002). 'Sachs, Chavafambira, Maggie: Prurience or the pathology of social relations?' *South African Journal of Psychology,* 32(2), June: 43–48.

Hayes, W.A. (1980). 'Radical black behaviorism.' In R.L Jones (ed), *Black psychology.* 2nd edition. 37–47. New York: Harper and Row.

Heelas, P. (1981). 'Introduction: Indigenous psychologies.' In P. Heelas & A. Lock (eds), *Indigenous psychologies: The anthropology of the self.* 3–18. London: Academic Press.

Hegel, G.W.F. (1956). *The philosophy of history.* Dover, MA: Dover.

Hekman, S. (1995). *Moral voices, moral selves.* Cambridge, UK: Polity Press.

Hendricks, C., & Lewis, D. (1994). 'Voices from the margins.' *Agenda,* 20: 61–75.

Henriques, J., Hollway, W., Urwin, C., Venn, C., & Walkerdine, V. (1984/1998). *Changing the subject: Psychology, social regulation and subjectivity.* London: Methuen/Routledge.

Herman, J. (1994). *Trauma and recovery.* London: Harper-Collins & Pandora.

Hermans, H.J.M. (1996). 'Voicing the self: From information processing to dialogical interchange.' *Psychological Bulletin,* 119: 31–50.

Hermans, H.J.M. (1997). 'Dialogue shakes narrative: From temporal storyline to spatial juxtaposition.' *Journal of Narrative and Life History,* 7: 387–394.

Hermans, H.J.M. (2001a). 'Mixing and moving cultures require a dialogical self.' *Human Development,* 44: 24–28.

Hermans, H.J.M. (2001b). 'The dialogical self: Toward a theory of personal and cultural positioning.' *Culture and Psychology,* 7(3): 243–281.

Hermans, H.J.M., & Kempen, H.J.G. (1993). *The dialogical self: Meaning as movement.* San Diego, CA: Academic Press.

Hermans, H.J.M., & Kempen, H.J.G. (1998). 'Moving cultures: The perilous problems of cultural dichotomies in a globalizing society.' *American Psychologist,* 53: 1111–1120.

Hermans, H.J.M., Kempen, H.G.C., & Van Loon, R.J.P. (1992). 'The dialogical self: Beyond individualism and rationalism.' *American Psychologist,* 47: 23–33.

Hermes, J. (1995). *Reading women's magazines: An analysis of everyday media use.* Cambridge, UK: Polity Press.

Hess, R.D. (1970). 'Social class and ethnic influences upon socialization.' In P.H. Mussen (ed), *Carmichael's manual of child psychology.* New York: Wiley.

Higgins, E.T. (1987). 'Self-discrepancy theory: A theory relating self and affect.' *Psychological Review,* 94: 319–340.

Hinsdale, M.A., Lewis, H.M., & Waller, S.M. (1995). *It comes from the people: Community development and local theology.* Philadelphia, PA: Temple University Press.

Hinshelwood, R.D., & Chiesa, M. (2002). 'Introduction to the span of the British tradition.' In R.D. Hinshelwood & M. Chiesa (eds), *Organisations, anxieties and defences: Towards a psychoanalytic social psychology.* 145–157. London: Whurr.

Ho, D.Y. (1998). 'Indigenous perspectives: Asian perspectives.' *Journal of Cross-Cultural Psychology,* 29(1): 88–103.

Hobson, J.A. (1901). *The psychology of jingoism.* London: Grant Richards.

Hoff, J. (1996). 'Gender as a postmodern category of paralysis.' In *Women's History Review,* 3: 149–168.

Holdstock, L.T. (2000). *Re-examining psychology: Critical perspectives and African insights.* London and New York: Routledge.

Hollway, W. (1984). 'Gender difference and the production of subjectivity.' In J. Henriques, W. Hollway, C. Urwin, C. Venn & V. Walkerdine (eds), *Changing the subject: Psychology, social regulation and subjectivity.* 227–263. London: Metheun.

Hollway, W. (1989). *Subjectivity and method in psychology: Gender, meaning and science.* London: Sage.

Hollway, W., & Jefferson, T. (2000). *Doing qualitative research differently: Free association, narrative and the interview method.* London: Sage.

Holmes, J., & Lindley, R. (1989). *The values of psychotherapy.* Oxford: Oxford University Press.

Holquist, M. (1983). 'Answering as authoring: Mikhail Bakhtin's trans-linguistics.' *Critical Inquiry,* 10: 307–319.

Holquist, M. (1990). *Dialogism: Bakhtin and his world.* London: Routledge.

Homer, S. (1998). *Fredric Jameson: Marxism, hermeneutics, postmodernism.* Cambridge, UK: Polity Press.

Hoogvelt, A.M. (1976). *The sociology of developing societies.* London: MacMillan.

Hook, D. (2001). 'Discourse, knowledge, materiality, history.' *Theory and Psychology,* 11(4): 521–547.

Hook, D. (2001). 'Editorial 2: Critical Psychology in South Africa: Applications, limitations, possibilities.' *Psychology in Society (PINS),* 27: 3–17.

Hook, D. (2001). 'Therapeutic discourse, co-construction, interpellation, role-induction: Psychotherapy as iatrogenic treatment modality?' *The International Journal of Psychotherapy,* 6(1): 47–66.

Hook, D. (2002). 'Bronfenbrenner's ecological theory of development.' In D. Hook, J. Watts & K. Cockcroft (eds), *Developmental psychology.* Cape Town: UCT Press.

Hook, D. (2002). 'Critical issues in developmental psychology.' In D. Hook, J. Watts, & K. Cockcroft (eds), *Developmental psychology.* Cape Town: UCT Press.

Hook, D., & Cockcroft, K. (2002). *Cognitive and psychosocial developmental psychology: A workbook.* Johannesburg: Wooden Tree Publishers.

Hook, D., & Eagle, G. (2002). *Psychopathology and social prejudice.* Cape Town: UCT Press.

Hook, D., Terre Blanche, M., & Bhavnani, K. (eds) (1999). *Body politics.* Johannesburg: Histories of the Present Press.

Hook, D., Watts, J., & Cockcroft, K. (eds). *Developmental psychology.* Cape Town: UCT Press.

hooks, b. (du). *Killing rage: Ending racism.* New York: Penguin.

Howard, P. (1994). 'The confrontation of modern and traditional knowledge systems in development.' *Canadian Journal of Communications,* 19(2). Available: http://www.wlu.ca/~wwwpress/jrls/cjc/BackIssues/19.2/howard.html [2001, 10 February].

Howitt, D., & Owusu-Bempah, J. (1994). *The racism of psychology: Time for change.* New York: Harvester Wheatsheaf.

Huebner, A., & Garrod, A. (1991). 'Moral reasoning in a karmic world.' *Human Development,* 34: 241–352.

Hunt, J.C. (1989). *Psychoanalytic aspects of fieldwork* (Sage University Paper Series on Qualitative Methods, Volume 18). Beverley Hills, CA: Sage.

Ikuenobe, P. (1998). 'Moral education and moral reasoning in traditional African cultures.' *The Journal of Value Inquiry,* 32: 25–42.

Ingelby, D. (1972). 'Ideology and the human sciences.' In T. Paterman (ed), *Counter course.* 45–46. Harmondsworth, UK: Penguin.

Ingleby, D. (ed) (1981). *Critical psychiatry: The politics of mental health.* London: Penguin.

Ingelby, D. (1985). 'Professionals as socializers.' *Research in Law, Deviance, and Social Control,* 7: 79–109.

Ivey, A.E. (1993). *Developmental strategies for helpers.* North Amherst, MA: Microtraining Associates.

Ivey, A.E., Ivey, M.B., & Simerk-Morgan, L. (1997). *Counseling and psychotherapy: A multi-cultural perspective.* Boston: Ally-Bacon.

Ivey, G. (1986) 'Elements of a critical psychology.' *Psychology in Society (PINS),* 5, 4–27.

Jackson, C.A., & Van Vlaenderen, H. (1994). 'Participatory research: A feminist critique.' *Psychology in Society (PINS),* 18: 3–20.

Jahoda, G. (1973). 'Psychology and the developing countries: Do they need each other?' *International Social Science Journal,* 25(4): 461–474.

Jahoda, G. (1982). *Cross-cultural research in developmental psychology.* India: Centre of Advanced Study in Psychology.

Jahoda, G. (1983). 'European "lag" in the development of an economic concept: A study in Zimbabwe.' *British Journal of Developmental Psychology,* 1: 2, 113–120.

Jameson, F. (1997). 'Five theses on actually existing Marxism.' In E. Meiksins Wood & J. Bellamy Foster (eds), *In defense of history: Marxism and the postmodern agenda.* New York: Monthly Review Press.

Jansen, J. (1991). 'Knowledge and power in South Africa: An overview and orientation.' In J. Jansen (ed), *Knowledge and power in South Africa.* Braamfontein: Skotaville.

Jensen, L.A. (1997). 'Different world-views, different morals: America's culture war divide.' *Human Development,* 40: 325–344.

Joffe, H. (1999). *Risk and 'The other'.* Cambridge, UK: Cambridge University Press.

Jones, R.L. (ed) (1980). *Black psychology.* 2nd edition. New York: Harper and Row.

Josephs, I.E. (1997). 'Talking with the dead: Self-construction as dialogue.' *Journal of Narrative and Life History,* 7: 359–367.

Jovchelovitch, S. (1997). 'Peripheral communities and the transformation of social representations: Queries on power and recognition.' *Social Psychological Review,* 1(1): 16–26.

Julien, I. (1995) (dir). *Frantz Fanon: Black skin, white mask.* n.p.

Kagarlitsky, B. (2000). *The return of radicalism: Reshaping the left institutions.* London: Pluto Press.

Kagitcibasi, G. (1973). 'Psychological aspects of modernization in Turkey.' *Journal of Cross-Cultural Psychology,* 4(2): 157–172.

Kardiner, A., & Ovesey, L. (1951). *The mark of oppression.* Cleveland: World Publishing.

Kasenene, P. (1992). 'Ethics in African theology.' In C. Villa-Vicencio & J.W. de Gruchy (eds), *Doing ethics in context: South African perspectives.* 138–147. Maryknoll, New York: Orbis Books.

Katz, P. (1976). 'Racism and social science: Toward a new commitment.' In P.A. Katz (ed), *Towards the elimination of racism.* New York: Pergamon Press.

Kelly, C., & Breinlinger, S. (1996). *The social psychology of collective action.* Basingstoke, UK: Taylor & Francis.

Kelly, K., & Van Vlaenderen, H. (1996). 'Dynamics of participation in a community health project.' *Social Science and Medicine,* 42: 1235–1246.

Kelly, K., & Parker, W. (2001). 'From people to places: Prioritizing contextual research for social mobilization against HIV/Aids.' Paper presented at the Aids in Context Conference, University of the Witwatersrand, Johannesburg, 4–7 April.

Kelly, K., & Van Vlaenderen, H. (1997). 'Dialogue, inter-subjectivity and the analysis of discourse.' In A. Levett, A. Kottler, E. Burman & I. Parker (eds), *Culture, power and difference: Discourse analysis in South Africa*. 159–172. London: Zed Books.

Kendall, G., & Wickham, G. (1999). *Using Foucault's methods*. London: Sage.

Kim, U. (1990). 'Indigenous psychologies and the cultural sciences tradition.' In V.G. Enriquez (ed), *Indigenous psychology: A book of readings*. Quezon City, Philippines: New Horizons Press.

Kindervatter, S. (1979). *Non-formal education as an empowering process*. Massachusetts: Centre for International Education.

King, L. (1999). 'Community participation in healthcare delivery.' In K. Dennill, L. King, & T. Swanepoel (eds), *Aspects of primary health care: Community healthcare in Southern Africa*. 2nd edition. 81–113. Cape Town: Oxford University Press.

Kinoti, H.W. (1992). 'African morality: Past and present.' In J.N.K. Mugambi & A. Nasimiyu-Wasike (eds), *Moral and ethical issues in African Christianity: Exploratory essays in moral theory*. 73–82. Nairobi: Initiative.

Kitzinger, C. (1987). *The social construction of lesbianism*. London: Sage.

Kitzinger, C., & Wilkinson, S. (1993). 'Theorizing heterosexuality.' In S. Wilkinson & C. Kitzinger (eds), *Heterosexuality: A feminism and psychology reader*. 1–32. London: Sage.

Kitzinger, J. (1998). 'Resisting the message: The extents and limits of media influence.' In D. Miller, J. Kitzinger, K. Williams & P. Beharrell (eds). *The circuit of mass communication: Media strategies, representation and audience reception in the Aids crisis*. Sage: London.

Klandermans, B. (1997). *The social psychology of protest*. Oxford: Blackwell.

Klein, M. (1959). 'Our adult world and its roots in infancy.' *Human Relations*, 12: 291–303.

Klein, M. (1986). *The selected Melanie Klein*. Harmondsworth, UK: Peregrine.

Kohlberg, L. (1981). *Essays in moral development. Volume I: The philosophy of moral development*. New York: Harper & Row.

Kohlberg, L. (1984). *Essays in moral development. Volume II: The psychology of moral development: Moral stages, their nature and validity*. San Francisco: Harper & Row.

Kontinen, T. (1999). 'The activity theoretical approach for studying NGOs in the process of development cooperation.' Unpublished working paper.

Korten, D. (1980). 'Community organisation and rural development: A learning process approach.' *Public Administration Review*, Sep.-Oct.: 480–503.

Korten, D. (1990). *Getting to the 21st Century: Voluntary action and the global agenda*. Connecticut: Kumarian Press.

Kottler, A. (1997). 'Homosexuality and psychoanalytic training: Struggles in England and North America – what implications for South Africa?' *Psychology in Society (PINS)*, 22: 5–26.

Kottler, A., & Swartz, S. (1993). 'Conversation analysis: What is it, can psychologists use it?' *South African Journal of Psychology*, 23: 103–110.

Kozulin, A. (1986). 'The concept of activity in Soviet psychology.' *American Psychologist*, 4(3): 264–274.

Kozulin, A. (1991). 'Life as authoring: The humanistic tradition in Russian psychology.' *New Ideas in Psychology*, 9: 335–351.

Kriegler, S.M. (1988). 'Opleiding van opvoedkundige sielkundiges vir die bevordering van geestesgesondheid in Suid-Afrika.' ('The training of educational psychologists for the advancement of mental health in South Africa.'). *South African Journal of Psychology,* 18(3): 84–90.

Kros, C. (1999). 'Putting the history books straight: Reflections on rewriting Biko.' Unpublished paper presented at the History Workshop Conference: The TRC: Commissioning the Past. University of the Witwatersrand, 11–14 June.

Kuhn, T.S. (1962). *The structure of scientific revolutions.* Chicago: University of Chicago Press.

Kuper, L. (1974). *Race, class and power: Ideology and revolutionary change in plural societies.* London: Duckworth.

Lacan, J. (1979). *The four fundamental concepts of psycho-analysis.* Harmondsworth, UK: Penguin.

Laclau, E. (1990). *New reflections on the revolution of our time.* London: Verso.

Laing, R.D. (1959). *The divided self.* London: Tavistock Publications.

Laing, R.D., & Esterson, A. (1964). *Sanity, madness and the family.* London: Tavistock Publications.

Lambley, P. (1980). *The psychology of apartheid.* London: Secker & Warberg.

Laubscher, L., & McNeil, J.D. (1995). 'Climbing Kilimanjaro: The case for an African philosophy and psychology.' *Psychology Bulletin,* 5: 1–10.

Lave, J. (1988). *Cognition in practice: Mind, mathematics and culture in everyday life.* Cambridge, UK: Cambridge University Press.

Le Bon, G. (1896). *The crowd.* London: Ernest Benn.

Lebeau, V. (1998). 'Psycho-politics: Frantz Fanon's *Black skin, white masks.*' In J. Campbell & L. Harbord (eds), *Psycho-politics and cultural desires.* London: UCL Press.

Leclerc-Madlala, S. (2001). 'Virginity-testing diverts attention from the lack of male sexual responsibility.' In *Women's Health Project,* 40: 3–6.

Legassick, M. (1967). *The NUSAS: Ethnic cleavage and ethnic integration in the universities.* Los Angeles: African Studies Centre (UCLA).

Leont'ev, A.N. (1978). *Activity, consciousness and personality.* Englewood Cliffs, NJ: Prentice Hall.

Levett, A. (1988). 'Psychological trauma: discourses of childhood sexual abuse.' Unpublished PhD thesis, University of Cape Town.

Levett, A., & Kottler, A. (1997) 'Through a lens, darkly.' In E. Burman (ed), *Deconstructing feminist psychology.* 184–205. London: Sage.

Levett, A., Kottler, A., Burman, E., & Parker, I. (eds) (1997). *Culture, power and difference.* Cape Town: UCT Press.

Levine, M., & Perkins, D.V. (1997). *Principles of community psychology: Perspectives and applications.* 2nd edition. New York: Oxford University Press.

Lewis, J.A., Lewis, M.D., Daniels, J.A., & D'Andrea, M.J. (1998). *Community counselling: Empowerment strategies for diverse society.* 2nd edition. Boston: Brooks/Cole.

Leyendecker, B., Harwood, R.L., & Schoelmecker, A. (2002). 'Mothers' socialisation goals and evaluations of desirable and undesirable everyday situations in two diverse cultural groups.' *International Journal of Behavioural Development,* 26: 3, 248–258.

Lifton, R.J. (1993). *The protean self.* New York: Basic Books.

Lightfoot, N. (1997). 'This is not a pipe.' *South African Journal of Psychology,* 27: 89–98.

Linell, P. (1990). 'The power of dialogue.' In I. Markova & K. Foppa (eds), *The dynamics of dialogue.* 147–177. New York: Harvester Wheatsheaf.

Lobban, M. (1996). *White man's justice. South African political trials in the black consciousness era.* New York: Oxford University Press.

Lock, A. (1981). 'Universals in human conception.' In P. Heelas & A. Lock (eds), *Indigenous psychologies: The anthropology of the self.* 19–36. London: Academic Press.

Lombard, A., Meyers, L.M., & Schoeman, J.H. (1991). *Community work and community development: Perspective on social development.* Pretoria: HAUM – Tertiary.

Lott, B. (1990). 'Dual natures or learned behaviour: The challenges to feminist psychology.' In R.T. Hare-Mustin & J. Maracek (eds), *Making a difference: Psychology and the construction of gender.* 65–101. New Haven, CT: Yale University Press.

Louw J. (1986). 'White poverty and psychology in South Africa: The poor white investigation of the Carnegie Commission.' *Psychology in Society (PINS),* 6: 47–62.

Louw, D.A. (1987). *Inleiding tot die psigologie (Introduction to psychology).* Isando: Lexicon.

Louw, D.J. (1999). '*Ubuntu:* An African assessment of the religious Other.' Noesis: Philosophical Research Online. Available: http://noesis.evansville.edu/Author_Index/L/Louw,_Dirk_J./>. [2001, 01 March].

Louw, D.J. (2001). '*Ubuntu* and the challenges of multi-culturalism in post-apartheid South Africa.' Available: http://www.phys.uu.nl/~unitwin/ubuntu.html [2001, 02 October].

Louw, J., & Foster, D. (1992). 'Historical perspective: Psychology and group relations in South Africa.' In D. Foster & J. Louw-Potgieter (eds), *Social psychology in South Africa.* 57–92. Johannesburg: Lexicon.

Louw, J. (1986). 'This is thy work.' Unpublished PhD thesis, University of Amsterdam.

Louw, J. (1987). 'From separation to division: The origin of the two psychological associations in South Africa.' *Journal of the History of the Behavioural Sciences,* 23: 341–352.

Lubeck, S. (1986). *Sandbox society: Early education in black and white America – A comparative ethnography.* London and Philadelphia: Falmer.

Lupton, D., & Tulloch, J. (1998). 'The adolescent unfinished body: Reflexivity and HIV/Aids risk.' *Body & Society,* 4(2): 19–34.

Luyt, R., & Foster, D. (2001). 'Hegemonic masculine conceptualisation in gang culture.' *South African Journal of Psychology,* 31(3): 1–11.

Lykes, M.B. (1997). 'Activist participatory research among the Maya of Guatemala: Constructing meanings from situated knowledge.' *Journal of Social Issues,* 53(4), 7: 25–746.

Lykes, M.B. (2000). 'Creative arts and photography in participatory action research in Guatemala.' In P. Reason & H. Bradbury (eds), *Handbook of Action Research.* 363–371. Boston: Sage.

MacCrone, I.D. (1937). *Race attitudes in South Africa.* Cape Town: Oxford University Press.

MacCrone, I.D. (1949). 'Race attitudes.' In E. Hellman (ed), *Handbook on race relations in South Africa.* 669–705. Cape Town: Oxford University Press.

Macey, D. (2000a). *Frantz Fanon: A life.* London: Granta.

Macey, D. (2000b). *The Penguin dictionary of critical theory.* London: Penguin Books.

MacGregor, K. (1997, August 3). 'Plans for black universities to rise above their second-class legacy', *The Sunday Independent,* 6.

Macheke, C., & Campbell, C. (1998). 'Perceptions of health on a Johannesburg goldmine.' *South African Journal of Psychology.* 28(3): 146–153.

MacIntyre, A. (1984). 'The virtues, the unity of human life, and the concept of a tradition.' In M. Sandel (ed), *Liberalism and its critiques.* 125–148. New York: New York University Press.

Macleod, C. (1999). 'The governmentality of teenage pregnancy: Scientific literature and professional practice in South Africa.' Unpublished PhD thesis, University of Natal, Pietermaritzburg, South Africa.

Macleod, C. (2001). 'Teenage motherhood and the regulation of mothering in the scientific literature: the South African example.' *Feminism and Psychology*, 11: 493–511.

Macleod, C. (2002). 'Economic security and the social science literature on teenage pregnancy in South Africa.' *Gender & Society*, 16: 647–664.

Macleod, C. (In press a). 'Teenage pregnancy and the construction of adolescence: Scientific literature in South Africa.' *Childhood: A Global Journal of Child Research*.

Macleod, C. (In press b). 'The management of risk: Adolescent sexual and reproductive health in South Africa.' *International Journal of Critical Psychology*.

Macleod, C., & Durrheim, K. (2002). 'Racializing teenage pregnancy: "Culture" and "tradition" in the South African scientific literature.' *Ethnic and Racial Studies*, 25: 778–801.

Macleod, C., & Durrheim, K. (In press). 'Psycho-medical discourse in South African research on teenage pregnancy', *Transformation*.

Macleod, C., Masilela, T.C., & Malomane, E. (1998). 'Feedback of research results: Reflections from a community-based mental health programme.' *South African Journal of Psychology*, 28: 215–221.

MacPhail, C. (1998). 'Adolescents and HIV in developing countries: New research directions.' *Psychology in Society*, 24: 69–87.

Maffi, L. (1998). 'Indigenous languages and knowledge and intellectual property rights.' Available: http://www.cougar.ucdavis.edu./nas/terralin/wip098.html [2001, 26 January].

Magona, S. (1990). *To my children's children*. Cape Town: David Philip.

Maguire, P. (1987). *Doing participatory research: A feminist approach*. Massachusetts: Centre for International Education.

Magwaza, A. (2001). 'Submissions to the South African Truth and Reconciliation Commission: The reflections of a commissioner on the culpability of psychology.' In N. Duncan, A. van Niekerk, C. de la Rey, & M. Seedat (eds), *'Race', racism, knowledge production and psychology in South Africa*. 37–44. New York: Nova Science Publishers.

Maiers, W. (1991). 'Critical psychology: Historical background and task.' In C.W. Tolman & W. Maiers (eds), *Critical psychology: Contributions to an historical science of the subject*. 23–49. Cambridge: Cambridge University Press.

Mama, A. (1995). *Beyond the masks: Race, gender and subjectivity*. London: Routledge.

Mama, A. (2001). 'Is psychology critical to Africa in the new millennium?' *Critical psychology: The International Journal of Critical Psychology*, 1: 97–105.

Mama, A. (2002). *Challenging subjects: Gender, power and identity in African contexts*. Cape Town: AGI Publications

Manganyi, N.C. (1973). *Being-black-in-the-world*. Johannesburg: Ravan Press.

Manganyi, N.C. (1977). *Mashangu's reverie and other essays*. Johannesburg: Ravan Press.

Manganyi, N.C. (1981). *Looking through the keyhole*. Johannesburg: Ravan Press.

Manganyi, N.C. (1991). *Treachery and innocence*. Johannesburg: Ravan Press.

Mannoni, O. (1990). *Prospero and Caliban: The psychology of colonization*. (trans Pamela Powesland). Ann Arbor, MI: University of Michigan Press.

Marcuse, H. (1969). *Eros and civilization*. London: Sphere Books.

Markus, H.R., & Kitayama, S. (1991). 'Culture and self: Implications for cognition, emotion, and motivation.' *Psychological Review*, 98: 224–253.

Markus, H.R., & Kitayama, S. (1994). 'A collective fear of the unconscious: Implications for selves and theories of selves.' *Personality and Social Psychology Bulletin*, 20: 568–579.

Markus, H.R., & Nurius, P. (1986). 'Possible selves.' *American Psychologist,* 41: 954–969.

Markus, H.R., & Wurf, E. (1987). 'The dynamic self-concept: A social psychological perspective.' *Annual Review of Psychology,* 38: 299–337.

Martin-Baro, I. (1994). *Writings for a liberation psychology.* Cambridge, MA: Harvard University Press.

Marx, K. (1959/1977). *Economic and philosophic manuscripts of 1844.* Moscow: Progress.

Marx, K. (1976/1979). *Capital, Volume 1.* Harmondsworth, UK: Penguin Books.

Marx, K., & Engels, F. (1938). *The German ideology.* London: Lawrence & Wishart.

Masson, J. (1989). *Against therapy.* London: Harper Collins.

Masson, J. (1994). 'The tyranny of psychotherapy.' In W. Dryden & C. Feltham (eds), *Psychotherapy and its discontents.* 7–28. Buckingham & Philadelphia: Open University Press.

Mathur, H.M. (1986). *Administering development in the 'Third World': Constraints and choices.* New Dehli: Sage.

Max-Neef M., Elizalde, A., & Hopenhayn, M. (1989). 'Human scale development: An option for the future.' *Development Dialogue,* 1: 5–80.

Mazrui, A. (1986). *The Africans: A triple heritage.* London: BBC Publications.

Mbiti, J.S. (1969). *African religions and philosophy.* London: Heinemann.

Mbiti, J.S. (1991). *African religions and philosophy.* 2nd edition. Portsmouth, NH: Heinemann.

McClintock, A. (1995). *Imperial leather.* New York: Routledge.

McCulloch, J. (1983). *Black soul white artifact: Fanon's clinical psychology and social theory.* Cambridge, UK: Cambridge University Press.

McHoul A., & Grace, W. (1997). *The Foucault primer.* New York: New York University Press.

McLoyd, V. (1990). 'The impact of economic hardship on black families and children: Psychological distress, parenting and socioemotional development.' *Child Development,* 61: 311–246.

McNay, L. (1992). *Foucault and feminism: Power, gender and the self.* Polity Press: Cambridge.

McNay, L. (1994). *Foucault: A critical introduction.* New York: Continuum.

Mda, Z. (1993). *When people play people: Development communication through theatre.* Johannesburg, South Africa: Witwatersrand University Press.

Mehmet, O. (1995). *Westernizing the 'Third World': The eurocentricity of economic development theories.* London: Routledge.

Melucci, A. (1995). 'The process of collective identity.' In H. Johnston & B. Klandermans (eds), *Social movements and culture.* London: UCL Press.

Memmi, A. (1957/1967). *The colonizer and the colonized.* Boston: Beacon Press.

Memmi, A. (1982). *Le racisme.* Brassiére Saint-Armand, Fr: Gallimard.

Menkiti, I.A. (1984). 'Person and community in African traditional thought.' In R.A. Wright (ed), *African philosophy: An introduction.* 3rd edition. 171–181. Lanham, MD: University Press of America.

Merquior, J.G. (1985). *Foucault.* London: Fontana Press.

Miller, J. (1994). *The passion of Michel Foucault.* London: Flamingo.

Miller, J.-A. (1986). '*Extimité.*' In *Lacanian theory of discourse: Subject, structure and society,* edited by M. Bracher, M.W. Alcorn Jnr, R.J. Corthell & F. Massardier-Kenney. 74–87. New York: NYU Press.

Miller, N. (1973). 'Letter to her psychiatrist.' In P. Brown (ed), *Radical psychology*. 7–24. New York, Evanston, San Francisco, London: Harper Colophon Books.

Minsky, R. (1996). *Psychoanalysis and Gender*. London and New York: Routlegde.

Mitchell, J. (1974). *Psychoanalysis and feminism*. London: Allen Lane.

Mitchell, J. (1975). *Psychoanalysis and feminism*. Harmondsworth, UK: Penguin Books.

Mkhize, N.J. (1999). 'Collective child-rearing: Becoming a person in an impersonal world.' *Children First*, 3: 12–14.

Moane, G. (1999). *Gender and colonialism*. Basingstoke, UK: MacMillan Press.

Moghaddam, F.M. (1990). 'Modulative and generative orientations in psychology: Implications for psychology in the Three Worlds.' *Journal of Social Issues*, 46(3): 21–41.

Moghaddam, F.M. (1993). 'Traditional and modern psychologies in competing cultural systems: Lessons from Iran 1978–1981.' In U. Kim & J.W. Berry (eds), *Indigenous Psychologies: Research and experience in cultural context*. 118–131. Newbury Park, CA: Sage.

Mohanty, C. (1987). 'Feminist encounters: Locating the politics of experience.' *Copyright*, 1: 30–44.

Moll, I. (2002). 'African psychology: Myth or reality.' *South African Journal of Psychology*, 32: 1, 9–16.

Moore-Gilbert, B. (1997). *Postcolonial theory: Contexts, practices, politics*. London and New York: Verso.

Morawski, J. (1994). *Practicing feminism, reconstructing psychology*. Ann Arbor: University of Michigan Press.

Morawski, J.G. (1990) 'Toward the unimagined: Feminism and epistemology in psychology.' In R.T. Hare-Mustin & J. Maracek (eds), *Making a difference: Psychology and the construction of gender*. 150–183. NewHaven, CT: Yale University Press.

Morelli, G.A., Rogoff, B., Oppenheim, D., & Goldsmith, D. (1992). 'Cultural variation in infants' sleeping arrangements: Questions of independence.' *Developmental Psychology*, 28: 4, 604–613.

Morrell, R. (ed) (2001). *Changing men in South Africa*. Pietermaritzburg: University of Natal Press.

Morson, G.S., & Emerson, C. (1990). *Mikhail Bakhtin: Creation of a prosaics*. Palo Alto, CA: Stanford University Press.

Morss, J.R. (1996). *Growing critical: Alternatives to developmental psychology*. London: Routledge.

Moscovici, S. (1976). *Social influence and social change*. London: Academic Press.

Moyo, A. (1992). 'Material things in African society: Implications for Christian ethics.' In J.N.K. Mugambi & A. Nasimiyu-Wasike (eds), *Moral and ethical issues in African Christianity: Exploratory essays in moral theology*. 49–57. Nairobi: Initiative.

Myers, L.J. (1988). *Understanding an Afrocentric worldview: Introduction to an optimal psychology*. Dubuque, IA: Kendal/Hunt Publishing.

Ndlovu, T.M., Ndlovu, D.N. and Ncube, B.S. (1995). *Imikhuba lamasiko Ama Ndebele*, Gweru, Mambo Press.

Nell, V. (1990). 'Oppression, interpersonal violence and the psychology of colonialism.' In L.J. Nicholas & S. Cooper (eds), *Psychology and apartheid*. Johannesburg: Vision Publications.

Nelson, N., & Wright, S. (eds) (1995). *Power and participatory development: Theory and practice*. London: Intermediate Technology Publications.

Neuman, W. (2000). *Social research methods: Qualitative and quantitative approaches*. Boston: Allyn & Bacon.

Neves, D. (2002). 'Dialogue and participation in development.' Unpublished masters thesis, Rhodes University, Grahamstown, South Africa.

Ngubane, H. (1977). *Body and mind in Zulu medicine: An ethnographic study of health and disease in Nyuswa-Zulu thought and practice.* London: Academic Press.

Ngudle, A. (1998, March). 'Fine feathers: What do women think of the way men dress?' *True Love,* 229: 74–75.

Nicholas, L. (ed) (1993). *Psychology and oppression: Critiques and proposals.* Johannesburg: Skotaville.

Nicholas, L., & Cooper, S. (eds) (1990). *Psychology and apartheid.* Johannesburg: Vision Publications.

Nicholas, L.J. (1990). 'The response of South African professional psychology associations to apartheid.' In L.J. Nicholas & S. Cooper (eds), *Psychology and apartheid.* Johannesburg: Vision Publications.

Nicholas, L.J. (2001). 'The history of racism in professional South African psychology.' In N. Duncan, A. van Niekerk, C. de la Rey, & M. Seedat (eds), *'Race', racism, knowledge production and psychology in South Africa.* 17–26. New York: Nova Science.

Nicholas, L.J., & Cooper, S. (eds) (1990). *Psychology and apartheid.* Cape Town: Vision Publications.

Nightingale, D. & Nielands, T. (1997). 'Understanding and practising critical psychology.' In D. Fox & I. Prilleltensky (eds), *Critical psychology: An introduction.* 68–84. London: Sage.

Nobles, W. (1980). 'African philosophy: Foundations for black psychology.' In R.L Jones (ed) *Black psychology.* 2nd edition. 23–36. New York: Harper and Row.

Norman, P., Abraham, C., & Conner, M. (2000). *Understanding and changing health behaviour: From health beliefs to self-regulation.* Sydney: Harwood.

Nsamenang, A.B. (1992). *Human development in cultural context: A Third World perspective.* Newbury Park, NY: Sage.

Nsamenang, A.B. (2000). 'African view on social development: Implications for cross-cultural developmental research.' Paper presented at the Fifth Biennial Africa Regional Workshop of the ISSBD, 25–30 September, Kampala.

Nsamenang, B. (2000). 'Critical psychology: A sub-Saharan African voice from Cameroon.' In T. Sloan (ed), *Critical psychology: Voices for Change.* 91–102. Basingstoke, UK: MacMillan Press.

Nsamenang, B. (1993). 'Psychology in sub-Saharan Africa.' *Psychology and Developing Societies,* 5(2): 171–184.

Nugent, C.D. (1994). 'Blaming the victims: Silencing women sexually exploited by psychotherapists.' *Journal of Mind and Behaviour,* 15(1–2): 113–138.

O'Meara, D. (1983). *Volkskapitalisme. Class, capital and ideology in the development of Afrikaner nationalism: 1934–1948.* Braamfontein: Ravan Press.

O'Sullivan, G. (1993). 'Behavioural therapy.' In W. Dryden (ed), *Individual therapy: A handbook.* 252–272. Milton Keynes, Philadelphia: Open University Press.

Oakes, D. (ed) (1989). *Illustrated history of South Africa. The real story.* Cape Town: Reader's Digest Association.

Oakley, P. & Marsden, D. (1985). *Approaches to participation in rural development.* Geneva: ILO.

Ogbonnaya, A.O. (1994). 'Person as community: An African understanding of the person as an intrapsychic community.' *Journal of Black Psychology,* 20: 75–87.

Ogbu, J. (1981). 'Origins of human competence: A cultural ecological perspective. *Child development* 52: 413–429.

Ogundipe-Leslie, M.M. (1994). *Re-creating ourselves: African women and critical transformations.* Trenton, NJ: Africa World Press.

Onyewuenyi, I.C. (1993). *The African origins of Greek philosophy: An exercise in Africocentrism.* Nsukka, Nigeria: University of Nigeria Press.

Oosthuisen, G.C. (ed) (1989). *Afro-Christian religion and healing in southern Africa.* Lewiston, NY: Mellen.

Owusu-Bempah, J.M. & Howitt, D. (1995). 'How Eurocentric psychology damages Africa.' *The Psychologist,* October: 462–465.

Painter, D., & Theron, W.H. (2001). 'Heading South! Importing discourse analysis.' *South African Journal of Psychology,* 31(1): 1–9.

Panitch, L., & Ginden, S. (1999). 'Transcending pessimism.' In L. Panitch & C. Leys (eds), *Necessary and unnecessary utopias.* 1–29. Rendlesham, UK: Merlin Press.

Paris, P.J. (1995). *The spirituality of African peoples: The search for a common moral discourse.* Minneapolis, MN: Fortress.

Parker, I. (1989). *The crisis in modern social psychology – and how to end it.* London: Routledge.

Parker, I. (1990). 'Discourse: Definitions and contradictions.' *Philosophical Psychology,* 3: 189–204.

Parker, I. (1992). *Discourse dynamics: Critical analysis for social and individual psychology.* London: Routledge.

Parker, I. (1994). 'Discourse analysis.' In P. Banister, E. Burman, I. Parker, M. Taylor & C. Tindall (eds), *Qualitative methods in psychology.* Milton Keynes, Philadelphia: Open University Press.

Parker, I. (1997). *Psychoanalytic culture: Psychoanalytic discourse in Western society.* London: Sage.

Parker, I. (ed) (1998). *Social constructionism, discourse and realism.* London: Sage.

Parker, I. (1999). 'Critical psychology: Critical links.' *Annual Review of Critical Psychology,* 1: 3–18.

Parker, I. (ed) (1999). *Critical textwork: An introduction to varieties of discourse and analysis.* Buckingham: Open University Press.

Parker, I. (2002). *Critical discursive psychology.* Basingstoke, UK: Palgrave Macmillan.

Parker, I., & Burman, E. (1993). 'Against discursive imperialism, empiricism and constructionism: Thirty-two problems with discourse analysis.' In E. Burman & I. Parker (eds), *Discourse analytic research: Repertoires and readings of texts in action.* 155–172. Routledge: London.

Parker, I., & Spears, R. (eds) (1996). *Psychology and society: Radical theory and practice.* London: Pluto Press.

Parlett, M., & Page, F. (1993). 'Gestalt Therapy.' In W. Dryden (ed), *Individual therapy: A handbook.* 175–198. Milton Keynes, Philadelphia: Open University Press.

Patton, C. (1996). *Fatal advice: How safe sex education went wrong.* London: Duke University Press.

Pelling, J.N. (1977). *Ndebele proverbs and other sayings.* Gweru: Mambo Press in association with The Literature Bureau.

Phillips, L., & Jorgensen, M.W. (2002). *Discourse analysis as theory and method.* London: Sage.

Phoenix, A., Woolett, A., & Lloyd, E. (eds) (1991). *Motherhood: Meanings, practices and ideologies.* London: Sage.

Piaget, J. (1924/1969). *Judgment and reasoning in the child*. London: Routledge & Kegan Paul.

Pilgrim, D. (1991). 'Psychotherapy and social blinkers.' *The Psychologist*, 2: 52–55.

Pilgrim, D. (1994). 'Psychotherapy and political evasions.' In W. Dryden & C. Feltham (eds), *Psychotherapy and its discontents*. 225–242. Buckingham and Philadelphia: Open University Press.

Potgieter, C., & De la Rey, C. (1997). 'Gender and race: Whereto psychology in South Africa?' *Feminism and Psychology*, 7(1): 138–142.

Potter, J. (1996). *Representing reality: Discourse, rhetoric and social construction*. London: Sage.

Poulantzas (1978). *State, power, socialism*. London: NLB.

Powell, J. (1997). *Derrida for beginners*. New York: Writers and Readers Publishers.

Prestby, J., Wandersman, A., Florin, P., Rich, R., & Chavis, D. (1990). 'Benefits, costs, incentive management and participation in voluntary organisations: A means to understanding and promoting empowerment.' *American Journal of Community Psychology*, 18(1): 117–149.

Prilleltensky, I. (1997). 'Values, assumptions, and practice: Assessing the moral implications of psychological discourse and action.' *American Psychologist*, 52: 517–535.

Prilleltensky, I. (2001). 'Value-based praxis in community psychology: Moving toward social justice and social action.' *American Journal of Community Psychology*, 29: 747–778.

Prilleltensky, I., & Austin, S. (2001). 'Critical psychology for critical action.' *The International Journal of Critical Psychology*, 2: 39–60.

Prilleltensky, I., & Nelson, G. (1997). 'Community psychology: Reclaiming social justice.' In D. Fox & I. Prilleltensky (eds), *Critical psychology: An introduction*. 166–184. London: Sage.

Psygram (1960). 'Verbatim report of the 12th Annual General Meeting.' *Psygram*, 2(27), 202–221.

Putman, R. (2000). *Bowling alone: The collapse and revival of American community*, New York: Simon Schuster.

Quinn, N., & Holland, D. (1987). 'Culture and cognition.' In D. Holland & N. Quinn (eds), *Cultural models in language and thought*. 3–40. Cambridge, UK: Cambridge University Press.

Rajakutty, S. (1991). 'People's participation in monitoring and evaluation of rural development programmes: Concepts and approaches.' *Journal of Rural Development*, 10(1): 35–53.

Ralekheto, M. (1991). 'The black university in South Africa: Ideological captive or transformative agent?' In J. Jansen (ed), *Racism and colonialism*. The Hague: Leiden University Press.

Ramazanoglu, C. (1996). 'Unraveling postmodern paralysis: A response to Joan Hoff.' *Women's History Review*, 5: 19–23.

Ramose, M.B. (1999). *African philosophy through ubuntu*. Harare: Mond Books.

Ratele, K. (2001). 'The sexualisation of apartheid.' Unpublished doctoral dissertation. University of the Western Cape, Bellville.

Rawls, J. (1972). *A theory of justice*. Oxford: Clarendon Press.

Reich, W. (1970). *The mass of psychology of fascism*. New York: Penguin.

Rhoads, R.A. (1997). *Community service and higher learning: Explorations of the caring self*. New York: State University of New York Press.

Richards, G. (1997). *Race, racism, and psychology: Toward a reflective perspective*. London: Routledge.

Richardson, D. (1996). 'Heterosexuality and social theory.' In D. Richardson (ed), *Theorising heterosexuality*. 1–20. Milton Keynes, UK: Open University Press.

Richardson, F.C., & Fowers, B.J. (1998). 'Interpretive social science: An overview.' *American Behavioral Scientist*, 41: 465–495.

Richardson, F.C., Rogers, A., & McCarroll, J. (1998). 'Toward a dialogical self.' *American Behavioral Scientist*, 41: 496–515.

Richter, L.M. (1994). 'Economic stress and its influence on the family and caretaking patterns.' In A. Dawes & D. Donald (eds), *Childhood and adversity: Psychological perspectives from South African research*. Cape Town: David Philip.

Richter, L.M. (1999). 'Parenting in poverty: Young children and their families in South Africa.' In L. Eldering & P. Leseman (eds), *Effective early education: Cross-cultural perspectives*. New York: Falmer Press.

Robbertse, P.M. (1967). 'Rasseverskille en die sielkundige.' *PIRSA Monographs*, 72: 1–11.

Roberts, V.Z. (1994). 'The self-assigned impossible task.' In A. Obholzer & V.Z. Roberts (eds), *The unconscious at work: Individual and organizational stress in the human services*. 110–120. London and New York: Routledge.

Rodney, W. (1988). *How Europe underdeveloped Africa*. Washington: Howard University.

Rogers, C. (1961). *On becoming a person*. Boston: Houghton Mifflin.

Rogoff, B. (1984). 'Introduction: Thinking and learning in social contexts.' In B. Rogoff & J. Lave (eds), *Everyday cognition*. Cambridge, MA: Harvard University Press.

Rogoff, B. (1990). *Apprenticeship in thinking: Cognitive development in social context*. New York: Oxford University Press.

Rogoff, B. (1995). 'Observing cultural activity on three planes: Participatory appropriation, guided participation, and apprenticeship.' In J.V. Wertsch, P. Del Rion, & A. Alvarez (eds), *Sociocultural studies of mind*. 139–164. Cambridge, UK: Cambridge University Press.

Rogoff, B., & Morelli, G. (1998). 'Perspectives on children's development from cultural psychology.' In D. Messers & J. Dockrell (eds), *Developmental Psychology*. London: Arnold.

Rose, N. (1985). *The psy complex: Psychology, politics and society in England 1869–1939*. London: Routledge & Kegan Paul.

Rose, N. (1989). 'Individualizing psychology.' In J. Shotter & K. Gergen (eds), *Texts of identity*. 119–131. London: Sage.

Rose, N. (1990). 'Psychology as a "social" science.' In I. Parker & J. Shotter (eds), *Deconstructing social psychology*. 103–116. London and New York: Routledge.

Rose, N. (1990, 1991). *Governing the soul: The shaping of the private self*. London and New York: Routledge.

Rose, N. (1995). *Inventing our selves*. London and New York: Routledge.

Rose, N. (1996). *Inventing our selves*. Cambridge: Cambridge University Press.

Rose, N. (1996). 'Identity, genealogy, history.' In S. Hall & P. du Gay (eds), *Questions of cultural identity*. 128–150. London: Sage.

Rose, N. (1998). *Inventing our selves: Psychology, power and personhood*. Cambridge: Cambridge University Press.

Rubin, G. (1984). 'Thinking sex: Notes for a radical theory of the politics of sexuality.' In C.S. Vance (ed), *Pleasure and danger: Exploring female sexuality*. 267–319. Boston: Routledge & Kegan Paul.

Ruble, D. (1988). 'Sex-role development.' In M. Bornstein & M.E. Lamb (eds), *Developmental psychology: An advanced textbook*. 2nd edition. Hillsdale, NJ: Erlbaum.

Ruch, E.A., & Anyanwu, K.C. (1981). *African philosophy: An introduction to the main philosophical trends in contemporary Africa*. Rome: Catholic Book Agency.

Rustin, M. (1991). *The good society and the inner world: Psychoanalysis, politics and culture*. London and New York: Verso.

Rutter, D., & Quine, L. (2002). *Changing health behaviour*. Buckingham, Philadelphia: Open University Press.

S.A. Institute of Clinical Psychology. (1986). 'PASA policy statement.' *Psychiatry and Clinical Psychology*, 1(1): 34.

Sabatier, R. (1988). *Blaming others: Prejudice, race and world-wide Aids*. London: Panos Publications.

Sachs, W. (1996). *Black Hamlet*. Johannesburg: Witwatersrand University Press.

Saegert, S., Thompson, J., & Warren, M. (2001). *Social capital and poor communities*. New York: Russell Sage Foundation.

Said, E. (1978). *Orientalism*. New York & London: Routledge & Kegan Paul.

Said, E. (1983). *The World, the Text and the Critic*. Cambridge, MA: Harvard University Press.

Said, E. (1993). *Culture and imperialism*. London: Chatto & Windus.

Salmon, P. (1991). 'Psychotherapy and the wider world.' *The Psychologist*, 2: 50–51.

Sampson, E.E. (1988). 'The debate on individualism: Indigenous psychologies of the individual and their role in personal and societal functioning.' *American Psychologist*, 43: 15–22.

Sampson, E.E. (1993, 1993b). *Celebrating the Other: A dialogical account of human nature*. New York: Harvester Wheatsheaf.

Sampson, E.E. (1993a). 'Identity politics.' *American Psychologist*, 48: 1219–1230.

Santiago-Rivera, A.L., Morse, G.S., & Hunt, A. (1998). 'Building a community-based research partnership: Lessons from the Mohawk Nation of Akwesasne.' *Journal of Community Psychology*, 26(2): 163–174.

Santrock, J.W. (2001). *Adolescence*. 8th edition. Boston: McGraw-Hill.

Savage, M. (1981). 'Constraints in research sociology and psychology in South Africa.' In J. Rex (ed), *Apartheid and social research*. Lausanne: UNESCO.

Schalet, A. (2000). 'Raging hormones, regulated love: Adolescent sexuality and the constitution of the modern individual in the United States and The Netherlands.' *Body & Society*, 6(1): 75–105.

Scheff, T. (1966). *Being mentally ill: A sociological approach*. London: Weidenfeld & Nicholson.

Sears, D.O. (1988). 'Symbolic racism.' In P.A. Katz & D.A. Taylor (eds), *Eliminating racism: Profiles in controversy*. New York: Plenum Press.

Seedat, M. (1990). 'Programmes, trends and silences in South African psychology: 1983–1988.' In L.J. Nicholas & S. Cooper (eds), *Psychology and apartheid*. Johannesburg: Vision Publications.

Seedat, M. (1992, 1993). 'Topics, trends and silences in South African psychology 1948–1988.' Unpublished PhD thesis, University of the Western Cape, Bellville, South Africa.

Seedat, M. (1997). 'The quest for a liberatory psychology.' *South African Journal of Psychology*, 27(4): 261–270.

Seedat, M. (1998). 'A characterisation of South African psychology (1948–1988): The impact of exclusionary ideology.' *South African Journal of Psychology*, 28(2): 74–84.

Seedat, M. (2001). 'Invisibility in South African psychology (1948–1988). A trend analysis.' In N. Duncan, A. van Niekerk, C. de la Rey & M. Seedat (eds), *'Race', racism, knowledge production and psychology in South Africa*. 83–102. New York: Nova Science.

Seedat, M. (2001). *Community psychology: Theory, method and practice. South African and other perspectives*. Oxford: Oxford University Press.

Seedat, M., Cloete, N., & Shochet, I. (1988). 'Community psychology: Panic or panacea.' *Psychology in Society (PINS)*, 11: 39–54.

Seedat, M., Duncan, N., & Lazarus, S. (2001). 'Community psychology: Theory, method and practice.' In M. Seedat, S. Lazarus & N. Duncan (eds), *Community psychology: Theory, method and practice. South African and other perspectives*. 3–14. Cape Town: Oxford University Press.

Senghor, L. (1965). *On African Socialism*. London: Preager.

Senghor, L. (1966). 'Négritude.' *Optima*, 16: 8.

Serequeberhan, T. (1991). *African philosophy: The essential readings*. New York: Paragon House.

Serpell, R. (1996). 'Cultural models of childhood in indigenous socialization and formal schooling in Zambia.' In C.P. Hwang & M.E. Lamb (eds), *Images of Childhood*. Hillsdale, NJ: Erlbaum.

Sève, L. (1978). *Man in Marxist theory and the psychology of personality*. Brighton: Harvester Press. (1974 French).

Sey, J., & Moss, D. (eds) (1998). 'South Africa Special Issue.' *American Imago*, 55: 1.

Shaeffer, S. (1994). 'Participatory Development: What it is and what it can and cannot do.' Unpublished manuscript, University of Cape Town.

Shefer, T. (1998). 'Gender (dis)order.' In M. Terre Blanche (ed), *Touch me I'm sick: Proceedings of the 3rd Annual South African Qualitative Methods Conference*, 22–35.

Shefer, T. (1999). 'Discourses of heterosexual negotiation and relation.' Unpublished PhD thesis, University of the Western Cape, Bellville.

Shefer, T. (2001). 'Ordering gender: Revisiting the role of psychology.' *Psychology in Society (PINS)*. n.d.

Shefer, T., Van Niekerk, A., Duncan, N., & De la Rey, C. (1997). 'Authorship and authority in psychology: A publishing initiative.' *Psychology in Society (PINS)*, 22: 37–46.

Shotter, J. (1989). 'Vygotsky's psychology: Joint activity in a developmental zone.' *New Ideas in Psychology*, 7: 185–204.

Shotter, J. (1993a). 'Bakhtin and Vygotsky: Internalisation as a boundary phenomenon.' *New Ideas in Psychology*, 11(3): 379–390.

Shotter, J. (1993b). 'Vygotsky: The social negotiation of semiotic mediation.' *New Ideas in Psychology*, 11(1): 61–75.

Shutte, A. (1993). *Philosophy for Africa*. Cape Town: UCT Press.

Shutte, A. (2001). *Ubuntu: An ethic for a new South Africa*. Pietermaritzburg: Cluster Publications.

Shweder, R.A. (1982). 'Beyond self-constructed knowledge: The study of culture and morality.' *Merrill-Palmer Quarterly*, 28: 41–69.

Shweder, R.A. (1991). *Thinking through cultures: Expeditions in cultural psychology*. Cambridge: Harvard University Press.

Sidanius, J., & Pratto, F. (1999). *Social dominance*. Cambridge, UK: Cambridge University Press.

Simanski, J. (1998). 'The birds and the bees: An analysis of advice given to parents through the popular press.' *Adolescence*, 33: 33–45.

Simbayi, L.C. (1997). 'Challenges and difficulties of psychology departments at historically black universities concerning research and scholarship.' Paper presented at the PsySSA Western Cape regional Conference, *Psychology in a changing South Africa*, University of the Western Cape, Bellville, 19 April.

Simon, R. (1982). *Gramsci's political thought*. London: Lawrence & Wishart.

Simpson, E.L. (1974). 'Moral development research: A case study of scientific cultural bias.' *Human Development*, 17: 81–106.

Singer, L. (1993). *Erotic welfare: Sexual theory and politics in the age of epidemic*. Routledge: New York.

Sinha, D. (1973). 'Psychology and the problems of developing countries: A general overview.' *International Review of Applied Psychology*, 22: 5–7.

Sinha, D. (1983). 'Applied social psychology and the problems of national development.' In Blackler, F. (ed), *Social psychology and developing countries*. London: Wiley.

Sinha, D. (1984). 'Psychology in the context of "Third World" development.' *International Journal of Psychology*, 19: 17–29.

Sinha, D. (1986). 'Motivational syndrome of farmers, education and rural development.' *Indian Journal of Current Psychological Research*, 1(2): 65–72.

Sinha, D. (1986). *Psychology in a Third World country: The Indian perspective*. New Delhi: Sage.

Sinha, D. (1990). 'The impact of psychology on Third World development.' *International Journal of Psychology*, 19: 169–178.

Sinha, D. (1993). 'Indigenisation of psychology in India and its relevance.' In U. Kim & J.W. Berry (eds), *Indigenous psychologies: Research and experience in cultural context*. 30–43. Newbury Park, CA: Sage.

Skinner, D., Valsiner, J., & Holland, D. (2001, September). 'Discerning the dialogical self: A theoretical and methodological examination of a Nepali adolescent's narratives' [34 paragraphs] Forum Qualitative Sozialforschung/Forum: Qualitative Social Research [On-line journal], 2(3). Available at: http://www.qualitative- research.net/fqs/fqs-eng. htm [2001, 04 December].

Sloan, T.S. (1996). *Damaged life*. London: Routledge.

Sloan, T.S. (1990). 'Psychology for the "Third World"?' *Journal of Social Issues*, 46(3): 1–20.

Smail, D. (1994). 'Community psychology and politics.' *Journal of community & applied psychology*, 42: 3–10.

Smith, B. (1998). *Psychology: Science & understanding*. Boston: McGraw-Hill.

Smith, D.L. (1991). *Hidden conversations: An introduction to communitive psychoanalysis*. London: Routledge.

Smith, D.L. (1993). 'Psychodynamic therapy: The Freudian approach.' In W. Dryden (ed), *Individual therapy: A handbook*. 18–38. Milton Keynes, Philadelphia: Open University Press.

Sodi, T. (1999). 'The meeting of a psychoanalyst and an indigenous healer.' *Psychology in Society (PINS)*, 25: 81–83.

Sogolo, G. (1993). *Foundations of African philosophy*. Ibadan: Ibadan University Press.

Southall, R., & Cobbing, J. (2001). 'From racial liberalism to corporate authoritarianism: The Shell affair and the assault on academic freedom in South Africa.' *Social Dynamics*, 27(2): 1–42.

Sow, I. (1980). *Anthropological structures of madness in black Africa*. (trans Joyce Diamanti). New York: International University Press.

Squire, C. (1989). *Significant differences.* London: Routledge.

Stadler, J. (1995). 'Development, research and participation: towards a critique of participatory rural appraisal methods.' *Development Southern Africa,* 12: 805–814.

Stenner, P. (1993). 'Discoursing jealousy.' In E. Burman & I. Parker (eds), *Discourse analytic research: Repertoires and readings of texts in action.* Routledge: London.

Stevens, G. (2001). 'Racism and cultural imperialism in the training of black psychologists in South Africa: Identity, ambiguity and dilemmas of praxis.' In N. Duncan, A. van Niekerk, C. de la Rey & M. Seedat (eds), *'Race', racism, knowledge production and psychology in South Africa.* 45–60. New York: Nova Science.

Stevens, G. (2002). 'Academic representations of "race" and racism in psychology: Knowledge production, historical context and dialectics in transitional South Africa.' *International Journal of Intercultural Relations,* 27(2): 189–207.

Steyn, M. (2001). *Whiteness just isn't what it used to be.* Albany: State University of New York Press.

Stockdale, J. (1995). 'The self and media messages: Match or mismatch?' In I. Markova & R. Farr, (eds), *Representations of health, illness and handicap.* 31–48. London: Harwood.

Straker, G. (1988). 'Child abuse, counselling and apartheid: The work of the Sanctuary Counselling Team.' *Free Associations,* 14: 7–38.

Straker, G. (1992). *Faces in the revolution.* Cape Town: David Philip.

Strümpfer, D.J.W. (1993). 'A personal history of psychology in South Africa.' Opening address PASA Congress, Durban, 22 September.

Sue, D.W. (1978). 'Eliminating cultural oppression in counseling: Toward a general theory.' *Journal of Counseling Psychology,* 25: 419–428.

Sue, D.W., & Sue, D. (1999). *Counseling the culturally different: Theory and practice.* New York: Wiley.

Suffla, S., Stevens, G., & Seedat, M. (2001). 'Mirror reflections: The evolution of organised professional psychology in South Africa.' In N. Duncan, A. van Niekerk, C. de la Rey & M. Seedat (eds), *'Race', racism, knowledge production and psychology in South Africa.* 27–36. New York: Nova Science.

Swannell, J. (ed) (1992). *The Oxford modern English dictionary.* Oxford, UK: Clarendon Press.

Swartz, L. (1997). *Culture and mental health.* Cape Town: Oxford University Press.

Swartz, L., & Gibson, K. (2001). 'The "old" versus the "new" in South African community psychology: The quest for appropriate change.' In M. Seedat, N. Duncan & S. Lazarus (eds), *Community psychology: Theory, method and practice – South African and other perspectives.* 37–50. Cape Town: Oxford University Press.

Swartz, L., Gelman, T., & Gibson, K. (2002). 'Introduction.' In L. Swartz, K. Gibson & T. Gelman (eds*), Reflective practice: Psychodynamic ideas in the community.* 1–8. Cape Town: Human Sciences Research Council.

Swartz, S. (1999). 'Lost lives: Gender, history and mental illness in the Cape, 1891–1910. *Feminism & Psychology,* 9(2): 152–158.

Swift, C., & Levin, G. (1987). 'Empowerment: An emerging mental health technology.' *Journal of Primary Prevention,* 8(1&2): 71–94.

Szasz, T. (1973). 'The myth of mental illness.' In P. Brown (ed), *Radical psychology.* 7–24. New York, Evanston, San Francisco, London: Harper Colophon Books.

Szasz, T.S. (1973). *The second sin.* New York: Columbia University Press.

Szasz, T.S. (1979). *The myth of psychotherapy.* London: Oxford University Press.

Szasz, T.S. (1984). *The myth of mental illness.* London: Paladin Books.

Tajfel, H. (1959). 'Quantitative judgement in social perception.' *British Journal of Psychology*, 10: 16–29.

Tajfel, H. (ed) (1981). *Human groups and social categories*. Cambridge: Cambridge University Press.

Tappan, M.B. (1998). 'Moral education in the zone of proximal development.' *Journal of Moral Education*, 27: 141–160.

Tawil, O., Verster, A., & O'Reilly, K. (1995). 'Enabling approaches for HIV/Aids promotion: Can we modify the environment and minimize the risk?' *Aids*, 9: 1299–1306.

Teffo, L.J., & Roux, A.P.J. (1998). 'Metaphysical thinking in Africa.' In P.H. Coetzee & A.P.J. Roux (eds), *Philosophy from Africa: A text with readings*. 134–148. Halfway House, South Africa: International Thomson Publishing.

Teffo, L.J. (1996). 'The other in African experience.' *South African Journal of Philosophy*, 15(3): 101–104.

Tempels, P. (1959). *Bantu philosophy*. (trans C. King). Paris: Présence Africaine.

Teo, T. (1999). 'Methodologies of critical psychology: Illustrations from the field of racism.' *Annual Review of Critical Psychology*, 1: 119–134.

Terre Blanche, M. (1998). 'This is war. Reply to Fred van Staden.' *South Africa Journal of Psychology*, 28: 44–46.

Terre Blanche, M. (1999). 'Crash.' *South African Journal of Psychology*, 27: 59–63.

Terre Blanche, M., & Durrheim, K. (1999). *Research in practice: Applied methods for the social sciences*. Cape Town: UCT Press.

Terre Blanche, M., & Seedat, M. (1994). 'Martian landscapes: The social construction of race and gender at the National Institute for Personnel Research.' Paper presented at the Psychology and Societal Transformation Conference, 24–28 January, University of Western Cape, Bellville, South Africa.

Terre Blanche, M., & Durrheim, K. (1999). 'Social constructionist methods.' In M. Terre Blanche & K. Durrheim (eds), *Research in practice: Applied methods for the social sciences*. Cape Town: UCT Press.

Terreblanche, S. (2002). *A history of inequality in South Africa*. Scottsville: University of Natal Press.

The Monitor, 13 October 1999. 'A voice against rape rattles South Africa.'

Therborn, G. (1980). *The ideology of power and the power of ideology*. London: Verso.

The Sunday Times, 10 October 1999. 'You be the Judge.'

The Sunday Times, 31 October 1999. 'Primary school pupils are to be taught about rape and sexual violence.'

Thiong'o, N.W. (1986). *Decolonising the mind: The politics of language in African literature*. London: J. Currey.

Thomen, C. (2002). 'Policy and practice: An Activity system's analysis of a further diploma in educational technology.' Unpublished PhD thesis, Rhodes University, East London, South Africa.

Thompson, J.B. (1984). *Studies in the theory of ideology*. Cambridge, UK: Polity Press.

Thompson, S. (1990). 'Putting a big thing into a little hole: Teenage girls' accounts of sexual initiation.' *Journal of Sex Research*, 27(3): 341–361.

Thorogood, N. (1992). 'Sex education as social control.' *Critical Public Health*, 3(2), 43–50.

Tiefer, L. (1992). 'Social constructionism and the study of human sexuality.' In E. Stein (ed), *Forms of desire: Sexual orientation and the social constructionist controversy*. 295–324. New York: Routledge.

Tolman, C.W. (1994). *Psychology, society, and subjectivity: An introduction to German critical psychology.* London and New York: Routledge.

Tong, R. (1998). *Feminist thought: A more comprehensive introduction.* 2nd edition. Oxford: Westview Press.

Touraine, A. (2000). *Can we live together?: Equality and difference.* Cambridge, UK: Polity Press. (1997 French).

Triandis, H.C. (1972). 'Some psychological dimensions of modernisation.' *Proceedings of the 17th International Congress of Applied Psychology.* Bruxelles: Editest.

Triandis, H.C. (1984). 'Toward a psychological theory of economic growth.' *International Journal of Psychology,* 19: 79–95.

Tulkin (1972). 'An analysis of the concept of cultural deprivation.' *Developmental Psychology,* 6: 326–339.

Tyson, G.A. (1987). *Introduction to psychology: A South African perspective.* Johannesburg: Westro Educational Books.

UN Aids. (1999). *Peer education and HIV/Aids: Concepts, uses and challenges.* Geneva: UN Aids.

UN Aids. (2000). *Report on the global HIV/Aids epidemic.* Geneva: UN Aids.

UNFPA (United Nations Population Fund) (2001). Population, environment and poverty linkages: Operational challenges. *Population and Development Strategies Series Number 1.* New York: UNFPA.

Unger, R.K. (1979). *Female and male.* New York: Harper & Row

Unger, R.K. (1990). 'Imperfect reflections of reality: Psychology constructs gender.' In R.T. Hare-Mustin & J. Maracek (eds), *Making a difference: Psychology and the construction of gender.* 102–149. New Haven, CT: Yale University Press.

Ussher, J. (1991). *Women's madness, misogyny or mental illness?* London: Harvester Wheatsheaf.

Van der Merwe, W.L. (1996). 'Philosophy and the multicultural context of (post)apartheid South Africa.' *Ethical perspectives,* 3: 1–15.

Van der Vliet, V. (1996). *The politics of Aids.* London: Bowerdean.

Van Deuzen-Smith. (1993). 'Existential therapy.' In W. Dryden (ed), *Individual therapy: A handbook.* 149–174. Milton Keynes, Philadelphia: Open University Press.

Van Dijk, T.A. (1987). *Discourse and the reproduction of racism.* Amsterdam: CRES.

Van Dijk, T.A. (1991). *Elite discourse and the reproduction of racism.* Amsterdam: University of Amsterdam.

Van Niekerk, A. (1991). 'Towards a South African feminism'. Unpublished Conference Paper, University of Cape Town.

Van Staden, F. (1998). 'The "new discursive paradigm": as yet an elitist European import? Comment on special edition of the *SAJP.*' *South African Journal of Psychology,* 28: 44

Van Vlaenderen, H., & Gilbert, A. (1993). 'Participatory research for capacity building in rural development: A case study.' In P. Stygen & M. Cameron (eds), *Development in transition: Opportunities and challenges.* Pretoria: Development Society of Southern Africa.

Van Vlaenderen, H., & Nkwinti, G. (1993). 'Participatory research as a tool for community development.' *Development Southern Africa,* 10: 211–228.

Van Vlaenderen, H. (1993). 'Psychological research in the process of rapid social change: A contribution to community development.' *Psychology in Developing Societies,* 5(1): 96–110.

Van Vlaenderen, H. (1999). 'Community water management.' *PLA notes,* June: 3–6.

Van Vlaenderen, H. (2001). 'Evaluating development programmes: Building joint activity.' *Evaluation and Programme Planning*, 24: 343–352.

Van Vlaenderen, H. (2001). 'Psychology in developing countries: People centred development and local knowledge.' *Psychology in Society (PINS)*, 27: 88–108.

Van Zyl, S. (1998). 'The Other and other Others: Post-colonialism, psychoanalysis and the South African question.' *American Imago*, 55(10), Spring 1998: 77–100.

Vance, C.S. (1984). 'Pleasure and danger: Toward a politics of sexuality.' In C.S. Vance (ed), *Pleasure and danger: exploring female sexuality*. 1–27. Boston: Routledge & Kegan Paul.

Vanderslice, V.J. (1984). 'Empowerment: A definition in process.' *Human Ecology Forum*, 14(1): 2–3.

Vasil'eva, I.I. (1985). 'The importance of M.M. Bakhtin's idea of dialogue and dialogic relations for the psychology of human communication.' In B.F. Lomov, A.V. Belyaeva & V.N. Nosulenko (eds), *Psychological Studies of communication*. 81–93. (trans E. Lockwood). Moscow: Nauka.

Vasudev, J., & Hummel, R.C. (1987). 'Moral stage sequence and principled reasoning in an Indian sample.' *Human development*, 30: 105–118.

Vaughan, M. (1991). *Curing their ills: Colonial power and African illness*. Cambridge, UK: Polity Press.

Venn, C. (2000). *Occidentalism: Modernity and subjectivity*. London: Sage.

Verhoef, H., & Michel, C. (1997). 'Studying morality within the African context: A model of oral analysis and reconstruction.' *Journal of Moral Education*, 26: 389–407.

Vetten, L., & Bhana, K. (2001). *Violence, vengeance and gender: An investigation into the links between violence against women and HIV/Aids in South Africa*. Johannesburg: Centre for the Study of Violence and Reconciliation.

Vygotsky, L.S. (1966). 'Development of the higher mental functions.' In A.N. Leont'ev, A.R. Luria, & A. Smirnov (eds), *Psychological research in the USSR*. Moscow, USSR: Progress.

Vygotsky, L.S. (1978). *Mind in society: The development of higher psychological processes*. Cambridge, MA: Harvard University Press.

Vygotsky, L.S. (1981). 'The genesis of higher mental functions.' In J.V. Wertsch (ed), *The concept of activity in Soviet psychology*. Armonk, NY: Sharpe.

Waldo, C.R., & Coates, T.J. (2000). 'Multiple levels of analysis and intervention in HIV prevention science: Exemplars and directions for new research.' *Aids, 14* (Suppl 2), Ss18–26.

Walkerdine, V. (1986). 'Post-structuralist theory and everyday social practices: The family and the school.' In S. Wilkinson (ed), *Feminist social psychology: Developing theory and practice*. 57–76. Milton Keynes, UK: Open University Press.

Wallerstein, N. (1992). 'Powerlessness, empowerment and health: Implications for health promotion programmes.' *American Journal of Health Promotion*, 6(3): 197–205.

Walters, S. (1983). 'Participatory research: Theory and practice.' *Perspectives in Education*, 7(3): 170–175.

Warwick, I., & Aggleton, P. (1990). 'Adolescents, young people and Aids research.' In P. Aggleton, P. Davies & G. Hart (eds), *Aids: Individual, cultural and policy dimensions*. London: Falmer Press.

Weedon, C. (1987). *Feminist practice and poststructuralist theory*. London: Blackwell.

Weeks, J. (1985). *Sexuality and its discontents*. London: Routledge & Kegan Paul.

Weisstein, N. (1996). 'Psychology constructs the female.' In M. Martin & L.C. McIntyre (eds), *Readings in the philosophy of social science*. 597–608. London: MIT Press.

Weiten, W. (1998). *Psychology: Themes and variations.* 4th edition. Pacific Grove: Brooks/Cole.

Weiten, W. (2001). *Psychology: Themes and variations.* 5th edition. Wadsworth: Thomson Learning.

Welsh, D. (1981). 'Social research in a divided society: The case of South Africa.' In J. Rex (ed), *Apartheid and social research.* Lausanne: UNESCO.

Wertsch, J.S. (1990). 'The voice of rationality in a sociocultural approach to mind.' In L. Moll (ed), *Vygotsky and education: Instrumental implications and applications of sociohistorical psychology.* 111–126. Cambridge, UK: Cambridge University Press.

Wertsch, J.S. (1995). 'Socio-historical research in the copyright age.' *Culture and Psychology,* 1: 81–102

Wertsch, J.V. (1990). 'Dialogue and dialogism is a sociocultural approach to mind.' In I. Markova & F. Foppa (eds), *The dynamics of dialogue.* 62–82. New York: Harvester Wheatsheaf.

Wertsch, J.V. (1991). *Voices of the mind: A sociocultural approach to mediated action.* Cambridge, MA: Harvard University Press.

Wertsch, J.V., & Stone, C.A. (1985). 'The concept of internalization in Vygotsky's account of the genesis of higher mental functions.' In J.V. Wertsch (ed), *Culture, communication, and cognition: Vygotskian perspectives.* 162–179. Cambridge, UK: Cambridge University Press.

Wertsch, J.S. & Tulviste, P. (1992). 'L.S. Vygotsky and contemporary developmental psychology.' *Developmental Psychology,* 28(4): 548–557.

West, C., & Zimmerman, D.H. (1992). 'Doing gender.' In J.S. Bohan (ed), *Seldom seen, rarely heard: Women's place in psychology.* 379–403. Boulder, Colorado: Westview Press.

Wetherell, M. (1986). 'Linguistic repertoires and literary criticism: new directions for a social psychology of gender.' In S. Wilkinson (ed), *Feminist social psychology: Developing theory and practice.* 77–95. Milton Keynes, UK: Open University Press.

Wetherell, M. (1998). 'Positioning and interpretative repertoires: conversation analysis and post-structuralism in dialogue.' *Discourse & Society,* 9(3): 387–412.

Wetherell, M., Taylor, S. & Yates, S. (eds) (2001). *Discourse theory and practice: A reader.* London: Sage.

Wetherell, M., Taylor, S., & Yates, S. (eds) (2001). *Discourse as data: A guide for analysis.* London: Sage.

White J.L. (1980). 'Toward a black psychology.' In R.L. Jones (ed), *Black psychology.* 2nd edition. 5–12. New York: Harper and Row.

Whittaker, S.R. (1990). 'Education for oppression: The case of psychology in Azania/South Africa.' *Psychology Quarterly,* 1(2): 5–14.

Whittaker, S.R. (1991). 'A critical historical perspective on psychology in Azania/South Africa.' In J. Jansen (ed), *Knowledge and power in South Africa: Critical perspectives across the disciplines.* Johannesburg: Skotaville.

Wilbraham, L. (1996, 1996b). '"Avoiding the ultimate break-up" after infidelity: The marketisation of counselling and relationship-work for women in a South African advice column.' *Psychology in Society (PINS),* 21: 27–48.

Wilbraham, L. (1996). 'Orgasms, needs, fun and romance: Dr David Delvin's Sexpert's Guide.' *Conference Proceedings of The Body Politic: Second South African Qualitative Methods Conference,* Old Wits Medical School, Johannesburg, September 1996.

Wilbraham, L. (1996a). 'Few of us are potential Miss South Africas, but ...: Psychological discourses about women's bodies in advice columns.' *South African Journal of Psychology,* 26(3): 162–171.

Wilbraham, L. (1996c). 'Dear Doctor Delve-in: A feminist analysis of a sex advice column for women.' *Agenda*, 30: 51–65.

Wilbraham, L. (1997). 'The psychologization of monogamy in advice columns: Surveillance, subjectivity and resistance.' In A. Levett, A. Kottler, E. Burman & I. Parker (eds), *Culture, power and difference: Discourse analysis in South Africa*. London: Zed Books.

Wilbraham, L. (1999). 'What is the risk of the wife getting Aids?: Psychological regimes of body-regulation in talk about HIV/Aids and monogamy-rules in advice columns.' In M. Terre Blanche, K. Bhavnani & D. Hook (eds), *Body politics: Power, knowledge and the body in the social sciences*. Johannesburg: Histories of the Present Press.

Wilcocks, R.W. (1932). *The poor white problem in South Africa: The report of the Carnegie Commission*. Stellenbosch: Pro Ecclesia Press.

Wilkinson, S. (1986). 'Sighting possibilities: Diversity and commonality in feminist research.' In S. Wilkinson (ed), *Feminist social psychology: Developing theory and practice*. 7–24. Milton Keynes, UK: Open University Press.

Wilkinson, S. (ed) (1986). *Feminist social psychology: Developing theory and practice*. Milton Keynes, UK: Open University Press.

Wilkinson, S. (ed) (1996). *Feminist social psychologies*. Milton Keynes, UK: Open University Press.

Wilkinson, S., & Kitzinger, C. (eds) (1993). *Heterosexuality: A feminism and psychology reader*. London: Sage.

Wilkinson, S., & Kitzinger, C. (eds) (1995). *Feminism and discourse: Psychological perspectives*. London: Sage.

Williams, P., & Chrisman, L. (eds) (1994). *Colonial discourse and post-colonial theory*. New York: Columbia University Press.

Williamson, R.C. (1982). 'Attitudes accompanying modernisation in advanced and developing societies.' In L.L. Adler (ed), *Cross-cultural research at issue*. New York: Academic Press.

Wilton, T. (1997). *Engendering Aids: Deconstructing sex, text and epidemic*. London: Sage.

Wiredu, K. (1984). 'How not to compare African thought with Western thought.' In R.A. Wright (ed), *African philosophy*. 149–162. Toledo: University Press of America.

Wiredu, K. (1991). 'Morality and religion in Akan thought.' In R. Allen, Jnr (ed), *African-American humanism: An anthology*. 210–225. Buffalo, New York: Prometheus Books.

Wiredu, K. (1992). 'The moral foundations of an African culture.' In K. Wiredu & K. Gyekye (eds), *Person and community: Ghanaian philosophical studies*, Volume I. Available: http://www.crvp.org/book/Series02/II-01.htm [2000, 18 September].

Wolberg, L.R. (1977). *The technique of psychotherapy*. New York, San Francisco, London: Grune & Stratton.

Wolpe, H. (1975). 'The theory of internal colonialism: The South African case.' In I. Oxaal, T. Barnett & D. Booth (eds), *Beyond the sociology of development*. 229–252. London: Routledge & Kegan Paul.

World Bank (1992). *World Bank Report 1992*. New York: Oxford University Press.

Wyrick, D. (1998). *Fanon for beginners*. London & New York: Writers and Readers.

Yeich, S., & Levine, R. (1992). 'Participatory research's contribution to a conceptualisation of empowerment.' *Journal of Applied Social Psychology*, 22(24): 1894–1908.

Young, I. (1990). *Justice and the politics of difference*. Princeton: Princeton University Press.

Young, R. (1993). 'Racism: Projective identification and cultural processes.' *Psychology in Society (PINS)*, 17: 5–18.

Young, R.M. (1994). *Mental Space*. Retrieved 10 February 2002 from http://human-nature.com/rmyoung/papers/paper55.html.

Zahan, D. (1979). *The religion, spirituality and thought of traditional Africa* (trans K.E. Martin & L.M. Martin). Chicago: University of Chicago Press.

Zahar, R. (1969). *Frantz Fanon: Colonialism and alienation.* New York & London: Monthly Review Press.

Zimmerman, A.A. (1990). 'Taking aim on empowerment research: On the distinction between individual and psychological conceptions.' *American Journal of Community Psychology*, 18(1): 169–177.

Social Psychology: References

Abdool Karim, S.S., Abdool Karim, Q., Preston-Whyte, E. & N. Sankar (1992). 'Reasons for lack of condom use among high school students'. *South African Medical Journal*, 82:107–110.

Abdool Karim, Q., Preston-Whyte, E. & S.S. Abdool Karim (1992). 'Teenagers seeking condoms at family planning services: Part I. A user's perspective'. *South African Medical Journal*, 82:356–359.

Abdool Karim, Q., Abdool Karim, S.S. & E. Preston-Whyte (1992). 'Teenagers seeking condoms at family planning services: Part II. A provider's perspective'. *South African Medical Journal*, 82:360–362.

Aboud, F. (1987). 'The development of ethnic self-identification and attitudes'. In Phinney, J. & M. Rotheram (Eds.) *Children's Ethnic Socialisation: Pluralism and Development*, pp. 32–35. Newbury Park: Sage.

Aboud, F.E. & S.R. Levy (1999). 'Are we ready to translate research into programs?' *Journal of Social Issues*, 55(4):621–625.

Abraham, M. (2000). *Speaking the Unspeakable. Marital Violence among South Asian Immigrants in the United States*. New Brunswick: Rutgers University Press.

Abrahams, N., Jewkes, R. & R. Laubsher. (1999). *'I Do Not Believe in Democracy in the Home.' Men's Relationships With and Abuse of Women*. Tygerberg: CERSA (Women's Health) Medical Research Council.

Abrahams, Y. (2000). *Colonialism, Dysfunction and Dysjuncture: The Histiography of Sarah Baartman*. Unpublished doctoral thesis, University of Cape Town.

Achmat, Z. (1993). '"Apostles of civilised vice": "Immoral practices" and "unnatural vice" in South African prisons and compounds, 1890–1920'. *Social Dynamics*, 19(2):92–110.

Adam, H. (1995). 'The politics of ethnic identity: Comparing South Africa'. *Ethnic and Racial Studies*, 18(3):457–475.

Adebayo, D. (1996). *Some Kind of Black*. London: Virago.

Adelman, M. (1980). *Adjustment to Aging and Styles of Being Gay: A Study of Elderly Gay Men and Lesbians*. Unpublished doctoral dissertation, University of California, Berkeley.

Adler, M. (1996). 'Skirting the edges of civilisation: Two Victorian women travelers and "colonial spaces" in South Africa'. In Darian-Smith, E., Gunner, L. & S. Nuttall (Eds.) *Text, Theory, Space: Land, Literature and History in South Africa and Australia*, pp. 83–98. London: Routledge.

Adler, N.J. (1996). 'Global women political leaders: An invisible history, an increasingly important future'. *Leadership Quarterly*, 7(1):133–161.

Adorno, T.W., Frenkel-Brunswik, E., Levinson, D.J. & R.N. Sanford (1950). *The Authoritarian Personality*. New York: Harper.

Agence France-Presse (1998). 'South African players face sanction over racism claims'. *Internet Sports Features Page*: www.afp.com/english (accessed 6 May 1998).

Alessandri, A.C. (Ed.) (1999). *Frantz Fanon: Critical Perspectives*. London: Routledge.

Alexander, N. (1985). *Sow the Wind: Contemporary Speeches*. Johannesburg: Skotaville.

Alexander, N. (1992). 'National liberation and socialist revolution'. In A. Callinicos (Ed.) *Between Apartheid and Capitalism*, pp. 114–136. London: Bookmarks.

Alexander, N. (1996). *Towards a National Plan for South Africa: Report of the Language Plan Task Group (LANGTAG)*. Pretoria: Department of Arts and Culture, Science and Technology.

Alexander, N. (2001). 'Language politics in South Africa'. In Bekker, S., Dodds, M. & M. Khosa (Eds.) *Shifting African Identities*, Vol. 2, pp. 141–152. Pretoria: Human Sciences Research Council.

Allport, G. (1954). *The Nature of Prejudice*. Reading: Addison-Wesley.

Allport, G.W. (1968). 'The historical background of modern social psychology'. In Lindzey, G. & E. Aronson (Eds.) *The Handbook of Social Psychology*, Vol. 1, 2nd Edition, pp. 1–80. Reading: Addison-Wesley.

Alwood, E. (1996). *Straight News: Gays, Lesbians, and the News Media*. New York: Columbia University Press.

Amadiume, I. (1987). *Male Daughters, Female Husbands: Gender and Sex in an African Society*. London: Zed Books.

ANC (African National Congress) (2000). 'Stereotypes steer the news'. Submission to the HSRC Inquiry into Racism in the Media. *Rhodes Journalism Review*, 19:21.

Anderson, K. (1997). 'Gender, status, and domestic violence. An integration of feminist and family violence approaches'. *Journal of Marriage and the Family*, 59:655–669.

Anzieu, D. (1985). *Le Moi Peau* [The Ego Skin]. Paris: Dunod.

Apteker, L. (1994). 'Street children in the developing world: A review of their condition'. *Cross-Cultural Research*, 28(3):195–224.

Armon, V. (1960). 'Some personality variables in overt female homosexuality'. *Journal of Projective Techniques and Personality Assessment*, 24:292–309.

Arnold, M. (Ed.) (1979). *Steve Biko: Black Consciousness in South Africa*. New York: Vintage.

Aronson, E. (1984). *The Social Animal*, 4th Edition. New York: W.H. Freeman & Company.

Aronson, E., Stephan, C., Sikes, J., Blaney, N. & M. Snapp (1978). *The Jigsaw Classroom*. Beverley Hills: Sage.

Artz, L. (2001). 'Policing the Domestic Violence Act: Teething troubles or system failure'. *Agenda*, 47:4–13.

Ashcroft, B. Griffiths, G. & H. Tiffin (Eds.) (1995). *The Post-colonial Studies Reader*. London & New York: Routledge.

Atkinson, D., Morten, G. & D.W. Sue. (1983). *Counselling American Minorities*. Dubuque, Iowa: W. C. Brown.

Bakare-Yusuf, B. (2003). '"Yorubas don't do gender": A critical review of Oyerunke Oyewumi's *The Invention of Woman: Making African Sense of Western Gender Discourses'*. *African Identities* (in press).

Baker, P.L. (1997). 'And I went back: Battered women's negotiation of choice'. *Journal of Contemporary Ethnography*, 26(1):55–74.

Balier, C. (1988). *Psychanalyse des Comportements Violents*. Paris: PUF.

Balogun, M.J. (1997). 'Enduring clientelism, governance reform and leadership capacity: A review of the democratisation process in Nigeria'. *Journal of Contemporary African Studies*, 15(2):237–260.

Bandura, A. (1977). *Social Learning Theory*. New Jersey: Prentice-Hall.

Banton, M. (1988). *Racial Consciousness*. London: Longman.

Banyard, V.L. & S.A. Graham-Bermann (1993). 'Can women cope? A gender analysis of theories of coping with stress'. *Psychology of Women Quarterly*, 17:303–318.

Barnes, T. (1999). *We Women Worked so Hard: Gender, Urbanization and Social Reproduction in Colonial Harare, Zimbabwe, 1930–1956*. Portsmouth: Heinemann.

Baron, R.A. & D. Byrne (1981). *Social Psychology*, 3rd Edition. Boston: Allyn and Bacon.

Baron, R.A. & D. Byrne (1997). *Social Psychology*, 8th Edition. Boston: Allyn and Bacon.

Barr, C. (1995). 'Saigon's street kids stand up for themselves'. *The Child Care Worker*, 13(8).

Barrette, M. (1995). *Street Children Need Our Care*. Pretoria: Kagiso Publishers.

Barthes, R. (1964). *Critique et Véréte*. Paris: Seuil.

Bassett, M. & J. Sherman (1994). 'Female sexual behaviour and the risk of HIV infection: an ethnographic study in Harare, Zimbabwe'. *Women and AIDS Program Research Report Series*. Washington DC: International Center for Research on Women.

Beach, B. (1980). *Lesbian and Non-lesbian Women: Profiles of Development and Self-actualization*. Unpublished doctoral dissertation, University of Iowa.

Bekker, S. (2001). 'Identity and ethnicity'. In Bekker, S., Dodds, M. & M. Khosa (Eds.) *Shifting African Identities*, Vol. 2, pp. 1–6. Pretoria: HSRC.

Benokraitis, N.V. & Feagin, J.R. (1995). *Modern Sexism: Blatant, Subtle and Covert Discrimination*. Englewood Cliffs, New Jersey: Prentice Hall.

Benson, S. (1997). 'The body, health and eating disorders'. In Woodward, K. (Ed.) *Identity and Difference*, pp. 121–181. London: Sage Publications/The Open University.

Bergler, E. (1956). *Homosexuality: Disease or Way of Life?* New York: Collier Boales.

Bergman, L. (1992). 'Dating violence among high school students'. *Social Work*, 37(1):21–27.

Berman, K. (1993). 'Lesbians in South Africa: Challenging the invisibility'. In Krouse, M. & K. Berman (Eds.) *The Invisible Ghetto: Lesbian and Gay Writing from South Africa*, pp. xvii–xxi. Johannesburg: COSAW Publishing.

Bertelsen, E. (2000). 'Race, class and other prejudices'. *Rhodes Journalism Review*, 19:19–20.

Bertoldi, A. (1998). 'Oedipus in (South) Africa? Psychoanalysis and the politics of difference'. *American Imago*, 55(1):101–134.

Bhabha, H.K. (1994). *The Location of Culture*. London & New York: Routledge.

Bhende, A. (1995). 'Evolving a model for AIDS prevention education among underprivileged adolescent girls in urban India'. *Women and AIDS Program Research Report Series*. Washington DC: International Center for Research on Women.

Biko, S. (1978). *I Write What I Like*. Randburg: Ravan Press.

Biko, S. (1988). *I Write What I Like*. London: Penguin.

Biko, S. (1996). *I Write What I Like*. London: The Bowerdean Publishing Company.

Billig, M. (1976). *Social Psychology and Intergroup Relations*. London: Academic Press.

Billig, M. (1988). 'Methodology and scholarship in understanding ideological explanation'. In C. Antaki (Ed.) *Analysing Everyday Explanation*, pp. 199–215. London: Sage Publications.

Billig, M. (1998). 'Rhetoric and the unconscious'. *Argumentation*, 12:199–216.

Bion, W. (1962). *Learning from Experience*. London: Heinemann.

Bion, W. (1963). *Elements of Psychoanalysis*. London: Heinemann.

Blumenfeld, W. & D. Raymond. (1989). *Looking at Gay and Lesbian Life*. Boston: Beacon Press.

Blummer, H. (1971). 'Social problems as collective behaviour'. *Social problems*, 18:298–306.

Blyth, S. (1989). *An Exploration of Accounts of Lesbian Identities*. Unpublished Master's thesis, University of Cape Town.

Blyth, S. & G. Straker (1996). 'Intimacy, fusion and frequency of sexual contact in lesbian couples'. *South African Journal of Psychology*, 26(4):253–256.

Bobo, L. (1988). 'Group conflict, prejudice, and the paradox of contemporary racial attitudes'. In Katz, P.A. & D.A. Taylor (Eds.) *Eliminating Racism. Profiles in Controversy*, pp. 85–114. New York: Plenum Press.

Bodiba, L.J. (nd.). *The Coloured-African Divide in the Western Cape: A Legacy of Apartheid.* Unpublished paper.

Bograd, M. (1990). 'Feminist perspectives on wife abuse: An introduction'. In Yllö, K. & M. Bograd (Eds.) *Feminist Perspectives on Wife Abuse,* pp. 11–26. Newbury Park: Sage.

Bograd, M. (1999). 'Strengthening domestic violence theories: Intersections of race, class, sexual orientation, and gender'. *Journal of Marital and Family Therapy,* 25(3):275–289.

Boloka, G. (2000). 'Not yet uhuru'. *Rhodes Journalism Review,* 19:35.

Bond, P. (1994). 'RDP versus World Bank'. *International Viewpoint,* 257:16–17.

Bond, P. (2000). *Elite Transition.* London: Pluto Press.

Boonzaier, F. (2001). *Woman Abuse: Exploring Women's Narratives of Violence and Resistance in Mitchell's Plain.* Unpublished Master's thesis, University of Cape Town.

Bornman, E. (1998). 'Group membership as determinant of violence and conflict: The case of South Africa'. In Bornman, E., van Eeden, R. & M. Wentzel (Eds.) *Violence in South Africa: A Variety of Perspectives,* pp. 85–116. Pretoria: HSRC.

Bornman, E. (1999). 'The individual and the group in the social, political and economic context: Implications for South Africa'. In Bekker, S. & R. Prinsloo (Eds.) *Identity? Theory, Politics, History,* Vol. 1, pp. 39–66. Pretoria: Human Sciences Research Council.

Botha, A.H. (1975). *Pastorale Sorg aan die Homoseksuele Mens.* Unpublished doctoral dissertation, University of Pretoria.

Bourdillon, M. (1995). 'The children on our streets'. *The Child Care Worker,* 13:12–13.

Bowlby, J. (1988). *A Secure Base: Parent-child Attachment and Healthy Human Development.* New York: Basic Books.

Bozzoli, B. (1987). *Class, Community and Conflicts.* Johannesburg: Ravan Press.

Brah, A. (1996). *Cartographies of Diaspora: Contesting Identities,* London: Routledge.

Brah, A. (2000). 'Difference, diversity, differentiation'. In Back, L. & J. Solomons (Eds.) *Theories of Race and Racism: A Reader,* pp. 431–446. London: Routledge.

Braude, C. (1999). *Cultural Bloodstains: Towards Understanding the Legacy of Apartheid and the Perpetuation of Racial Stereotypes in the Contemporary South African Media.* Parktown: SAHRC.

Brecker, C. (1994). 'Left faces new challenge'. *International Viewpoint,* 257:6–12.

Breckinridge, K. (1998). 'The allure of violence: Men, race and masculinity on the South African goldmines, 1900–1950'. *Journal of Southern African Studies,* 24(4):669–693.

Bremridge, C. (2000). *Constructions of Male Adolescent Sexuality: An Exploratory Study in a Coloured, Rural Community.* Unpublished Master's thesis, University of Stellenbosch.

Brett, J. (2000). 'Culture and negotiation'. *International Journal of Psychology,* 35(2):97–104.

Brown, L. (Ed.) (1993). *The New Shorter Oxford English Dictionary on Historical Principles.* Oxford: Clarendon Press.

Browne, A. (1987). *When Battered Women Kill.* New York: Free Press.

Browne, A. (1997). 'Violence in marriage: Until death do us part'? In Cardarelli, A.P. (Ed.) *Violence between Intimate Partners: Patterns, Causes, and Effects,* pp. 48–69. Boston: Allyn and Bacon.

Buga, G., Amoko, D. & D. Ncayiyana (1996). 'Sexual behaviour, contraceptive practice and reproductive health among school adolescents in rural Transkei'. *South African Medical Journal,* 86(5):523–527.

Bulhan, H.A. (1979). 'Black psyches in captivity and crisis'. *Race and Class,* 20(3):243–261.

Bulhan, H.A. (1980a). 'Frantz Fanon: The revolutionary psychiatrist'. *Race & Class,* 21(3):251–271.

Bulhan, H.A. (1980b). 'Dynamics of cultural in-betweenity: An empirical study'. *International Journal of Psychology,* 15:105–121.

Bulhan, H.A. (1985). *Frantz Fanon and the Psychology of Oppression.* New York: Plenum Press.

Bulhan, H.A. (1992). 'Imperialism in studies of the psyche'. In Nicholas, L. (Ed.) *Psychology and Oppression,* pp. 1–34. Johannesburg: Skotaville.

Bundy, C. (2000). 'The beast of the past'. In James, W. & D.P. van der Vijver (Eds.) *After the TRC: Reflections on Truth and Reconciliation in South Africa,* pp. 9–20. Cape Town: David Phillip.

Burrows, S., Bowman, B., Matzopoulos, R. & A. van Niekerk (2001). *A Profile of Fatal Injuries in South Africa 2000.* Tygerberg: Medical Research Council.

Burstyn, V. (1999). *The Rites of Men: Manhood, Politics and the Culture of Sport.* Toronto: University of Toronto Press.

Busch, A. (1999). *Finding Their Voices: Listening to Battered Women Who've Killed.* New York: Kroshka Books.

Butchart, A. & J. Kruger (2001). 'Public health and community psychology: A case study in community-based injury prevention'. In Seedat, M., Duncan, N. & S. Lazarus (Eds.) *Theory, Method and Practice in Community Psychology: South African and Other Perspectives,* pp. 215–241. Cape Town: Oxford University Press.

Butchart, A. (1996). 'Violence prevention in Gauteng: The public health approach'. *Acta Criminologica,* 9(2):5–15.

Butchart, A. (1998). *The Anatomy of Power: European Constructions of the African Body.* Pretoria: Unisa.

Butchart, A., Nell, V. & M. Seedat (1996). 'Violence in South Africa: Its definition and prevention as a public health problem'. In Seager, J. & C. Parry (Eds.) *Urbanisation and Health in South Africa,* pp. 1–41. Tygerberg: Medical Research Council.

Butchart, A., Terreblanche, M., Hamber, B. & M. Seedat (2000). 'Violence and violence prevention in South Africa: A sociological and historical perspective'. In Emmett, T. & A. Butchart (Eds.) *Behind the Mask,* pp. 29–54. Pretoria: HSRC.

Butler, J. (1990a). *Gender Trouble: Feminism and the Subversion of Identity.* New York: Routledge.

Butler, J. (1990b). 'Gender trouble, feminist theory, and psychoanalytic discourse'. In Nicholson, L.J. (Ed.) *Feminism/Postmodernism,* pp. 324–340. New York and London: Routledge.

Butler, J. (1993). *Bodies That Matter.* New York: Rouledge.

Butulia, U. (2000). *The Other Side of Silence: Voices from the Partition of India.* London: Hurst and Company.

CAL (Cape Action League). (1987). *Introduction to 'Race' and Racism.* Cape Town: CAL.

Callaghan, N., Hamber, B. & S. Takura (1997). *A Triad of Oppression: Violence, Women, and Poverty.* Johannesburg: South African NGO Coalition.

Callinicos, L. (1987). *Working Life 1886–1940.* Johannesburg: Ravan Press.

Cameron, E. (1994). '"Unapprehended felons": Gays and lesbians and the law in South Africa'. In Gevisser, M. & E. Cameron (Eds.) *Defiant Desire: Gay and Lesbian Lives in South Africa,* pp. 89–98. Braamfontein: Ravan.

Camilleri, C. (1990). 'Identité collective et gestion de la disparité culturelle: essai d'une typologie' [Collective identity and the management of cultural disparity: Towards a typology]. In Camilleri, C., Kasterszein, J., Lipiansky, M.E., Malewska-Peyre, H., Taboada-Leonetti, I. and A. Vasquez (Eds.) *Stratégies Identitaires,* pp. 85–110. Paris: PUF.

Campbell, C. (1995). 'Identity and difference'. *Agenda*, 4:45–63.

Campbell, C. (2001). 'Going underground and going after women: Masculinity and HIV transmission amongst black workers on the gold mines'. In Morrell, R. (Ed.) *Changing Men in Southern Africa*, pp. 275–286. Pietermaritzburg: University of Natal Press.

Campbell, C., Mzaidume, Y. & B. Williams (1998). 'Gender as an obstacle to condom use: HIV prevention amongst commercial sex-workers in a mining community'. *Agenda*, 39:50–57.

Campbell, J. (1992). 'If I can't have you, no one can: Power and control in homicide of female partners'. In Radford, J. & D. Russel (Eds.) *Femicide: The Politics of Woman Killing*, pp. 99–113. New York: Twayne/Gale Group.

Campbell, J.C., Miller, P., Cardwell, M.M. & A. Belknap (1994). 'Relationship status of battered women over time'. *Journal of Family Violence*, 9(2):99–111.

Caprio, F.S. (1954). *Female Homosexuality: A Psychodynamic Study of Lesbianism*. New York: Citadel Press.

Carby, H. (1987). *Reconstructing Womanhood: The Emergence of the Afro-American Woman Novelist*. New York: Oxford University Press.

Cario, R. (1997). *Les Femmes Résisten au Crime*. Paris: L'Harmattan.

Carrim, N. (2000). 'Critical anti-racism and problems in self-articulated forms of identities'. *Race, Ethnicity and Education*, 3(1):25–44.

Caute, D. (1970). *Frantz Fanon*. New York: Viking Press.

Césaire, A. (1995). *Notebook of a Return to My Native Land*. Newcastle-upon-Tyne: Bloodaxe Books.

Chan, C. (1989). 'Issues of identity development among Asian American lesbians and gay men'. *Journal of Counseling and Development*, 68(1):16–20.

Chan-Sam, T. (1994). 'Profiles of black lesbian life on the Reef'. In Gevisser, M. & E. Cameron (Eds.) *Defiant Desire: Gay and Lesbian Lives in South Africa*, pp. 186–192. Johannesburg: Ravan Press.

Chapman, M.D. (1997). *The Group Psychotherapeutic Effects of Human Modelling Psychotherapy on the Self-esteem of Street Children Identified as Having Low Self-esteem*. Unpublished Master's dissertation, University of North-West.

Chesler, M.A. (1976). 'Contemporary sociological theories of racism'. In Katz, P.A. (Ed.) *Towards the Elimination of Racism*, pp. 21–72. New York: Pergamon.

Chetty, D. (1994). 'Lesbian gangster: the Gertie William story'. In Gevisser, M. & E. Cameron (Eds.) *Defiant Desire: Gay and Lesbian Lives in South Africa*, pp. 128–133. Johannesburg: Ravan Press.

Chetty, V.R. (1997). *Street Children in Durban: An Exploratory Investigation*. Pretoria: HSRC.

Chipkin, I. (2002). *The South African Nation*. Unpublished manuscript.

Christian, B. (2000). 'Black feminism and the academy'. In Back, L. & J. Solomons (Eds.), *Theories of Race and Racism: A Reader*, pp. 462–472. London: Routledge.

Christopher, A.J. (1994). *The Atlas of Apartheid*. London: Routledge.

Clark, D. (1993). '"With my body I thee worship": The social construction of marital sex problems'. In Scott, S. & D. Morgan (Eds.) *Body Matters*, pp. 22–34. London: The Falmer Press.

Clarke, C. (1981). 'Lesbianism: An act of resistance'. In Moraga, C. & G. Anzaldua (Eds.) *This Bridge Called My Back: Writings by Radical Women of Color*, pp. 128–137. Massachusetts: Persephone Press.

Cockburn, A. (1991). 'Street children: Victims of multiple abuses'. Paper presented at the South African Society for the *Prevention of Child Abuse and Neglect Conference*, Durban, nd.

Cockburn, A. (1994). 'Who cares? Sexual abuse and the street child'. *The Child Care Worker*, 12(7):11–12.

Cockburn, A. (1995). 'Looking after street children: A model indigenous to South Africa'. Paper presented at the *Tenth Biennial Conference of the National Association of Child Care Workers*. Cape Town, nd.

Collins, A. (2001). 'How the social psychologist got his facts: A postcolonial tale'. *Psychology in Society*, 27:53–60.

Collins, P.H. (1990). *Black Feminist Thought: Knowledge, Consciousness and the Politics of Empowerment*. New York: Routledge.

Connell, R. (1995). *Masculinities*. Cambridge: Polity Press.

Cooper, S. (1990). 'The violence of apartheid on the family'. *University of the Western Cape Psychology Resource Centre Bulletin*, 1(1):2–3.

Cornwell, A. (1983). *Black Lesbian in White America*. Tallahassie, Florida: Naiad.

Cronin, J. (1999). 'We're right here, in the South – Chris Hani's legacy': www.sacp.org.za/pr/press/1999/nw0411.htm (accessed 6 June 2000).

Cronjé, C.J. (1979). *Lesbinisme: Etiologie in Psigodinamika*. Unpublished Master's thesis, Rand Afrikaans University, Johannesburg.

Curran, J., Morley, D. & V. Walkerdine (Eds.) (1996). *Cultural Studies and Communications*. New York: Halstead Press.

Dangor, Z., Hoff, L.A. & R. Scott (1996). *Woman Abuse in South Africa: An Exploratory Study*. Johannesburg: Nisaa Institute for Women' Development.

Das, A. (1996). 'Language and body: Transactions in the construction of pain'. *Daedelus*, 125(1):67–92.

Davis, F.J. (1992). *Who is Black? One Nation's Definition*. Pennsylvania: Pennsylvania State University Press.

Davis, K. (Ed.) (1997a). *Embodied Practices: Feminist Perspectives on the Body*. London: Sage Publications.

Davis, K. (1997b). '"My body is my art": Cosmetic surgery as feminist utopia?' *The European Journal of Women's Studies*, 4(1):23–37.

Dawes, A. & D. Donald (Eds.) (1994). *Childhood and Adversity*. Cape Town: David Phillip.

Dawes, A. (1994). 'The emotional impact of political violence'. In Dawes, A. & D. Donald (Eds.) *Childhood and Adversity*, pp. 177–199. Cape Town: David Phillip.

Dayile, N.M. (1998). *The Representation of Inter-ethnic/Racial Life Stories*. Unpublished Honours Research Project, Women and Gender Studies, University of the Western Cape, Cape Town.

De Beer, A.S. (1997). 'Mass communication in society: Pervasive images and images of our time'. In de Beer, A.S. (Ed.) *Mass Media for the Nineties: A South African Handbook of Mass Communication*, pp. 5–25. Pretoria: van Schaik.

De la Rey, C. (1991). 'Intergroup relations: Theories and positions'. In Foster, D. & J. Louw-Potgieter (Eds.) *Social Psychology in South Africa*, pp. 26–53. Johannesburg: Lexicon.

De la Rey, C. (1997). 'South African feminism, race and racism'. *Agenda*, 32:6–10.

De Waal Malefijt, A. (1976). *Images of Man: A History of Anthropological Thought*. New York: Knopf.

Degenaar, J.J. (1980). 'The concept of violence'. *Politikon*, 7(1):14–27.

Derrida, J. (1978). *Writing and Difference*. London: Routledge.

Descartes, R. (1968). *Discourse on Method and the Meditations*. London: Penguin Books.

Diederichs, P. (1997). 'Newspapers: The fourth estate'. In de Beer, A.S. (Ed.) *Mass Media for the Nineties: A South African Handbook of Mass Communication*, pp. 71–100. Pretoria: van Schaik.

Dimenstein, G. (1991). *Brazil. War on Children*. London: Latin America Bureau.

Dobash, R.E. & R. Dobash (1979). *Violence against wives: A Case against Patriarchy*. New York: The Free Press.

Dobash, R.P., Dobash, R.E., Wilson, M. & M. Daly (1992). 'The myth of sexual symmetry in marital violence'. *Social Problems*, 39(1):71–85.

Dolby, N.E. (2000). *Constructing Race: Youth, Identity and Popular Culture in South Africa*. New York: State University of New York Press.

Dollard, J., Doob, L.W., Miller, N.E., Mower, O.H. & R.R. Sears (1939). *Frustration and Aggression*. New Haven: Yale University Press.

Donald, D. & J. Swart-Kruger (1994). 'The South African street child: Developmental implications'. *South African Journal of Psychology*, 24(4):169–174.

Dovidio, J.F. & S.L. Gaertner (1986). *Prejudice, Discrimination and Racism*. London: Academic Press.

Du Bois, W.E.B. (1995). *W.E.B du Bois Reader*. New York: H. Holt.

Du Toit, P. (1989). 'Bargaining about bargaining: Inducing the self-negating prediction in deeply divided societies – the case of South Africa'. *Journal of Conflict Resolution*, 33(2):210–230.

Dubow, S. (1995). *Illicit Union: Scientific Racism in South Africa*. Johannesburg: Witwatersrand University Press.

Duckitt, J.H. (1984). 'Attitudes of white South Africans toward homosexuality'. *South African Journal of Sociology*, 15(2):89–93.

Duffy, A. (1995). 'The feminist challenge: Knowing and ending the violence'. In Mandell, N. (Ed.) *Feminist Issues: Race, Class and Sexuality*, pp. 152–184. Scarborough, Canada: Prentice Hall.

Dunbar Moodie, T. (2001). 'Black migrant mine labourers and the vicissitudes of male desire'. In Morrell, R. (Ed.) *Changing Men in Southern Africa*, pp. 297–315. Pietermaritzburg: University of Natal Press.

Dunbar Moodie, T. with Ndatshe, V. & B. Sibuyi (1988). 'Migrancy and male sexuality on the South African goldmines'. *Journal of Southern African Studies*, 14(2):228–256.

Dunbar Moodie, T. with V. Ndatshe. (1994). *Going for Gold: Men, Mines & Migration*. Berkeley: University of California Press.

Duncan, N. & B. Rock (1994). *Inquiry into the Effects of Public Violence on Children: Preliminary Report*. Sandton: Goldstone Commission.

Duncan, N. & B. Rock. (1995). 'South African children and public violence: Quantifying the damage'. *Psychology Resource Centre Occasional Publication Series*, No. 9. University of the Western Cape, Cape Town.

Duncan, N. & C. de la Rey (2000). 'Racism: A psychological perspective'. Paper presented at the South African Human Rights Commission's *National Conference on Racism and Related Forms of Intolerance*, Sandton, 30 September–2 October.

Duncan, N. (1991). 'The black family and child development'. *Psychology Quarterly*, 2(1):2–5.

Duncan, N. (1993). *Discourses of Racism*. Unpublished doctoral dissertation, University of the Western Cape, Cape Town.

Duncan, N. (1996). 'Discourses on public violence and the reproduction of racism'. *South African Journal of Psychology*, 26(3):172–182.

Duncan, N. (2001). 'Discourses on race and racial difference'. Paper presented at the meeting of the *Second Biannual Congress of the International Academy of Intercultural Research*, Mississippi, 18–22 April.

Duppong, K. (1999). *Intimate Partner Homicide: The Role of Gender Equality and Type of Intimate Relationship*. Unpublished doctoral thesis, Southern Illinois University, Carbondale.

Durkheim, E. (1998). 'Functions of crime'. In Macionis, J.J. & N.V. Benokraitis (Eds.) *Seeing Ourselves: Classic, Contemporary and Cross-cultural Readings in Sociology*, pp. 150–152. New Jersey: Prentice-Hall.

Durrheim, K. (1999). 'Research design'. In Terre Blanche, M. & K. Durrheim (Eds.) *Research in Practice*. Cape Town: University of Cape Town Press.

Edley, N. & M. Wetherell (1995). *Men in Perspective: Practice, Power and Identity*. London: Prentice Hall.

Edwards, J. & L. McKie (1997). 'Women's public toilets: a serious issue for the body politic'. In K. Davis (Ed.) *Embodied Practices: Feminist Perspectives on the Body*, pp. 135–149. London: Sage Publications.

Eiguer, A. (1998). *Clinique Psychanalytique du Couple*. Paris: Dunod.

Eiguer, A., Ruffiot, A. & Associates (1984). *La Thérapie Psychanalytique du Couple*. Paris: Dunod.

Ellison, G. & T. de Wet (2002). '"Race", ethnicity and psychopathology of social identity'. In Hook, D. & G. Eagle (Eds.) *Psychopathology and Social Prejudice*, pp. 139–149. Cape Town: University of Cape Town Press.

Ellsberg, M., Caldera, T., Herrera, A., Winkvist, A. & G. Kullgren (1999). 'Domestic violence and emotional distress among Nicaraguan women. Results from a population-based study'. *American Psychologist*, 54(1):30–36.

Emmett, T. & A. Butchart (Eds.) (2000). *Behind the Mask*. Pretoria: HSRC Publishers.

Epprecht, E. (1998). 'The "Unsaying" of indigenous homosexualities in Zimbabwe: Mapping a blind spot in an African masculinity'. *Journal of Southern African Studies*, 24(4):631–651.

Erasmus, Z. (2000). 'Hair Politics'. In Nuttall, S. and C. Michael (Eds.) *Sense of Culture: South African Culture Studies*. London: Oxford University Press.

Erikson, E.H. (1963). *Childhood and Society*. New York: Norton.

Erikson, E.H. (1968). *Identity: Youth and Crisis*. New York: Norton.

Essed, P. (1986). *The Dutch as Everyday Problem*. Amsterdam: CRES Publications.

Essed, P. (1987). *Academic Racism*. Amsterdam: CRES Publications.

Etheridge, L.S. (1992). 'Wisdom and good judgment in politics'. *International Society for Political Psychology*, 13(3):497–516.

Evans, I. (1990). 'The racial question and intellectual production in South Africa'. *Perspectives in Education*, 11:21–35.

Evans-Pritchard, E.E. (1970). 'Sexual inversion among the Azande'. *American Anthropologist*, 72:1428–1434.

Ewing, C. (1990). 'Psychological self-defence: A proposed justification for battered women who kill'. *Law and Human Behaviour*, 14(6):579–594.

Eyber, C., Dyer, D. & R. Versveld (1997). *Resisting Racism. A Teacher's Guide to Equality*. Cape Town: TLRC & IDASA.

Faderman, L. (1981). *Surpassing the Love of Men: Romantic Friendship and Love Between Women from the Renaissance to the Present*. New York: William Morrow.

Fanon, F. (1968) [1961]. *Toward the African Revolution*. New York: Grove.

Fanon, F. (1968). *The Wretched of the Earth*. New York: Grove Press.

Fanon, F. (1970) [1959]. *A Dying Colonialism*. New York: Grove.

Fanon, F. (1986) [1952]. *Black Skin, White Masks*. London: Pluto.

Fanon, F. (1990) [1963]. *The Wretched of the Earth*. London: Penguin.

Farrington, D.P. (1991). 'Childhood aggression and adult violence: Early precursors and later-life outcomes'. In Pepler, D.J. & K.H. Rubin (Eds.) *The Development and Treatment of Childhood Aggression*, pp. 5–29. New Jersey: Lawrence Erlbaum Associates.

Feldman, A. (2000). 'Violence and vision: The prosthetics and asthetics of terror'. In Das, V., Kleinman, A., Ramphele, M. & P. Reynolds (Eds.) *Violence and Subjectivity*, pp. 46–78. Berkeley: University of California Press.

Ferber, A. (1999). *White Man Falling*. Lanham: Rowman & Littlefield.

Ferguson, A. (1982). 'Patriarchy, sexual identity and the sexual revolution'. *Agenda*, 28:48–53.

Ferguson, A., Zita, J. & K. Addelson (1981). 'On compulsory heterosexuality and lesbian existence: Defining the issues'. *Signs*, 7:158–199.

Festinger, L., Pepitone, A. & T. Newcomb (1952). 'Some consequences of deindividuation in a group'. *Journal of Abnormal and Social Psychology*, 47:38–389.

Fiffer, S.S. & S. Fiffer (Eds.) (1999). *Body*. New York: Avon Books.

Finchilescu, G. & G. Nyawose (1998). 'Talking about language: Zulu students' views on language in the new South Africa'. *South African Journal of Psychology*, 28(2):53–61.

Finn, J. (1985). 'The stresses and coping behavior of battered women'. *Social Casework: The Journal of Contemporary Social Work*, 51:341–349.

Fleury, R.E. (2000). 'When ending the relationship does not end the violence: Women's experiences of violence by former partners'. *Violence Against Women*, 6(12):1363–1383.

Foster, D. (1991a). 'Introduction'. In Foster, D. & J. Louw-Potgieter (Eds.) *Social Psychology in South Africa*, pp. 3–23. Johannesburg: Lexicon Publishers.

Foster, D. (1991b). *On Racism: Virulent Mythologies and Fragile Threads*. Inaugural lecture, University of Cape Town.

Foster, D. (1991c). 'Social influence I: Ideology'. In D. Foster & J. Louw-Potgieter (Eds.) *Social Psychology in South Africa*, pp. 345–391. Johannesburg: Lexicon Publishers.

Foster, D. & E. Nel (1991). 'Attitudes and related concepts'. In Foster, D. & J. Louw-Potgieter (Eds.) *Social Psychology in South Africa*, pp. 121–167. Isando: Lexicon Publishers.

Foster, D. & J. Louw-Potgieter (Eds.) (1991). *Social Psychology in South Africa*. Johannesburg: Lexicon Publishers.

Foster, D. & K. Durrheim (1998). 'Crowds, psychology and crowd control'. In Bornman, E., van Eeden, R. & M. Wentzel (Eds.) *Violence in South Africa: A Variety of Perspectives*, pp. 117–146. Pretoria: HSRC.

Foucault, M. (1973). *The Order of Things*. New York: Random House.

Foucault, M. (1979). *Discipline and Punish*. Harmondsworth: Penguin.

Foucault, M. (1980). 'Power/knowledge'. In Gordon, C. (Ed.) *Power/Knowledge: Selected Interviews and other Writings by Michel Foucault, 1972–1977*. New York: Pantheon Books.

Foucault, M. (1981). *The History of Sexuality, Vol 1: Introduction*. Harmondsworth: Penguin.

Franchi, V. (1999). *Approche Clinique et Sociocognitive des Processus Identitaires et de la Représentation de Soi en Interculturel* [A Clinical and Intercultural Study of the Construction of Identity at the Interface of Cultural Affiliations]. Unpublished doctoral thesis. Nanterre: Laboratoire IPSE, University of Paris X.

Franchi, V. 2000. 'Positioning of self at the intersection of differing acculturation discourses, cross-cultural study of identity strategies among youth schooled in Paris'. Paper presented at the *15th Congress of the International Association for Cross-Cultural Psychology*, Pultusk, Poland, 16–21 July.

Franchi, V. & A. Andronikof-Sanglade (1998). 'Debating interpretive frameworks for conceptualizing self, identity and culture: The case of French-born youth of second generation immigrant descent, schooled in France'. Paper presented at the *25th International Conference of Cross-Cultural Psychology*, Bellingham, USA, 4–8 August.

Franchi, V. & A. Andronikof-Sanglade (2001). 'Intercultural identity structure of second generation French women of African descent'. In Bekker, S., Dodds, M. & M. Khosa (Eds.) *Shifting African Identities*, Vol. 2, pp. 115–132. Pretoria: Human Sciences Research Council.

Franchi, V. & T.M. Swart (2003). 'From apartheid to affirmative action: The use of 'racial' markers in past, present and future articulations of identity among South African students'. *International Journal of Intercultural Relations*, 27:209–36.

Frankenberg, R. (1993). *White Women, Race Matters: The Social Construction of Whiteness.* Minneapolis: University of Minneapolis Press.

Freud, S. (1912). 'On the universal tendency to debasement in the sphere of love'. *Standard Edition XI*, pp. 179–190. London: Hogarth Press.

Freud, S. (1913). 'Totem and taboo'. *Standard Edition XIII*, pp. 1–161. London: Hogarth Press.

Freud, S. (1914). 'On narcissism: An introduction'. *Standard Edition XIV*, pp. 73–102. London: Hogarth Press.

Freud, S. (1918). 'The taboo of virginity'. *Standard Edition XI*, pp. 193–208. London: Hogarth Press.

Freud S. (1921). 'Group psychology and the analysis of the Ego'. *Standard Edition XVIII*, pp. 65–143. London: Hogarth Press.

Freud, S. (1922). 'Some neurotic mechanisms in jealousy, paranoia and homosexuality'. *Standard Edition XVIII*, pp. 221–232. London: The Hogarth Press.

Freud, S. (1932). 'Femininity'. *Standard Edition XXII*, pp. 112–135. London: Hogarth Press.

Freud, S. (1938). *The Basic Writings of Sigmund Freud.* New York: Modern Library.

Frye, M. (1992). 'Oppression'. In Andersen, M.L. & P. Hill Collins (Eds.) *Race, Class and Gender.* Belmont, California: Wadsworth.

Fuss, D. (1994). 'Interior colonies: Frantz Fanon and the politics of identification'. *Diacritics*, 24(2):20–42.

Garling, T., Kristensen, H., Backenroth-Ohsako, G., Ekehammar, B. & M.G. Wessells (2000). 'Diplomacy and psychology: Psychological contributions to international negotiations, conflict prevention, and world peace'. *International Journal of Psychology*, 35(2):81–86.

Gartner, R., Dawson, M. & M. Crawford (2001). 'Woman killing: Intimate femicide in Ontario, 1974–1994'. In Russel, D. & R. Harmes (Eds.) *Femicide in Global Perspective*, pp. 147–165. New York: Columbia University.

Gates, H.L. Jr & C. West (1996). *The Future of the Race.* New York: Alfred A. Knopf.

Gatrell, N. (1984). 'Combating homophobia in the psychotherapy of lesbians'. *Women and Therapy*, 3:13–29.

Gavey, N. (1996). 'Women's desire and sexual violence discourse'. In Wilkinson, S. (Ed.) *Feminist Social Psychologies. International Perspectives*, pp. 51–65. Buckingham: Open University Press.

Gavey, N. (1997). 'Feminist poststructuralism and discourse analysis'. In Gergen, M.M. & S.N. Davis (Eds.) *Toward a New Psychology of Gender*, pp. 49–60. New York: Routledge.

Gay, G. (1985). 'Implications of the selected models of ethnic identity development for educators'. *Journal of Negro Education*, 54:43–55.

Gay, J. (1985). '"Mummies and babies" and friends and lovers in Lesotho'. *Journal of Homosexuality*, 2(3–4):97–116.

Gergen, K. & M. Gergen (1981). *Social Psychology*. New York: Harcourt Brace Jovanovitch.

Gergen, K. (1973). 'Social psychology as history'. *Journal of Personality and Social Psychology*, 26:309–320.

Gergen, K. (1995). 'Social construction and the transformation of identity politics': www.swarthmore.edu/SocSci/kgergen1/text8.html (accessed 10 August 2001).

Gergen, K. (1996). 'Social psychology as social construction: the emerging vision': www.swarthmore.edu/SocSci/ kgergen1/ (accessed 10 August 2001).

Gergen, K. (2002). 'From identity to relational politics'. In Holzman, L. & J. Morss (Eds.) *Postmodern Psychologies, Social Practice, and Political Life*, pp. 130–150. New York: Routledge.

Gergen, K.J (1985). 'The social constructionist movement in modern psychology'. *American Psychologist*, 40:266–275.

Gevisser, M. (1994). 'A different fight for freedom'. In Gevisser, M. & E. Cameron (Eds.) *Defiant Desire: Gay and Lesbian Lives in South Africa*, pp. 14–73. Johannesburg: Ravan Press.

Giesbrecht, N. & I. Sevcik (2000). 'The process of recovery and rebuilding among abused women in the conservative evangelical subculture'. *Journal of Family Violence*, 15(3):229–248.

Gillespie, C. (1989). *Justifiable Homicide: Battered Women, Self-defense, and the Law*. Colombus: Ohio State University Press.

Gilman, S. (1985). *Difference and Pathology: Stereotypes of Sexuality, Race, and Madness*. New York: Cornell University Press.

Gilroy, P. (1994). *The Black Atlantic: Modernity and Double Consciousness*. Cambridge, Massachusetts: Harvard University Press.

Gilroy, P. (1997). 'Diaspora and the detours of identity'. In Hall, S. & K. Woodward (Eds.) *Identity and Difference*, pp. 276–300. London: Sage.

Gilroy, P. (2000). *Between Camps: Nations, Cultures and the Allure of Race*. Cambridge, Massachusetts: Harvard University Press.

Gobodo-Madikizela, P. (1995). 'Remembering and the politics of identity'. *Psychoanalytic Psychotherapy in South Africa*, 3:57–62.

Goldberg, D.T. (1988). *The Social Formation of Racist Discourse*. Unpublished paper.

Golden, C. (1987). 'Diversity and variability in women's sexual identities'. In The Boston Lesbian Psychologies Collective (Eds.) *Lesbian Psychologies: Explorations and Challenges*, pp. 18–34. Urbana and Chicago: University of Illinois Press.

Gondolf, E. & E. Fisher (1988). *Battered Women as Survivors: An Alternative to Treating Learned Helplessness*. Lexington: DC Heath & Co.

Gordon, L.R., Sharpley-Whiting, T.D. & R.T. White (Eds.) (1996). *Fanon: A Critical Reader*. London: Blackwell.

Gore, J.P., Miller, J.P. & J. Rappaport (1999). 'Conceptual self as normatively oriented: The suitability of past narrative for the study of cultural identity'. *Culture and Psychology*, 5(4):371–398.

Govinden, D.B. (1997). '"Dominion to rule": The abuse of women in Christian homes'. *Journal of Constructive Theology*, 3(2):23–38.

Greene, B. (1994). 'Lesbian women of color: Triple jeopardy'. In Comas-Diaz, L. & B. Greene (Eds.) *Women of Color: Integrating Ethnic and Gender Identities in Psychotherapy*, pp. 389–427. New York: Guildford.

Greer, G. (1999). *The Whole Woman.* London: Doubleday.

Gregg, N. (1993). '"Trying to put first things first": Negotiating subjectivities in a workplace organizing campaign'. In Davis, K. & S. Fisher (Eds.) *Negotiating at the Margins: The Gendered Discourses of Power and Resistance,* pp. 172–204. New Brunswick: Rutgers University Press.

Gross, L. (1995). 'Out of the mainstream: Sexual minorities and the mass media'. In Dines, G. & J.M. Humez (Eds.) *Gender, Race and Class in Media,* pp. 61–69. Thousand Oaks: Sage.

Grosz, E. (1994). *Volatile Bodies: Toward a Corporeal Feminism.* Bloomington: Indiana University Press.

Guillais, J. (1986). *La Chair de l'Autre.* Paris: Orban.

Gurr, T.R. (1970). *Why Men Rebel.* Princeton: Princeton University Press.

Haddon, W. & S. Baker (1981). 'Injury control'. In Clark, D. & C. MacMahon (Eds.) *Preventive and Community Medicine,* pp. 109–140. Boston: Little Brown and Company.

Haffajee, F. (1998). 'Wanted: A woman newspaper editor'. *Tribute,* (March):40–45.

Haj-Yahia, M.M. (2000). 'Wife abuse and battering in the sociocultural context of Arab society'. *Family Process,* 39(2):237–255.

Halford, W.K., Sanders, M.R. & B.C. Behrens (2000). 'Repeating the errors of our parents? Family-of-origin spouse violence and observed conflict'. *Family Process,* 39(2):219–235.

Hall, G.S. (1919). 'Some possible effects of the war on American psychology'. *Psychology Bulletin,* 16:48–9.

Hall, S. (1995). 'The white of their eyes'. In Dines, G. & J.M. Humez (Eds.) *Gender, Race and Class in Media,* pp. 18–22. Thousand Oaks: Sage.

Hall, S. (1996). 'Introduction: Who needs "identity"?' In Hall, S. & P. du Gay (Eds.), *Questions of Cultural Identity,* pp. 1–17. London: Sage.

Hall, S. (1996). 'The question of cultural identity'. In Hall, S., Held, D., Hubert, D. & K. Thompson (Eds.) *Modernity: An Introduction to Modern Societies,* pp. 595–634. Cambridge, Massachusetts: Blackwell.

Hall, S. (1997). 'The rediscovery of "ideology": Return of the repressed in media studies'. In Boyd Barret, O. & C. Newbold (Eds.) *Approaches to Media,* pp. 354–364. London: Arnold.

Hallowell, A.I. (1955). *Culture and Experience.* Philadelphia: University of Pennsylvania Press.

Hamber, B. & T. Mofokeng (Eds.) (2000). *From Rhetoric to Responsibility: Making Reparations to the Survivors of Past Political Violence in South Africa.* Johannesburg: Centre for the Study of Violence and Reconciliation.

Hampton, R.L., Vandergriff-Avery, M. & J. Kim (1999). 'Understanding the origins and incidence of spousal violence in North America'. In Gullotta, T.P. & S.J. McElhaney (Eds.) *Violence in Homes and Communities: Prevention, Intervention, and Treatment,* pp. 39–70. Thousand Oaks: Sage.

Hanmer, J. (1996). 'Women and violence: Commonalities and diversities'. In Fawcett, B., Featherstone, B., Hearn, J. & C. Toft (Eds.) *Violence and Gender Relations: Theories and Interventions,* pp. 7–21. London: Sage.

Hansonn, D. (1991). *We the Invisible Face: A Feminist Analysis of the Conception of 'Street Children' in South Africa.* Cape Town: University of Cape Town Press.

Harré, R. (1989). 'Language games and the texts of identity'. In Shotter, J. & K. Gergen (Eds.) *Texts of Identity,* pp. 20–35. London: Sage.

Harré, R. (1998). *The Singular Self: An Introduction to the Psychology of Personhood.* London: Sage.

Harries, P. (1990). 'Symbols and sexuality: Culture and identity in the early Witwatersrand mines'. *Gender & History*, 11(3):318–336.

Henriques, J., Hollway, W., Urwin, C., Venn, C. & V. Walkerdine (1984). *Changing the Subject*. New York: Methuen.

Herek, G. (1994). 'Assessing heterosexuals' attitudes toward lesbians and gay men'. In Greene, B. & G. Herek (Eds.) *Lesbian and Gay Psychology: Theory, Research and Clinical Applications*, pp. 206–228. Thousand Oaks, California: Sage.

Herman, E. & N. Chomsky (1988). *Manufacturing Consent: The Political Economy of the Mass Media*. New York: Pantheon.

Hill, M. (1987). 'Child-rearing attitudes of black lesbian mothers'. In The Boston Lesbian Psychologies Collective (Eds.) *Lesbian Psychologies: Explorations and Challenges*, pp. 215–226. Urbana and Chicago: University of Illinois Press.

Hoff, L.A. (1990). *Battered Women as Survivors*. London: Routledge.

Holland, J., Ramazanoglu, C. & S. Scott (1990). 'Sex, risk, danger: AIDS education policy and young women's sexuality'. *Women Risk and Aids Project (WRAP)*, Paper 1. London: Tufnell Press.

Holland, J., Ramazanoglu, C., Scott, S., Sharpe, S. & R. Thomson (1991). 'Pressure, resistance, empowerment: Young women and the negotiation of safer sex'. *Women Risk and Aids Project (WRAP)*, Paper 6. London: Tufnell Press.

Hollway, W. (1989). *Subjectivity and Method in Psychology: Gender, Meaning and Science*. London: Sage.

Hollway, W. (1995). 'Feminist discourses and women's heterosexual desire'. In Wilkinson, S. & C. Kitzinger (Eds.) *Feminism and Discourse: Psychological Perspectives*, pp. 86–105. London: Sage.

Hollway, W. (1996). 'Recognition and heterosexual desire'. In Richardson, D. (Ed.) *Theorising Heterosexuality*, pp. 91–108. Milton Keynes: Open University Press.

Holmes, R. & S. Holmes (1994). *Murder in America*. Thousand Oaks: Sage.

Holmes, R. (1994). '"White rapists made coloureds (and homosexuals)": The Winnie Mandela trial and the politics of race and sexuality'. In Gevisser, M. & E. Cameron (Eds.) *Defiant Desire: Gay and Lesbian Lives in South Africa*, pp. 284–294. Johannesburg: Ravan Press.

Holtzworth-Munroe, A. (2000). 'A typology of men who are violent toward their female partners: Making sense of the heterogeneity in husband violence'. *Current Directions in Psychological Science*, 9(4):140–143.

Hook, D. (2002). 'Introduction: A "social psychology" of psychopathology'. In Hook, D. & G. Eagle (Eds.) *Psychopathology and Social Prejudice*, pp. 1–18. Cape Town: University of Cape Town Press.

hooks, b. (1990). *Yearning: Race, Gender and Cultural Politics*. Boston: South End Press.

hooks, b. (1995). *Killing Rage: Ending Racism*. New York: Penguin.

hooks, b. (1995). 'Doing it for Daddy'. In Berger, M., Wallis, B. & S. Watson (Eds.) *Constructing Masculinity*, pp. 98–106. New York: Routledge.

Hoosen, S. & A. Collins (2001). 'Women and AIDS: how discourses of gender and sexuality affect safe sex behaviour'. *Journal of the Islamic Medical Association of South Africa*, 8(3):62.

Hopkins, J. (1969). 'The lesbian personality'. *British Journal of Psychiatry*, 115:1436.

Horne, S. (1999). 'Domestic violence in Russia'. *American Psychologist*, 54(1):55–61.

Hotaling, G.T. & D.B. Sugarman (1986). 'An analysis of risk markers in husband to wife violence: The current state of knowledge'. *Violence and Victims*, 1(3):101–124.

Howitt, D. (1989). *Social Psychology: Conflicts and Continuities – An Introductory Textbook.* Milton Keynes: Open University Press.

Hunt, S.W. (1989). 'Migrant labour and sexually transmitted diseases: AIDS in Africa'. *Journal of Health and Social Behaviour*, 30:353–373.

Hydén, M. (1994). *Woman Battering as Marital Act. The Construction of a Violent Marriage.* Oslo: Scandinavian University Press.

Hydén, M. (1999). 'The world of the fearful: Battered women's narratives of leaving abusive husbands'. *Feminism & Psychology*, 9(4):449–469.

Ickes, W. & S. Duck (Eds.) (2000a). *The Social Psychology of Personal Relationships.* Chichester: John Wiley & Sons.

Ickes, W. & S. Duck (2000b). 'Personal relationships and social psychology'. In Ickes, W. & S. Duck (Eds.) *The Social Psychology of Personal Relationships*, pp. 1–8. Chichester: John Wiley & Sons.

IMF (International Monetary Fund) (2000). *International Statistics.* Bloomberg: IDEA-global.com.

Immelman, A. (1993). 'The assessment of political personality: A psychodiagnostically relevant conceptualisation and methodology'. *International Society for Political Psychology*, 14(4):725–741.

Isaacs, G. & B. McKendrick (1992). *Male Homosexuality in South Africa: Identity Formation, Culture and Crisis.* Cape Town: Oxford University Press.

Jackson, S. (1996). 'Heterosexuality and feminist theory'. In Richardson, D. (Ed.) *Theorising Heterosexuality*, pp. 21–38. Milton Keynes: Open University Press.

Jackson, S. (2001). 'Happily never after: Young women's stories of abuse in heterosexual love relationships'. *Feminism & Psychology*, 9(4):449–469.

Jacobs, M. (1975). *Conditioned Aversion Applied to the Treatment of Homosexuality and Compulsive Ruminations.* Unpublished Master's thesis, University of the Witwatersrand, Johannesburg.

Jacobs, T. & F. Suleman (1999). 'Breaking the silence: A profile of domestic violence in women attending a community health centre.' Health Systems Trust: www.hst.org.za/research/violence/ (accessed 5 October, 2000).

Jamieson, L. (1998). *Intimacy: Personal Relationships in Modern Societies.* Cambridge: Polity Press.

Jansen, J. (Ed.) (1991). *Knowledge and Power in South Africa: Critical Perspectives across the Disciplines.* Johannesburg: Skotaville.

Jansen, P., Richter, L.M., Griesel, R.D. & J. Joubert (1990). 'Glue sniffing: A description of social, psychological and neuropsychological factors in a group of South African street children'. *South African Journal of Psychology*, 20(3):150–158.

Jeffreys, S. (1985). *The Spinster and her Enemies: Feminism and Sexuality 1880–1930.* Oxford: Pandora.

Jeffreys, S. (1990). *Anticlimax: A Feminist Perspective on the Sexual Revolution.* London: The Women's Press.

Jeffreys, S. (1993). *The Lesbian Heresy: A Feminist Perspective on the Lesbian Sexual Revolution.* Australia: Spinifex Press.

Jennings, J. & C. Murphy (2000). 'Male–male dimensions of male–female battering: a new look at domestic violence'. *Psychology of Men and Masculinity*, 1(1):21–29.

Jensen, V. (1996). *Why Women Kill: Homicide and Gender Equality.* London: Lynne Rienner.

Jewkes, R. & N. Abrahams (2000). *Violence against Women in South Africa: Rape and Sexual Coercion.* Pretoria: Crime Prevention Research Resources Centre, CSIR.

Jewkes, R., Penn-Kekana, L., Levin, J., Ratsaka, M. & M. Schrieber (1999). 'He Must Give Me Money, He Mustn't Beat Me'. Violence against Women in Three South African Provinces. Tygerberg: CERSA (Women's Health) Medical Research Council.

Johns, L. (1995). 'Racial vilification and ICERD in Australia'. Murdoch University Electronic Journal of Law, 2(1): www.murdoch.edu.au/elaw/indices/title/johns21_abstract.html (accessed 17 April 2003).

Johnson, A.D. (1994). Journey Magazine, Spring. New York: Rochester.

Johnson, H. (1996). Dangerous Domains: Violence Against Women in Canada. Toronto: Nelson Canada.

Jones, J.M. (1986). Prejudice and Racism. London: Addison-Wesley.

Jones, J.M. (1997). Prejudice and Racism, 2nd edition. New York: McGraw-Hill.

Julien, I. (Director) (1996). Frantz Fanon: Black Skin, White Masks. Arts Council of England, BFI/K Films, UK.

Kaarbo, J. & M.G. Hermann (1998). 'Leadership styles of prime ministers: How individual differences affect the foreign policymaking process'. Leadership Quarterly, 9(3):243–263.

Kane, T.A. & P.K. Staiger (2000). 'Male domestic violence'. Journal of Interpersonal Violence, 15(1):16–29.

Katz, J. (1976). Gay American History: Lesbians and Gay Men in the USA. New York: Crowell.

Katz, P.A. & D.A. Taylor (Eds.) (1988). Eliminating Racism: Profiles in Controversy. New York: Plenum Press.

Katz. J. (1983). Gay/Lesbian Almanac. New York, Harper & Row.

Kendall (1998). '"When a woman loves a woman" in Lesotho: Love, sex and the Western construction of homophobia'. In Murray, S. & W. Roscoe (Eds.) Boy-Wives and Female Husbands, pp. 223–241. New York: St. Martins Press.

Kendall, K. (1999). 'Women in Lesotho and the (Western) construction of homophobia'. In Blackwood, E. & S. Wieringa (Eds.) Female Desires: Same Sex Relations and Transgendere Practices Across Cultures, pp. 157–178. New York: Columbia University Press.

Keseredy, W. & M. Schwartz (1996). Contemporary Criminology. New York: Wadsworth.

Khmelkov, V.T. & M.T. Hallinan (1999). 'Organizational effects on race relations in schools'. Journal of Social Issues, 55(4):627–645.

Kimmel, M. (1994). 'The contemporary "crisis" of masculinity in historical perspective'. In Brod, E. (Ed.) The Making of Masculinities: The New Men's Studies, pp. 120–138. Boston: Allen & Unwin.

Kingdom, M.A. (1979). 'Lesbians'. Counseling Psychologist, 8(1):44–45.

Kirkwood, C. (1993). Leaving Abusive Partners. London: Sage.

Kitzinger, C. (1987). The Social Construction of Lesbianism. London: Sage.

Kitzinger, C. & S. Wilkinson (1993). 'Theorizing heterosexuality'. In Wilkinson, S. & C. Kitzinger (Eds.) Heterosexuality: A Feminism and Psychology Reader, pp. 1–32. London: Sage.

Klaaren J. & J. Ramji (2001). 'Inside illegality: Migration policing in South Africa after apartheid'. Africa Today, 48(3):35–47.

Klein, M. (1946). 'Notes on some schizoid mechanisms'. In Envy and Gratitude and Other Works 1946–1963. London: Hogarth Press.

Knight, S. (1989). Towards an Understanding of an Invisible Minority. Unpublished Master's thesis, University of the Witwatersrand, Johannesburg.

Koss, M. (1994). No Safe Haven: Male Violence Against Women at Home, at Work, and in the Community. Washington DC: American Psychological Association.

Kotze, C.G. (1974). 'n Diepteigologiese Ondersoek na die Verskynsel van Homoseksuele Gedrag. Unpublished doctoral dissertation, University of Pretoria.

Kozu, J. (1999). 'Domestic violence in Japan'. American Psychologist, 54(1):50–54.

Krige, E.J. (1974). 'Women-marriage with special reference to the Lovedu – its significance for the definition of marriage'. Africa, 44(11):11.

Krige, E.J., & J.D. Krige (1943). The Realm of a Rain Queen. London: Oxford University Press.

Kritzinger, A. & F. van Aswegen (1994). 'Problems associated with stigmatization: The case of lesbianism'. South African Sociological Review, 5(1):83–98.

Krog, A. (1998). Country of My Skull. Johannesburg: Random House.

Kruger, J., Butchart, A., Seedat, M. & A. Gilchrist (1998). 'A public health approach to violence in South Africa'. In Bornman, E., van Eeden, R. & M. Wentzel (Eds.) Violence in South Africa: A Variety of Perspectives, pp. 399–424. Pretoria: HSRC.

Kuper, L. (1974). Race, Class and Power: Ideology and Revolutionary Change in Plural Societies. London: Duckworth.

Lancaster, R.N. (1987). 'Subject honor and object shame: The construction of male homosexuality and stigma in Nicaragua'. Ethnology, 27:111–125.

Lancaster, R.N. (1997). 'Guto's performance: Notes on the transvestism of everyday life'. In Lancaster, R.N. & M. di Leornado (Eds.) The Gender Sexuality Reader, pp. 558–570. New York: Routledge.

LaTorre, R. & K. Wendenburg (1983). 'Psychological characteristics of bisexual, heterosexual and homosexual women'. Journal of Homosexuality, 9(1):87–97.

Laville, R. (2000). 'An anthropology of race'. Rhodes Journalism Review, 19:9.

Legassick, M. (1980). 'The frontier tradition in South African historiography'. In Marks, S. & A. Atmore (Eds.) Economy and Society in Pre-industrial South Africa, pp. 44–79. London: Longman.

Lelyveld, J. (1987). Move Your Shadow: South Africa, Black and White. London: Abacus.

Lempert, L. B. (1996). 'Women's strategies for survival: Developing agency in abusive relationships'. Journal of Family Violence, 11(3):269–289.

Lesch, E. (2000). Female Adolescent Sexuality in a Coloured Community. Unpublished doctoral dissertation, University of Stellenbosch.

Letlaka-Rennert, K. (1990). 'Soweto street children: Implications of family disintegration for South African psychologists'. In Nicholas, L.J. & S. Cooper (Eds.) Psychology and Apartheid, pp. 100–114. Cape Town: Vision Publications.

Levett, A. (1988). Psychological Trauma: Discourses of Childhood Sexual Abuse. Unpublished doctoral thesis. University of Cape Town.

Lewis, G. (1987). Between the Wire and the Wall: A History of South African 'Coloured' Politics. Cape Town: David Phillip.

Lewis, J. & F. Loots (1994). '"Moffies en manvroue": Gay and lesbian life histories in contemporary Cape Town'. In Gevisser, M. & E. Cameron (Eds.) Defiant Desire: Gay and Lesbian Lives in South Africa, pp. 140–157. Johannesburg: Ravan Press.

Liddicoat, R. (1956). Homosexuality: Results of a Survey Related to Various Theories. Unpublished doctoral dissertation, University of the Witwatersrand, Johannesburg.

Liebenberg, I. (1993). Transition from Authoritarian Rule to Democracy in South Africa: The Role of Political Leadership and Some Strategies to Attain Democracy. Unpublished Master's thesis, University of the Western Cape, Cape Town.

Lockhat, R. & A. van Niekerk (2000). 'South African children and mental health: A history of adversity, violence and trauma'. Ethnicity and Health, 5(3/4):291–302.

Loedolff, J.J. (1951). *Homosexualiteit: 'n Sosiologiese Studie*. Unpublished Master's thesis, University of Pretoria.

Lorde, A. (1984). *Sister Outsider*. Trumansberg, New York: The Crossing Press.

Lorde, A. (1988). *A Burst of Light*. London: Sheba Feminist Publishers.

Louw-Potgieter, J. (1988). 'The authoritarian personality: An inadequate explanation for inter-group conflict in South Africa'. *Journal of Social Psychology*, 128(1):75–87.

Louw-Potgieter, J., Kamfer, L. & R.G. Boy (1991). 'Stereotype reduction workshop'. *South African Journal of Psychology*, 21(4):219–224.

LoveLife (2000). *Hot Prospects, Cold Facts*. Cape Town: Colorpress.

Lowe, K.B. & K. Galen Kroeck (1996). 'Effective correlates of transformational and transac-tional leadership: A meta-analytic review of the MLQ literature'. *Leadership Quarterly*, 7(3):385–425.

Lui, M. (1999). 'Enduring violence and staying in marriage: Stories of battered women in rural China'. *Violence against Women*, 5(12):1469–1492.

MacDonald, A. & R. Games (1974). 'Some characteristics of those who hold positive and negative attitudes toward homosexuals'. *Journal of Homosexuality*, 2(1):3–10.

MacDonald, A. (1976). 'Homophobia: Its roots and meanings'. *Homosexual Counselling Journal*, 3:23–33.

Macdonell, D, (1987). *Theories of Discourse*. Worcester: Basil Blackwell.

Macey, D. (2000a). *Frantz Fanon: A Life*. London: Granta.

Macey, D. (2000b). *The Penguin Dictionary of Critical Theory*. London: Penguin Books.

MacKinnon, C. (1989). *Toward a Feminist Theory of the State*. Harvard: Harvard University Press.

Mager, A. (1996). 'Sexuality, fertility and male power'. *Agenda*, 28:12–24.

Malepa, M. (1990). 'The effects of violence on the development of young children in Soweto'. *Centre for Intergroup Studies Occasional Papers*, No.13. Cape Town: Centre for Inter-group Studies.

Mama, A. (1995). *Beyond the Masks. Race, Gender and Subjectivity*. London: Routledge.

Mama, A. (1996). *The Hidden Struggle. Statutory and Voluntary Sector Responses to Violence Against Black Women in the Home*. London: Whiting & Birch.

Mandaza, I. (2000). 'White heroes & bêtes noires'. *Rhodes Journalism Review*, 19:23.

Mandaza, I. (2001). 'Southern African identity: A critical assessment'. In Bekker, S., Dodds, M. & M. Khosa (Eds.) *Shifting African Identities*, Vol. 2, pp. 133–140. Pretoria: HSRC.

Mandela, W. (1985). *Part of My Soul*. London: Penguin.

Manganyi, N.C. (1973). *Being-Black-in-the-World*. Johannesburg: Skotaville.

Manganyi, N.C. (1981). *Looking through the Keyhole*. Johannesburg: Ravan Press.

Mannoni, O. (1962). *Prospero and Caliban: The Psychology of Colonisation*. New York: Praeger.

Marais, H. (1998). *South Africa: Limits to Change – The Political Economy of Transition*. London: Zed Books.

Marcia, J.E. (1966). 'Development and validation of ego identity status'. *Journal of Personality and Social Psychology*, 3:551–558.

Marcia, J.E. (1980). 'Identity in adolescence'. In Adelson, J. (Ed.) *Handbook of Adolescent Psychology*, pp. 159–187. New York: Wiley.

Markus, H. & D. Oyserman (1989). 'Gender and thought: The role of the self-concept'. In Crawford, M. & M. Hamilton (Eds.) *Gender and Thought*, pp. 100–127. New York: Springer-Verlag.

Markus, H. & E. Wurf (1987). 'The dynamic self-concept: A social psychological perspective'. *Annual Review of Psychology*, 38:299–337.

Markus, H. (1977). 'Self-schemas and processing information about the self'. *Journal of Personality and Social Psychology*, 35:63–78.

Markus, H., & A.R. Herzog (1991). 'The role of the self-concept in ageing'. In K.W. Schaie (Ed.) *Annual Review of Gerontology and Geriatrics*, Vol. 11. New York: Springer-Verlag.

Markus, H., & S. Kitayama (1991). 'Culture and the self: Implications for cognition, emotion and motivation'. *Psychological Review*, 98:224–253.

Markus, H., Cross, S., & E. Wurf (1990). 'The role of the self system in competence'. In Sternberg, R.J. & J. Kolligian, Jr (Eds.) *Competence Considered*, pp. 205–25. New Haven, Connecticut: Yale University Press.

Marquard, L. (1957). *South Africa's Colonial Policy*. Johannesburg: South African Institute of Race Relations.

Martin, D. & M. Wilson (1988). *Homicide*. New York: Aldine de Gruyter.

Mathiti, V. (2000). *The Quality of Life of Street Children in Pretoria: An Exploratory Study*. Unpublished Master's dissertation, University of Pretoria.

Matshazi, N.S. (1996). *Magona's Autobiography: A Recognition of the Interconnectedness of Race, Class, and Gender in the Lives of Black South African Women*. Unpublished Master's thesis, University of the Witswatersrand, Johannesburg.

May, J., Woolard, I. & S. Klasen (2000). 'The nature and measure of poverty and inequality'. In J. May (Ed.) *Poverty and Inequality in South Africa: Meeting the Challenge*, pp. 19–50. Cape Town: David Phillip.

Mbeki, T. (1998). 'I am an African'. In *Africa: The Time has Come. Selected Speeches*. Cape Town: Mafube Publishing.

Mbembe, A. (2002). 'African Modes of Self-Writing'. *Public Culture*, 14(1):239–273.

McCloskey, L.A. (1996). 'Socioeconomic and coercive power within the family'. *Gender & Society*, 10(4):449–463.

McCulloch, J. (1983). *Black Soul White Artifact: Fanon's Clinical Psychology and Social Theory*. Cambridge: Cambridge University Press.

McDougall, W. (1908). *An Introduction to Social Psychology*. London: Methuen.

McFadden, P. (1992). 'Sex, sexuality and the problems of AIDS in Africa'. In Meena, R. (Ed.) *Gender in Southern Africa: Conceptual and Theoretical Issues*, pp. 157–195. Harare: SAPES.

McGrath, J.E. (1970). *Social Psychology: A Brief Introduction*. London: Holt, Rinehart, Winston.

McWhirter, P.T. (1999). 'La violencia privada. Domestic violence in Chile'. *American Psychologist*, 54(1):37–40.

Meintjies, S. (1993). 'Dilemmas of difference'. *Agenda*, 19:37–44.

Memmi, A. (1982). *Le Racisme*. Brassière Saint-Amand: Gallimard.

Mercader, P., Houel, A. & H. Sobota (2003). *Crime Passionnel, Crime Ordinaire*. Paris: Presses Universitaires de France. ·

Meyer, W.F., Moore, C. & H.G. Viljoen (1997). *Personology: From Individual to Ecosystem*. Johannesburg: Heinemann.

Mhlambo, M.G. (1993). *Violence as an Impediment in the Actualisation of the Psychic Life of the Child in Education: A Psycho-pedagogic Perspective*. Unpublished Master's thesis. University of Zululand, Durban.

Mhone, G., Humber, J.L., Gault, R.T., & D. Mokhobo (1998). 'Affirmative action – Is South Africa heading down a route which many African Americans are re-thinking?' *CDE Debate*, No. 10.

Miles, L. (1992). 'Women, AIDS, power and heterosexual negotiation: A discourse analysis'. *Agenda*, 15:14–27.

Miles, R. (1989). *Racism*. London: Routledge.

Miles-Doan, R. (1998). 'Violence between spouses and intimates: Does neighbourhood context matter?' *Social Forces*, 77(2):623–645.

Milgram, S. (1963). 'Behavioural study of obedience'. *Journal of Abnormal and Social Psychology*, 67:371–378.

Milgram, S. (1974). *Obedience to Authority*. New York: Harper & Row.

Mills, C.W. (1978). *The Sociological Imagination*. Harmondsworth: Penguin.

Mills, S.W. (2001). 'Intimate femicide and abused women who kill'. In Russel, D. & R. Harmes (Eds.) *Femicide in Global Perspective*, pp. 71–87. New York. Columbia University.

MMP (Media Monitoring Project) (1999). *The News in Black and White: An Investigation into Racial Stereotyping in the Media*. Parktown: SAHRC.

Mohan, D. (1996). 'Control of injuries in large cities: Dealing with plurality and complexity'. *Karolinska Institute Summary of International Congress, Safe Communities: The Application to Large Urban Environments*, Dallas, Texas, 14–26 November.

Mohanty, C.T. (1988). 'Under Western eyes: Feminist scholarship and colonial discourses'. *Feminist Review*, 30:61–89.

Mokoe, A. (2000). 'Beating the black drum'. *Rhodes Journalism Review*, 19:15.

Moloi, G. (1987). *My Life*, Vol. 1. Johannesburg: Ravan Press.

Mona, V. (1999). 'Racism in the fourth estate'. *Tribute*, (January):57–59.

Moore-Gilbert, B. (1997). *Postcolonial Theory: Contexts, Practices, Politics*. London & New York: Verso.

Moosa, F., Moonsamy, G. & P. Fridjohn (1997). 'Identification patterns among black students at a predominantly white university'. *South African Journal of Psychology*, 27(4): 256–260.

Moran, C.T. (1994). *Coping Strategies and Personality Traits in Street Children: An Exploratory Study*. Unpublished Master's dissertation, University of Natal, Durban.

Morgan, D. & S. Scott (1993). 'Afterward: Constructing a research agenda'. In Scott, S. & D. Morgan (Eds.) *Body Matters*, pp. 135–139. London: The Falmer Press.

Morrell, R. (Ed.) (2001). *Changing Men in Southern Africa*. Pietermaritzburg: University of Natal Press.

Moscovici, S. (1972). 'Society and theory in social psychology'. In Israel, J. & H. Tajfel (Eds.) *The Context of Social Psychology: Critical Assessment*, pp. 17–68. London: Academic Press.

Moskop, W.W. (1996). 'Prudence as a paradigm for political leaders'. *International Society for Political Psychology*, 17(4):619–642.

Motsei, M. (1993). *Detection of Woman Battering in Health Care Settings: The Case of Alexandra Health Clinic*. Johannesburg: Centre for Health Policy.

Motsemme, N. (1999). *Voices of Loss and Voices of Nation: The Truth and Reconciliation Commission and Women's Testimonies*. Unpublished Master's thesis, University of Sussex, Falmer.

Motsemme, N. (2002). 'Gendered experiences of Blackness in post apartheid South Africa'. *Social Identities*, 8(4):647–673.

Motz, A. (2001). *The Psychology of Female Violence*. Philadelphia: Taylor and Francis.

Mouton, J. (1996). *Understanding Social Research*. Pretoria. Van Schaik.

Mthembu, P. (1998). 'A positive view'. *Agenda*, 39:26–29.

Muckler, B. & G. Phelan (1979). 'Lesbian and traditional mothers' responses to adult response to child behaviour and self-concept'. *Psychological Reports*, 44(3):880–882.

Murray, C.J.L. & A.D. Lopez (Eds.) (1996). *The Global Burden of Disease*. Boston: Harvard University Press.

Murray, K. (1989). 'The construction of identity in the narratives of romance and comedy'. In Shotter, J. & K. Gergen (Eds.) *Texts of Identity*, pp. 176–205. London: Sage.

Murray, S. (1998). 'Sexual politics in contemporary Southern Africa'. In Murray, S. & W. Roscoe (Eds.) *Boy-Wives and Female Husbands*, pp. 243–254. New York: St. Martin's Press.

Murray, S. & W. Roscoe (Eds.) (1998). *Boy-Wives and Female Husbands*. New York: St Martin's Press.

Mutongi, K. (2000). 'Dear Dolly's advice: Representations of youth, courtship, and sexualities in Africa, 1960–1980'. *International Journal of African Historical Studies*, 33(1):1–23.

Nast, H.J. & S. Pile (Eds.) (1998). *Places Through the Body*. London: Routledge.

Ndebele, N. (1991). *Rediscovery of the Ordinary: Essays on South African Literature and Culture*. Johannesburg: Cosaw.

Neil, W. (1999). *Understanding Domestic Homicide*. Boston: North-Eastern University Press.

Neisser, U. (1988). 'Five kinds of self-knowledge'. *Philosophical Psychology*, 1(1):35–59.

Nell, V. & F. van Staden (1988). 'An affirmative action prospectus for South African universities'. *South African Journal of Psychology*, 84:19–22.

Nice, D.C. (1998). 'The warrior model of leadership: Classic perspectives and contemporary relevance'. *Leadership Quarterly*, 9(3):321–332.

Nicholas, L.J. & S. Cooper (Eds.) (1990). *Psychology and Apartheid*. Johannesburg: Vision Publications.

Nix, J. (1998). 'To protect and abuse: An exploratory study discussing intimate partners of police as victims of domestic abuse'. *Centre for the Study of Violence and Reconciliation, Seminar*, No. 4: www.wits.ac.za/csvr/papers/papnix.htm (2 August 2001).

Nodoba, G. (2002). 'Many languages, different cultures. The effects of linguicism in a changing society'. In Duncan, N., Gqola, P., Hofmeyer, M. *et al.* (Eds.) *Discourses on Difference, Discourses on Oppression*, pp. 331–358. Plumstead: CASAS Book Series.

Norval, A.J. (1996). *Deconstructing Apartheid Discourse*. London: Verso.

NPPHCN (National Progressive Primary Health Care Network) (1995). *Youth Speak out for a Healthy Future: A Study on Youth Sexuality*. Braamfontein: NPPHCN/UNICEF.

Ntshangase D.K. (1993). *The Social History of Iscamtho*. Unpublished Master's thesis, University of the Witwatersrand, Johannesburg.

Nurius, P.S., Furrey, J. & L. Berliner. (1992). 'Coping capacity among women with abusive partners'. *Violence and Victims*, 7(3):229–243.

Nuttall, S. (2000). 'Telling "free" stories? Memory and democracy in South African autobiography since 1994'. In Nuttall, S. & C. Coetzee (Eds.) *Negotiating the Past: The Making of Memory in South Africa*, pp. 75–88. Cape Town: Oxford University Press.

Nuttall, S. (2001). 'Subjectivities of Whiteness'. *African Studies Review*, 24(2):115–40.

O'Meara, D. (1983). *Volkskapitalisme*. Braamfontein: Ravan Press.

O'Neill, D. (1998). 'A post-structuralist review of the theoretical literature surrounding wife abuse'. *Violence against Women*, 4(4):457–490.

Oetting, E.R., & F. Beauvais (1991). 'Orthogonal cultural identification theory: The cultural identification of minority adolescents'. *Journal of the Addictions*, 25(5A & 6A): 655–85.

Olivier, J. (1991). 'The South African Police: Managers of conflict or party to the conflict'. *Centre for the Study of Violence and Reconciliation Seminar*, No. 1, Johannesburg.

Oyewumi, O. (1997). *The Invention of Woman: Making African Sense of Western Gender Discourses*. Minneapolis: University of Minnesota Press.

Oyserman, D. (1993). 'The lens of personhood: Viewing self and others in a multicultural society'. *Journal of Personality and Social Psychology*, 65(5):993–1009.

Page, C. (1996). *Showing My Color: Impolite Essays on Race and Identity*. New York: Harper-Collins.

Parker, I. (1989). *The Crisis in Modern Social Psychology – and How to End It*. London: Routledge.

Parker, I. (1999). 'Introduction: varieties of discourse and analysis'. In Parker, I. & The Bolton Discourse Network (Eds.) *Critical Textwork. An Introduction to Varieties of Discourse and Analysis*, pp. 1–12. Buckingham: Open University Press.

Parmenter, T.R. (1994). 'Quality of life as a concept and measurable entity'. *Social Indicators Research*, 33:9–46.

Passerini, L. (1992). *Memory and Totalitarianism*. Oxford: Oxford University Press.

Peden, M. & J. van der Spuy. (1998). 'The cost of treating firearm victims'. *Trauma Review*, 6(2):4–5.

Perilla, J.L., Bakeman, R. & F.H. Norris (1994). 'Culture and domestic violence: The ecology of abused Latinas'. *Violence and Victims*, 9(4):325–339.

Perkel, A., Strebel, A. & G. Joubert (1991). 'The Psychology of AIDS Transmission: Issues for Intervention'. *South African Journal of Psychology*, 21(3):148–152.

Petrik, N.D., Petrik Olson, R.E. & L.S. Subotnik (1994). 'Powerlessness and the need to control. The male abuser's dilemma'. *Journal of Interpersonal Violence*, 9(2):278–285.

Pettigrew, T. (1958). 'Personality and sociocultural factors in intergroup attitudes: A cross-national comparison'. *Journal of Conflict Resolution*, 2:29–42.

Phinney, J.S. (1990). 'Ethnic identity in adolescents and adults: Review of research'. *Psychological Bulletin*, 108:499–514.

Pickel, B. (1996). *Ethnicity and Ethnic Awareness in the Former Coloured Areas*. Unpublished research report. Cape Town: Human Sciences Research Council.

Pityana, S.M. (1992). 'The role and place of research and intellectual discourse in the reproduction of social relations of racial domination in South Africa'. *Development South Africa*, 9:481–486.

Plummer, K. (1981). 'Homosexual categories: Some research problems in the labelling perspective of homosexuality'. In Plummer, K. (Ed.)*The Making of the Modern Homosexual*, pp. 53–75. London: Hutchinson.

Posel, D. & G. Simpson (Eds.) (2002). *Commissioning the Past: Understanding South Africa's Truth and Reconciliation Commission*. Johannesburg: Witwatersrand University Press.

Posel, D. (2001). 'Race as common sense'. *African Studies Review*, 44(2):87–114.

Potgieter, C. (1997). 'From apartheid to Mandela's constitution: Black South African lesbians in the nineties'. In Greene, B. (Ed.) *Ethnic and Cultural Diversity Among Lesbians and Gay Men*, pp. 88–116. Thousand Oaks, California: Sage.

Potgieter, C. (2003). 'Black South African lesbians: Discourses on motherhood and women's roles'. *Journal of Lesbian Studies*, in press.

Potgieter, C. & L. Fredman (1997). 'Childhood sexuality'. In de la Rey, C., Duncan, N., Shefer, T. & A. Van Niekerk (Eds.) *Contemporary Issues in Human Development: A South African Focus*, pp. 99–109. Halfway House: International Thomson Publishing.

Prinsloo, S.W. (1973). *'n Vergelykende Persoonlikeheidstudie Tussen 'n Groep Passiewe Homoseksuele en 'n Kontrole Groep*. Unpublished Master's thesis, University of Pretoria.

Profitt, N.J. (2000). *Women Survivors, Psychological Trauma, and the Politics of Resistance*. New York: The Haworth Press.

Ramphele, M. (1995a). *Across Boundaries: The Journey of a South African Leader*. New York: Feminist Press.

Ramphele, M. (1995b). *A Life*. Cape Town: David Phillip.

Ramphele, M. (2000). 'Teach me how to be a man: An exploration of the definition of masculinity'. In Das, V., Kleinman, A., Ramphele, M. & P. Reynolds (Eds.) *Violence and Subjectivity*, pp. 102–119. Berkeley: University of California Press.

Rapholo, J.C. (1996). *The Self-concept of Street Children Compared to that of Placement Children*. Unpuplished Master's dissertation, University of Natal, Durban.

Ratele, K. & T. Shefer (2002). 'Stigma in the social construction of sexually transmitted diseases'. In Hook, D. & G. Eagle (Eds.) *Psychopathology and Social Prejudice*. Cape Town: UCT Press.

Ratele, K. (1998a). 'The end of the black man'. *Agenda*, 37:60–64.

Ratele, K. (1998b). 'Relating to whiteness: Writing about the black man'. *Psychology Bulletin*, 8(2):35–40.

Ratele, K. (2002). 'Interpersonal relationships around race'. In Duncan, N., Gqola, P.M., Hofmeyer, M., Shefer, T., Malunga, F. & M. Mashige (Eds.) *Discourses on Difference, Discourses on Oppression*, pp. 371–406. Cape Town: Centre for Advanced Studies of African Society.

Read, A. (Ed.) (1996). *The Fact of Blackness: Frantz Fanon and Visual Representation*. Seattle: Bay Press.

Redlinghuys, J.L. (1978). *'n Psignodinamiese Ondersoek na die Verskynsel van Lesbinisme Binne 'n Gesinstruktuur*. Unpublished Master's thesis, University of Pretoria.

Rees, H. (1998). 'The search for female-controlled methods of HIV prevention'. *Agenda*, 39:44–49.

Renshon, S.A. (1992). 'The psychology of good judgment: A preliminary model with some application to the Gulf War'. *Political Psychology*, 13(3):477–495.

Retief, G. (1994). 'Keeping Sodom out of the lager'. In Gevisser, M. & E. Cameron (Eds.) *Defiant Desire: Gay and Lesbian Lives in South Africa*, pp. 99–111. Braamfontein: Ravan.

Reynolds, P. (1989). *Childhood in Crossroads*. Cape Town: David Phillip.

Rhodes Journalism Review (2000). *Racism in the Media*. Grahamstown: Rhodes University.

Rich, A. (1979). *On Lies, Secrets, and Silences: Selected Prose 1966–1978*. New York: W.W. Norton.

Rich, A. (1980). 'Compulsory heterosexuality and lesbian existence'. *Signs*, 5(4):631–660.

Richards, C.C. (1996). 'Female condom acceptability study'. *Women's Health News*, 18:23.

Richardson, D. (1996). 'Heterosexuality and social theory'. In Richardson, D. (Ed.) *Theorising Heterosexuality*, pp. 1–20. Milton Keynes: Open University Press.

Richie, B.E. & V. Kanuha (1997). 'Battered women of color in public health care systems'. In Zinn, M.B., Hondagneu-Sotelo, P. & M. Messner (Eds.) *Through the Prism of Difference: Readings on Sex and Gender*, pp. 121–129. Boston: Allyn and Bacon.

Richter, L. (1994). 'Economic stress and its influence on the family and caretaking patterns'. In Dawes, A. & D. Donald (Eds.) *Childhood and Adversity*, pp. 28–50. Cape Town: David Phillip.

Richter, L. (1996). *A Survey of Reproductive Health Issues among Urban Black Youth in South Africa*. Unpublished final grant report for the Society for Family Health.

Richter, L.M. (1988). *Street Children. The Nature and Scope of the Problem in Southern Africa*. Report no. 88–02. Pretoria: Institute for Behavioural Sciences, University of South Africa.

Rose, N. (1989). 'Individualizing psychology'. In Shootter, J. & K. Gergen (Eds.) *Texts of Identity*, pp. 176–205. London: Sage.

Rose, N. (1996). 'Identity, genealogy, history'. In Hall, S. & P. du Gay (Eds.) *Questions of Cultural Identity*, pp. 1–17. London: Sage.

Rosenberg, S. (1990). 'Une stratégie de recherche pour l'analyse structurale et fonctionnelle de l'identité de la personne' [A research strategy for the structural and functional analysis of personal identity]. *Psychologie Française*, 35(1):51–57.

Rosenthal, D. (1987). 'Ethnic identity development in adolescents'. In Phinney, I.S. & M.S. Rotherman (Eds.) *Children's Ethnic Socialisation, Pluralism and Development*, pp.156–179. Newbury Park, California: Sage.

Ross, E.A. (1908). *Social Psychology: An Outline and a Source Book*. New York: Macmillan.

Ross, F. (1996). 'Existing in secret places: Women's testimony in the first five weeks of public hearings of the Truth and Reconciliation Commission'. Paper presented at the *Faultiness Conference*, Cape Town, 25–26 July.

Ross, M.H. (1995). 'Psychocultural interpretation theory and peacemaking ethnic conflicts'. *International Society for Political Psychology*, 16(3):523–543.

RSA (Republic of South Africa) (1957). *Sexual Offences Act*, No. 23 of 1957. Pretoria: Government Printer.

RSA (Republic of South Africa) (1969). *Immorality Amendment*, No. 57 of 1969. Pretoria: Government Printer.

RSA (Republic of South Africa) (1986). *Hansard Debates of the House of Assembly*. (A) 2q col 28, (A) 7q col 664, 20 March. Cape Town: The Government Printers.

RSA (Republic of South Africa) (1987). *Hansard Debates of the House of Assembly*. (A) 3q col 162, 19 February. Cape Town: The Government Printers.

Rusbult, C.E. (1980). 'Commitment and satisfaction in romantic associations: A test of the investment model'. *Journal of Experimental and Social Psychology*, 16:172–186.

Russel, D. & R. Harmes (Eds.) (2001). *Femicide in Global Perspective*. New York: Columbia University.

SABC (South African Broadcasting Corporation) (1993). *Chris Hani: 1942–1993* (video recording). Johannesburg: SABC.

Saghir, M.T. & E. Robins (1971). 'Male and female homosexuality: Natural history'. *Comparative Psychiatry*, 12:503–510.

Samuels, A. (1996). 'The politics of transformation/the transformation of politics'. *International Journal of Psychotherapy*, 1(1):79–89.

Sang, B. (1989). 'New directions in lesbian research, theory and education'. *Journal of Counseling and Development*, 68:92–96.

Sansome. L. (1997). 'The new Blacks from Bahia: Local and global in Afro-Bahia'. *Social Identities*, 3(4):457–93.

Sasaki, B. (1998). 'Reading silence in Joy Kogawa's *Obsan*'. In Fisher, J. & E. Silber (Eds.) *Analysing a Different Voice*, pp. 117–140. Oxford: Rowan and Littlefield.

Saul, J.S. (1986). 'Introduction: The revolutionary prospect'. In Saul, J.S. & S. Gelb (Eds.) *The Crisis in South Africa*, pp. 9–52. New York: Monthly Review Press.

Saunders, D.G. (1990). 'Wife abuse, husband abuse, or mutual combat? A feminist perspective on the empirical findings'. In Yllö, K. & M. Bograd (Eds.) *Feminist Perspectives on Wife Abuse*, pp. 90–113. Newbury Park: Sage.

Scharf, W., Powell, M. & E. Thomas (1986). 'Strollers: Street children of Cape Town'. In Burman, S. & P. Reynolds (Eds.) *Growing up in a Divided Society: The Context of Childhood in South Africa*. Johannesburg: Ravan Press.

Schiebinger, L. (Ed.) (2000). *Feminism and the Body*. Oxford: Oxford University Press.

Schneider, J.W. (1985). 'Social problem theory: The constructionist's view'. *Annual Review of Sociology*, 11:209–229.

Schoepf, B.G. (1988). 'Women, AIDS and economic crisis in Central Africa'. *Canadian Journal of African Studies*, 22(3):625–644.

Schornstein, S.L. (1997). *Domestic Violence and Health Care: What Every Professional Needs to Know*. Thousand Oaks: Sage.

Schulman, N. (1995). 'Laughing across the color barrier: In living color'. In Dines, G. & J.M. Humez (Eds.) *Gender, Race and Class in Media*, pp. 438–444. Thousand Oaks: Sage.

Schulze, S (1991). 'Homoseksuele identiteitsvorming by 'n groep Suid-Afrikaanse mans'. *South African Journal of Sociology*, 22(3):78–83.

Schurink, W. (Ed.) (1993). *Street Children*. Pretoria: Human Sciences Research Council.

Schurink, W.J. (1981). *Gay-Vroue: 'n Sosiologiese Verkenning van die Leefwyse van 'n Aantal Lesbieërs aan die Hand van Outobiografiese Sketse*. Pretoria: HSRC.

Sears, D.O. (1988). 'Symbolic racism'. In Katz, P. and D. Taylor (Eds.) *Eliminating Racism. Profiles in Controversy*, pp. 53–84. New York: Plenum Press.

Seedat, M. (1990). 'Programmes, trends and silences in South African psychology'. In Nicholas, L. & S. Cooper (Eds.) *Psychology and Oppression*, pp. 23–49. Johannesburg: Vision/Madiba Publications.

Seedat, M. (1995). 'Creating safe communities in the context of reconstruction and development: The Centre for Peace Action'. *Psychosocial Research and Practice*, 2:27–32.

Seedat, M.A. (1992). *Topics, Trends and Silences in South African Psychology, 1948–1988*. Unpublished doctoral thesis, University of the Western Cape, Cape Town.

Seepe, S. (1998). *A Critical Look at the South African Media*. Unpublished article, University of Venda, Thohoyandou.

Seidel, G. (1993). 'Women at risk: Gender and AIDS in Africa'. *Disasters*, 17(2):133–142.

Seigelman, M. (1972). 'Adjustment of homosexual and heterosexual women'. *British Journal of Psychiatry*, 120:479.

Sennet, J. & D. Foster (1996). 'Social identity: Comparing white English-speaking South African students in 1975 and 1994'. *South African Journal of Psychology*, 26(4):203–11.

Shamir, B. (1994). 'Ideological position, leaders' charisma, and voting preferences: Personal vs. partisan elections'. *Political Behaviors*, 16(2):265–287.

Sharp, J. (1997). 'Non-racialism and its discontents: A post-apartheid paradox'. Paper presented at the *Conference on Identity, Theory, Politics and History*, Human Sciences Research Council, Pretoria, 3–4 July.

Shefer, T. (1998). '"Girl's stuff": Stories of gender development in a local context'. *Psychology Bulletin*, 8(2):1–11.

Shefer, T. (1999). *Discourses of Heterosexual Negotiaton and Relation*. Unpublished doctoral thesis, University of the Western Cape, Cape Town.

Shefer, T. (2000). 'Discourses of culture in students' talk on heterosex'. Paper presented at the conference *Discourses on Difference and Oppression*, University of Venda, Makhado, 20–22 July.

Shefer, T. (2002). 'Discourses of culture and difference in the construction of heterosex'. In Duncan, N., Gqola, P., Hofmeyer, M., Shefer, T., Malunga, F. & M. Mashige (Eds.) *Discourses on Difference, Discourses on Oppression: Centre for Advanced Studies of African Society (CASAS) Book Series*, No. 24, pp. 427–441. Cape Town: CASAS.

Shefer, T. & A. Strebel (2001). 'Re-negotiating sex: Discourses of heterosexuality among young South African women students'. *Journal of Psychology in Africa*, 11(1):38–59.

Shefer, T. & D. Foster (2001). 'Discourses on women's (hetero)sexuality and desire in a South African local context'. *Culture, Health and Sexuality*, 3(4):375–390.

Shefer, T. & K. Ruiters (1998). 'The masculine construct in heterosex'. *Agenda*, 27:39–45.

Shefer, T., Potgieter, C. & A. Strebel (1999). 'Teaching gender in psychology at a South African university'. *Feminism and Psychology*, 9(2):127–133.

Shefer, T., Strebel, A. & D. Foster (2000). '"So women have to submit to that..." Discourses of power and violence in student's talk on heterosexual negotiation'. *South African Journal of Psychology*, 30(2):11–19.

Sherif, M. & C.W. Sherif (1969). *Social Psychology*. Evanston & London/Toyko: Harper & Row/John Weatherill, Inc.

Sherif, M. (1966). *Group Conflict and Co-operation*. London: Routledge & Kegan Paul.

Sherif, M., Harvey, O., White, B., Hood, W. & C. Sherif (1961). *Intergroup Conflict and Cooperation: The Robber's Cove Experiment*. Norman: University of Oklahoma, Institute of Group Relations.

Sherlock, J. (1993). 'Dance and the culture of the body'. In Scott, S. & D. Morgan (Eds.) *Body Matters*, pp. 35–48. London: The Falmer Press.

Shilling, C. (1997). 'The body and difference'. In Woodward, K. (Ed.) *Identity and Difference*, pp. 63–120. London: Sage Publications/The Open University.

Shire, C. (1994). 'Men don't go to the moon: Language, space and masculinities in Zimbabwe'. In Cornwall, A. & N. Lindisfarne (Eds.) *Dislocating Masculinity: Comparative Ethnographies*, pp. 147–158. London: Routledge.

Shotter, J. (2000). 'At the boundaries of being: Refiguring our intellectual lives together.' Draft paper of plenary address given at the *Psychology 2000 Congress*, Joensuu, Finland, 1 September: www.pubpages.uhn.edu/~jds/Finland.htm

Shotter, J. (nd.). 'Wittgenstein and the everyday: From radical hiddenness to "nothing is hidden" from representation to participation': www.pubpages.uhn.edu/~jds/JMB.htm

Simbayi, L., Strebel, A., Wilson, T., Andipatin, M., Msomi, N., Potgieter, C., Ratele, K. & T. Shefer (1999). *Sexually Transmitted Diseases in the South African Public Health Sector*. Unpublished report compiled for the National Department of Health. University of the Western Cape, Cape Town.

Skutnabb-Kangas, T. (1990). 'Legitimating or delegitimating new forms of racism: The role of researchers'. *Journal of Multilingual and Multicultural Development*, 11(1/2):77–99.

Slovo, J. (1989). *The South African Working Class and the National Democratic Revolution*. London: South African Communist Party.

Smart, C. (1996). 'Collusion, collaboration and confession: On moving beyond the heterosexuality debate'. In Richardson, D. (Ed.) *Theorising Heterosexuality*, pp. 161–195. Milton Keynes: Open University Press.

Smit, B. & C. Cilliers (1998). 'Violence and the criminal justice system'. In Bornman, E., van Eeden, R. & M. Wentzel (Eds.) *Violence in South Africa: A Variety of Perspectives*, pp. 201–226. Pretoria: HSRC.

Smith, C.S. (1996). *The Life-world of Street Children in the Durban Metropolitan Area*. Unpuplished doctoral thesis, University of Pretoria.

Smith, G. (2000). 'From suffering in silence, to drawing strength from the margins'. *Agenda*, 46:34–41.

Smith, K.T. (1971). 'Homophobia: A tentative personality profile'. *Psychological Reports*, 29:1091–1094.

Smith, T.B., & C.R. Stones (1999). 'Identities and racial attitudes of South African and American adolescents: A cross-cultural examination'. *South African Journal of Psychology*, 29(1):23–9.

Smitherman-Donaldson, G. & T. van Dijk (1988). *Discourse and Discrimination*. Detroit: Wayne State University Press.

Sobukwe, R. (1959). *Opening Address to the Africanist Inaugural Convention*. Karis Carter Collection, UCT 2:DP1:30/1. Cape Town: University of Cape Town.

Sole, K.E. (1993). *Authority, Authenticity and the Black Writer: Depictions of Politics and Community in Selected Fictional Black Consciousness Texts*. Unpublished doctoral thesis, University of the Witswatersrand, Johannesburg.

Solomon, R.C. (1988). *Continental Philosophy since 1750: The Rise and Fall of the Self*. Oxford: Oxford University Press.

Sonking, D. (1985). *The Male Batterer*. New York: Springer.

South African Human Rights Commission (SAHRC) (2000). *Faultlines: Inquiry into Racism in the Media*. Parktown: SAHRC.

South African Institute of Race Relations (1984). *Race Relations Survey 1983, Volume 37*. Johannesburg: South African Institute of Race Relations.

South African Institute of Race Relations (1986). *Race Relations Survey 1985*. Johannesburg: South African Institute of Race Relations.

South African Institute of Race Relations (1987). *Race Relations Survey 1986, Part 1*. Johannesburg: South African Institute of Race Relations.

Soyinka, W. (1988). *Art, Dialogue and Outrage*. Ibadan: New Horn Press.

Speake, J. (Ed.) (1979). *A Dictionary of Philosophy*. London: Pan Books.

Spears, R. & I. Parker (1996). 'Marxist theses and psychological themes'. In Parker, I. & R. Spears (Eds.) *Psychology and Society: Radical Theory and Practice*, pp.1–17. London: Pluto Press.

Spry-Leverton, J. (1996). 'Lessons in survival for children of war'. *Child and Youth Care*, 14:11–13.

Squire, C. (1998). 'Women and men talk about aggression: An analysis of narrative genre'. In Henwood, K., Griffin, C. & A. Phoenix (Eds.) *Standpoints and Differences. Essays in the Practice of Feminist Psychology*, pp. 65–90. London: Sage.

Stacey, M. (1998). 'Mixed blessings: Experience of mixed race couples in South Africa'. *Psychology Bulletin*, 8(2):41–46.

Stark, E. & A. Flitcraft (1996). *Women at Risk. Domestic Violence and Women's Health*. Thousand Oaks: Sage.

Statutes of the Union of South Africa (1927). *The Immorality Act*, No. 5 of 1927. Pretoria: Government Printer.

Statutes of the Union of South Africa (1949). *The Prohibition of Mixed Marriages Act*, No. 55 of 1949. Pretoria: Government Printer.

Statutes of the Union of South Africa (1950a). *The Immorality Amendment Act*, No. 21 of 1950. Pretoria: Government Printer.

Statutes of the Union of South Africa (1950b). *The Population Registration Act*, No. 30 of 1950. Pretoria: Government Printer.

Steenveld, L. (2000a). 'Defining the undefinable'. *Rhodes Journalism Review*, 19:11.

Steenveld, L. (2000b). 'Cricket's infamous coolie creeper'. *Rhodes Journalism Review*, 19:25.

Steenveld, L. (2000c). 'Equality and expression'. *Rhodes Journalism Review*, 19:26.

Stefan, S. (1993). 'Power of discourse and discourse of power in making an issue of sexual abuse in South Africa: The rise and fall of social problems'. *Critical Arts*, 7(2):1–18.

Stein, E. (1999). *The Mismeasure of Desire: The Science, Theory, and Ethics of Sexual Orientation*. New York: Oxford University Press.

Stein, P. & R. Jacobsen. (1986). *Sophiatown Speaks*. Johannesburg: Junction Avenue Press.

Stevens, G. & R. Lockhat (1997). '"Coca-cola kids" – Reflections on black adolescent identity development in post-apartheid South Africa'. *South African Journal of Psychology*, 27(4):250–55.

Stevens, G. (1996). *The 'Racialised' Discourses of a Group of Black Parents and Adolescents in a Western Cape Community*. Unpublished Master's thesis. University of the Western Cape, Cape Town.

Stevens, G. (1997). *Understanding 'Race' and Racism: A Return to Traditional Scholarship*. PRC Occasional Publications Series. Bellville: University of the Western Cape.

Stevens, G., Seedat, M., Swart, T. & C. van der Walt (2003). 'Promoting methodological pluralism, theoretical diversity and interdisciplinarity in a multi-levelled violence prevention initiative in South Africa'. *Journal of Prevention and Intervention in the Community*, in press.

Steyn, M.E. (2002). *'Whiteness Just isn't What it Used to Be'. White Identity in a Changing South Africa*. New York: State University of New York Press.

Stout, K. (1992). 'Intimate femicide, an ecological analysis'. *Journal of Sociology and Social Welfare*, 19(3):29–50.

Straker, G. (1992). *Faces in the Revolution*. Cape Town: David Philip.

Straker, G. (1992). *Faces in the Revolution*. Cape Town: David Phillip.

Strebel, A. & G. Lindegger (1998). 'Power and responsibility: Shifting discourses of gender and HIV/AIDS'. *Psychology in Society*, 24:4–20.

Strebel, A. (1992). '"There's absolutely nothing I can do, just believe in God": South African women with AIDS'. *Agenda*, 12:50–62.

Strebel, A. (1993). *Women and Aids: A Study of Issues in the Prevention of HIV Infection*. Unpublished doctoral thesis, University of Cape Town.

Strebel, A., & G. Lindegger (1998). 'Power and responsibility: shifting discourses of gender and HIV/AIDS'. *Psychology in Society*, 24:4–20.

Sullivan, J.L. & J.E. Transue (1999). 'The psychological underpinnings of democracy: A selective review of political tolerance, interpersonal trust, and social capital'. *Annual Review of Psychology*, 50:625–650.

Sunde, J. & V. Bozalek, V. (1993). '(Re)searching difference'. *Agenda*, 19:29–36.

Swart, J. (1990). *Malunde: The Street Children of Hillbrow*. Johannesburg: Witwatersrand University Press.

Swart, T.M. (2001). *A Study of Identity Articulations among University-attending Students in South Africa*. Unpublished Master's dissertation. Johannesburg: University of the Witwatersrand.

Swartz, L. & A. Levett. (1989). 'Political repression and children in South Africa: The social construction of damaging effects'. *Social Science and Medicine*, 28:741–750.

Szesnat, H. (1997). 'The essentialist-social constructionist debate and biblical research'. In Germond, P. & S. de Gruchy (Eds.) *Aliens in the household of God*, pp. 270–294. Cape Town: David Philip.

Tajfel, H. (1959). 'Quantitative judgement in social perception'. *British Journal of Psychology*, 10:16–29.

Tajfel, H. (1972). 'Introduction'. In Israel, J. & H. Tajfel (Eds.) *The Context of Social Psychology: Critical Assessment*, pp.1–13. London: Academic Press.

Tajfel, H. (1981). *Human Groups and Social Categories*. Cambridge: Cambridge University Press.

Tajfel, H. (1982). *Social Identity and Intergroup Relations*. Cambridge: Cambridge University Press.

Tajfel, H. & C. Fraser (Eds.) (1978). *Introducing Social Psychology*. Middlesex: Penguin.

Tajfel, H. & J. Turner (1979). 'An integrative theory of inter-group conflict'. In Austin, W. & S. Worchel (Eds.) *The Social Psychology of Inter-group Relations*. California: Brooks/Cole.

Tambo, A. (1987). *Preparing for Power: Oliver Tambo Speaks*. London: Heinemann.

Tarrant, S. (1992). *Psychotherapy with Gay Clients: Therapeutic Approaches of Clinical Psychologists in Durban*. Unpublished Master's thesis, University of Durban Westville, Durban.

Terman, L. & C. Miles (1936). *Sex and Personality: Studies in Masculinity and Feminity*. New York: McGraw-Hill.

Terre Blanche, M. & K. Durrheim (1999). 'Histories of the present: Social science research in context'. In Terre Blanche, M. & K. Durrheim (Eds.) *Research in Practice: Applied Methods for the Social Sciences*, pp. 1–16. Cape Town: University of Cape Town Press.

Terre Blanche, M., Bhavanani, K. & D. Hook (Eds.) (1999). *Body Politics: Power, Knowledge & the Body in Social Sciences*. WITS: Histories of the Present Press.

Terreblanche, S. & N. Nattrass (1990). 'A periodisation of the political economy from 1910'. In Nattrass, N. & E. Ardingon (Eds.) *The Political Economy of South Africa*, pp. 6–23. Cape Town: Oxford University Press.

Terreblanche, S. & N. Nattrass (1990). 'A periodisation of the political economy from 1910'. In Nattrass, N. & E. Ardington (Eds.) *The Political Economy of South Africa*, pp. 6–23. Cape Town: Oxford University Press.

Therborn, G. (1980). *The Ideology of Power and the Power of Ideology*. London: Verso.

Theron, A. (1984). 'Meningsverskil rondom die Amerikaanse Psigiatriese Vereniging se besluit om homoseksualiteit as psigopatologiese versteuring te skrap'. *South African Journal of Psychology*, 14(3):106–112.

Thomson, R. & S. Scott (1991). 'Learning about sex: Young women and the social construction of sexual identity'. *Women Risk and Aids Project (WRAP)*, Paper 4. London: Tufnell Press.

Thompson, J.B. (1984). *Studies in the Theory of Ideology*. Cambridge: Polity Press.

Thompson, J.B. (1990). *Ideology and Modern Culture*. Cambridge: Polity Press.

Thompson, N., McCandless, R. & B. Strickland (1971). 'Personal adjustment of male and female homosexuals and heterosexuals'. *Journal of Abnormal Psychology*, 78(2):237–240.

Thornton, R. (1996). 'The potentials and boundaries in South Africa: Steps towards a theory of social change'. In Webner, R. & T. Ranger (Eds.) *Postcolonial Identities in Africa*. London: Zed Books.

Tiefenthaler, J. & A. Farmer (2000). 'The economics of domestic violence'. In Park, Y.J., Fedler, J. & Z. Dangor (Eds.) *Reclaiming Women's Spaces: New Perspectives on Violence Against Women and Sheltering in South Africa*, pp. 177–199. Johannesburg: Nisaa Institute for Women's Development.

Tosh, J. (1994). 'What should historians do with masculinity? Reflections on nineteenth-century Britain'. *History Workshop Journal*, 38:179–202.

Tucker, C. (1986). *A Medico-legal Examination of Homosexual Women and Their Children: Ethical Considerations and the Role of the Clinical Psychologist*. Unpublished Master's thesis, University of Cape Town.

Turner, B.S. (1984). *The Body and Society*. New York: Basil Blackwell.

Tutu, D. (2000). 'No future without forgiveness'. *Essence*, 30(9):58–60.

UNAIDS. (1999). *Trends in HIV Incidence and Prevalence: Natural Course of the Epidemic or Results of Behavioural Change?* UNAIDS/99.12 E. Geneva: UNAIDS.

UNICEF (1986). *Approaches to Improving the Lives of Working Children and Street Children*. New York: UNICEF.

Union of South Africa (1950). *Debates of the House of Assembly (Hansard) Third Session Tenth Parliament, 20 January–24 June. Vol. 71*. Cape Town: Unie-Volkspers.

United Nations (1993). *The United Nations' Convention on the Rights of the Child*. Geneva, United Nations.

United Nations (2000). *International Convention on the Elimination of all Forms of Racial Discrimination*: www.unhchr.ch (accessed 6 October).

United States Department of Justice (1996). *Violence by Intimates*. Federal Bureau of Investigations Supplementary Homicide Reports (SHR): 1976–1996.

Uwakwe, C.B.U., Mansaray, A.A. & G.O.M. Onwu (1994). *A Psycho-educational Program to Motivate and Foster AIDS Preventative Behaviors among Female Nigerian University Students*. Unpublished final technical report, Women and AIDS Research Program. Washington DC: International Center for Research on Women.

Valentine-Daniel, E. (2000). 'Mood, moment, and mind'. In Das, V., Kleinman, A., Ramphele, M. & P. Reynolds (Eds.) *Violence and Subjectivity*, pp. 333–366. Berkeley: University of California Press.

Van der Merwe, H.W. (1989). *Pursuing Justice and Peace in South Africa*. New York: Routledge.

Van der Ross, R.E. (1979). *Myths and Attitudes: An Inside Look at the Coloured People*. Cape Town: Tafelberg.

Van der Walt, C. Franchi, V. & G. Stevens (2003). 'The South African Truth and Reconciliation Commission: "Race", historical compromise and transitional democracy'. *International Journal of Intercultural Psychology*, 27:251–67.

Van Dijk, T. (1987). *Communicating Racism. Ethnic Prejudice in Thought and Talk*. Newbury Park: Sage.

Van Dijk, T. (1987). *Communicating Racism*. Newbury Park: Sage.

Van Dijk, T. (1989). 'Structures and strategies of discourse and prejudice'. In van Oudenhoven, J.P. & T.M. Willemsen (Eds.) *Ethnic Minorities. Social Psychological Perspectives*, pp. 115–138. Amsterdam: Swets & Zeitlinger.

Van Dijk, T. (1990). 'Discourse and inequality'. Unpublished keynote address presented at the *International Communication Association Conference*, Dublin, 25–30 June.

Van Dijk, T. (1991). *Elite Discourse and the Reproduction of Racism*. Amsterdam: University of Amsterdam.

Van Zyl, S. (1998). 'The Other and other Others: Post-colonialism, psychoanalysis and the South African question'. *American Imago,* 55(1):77–100.

Vance, C. (1989). 'Social construction theory: problems in the history of sexuality'. In Altman, D., Vance, C., Vicinus, M. & J. Weeks (Eds.) *Homosexuality, Which Homosexuality?,* pp. 13–34. London: GMP Publishers.

Vance, C.S. (1984). 'Pleasure and danger: Toward a politics of sexuality'. In Vance, C.S. (Ed.) *Pleasure and Danger: Exploring Female Sexuality,* pp. 1–27. Boston: Routledge.

Varga, C. & L. Makubalo (1996). 'Sexual non-negotiation'. *Agenda,* 28:31–38.

Vasconcelos, A., Neto, A., Valenca, A., Braga, C., Pacheco, M., Dantas, S., Simonetti, V. & V. Garcia (1995). 'Sexuality and AIDS prevention among adolescents from low-income communities in Recife, Brazil'. *Women and AIDS Program Research Report Series.* Washington DC: International Center for Research on Women.

Vetten, L. (1999). 'Violence Against Women in Metropolitan South Africa: A Study on Impact and Service Delivery'. *Institute for Security Studies Monograph Series,* No. 41: www.wits.ac.za/csvr/pubsgend.htm (28 September, 2000).

Vetten, L. (2000). 'Gender, race and power dynamics in the face of social change. Deconstructing violence against women in South Africa'. In Park, Y.J., Fedler, J. & Z. Dangor (Eds.) *Reclaiming Women's Spaces. New Perspectives on Violence Against Women and Sheltering in South Africa,* pp. 47–80. Johannesburg: Nisaa Institute for Women's Development.

Vetten, L. & J. Dladla (2000). 'Women's fear and survival in inner-city Johannesburg'. *Agenda,* 44:70–75.

Vetten, L. & K. Bhana (2001). *Violence, Vengeance and Gender: A Preliminary Investigation into the Links Between HIV/AIDS and Violence Against Women in South Africa.* Johannesburg: The Centre for the Study of Violence & Reconciliation.

wa Machwofi, N. (1998). *On Capitalism, Ethnic Dominance and Racism: The Elite Media and the 'Million Man March'.* Kenosha: University of Wisconsin-Parkside.

waThiong'o, N. (1986). *Decolonising the Mind: The Politics of Language in African Literature.* London: James Currey.

Waldby, C., Kippax, S. & J. Crawford (1993). *'Cordon sanitaire:* "clean" and "unclean" women in the AIDS discourse of young heterosexual men'. In Aggleton, P., Davies, P. & G. Hart (Eds.) *AIDS: Facing the Second Decade,* pp. 29–39. London: Falmer Press.

Waldman, L. (1995). '"This house is a dark room". Domestic violence on farms in the Western Cape'. *African Anthropology,* 11(2):60–81.

Walker, L. (1979). *The Battered Woman.* New York: Harper and Row.

Walker, L. (1984). *The Battered Woman Syndrome.* New York: Springer.

Walker, L. (1989). *Terrifying Love: Why Battered Women Kill and How Society Responds.* New York: Harper & Row.

Walker, L.E. (2000). *The Battered Woman Syndrome,* 2nd Edition. New York: Springer.

Watts, C., Osam, S. & E. Win (1995). *The Private is Public. A Study of Violence Against Women in Southern Africa.* Harare: Women in Law and Development in Africa (WiLDAF).

Weber, M. (1969). *Max Weber on Law and Economy in Society.* Harvard: Harvard University Press.

Weedon, C. (1987). *Feminist Practice and Poststructuralist Theory.* Oxford: Blackwell Publishers.

Weeks, J. (1986). *Sexuality.* London: Ellis Horwood.

Weeks, J. (1987). 'Question of identity'. In Caplan, P. (Ed.) *The Cultural Construction of Sexuality*, pp. 31–51. London: Tavistock.

Weinberg, G. (1972). *Society and the Healthy Homosexual*. New York: St Martin's Press.

Weinreich, P. (1989a). 'Variations in ethnic identity: Identity Structure Analysis'. In K. Leibkind (Ed.) *New Identities in Europe: Immigrant Ancestry and the Ethnic Identity of Youth*, pp. 41–75. London: Gower.

Weinreich, P. (1989b). 'Conflicted identifications: A commentary on Identity Structure Analysis concepts'. In K. Leibkind (Ed.) *New Identities in Europe: Immigrant Ancestry and the Ethnic Identity of Youth*, pp. 219–36. London: Gower.

Weinreich, P., Chung, L.L., & M.H. Bond (1991). 'Ethnic stereotyping and identification in a multicultural context: "Acculturation", self-esteem and identity diffusion in Hong Kong Chinese university students'. *Psychology and Developing Societies*, 8(1):107–67.

Weiss, E., Whelan, D. & G.R. Gupta (1996). *Vulnerability and Opportunity: Adolescents and HIV/AIDS in the Developing World*. Washington DC: International Center for Research on Women.

Wekker, G (1999). '"What's identity got to do with it?" Rethinking identity in the light of the Mati work in Suriname'. In Blackwood, E. & S. Wieringa (Eds.) *Female Desires: Same-sex Relations and Transgender Practices Across Cultures*, pp. 119–139. New York: Columbia University Press.

West, C. (1992). 'Black Leadership and the Pitfalls of Racial Reasoning'. In Morrison, T. (Ed.) *Race-ing Justice and En-gendering Power: Essays on Anita Hill, Clarence Thomas, and the Constructions of Social Reality*. New York: Pantheon.

West, C. (1995). *Race Matters*. New York: Vintage.

Westlund, A. C. (1999). 'Pre-modern and modern power: Foucault and the case of domestic violence'. *Signs: Journal of Women in Culture and Society*, 24(4):1045–1066.

Wetherell, M. & J. Potter (1988). 'Discourse analysis and the identification of interpretative repertoires'. In Antaki, C. (Ed.) *Analyzing Everyday Explanations*, pp. 168–183. London: Sage.

Wetherell, M. (Ed.) (1996). *Social Psychology: Identities, Groups and Social Issues*. London: Sage.

Whitfield, C. (2000). 'Words and wounds'. *Rhodes Journalism Review*, 19:30.

Whitlock, G. (1996). 'A "White-Souled State": Across the "South" with Lady Barker'. In Darian-Smith, E., Gunner, L. & S. Nuttall (Eds.) *Text, Theory, Space: Land, Literature and History in South Africa and Australia*, pp. 65–80. London: Routledge.

WHO (World Health Organisation) (1994). *Women and AIDS: Agenda for Action*. Global Programme on AIDS. Geneva: World Health Organisation.

WHO (World Health Organisation) (1996). *Violence: A Public Health Priority*. EHA/SPI/POA.2. Geneva: World Health Organisation.

WHO (World Health Organisation) (2001). *Proceedings of WHO Meeting to Develop a Five-year Strategy*. Unpublished document WHO/NMH/VIP/01.04. Geneva: Department of Injuries and Violence Prevention, World Health Organisation.

Wiegman, R. (1995). *American Anatomies: Theorising Race and Gender*. Durham: Duke University Press.

Wilkinson, S. & C. Kitzinger (Eds.) (1993). *Heterosexuality: A 'Feminism & Psychology' Reader*. London: Sage.

Williams, P. & L. Chrisman (Eds.) (1994). *Colonial Discourse and Post-colonial Theory*. New York: Columbia University Press.

Williams, P.J. (2000). 'Race and rights'. In Back, L. & J. Solomons (Eds.) *Theories of Race and Racism: A Reader*, pp. 410–425. London: Routledge.

Williams, R. (1997). 'Texts and discourses'. In de Beer, A.S. (Ed.) *Mass Media for the Nineties. A South African Handbook of Mass Communication*, pp. 341–362. Pretoria: van Schaik.

Wilson, F. & M. Ramphele (1989). *Uprooting Poverty*. Cape Town: David Phillip.

Wilson, M. & M. Daly (1992). 'Till death us do part'. In Radford, J. & D. Russel (Eds.) *Femicide: The Politics of Woman Killing*, pp. 83–93. New York: Twayne/Gale Group.

Winnicott, D. W. (1965) [1963]. 'The development of the capacity for concern'. In *The Maturational Processes and the Facilitating Environment: Studies in the Theory of Emotional Development*, pp. 73–82. New York: International Universities Press.

Winnicott, D.W. (1960). *Le Processus de Maturation Chez l'Enfant* [The process of development in the child]. Paris: Payot.

Winnicott, D.W. (1965) [1958]. 'The capacity to be alone'. In *The Maturational Processes and the Facilitating Environment: Studies in the Theory of Emotional Development*, pp. 29–36. New York: International Universities Press.

Winnicott, D.W. (1965) [1960]. 'The theory of the parent-infant relationship'. In *The Maturational Processes and the Facilitating Environment: Studies in the Theory of Emotional Development*, pp. 37–55. New York: International Universities Press.

Winnicott, D.W. (1965) [1962]. 'Ego integration in child development'. In *The Maturational Processes and the Facilitating Environment: Studies in the Theory of Emotional Development*, pp. 56–63. New York: International Universities Press.

Woelz-Stirling, N.A., Kelaher, M. & L. Manderson (1998). 'Power and the politics of abuse: Rethinking violence in Filipina-Australian marriages'. *Health Care for Women International*, 19:289–301.

Wolfe, S. & J. Penelope (1993). 'Sexual identity/textual politics: Lesbian decomposition'. In Wolfe, S. & J. Penelope (Eds.) *Sexual Practice, Textual Theory: Lesbian Cultural Criticism*, pp. 1–24. Cambridge, Massachusetts: Blackwell.

Wolpe, H. (1975). 'The theory of internal colonialism: The South African case'. In Oxaal, I., Barnett, T. & D. Booth (Eds.) *Beyond the Sociology of Development*, pp. 229–252. London: Routledge and Kegan Paul.

Wolpe, H. (1988). *Race, Class and the Apartheid State*. Addis Ababa: Organisation for African Unity.

Women's Health and Development (WHD) (1997). *Violence Against Women. A Priority Health Issue*. Geneva: Family and Reproductive Health, World Health Organisation.

Wood, K. & D. Foster (1995). '"Being the Type of Lover ...": Gender-differentiated reasons for non-use of condoms by sexually active heterosexual students'. *Psychology in Society*, 20:13–35.

Wood, K. & R. Jewkes (1998). *'Love is a Dangerous Thing': Micro-dynamics of Violence in Sexual Relationships of Young People in Umtata*. Tygerberg: Medical Research Council.

Wood, K. & R. Jewkes (2001). '"Dangerous" love. Reflections on violence among Xhosa township youth'. In Morrell, R. (Ed.) *Changing Men in Southern Africa*, pp. 317–336. Pietermaritzburg: University of Natal Press.

Wood, K., Maforah, F. & R. Jewkes (1996). *Sex, Violence and Constructions of Love among Xhosa Adolescents: Putting Violence on the Sexuality Education Agenda*. Tygerberg: Medical Research Council.

Woodward, W. (1999). 'Disturbing difference: Some literary representations of inter-racial relationships in the "new" South Africa'. Paper presented at the *Utrecht University–*

University of the Western Cape UNITWIN Colloquium, University of the Western Cape, Cape Town.

Woolfson, L. (1975). *Aetiological and Personality Factors Relating to Homosexual Behaviour in Adult Females*. Unpublished Master's thesis, University of South Africa, Pretoria.

Worchel, S., Cooper, J. & G.R. Goethals (1988). *Understanding Social Psychology*, 4th Edition. Chicago: The Dorsey Press.

Wyrick, D. (1998). *Fanon for Beginners*. London & New York: Writers and Readers.

Yllö, K. & M. Bograd (Eds.) (1990). *Feminist Perspectives on Wife Abuse*. Newbury Park: Sage.

Young, R. (1990). *White Mythologies: Writing History and the West*. London: Routledge.

Zahar, R. (1969). *Frantz Fanon: Colonialism and Alienation*. New York & London: Monthly Review Press.

Zaman, H. (1999). 'Violence against women in Bangladesh: Issues and responses'. *Women's Studies International Forum*, 22(1): 37–48.

Zarkov, D. (1997). 'Sex as usual: Body politics and the media war in Serbia'. In Davis, K. (Ed.) *Embodied Practices: Feminist Perspectives on the Body*, pp. 110–127. London: Sage Publications.

Zimbardo, P.C. (1974). 'On the ethics of intervention in human psychological research: With special reference to the Stanford prison experiment'. *Cognition*, 2:243–256.

Zimmerman, B. (1993). 'What has never been: An overview of lesbian feminist criticism'. In Wolfe, S. & J. Penelope (Eds.) *Sexual Practice, Textual Theory: Lesbian Cultural Criticism*, pp. 33–54. Cambridge Massachusetts: Blackwell.

Zur, J.N. (1998). *Violent Memories: Mayan War Widows in Guatemala*. Oxford: Westview Press.